Lecture Notes in Artificial Intelligence 1902

Subseries of Lecture Notes in Computer Science
Edited by J. G. Carbonell and J. Siekmann

Lecture Notes in Computer Science

Edited by G. Goos, J. Hartmanis and J. van Leeuwen

Springer
Berlin
Heidelberg
New York
Barcelona
Hong Kong
London
Milan
Paris
Singapore
Tokyo

Petr Sojka   Ivan Kopeček
Karel Pala (Eds.)

Text, Speech and Dialogue

Third International Workshop, TSD 2000
Brno, Czech Republic, September 13-16, 2000
Proceedings

Springer

Series Editors

Jaime G. Carbonell, Carnegie Mellon University, Pittsburgh, PA, USA
Jörg Siekmann, University of Saarland, Saabrücken, Germany

Volume Editors

Petr Sojka
Masaryk University, Faculty of Informatics
Department of Programming Systems and Communication
Botanická 68a, 602 00 Brno, Czech Republic
E-mail: sojka@informatics.muni.cz

Ivan Kopeček
Karel Pala
Masaryk University, Faculty of Informatics, Department of Information Technologies
Botanická 68a, 602 00 Brno, Czech Republic
E-mail: {kopecek/pala}@informatics.muni.cz

Cataloging-in-Publication Data applied for

Die Deutsche Bibliothek - CIP-Einheitsaufnahme

Text, speech and dialogue : third international workshop ; proceedings /
TSD 2000, Brno, Czech Republic, September 13 - 16, 2000. Petr Sojka
... (ed.). - Berlin ; Heidelberg ; New York ; Barcelona ; Hong Kong ;
London ; Milan ; Paris ; Singapore ; Tokyo : Springer, 2000
  (Lecture notes in computer science ; 1902 : Lecture notes in
  artificial intelligence)
  ISBN 3-540-41042-2

CR Subject Classification (1998): I.2.7, H.3, H.4, I.7

ISBN 3-540-41042-2 Springer-Verlag Berlin Heidelberg New York

Springer-Verlag Berlin Heidelberg New York
a member of BertelsmannSpringer Science+Business Media GmbH
© Springer-Verlag Berlin Heidelberg 2000
Printed in Germany

Typesetting: Camera-ready by editors from source files provided by authors, data conversion by Steingräber
Satztechnik GmbH, Heidelberg
Printed on acid-free paper   SPIN: 10722638   06/3142   5 4 3 2 1 0

Preface

The workshop series on Text, Speech and Dialogue originated in 1998 with the first TSD 1998 held in Brno, Czech Republic. This year's TSD 2000, already the third in the series, returns to Brno and to its organizers from the Faculty of Informatics at the Masaryk University. As shown by the ever growing interest in TSD series, this annual workshop developed into the prime meeting of speech and language researchers from both sides of the former Iron Curtain, which provides a unique opportunity to get acquainted with the current activities in all aspects of language communication and to witness the amazing vitality of researchers from the former East Block countries. Thanks need to be extended to all who continue to make the TSD workshop series such a success: first, to the authors themselves, without whom TSD 2000 would not exist; next, to all organizations that support TSD 2000, among them the International Speech Communication Association, the Faculty of Informatics at the Masaryk University in Brno and the Faculty of Applied Sciences, West Bohemia University in Plzeň; and last but not least, to the organizers and members of the Program Committee who spent much effort to make TSD 2000 success and who reviewed 131 contributions submitted from all corners of the world and accepted 75 out of them for presentation at the workshop. This book is evidence of the success of all involved.

June 2000   Hynek Hermansky

Organization

TSD 2000 was organized by the Faculty of Informatics, Masaryk University, in cooperation with the Faculty of Applied Sciences, University of West Bohemia in Plzeň. The workshop's Web page is located at http://www.fi.muni.cz/tsd2000/.

Program Committee

Jelinek, Frederick (USA), *general chair*
Hermansky, Hynek (USA), *executive chair*
Baudoin, Geneviève (France)
Čermák, František (Czech Republic)
Ferencz, Attila (Romania)
Hajičová, Eva (Czech Republic)
Hanks, Patrick (Great Britain)
Kilgarriff, Adam (Great Britain)
Kopeček, Ivan (Czech Republic)
Kučera, Karel (Czech Republic)
Matoušek, Václav (Czech Republic)
Moon, Rosamund (Great Britain)
Nöth, Elmar (Germany)
Pala, Karel (Czech Republic)
Pavesić, Nikola (Slovenia)
Petkevič, Vladimír (Czech Republic)
Psutka, Josef (Czech Republic)
Schukat-Talamazzini, E. Günter (Germany)
Skrelin, Pavel (Russia)
Vintsiuk, Taras (Ukraine)
Wilks, Yorick (Great Britain)

Organizing Committee

Luděk Bártek, Robert Batůšek, Pavel Gaura, Aleš Horák, Dagmar Janoušková, Dana Komárková *(secretary)*, Ivan Kopeček *(co-chair)*, Václav Matoušek, Pavel Nygrýn, Karel Pala *(co-chair)*, Pavel Smrž, Petr Sojka *(Proceedings)*, Jan Staudek, Marek Veber, Eva Žáčková

Supported by:

International Speech Communication Association

Table of Contents

II Speech

III   Dialogue

The Linguistic Basis of a Rule-Based Tagger of Czech*

Karel Oliva[1], Milena Hnátková[2], Vladimír Petkevič[2], and Pavel Květoň[2]

[1] Computational Linguistics, University of Saarland, Saarbrücken, Germany
oliva@coli.uni-sb.de
[2] Faculty of Arts, Charles University, Prague, Czech Republic
Milena.Hnatkova@ff.cuni.cz, Pavel.Kveton@ff.cuni.cz, Vladimir.Petkevic@ff.cuni.cz

Abstract. This paper describes the conception of a rule-based tagger (part-of-speech disambiguator) of Czech currently developed for tagging the *Czech National Corpus* (cf. [2]). The input of the tagger consists of sentences whose words are assigned all possible morphological analyses. The tagger disambiguates this input by successive elimination of tags which are syntactically implausible in the sentential context of the particular word. Due to this, the tagger promises substantially higher accuracy than current stochastic taggers for Czech. This is documented by the results concerning the disambiguation of the most frequent ambiguous word form in Czech – the word *se*.

1 Introduction

An automatic morphological disambiguation of large textual corpora is one of the main tasks in contemporary corpus linguistics. The majority of corpora are in English and they are morphologically disambiguated by stochastic taggers with accuracy over 97%. Unlike English, Czech is characterised by a high degree of free-word order and by the absence of the abundant usage of unambiguous "small" words (articles, auxiliary verbs, etc.). Hence in Czech a stochastic tagger, selecting the most likely tag for a word by considering the immediately neighbouring words, often makes incorrect choice because it cannot base its decision on the dense sentence skeleton induced by the fixed word order in combination with frequent occurrences of functional words (as is the case in English).

On the contrary, the decisions of a rule-based tagger (in the spirit of [8]) can be based on the entire sentential context and hence they can very often profit from the rich inflection of Czech.

2 Assessment of the Stochastic Disambiguation of Czech

The highest correctness rate hitherto achieved by statistical-based tagging for Czech is 93.85% (cf. [6]). This number is to be understood, however, as resulting from the combination of performance of the stochastic tagger used *and* the ambiguity of the text.

---

* The work described is funded by the *GAČR* grant No. 405/96/K214.

P. Sojka, I. Kopeček, and K. Pala (Eds.): TSD 2000, LNAI 1902, pp. 3–8, 2000.

As about 66% of the tokens in the *Czech National Corpus* are unambiguous (i.e. the tagger has nothing to decide on these tokens), the actual success rate of the tagger is in fact about 71%. After careful inspection of a portion of stochastically disambiguated data, we can summarise the main reasons for such a state of affairs as follows:

- Stochastic methods seem to be very primitive when applied on a syntactically complex, free word-order language without an abundance in syntactically fixed points (such as Czech).
- Stochastic taggers are dependent on the training data. If they have not "seen" a particular configuration of tags in the training corpus, they cannot cope with this configuration properly. In other words, stochastic taggers model *parole* (in the de Saussurean wording) rather than *langue*. As there are immense quantities of distinct complex manifestations of phenomena (esp. due to their different combinations and word order variants) in any Czech text, the modelling of *parole* – unlike the modelling of *langue* – cannot be adequate. In other words, the source of many problems of stochastic tagging is its underlying assumption that texts of a language can be viewed as accidental sequences of word forms, an assumption standing in opposition to the obvious fact that natural languages are systems *sui generis*.
- Stochastic taggers are dependent on the size and the repertory of tags. This dependency turns to be fatal: the more fine-grained input the morphological analysis provides (i.e. the more refined information is contained in the tagset), the worse the overall results are. Closely related to this is also the fact that a stochastic tagger for a flective language has to use a large tagset (1100+ tags are reported in [5]) and hence it should be trained on a very large manually disambiguated corpus (millions of word forms), but creating such a corpus is infeasible in practice.
- It is very difficult to localise and fix the sources of errors which a stochastic tagger commits (to *debug* the tagger); these taggers are black boxes driven only by the data they encountered, and as such they often behave contrary to expectations. For one instance out of many: in Czech a preposition can never be followed by a word form in the nominative case but the most successful stochastic tagger of Czech sometimes does disambiguate such a word form as nominative (though the sequence could not occur in the training corpus!).
- Stochastic taggers of Czech do not make use of information about the structure of language which is, however, available in the data. For instance, they do not use the systemic phenomenon consisting in the vocalisation of those occurrences of prepositions that are immediately followed by word forms beginning with specific consonant clusters.

As a matter of fact, we consider all these points to be true in general, not only in the particular case of Czech – even though they get a substantial confirmation on Czech as a test case. The conclusions which we draw from this are that the morphological disambiguation of Czech must be performed in such a way that it will have none of the above-mentioned drawbacks of currently available stochastic taggers of Czech, and, fundamentally, that the disambiguation must be based on exploiting as much linguistic information provided by the system of language as possible.

3 General Conception of the Rule-Based Tagger

The core idea of the rule-based tagging process is the combination of a morphological analyser (lemmatizer) with linguistically-based tag-elimination rules, which has been presented for the first time in [8]. In particular, the point is that for a language with rich inflection such as Czech, the morphological analysis of the text is an indispensable basis of any tagging (even a statistics-based one, cf. [5]). To put things clearly, we consider the morphological analysis to be a process assigning each word form in the text the set of all possible tags appurtenant to this word form, irrespective of its environment (neighbouring words) as well as of the probability of an occurrence of the particular form with the particular tag (i.e. word form with its "morphological meaning") in a real text (as an example of an intuitively very unrealistic – i.e. improbable – meaning, let us take the word form *čas* as the form of the imperative of the verb *časiti (se)*). For this purpose, we use the morphological analyser and a tagset developed by Jan Hajič (cf. [3,4]).

In the entire tagging process, the morphological analysis (i.e. multiple tag assignment) is then followed by tag elimination, that is, by a set of procedures (rules) trying to narrow down the set of tags associated (by the morphological analysis) with a particular word form, ideally achieving the situation in which only the correct tag is associated with each word of the input. Unlike morphological analysis, this elimination makes use of context of the word form whose tags are to be eliminated, and it is, in fact, based on this context.

Provided that the morphological analysis has been already implemented, the true task of rule-based tagging consists in the development of the tag-elimination procedures.

As the first step in solving this task, we studied the types of morphological ambiguity occurring in Czech. Classified broadly, there are two types of such ambiguity: provisionally, we call them *regular (paradigm-internal)* and *casual (lexical)*.

The regular (paradigm-internal) ambiguities are those which occur within a paradigm, i.e. which are common to all lexemes belonging to a particular inflection class. As an example, we might take the paradigm of masculine inanimate nouns with stems ending in a non-soft consonant (declension pattern *hrad*), with systemic ambiguity among nominative, accusative and instrumental case of plural number (e.g., *hrady*). (In this respect, the inflection is to be taken rather broadly, including, e.g., regular derivation of verbal nouns and adjectives, cf. the example of the word form *stavění*, where the ambiguity goes also between a nominal and an adjectival reading.)

Massive as this kind of ambiguity is, it is relatively easy to discover and classify since it is paradigmatical and hence it can be read off the inflection tables of Czech morphology.

More intricate is the study of the casual (lexical, paradigm-external) morphological ambiguity. This ambiguity is lexically specific and hence cannot be investigated via paradigmatics. Nevertheless, a detailed knowledge of this ambiguity is essential for the aim of tagging, since only after grasping the ambiguity classes, it becomes clear *which* ambiguities are to be resolved, and strategies can be developed *how* to do this. As a result of work in this field we arrived at a listing of approximately 125 classes of such ambiguous word forms (where a class is constituted by word forms displaying the same kind of ambiguity, e.g., the forms which have a reading as a noun in a particular case and number, and a verbal reading, or nominal feminine and masculine reading, etc.), apart from hundreds of forms which are, as a rule, unique (the "class" has just one member) but display triple or more ambiguity[1].

The general idea following from this is then that the rules of the tagger are organised into packages, each aimed at resolving one ambiguity class by stepwise discarding the contextually impossible tags of a word (cf. again [8]). The set of all (packages of) elimination rules we use can be classified according to two criteria: according to locality/nonlocality of their operation and according to the level of reliability a rule can be assigned.

The most important feature of the approach is the possibility for the tag elimination process to operate on a context whose range is not fixed in advance. The beneficial impact of this becomes clear in comparison with both the statistical taggers and the Brill taggers [1], where in both cases the limitation of the operational scope of the tagger to a local context (window of a fixed size) seems to be the source of most errors.

The importance of non-locality, obvious even for English, becomes truly crucial for languages with so-called "free word-order" (such as Czech). Thus, for example, in deciding the status of the word *se* which is ambiguous between a preposition and a reflexive particle/pronoun, a rule-based tagger can take into consideration the presence/absence of a reflexive tantum verb in the sentence (in any position of the sentence, not just in the immediate neighbourhood of *se*), which brings along a decisive advantage over the locally operating methods which commit errors in this point exactly due to the lack of globality.

However, obviously nothing prevents us also from the use of purely local linguistic strategies: to take another example from the package of rules devoted to solving the ambiguity of *se*, it is a linguistically trivial fact that the prepositional reading of *se* can be available only in local contexts requiring the vocalisation of the basic form of the preposition *s* resulting in the form *se*.

Another profound conceptual difference between a rule-based tagger and a stochastic one is that the rules (and hence also results) of the former can be assigned reliability (either as binary opposition "fully reliable"/"not fully reliable" or on a more fine-grained scale, discrete or continuous[2]) which seems to be in principle impossible with the latter (this is to say, the results of a stochastic tagger can never be claimed as fully reliable).

It is obvious that it is desirable to perform the tagging with as many fully reliable rules as possible. As a matter of fact, our rules are currently divided into two classes ("fully reliable"/"not fully reliable") as follows:

– All tag-elimination rules reflecting general syntactic regularities of Czech belong to the class of fully reliable rules (not only wrt. some testing corpus, but generally).
– Apart from these general rules, we have implemented a number of rules coping with idioms and collocations; since it is (next to) always possible to construct an example

---

[1] The highest level of lexical ambiguity, fivefold, which has been discovered is represented by the word *kose*; together with paradigmatical ambiguity, this adds up to seven different morphological analyses of this word form.

[2] Currently we use only the binary scale, and we set the reliability manually – however, there is work in progress which should result in a continuous scale of reliability of rules measured automatically by the percentage of errors a rule makes when resolving ambiguity within a testing corpus.

where the construction otherwise interpreted as an idiom or a collocation can also get a literal meaning, this module cannot be considered as fully reliable[3].

4   First Implemented Results

Although the work on the tagger started only in spring this year, we can already present the first results and compare them to those obtained by the stochastic and Brill-like taggers developed for Czech [5,6].

The first package of rules created concerns the disambiguation of the word form *se* (ambiguous between a reflexive particle/pronoun and a preposition), since this is the most frequent ambiguous form in Czech (according to [7], *se* is the eighth most frequent Czech word, and the most frequent one among all ambiguous words; in the corpus formed by the current Czech translation of George Orwell's *1984*, it is the most frequent Czech word form at all – cf. [9]. After implementing slightly more than twenty general syntactic rules concerning *se*, we arrived at disambiguating 94.34% of occurrences of *se* (700 out of 742) within a sample text of 39,000+ words (one issue of the scientific magazine *Vesmír* dated 1992). These figures are to be interpreted as follows: 94.34% of occurrences of *se* are decided correctly, while the rest, i.e. 5.66%, remains ambiguous[4]. In the particular task of the disambiguation of *se*, the incorporation of the module processing idioms and collocations did not bring much progress in this case, as the number of disambiguated occurrences of *se* rose to 702 only, thus yielding the total of 94.60% success rate and leaving 5.40% unresolved. However, after inspecting the undecided cases we are developing additional rules, with the prospect of arriving finally at the stage where only genuinely syntactically ambiguous cases are left undecided at last.

5   Remarks on Computer Implementation

The system (i.e. the rules and the software environment needed for their application) is currently implemented in C++ under the Linux operating system. In particular, the rules are created by linguists in a semi-formal format and only then they are programmed in C++. This makes the implementation of a rule slow and above all error-prone as well as slightly difficult to debug (redecoding C++ program code back to a "human" language is not entirely simple). Therefore we are currently developing a "rule language", i.e. a language in which the linguist can write the rules directly. The development of such a rule language involves the definition of the language itself and the interpreter or compiler of the rules for transforming them to their executable form.

---

[3] Let us remark, however, that in the body of the *Czech National Corpus* comprising 100,000,000+ words we did not encounter a construction where an incorrect tag would be assigned by using this module (and hence it is obvious that the counterexamples are of only rather theoretical nature).

[4] This is to be compared with the statistical tagger currently in experimental use for tagging the *Czech National Corpus*, where the success rate of resolving the ambiguity of *se* ranks at the level of about 61% of occurrences, while the remaining cca 39% are not left unresolved but are disambiguated incorrectly.

References

1. Brill, E.: A Simple Rule-Based Part-of-Speech Tagger. Proceedings of the Third Conference on Applied Natural Language Processing. Trento (1992).
2. Czech National Corpus. Faculty of Arts, Charles University. http://ucnk.ff.cuni.cz.
3. Hajič, J.: Unification Based Morphology Grammar. Ph.D. Thesis. MFF UK (1994).
4. Hajič, J.: Morfologické značky pro užití v Českém národním korpusu. ms.
5. Hajič, J., Hladká, B.: Probabilistic and Rule-Based Tagger of an Inflective Language – a Comparison. Proceedings of the Fifth Conference on Applied Natural Language Processing. Washington D.C. (1997).
6. Hladká, B.: Czech Language Tagging. Ph.D. Thesis. MFF UK (2000).
7. Jelínek, J., Bečka, J. V., Těšitelová, M.: Frekvence slov, slovních druhů a tvarů v českém jazyce. Praha (1961).
8. Karlsson, F., Voutilainen, A., Heikkilä, J., Antilla, A. (Eds.): Constraint Grammar. A Language-Independent System for Parsing Unrestricted Text. Mouton de Gruyter, Berlin New York (1995).
9. Petkevič, V.: Korpus románu George Orwella '1984'. In preparation.

Harnessing the Lexicographer in the Quest for Accurate Word Sense Disambiguation

David Tugwell and Adam Kilgarriff

ITRI, University of Brighton, UK

Abstract. This paper outlines a novel architecture for the development of a word sense disambiguation (WSD) system. It is based on the premiss that one way to improve the performance of such systems is through increased, and more flexible, human intervention. To this end a human-WSD program interface, WASPS[1] is being developed for use by lexicographers in organising corpus data in the drawing up of new dictionary entries. A by-product of this activity will be an accurate sense disambiguation program.

1 Background

Human languages are, to a varying degree, prone to *polysemy*: the phenomenon where the same outward word form may give rise to different meanings. To illustrate, consider two sentences containing one of the standard examples, the English noun *bank*.

1. He dived into the water and set off strongly towards the opposite *bank*.
2. Requiring traveller's cheques, she popped into the nearest *bank*.

Hearing sentence (1) should be enough to evoke the meaning paraphrasable by *raised strip of land along a river or canal*. Whereas in (2), the meaning *establishment providing financial services* will undoubtedly come to mind. Although going largely unnoticed by human users, this phenomenon places an extra burden on the automatic analysis of language, such as machine translation, information extraction and parsing, so the achievement of high-accuracy sense disambiguation may improve performance in these tasks.[2]

Great efforts have been made over the years to develop automatic techniques to perform this task. An overview of the approaches taken, both statistical and non-statistical, is given in [2]. The recent evaluation exercise SENSEVAL (described in [3]) was a good opportunity to assess current levels of performance and determine future directions. SENSEVAL clearly established that the sense discrimination task in itself was achievable to a high degree of precision by human judges ($> 95\%$ inter-judge agreement) even where words had a large number of senses.

---

[1] A Semi-Automatic Lexicographer's Workbench for Writing Word Sense Profiles, funded by EPSRC

[2] For a discussion of this point, see [1].

P. Sojka, I. Kopeček, and K. Pala (Eds.): TSD 2000, LNAI 1902, pp. 9–14, 2000.

The best results for automatic systems were achieved by *supervised* systems, i.e. those which made use of the varying amounts of pre-tagged training data available in the SENSEVAL task. This data was used to find relevant patterns characteristic of particular senses. However, even with this data, state of the art performance for automatic systems was still significantly lower than human performance, achieving accuracy in the region 75–80%. Furthermore, the performance of such supervised systems appears to cluster in this range, suggesting perhaps that a ceiling on performance may be being reached using existing techniques.

One obvious way to improve disambiguation accuracy is to substantially increase the amount of sense-disambiguated training data available. One obvious problem with this is the prohibitive expense of manually disambiguating training data in the depth and for the range of words required for real-world applications. However, this paper will propose that an alternative course of action might be to harness the skills and energies of another group of people for whom WSD is an important task, namely lexicographers. Modern lexicographers typically draw up dictionary entries with reference to a large on-line database of examples. To make this task less labourious and to reduce the number of examples they have to inspect, they require ways to automatically divide large numbers of example sentences into the senses they are interested in. Given these limitations, the availability of semi-automatic techniques to bring out interesting and typical examples are of great interest to them. This paper will explore how it might be possible to establish a synergy between lexicographers and language engineers serving the interests of both parties and with the aim from the engineering perspective of increasing the potential range and precision of WSD.

2   Method

The central concern of the approach is to make use of human input and decision-making in as efficient way as possible, leaving analysis to automatic techniques wherever possible. The proposed scenario of interaction may be divided into the following stages.

Stage 1: Automatic preanalysis

Given a large corpus[3] containing many instances of the word we are interested in, we can find out much about its behaviour using completely automatic techniques. As a first step in disambiguation procedure, we find characteristic patterns which the word occurs in ranked by their statistical significance, that is to what extent the behaviour of this word diverges from that of the vocabulary (or more precisely, the wordclass) as a whole. These patterns include a range of grammatical relations (found by regular expression matching over the BNC), as well as the looser pattern of *word in proximity*, i.e. cooccurrence in an n-word window. The set of patterns is currently under development, but a subset of them is given in the following table, which gives an idea of what partial results of this automatic procedure might look like for the word *bank*.

---

[3] The WASPS project uses the resource of the 100 million+ word British National Corpus, available with part-of-speech tags.

relation	significant items for *bank*
subject-of	*lend, announce, borrow, refuse, . . .*
object-of	*rob, burst, repay, overflow, . . .*
modifying adjective	*central, opposite, steep, commercial, . . .*
modifying noun	*merchant, river, piggy, canal, . . .*
modifies	*manager, account, holiday, robber, . . .*
preposition *of* + NP head	*England, river, America, Danube, . . .*
word in proximity	*money, mud, debt, water, . . .*

It will be seen that these characteristic patterns automatically extracted in this way will in general be relevant to only one of the senses of the word, that is they may be thought of as *clues* for that sense. The assignment of senses to clues is where the human input comes in at the next stage.

Stage 2: Initial interaction with lexicographer

The characteristic patterns (relation-lexeme pairs) for the word in question are then presented to the lexicographer. It is then the lexicographer's task to draw up an initial list of potential senses for the word, which may be modified and extended as the interaction progresses. This could either be done with reference to the automatically-extracted patterns, be based on pre-existing dictionaries, or be sensitive to special requirements of the task in hand, for example correspondence to possible targets in the machine translation task.

Having decided on a sense inventory, the lexicographer then runs through the patterns selecting the appropriate sense with the click of a mouse. As will become apparent later this procedure does not have to be lengthy or exhaustive, as even a small number of sense assignments should be sufficient to bootstrap the WSD algorithm described below. To check on the appropriate sense assignment, access is available to the actual sentences in the corpus where the patterns occur.[4]

The patterns with senses assigned are then used as input to the next stage: the sense disambiguation algorithm.

Stage 3: Disambiguation algorithm

The core of the automatic disambiguator is an iterative bootstrapping procedure, based on that described by Yarowsky in [4]. In that paper, Yarowsky uses a few seed collocations, which have been assigned senses, to bootstrap the finding of new good indicators for particular senses. Yarowsky proposes a number of techniques for the initial sense assignment, the one used here is an elaboration of his proposal for limited human intervention to set a small number of seeds. The number to be set here is under the control of the lexicographer in Stage 2.

---

[4] The option is also available to mark individual corpus instances with a particular sense, if so desired, although doing this extensively will slow the process.

The essential idea of this algorithm is to extract from the seed, "sense-defined", example sentences a decision list of commonly occurring syntactic patterns which are good indicators of a particularly sense. The best clues on the decision list are then used to increase the data set by classifying more of the unclassified examples, and a new decision list is calculated from the increased dataset that results. This process is repeated in a bootstrapping manner until the dataset is divided between the different senses. The resulting decision list can then be applied to disambiguate an unseen dataset. It has certainly been well demonstrated that this is a very effective technique where the number of senses is small in number.

Stage 3a (concurrent with Stage 3): Continued human interaction

In the standard Yarowsky technique, the algorithm runs without further human input until all examples are classified into one sense or another. The distinguishing feature of the present approach is the assumption that to achieve a higher level of precision in more difficult conditions (i.e. where there are a greater number of senses or less distinct senses to be distinguished), then it will require a more detailed interaction with a lexicographer and possibly a repeated series of interactions to arrive at a high-precision decision list.

To that end new clues for senses are shown to the lexicographer as they are found, so that they can be verified, again with reference to the original sentences from where they derived if necessary. One interesting avenue to explore is that of not finding best clues overall but best clues for each sense and using these, subject to their satisfying some threshold criterion. Clues can be rejected at any time, and the lexicographer is kept informed of the progress of the disambiguation process, that is how many examples have been assigned to each sense and how many remain unassigned.

It is this "rump" of examples that are not easy to assign to any of the senses that may be of great interest to the lexicographer, since it is likely to contain examples of rare senses and uses, of great interest in compiling a dictionary. The task of wading through all examples to find such interesting cases may thus be significantly reduced.

Stage 4: Final outcome

The final outcome of this hopefully relatively brief and non-labourious man-machine interaction may be summarised as follows.

- For the lexicographer, the interaction has been of assistance in preparing the lexical entry: providing a semi-automatic sorting of the examples into senses, quick and discriminating access to the corpus evidence, and an efficient paring away of standard and repetitive examples.
- For the language engineer, we end up with a decision list of clues for the various senses that can directly be applied to the disambiguation of a new test.
- Finally, we are also left with a potentially reusable resource for other NLP tasks: a (partially) sense-disambiguated corpus.

3   Towards a Divide and Rule Strategy?

One common problem facing word sense disambiguation programs is that the distribution of senses is typically highly skewed, with a few very common senses and a long tail of increasingly rare senses. It is difficult to get sufficient training data to establish good clues for these rarer senses, since they tend to be swamped by the more common ones. However, to the lexicographer these rare senses are equally, if not disproportionately, interesting and important, so it is vital that any automatic techniques that might be employed will bring such examples out of the mass of more common ones. To this end, the simple bootstrapping techniques set out above may be modified by aiming for a gradual refinement of senses as the lexicographer interacts with the program.

To give a concrete example of how this might work, let us return to our example word: *bank*. The "financial institution" sense accounts for well over 85% of the $\approx 21,000$ tokens of *bank* in the BNC, with the sense "bank of waterway" accounting for the majority of the remaining examples. A glance in a dictionary, however, shows a range of other senses such as "ridge of earth" (i.e. not by a river), "mass" as in *bank of snow*, "row or series" as in *bank of pumps*, "store" as in *blood bank, bank of data*, and even "degree of banking" as in *the plane went into a steep bank*.[5]

One way that we might overcome the swamping effect of overly-dominant senses is to approach the sense division in stages. For example, we could attempt to first make an initial cut of the data between the "financial institution" sense on the one hand and a single grouping of "other senses" on the other. Having classified the patterns in this broad way, removing those examples that can be safely classified as "finance" leaves a smaller set of examples from which statistically-significant patterns may again be calculated and the approach can be applied to this reduced dataset. With the swamping effect of the "financial institution" sense of bank largely removed, there is a good chance that patterns associated with less frequent senses can come to the fore.

It will be seen that the approach provides the flexibility for a number of different approaches, and it remains an empirical problem to discover which are the most effective strategies.

4   Evaluation

As outlined above, the finished system should produce results of various types. In the first instance, it will be possible to judge it for its usefulness as a lexicographic tool, although evaluation of this is bound to have a degree of subjectivity, tests are planned and should provide useful feedback on the design and functionality of the system.

A more objective evaluation will be possible for the resulting disambiguation program, which can be applied to fresh text. Trials have already been carried out with a

---

[5] There are clearly problems in defining these separate senses with any clarity, for the meanings often appear to run into the other without clear boundaries, for example a mound of earth by the side of a river may be thought of as a bank in two different senses, possibly both at the same time. However, although the concept of "word sense" may be undefinable in any absolute way, it may nevertheless still be a useful concept for specific tasks. For discussion of these problems, see for example [5].

small subset of the data in the first SENSEVAL competition and preliminary results are encouraging. Starting with the sense inventory provided for the task, and brief human interaction, it seems to be possible to obtain results rivalling the best supervised systems, without using the pre-prepared training data that these systems rely on. The question of whether this performance can be consistently replicated and whether the further addition of "gold standard" training data can increase this performance level awaits further investigation.

5   Conclusion

This paper has presented a proposal for an interactive architecture to improve the accuracy of word sense disambiguation by recruiting the input of lexicographers to the task. Although many of the details of the proposal remain to be worked out, we hope that it can become a flexible tool for all those with an interest in word senses and eventually offer the prospect of increased accuracy in automatic sense disambiguation systems.

References

1. Kilgarriff, Adam. "What is word sense disambiguation good for?". In Proceedings of NLP Pacific Rim Symposium 1997, Phuket, Thailand.
2. Ide, Nancy and Jean Véronis. Introduction to the special issue on word sense disambiguation: The state of the art. *Computational Linguistics* **24** (1998) 1–40.
3. Kilgarriff, Adam and Joseph Rosenzweig. English SENSEVAL: report and results. Proceedings of LREC, Athens, May–June 2000 (to appear).
4. Yarowsky, David. Unsupervised word sense disambiguation rivalling supervised methods. In Proceedings of ACL 33 (1995) 189–196.
5. Kilgarriff, Adam. "I don't believe in word senses". *Computers and the Humanities* **31 (2)** (1997) 91–113.

An Integrated Statistical Model
for Tagging and Chunking Unrestricted Text*

Ferran Pla, Antonio Molina, and Natividad Prieto

Universitat Politècnica de València
Departament de Sistemes Informàtics i Computació
Camí de Vera s/n 46020 València
fpla@dsic.upv.es, amolina@dsic.upv.es, nprieto@dsic.upv.es

Abstract. In this paper, we present a corpus-based approach for tagging and chunking. The formalism used is based on stochastic finite-state automata. Therefore, it can include n-grams models or any stochastic finite-state automata learnt using grammatical inference techniques. As the models involved in our system are learnt automatically, it allows for a very flexible and portable system for different languages and chunk definitions. In order to show the viability of our approach, we present results for tagging and chunking using different combinations of bigrams and other more complex automata learnt by means of the Error Correcting Grammatical Inference (ECGI) algorithm. The experimentation was carried out on the Wall Street Journal corpus for English and on the Lexesp corpus for Spanish.

1   Introduction

Part of Speech Tagging and Shallow Parsing are two well-known problems in Natural Language Processing. A tagger can be considered as a translator that reads sentences from a certain language and outputs the corresponding sequences of part-of-speech (POS) tags, taking into account the context in which each word of the sentence appears. A Shallow Parser involves dividing sentences into non-overlapping segments on the basis of a very superficial analysis. It includes discovering the main constituents of the sentences (NPs, VPs, PPs, . . .) and their heads. Shallow Parsing usually identifies non-recursive constituents, also called chunks (such as non-recursive Noun Phrases or base NP, base VP, and so on) [1]. Shallow Parsing is used as a fast and reliable pre-processing phase for full or partial parsing. It can be used for Information Retrieval Systems, Information Extraction, Text Summarisation, Bilingual Alignment, etc. The different approaches for solving Tagging problem can be classified into two main groups, depending on the tendencies followed for establishing the Language Model: the linguistic approach, which is based on hand-coded linguistic rules [6,22], and the learning approach which is derived from a corpora (labelled or non-labelled), using different formalisms: HMM [8,15], Decision Trees [11,13], Maximum Entropy [20]. Other approximations that use hybrid methods have also been proposed [23]. Shallow parsing techniques can also be classified

* This work has been supported by the Spanish Research Project TIC97-0671-C02-01/02.

P. Sojka, I. Kopeček, and K. Pala (Eds.): TSD 2000, LNAI 1902, pp. 15–20, 2000.
© Springer-Verlag Berlin Heidelberg 2000

into the same two groups as above. These approaches have a common characteristic: they take the sequence of lexical tags proposed by a POS tagger as input for the chunking process. Most linguistic approaches use finite state methods for detecting chunks or for accomplishing other linguistic tasks [2,4,12]. Other works use different grammatical formalisms (such as constraint grammars) [21], or combine the grammar rules with a set of heuristics [5]. Learning technique approaches automatically construct a language model from a labelled and bracketed corpus. In [8], a stochastic model for detecting simple noun phrases is learnt. Transformation-based learning was used in [19] to detect base NP. The Memory-Based Learning algorithm [10] takes into account lexical and POS information. The Memory-Based Sequence Learning algorithm [3] learns substrings or sequences of POS and brackets.

2   General Description of Our System for Tagging and Chunking

In this work, we present an integrated system that combines different knowledge sources (lexical probabilities, models for chunks and a contextual model for the sentences) for tagging and chunking texts from a certain language. The approach is based on stochastic finite-state models that are learnt automatically, so we achieved a very flexible and portable system. The models that we have used are based on bigrams and other finite-state automata which were learnt using grammatical inference techniques [17,18]. Our system can be considered as a two-level transducer. The upper one describes contextual information about the structure of the sentences, and the lower one modelises the structure of the chunks considered.

All these models have been estimated from labelled and bracketed corpora. The training set is composed by sentences which are marked with a begin label and an end label for each chunk, and each word is labelled with its corresponding part-of-speech tag. Once the different models have been learnt, a regular substitution of the lower models into the upper one is made. In this way, we get a single integrated model which shows the possible concatenations of lexical tags and syntactical units. This integrated model includes the transition probabilities as well as the lexical probabilities.

The lexical probabilities are estimated from the word frequencies, the tag frequencies and the word-per-tag frequencies. For English, we used a tag dictionary which was built from the entire corpus. It gives us all the possible lexical categories (POS tags) for each word; this is equivalent to having an ideal morphological analyser. For the Spanish task, we have incorporated the morphological analyser MACO [7]. In both cases, the probabilities for each possible tag were assigned from this information taking into account the obtained statistics. Due to the fact that a word may not have been seen at training, or it may have only been seen in some of the possible categories (not all), it is necessary to apply a smoothing mechanism. In our approach, if the word has not previously been seen, the same probability is assigned to all the categories given by the dictionary; if it has been seen, but not in all the categories, the smoothing mechanism called "add one" is applied. Afterwards, a renormalisation process is carried out.

The tagging and shallow parsing process consists of finding out the sequence of states of maximum probability on the integrated model for an input sentence. Therefore, this sequence must be compatible with the contextual, syntactical and lexical constraints.

This process can be carried out by Dynamic Programming using the Viterbi algorithm, which we modified to adapt to our models. From the Dynamic Programming trellis, we can not only obtain the maximum probability path for the input sentence through the model and the best sequence of lexical tags, but also the best segmentation into chunks.

3   Experimental Work

In order to evaluate the approach proposed here, we conducted some experiments to estimate the tagging accuracy rate and the precision and recall rates for NP-chunk detection. The models that represent contextual information and NP-chunks structure were learnt from training data using the SLM-toolkit developed by CMU [9] or using the ECGI algorithm. In the first case, we used smoothed bigrams (BIG), and in the second one, we used the so-called ECGI automata which were also smoothed. The experiments were carried out on the WSJ corpus, using the lexical tags defined in [14], taking only the NP chunks defined by [8] into account. Nevertheless, the use of this approach on other corpora (changing the reference language), other lexical tag sets or other kinds of chunks could be done in a direct way. In particular, we conducted some experiments on the Lexesp Spanish Corpus [7] using a different tag set, and a different chunks definition.

For the experiments, we used 900,000 words out of the entire WSJ corpus (800,000 words for training and 100,000 words for testing). In Table 1, we show the results for tagging and NP-chunking on the test set. Each row in the table corresponds to a certain kind of model for the upper level and for the lower level. For example, the first row (BIG-BIG) shows the results using the integrated model when we used bigrams in order to modelise the two levels; the second one (BIG-ECGI) corresponds to an integrated model where we used a bigram to modelise the contextual information and the ECGI automata to describe the structure of NP chunks, and so on.

Table 1. Tagging and NP-chunking on WSJ corpus. Results using the two-level transducer (800 kwords for training and 100 kwords for testing).

Method	NP-Precision	NP-Recall	Tagging Accuracy
BIG-BIG	94.55%	93.60%	96.76%
BIG-ECGI	93.74%	93.09%	96.66%
ECGI-ECGI	93.17%	91.44%	96.56%
ECGI-BIG	93.75%	91.80%	96.61%

The best results for tagging were obtained on BIG-BIG models (96.8%), This value was slightly lower than the obtained using a simple bigram model (96.9%) and was the same using a simple ECGI automaton. The results obtained for NP chunking were very satisfactory: achieving a precision rate of 94.5% and a recall rate of 93.6%.

We conducted similar experiments on the Spanish Corpus LexEsp, using a smaller data set: 70,000 words for training and 25,000 words for testing. The results are presented in Table 2. In this case, we obtained a tagging accuracy rate of 96.9% using BIG-BIG or BIG-ECGI integrated models. When we used a simple bigram model, we obtained a rate of 97.0% (96.8% using a single ECGI automaton). The results obtained for NP-chunking achieved a precision rate of 93.2% and a recall rate of 92.7%.

When we worked on simpler tasks (simple syntax and reduced vocabulary), the approach based on ECGI was a bit better. For instance, over the Spanish corpus BDGEO [16], the tagging accuracy was 99.2% using ECGI models and 99.0% using BIG.

Table 2. Tagging and NP-chunking on the Spanish Lexesp corpus. Results using the two-level transducer (70 kwords for training and 25 kwords for testing).

Method	NP-Precision	NP-Recall	Tagging Accuracy
BIG-BIG	93.18%	92.74%	96.92%
BIG-ECGI	92.46%	91.97%	96.92%
ECGI-ECGI	91.82%	91.42%	96.80%
ECGI-BIG	91.79%	91.52%	96.74%

Even though the results presented using ECGI automata were, in general, slightly worse than those obtained using only bigrams, more work should be done in order to further develop all the capabilities of the ECGI approach. We are working currently in order to introduce certain adjustment factors between the probability distributions involved in the process.

4   Conclusions and Future Work

The proposed framework constitutes an attractive approach for tagging and shallow parsing in a single process. It is based on stochastic finite-state automata that are learnt automatically from data. It allows for a very flexible and portable system.

The comparison of results among different approaches proposed by other authors is difficult due to the multiple factors that must be considered: the language, the number and kinds of tags, the size of the vocabulary, the ambiguity, the difficulty of the test set, etc. Nevertheless, we believe that the results reported here are competitive (96.9% for part-of-speech tagging accuracy and a 94.9% of precision rate of NP-chunking, on the WSJ corpus).

In addition, the usual sequential process for chunking a sentence can also be used. That is, first we tag the sentence (using a single bigram model or other available tagger) and then we use the integrated model to carry out the chunking from the output of the tagger. In this case, only the contextual models are taken into account in the decoding process (without lexical probabilities). The performance of this sequential process slightly improves the recall rate (94.1%). We think that this is due to the way we combined the probabilities of the different models.

In general, tagging and chunking results obtained using ECGI models are worse than those obtained using bigrams. We have observed that the differences in the tagging errors are around 3%, even if the accuracy is the same. This fact encourages us to deeply study the kind of errors in order to characterise them. We are working on the possibility of combining this information in order to increase the performance of the system.

Also, the system can easily incorporate the contextual information of the words using structural tags. That is, we can specialise certain part-of-speech tags using lexical information. Preliminary results obtained using this approach show that precision and recall rates for certain kinds of chunks are improved.

References

1. S. Abney. *Parsing by Chunks*. R. Berwick, S. Abney and C. Tenny (eds.) Principle-Based Parsing . Kluwer Academic Publishers, Dordrecht, 1991.
2. S. Abney. Partial Parsing via Finite-State Cascades. In *Proceedings of the ESSLLI'96 Robust Parsing Workshop*, Prague, Czech Republic, 1996.
3. S. Argamon, I. Dagan, and Y. Krymolowski. A Memory-Based Approach to Learning Shallow Natural Language Patterns. In *Proceedings of the joint 17th International Conference on Computational Linguistics and 36th Annual Meeting of the Association for Computational Linguistics, COLING-ACL*, pp. 67–73, Montréal, Canada, 1998.
4. S. Aït-Mokhtar and J.-P. Chanod. Incremental Finite-State Parsing. In *Proceedings of the 5th Conference on Applied Natural Language Processing*, Washington D.C., USA, 1997.
5. D. Bourigault. Surface Grammatical Analysis for the Extraction of Terminological Noun Phrases. In *Proceedings of the 15th International Conference on Computational Linguistics*, pp. 977–981, 1992.
6. E. Brill. Transformation-Based Error-Driven Learning and Natural Language Processing: A Case Study in Part-Of-Speech Tagging. *Computational Linguistics*, 21(4):543–565, 1995.
7. J. Carmona, S. Cervell, L. Màrquez, M. Martí, L. Padró, R. Placer, H. Rodríguez, M. Taulé, and J. Turmo. An Environment for Morphosyntactic Processing of Unrestricted Spanish Text. In *Proceedings of the 1st International Conference on Language Resources and Evaluation, LREC*, pp. 915–922, Granada, Spain, May 1998.
8. K. W. Church. A Stochastic Parts Program and Noun Phrase Parser for Unrestricted Text. In *Proceedings of the 1st Conference on Applied Natural Language Processing, ANLP*, pp. 136–143. ACL, 1988.
9. P. Clarksond and R. Ronsenfeld. Statistical Language Modelling using the CMU-Cambridge Toolkit. In *Proceedings of Eurospeech*, Rhodes, Greece, 1997.
10. W. Daelemans, S. Buchholz, and J. Veenstra. Memory-Based Shallow Parsing. In *Proceedings of EMNLP/VLC-99*, pp. 239–246, University of Maryland, USA, June 1999.
11. W. Daelemans, J. Zavrel, P. Berck, and S. Gillis. MBT: A Memory-Based Part-Of-Speech Tagger Generator. In *Proceedings of the 4th Workshop on Very Large Corpora*, pp. 14–27, Copenhagen, Denmark, 1996.
12. E. Ejerhed. Finding Clauses in Unrestricted Text by Finitary and Stochastic Methods . In *Proceedings of Second Conference on Applied Natural Language Processing*, pp. 219–227. ACL, 1988.
13. D. M. Magerman. Learning Grammatical Structure Using Statistical Decision-Trees. In *Proceedings of the 3rd International Colloquium on Grammatical Inference, ICGI*, pp. 1–21, 1996. Springer-Verlag Lecture Notes Series in Artificial Intelligence 1147.
14. M. P. Marcus, M. A. Marcinkiewicz, and B. Santorini. Building a Large Annotated Corpus of English: The Penn Treebank. *Computational Linguistics*, 19(2), 1993.

15. B. Merialdo. Tagging English Text with a Probabilistic Model. *Computational Linguistics*, 20(2):155–171, 1994.

16. F. Pla and A. Molina. Etiquetado Morfosintáctico del Corpus BDGEO. In *Proceedings of the CAEPIA*, Murcia, España, November 1999.

17. F. Pla and N. Prieto. Using Grammatical Inference Methods for Automatic Part-Of-Speech Tagging. In *Proceedings of 1st International Conference on Language Resources and Evaluation, LREC*, Granada, Spain, 1998.

18. N. Prieto and E. Vidal. Learning Language Models through the ECGI Method. *Speech Communication*, 1:299–309, 1992.

19. L. Ramshaw and M. Marcus. Text Chunking Using Transformation-Based Learning. In *Proceedings of third Workshop on Very Large Corpora*, pp. 82–94, June 1995.

20. A. Ratnaparkhi. A Maximum Entropy Part-Of-Speech Tagger. In *Proceedings of the 1st Conference on Empirical Methods in Natural Language Processing, EMNLP*, 1996.

21. A. Voutilainen. NPTool, a Detector of English Noun Phrases. In *Proceedings of the Workshop on Very Large Corpora*. ACL, June 1993.

22. A. Voutilainen. A Syntax-Based Part-Of-Speech Analyzer. In *Proceedings of the 7th Conference of the European Chapter of the Association for Computational Linguistics, EACL*, Dublin, Ireland, 1995.

23. A. Voutilainen and L. Padró. Developing a Hybrid NP Parser. In *Proceedings of the 5th Conference on Applied Natural Language Processing, ANLP*, pp. 80–87, Washington DC, 1997. ACL.

Extending Bidirectional Chart Parsing
with a Stochastic Model

Alicia Ageno and Horacio Rodríguez

LSI Department, Universidad Politècnica de Catalunya (UPC)
Jordi Girona, 1-3. E-08034 Barcelona, Spain
ageno@lsi.upc.es, horacio@lsi.upc.es

Abstract. A method for stochastically modelling bidirectionality in chart parsing is presented. A bidirectional parser, which starts analysis from certain dynamically determined positions of the sentence (the *islands*), has been built. This island-driven parser uses the stochastic model to guide the recognition process. The system has been trained and tested over two wide-coverage corpus: Spanish Lexesp and English Penn Treebank. Results regarding comparison of our approach with the basic Bottom-Up are encouraging.

1   Introduction

Although most methods for CFG parsing are based on a uniform way of guiding the parsing process (e.g. top-down, bottom-up, left-corner, ...), there have recently been several attempts to introduce more flexibility, for instance allowing bidirectionality, in order to make parsers more sensitive to linguistic phenomena (see [1,2,3]).

We can roughly classify such approaches into *head-driven* and *island-driven* parsing. They respectively assume the existence of a distinguished symbol in each rule, the *head*, and certain distinguished words in the sentence to be parsed, the *islands*, playing a central role on the respective parsing approach.

While assigning *heads* to rules is a heavy knowledge intensive task, selecting *islands* can be carried out quite straightforwardly: unambiguous words, base NPs (in the case of textual input), accurately recognised fragments (in the case of speech), might be considered *islands*. The problem is, however, that simply starting with *islands* or *heads* does not assure improvements over the basic parsing schemata. Only with appropriate heuristics for deciding where and in which direction to proceed, we can restrict the syntactic search space and therefore obtain better results, coming through the obvious overhead that these more complex algorithms supposed.

What we present here is a method for modelling bidirectionality in parsing, as well as a bidirectional island-driven chart parser that uses such a stochastic model. Our framework accounts for bidirectional expansion of partial analysis, which improves the predictive capabilities of the system.

In the remainder of this paper, we describe the parsing algorithm we have built for testing the stochastic model in Section 2, present this model in Section 3, discuss the planning of the experiments and their results in Section 4, and give conclusions in Section 5.

P. Sojka, I. Kopeček, and K. Pala (Eds.): TSD 2000, LNAI 1902, pp. 21–26, 2000.
© Springer-Verlag Berlin Heidelberg 2000

2   The Parsing Algorithm

The conventional left-to-right approach of chart parsing is enriched with bidirectionality: parsing is started from several dynamically determined positions of the sentence (the *islands*), and then proceed outward in both directions. Island-driven flexibility allows for the use of optimal heuristics that could not be applied to unidirectional strategies. These heuristics are based on a stochastic model, which will be described below.

In island-driven parsing, one must deal with cases in which no island at all has been selected within the portion of the input where a constituent is required by the surrounding analyses. Hence the parser must employ *top-down prediction* to be sure that no constituent is lost. Obviously, this *prediction* may take place either at the constituent's left or right boundary. Therefore, we'll talk about *prediction* to the right or to the left.

The parsing algorithm works by following an agenda-based approach. A priority queue, implemented as a heap, is used to deal with the idea of choosing the most probable *island*, according to the stochastic model, to be extended in the most probable side. In fact, the heap's sorting criterion will always be a real number representing a probability attached in a way or another to each chart edge. Two different instances of heap are currently used by the algorithm (though with identical type of contents): the *extension heap* and the *prediction heap*. An element of any of both heaps consists of a bidirectional chart edge (either active or inactive at the *extension heap*, always active at the *prediction* one), a direction attribute indicating whether the edge must be extended/used for prediction to the left or to the right, and a probability attribute stating the probability of extension/fruitful prediction of the edge in question to the indicated direction. Null probabilities are not dealt with at all. The algorithm consists of a loop composed by two stages:

1. A purely bottom-up phase which operates with the *extension heap* as an agenda. It extends the bidirectional chart edges contained in the heap and in turn might add new elements to it, always according to the attached probability. At the very first step of this phase, only those inactive edges representing *islands* are taken into account. The order in which the *extension* (if any) of the existing *islands* to the possible sides will be carried out is therefore determined by the computed probabilities (though once the process started up, new elements with higher probabilities may be added that would delay the *extension* of certain *islands*).

2. Whenever the first phase does not lead to a complete analysis, a top-down *prediction* phase is started. It uses a *prediction heap* which will be updated at the beginning of every step of this type, only with those active edges adjacent to a *gap*[1] (and not used in a previous *prediction* phase yet), always according to a computed probability for each edge and direction. Therefore, a *coverage* structure must be maintained, storing which elements of the sentence form part of an *island*. This second phase lasts until *coverage* is incremented (i.e. one of the *islands* grows a word to one side), which is when we will go back to the first stage, presumably with a non empty *extension heap*. The key idea is to limit *prediction* as much as possible, going back to the *extension* phase as soon as an increment of *coverage* is detected.

---

[1] *Gaps* are segments of the input sentence spanning between adjacent *islands*.

3   The Stochastic Model

Given a stochastic CFG, what we try to model is the likelihood of extending (either to the right or to the left) an (either inactive or active) arc, or partial analysis. Two basic models have been studied. The first one, the *local* model, is static, as it just takes into account grammatical information. The second one considers as well the immediate environment around the *island* being dealt with, that is, the *islands* and *gaps* immediately surrounding each *island* (in fact, bidirectional strategies can be used in restricting the syntactic search space for gaps surrounded by two partial analyses). The results obtained for this latter method, the *neighbouring* model, have not entailed relevant improvement over the *local* one yet. Therefore, we'll concentrate on the first one.

The *local* approach is based on regarding the probability of an arc to be extended (and the same applies to the *prediction*) as the probability of the next symbol to be expanded having the terminal(s) symbol(s) in the corresponding position of the sentence as either left or right corner (according to the *expansion/prediction* direction)[2]. We'll employ the usual (two-)dotted rule notation for the arcs. Being G a stochastic Context Free Grammar, T the set of terminal symbols of G, N the set of non terminal symbols of G, R_i the i-th production of G and $P(R_i)$ its attached probability, $[A, i, j]$ is an *island* of category A spanning positions i to j, and $\{left|right\}\_corner$ are functions from $N \times T$ to $[0, 1]$, being $\{left|right\}\_corner\,(A, a)$ the probability that a derivation tree rooted A could have symbol a as a $\{left|right\}\_corner$. $\{left|right\}\_corner^*$ are functions from $N \times T^*$ to $[0, 1]$, being $\{left|right\}\_corner^*\,(A, la)$ the probability that a derivation tree rooted A could have any of the symbols of list la as a $\{left|right\}$ corner.

$$\forall A \in N,\, a \in T : right\_corner(A, a) = P(A \gg a/G) \tag{1}$$

$$right\_corner^*(A, la) = \sum_{a \in la} right\_corner(A, a) \tag{2}$$

Left-corner probabilities are symmetrically defined.

These probabilities are pre-computed and stored in two structures (the *Lreachability* and the *Rreachability* tables), which can be efficiently accessed:

– For *expansion* to the left of an *island* (inactive arc) labelled A:

$$P^{left}_{island}\,([A, i, j]/G, w) = \sum_{R_i : X \to \alpha A} P(R_i) \tag{3}$$

– For *expansion* to the left of (or prediction to the left from) an active arc[3]:

$$P^{left}_{arc}\,([A \to \alpha B.\beta.\gamma, i, j]/G, w) = right\_corner^*(B, lt) \tag{4}$$

Expansions and *predictions* to the right are symmetrically defined.

---

[2] Following [4]'s notation
[3] *lt* being the list of terminal categories attached to w_{i-1}.

4   The Experiments

In order to compare the performance of the *local* approach with the classical left-to-right *bottom-up*[4], we have carried out a series of experiments. On one hand, we have used the Lexesp Spanish corpus (5.5Mw), and a grammar for Spanish including 704 rules, 123 non-terminal symbols and 310 terminal (Parole compliant) ones [5]. The corpus was simply morphologically analysed. Hence it had to be syntactically analysed with the bottom-up chart parser in order to produce a training corpus. Probabilities attached to the grammar rules were learnt by means of this corpus of 10000 sentences, while a corpus of 1000 sentences was reserved for testing.

On the other hand, we have used English Penn Treebank II [6], 1.25Mw. The grammar underlying the bracketing has been extracted, but its size (17534 rules) is simply too big to contemplate for our parser. Therefore, and given that many of the rules occur so infrequently, we have applied a simple thresholding mechanism to prune rules from the grammar [7]. This mechanism consists simply of removing all rules that account for fewer than $n\%$ of rule occurrences of rules in each category. In our case we have used $n = 22$, obtaining a grammar with 941 rules, 26 non-terminal symbols and 45 terminal ones. This reduction of the grammar has shown to keep a coverage of 60% over the test corpus. Probabilities attached to the grammar rules have also been learnt using, for the training process, the complete corpus (49208 sentences). A corpus of 1000 sentences extracted randomly from directories 13 and 23 was used for testing.

The criterion chosen for the selection of the *islands* has been considering all unambiguous words, taking into account that we are dealing with a categorised but non tagged corpus. Efficiency has been measured in terms of the number of inactive and active arcs created during the parsing process.

Global results corresponding to both corpus are shown in Table 1. In general, the use of SCFG has proven to be successful if a "good" grammar for a given language is available, together with a large enough labelled corpus of written sentences so that productions can be estimated with acceptable precision. In the case of the *Spanish experiments*, the quality of the grammar, as well as the fact that the training process had to be performed from analyses of the bottom-up parser, has shown to be relevant for the global results.

Table 1. Comparative results for corpus PTBII and Lexesp

PTBH	Local	Bottom-Up		Lexesp	Local	Bottom-Up
Inactive arcs	2569	6679		Inactive arcs	116	143
Active arcs	13777	53164		Active arcs	648	645

The corpus has been divided into groups according to the length of the sentences starting from group 0 (length < 10) to group 9 (length > 38). The tendencies for both corpus and languages have been similar. Part of the relevant results obtained for PTBII are shown in Figure 1. It is obvious that, while *bottom-up's* performance degrades as the length increases, *local's* remains rather constant.

---

[4] Trying Top-Down approach led, as expected, to far worse results.

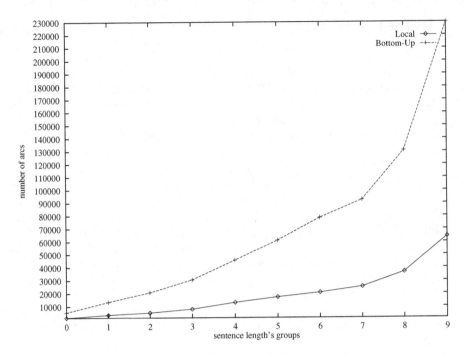

Fig. 1. Average number of arcs for each method and group of sentences of a certain length

Other criteria of classification of sentences have been tested, including *ambiguity rate*, *MID* (Maximum Island Distance) and *island density*. The results corresponding to PTBII and the latter measure are shown in Figure 2.

5   Conclusions

A stochastic model for dealing with bidirectionality in island-driven chart parsing has been presented. The model, a static one, provides for the probability of extension of each *island* given the stochastic grammar. A chart parser that uses such a model has been built. Several experiments with broad coverage grammars of English and Spanish have been carried out. Parsing performance has been analysed according to several metrics (sentence length, ambiguity rate, MID and island density). Our approach clearly outperforms the baseline bottom-up strategy.

References

1. Satta, G., Stock, O.: Bidirectional Context-Free Grammar Parsing for Natural Language Processing. Artificial Intelligence, 69 (1994) 123–164.
2. Sikkel, K., op den Akker, R.: Predictive Head-Corner Chart Parsing. Recent Advances in Parsing Technology. Harry Bunt and Masaru Tomita (Eds.), Kluwer Academic, Netherlands, chapter 9 (1996) 169–182.

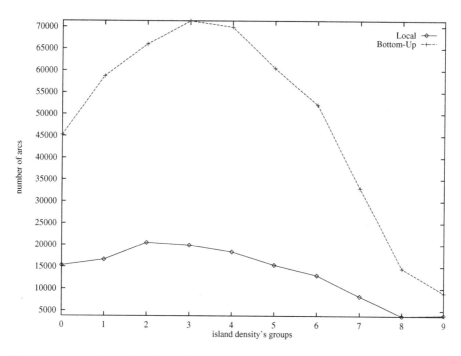

Fig. 2. Average number of arcs for each method and group of sentences of a certain island density

3. Ritchie, G.: Completeness Conditions for Mixed Strategy Bidirectional Parsing. Computational Linguistics, vol. 25, Number 4 (1999) 457–486.
4. Jelinek, F., Lafferty, J.D.: Computation of the Probability of Initial Substring Generation by Stochastic Context-Free Grammars. Computational Linguistics, vol. 17, Number 3 (1991) 315–323.
5. Castellón, I., Civit, M., Atserías, J.: Syntactic Parsing of Unrestricted Spanish Text. Proceedings of the First International Conference on Language Resources and Evaluation, Granada (1998) 603–609.
6. Marcus, M., Kim, G., Marcinkiewicz, M.A., MacIntyre, R., Bies, A., Ferguson, M., Katz, K., Schasberger, B.: The Penn Treebank: Annotating Predicate Argument Structure. Distributed on The Penn Treebank Release 2 CD-ROM by the Linguistic Data Consortium (1995).
7. Gaizauskas, R.: Investigations into the Grammar Underlying the Penn Treebank II. Research Report CS-95-25, University of Sheffield (1995).

Ensemble of Classifiers for Noise Detection in PoS Tagged Corpora

Harald Berthelsen[1,2] and Beáta Megyesi[2]

[1] Telia Promotor, Infovox, 169 02, Solna, Sweden
harald@ling.su.se
http://www.ling.su.se/staff/harald
[2] Computational Linguistics, Dept. of Linguistics, Stockholm University,
106 91, Stockholm, Sweden
bea@ling.su.se
http://www.ling.su.se/staff/bea

Abstract. In this paper we apply the ensemble approach to the identification of incorrectly annotated items (noise) in a training set. In a controlled experiment, memory-based, decision tree-based and transformation-based classifiers are used as a filter to detect and remove noise deliberately introduced into a manually tagged corpus. The results indicate that the method can be successfully applied to automatically detect errors in a corpus.

1 Introduction

In recent years there has been an increase in the application of several machine learning techniques to Natural Language Processing (NLP). They have proven to be successful in a large number of tasks, such as Part of Speech (PoS) tagging. Part of speech (PoS) taggers are classifiers, used to assign the appropriate, i.e. contextually correct, part of speech label with or without morphological information to every word token in a corpus.

The purpose of this study is to investigate a method to automatically improve the quality of the training data by identifying and correcting the wrongly annotated items in order to achieve a higher accuracy of the learning system. If a method along these lines can be shown to work, it could be used to great advantage in the creation of corpora.

Automatic identification and elimination of noise in data sets is a well-known problem in the machine learning community. Several studies show that the elimination of noise in the training set results in higher accuracy. For example, Quinlan [6] showed that cleansing the training data from mislabelled training instances results in a classifier with significantly higher accuracy. This is illustrated by Brodley and Friedl [3], by adding class noise levels of less than 40% and then removing wrongly labelled items from the training data. The result is higher predictive accuracy compared to classification accuracy achieved without removing the mislabelled instances in the training data.

To improve system performance several methods have been suggested for the automatic recognition of noise in data sets[1]. One of these techniques is based on creating

---

[1] See [3] for a summary of these methods.

P. Sojka, I. Kopeček, and K. Pala (Eds.): TSD 2000, LNAI 1902, pp. 27–32, 2000.

ensembles of classifiers. The advantage of using ensembles of classifiers is that they can improve performance, i.e. errors made by an individual classifier can be removed by voting.

In 1999, Brodley & Friedl developed a general method for removing instances that do not follow the same model as the rest of data. Their method for removing outliers differs from the technique used in, e.g., regression analysis in the way that the errors in the class labels are independent of the particular learning model being fit to the data. By using m learning algorithms, they create m classifiers that together act as a filter. A classifier is defined as the output of a learning algorithm, given a set of training examples. An ensemble of classifiers, i.e. a set of classifiers where the decisions of each individual classifier are combined by weighted or non-weighted voting to classify new examples is created. The vote of the ensemble is used to remove or reclassify instances that are assumed to be mislabelled. Brodley & Friedl use the filtered data to train a classifier, and show that the performance is better than for a classifier trained on the unfiltered data. The general procedure is shown in Figure 1, see [4].

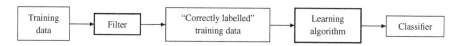

Fig. 1. Method for eliminating incorrectly labelled instances

Thus, by using a set of classifiers formed from part of the training data, it is possible to test whether instances in the remaining part of the training data are mislabelled.

In the domain of NLP, Brill and Wu [2] combined multiple classifiers (based on unigram, n-gram, transformation-based, and maximum entropy tagging) for improved lexical disambiguation. They showed that errors made by different PoS tagger are complementary and hence the taggers can be combined to a single, new tagger for achieving higher accuracy.

2   Method for Noise Detection for PoS Tagging

In this section, we describe an approach, based on Brodley & Friedl [4], for the detection of noise in a training corpus. First, we build classifiers, based on different learning algorithms for varying levels of inserted noise to the training set to act as a filter. Next, we filter the training data using standard ensemble vote procedure: consensus and majority vote filters.

2.1   Learning Algorithms

We used three widespread and successful learning algorithms in the experiment: nearest neighbour, decision tree induction, and transformation-based learning. The implementations used are TiMBL [5] for nearest neighbour and decision trees. We choose this system because it has been used in the past and it produces good results in developing PoS-taggers (see [8]). TBL is represented by the PoS-tagger developed by Eric Brill [1].

The *memory-based learning* (MBL) algorithm implemented in the TiMBL system is an example of the k-nearest neighbour algorithm. Features of an instance are represented as elements in a vector. Training consists of storing the selected training instances in memory, and an instance to be classified is compared to all the stored instances. An information gain measure is used to determine the relative weights of different features. The TiMBL system also includes an implementation of *decision tree* induction, called ig-tree. Here, as in MBL, an instance is represented by a vector, where the elements are the different features of the instance. Information gain is used to determine, at each node in the tree, which feature should be used to create new branches. Each of the two algorithms is used with one and three words of context to create four classifiers.

Transformation-based Error-driven Learning (TBL), developed by Eric Brill [1] is based on transformations or rules, and learns by detecting errors. Roughly, the TBL begins with an unannotated text as input which passes through the 'initial state annotator'. It assigns tags to the input in a heuristic fashion. The output of the initial state annotator is a temporary corpus, which is then compared to a goal corpus, i.e. the correctly annotated training corpus. For each time the temporary corpus is passed through the learner, the learner produces one new rule, i.e. the single rule that improves the annotation the most when compared with the goal corpus. It replaces the temporary corpus with the analysis that results when this rule is applied to it. By this process the learner produces an ordered list of rules.

2.2 Training and Test Data

The corpus used in this study is the SUSANNE corpus (freely available at `ftp://ftp.cogsci.ed.ac.uk/pub/susanne/` which comprises a 152,332 tagged tokens subset of the Brown Corpus of American English consisting of different text types annotated with PoS tags only. Other morpho-syntactical features that belong in the SUSANNE annotation scheme [7] have been removed. The corpus was randomly divided into approximately two equal parts; one for training and one for testing in order to get different text types both for training and testing. The training corpus contains 3598 sentences with 76221 words; while the test corpus consists of 3596 sentences with 76111 words.

2.3 Adding Noise to the Data

In order to allow a controlled simulation of the effects of noise in the data, the following procedure was adopted. Words belonging to four ambiguity classes, i.e. words that may be classified into two different ways depending on context, were selected as candidates for noise insertion. The ambiguity classes selected were (1) noun-verb, (2) adverb-preposition, (3) adjective-noun and (4), adjective-adverb. These classes are all known to be error prone in manual tagging and automatic classification alike. A lexicon was built out of the entire corpus, and used to identify all individual words belonging to the four ambiguity classes. A total of 10978 such cases were found in the corpus: 5445 in the training set and 5533 in the test set. In the noise insertion procedure, a percentage of the words belonging to the selected ambiguity classes had their tags altered. In one particular case, for example, the word 'answer' was found in the corpus, with the PoS tag VB, for verb. This word is of course ambiguous between a noun reading and a verb reading, so it belongs to one of the selected ambiguity classes. A random number (between 1 and 100) was drawn and if this number was less than or equal to the noise level set, the PoS tag for this word was changed to NN, i.e. the other possible tag in this ambiguity class. In this way the original training and test sets were converted to five new training sets and five new test sets with different levels of noise, from 0 through 40. The noise level is thus the percentage of words, belonging to the selected ambiguity classes, that were actually changed.

2.4   Constructing Classifiers

First, the original training corpus and the four training corpora with varying levels of inserted noise were used as training data for five classifiers, where MBL and ig-tree was used in two each, with respectively one and three words as right and left context. The fifth classifier used was Brill's tagger. The ambiguity class for the current word was retrieved from a lexicon of the entire corpus.

The classification task, then, consisted of assigning one PoS tag to each word, based on the ambiguity class of the word and the tags of the surrounding words.

Individual Classifier Precision   In the basic classification task, the accuracy of the classifiers was computed on the entire test set. The outcome is shown in the second column of Table 1. The five classifiers perform at very much the same level when assigning a part-of-speech label to each word in the test set without any introduced noise in the training data. MBL, with only one word of left and right context, turns out to be the best, but the difference is small and hardly significant.

Table 1. Accuracy of the five classifiers, trained and tested on original data. Accuracy on the entire test set (ACCURACY 1), accuracy on the selected ambiguity classes (ACCURACY 2).

CLASSIFIER	ACCURACY 1	ACCURACY 2
MBL, 1-W CONTEXT	97.93%	90.31%
IG-TREE, 1-W CONTEXT	97.88%	90.04%
MBL, 3-W CONTEXT	97.88%	89.93%
IG-TREE, 3-W CONTEXT	97.85%	89.75%
TBL	97.87%	90.11%
AVERAGE	97.88%	90.03%

However, it is interesting to compare the error rates not on the entire test set, but on only the words belonging to the ambiguity classes selected as candidates for noise insertion. The accuracy of the five classifiers when measured on these words is shown in the third column of Table 1. It is immediately obvious that the accuracy is much lower on this subset than on the entire test set. This reflects the fact that these words belong to difficult ambiguity classes, the very reason why they were selected for this experiment.

2.5 Filtering

The second part of this study involves the standard ensemble voting procedure to finally classify an instance.

As we have shown in Table 1, the difference in accuracy over the entire test set is minimal between the five classifiers. For this reason, assigning different voting weights to the classifiers was deemed inappropriate. Instead, we used two types of non-weighted filters: majority vote filter and consensus filter. A majority vote filter annotates an item as mislabelled if more than 50% of the five individual classifiers agree on assigning a tag different from the original. A consensus filter, on the other hand, is used when all individual classifiers agree to classify an instance as the target label. In case all classifiers disagree, the decision of MBL (one-word context) algorithm is chosen, since this algorithm has the highest overall accuracy (see Table 1).

Voting Results for the Different Filters If the filtering is completely successful, the tag given by the voting should always be the correct tag and not the erroneous tag that was assigned by the noise insertion procedure. Table 2 shows the extent to which the filtering is successful, using consensus or majority vote filters.

Table 2. Filtering by consensus (CON) and majority (MAJ) vote filters

	NOISE LEVEL	NOISE REMOVED: NO.OF CASES	NOISE REMOVED: PERCENTAGE OF INSERTED NOISE	CORRECT TAGS REMOVED: NO. OF CASES	CORRECT TAGS REMOVED: PERCENTAGE OF ALL CASES
	0	0	–	209	3.8%
C	10	407	75.9%	190	3.4%
O	20	749	68.0%	183	3.3%
N	30	842	52.7%	179	3.2%
	40	787	36.1%	272	4.9%
	0	0	–	533	9.6%
M	10	474	88.4%	590	10.7%
A	20	937	85.1%	674	12.2%
J	30	1266	79.3%	800	14.4%
	40	1459	66.9%	982	17.7%

As Table 2 shows, there is a trade off between the removal of noise and the elimination of correct tags. The majority vote filter succeeds better in choosing the correct class among the possible classes but it also removes the correct tag in many cases. On the other hand, the consensus filter takes up a more cautious attitude since it does not remove as many correct tags, but instead removes less noise, compared to the majority vote filter.

At a lower noise level, consensus vote can perhaps be said to perform better than majority vote. This trade off could possibly be exploited if one has a general idea of the error level in a corpus.

3   Conclusions and Future Directions

In this small study, we have applied a method for the automatic detection of noise in a part-of-speech tagged training corpus. The results show that a filter can successfully be created, by combining classifiers based on different learning algorithms, using standard ensemble vote procedures.

Without performing the final step of Brodley & Friedl, the training of a classifier on the filtered data, the filter can be used as an aid in identifying and correcting misclassified data. This method can be put to use in the development of large corpora. A boot-strapping procedure is envisaged, where a PoS-tagger is trained on a smaller corpus, the tagger is used to tag new text, and the filter is applied to identify errors. In this iterative way, larger corpora and better PoS-taggers can be constructed.

References

1. Brill, E.: Transformation-Based Error-Driven Learning and Natural Language Processing: A Case Study in Part of Speech Tagging. In Computational Linguistics. 21:4. (1995).
2. Brill, E. & Wu, Y.: Classifier Combination for Improved Lexical Disambiguation. In Proceedings of COLING-ACL'98, 1, pp. 191–195. (1998).
3. Brodley, C. E., & Friedl, M. A.: Identifying and eliminating mislabelled training instances. In Proceedings of the Thirteenth National Conference on Artificial Intelligence, pp. 799–805 Portland, OR. AAAI Press. (1996).
4. Brodley, C. E., Friedl, M. A.: Identifying Mislabelled Training Data. Journal of Artificial Intelligence Research, 11, pp. 131–167. (1999).
5. Daelemans, W., Zavrel, J., Sloot, K, Bosch, A.: TiMBL: Tilburg Memory Based Learner. Reference Guide. ILK Technical Report - ILK 99-01. (1999).
6. Quinlan, J. R.: Induction of decision trees. Machine Learning, 1 (1), 81–106. (1986).
7. Sampson, G.: English for the Computer. Oxford University Press. (1995).
8. Zavrel, J and Daelemans, W.: Recent Advances in Memory-Based Part-of-Speech Tagging. VI Simposio Internacional de Comunicacion Social, Santiago de Cuba, pp. 590–597, 1999. ILK-9903. (1999).

Towards a Dynamic Syntax for Language Modelling

David Tugwell

ITRI, University of Brighton

Abstract. This paper argues that a dynamic, "left-to-right" approach to modelling syntax is best suited to the demands of the language modelling task. An outline of a dynamic grammar is presented, which is based on word-by-word transitions between incomplete "prefix" semantic structures. It is argued that a further advantage of this approach is that it dispenses with the need for any notion of syntactic structure, whether based on constituents or dependencies, and is thus preferable by the argument of Occam's razor.

1 Background

Probabilistic language modelling, the prediction of the next word in a string, has obvious importance in the task of speech recognition and other domains. Important recent work [1,2] has demonstrated that exploiting the information in an incrementally constructed syntactic structure has benefits for language modelling, achieving decreases in perplexity and word-error rate over existing n-gram techniques. Given the nature of language, where statistically significant relations regularly hold between words which are more than two or three words apart, such demonstrations of the usefulness of syntax are long overdue. It is argued in [1] that one reason for this may be that standard approaches to natural language syntax, based on a static syntactic structure, have obvious disadvantages when applied to the task of language-modelling and that dynamic, "left-to-right" grammars are desirable for this task.

Given this, let us consider what properties we might desire from our syntactic model from the perspective of language modelling.

1. **"Deep" rather than "surface" relations**. A little consideration will show that the most significant relations for prediction of words are essentially semantic, rather than the surface syntactic ones such as subject or object. Consider the sentence: *The dog seemed to be about to bark*. The relation of surface subject between *dog* and *seem* is of little use here, we need to construct the deeper relation that *dog* is the theme of the verb *bark*. Of course, in many cases the two relations will coincide, but a syntactic model which only constructs surface syntactic structure will consistently miss important relations with a consequent loss of predictive power.
2. **Incrementality**. It is also of paramount importance that such information can be employed as soon as possible in the left-to-right processing of the sentence, both in order to make a good prediction of the next word in the string and also to prune sub-optimal paths as early as possible. Approaches based on syntactic constituency

P. Sojka, I. Kopeček, and K. Pala (Eds.): TSD 2000, LNAI 1902, pp. 33–38, 2000.

often do not allow this, even in cases where it is clear that human language users are in a position to make such early decisions. For example, in the sentence: *The dog barked and growled*, a constituency-based syntax would typically force us to wait until the entire VP *barked and growled* is constructed before we can add this to the NP *the dog* and recover the relation between *bark* and *dog*. Note that the same problem holds for dependency-based approaches such as [3] and even approaches based on categorial grammar with flexible constituents, such as [4].

Now let us turn our attention to how we might build a model of syntax that satisfies these conditions.

2   How to Construct a Dynamic Model of Syntax

A model of syntax must specify the relation between form and meaning, broadly speaking the relation between a string of words $(w_1, w_2, w_3, \ldots, w_n)$ and its possible interpretation $(\mathbf{M}_{w_{1..n}})$.

It has been standardly assumed since the inception of generative grammar that this relation must be specified by introducing some abstract level of syntactic structure or derivation. However, it is also possible to make use of the knowledge that the meaning of sentence does not arise spontaneously at the end of a sentence but is built up on a word-by-word basis. So, given any sentence prefix $(w_1, \ldots, w_i)$, we can use as objects of our grammar the associated potential meanings of that prefix $(\mathbf{M}_{w_{1..i}})$, which we will refer to as prefix meanings.

$$\mathbf{M}_{w_0} \xrightarrow{w_1} \mathbf{M}_{w_{0,1}} \xrightarrow{w_2} \mathbf{M}_{w_{0..2}} \cdots \mathbf{M}_{w_{0..n-1}} \xrightarrow{w_n} \mathbf{M}_{w_{0..n}}$$

Assuming such an approach, the whole of the grammar is reduced to specifying the change a word can make to the growing semantic/conceptual interpretation of the sentence, that is the grammar has to define all possible transitions of the form: $\{w_i, \mathbf{M}_j, \mathbf{M}_k\}$.

As such transitions do not depend on previous transitions, but only the present "prefix meaning", we have a simple Markov process. Of course, since the size of prefix meanings increases with the length of the sentence, they do not belong to a finite set, and we do not have a finite-state Markov process.

It should be stressed that this is a declarative grammar, not a model of processing. The above represents a *possible* derivation of the meaning of the sentence. At any word there may be multiple transitions possible and it is not the job of the grammar to decide which path or paths to pursue. The distinction is thus preserved between a competence grammar and the use of this grammar in a processing system. This point often leads to confusion since the grammar is referring to objects (prefix meanings) that in a typical architecture are outside the realm of grammar and have to be specified and constructed by the processor. By putting these objects in the grammar, we are in effect reslicing the competence/performance cake. It is argued that such a redistribution not only simplifies the grammar in that it only deals with objects which are conceptually necessary[1], but

---

[1] Unlike syntactic structures, for which it is generally admitted, there is little direct evidence.

that it also greatly simplifies the extra work that the processor has to do in employing the grammar, reducing it to specifying which path or paths to take, when to backtrack and so on.

Although the relation between grammar and processor is therefore much more transparent than in approaches based on constituent structure, it clearly separates the two. This contrasts the approach with models such as ATN's and deterministic parsers such as that described in [5], where with hindsight the unclear relation between grammar and parser was held to be a major drawback to their usability.

To see how such a dynamic grammar might look in practise, we must first look at how the building blocks of the grammar, the prefix meanings, are to be represented.

2.1 Semantic Structures

We shall assume a psychologically-real, representationalist conception of semantic structures, akin to that of [6,3] and others, and that we can represent these in complex hierarchical networks of conceptual constituents linked by semantic/thematic relations. To illustrate, suppose that we can represent important elements of the meaning of the simple sentence *he fed the horse today* in the following network:

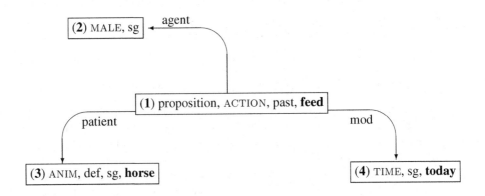

We are using here a relatively "flat" representation of the semantic network, which allows us to focus on individual elements: events, entities, states, propositions and so forth. This will be important when we consider how syntactic rules, specifying transitions between such structures, are to be formulated.

2.2 How to Specify Transition Rules

The first problem facing us in formulating transition rules is that prefix meanings are (potentially vast) hierarchical structures. Clearly we need some way to pick out from such structures a small subset of salient information. To this end, we assume that the semantic constituents, in addition to being related by thematic relations with other constituents, are at the same time subject to a salience ordering, that is an ordering of constituents on what we will term an *active stack*, which is employed in the following way:[2]

- Incomplete constituents are placed on the active stack.
- Newly-completed constituents may be removed from this stack.
- The topmost constituent on the stack is termed the *active constituent*.

Syntactic transition rules will then add new structure ($\approx$ the semantic content of the present word), conditional on the present active constituent and the syntactic category of the word. To illustrate this, let us consider the word-by-word derivation of our earlier example: *he fed the horse today*.

Active stack	**Inactive constituents**
$\mathbf{M}_{w_0}$: [1, proposition]	
he	
$\mathbf{M}_{w_{0,1}}$: [1, proposition, [+2]]	[2, MALE, sg]
fed	
$\mathbf{M}_{w_{0..2}}$: [1, prop, **feed**, past, agent:2, patient: , [+$\underline{2}$]]	[2, MALE, sg]
the	
$\mathbf{M}_{w_{0..3}}$: [3, def] [1, prop, **feed**, past, agent:2, patient:3, [+$\underline{2}$]]	[2, MALE, sg]
horse	
$\mathbf{M}_{w_{0..4}}$: [1, prop, **feed**, past, agent:2, patient:3, [+$\underline{2}$]]	[3, def, sg, **horse**] [2, MALE, sg]
today	
$\mathbf{M}_{w_{0..5}}$: [1, prop, **feed**, past, agent:2, patient:3, mod:4, [+$\underline{2}$]]	[4, TIME, **today**] [3, def, sg, **horse**] [2, MALE, sg]

It will be seen that the first transition (for *he*) adds a constituent which cannot yet be related semantically to the active constituent (the empty proposition). Until such time as it can be interpreted (in this case at the next word) the constituent address is placed on the *store* of the proposition and marked with the *syntactic relation* of subject ("+"). The store will be used in such a way for all temporarily uninterpretable items, not only subjects, but also topics and *wh*-constituents.

The actual transitions in the derivation may be seen to be instances of particular transition rules, which are outlined in the following table. Here, the top of the active stack is shown before and after the transition: **X** stands for the information in the old active constituent and **N** for the new information supplied by the lexical entry for the current word.

---

[2] This has an obvious correlation with the parse stack of familiar left-to-right parsing algorithms. As discussed above, in the present approach prefix meanings are objects of the grammar and not relegated entirely to the processor.

rule	applies at	lexical entry	top of stack (S_n)	top of stack (S_{n+1})
add-subject	*he*	{nominative}	(X, prop)	(N) (X, prop, [+N]
finite-verb	*fed*	{verb, fin}	(X, prop, [+α])	(X ∪ N, prop, arg1: α)
add-arg	*the*	{det}	(X, arg:)	(N) (X, arg:N)
add-head	*horse*	{ noun}	(X)	(X ∪ N)
modify	*today*	{adv}	(X)	(N) (X, mod:N)

A manageably small number of such transition rules may be produced to cover a significantly large range of English constructions, including *wh*-movement, coordination, raising and others.

2.3 Does Dynamic Syntax Fit the Data?

Another constraint on how useful a grammar is, and how interesting from a theoretical point of view, is how faithfully it models the data, here the relationship between strings of words and possible meanings. It has been extensively argued[3] that the dynamic approach offers clear advantages in a number of syntactic phenomena, such as problems of non-constituent coordination, binding, scrambling and many others. From consideration of this range of constructions, it will be seen that the key advantage of the dynamic approach is that it avoids unnecessary problems introduced by the supposition that there is some level of representation (syntactic structure) relating the levels of form and meaning and therefore containing elements of both. The dynamic approach introduces no such level.[4]

3   Constructing a Probabilistic Language Model

If we have a dynamic grammar of the type described with a reasonable coverage of grammatical constructions, how can we extend this into a language model?

The syntactic rules and the lexicon will provide us with possible transitions $\{w_i, S_j, S_k\}$, but we need to estimate the probability of such transitions occurring $P(S_k|w_i, S_j)$. The basic factors to be used in such calculations will be collocations between the head of a constituent and the head of its arguments or modifiers. Thus, in the example *the stray dog was barking loudly*, we will need estimates for the collocations: *bark'(theme=dog')*, *bark'(manner=loudly')* and *dog'(quality=stray')*.

If we factor in estimates of the probability of such relations we are then in the position to make predictions of the next word. Luckily, such counts can be obtained from large corpora to a usable degree of accuracy with simple regular expression techniques. To counter problems of data sparseness there will be a need for smoothing, possibly using similarity metrics.

---

[3] See, for example, in [7,8,9,10] and [11].

[4] A thought-provoking modern take on Occam's razor is given as: "Whatever happens, try all possible ways of explaining it in terms of things we already know about, before introducing aliens or dark matter." Mike Holderness, New Scientist 3rd June, 2000.

The final requirement for a processor is a suitable control structure, determining which potential paths of the derivation to pursue and which to reject. The processor in [1] employs the beam search algorithm, where a number of paths are pursued in parallel subject to them satisfying some threshold criteria.

4   Conclusion

This paper has outlined the architecture of a dynamic model of syntax. Although very much in their infancy, such models offer the enticing prospect of a useful approach being used both for the practical task of language modelling for speech recognition, as well as for addressing some outstanding problems in theoretical linguistics.

References

1. Chelba, Ciprian & Frederick Jelinek: Exploiting syntactic structure for language modelling. COLING-ACL (1998) Vol. I 225–231.
2. Wu, Jun & Sanjeev Khudanpur: Combining nonlocal, syntactic and n-gram dependencies in language modelling. Proceedings of Eurospeech '99, Vol. 5 (1999) 2179–2182.
3. Hudson, Richard: *English word grammar*. Oxford: Blackwell (1990).
4. Steedman, Mark: *The syntactic process*. MIT Press/Bradford Books (2000).
5. Marcus, Mitchell P.: *A theory of syntactic recognition for natural language*. MIT Press (1980).
6. Jackendoff, Ray: *Semantic structures*. MIT Press (1990).
7. Hausser, Roland: *Foundations of computational linguistics*. Berlin: Springer (1999).
8. Kempson, Ruth, Wilfried Meyer-Viol & Dov Gabbay: *Dynamic Syntax: The Flow of Language Understanding*. Oxford: Blackwell (to appear).
9. Milward, David: Dynamic Dependency Grammar. Linguistics and Philosophy **17** (1995) 561–615.
10. Philips, Colin: Order and Structure. Ph.D. thesis, MIT (1996).
11. Tugwell, David: Dynamic Syntax. Ph.D. thesis, University of Edinburgh (1999).

A Word Analysis System for German Hyphenation, Full Text Search, and Spell Checking, with Regard to the Latest Reform of German Orthography*

Gabriele Kodydek

Institute of Computer Graphics, Algorithms and Data Structures Group,
Vienna University of Technology, Favoritenstraße 9–11/186, A–1040 Vienna, Austria
kodydek@apm.tuwien.ac.at
http://www.apm.tuwien.ac.at/

Abstract. In text processing systems, German words require special treatment because of the possibility to form compound words as a combination of existing words. To this end, a universal word analysis system will be introduced which allows an analysis of all words in German texts according to their atomic components. A recursive decomposition algorithm, following the rules for word flexion, derivation, and compound generation in the German language, splits words into their smallest relevant parts (= atoms), which are stored in an atom table. The system is based on the foundations described in this article, and is being used for reliable, sense-conveying hyphenation, as well as for sense-conveying full text search, and in limited form also as a spelling checker.

1 Introduction

An essential feature of the German language is the possibility to form compound words as a combination of existing words. This peculiarity requires special treatment of German words in text processing systems. To this end, we introduce a universal word analysis system which allows the analysis of all words in German texts according to their smallest relevant components, the so-called *atoms*. The notion of the atom roughly corresponds to the linguistic expression *morpheme*, which denotes the smallest meaningful unit of a language. The word analysis system consists of two major parts: an atom table and a recursive decomposition algorithm. The atom table contains a set of approximately 6000 atoms. This number suffices for the analysis of almost all German words and the most common naturalised foreign-language words. The recursive decomposition algorithm, following the rules for word flexion, derivation, and compound generation in the German language, splits words into their atoms. The word analysis system is being used for reliable, sense-conveying hyphenation (called SiSiSi from the German "Sichere Sinnentsprechende Silbentrennung"), as well as for sense-conveying full text search, and in limited form also as a spelling checker. It can also be applied to other problems that arise in the context of processing German texts, e.g. capitalisation.

---

* This project was in part supported by *Hochschuljubiläumsstiftung der Stadt Wien* under the grant number H-75/99.

P. Sojka, I. Kopeček, and K. Pala (Eds.): TSD 2000, LNAI 1902, pp. 39–44, 2000.

2 Principles of Word Analysis

In an original version [1], atoms are being classified by their functionality into prefixes (P), stems (S), and suffixes (E). Accordingly, there are simple rules for forming legal words: a single word consists of an arbitrary number of prefixes, one stem, and an arbitrary number of suffixes; a compound word consists of an arbitrary number of single words. However, this primitive grammar allows for a large number of nonsensical words (e.g. stems followed by any number of copies of the same suffix). Figure 1 illustrates the grammar with the compound word *Wortzerlegungsverfahren*, which is made up by three single words meaning "word", "decomposition" and "method":

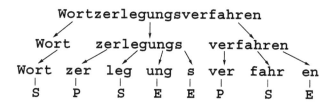

Fig. 1. Example for the decomposition of a compound word

Each atom is stored in the atom table along with a set of attributes according to its classification. An atom can be used for different purposes, e.g. *end* can be used as a stem as in *enden* (to end) or as suffix as in *gehend* (going).

The decomposition algorithm (see Figure 2) consists of trying to find substrings of the given word in the atom table and to combine all found atoms according to the grammar rules. The outer loop tests for each possible beginning of partial_word whether it is an atom. If that is the case and the atom may be appended at the current position, the rest of the word is decomposed in the same way. Whether or not an atom may be appended at a certain position is determined by its atom class and the current state, which depends on the function of the previously appended atom. At the beginning of a word, only prefixes and stems are allowed. As an atom can be a member of more than one atom class, all of them need to be considered one after the other. Each of the atom classes causes a recursive call with the resulting new_state. Inside the inner loop, the results for any application specific task (e.g. marking component boundaries) can be stored in appropriate data structures. A valid decomposition is obtained when the state that is reached after processing the whole word qualifies as a final state. Note that the algorithm does not stop when one valid decomposition is found but rather looks for all valid decompositions of the given word.

Using and extending the work presented in [7,8], the method was significantly improved by classifying atoms into word categories (e.g. noun, verb, adjective, inflective ending for nouns, inflective ending for verbs, derivative ending, and a lot of special others) and coding appropriate grammar rules for the composition of these elements. For further improvement, the stem classes are sub-classified according to their inflected forms, which can be formed in different ways: e.g. the noun *Kind/Kinder* (child/children)

```
procedure decompose(state, partial_word,
app_spec_info)
      var
        i, n, new_state: integer;
      begin
        if (partial_word is empty_string) and (state is final_state) then
           { call post-processing method for the desired application; }
        else
           n := length of partial_word;
           for i := n downto 1 do
              if partial_word[1..i] is atom then
                 for atom_class in atom_classes_of_this_atom do
                    if transition(state, atom_class, new_state) then
                       { store application specific information app_spec_info;
}
                       decompose(new_state, partial[i+1..n], app_spec_info);
      end.
```

Fig. 2. Pseudo-code for the recursive decomposition algorithm

belongs to a different subclass than the noun *Bett/Betten* (bed/beds). The suffix classes are subdivided accordingly. Along with proper grammar rules this guarantees that only the correct inflection endings may be used with a stem of a certain subclass. A number of classes for derivative endings is used for changing a stem of a certain class to another class. For example, a verb stem followed by the derivative ending *ung* is further treated as a noun: *trenn/trennung* (divide/division). In the improved version, a compound word can consist of a sequence of single words with the restriction that an inflectional suffix may only be used with the last stem occurring in the compound word.

While in the original version only a few grammar rules existed, which could easily be directly implemented as part of the decomposition algorithm, the large number of grammar rules necessary for the improved version needed to be incorporated into the system in a different way. The atom classes have been combined with a number of states to rules such that they form an automaton for word decomposition. A rule has the following syntax: *start state* → *atom class* → *target state*. A special state serves as initial start state; all states that qualify as final states are marked as such.

3   Reliable and Sense-Conveying Hyphenation

Hyphenation supports the reading process by avoiding large inter-word gaps, and is therefore vital in the generation of high-quality print documents. Common hyphenation methods, e.g. the pattern method as presented by Liang [4] are based on complete dictionaries and therefore not applicable to the German language with its unlimited number of compound words. The intrinsic incompleteness of dictionaries leads to problems in the recognition of word boundaries in compound words, which in turn can lead to serious hyphenation errors. For the same reason, hyphenation based on looking up words in large dictionaries does not lead to satisfactory results. Other methods make use of the combinations of vowels and consonants in order to generate rules derived from grammar books [3] for finding suitable hyphen points. Often prefixes and suffixes are considered separately. Nevertheless, these methods only work well for single words since they fail to recognise component boundaries in compound words.

In contrast, the SiSiSi method of hyphenation is based on the decomposition of compound words into their building parts. Word boundaries can always be recognised in the course of the decomposition process and are immediately marked as major hyphenation points ("Haupttrennstellen", represented by "="). Hyphenation points within the single words are then found by an additional algorithm which is based on the sequence of consonants and vowels, and are marked as minor hyphenation points ("Nebentrennstellen", marked by "–"). A preferred use of major hyphenation points promotes the sense-conveying hyphenation of compound words at the component boundaries.

The main emphasis of SiSiSi lies in the reliability of hyphenation: based on the fact that all valid decompositions are determined, the set of all possible positions for hyphens is generated, e.g. *Mes–ser=at–ten–tat* (formed by the words meaning "knife" and "assassination"), *Mes–se=rat–ten=tat* (of the components meaning "mass", "rat" and "deed"); only the hyphens which occur in all variants are safe, i.e. never incorrect; any others should only be used very restrictively, e.g. after consulting the user because it is possible that such an unsafe hyphen belongs only to an unintentional decomposition.

4   Sense-Conveying Full Text Search

The search for documents containing certain keywords is often realized using *pattern-matching* methods. This method has the disadvantage that sometimes documents are found which do not meet the user's expectations (e.g., searching for the keyword *car* may find a document containing *card*). Sense-conveying full text search [2] is based on the decomposition of keywords and the words in searched text documents into the atoms which contribute to their meaning. The meaning of a compound word is determined by the meaning of its components, e.g. *Textverarbeitungssystem* (text processing system) → *text, verarbeitung, system*; the meaning of a single word is given by its stem, possibly in conjunction with a prefix, while suffixes are in general irrelevant, e.g. *ver+arbeit* (process) without the suffix *ung* (ing).

Usually inflected forms of nouns, verbs, or adjectives, are created in a manner considered regular by adding specific suffixes to the stem. There is however a considerable number of words where the stem is changed when the word is inflected. This variant of the stem is often closely related to the original stem, yet spelled differently so that it needs to be represented by a different atom: e.g. the noun *Maus* (mouse) and its plural *Mäuse* (mice), the verb *gehen* (go) and its past tense *gingen* (went) or the adjective *gut* (good) and its comparative form *besser* (better). In these cases, particular attention needs to be devoted to relating different versions of the stem to each other, so searching for words which have the same meaning is still possible. This is achieved by the newly introduced concept of word families: a word family comprises all the different ways of spelling for a particular stem, e.g. the word family <gehen v> (to go, v denotes a verb) comprises the stems {*geh, ging, gang*}. For an irregular stem, the word analysis will therefore deliver the corresponding word family instead of the single stem.

5 Spell Checking

In a limited way, our system for word analysis can also be used as a spelling checker. If the word analysis mechanism is unable to split a given word into atoms according to the grammar rules, usually it is a construct containing an orthographical or grammatical error; the only other possibility is that its atoms are not in the table, e.g. when the word to be analysed is a biographical or geographical name or an uncommon foreign word. In this case, the atom in question can easily be added to the atom table with its appropriate attributes; then all future combinations with this atom will be recognised. However, the system cannot detect all spelling errors because sometimes a spelling error leads to another word for which the system finds a valid decomposition even though it might not be meaningful.

6 Incorporation of the Reform of German Orthography

The 1998 reform of German orthography [6] gave rise to a wide-reaching make-over of our word analysis system. The new rules assign different spelling to some words, e.g. *rau* instead of *rauh* (rough), *Fluss* instead of *Fluß* (river). Based on the improved version of the system, the analysis algorithm and atom table were adapted in a way that allows the word analysis to comply with both the old and the new rules, as the old rules continue to be valid until 2005. For new spellings, additional atoms have been introduced; all atoms which are only valid in one set of rules have been marked accordingly. The word formation rules are not affected by the reform and can therefore be immediately applied to the new version of the word analysis system.

Hyphenation rules have also been affected by the reform. The sequence *ck*, which was formerly hyphenated as *k-k*, remains now undivided, e.g. *Bä-cker* (baker), formerly *Bäk-ker*. On the other hand, *st* must not be divided according to the old rules, but may be divided now: *kos-ten* (to cost), formerly *ko-sten*. The algorithm for finding hyphens in single words was changed accordingly.

SiSiSi is able to hyphenate words according to both sets of rules. Therefore, according to the new hyphenation rules, it allows both the hyphenation according to spoken syllables as well as according to etymological considerations in certain words such as *Helikopter* (helicopter), which can be hyphenated as *He-li-kop-ter* (according to syllables) or as *He-li-ko-pter* (according to its Greek components *helix* and *pterón*). The old rules, however, only allow the latter hyphenation. Also, SiSiSi recognises compound words where, according to the old rules, one of three adjacent identical consonants has been dropped at a component boundary, and will still get the correct hyphenation, e.g. *Schiffahrt* (navigation) → *Schiff=fahrt*. The new rules do not require such special treatment as the rule for dropping consonants has been eliminated.

7   Outlook

The word analysis system has been tested on large text files, using a newly developed test environment, see [5]. Specifically developed test methods were used to filter the few problematic cases from the huge number of analysed words. Based on the test results, the atom table was extended by some missing, mostly foreign-language, stems. In its current state, SiSiSi can be used for pre-hyphenation of texts. Plans to directly incorporate the SiSiSi algorithm into the TEX type setting system are underway. However, the adaptation to TEX is not trivial because the concept of reliable hyphenation sometimes requires user interaction to correctly identify the intended meaning of ambiguous words. The word analysis system can readily be adapted to other languages that have to deal with compound words, such as Dutch. In general, only the language-specific parts of the system, i.e. the atom table and the rules, which are stored as text files, have to be replaced for this purpose.

References

1. Barth, W., Nirschl, H.: Sichere sinnentsprechende Silbentrennung für die deutsche Sprache. Angewandte Informatik 4, 1985, pp. 152–159.
2. Barth, W.: Volltextsuche mit sinnentsprechender Wortzerlegung. Wirtschaftsinformatik, vol. 32, no. 5, 1990, pp. 467–471.
3. Duden "Grammatik der deutschen Gegenwartssprache" (Duden Band 4). Fourth edition, ed. Günther Drosdowski, Bibliographisches Institut, Mannheim, 1984.
4. Liang, F. M.: Word Hy-phen-a-tion by Com-put-er. Ph.D. thesis, Department of Computer Science, Stanford University, Report No. STAN-CS-83-977, 1983.
5. Schönhacker, M., Kodydek, G.: Testing a Word Analysis System for Reliable and Sense-Conveying Hyphenation and Other Applications. Proc. of the Third Int. Workshop on Text, Speech and Dialogue, Brno, Czech Republic, 2000.
6. Sitta, H., Gallmann, P.: Duden, Informationen zur neuen deutschen Rechtschreibung, ed. Dudenredaktion, Dudenverlag, Mannheim, 1996.
7. Steiner, H.: Automatische Silbentrennung durch Wortbildungsanalyse. Ph.D. thesis, Institute of Computer Graphics, Vienna University of Technology, 1995.
8. Steiner, H., Barth, W.: Sichere sinnentsprechende Silbentrennung mit Berücksichtigung der deutschen Wortbildungsgrammatik. Tagungsband Konvens '94, ed. H. Trost, Vienna, 1994, pp. 330–340.

Automatic Functor Assignment
in the Prague Dependency Treebank[*]

Zdeněk Žabokrtský

Czech Technical University, Department of Computer Science
121 35 Praha 2, Karlovo nám. 13, Czech Republic
zabokrtz@cs.felk.cvut.cz

Abstract. This paper presents work in progress, the goal of which is to develop a
module for automatic transition from analytic tree structures to tectogrammatical
tree structures within the Prague Dependency Treebank project. Several rule-based
and dictionary-based methods were combined in order to be able to make maximal
use of both information extractable from the training set and a priori knowledge.
The implementation of this approach was verified on a testing set, and a detailed
evaluation of the results achieved so far is presented.

1 Introduction

The process of syntactic tagging in the Prague Dependency Treebank (PDT) is divided
into two steps. The first step results in *analytic tree structures* (ATS), in which every
word form and punctuation mark is explicitly represented as a node of rooted tree,
with no additional nodes added (except for the root of the tree of every sentence). The
second step results in *tectogrammatical tree structures* (TGTS), which approximate
the underlying sentence representations according to [4]. In contrast to the ATSs, only
autosemantic words have nodes of their own in TGTSs, information about functional
words (prepositions, subordinating conjunctions, etc.) are contained in the tags attached
to the autosemantics nodes. Figure 1 depicts an example of a TGTS.

Apart from slight changes in the topology of the input ATS (for instance, pruning
of synsemantic nodes), the transition from ATSs to TGTSs involves the assignment of
the tectogrammatical function (*functor*) to every node in the tree. There are roughly 60
functors divided into two subgroups (cf. [4]): (i) *actants* (<u>ACT</u>or, <u>PAT</u>ient, <u>ADDR</u>essee,
<u>EFF</u>ect, <u>ORIG</u>in) and (ii) *free modifiers*: <u>TWHEN</u> (time-when), <u>LOC</u>ation, <u>MEANS</u>,
<u>EXT</u>ent, <u>BEN</u>eficiary, <u>ATT</u>ribute ...).

At present, the topological conversion and the assignment of a few functors (e.g.,
ACT, PAR, PRED) are solved automatically by the procedure from Böhmová et al. [1].
However, most of the functors have to be assigned manually. The amount of labour
involved in the manual annotation obviously slows down the growth of the PDT on

---

[*] I would like to thank my advisor Ivana Kruijff-Korbayová for her permanent support. I am also
indebted to Alevtina Bémová for consultations about functor assignment, to Petr Pajas for the
help with the data preprocessing and to Julia Hockenmaier for her useful comments.

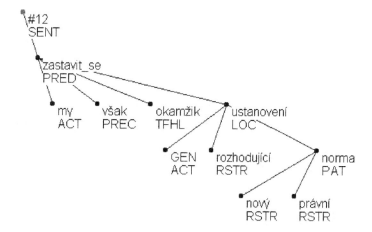

Fig. 1. TGTS of the sentence *Zastavme se však na okamžik u rozhodujících ustanovení nové právní normy.* (Let's however stop for a moment at the most important paragraphs of the new legal norm.)

the tectogrammatical level. Decreasing the amount of manual annotation has been the motivation for developing the more complex *automatic functor assignment system* (AFA) presented in this paper. Let us describe the starting position.

- No general unambiguous rules for functor assignment are known, human annotators use mostly only their language experience and intuition. We cannot reach 100% correctness of AFA since even the results of individual annotators sometimes differ.
- The annotators usually use the whole sentence context for their decision. It has not been measured how often it is really unavoidable to take the full context into account or how large the context must be.
- Preliminary measurements revealed that the distribution of functors is very non-uniform. The 15 most frequent functors cover roughly 90% of nodes. Conversely, there are hardly any examples for the least frequent functors.
- It would be very time consuming to test the performance AFA on randomly selected ATSs and find errors manually. Fortunately we can use the ATSs for which manually created TGTSs are already avaliable, annotate them automatically and compare the results against the manually annotated TGTSs.
- The available TGTSs contain imperfect data. Some errors are inherited from ATSs, and functor assignments are in some cases ambiguous (nodes with more than one functor) or incomplete (some nodes have no functor yet).

2   Materials

Training and Testing Sets. When I started working on AFA, 18 TGTS files were available, each containing up to 50 sentences from newspaper articles. This was a sufficient amount of data for knowledge mining, which can improve the AFA's performance. However, in order to reliably measure AFA's correctness, it is necessary to have a separate data set which has not been used for knowledge mining. Therefore I randomly selected 15 files for the training set and 3 files for the testing set. After removing incomplete and ambiguously assigned nodes, the training set contained 6049 annotated nodes, and the testing set 1089 annotated nodes.

Data Preprocessing. Neither the maximum degree of a node (i.e., the number of outgoing edges) nor the depth of a tree are limited in TGTSs. The trees thus can be very complex, and working with the whole tree context of the individual nodes would make AFA unnecessarily complicated. For the sake of the experiments described here, I assumed that reasonable correctness can be achieved using only information about the node to be annotated and about its governing node (i.e., about the edge in the tree). Thus the first step of the preprocessing was the *transformation from the tree structure into the list of edges*.

Each node in PDT can have tens of attributes, majority of them being useless for AFA. Hence, a selection of the relevant attributes is performed next (*feature selection*). I chose the following set: word form, lemma, full morphological tag and analytical function of both the governing and dependent node, preposition or conjunction which binds the governing and the dependent node, and the functor of the dependent node.

In order to make the subsequent processing easier, 3 additional simple attributes (the parts of speech of both nodes, the morphological case of the dep. node) were extracted from these 10 attributes (*feature extraction*). Finally, each accented character has been substituted with the corresponding ASCII character followed by "_". Having a vector of 13 symbolic attributes, the task of AFA can be now formulated as the *classification of the symbolic vectors into 60 classes*.

3   Implementation

The AFA system has been designed as a collection of small programs written mostly in Perl. Each method of functor assignment forms a separate program (script), the data to be assigned goes through a sequence of these scripts in a pipeline fashion. Each method can assign only those nodes which have not been assigned by any of the previous scripts yet. This approach enables flexible tuning of the AFA characteristics (precision, recall) simply by reordering or removing the individual methods. This advantage would be lost in the case of one compact complicated program.

Rule-Based Methods (RBM). The RBMs consist of simple hand written decision trees. They use no external data and therefore are independent of the quality of the training set. They do not bring any new information into the PDT, only transform the information contained in an ATS. Currently I have 7 methods with reasonable precision:

1. `verbs_active`: if the governing node is a verb in active form then
   - if the analytical function (afun) is subject, then the node is assigned the functor ACT ($\rightarrow$ ACT)
   - if afun is object and case is dative then $\rightarrow$ ADDR
   - if afun is object and case is accusative then $\rightarrow$ PAT

2. `verbs_passive`: if the governing node is a verb in passive form:
   - if afun is subject then → PAT
   - if afun is object and case is dative then → ADDR
   - if afun is object and case is instrumental then → ACT
3. `adjectives`: if the node corresponds to an adjective
   - if it is a possessive adjective then → RSTR
   - else → RSTR
4. `pronounposs`: if the node is a possessive pronoun then → APP
5. `numerals`: if the node is a numeral then → RSTR
6. `pnom`: if afun is PNOM then → PAT
7. `pred`: if afun is PRED then → PRED

Dictionary-Based Methods (DBM). It is not feasible to resolve all the remaining unassigned functors using only simple RBMs like those above, since we could not profit from the growing volume and diversity of the training set.

So far I have developed four methods using different types of dictionaries:

- `adverbs`: The couples *adverb–functor* were automatically extracted from the training set, and added to the list of adverbs from [2]; from the combined list, the *unambiguous* (accompanied always with the same functor) adverbs were extracted. Such a dictionary can be used to assign functors to adverbs.
  Examples from the dictionary: *výlučně* (exclusively) RHEM, *výrazně* (extensively) EXT
- `subconj`: A dictionary of unambiguous *subordinative conjunctions* was constructed in the same way as the dictionary of adverbs. If a verb is related to its governing node by one of these conjunctions, the functor can be easily assigned.
  Examples from the dictionary: *i když* (even when) CNCS,
  jelikož (because) CAUS, *jen co* (as soon as) TWHEN, *jestli* (if) COND
- `prepnoun`: All the *preposition–noun* pairs (a preposition followed by a noun) were extracted from the training set. The unambiguous couples which occurred at least twice were inserted into the dictionary.
  Examples from the dictionary: *v roce* (in year) TWHEN, *pro podnikatele* (for businessman) BEN, *od doby* (from time) TSIN, *z odvětví* (from branch) DIR1, *v zemích* (in countries) LOC
- `similarity`: The dictionary is formed by the entire training set. The functor of the most similar vector found in the training set is used for assignment. The (in)equality of individual attributes has different impact (weight) on the similarity function, e.g., the part of speech is more important than the lemma. The weights were determined experimentally. Example: for *zálohy na daně* (pre-payments of taxes), where the dependent node *daně* (taxes) is to be assigned a functor, the most similar record found is *návrh na stanovení* (proposal of determination), so the functor PAT of the dependent node is used.

4   Results

Testing Set. The testing set was not used in the mining of knowledge (dictionaries), therefore we can apply both rule-base and dictionary methods on it. For each method, six quantitative characteristics have been determined (Table 1):

- *Cover* = the number of all nodes assigned by the given method
- *Relative cover* = cover divided by number of all functors to be assigned (1089 in the training set). This number also reflects the frequency of several phenomena (e.g., possessive pronouns).
- *Errors* = the number of incorrectly assigned functors
- *Hits* = the number of correctly assigned functors
- *Recall* = the percentage of correct functor assignments by the given method among all functors to be assigned (hit/1089·100%)
- *Precision* = the percentage of correct functor assignments by the given method among all functors assigned by this method (hits/cover·100%)

Table 1. Results of AFA on the testing set

Method	Cover	Rel. cover	Hits	Recall	Errors	Precision
pred	104	9.5%	104	9.6%	0	100%
verbs_active	199	18.3%	184	16.9%	15	92.5%
verbs_passive	7	0.6%	6	0.6%	1	85.7%
pnom	34	3.1%	32	2.9%	2	94.1%
adjectives	177	16.3%	170	15.6%	7	96.0%
numerals	21	1.9%	15	1.4%	6	71.4%
pronounposs	16	1.5%	13	1.2%	3	81.3%
subconj	3	0.3%	2	0.2%	1	66.7%
adverbs	34	3.1%	30	2.8%	4	88.2%
prepnoun	9	0.8%	9	0.8%	0	100%
similarity	485	44.5%	287	26.4%	198	59.2%
Total	Σ=1089	Σ=100%	Σ=852	Σ=78.2%	Σ=237	78.2%

The methods listed in Table 1 are sorted in the same order as they were executed. This order permutation reaches the highest precision. The similarity method is handicapped by the fact that all easily solvable cases are assigned by its predecessors. If we use similarity alone, we get Recall=Precision=73%.

I believe that the results of this first implementation are satisfactory, I had expected lower overall precision. However, I cannot compare it to anything else, since there is no other AFA implementation with comparable recall within the PDT project.

Rule-Based Methods on Training Set. In order to verify the precision of RBMs, we can apply them on the training set as well (see Table 2). Note that the size of the training set is 6049 nodes.

Precision versus Recall. We have to decide whether we prefer to *minimise the number or errors* (i.e., maximising precision using only the methods with the best precision) or *maximise the number of correctly assigned nodes* (i.e., maximising recall using all the methods with admissible precision). The optimal compromise should be influenced by the *misclassification cost* which can be estimated as an amount of annotators' work for finding and correcting incorrectly assigned functors.

Table 2. Results of RBMs on the training set

Method	Cover	Rel. cover	Hits	Recall	Errors	Precision
pred	574	9.5%	554	9.2%	20	96.5%
verbs_active	973	16.1%	907	15.0%	66	93.2%
verbs_passive	34	0.6%	27	0.4%	7	79.4%
pnom	164	2.7%	152	2.5%	12	92.7%
adjectives	1063	17.6%	976	16.1%	87	91.8%
numerals	92	1.5%	66	1.1%	26	71.7%
pronounposs	64	1.1%	61	1.0%	3	95.3%
Total	Σ=2964	Σ=49.0%	Σ=2743	Σ=45.3%	Σ=221	92.5%

5   Conclusion and Future Work

I implemented several methods for automatic functor assignment, tested them and evaluated their characteristics. Methods based on rules had higher precision than dictionary-based methods. The possibility of combining individual approaches opened the question on whether we prefer to assign, e.g., 49% of functors with 92% precision or to assign everything with 78% precision.

All the available TGTSs are from newspaper articles. The distance between the training set and the testing set is thus rather small. If AFA were to be applied to other text than newspaper articles, it is likely that the resulting precision would be slightly lower.

As more manually annotated TGTSs become available, we can expect improvements on the dictionary-based methods. Moreover, it will hopefully be possible to discover some more rules for functor assignment by using the machine learning system C4.5; so far we have obtained promising preliminary results.

References

1. Böhmová, A., Panevová, J., Sgall, P.: *Syntactic Tagging: Procedure for the Transition from the Analytic to the Tectogrammatical Tree Structures.* Text, Speech and Dialogue, Springer (1999).
2. Hajičová, E., Panevová, J., Sgall, P.: *Manuál pro tektogramatické značkování.* ÚFAL MFF UK (1999).
3. Panevová, J.: *Formy a funkce ve stavbě české věty.* Academia (1980).
4. Petr Sgall, Eva Hajičová, and Jarmila Panevová: *The Meaning of the Sentence in its Semantic and Pragmatic Aspects.* Reidel, Dordrecht, The Netherlands (1986).

Categories, Constructions, and Dependency Relations

Geert-Jan M. Kruijff

Institute of Formal and Applied Linguistics
Faculty of Mathematics and Physics
Charles University, Prague
gj@cogsci.ed.ac.uk

Abstract. The paper discusses combining transparent intensional logic with (dependency-based) categorial grammars, based on the idea of a Curry-Howard correspondence between categories and semantics types.

1 Introduction

It is perhaps a geographical coincidence that one can draw a more or less straight line connecting Brno, Prague, Amsterdam and Edinburgh. But there are even more interesting connections to be made.

Edinburgh has been an important centre of developments in categorial grammar ever since the 1980's, side by side with Amsterdam where categorial grammar was (re-)married to Montague grammar to give rise to type-logical grammar; Prague has been a focal point of dependency grammar and information structure ever since the beginning of – already – last century, and Brno is the place where the spirit of transparent intensional logic (TIL) is kept high.

It seems that these approaches – dependency grammar, transparent intensional logic, and type-logical grammars – all can be considered to point to the following conception:

The linguistically realized meaning of a sentence relates the use of words in the sentence as an expression *to the* construction *of the sentence's (linguistic) meaning out of meanings of the individual words.*

The aim of this paper is to explore how these three approaches could possibly be combined. The advantages of a symbiosis of dependency grammar, TIL, and categorial grammar or categorial type logics can be briefly characterised as follows. Categorial type logics provide us with very powerful (formal *and* computational) means to describe intricate phenomena of surface structure, and using these logics to construct a dependency-based perspective on natural language grammar (DGL, [8]) enables us to model phenomena that arguably cannot be explained using a phrase-structure based approach. Furthermore, by using TIL we can tap into a considerable amount of research in formal semantics, whereas for TIL, DGL might provide the possibility for more fine-grained grammatical modelling.

P. Sojka, I. Kopeček, and K. Pala (Eds.): TSD 2000, LNAI 1902, pp. 51–56, 2000.

2   Three Strands

Dependency grammar, in its form as developed by Sgall et al. [19], describes linguistic meaning using dependency relations and the head/dependent distinction. Thus, linguistic meaning as a *representation* elucidates in a direct way who modifies what, and in what semantically relevant way. Sgall et al. describe various types of dependency relations that can hold between heads and dependents (see also Petkevič's [18] for a succinct overview). For the representation it is assumed that each dependent always has only one head (i.e. we are dealing with trees), and that each relation between a head and a dependent is classified as a *single* dependency relation.[1] Sgall et al., following Panevová's [16], describe (and distinguish) dependency relations in terms of syntactic behaviour.

Categorial grammar, particularly in its extended form as *categorial type logics* combining resource-sensitive proof systems with a typed λ-calculus (cf. work by Hepple [6], Moortgat [11], Morrill [12], and Oehrle [13,14]), gives rise to the above conception through the establishment of a Curry-Howard correspondence between proof formulas and λ-terms. A proof is not (just) a normative judgement – by virtue of the Curry-Howard correspondence, we build a representation of the sentence's linguistic meaning *in parallel* to establishing a syntactic structure, given the sentence's outer form. It is interesting and important to note that the λ-term representing linguistic meaning thus arrived at is – without exception – considered to be the *only* representation of the sentence. Syntactic structure in the Chomskyan sense is a useful but dispensable means to obtain our goal of relating the sentence's outer form to its (conceivable) linguistic meaning – a point that, we would argue, closely corresponds to the stress [19] lays on representing a sentence in terms of its linguistic meaning.

Finally, Tichý's transparent intensional logic as discussed by Materna in [9], describes meaning in terms of type-logical "constructions" that show how a meaning is constructed out of its components. A linguistic expression corresponds to a construction, which in turn can be evaluated to an object. An important characteristic is the distinction between constructions as representations of meaning, and the objects they can be associated to. Since we represent meaning as a *construction*, and not as an object, various semantic pitfalls are avoided. Moreover, the type logic is defined on a ramified hierarchy, meaning we can talk not just *in terms of* constructions, but also *about* constructions (without needing a metalanguage). That enables us to give – for example – a fairly straightforward logical account of propositional attitudes.

Available literature has pointed out various parallels between the above lines of thought. Categorial grammar and dependency grammar are closely related, as for example Bar-Hillel and Bach frequently pointed out. Montague Grammar and TIL have at occasion been compared, the latter often being argued for as preferable over the former – see for example Materna's [9]. And finally, TIL has been used in a couple of papers to provide a logical interpretation of core aspects of the representations used in Sgall et al.'s [19] – see for example [10,22].

Below we explore how we could try to weave these three lines of thought together. As the starting point for our exploration we take Dependency Grammar Logic (or DGL

---

[1] Observe that this is an *assumption* – cf. Dowty's discussion on the closely related thematic relations or θ-roles in [4].

for short), as introduced in [7] and described in detail in [8]. DGL is a categorial type logic that models dependency grammar, based on the intuitions behind the framework described by Sgall et al.[2]

3   Dependency Grammar Logic

DGL aims at describing the relation between a surface form and an (underlying) linguistic meaning that can be considered as being expressed by the outer form. The important questions there are of course, *how* form can be *indicative* of linguistic meaning, and what we consider to be the ingredients of linguistic meaning that can be expressed by form.

Following [19], the *structure* of linguistic meaning is phrased in terms of heads being modified by dependents, along particular dependency relations. When establishing the relation between surface form and linguistic meaning, we thus have to discern words (or word groups) as dependents and heads, making out what dependent modifies which head and along which type of relation. As Jakobson, Mathesius, and other authors in the Prague School have discussed at length (cf. [17,23]), *case* can assist us in that job (whereby we understand "case" to cover the various ways in which morphological case is realized across languages – cf. e.g. [3, Chapter 2]).

However, there are more aspects of form that are indicative of the underlying meaning of a sentence. For verbs, this concerns for example modality, tense and aspect. Steedman presents in [20] an elaborate model of tense and aspect (a model which DGL incorporates), explaining how tense and aspect give rise to *presuppositions* regarding relations holding between the meaning of the sentence and the context. These relations need not have to do primarily with temporality as such. Steedman advances the point that the relations are more generally concerned with aspects of causality and goal-directed action.

Finally, there are aspects of form that are indicative of a sentence's *information structure*. These *structural indications of informativity* [7,8] signify how the meaning of a particular word (or word group) is dependent on the already established context, or how it will affect that context (cf. Sgall et al.'s topic-focus articulation). Examples of structural indications are word order and intonation, cf. for example [19,21].

To recapitulate, we understand *form* here to be indicative of how the meanings of words and word groups relate to one another *structurally*, and how they relate to the preceding context or purport to affect the succeeding context. Dependency relations are "presupposition triggers" (in a loose sense of the word)[3], just as tense and aspect signify

---

[2] Needless to say, space limits us in how far we can take our exploration. For that reason, we will focus on pointing out the possibilities rather than discussing formal details. Where possible, we will refer to places where such details are available.

[3] Without any formal characterisation of what a presupposition is, we can only use the idea of presupposition triggers here in the loose sense. Whether a dependency relation will trigger a genuine presupposition in the sense as used in formal semantics or a weaker form, i.e. an allegation, will be dependent on information structure – cf. the discussion in [19]. Note that in [8], I characterise dependency relations primarily from this 'semantic' viewpoint, and conceive of syntactic behaviour as derived from that. On the contrary, Sgall et al. characterise

underlying presuppositions about, e.g., causal relations. Finally, form can be indicative of information structure.

Together this leads (in DGL) to an understanding of linguistic meaning as a structure indicating how meanings of words are related using dependency-relations, and how these meanings and their relations *project* presuppositions (and possibly, allegations) about referring to the preceding context, affecting the succeeding context, and presupposed temporal/causal/etc. relations. (See [8] for a detailed discussion.) The important point here is that, in keeping with for example [19] and dynamic approaches like Oehrle's [15], we do not *evaluate* the presuppositions against the larger context. Linguistic meaning only projects how, as far as the form has indicated it, the sentence "aims to" relate to the larger context. Whether it does (i.e. is felicitous) or not, is left for subsequent discourse interpretation.

In a sense, this appears to correspond to TIL's distinction between constructions and object – whereby DGL's linguistic meaning would correspond to the former, and the interpretation established by discourse interpretation could be considered to be like the latter.

To be able to represent linguistic meaning, DGL uses *hybrid logics* [2,1]. Traditionally, typed λ-calculi are used to represent "semantics" in categorial grammar, cf. e.g. [12,14]. As the above discussion already indicates, though, our linguistic meaning potentially contains a rich variety of information about modality, temporality, causality, reference, etc. For this purpose, DGL abandons the fairly monolithic traditional approach in favour for a system of modal logic that is capable of capturing the kind of ontological richness we need.

4   Weaving the Three Strands Together

In DGL, the underlying machinery for carrying out derivations establishing the relation between form and meaning is phrased as a resource-sensitive proof theory [11]. Traditionally, categorial type logics relate form and meaning through a Curry-Howard correspondence, established as follows. First, as Oehrle describes in detail in [14], the meanings of words are given in a (e, t)-typed λ-calculus. These definitions are translated into syntactic categories specifying the syntactic behaviour corresponding to the underlying meaning. Oehrle describes the translation as an isomorphism – in particular, there is an isomorphic relation between the number (and type) of arguments a verbal predicate takes and the corresponding syntactic functional category. Besides an isomorphism at the level of lexical meaning, there is also an isomorphism (or at least, a close correspondence) at the level of derivations. Fashioned after the original Curry-Howard isomorphism, each step in a proof (operating on a category) is reflected in the meaning. Thus, when we use natural deduction, composition (or elimination) corresponds to application at the level of meaning, and introduction corresponds to abstraction.

It is easy to see why this has lead various authors to claim that surface syntax is thus an artefact: this is a direct consequence of the correspondence between lexically assigned

---

dependency relations (strictly) in terms of their syntactic behaviour, without noting the influence that distinguishing different relations might have on a sentence's interpretation-in-context.

categories and meanings, and maintaining the correspondence between categories and meanings in a derivation.

Since DGL does not use a typed λ-calculus but a (many sorted or hybrid) modal logic, a correspondence is established in a slightly different fashion; namely, using a *linking theory*. The purpose of the linking theory is to relate dependency relations, specified in a predicate's valency frame, with a surface category. Naturally, it is for an important part based on the Praguian ideas about abstract case, how abstract case realizes dependency relations, and how different languages can realize case. The need for a more involved linking theory (rather than saying that "*e*'s map to N's") arises from the fact that we have a richer representation of meanings. At the same time, we broadly maintain the ideas expressed in Oehrle's [14] regarding the relation between categorial functions and predicate structure[4].

The way that we proceed in DGL to establish a relation between form and meaning is very different from Hadacz's proposal involving TIL. Hadacz discusses in [5] a so-called *translation procedure* translating forms into TIL-constructions. Contrary to DGL, syntactic composition appears to play little or no role in the translation procedure (possibly because Hadacz's model is based on a fragment of Czech that has a completely free word order). We would like to argue that this makes the approach too restricted to be generally applicable. For example, any phenomenon involving word order will be hard to model, like case realized through word order (cf. [3]), information structure, or restrictions on otherwise flexible word order (like clitic placement in Czech). Hadacz's model simply misses an explicit syntactic component.

At the same time, it is not difficult to imagine how we can overcome this problem, in almost exactly the same way as done in DGL. Like in DGL, we could establish a Curry-Howard correspondence – this time between (primitive) objects and constructions in TIL on the one hand, and syntactic categories on the other hand.

References

1. Patrick Blackburn. Internalizing labelled deduction. *Journal of Logic Computation*, 10(1):137–168, 2000.
2. Patrick Blackburn. Representation, reasoning, and relational structures: a hybrid logic manifesto. *Journal of the Interest Group in Pure Logic*, 8(3):339–365, 2000.
3. William Croft. *Typology and Universals*. Cambridge Textbooks in Linguistics. Cambridge University Press, Cambridge, United Kingdom, 1990.
4. David R. Dowty. On the semantic content of the notion "thematic role". In Giennaro Chierchia, Barbara H. Partee, and Raymond Turner, editors, *Properties, Types, and Meaning: Volume II, Semantic Issues*, volume 39 of *Studies in Linguistics and Philosophy*, pages 69–129. Kluwer Academic Publishers, Dordrecht, Boston, London, 1989.
5. Leo Hadacz. Semantic inference in the human-machine communication. In *Proceedings of Text, Speech and Dialogue '99*, Czech Republic, 1999. Springer Verlag.
6. Mark Hepple. A general framework for hybrid substructural categorial logics. Technical Report 94-14, IRCS, University of Pennsylvania, Philadelphia PA, September 1994.
7. Geert-Jan M. Kruijff. Dependency grammar logic: An introduction. Available from http://www.cogsci.ed.ac.uk/~gj/, November 1999.

---

[4] With some notable exceptions, as I noted in [7].

8. Geert-Jan M. Kruijff. *A Categorial Architecture of Informativity*. Ph.D. thesis, Institute of Formal and Applied Linguistics (ÚFAL), Faculty of Mathematics and Physics, Charles University, Prague, Czech Republic, f.c.

9. Pavel Materna. *Concepts and objects*, volume 63 of *Acta Philosophica Fennica*. Philosophical Society of Finland, Helsinki, Finland, 1998.

10. Pavel Materna, Eva Hajičová, and Petr Sgall. Redundant answers and topic-focus articulation. *Linguistics and Philosophy*, 10:101–113, 1987.

11. Michael Moortgat. Categorial type logics. In Johan van Benthem and Alice ter Meulen, editors, *Handbook of Logic and Language*. Elsevier Science B.V., Amsterdam New York etc., 1997.

12. Glyn V. Morrill. *Type Logical Grammar: Categorial Logic of Signs*. Kluwer Academic Publishers, Dordrecht, Boston, London, 1994.

13. Richard T. Oehrle. Multi-dimensional compositional functions as a basis for grammatical analysis. In Emon Bach, Richard T. Oehrle, and Deirdre Wheeler, editors, *Categorial Grammars and Natural Language Structures*, pages 349–389. D. Reidel, Dordrecht The Netherlands, 1988.

14. Richard T. Oehrle. Term-labelled categorial type systems. *Linguistics & Philosophy*, 17(6):633–678, December 1994.

15. Richard T. Oehrle. Binding as term rewriting. In Gosse Bouma, Erhard Hinrichs, Geert-Jan M. Kruijff, and Richard T. Oehrle, editors, *Constraints and Resources in Natural Language Syntax and Semantics*, pages 221–241. CSLI Press, Stanford CA, 1999.

16. Jarmila Panevová. On verbal frames in functional generative description I. *Prague Bulletin of Mathematical Linguistics*, 22:3–40, 1974.

17. Jarmila Panevová. Valency frames and the meaning of the sentence. In Philip Luelsdorff, editor, *The Prague School of Structural and Functional Linguistics*, volume 41 of *Linguistics and Literary Studies in Eastern Europe*, pages 223–243. John Benjamins, Amsterdam, 1994.

18. Vladimír Petkevič. A new formal specification of underlying structures. *Theoretical Linguistics*, 21(1):7–61, 1995.

19. Petr Sgall, Eva Hajičová, and Jarmila Panevová. *The Meaning of the Sentence in Its Semantic and Pragmatic Aspects*. D. Reidel Publishing Company, Dordrecht, Boston, London, 1986.

20. Mark Steedman. The productions of time. Draft 2.1, June 1998.

21. Mark Steedman. *The Syntactic Process*. The MIT Press, Cambridge Massachusetts, 2000.

22. Aleš Svoboda and Pavel Materna. Function sentence perspective and intensional logic. In René Dirven and Vilém Fried, editors, *Functionalism in Linguistics*, pages 191–205. John Benjamins, Amsterdam, The Netherlands, 1987.

23. Josef Vachek. *A Prague School Reader in Linguistics*. Indiana University Press, Bloomington, IN, 1964.

Local Grammars and Parsing Coordination of Nouns in Serbo-Croatian

Goran Nenadić

Faculty of Mathematics, University of Belgrade, Yugoslavia
goran@matf.bg.ac.yu

Abstract. Parsing coordination units is important as a part of preprocessing phase of an NLP tool. In this paper, a method for modelling and recognition of coordination of some noun phrase classes in Serbo-Croatian is presented. The model is based on local grammars and can be applied to a digital text by using an equivalent finite-state transducer. Therefore, the implementation of the model is efficient and can be embedded as a preprocessor in a system that performs further linguistic analysis of a digital text. In addition to the recognition of a coordination of noun phrases, we discuss possibilities to check some agreements between such a unit and other constituents of a sentence.

1 Introduction

The increasing production of electronically available texts (either on the Web or in other machine-readable forms such as digital libraries and archives) demands appropriate computer tools that can perform automatic processing of language resources. In the first place, a natural language processing (NLP) system needs to implement models for recognition and isolation of various lexical and syntactical units for further analysis. For example, an information extraction system or a Web search engine should implement procedures for extraction of strings of words which represent, for example, compound names [8], terms specific to a certain domain [2], etc. In this paper, we will analyse a method for modelling some types of coordination of nouns and/or noun phrases in Serbo-Croatian, and, additionally, an approach to automated recognition of string sequences which represent such units.

Since a coordination of noun phrases (abbr. CNP) usually plays a role as a subject or an object in a sentence, the problem of recognition and parsing coordination units is important as a part of preprocessing phase of an NLP tool. Using methods and procedures described in [5,6,8], we can recognise some classes of noun phrases (NPs) in a digital text, but the aim of this paper is to investigate a computational model for combining NPs in a wider syntactical unit that is grouped around a specific coordinating conjunction. The problem has been studied for both non-inflective (e.g. English [3]) and inflective languages (e.g. Czech [9]), although different approaches were undertaken.

A CNP can be very complex: such a unit can involve various noun phrases, prepositional phrases, names of people, companies, places, etc. In addition, since Serbo-Croatian is highly inflective, we have to use computationally effective way for recognition

P. Sojka, I. Kopeček, and K. Pala (Eds.): TSD 2000, LNAI 1902, pp. 57–62, 2000.

of lexical and syntactical units on one hand, and – on the other – we want to base our model on a formalism that is "well-adapted to model syntax of natural languages" [2]. Therefore, we have based the model on the system of electronic lexicons (abbr. **e-lexicon**) containing electronic dictionaries and local grammars [1]. In order to check some agreements that have to be followed, we have used extended regular expressions [6].

2   Background and Resources

The model for building a coordination of constituents of various types is usually described in detail in traditional grammar books [11]: a coordination consists of two or more comma separated units, which are coordinated by a specific relationship marked by using appropriate coordination conjunction. The type of the relationship determines the set of conjunctions, and vice versa. However, information presented in grammar books are incomplete for building corresponding computational procedure that can recognise a CNP in an unrestricted digital text. In order to complete the information needed, we have explored the corpus[1], and this revealed some additional examples of coordination usage. The model obtained by analysing both grammar books rules and the corpus, was compiled into **local grammars**.

We give a short overview of a notion of local grammar (for details, see [1,2]): a local grammar is a finite-state transducer that recognises "well formed" word sequences in a digital text and chooses the proper tags for them. It describes a set of related strings that have similar structures and that can be processed in a uniform way. A local grammar does not describe a sentence as a whole; however, it defines and applies lexical constraints to a local environment containing a sequence of several words. This way, local grammars can be used for lemmatisation, lexical disambiguation, recognition of syntactic units, etc. Some examples of local grammar application in Serbo-Croatian are presented in [4,5,6,8]. For example, the grammar <N> <ADJ:g> <N:g> denotes the set of three-word noun phrases that consist of a noun and frozen forms of an adjective and a noun in genitive case. This set includes phrases such as *Fakultet prime-njenih umetnosti* 'Faculty of Applied Arts', *Insitut društvenih nauka* 'Institute of Social Sciences', *operacija prirodnog spajanja* 'natural join operation', *jezik visokog nivoa* 'high level language', etc.

Since a local grammar is a finite-state transducer, it can be represented either by a graph [1,10] or by a regular expression, and is applied to a digital text after the initial tagging. The tagging is performed by the system of lexicons which consists of electronic dictionaries and pre-stored local grammars [1,10] used for reducing lexical ambiguities. An *electronic dictionary* is a specific database that models morphological characteristics of a specified language [1,10,12].

These resources are integrated into a corpus processing system INTEX [10], which is developed at the LADL (Laboratoire d'Automatique Documentaire et Linguistique), University Paris VII, and is adjusted for Serbo-Croatian at the University of Belgrade.

---

[1] The corpus we have been working with is a newspaper corpus containing news text taken from a few Yugoslav daily newspapers presented on the Internet. The bulk of it included text automatically collected from URLs http://www.blic.co.yu (home-page of daily newspaper "Blic") and http://www.politika.co.yu (home-page of daily newspaper "Politika").

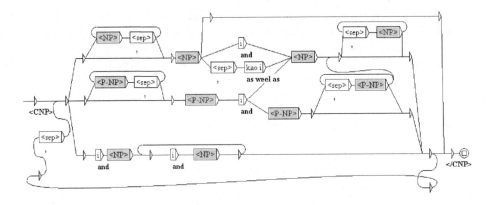

Fig. 1. A local grammar for CNPs containing coordinator *i* 'and'

3   Towards a Local Grammar for CNPs

Traditional grammar books describe several types of coordination of NPs: "conjunctive" coordination (marked by conjunctions *i, na, niti, pa, te, ...*), "disjunctive" coordination (conjunction *ili*), "adversative" coordination (conjunctions *a, ali, nego, već, ...*), "conclusive" coordination (marked by particles *dakle, prema tome, ...*), etc. The full list of *coordinators* (i.e. coordination conjunctions and particles) can be obtained from grammar books[2]. Grammar books additionally clearly state that – along with coordinators – comma is used as an obligatory separator of the constituents whenever there is no coordinator to separate two of them. This description, although informative for a native speaker, was not enough to construct the structure of a coordination. Therefore, we have applied an approach for constructing corresponding local grammars similar to those presented in [7] and [8], with coordinators being *keywords*. The initial step was to extract environments of coordinators from the part of the corpus[3], and to tag them using the system of e-lexicons (by means of the system INTEX).

During the next step, we have applied local grammars for NP recognition on the tagged extracted sequences, and kept only those that represented "well formed" CNPs.[4] Having isolated different types of CNP, corresponding structures were compiled into local grammars for CNP parsing. For the sake of obtaining local grammars which are reasonably complex and readable, we have clustered the structures into graphs that match the types of CNPs described in grammar books. However, by examining the corpus, some unlisted coordinators[5] and additional CNP structures appeared, and were compiled into local grammars as well.

---

[2] Our list initially contained 24 different coordinators.

[3] Since coordinators are not inflective, we did not have to lemmatise the corpus before extracting the environments.

[4] Extracted sequences contained coordinating sentences (clauses) as well, but they were discarded as we have restricted our research on CNPs.

[5] For example, some abbreviated forms of coordinators (e.g. *al', nit', il',* etc.) and colloquial forms (e.g. *jošte,* etc.) were found in the corpus.

60   G. Nenadić

In order to illustrate the results, we will present an example of a local grammar for coordinator *i* 'and' (Figure 1), and a graph that illustrates some specific CNP structures (Figure 2).[6] Figure 3 shows the sample of a text tagged using the local grammars for CNP parsing. The tags, obtained by means of output of the local grammars' transducers, mark CNPs as separate syntactical units in a SGML-manner.

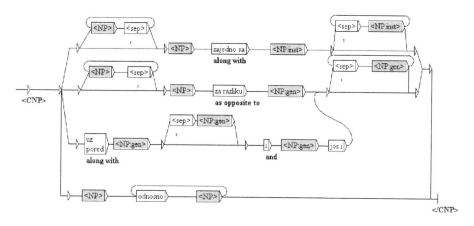

Fig. 2. A local grammar for CNPs containing various coordinators

The local grammars presented can recognise strings of words that form "potential" CNPs, as these local grammars do not check the agreements that constituents have to follow. First of all, NP constituents in a CNP have to agree in case, which can be modelled by extended morpho-syntactic regular expressions [6]. The general model (that is to be specialised for each of the graphs) is: (<NP:x> <sep>)* <NP:x> COORD_CONJ <NP> (<sep> <NP:x>))* denoting that a generic case (x) has to be the minimal morpho-syntactic feature that all constituents has to follow. In general, these agreements can be checked by procedures[7] described in [6]. On the other hand, when a COORD_CONJ is combined with a preposition (as illustrated by <NP:gen> nodes on Figure 3), the corresponding NPs have to appear in the fixed case determined by the preposition [7], which can be encoded in a corresponding local grammar.

Beside the case agreement of constituents, we have analysed the agreement between a CNP and corresponding adjectives and/or verb phrases. When an adjective or verb is to be "applied" to all constituents of a CNP, it is almost always in plural[8]. If all constituents have the same gender, an adjective or a verb could have the same

---

[6] The shaded boxes represent other graphs which describe noun phrases (subgraph <NP>) and prepositional phrases (subgraph <P-NP>). During the recognition process, the graphs are automatically invoked by INTEX.

[7] A procedure (written using `flex`) is used to check if there exists a feature that forms the intersection of features of the constituents.

[8] In some cases that are precisely determined by specific compound coordinators (e.g. *kao i* 'like'), the verb can appear in the singular form.

```
<CNP>Zatisxje i mir na Kosovu<CNP> traju vecy 48 sati, a
<CNP>vojska i policija</CNP> su se sa povukle u <CNP>kasarne i
baze</CNP>. Stanovnisxtvo je, prema oceni predstavnika MUP-a i
opsxtinskih vlasti, prepusxteno na <CNP>milost i nemilost</CNP>
ekstremistima, koji, kako nam rekosxe u ...

saznali smo od <CNP>profesora i roditelja</CNP> koji su takodye ...
... jer su profesori iz Beograda pokrivali sve ostale centre u
<CNP>Niksxicyu, Kragujevcu, Nisxu, Banjaluci i Palama</CNP>.

Ovakav govor silno zagolica <CNP>Kunigundu i Kandida</CNP>.
Kako je Kandid bio primoran da se rastavi <CNP>od lepe Kunigunde
i od starice</CNP>.

U sumraku njene sobe je tvrdio da zna visxe od nje<CNP>o Klajstu,
i Geteu, o SXeliju i Kitsu</CNP>. Njega, kome je poverila sve svoje
<CNP>uspomene i slutnje, sate i snove</CNP> ...
```

Fig. 3. A sample of a tagged text

gender (not obligatory); otherwise, the masculine is used regardless of the gender of constituents (e.g. *'nasi(A:p**m**) dragi(A:p**m**) dete(N:s**n**) i bake(N:p**f**)'* 'our dear child and grandmothers'). These agreements can be also checked by defining and applying extended regular expressions.

4   Conclusion and Further Research

This paper presents the initial stage of research in modelling coordination of noun phrases in a highly inflective language such as Serbo-Croatian. The method presented can be used for modelling new CNP structures and, consequently, for CNP parsing. Local grammars were constructed around typical keywords that denote coordinators. Since it is based on local grammars, i.e. finite-state tools, the implementation is efficient and can be embedded as a preprocessor in a system that performs further linguistic analysis of a digital text.

However, the local grammars presented are by no means complete, although they do not make false recognition. By examination of large corpora, local grammars can be improved: the percentage of successfully recognised coordination of nouns depends on the number of local grammars that are defined and applied to a digital text. For further research, we plan to enlarge and complete the local grammars presented.

Inserts that can occur between constituents of a CNP need to be parsed either as special "particles" (the list can be extracted only partially from grammar books) or as embedded sentences.[9] Further research includes parsing these complex inserts. Moreover, parsing some other types of coordination seems to be very important: in addition to coordination of NPs, coordination of adjectives (e.g. **Milanov i Petrov** *brat*) and adverbs (e.g. *išao je* **izmoreno ali sigurno**) have to be studied as well.

References

1. Gross M., Perrin D. (eds.): Electronic Dictionaries and Automata in Computational Linguistics, Lecture Notes in Computer Science, Berlin, Springer Verlag, 1989.
2. Gross M.: A Bootstrap Method for Construction Local Grammars, in Monograph on 125th anniversary of the Faculty of Mathematics, University of Belgrade, pp. 231-249, 1998.
3. Haugeneder H.: A Computational Model for Processing Coordinate Structures: Parsing Coordination will-out Grammatical Specification, Proc. of ECAI 92, Vienna, Austria, 1992.
4. Nenadić G.: Algorithms for compound word recognition in mathematical texts and applications, M.Sc. thesis, Faculty of Mathematics, University of Belgrade, 1997.
5. Nenadić G., Vitas D.: Formal Model of Noun Phrases in Serbo-Croatian, BULAG 23, Universite Franche-Compte, 1998.
6. Nenadić G., Vitas D.: Using Local Grammars for Agreement Modelling in Highly Inflective Languages, in Proc. of First Workshop TSD 98, Brno, 1998.
7. Nenadić G., Spasić I.: The Acquisition of Some Lexical Constraints from Corpora, in Text, Speech and Dialogue – TSD '99, Lecture Notes in Artificial Intelligence 1692, Springer Verlag, 1999.
8. Nenadić G, Spasić I: Recognition and Acquisition of Compound Names from Corpora, in NLP-2000, Lecture Notes in Artificial Intelligence, Berlin, 2000.
9. Petkevič V.: Nominal Subject and Verbal Predicate, in Proc. of Third European Conference on Formal Description of Slavic Languages FDSL-3, 1999.
10. Silberztein M.: Dictionnaries électroniques et analyse automatique de textes: le systéme INTEX, Masson, Paris, 1993.
11. Stanojčić Ž., Popović LJ.: Gramatika srpskoga jezika, Zavod za udžbenike i nastavna sredstva, Beograd, 1994.
12. Vitas, D.: Mathematical Model of Serbo-Croatian Morphology (Nominal Inflection), Ph.D. thesis, Faculty of Mathematics, University of Belgrade, 1993.

---

[9] Consider examples: *Pozvao je Peru, Marka* **a bogami čak** *i Milana* 'He invited Peter, Marko and even Milan as well', or *Pozvao je Peru, Marka,* **a juče je pozvao čak** *i Milana.* 'He invited Peter, Marko and yesterday he invited Milan as well'.

Realization of Syntactic Parser for Inflectional Language Using XML and Regular Expressions*

Marek Trabalka and Mária Bieliková

Slovak University of Technology
Department of Computer Science and Engineering
Ilkovičova 3, 812 19 Bratislava, Slovakia
trabalka@dcs.elf.stuba.sk, bielik@elf.stuba.sk
http://dcs.www.elf.stuba.sk/~trabalka/,
http://dcs.www.elf.stuba.sk/~bielik/

Abstract. In the paper we present a method of syntactic parsing for inflectional language. This method consists of several steps including morphological and syntactical levels of analysis. We proposed a bottom-up model of syntactic analysis of the sentence. Its advantage is in the case of ill-formed sentence because the analyser is still able to parse at least parts of the sentence. We describe also experimental implementation of the proposed method, which is based on the use of XML and regular expressions.

1 Introduction

Syntactic parsing plays an important role in natural language processing. Most of today's research and practice in syntactic parsing is concerned with the English language. The concentration on English has resulted in advances in solving its linguistic problems. However, parsing text written in other languages often requires solving different problems. Performance of syntactic parsers for the English language is often not satisfactory, in particular, for inflectional languages [4].

Inflectional languages (e.g., Slavonic languages such as the Slovak, Czech, or Russian languages) use more morphology than English does. Words in these languages have usually several different morphological forms that are created by changing a suffix. Each form represents some morphological attributes like case, number or gender. Morphology in inflectional languages strongly influences syntax. In an English sentence, meaning is determined by order of words while, e.g., in Slovak it depends primarily on the word form and word order is not so strict. On the other hand, syntactical analysis of a sentence in an inflectional language carried out after successful morphological analysis is a simpler task than that in English.

In this paper we present a method of syntactic parsing for inflectional language. This method consists of several steps including morphological and syntactical analyses.

---

* The work reported here was partially supported by Slovak Science Grant Agency, grant No. 95/5195/605 and project INCO Copernicus, No. 977069, European Research Network for Intelligent Support of Electromyographic Studies: EMG-Net.

P. Sojka, I. Kopeček, and K. Pala (Eds.): TSD 2000, LNAI 1902, pp. 63–68, 2000.

We proposed a bottom-up model of syntactic analysis of the sentence. This approach is suitable, in particular, for parsing an ill-formed sentence because the analyser is able to parse at least parts of the sentence. It can also be used for parsing grammatically correct text. One of the positive features of our approach is that it does not depend heavily on a morphological lexicon. It can extend existing approaches for morphological analysis (e.g., improve grammar checking of existing spell-checkers by considering the context of the whole sentence). The proposed method is suitable for using in a situation where unknown word form has to be analysed for its morphological category. We describe an experimental implementation of the proposed method, which is based on the use of XML and regular expressions.

2   Bottom-Up Syntactic Analysis

Relations between words and clauses in a sentence written in an inflectional language are primarily expressed by an agreement on the equality of some morphological categories. For example, a noun phrase in the Slovak language can be formed by a noun, preceded by one or more adjectives where these adjectives have the same gender, case and number. Such rules regarding regular phrases and sentences influence connections between words and disambiguate their alternative forms suggested by morphology.

For languages with a strong word order, the use of a top-down parser is highly recommended because of its prediction features. On the other hand, the order of sentence constituents in the inflectional language is not strict and often is driven more by human intuition than by the rigid regulations specified by linguists [4]. Therefore, the design of a top-down syntactic parser for inflectional language requires consideration of many possible combinations of words in the sentence. In this case, bottom-up syntactic parsing is more suitable.

With inflectional languages, it is possible to determine even the role of a word at the centre of the sentence when no analysis of previous words has been made. We use morphological categories of words and rules for connecting words into phrases. These phrases are then used to build longer and longer phrases and finally combine them into a sentence. Words are not processed from the left to the right (such as in [2]), but the processing depends on their potential role and priority of a syntactic rule used.

In the process of syntactic analysis, a parsing graph is created. A sentence is represented by the graph of connected words. At the beginning of the process, all possible morphological categories of each word are found. After this analysis, an initial parsing graph is created: all morphological categories become nodes, and edges are created between all forms of two neighbouring words. Next, a new node is created using syntactic rules about how to connect word forms into a phrase. Each new node is connected to all predecessors of the first node of the created phrase and also to all successors of the last node of this phrase. The parser has to remember application of each rule on each combination of words and finish when there is no other applicable rule available.

The process of analysis can be finished also when such a top node is created that has neither predecessors nor successors, i.e. the node representing the whole sentence, is created. In this case, the parsing process is successful.

The procedure of parsing consists of the following steps:

1. Perform morphological analysis on each word from the sentence (base form and grammatical categories of each word are determined; the result can be ambiguous).
2. Create list of nodes (a node represents base form together with grammatical categories; for each morphological alternative, a separate node is created). Create oriented edges that concatenate nodes representing neighbouring words in the sentence.
3. Put all syntactic rules into the set of applicable rules and sort them by defined priority.
4. If the set of applicable rules is empty, go to step 9.
5. Select the first applicable rule. Let its length be n.
6. Try to unify each n-tuple of concatenated nodes with the right hand side of the selected syntactic rule. Try only those n-tuples that were not tested with that rule before.
7. If the unification is successful, create a new node(s) using the left hand side of the rule with bound variables. Create oriented edges from each predecessor of the first node of the original n-tuple that ends in the first node of the new m-tuple. Similarly create also edges from the last node of the new m-tuple to all successors of the original n-tuple.
8. If there are some successful applications of the rule, continue by step 3, otherwise follow the next step.
9. If there is a node with neither predecessors nor successors, parsing will be successful. Such node represents a full sentence and its parse tree can be created by analysing the history of node creations. If there are no such nodes, parsing will be unsuccessful.

Figure 1 illustrates the parsing graph of the Slovak sentence *"Pekný veľký strom rastie"* ("A nice big tree grows"). Based on the syntactic rule, the node NOUNPHRASE(N,sg,m) is created from the nodes ADJ(sg,m) (the word *veľký*) and NOUN(N,sg,m) (the word *strom*). Next, this phrase is connected with the adverb *pekný* (its form ADV(N,sg,m)) and another noun phrase is created. Finally this phrase is connected to the verb *rastie* (in the form VERB(3,sg)) and the node represented the whole sentence SENTENCE() is created. The sentence is therefore parsed successfully.

The main advantage of the proposed bottom-up syntactic parser is to minimise necessary processing of rules over different groups of nodes (words in a sentence). Efficiency of the analysis is influenced by the quality of morphological analysis and its performance.

3   Morphological Analysis

The syntax of inflectional languages strongly depends on morphology, i.e. word form influences potential syntactic role of a word in a sentence. Morphology in such languages is based on suffixes that combine several morphological categories, e.g. gender, case or number.

Our approach to morphological analysis is based on subsequent refining of partial results. Our aim was to support the analysis of unknown words.

We proposed two levels of morphological analysis. The first level is based on suffix analysis and the second level on the definition of paradigms, which represent different word forms. To automate the process of binding an unknown word to an appropriate

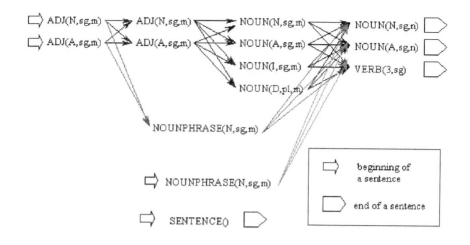

Fig. 1. An example of the parsing graph

paradigm, we devised a method of adaptive morphological analysis [6]. This method uses paradigms and heuristics to compute an acceptance probability of the particular word. The acceptance probability expresses a degree of belief in the correct determination of paradigm for the word.

An input to the method is a word, which is subject to the morphological analysis. The output is the determination of possible forms for this word (morphological tags) with an acceptance probabilities for each tag alternatives of the analysed word. These alternatives and their acceptance probabilities are computed by means of linguistic knowledge. Linguistic knowledge is either filled in advance by an expert, or learned by the system during the previous analysis.

For purposes of syntactic analysis, we do not need a base form of the word. To improve effectiveness of a paradigm check, we proposed an advanced suffix analysis, which precedes our adaptive morphological analysis. It is used when the analysed word is not found in the morphological lexicon. Suffix analysis is not a completely new idea. Many authors use such approach to increase performance of lemmatisation, but they usually check only grammatical suffix. However, in this case there is high ambiguity of the analysis.

In fact, many words have typical endings, which determine some of their morphological categories. However, these typical endings often contain also some letters before the actual grammatical suffix. Our approach is also applicable for checking letters before the grammatical suffix. For example, the (nongrammatical) suffix *-pcia* in the Slovak language is typical for feminine nouns in singular nominative. On the other hand, the grammatical suffix *-a* can determine verb, noun, or adjective in various numbers, cases and genders.

The main advantage of the proposed approach is that the process of suffix analysis is straightforward and fast. It can also disambiguate some alternatives in very early stage of analysis. However, such analysis can produce more results (possible word categories), because not all suffixes are unambiguous. In order to perform suffix analysis, we checked a stock of language words and introduced meaningful suffixes into a lexicon.

4   XML and Regular Expressions

The proposed method of syntactic analysis is realised using two technologies: XML and regular expressions. XML (eXtensible Markup Language) was developed as a universal tool for describing structures and documents [1]. We use XML to describe state of the process of analysis, lexicons and all necessary static structures. Regular expressions are used to represent rules, i.e. the dynamic character of the parser. Combination of these two approaches provides interesting and robust features. It enables the unified representation of static and dynamic aspects of natural language processing.

The static part (XML) is represented mainly by lexicons (morphological lexicon, paradigms definitions, suffix lexicon) and texts. It can be considered as knowledge base together with working memory of the knowledge-based system. There are many ways how different authors solve the storage of these data and knowledge. They often use some self-defined text formats or database tables (see e.g. how word can be tagged [3]).

The dynamic part (regular expressions) determines the way of change, manipulation, or transformation of the static part. We exploit the fact that the arbitrary change can be considered as transformation of strings. Such dynamic part is meaningful only if there exists a text form of processed entities. XML is an ideal candidate for this purpose.

In the following we illustrate several examples. Each word form in a node of the parsing graph is represented by an XML string, e.g.:

```
    <NOUN paradigm="otec" case="4" number="sg"
gender="m">mládenca</NOUN>
```

Rules are described using regular expression substitutions. They are represented by a tag RULE which consists of two parts:

```
    <RULE> s{left-hand-side}{right-hand-side} </RULE>
```

The left hand side of the rule determines the text to be substituted, the right hand side specifies the text used for substitution. An example below illustrates a syntactic rule which combines attribute and nounphrase into the nounphrase:

```
    <RULE cf="8.5">
     s{ <ATTRIBUTE
           (animate="\w*")  (case="\d*")
 (number="\w*")(gender="\w*")>(\r*)
       </ATTRIBUTE>
       <NOUNPHRASE \1 \2 \3 \4 (person="\d*")
          (compoundnumber="\w*")>(\r*)
       </NOUNPHRASE>
     }
     { <NOUNPHRASE $1 $2 $3 $4 $6 $7>$5 $8</NOUNPHRASE>
     }m
    </RULE>
```

Rules are exploited in all levels of the analysis. On the morphological level, rules are used for paradigm specification. In this case, a rule specifies transformation between different forms of the word. On the syntactical level, rules describe transformation of morphological categories of words into phrases and phrases into the sentence.

5   Conclusions

The proposed syntactic parsing method is aimed to be used for the Slovak language. However, it can also be used for other languages with a rich morphology. We emphasise differences between languages with a weak morphology where different algorithms and methods are used.

We implemented the proposed method of bottom-up syntactic parsing for performing grammar checking of sentences [5]. The system combines words into phrases and when it finally achieves only one top node, parsing is successful and the sentence is correct. On the other hand, when there are still more nodes after analysing all combinations, the sentence is probably incorrect.

Our approach takes advantage of a refined processing of the sentence in several adjoining phases. The analysis exploits the morphological information of particular suffixes. Suffix analysis often produces ambiguous results although in the particular context the word often has only one meaningful form. This limitation is resolved by including the adaptive morphological analysis [6] and the syntactic analysis that reduce the number of possible alternatives.

References

1. Bradley. N. The XML companion. Addison Wesley, Harlow, England, 1998.
2. Hausser, R.: Newcat: Parsing Natural Language using Left-Associative Grammar. Berlin, Springer-Verlag, 1986.
3. Nenadic, G., Vitas, D. Using Local Grammars for Agreement Modeling in Highly Inflective Languages. In Proceedings of TSD '98, P. Sojka, V. Matoušek, K. Pala, I. Kopeček (Eds.), Masaryk University Press, pp. 91–96, 1998.
4. Smrž, P., Horák, A. Implementation of Efficient and Portable Parser for Czech. In Proc. of TSD '99, V. Matoušek, P. Mautner, J. Ocelíková, P. Sojka (Eds.), Springer Verlag, LNAI 1692, pp. 105–108, 1999.
5. Trabalka, M. Grammar-checker for the Slovak Language. Diploma Thesis. Slovak University of Technology. 1999. (in Slovak).
6. Trabalka, M., Bieliková, M. Performing Adaptive Morphological Analysis Using Internet Resources. In Proc. of TSD '99, V. Matoušek, P. Mautner, J. Ocelíková, P. Sojka (Eds.), Springer Verlag, LNAI 1692, pp. 66–71, 1999.

A Rigoristic and Automated Analysis of Texts Applied to a Scientific Abstract by Mark Sergot and Others

Gregers Koch

Department of Computer Science (DIKU), Copenhagen University
Universitetsparken 1, DK-2100 Copenhagen, Denmark
gregers@diku.dk

Abstract. We discuss the automated construction of a translation mechanism capable of translating from any given textual input into some preferred logical notation. By constructing a syntax tree for the input text, we can augment it with semantic features through a data-flow analysis, in such a way that the parser in the shape of a (DCG) Prolog program may be extracted immediately. Over the years, our methods building on those principles, have been developed so that they seem to be mature for manipulating normal complicated texts meant for human communication now. Here scientific abstracts seem to be very interesting. We shall discuss the analysis of a particular scientific abstract, namely that from an article by M. Sergot et al. [10]. A highly tentative comparison is made with several important alternative approaches, known from the scientific literature.

1   Introduction

As an activity combining logic programming and language technology, we are studying certain problems in computational linguistics, in particular problems concerning the automation of data-flow analysis leading to the automatic synthesis of a special kind of data-flow structures. This automated approach may be applied for inductive purposes. The approach is sometimes called logico-semantic induction, and it constitutes an efficient kind of automated program synthesis.

Here we shall discuss the automated construction of such a translation mechanism which is capable of translating from any given textual input to some preferred logical notation. By means of a context-free grammar and using this for constructing a syntax tree for the input text, we can augment the syntax tree with semantic features through a data flow analysis [1].

This can be done in such a way that the parser in the shape of a Definite Clause Grammar (DCG) or Prolog program may be extracted immediately.

2   A Small Example

Before starting with the text, we might as well analyse at least one utterly simple example in order to present and understand the approach recommended here. The tiny example is the following sentence consisting of three words only:

```
Peter kicks Pluto
```

P. Sojka, I. Kopeček, and K. Pala (Eds.): TSD 2000, LNAI 1902, pp. 69–74, 2000.
© Springer-Verlag Berlin Heidelberg 2000

This sentence can trivially be described by the following context-free grammar:

```
S -> NP VP.
NP -> Prop.
VP -> TV NP.
```

The syntax tree corresponding to the sentence may be augmented into a data-flow structure.

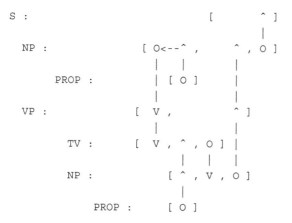

In this context, it makes sense to read the diagram in the following way. The structure constitutes an augmented syntax tree (the indentations hint at the form of the syntax tree), that is a tree structure where each node of the tree has the name of a syntactic category as its label. We consider it augmented because each node also has one or several attributes, and each attribute may have an entire logical formula as its value. The attributes are indicated in square brackets in the diagram.

The first line of the diagram shows that the node with label S (for Sentence) needs a single attribute only, let us call it AS. The node with the label NP (for Noun Phrase) needs four attributes, (if typographically possible separated by commas), let us call them ANP, BNP, CNP and DNP. The horizontal arrow shows that ANP and BNP have the same value. The vertical arrow between the first and the second lines shows that AS and DNP have the same value. The node with the label PROP (for Proper Name) has a single attribute APROP that has the same value as BNP, due to the vertical arrow. The node with the label VP (for Verb Phrase) has two attributes AVP and BVP. The vertical arrows over this line of the diagram show that AVP has the same value as ANP and BVP has the same value as CNP. The next node with the label TV (for Transitive Verb) has three attributes ATV, BTV and CTV. The leftmost vertical arrow over this line in the diagram shows that ATV has the same value as AVP. The next node with the label NP (for Noun Phrase as before) also has three attributes. In order to distinguish them from the attribute of the NP node mentioned before, we might call them ANP', BNP' and CNP'. The vertical arrows over this line indicate that ANP' has the same value as BTV, BNP' has the same value as CTV, and CNP' has the same value as BVP. Finally, as the last line of the diagram we have a node labelled PROP (again, for Proper Name) with a

single attribute APROP'. The vertical arrow over the last line shows that APROP' has
the same value as ANP'.

As we have seen here, this diagram contains an awful lot of information, but
nevertheless it can easily and mechanically be transformed into a tiny little Definite
Clause Grammar (DCG) that really is a small logic program:

```
s(Z)  --> np(X,Y,Z), vp(X,Y).
np(X,Y,Y) --> prop(X).
vp(X,W)  --> tv(X,Y,Z), np(Y,Z,W).
```

Supplied with suitable lexical information, for instance:

```
prop(peter) --> [peter].
prop(pluto) --> [pluto].
tv(X,Y,kicks(X,Y)) --> [kicks].
```

it constitutes a executable logic program, the parser.

If we execute this program with the given sentence as input, we shall get the matchings
(here we change the names of the variables to obtain unambiguity) as in Figure 1.

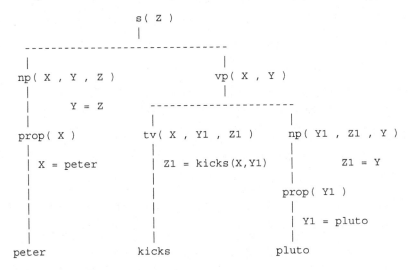

Fig. 1. Matchings of the logic program

The matchings (unifications) obtained through the execution of the program would
result in the following equations:

```
Y = Z
X = peter
Z1 = kicks(X,Y1)
Z1 = Y
Y1 = pluto
```

This small equational system will have the following solution:

```
[peter kicks pluto]
      = Z
      = Y
      = Z1
      = kicks(X,Y1)
      = kicks(peter,pluto)
```

And that gives us a precise suggestion for a semantic representation of the input sentence.

Instead, we might have obtained the logic program from the suggested input and output. This can be done automatically by means of one of our inductive meta programs [6,7,8].

This parser needs test runs, both forward and backward. In case all these have been successful, we definitely have made a very detailed scrutiny of the constructive situation.

And now, looking at the control aspects, let us make a list or schema of the analytical steps performed here. The steps are:

```
 1. example
 2. syntax
 3. data-flow
 4. definite clause grammar
 5. lexical information
 6. execution
 7. equations
 8. solution
 9. induction
10. forward test run.
11. backward test run.
```

The most important description levels in this example seem to be: 1) the text (input), 2) the formula (output or semantic representation), 3) the data-flow, 4) the parser.

3   Application to a Scientific Abstract

Over the years, our methods building on those principles, have been developed so that they seem now to be mature for manipulating normal complicated texts meant for human communication. Here we consider scientific abstracts to be highly interesting, mainly because they normally are concise and very complicated. In what follows, we shall discuss the analysis of a particular scientific abstract, namely that from an article by M. Sergot et al. [10]. The text simply reads:

```
"The formalisation of legislation and the development
 of computer systems to assist with legal problem
 solving provide a rich domain for developing and
 testing artificial-intelligence technology".
```

The resulting semantic structure became the following

```
result(empty(x,legislation(x)&
  the(y,of(formalisation(y),x)&
    empty(x1,computer(systems(x1))
      &empty(w,legal(problem(solving(w)))&with(assist(x1),w))
      &the(y1,of(development(y1),x1)
          &empty(v,artificialintelligence(technology(v))
            &exists(z,for(rich(domain(z)),
                developingAndTesting(t,v))
              &provide(y&y1,z)))))))).
```

4 Discussion

In a tentative comparison with some important alternative approaches, it makes sense to distinguish between the design of representation, manual programming, and automated program synthesis.

Hans Kamp and followers [2] seem to handle the design of representation very well. I do not know if they can produce the hand-coded programs. Roger Schank and followers [9] seem to be able to handle both the design and the hand-coded programming. However, we should notice that their software solutions seem to suffer from mediocre reproducibility. As to other approaches, including that of Professor Kawaguchi and others [4,11], they can handle the design of representation, but they seem unable to produce the hand-coded translation software. Some other alternatives were discussed in earlier papers (see [5]). None of the mentioned alternative approaches seems to be able to produce the automated program synthesis. In contrast, my project reported here seems to handle the design of representation rather well and to give partial solutions to the manual programming (Steps 3–8) and the automated program synthesis (Steps 9–11). In short, the method advocated here seems to be unique compared to today's scientific literature.

Acknowledgements

Acknowledgements are due to Dr. Laszlo Bela Kovacs of Copenhagen University and to the anonymous referees for their critical and constructive remarks and suggestions.

References

1. C. G. Brown and G. Koch, (Eds.), *Natural Language Understanding and Logic Programming, III*, (North-Holland, 1991).
2. H. Kamp, U. Reyle, *From Discourse to Logic*. Kluwer, Amsterdam, 1993.
3. H. Kangassalo et al., (Eds.), *Information Modelling and Knowledge Bases VIII*, IOS, 1997.
4. E. Kawaguchi et al., Toward development of multimedia database system for conversational natural language, 69–84 in [3].

5. E. Kawaguchi et al., (Eds.), *Information Modelling and Knowledge Bases XI*, IOS, 2000.
6. G. Koch, Some perspectives on induction in discourse representation, 318–327, in A. Gelbukh (Ed.), *Proceedings of CICLing-2000*, Mexico City, Mexico, 2000.
7. G. Koch, A method for making computational sense of Situation Semantics, 308–317, in A. Gelbukh (Ed.), *Proceedings of CICLing-2000*, Mexico City, Mexico, 2000.
8. G. Koch, A method of automated semantic parser generation with an application to language technology, 103–108 in [5].
9. R.C. Schank, *Dynamic Memory*, Cambridge University Press, 1982.
10. M. Sergot et al., The British Nationality Act as a logic program, *Communications of the ACM*, Vol. 29, no. 5, pp. 370–386.
11. S. Yoshihara et al., An experiment on Japanese sentence generation from SD-formed semantic data, 205–221, in [5].

Evaluation of Tectogrammatical Annotation of PDT
First Observations

Eva Hajičová and Petr Pajas

Faculty of Mathematics and Physics, Charles University, Prague, Czech Republic
hajicova@ufal.ms.mff.cuni.cz, pajas@ufal.ms.mff.cuni.cz

Abstract. Two phases of an evaluation of annotating a Czech text corpus on an underlying syntactic level are described and the results are compared and analysed.

1   Introduction: Tectogrammatical Annotation of the Prague Dependency Treebank

Tagging of the Prague Dependency Treebank (PDT in the sequel) on the underlying syntactic layer (resulting in tectogrammatical tree structures, TGTSs) is an ambitious task, the realization of which must be carefully supervised and regularly evaluated, in order to reach the proclaimed aims and to obtain (theoretically and applicationally) interesting and applicable results. In the present contribution, we describe one of the steps in the introduction of large-scale tagging of a very large corpus.

Tectogrammatical tagging of PDT is carried out in two phases:

(i) an automatic preprocessing transforming the analytic tree structures (ATSs) into structures that are half-way to the TGTSs,

(ii) manual "shaping" of the TGTSs into their final forms. The human annotators have at their disposal a manual [2] and there are regular (weekly) instructive sessions.

2   Description of the Evaluation Experiment

In order to evaluate the quality of the manual and the instructive sessions and to make estimates about the difficulty of the tagging task (as well as to predict the speed of tagging), we have carried out the following experiment.

Three annotators (all linguists with a university-level education, two having a Ph.D. in linguistics) were given one (randomly chosen) sample of (newspaper) text taken from the Czech National Corpus, which consisted of 50 sentences, with their ATSs preprocessed by the automatic preprocessing procedure mentioned above. They had the manual at their disposal and were asked to tag the sentences according to the manual without negotiations among themselves about the unclear issues. The task of the annotators was to check the dependency structure as such and to assign to the particular values of the dependency relations (functors). They were also supposed to check the lexical values

P. Sojka, I. Kopeček, and K. Pala (Eds.): TSD 2000, LNAI 1902, pp. 75–80, 2000.

of the nodes and to add appropriate lexical values in case they added some node in the TGTS that was deleted in the surface structure and therefore was missing also in the ATS. A special programme was written to compare the results of the three annotators sentence by sentence (actually, word by word (or node by node)) and to summarise some statistical and qualitative results.

After the evaluation of the results and after a thorough discussion during several instructive sessions about the points in which the annotators differed, we have repeated the same task with the same annotators annotating another randomly chosen set of 47 sentences, to compare the results in order to obtain some judgements about the degree of improvements of the quality of tagging and also to make some predictions about the speed.

3   The First Round of the Experiment

Out of the total of 50 sentences, only for 10 of them all the annotators gave the same TGTSs; since the number of occurrences of dependency relations in these sentences was not greater than 3, this is a negligible portion of the whole set. The distribution of the number of sentences and the number of differences (one difference means that one dependency relation or a part of a label of a node was assigned in a different way by one of the annotators) is displayed in Table 1.

Table 1. The distribution of the number of sentences and the number of differences

No. of diff.	1	2	3	4	5	6	7	9	10	11	13	14	20	21	27
No. of sent.	3	4	4	5	3	3	4	1	6	2	1	1	1	1	1

Table 2. Distribution of sentences according to the number of differences in each sentence ignoring the differences in lemmas

No. of diff.	1	2	3	4	5	6	7	8	9	10	11	18	20	21
No. of sent.	6	4	3	7	4	3	3	2	2	2	1	1	1	1

Let us note that the number of dependency relations is slightly smaller than the number of words in the sentence, due to the fact that more nodes get taken away than newly restored. The total number of occurrences of dependency relations (i.e. edges) in the test set was 720; the number of differences was 290. Out of this total number of differences, there were 56 differences in lemmas, 64 differences in the determination of which node depends on which node, and 58 differences in the restoration of nodes not appearing in the ATSs but restored – at least by one of the annotator – in the TGTSs. This leads us to the total of 178 differences in other features than the values of the dependency relations, i.e. out of the total of 720 occurrences of dependency relations (edges) in the first set of sentences, there were 112 differences in the assignment of the values of these relations, and 64 differences in the establishment of the edges. It is interesting to note that while the trees with difference 0 were more than simple, the trees with the number of differences $N = 1$ were rather complicated (including 13, 9 and 18 relations respectively), and the same holds about $N = 2$ (12, 5, 9, 15), and $N = 3$ (26, 11, 17, 4). The sentences with $N > 10$ were almost all complex sentences with one or more coordinated structures ($N = 11, 13, 20$), with several general participants expressed by a zero morph ($N = 21$), structures with focus-sensitive particles in combination with negation and with general participants ($N = 14$), and a structure with several surface deletions that should be restored in the TGTS ($N = 27$).

The following observations seem to be important:

(a) The dependency relations (i.e. edges) were correctly established in all cases with the following exceptions:
   (i) the position of focussing particles.
   (ii) the apposition relation was attached differently in one case
   (iii) in several cases, the edges for obligatory, though (superficially) deletable, complementations of verbs were missing with one or two annotators.
   Improvements to be done: for (i) and (ii), more specific instructions should be formulated in the manual; (iii) will improve once the basic lexicon is completed with the assignment of verbal frames specifying the kinds of obligatory complementations.
(b) Lexical labels: the differences concerned uncertainties in assigning the value Gen (for a general participant) and 'on' (pronoun 'he' used in pro-drop cases) and cor (used in cases of control). Improvement: these cases are well-definable and should be more clearly formulated in the manual.
(c) Values of dependency relations: The instructions give a possibility to put a question mark if the annotator is not sure or to use alternatives (two functors). The differences mostly concern uncertainties of the annotators when they try to decide in favour of a single value; other differences are rather rare and concern issues that are matters of linguistic discussions.

4   The Second Round of the Experiment

In the second round of the task, we have evaluated the assignment of TGTSs to 47 sentences in another randomly chosen piece of text (again, taken from the newspaper corpus). When analysing the results, we faced a striking fact (not so prominent in the first round): there was a considerable amount of differences in the shape rather than in the value of the lexical tags, esp. with lemmas of the general participants (Gen vs. gen) and of the added nodes for co-referring elements (Cor vs. cor). Also, other differences in the lemmas were rather negligible caused just by certain changes in the instructions for the annotators.

In Table 3, we count all differences and in Table 4 we ignore the differences in lemmas. A comparison of the two Tables, e.g., shows that if differences in lemmas are ignored, the number of sentences with the number of differences equal to 0 through 2 increases from 20 to 26, and that the number of sentences with the number of differences greater than 7 decreases from 10 to 5.

Table 3. Distribution of sentences according to the total number of differences in each sentence

No. of diff.	0	1	2	3	4	5	6	7	8	9	10	11	12	14	16	18	29
No. of sent.	5	8	7	4	4	5	2	2	1	1	1	2	1	1	1	1	1

Table 4. Distribution of sentences according to the number of differences in each sentence ignoring the differences in lemmas

No. of diff.	0	1	2	3	4	5	6	7	11	12	14	28
No. of sent.	8	7	11	2	6	4	2	2	2	1	1	1

The total number of occurrences of dependency relations (i.e. edges) in the second test set was 519; the number of differences was 239. Out of this total number of differences, there were 54 differences in lemmas, 1 difference in the assignment of modality, 35 differences in the determination of which node depends on which node, and 43 differences in the restoration of nodes not appearing in the ATSs but restored – at least by one of the annotator – in the TGTSs. This leads us to the total of 133 differences in other features than the values of the dependency relations, i.e. out of the total of 519 occurrences of dependency relations (edges) in the second set of sentences there were 106 differences in the functors.

In contrast to the first round of the experiment, in the second round the trees with differences 0 were comparatively rich in the number of relations they contained; having $2, 2, 4, 9$, and 10 relations if all differences are taken into account, and if the differences in lemmas are ignored, the set of sentences without differences is even enriched by sentences with $7, 11$, and 17 relations. The trees with the number of differences $N = 1$ were again rather complicated (including $4, 6, 7, 9, 9, 10, 11, 17$ relations, if all differences are taken into account), and the same holds about $N = 2$ $(5, 5, 7, 7, 8, 11, 15)$, and $N = 3$ $(8, 8, 11, 13)$. Similarly as in the first round, the sentences with $N > 10$ included differences in the assignment of general participants expressed by zero morphs (this is true about all sentences in this group), and in most of them the same differences were repeated because of the fact that the sentences included coordination.

5   Comparison

To make Tables 1 and 3 comparable, we exclude the number of sentences with $N = 0$. This group was of no importance in the first round because the sentences included there were very poor in the number of relations they contained, but in the second round this figure is rather important because the sentences belonging there are rather complex (having $2, 2, 4, 9$, and 10 relations if all differences are taken into account, and if the differences in lemmas are excluded, this set of sentences is even enriched by sentences with $7, 11$, and 17 relations). In total, there are 40 sentences taken into account in Table 1 and 42 in Table 3; out of this total number, 19 sentences in the first round contain less than 5 differences, the rest includes more differences; this number improves in the second round, in which there are 28 with less than 5 differences, i.e. an improvement of almost 50%.

There was a considerable improvement in the assignment of the values of the dependency relations if compared with the first round: out of the total of 123 differences, 21 are not real differences because they consist in an assignment of a "double functor" (or a "slashed" value) by some of the annotators and only one of the values of such a double functor by the other(s). The possibility of an assignment of two (or even more) alternatives to a simple node was introduced in order to make it possible for an annotator to express his/her uncertainty in case even the context does not make it clear what particular relation is concerned (e.g. ACMP/COND – Accompaniment or Condition; EFF/RESL – Effect of Result; AIM/BEN – Aim or Benefactive). The introduction of the slashed values is very important for the future research in the taxonomy of dependency relations (merging two current types into one, or making more distinctions) based on the corpus, or formulating the criteria for the distinction between particular values in a more explicit way. In any case, however, the agreement between the annotators on one of the values (and the disregard of the other value by other annotators) should not be really counted as a difference.

There remain, of course, differences which have to be reduced in the further course of the annotation task. The following observations seem to be important for the future development:

(i) As already noticed in (a)(iii) in Section 3 above, in several cases, the edges for obligatory, though (superficially) deletable, complementations of verbs or nouns were missing with one or two annotators. There has been a considerable improvement over the first round since the instructions in the manual have been made more precise in that the restoration of deletable complementations of nouns is restricted to deverbatives in the strict sense, specified by productive derivational means (endings such as *-ání, -ení*). However, there still were cases where the annotators added nodes in cases which were excluded by the instructions (*prodejce* 'seller', *rozhodnutí* 'decision') or were not certain if they are supposed to distinguish two meanings of the deverbative (*uznání* 'recognition' or 'recognising', *plánování* 'planning' or 'the result of planning'). This is really a difficult point and we may only hope that a better routine will be acquired by the annotators during the annotation process.

(ii) Another case of incorrect restoration is connected with the different types of 'reflexive' forms in Czech. In the TGTSs, a distinction should be made between cases where the reflexive form of the verb is equivalent to a passive (the so-called reflexive passive is very frequent especially in technical text), or whether the particle '*se*' is an integral part of the verb (esp. the so-called reflexivum tantum). Examples of the former type occurring in our sample are the forms *šlo se* 'they went', *vytváří se* '(it) is created'; in these cases, the lemma '*se*' of the corresponding node in the ATS is 'rewritten' to the lemma of a general participant (gen) and gets the functor of Act; the subject of the (surface) construction gets the functor Pat. In the latter type of reflexive verbs, the ATS node with the label '*se*' is deleted and the particle '*se*' is added to the lexical label of the verb; this is the case of verbs such as *specializovat se* 'specialise', *orientovat se* 'orientate oneself', *představit si* 'imagine', *pustit se* 'to get involved in', *zabývat se* 'occupy oneself with'. Improvement should be reached by more explicit (and more thoroughly exemplified) instructions in the manual.

(iii) Another considerable improvement concerned the cases of lexical labels assigning the value Gen (for a general participant), '*on*' (pronoun 'he' used in pro-drop cases) and cor (used in cases of control). The trivial mistake in the outer shape of the labels (Gen or gen, Cor or cor) will be removed by a macro assigning these values automatically.

(iv) A similar unifying measure should be taken for cases of the assignment of lemmas for pronouns (the lemma of a personal pronoun should be assigned also in cases of a possessive use of pronouns), for the assignment of lemmas to nodes representing certain (meaningful) punctuation marks, and for adding 'empty verbs' in cases when this is necessary for an adequate account of the dependency structure of the sentence.

To conclude, we believe that the results of both rounds of the evaluation and their comparison will help us to improve the manual for the further process of annotation in order to give better specifications and to help to speed up the work of the annotators. We have also gained several stimuli for linguistic research in areas that have not yet been adequately described in any Czech grammar.

Acknowledgements. We would like to thank our colleagues Jan Hajič for giving us an impetus for the evaluation experiments, Alena Böhmová for providing technical help in carrying them out, and Petr Sgall for an intensive and continuous collaboration on writing and modifying the manual. Research for this paper was supported mainly by the grant of the Czech Ministry of Education VS96151 and partly also by the grant of the Czech Grant Agency GAČR 405/96/K214.

References

1. Hajičová, E.: Prague Dependency Treebank: From analytic to tectogrammatical annotations. In: Text, Speech, Dialogue (eds. Petr Sojka, Václav Matoušek, Karel Pala and Ivan Kopeček), Brno: Masarykova univerzita, 1998, pp. 45–50.
2. Hajičová E., Panevová J., Sgall P.: Manuál pro tektogramatické značkování, ÚFAL Technical Report TR-1999-07, Universitas Carolina Pragensis, 1999.

Probabilistic Head-Driven Chart Parsing
of Czech Sentences

Pavel Smrž and Aleš Horák

NLP Laboratory, Faculty of Informatics, Masaryk University
Botanická 68a, 602 00 Brno, Czech Republic
smrz@fi.muni.cz, hales@fi.muni.cz

Abstract. In this paper we present the results of our work on an implementation of a fast head-driven chart parser for the Czech language and constructing the appropriate grammar covering all prevailing grammatical phenomena of Czech. We re-assume our previous work on syntactic analysis that was based on the GLR mechanism. We have extended our metagrammar formalism so as to reinforce the declarativeness of the linguistic description. With respect to the massive ambiguity of the grammar we have enriched the head-driven chart parsing mechanism with probabilities obtained from training tree-bank corpus.

1   Introduction

There are many grammar formalisms for representing the natural language phenomena that usually use feature structures. The most popular ones are probably HPSG [1], LFG [2] and LTAG [3]. These formalisms are well known for their linguistic adequacy, however, they suffer from problems with high complexity of parsing algorithms. To overcome this difficulty, we have introduced the concept of metagrammar [4] that is constructed on a context free grammar backbone which enables us to use a CFG parser modified for the sake of feature agreement satisfaction and other linguistic tests and actions essential for parsing a free word order language like Czech.

Taking into consideration the high ambiguity of free word order languages on the syntactic level, one soon comes to the need of a tool for choosing among the huge number of resulting parses. Such tools are often based on probabilities automatically acquired from syntactically tagged training sentences. A stochastic model of context free parsing with the longest tradition is the probabilistic CF grammar [5], which combines the classical CF rules with quantities characterising how likely the rule applications are. Nevertheless, this mechanism usually needs an extension that captures the context dependency in the derivation process. Our system described below exploits the probabilistic approach for assorting the set of output syntactic structures.

2   Grammar and Parser Design

In this section, we describe the insides of our system from the point of the grammar formalism and the actual parser implementation. We also present new combinatoric

P. Sojka, I. Kopeček, and K. Pala (Eds.): TSD 2000, LNAI 1902, pp. 81–86, 2000.

constructs that substantially reduce the number of verb part rules written by linguists (which form nearly 60% of our grammar).

The only grievance to the output of our parser from the linguistic point of view regarded the complexity of derivation trees, namely the high number of levels in trees. We have therefore provided the possibility to postprocess the output with the aim to specify the importance of selected nonterminals that are then displayed in the result.

2.1   Metagrammar Uplift

The metagrammar consists of a set of CF rules extended with global order constraints, combinatoric constructs and special flags restricting the generative process. The basic metagrammar constructs are order(), rhs() and first() as described in [4].

In the current version, we have added two generative constructs and the possibility to define rule templates to simplify the creation and maintenance of the grammar. The first construct is formed by a set of %list_* expressions, that automatically produce new rules for a list of the given nonterminals either simply concatenated or separated by comma and co-ordinative conjunctions:

```
/* (nesmim) zapomenout udelat - to forget to do */
%list_nocoord vi_list
vi_list -> VI

%list_nocoord_case_number_gender modif
/* velky cerveny - big red */
modif -> adjp

/* krute a drsne - cruelly and roughly */
%list_coord adv_list
adv_list -> ADV

%list_coord_case_number_gender np
/* krasny pes - beautiful dog */
np -> left_modif np
...
```

The endings *_case, *_number_gender and *_case_number_gender denote the kind of agreement between list constituents. The incorporation of this construct has decreased the number of rules by approximately 15%.

A significant portion of the grammar is made up by the verb group rules. Therefore we have been seeking for an instrument that would catch frequent repetitive constructions in verb groups. The obtained addition is the %group keyword illustrated by the following example:

```
%group verb={
    V:head($1,intr)
```

```
        add_verb($1),
    VR R:head($1,intr)
          add_verb($1)
          set_R($2)
  }

  /* ctu - I~am reading */
  /* ptam se - I~am asking */
  clause ====> order(group(verb),vi_list)
```

Here the group `verb` denotes two sets of non-terminals with the corresponding actions that are then substituted for the expression `group(verb)` on the right hand side of the `clause` non-terminal.

2.2 Large Scale Parsing

The choice of employed grammar formalism does not directly force us to use a particular parsing strategy. Our previous implementation was derived from generalised LR approach (Tomita parsing) [6]. The results we obtained have been excellent for common sentences, nevertheless we could find some examples that were not parsed in a feasible time. That is why we started to implement a head driven chart parser extended by three kinds of unification actions and probabilistic selection from agenda. This work has already been recompensed with admirable time response for all input sentences.

The number of rules may differ significantly in particular grammars. Extreme values are reached in grammars that are obtained automatically from corpus processing [7]. Our parser is designed in order to cope with drastic increases in number of rules without the loss of its speed. We use as an experiment a grammar of about 35000 rules that were expanded from the base rules plus the unification actions and the rise of analysis time is negligible. Even several hundred thousand rules (created by multiplying the ruleset) are no challenge for the analyser.

The chart parsing techniques for extended CFGs are often underspecified with respect to the way how and when the rule constraints are evaluated. An elegant solution is the conversion of the agreement fulfilment actions to the CF rules. For instance, a grammar rule

```
    pp -> prep np
      agree_case_and_propagate($1,$2)
```

is transformed to

```
    pp1 -> prep1 np1
    pp2 -> prep2 np2
    pp3 -> prep3 np3
    . . .
```

In Czech, similar to other Slavic languages, we have 7 grammatical cases (nominative, genitive, dative, accusative, vocative, locative and instrumental), two numbers (singular and plural) and three genders (masculine, feminine and neuter), where masculine exists in two forms – animate and inanimate. Thus, e.g., we get 56 possible variants for a full agreement between two constituents. The expanded grammar form consists of more than 10000 rules in our case.

Since the number of rules that we need to work with is quite big, we need efficient structures to store the parsing process state. For example, the chart parser implementation used in our experiments employs 6 hash structures – two for open edges, two for closed edges, one hash table for the grammar rules (needed in the prediction phase) and one for all edges in agenda or in chart (the hash key is made of all the attributes of an edge – the rule, the dot position and the surface range).

The gain of this rather complex structure is the linear dependency of the speed of analysis on the number of edges in the resulting chart. Each edge is taken into considerations two times – when it is inserted into the agenda and when it is inserted into the chart. The overall complexity is therefore $2k$, where k is the number of edges in the resulting chart.

In the next table, we present running times and the number of edges in the resulting chart. We have chosen a set of longer sentences (more than 40 words) from a Czech corpus to demonstrate the efficiency of our parser implementation.

Sentence number	number of words	number of edges	time (s)
1074	47	170941	2.88
1100	52	143044	2.53
1236	42	144286	2.77
1654	51	361072	6.81
1672	59	434430	7.13
1707	40	205345	3.44
2079	66	223063	3.75
2116	49	259899	3.91
2284	42	452797	7.55
2300	60	443022	7.28
2306	102	715835	10.95

3   Analysis Guided by Statistical Data

Ambiguity is the fundamental property of natural language. Perhaps the most oppressive case of ambiguity manifests itself on the syntactic level of analysis. In order to face up to the high number of obtained derivation trees, we define a sort order on the output trees that is specified by probabilities computed from appropriate edges in the chart structure. The statistics is also involved in the process of sorting out the edges from agenda in the order that leads directly to n most probable analyses.

A common approach to acquiring the statistical data for analysis of syntax employs learning the values from a fully tagged tree-bank training corpus. Building of such corpora is a tedious and expensive work and it requires a team cooperation of linguists and computer scientists. At present, the only source of Czech tree-bank data is the Prague Dependency Treebank (PDTB) [8], which catches dependency analyses of about 20,000 Czech sentences.

In order to be able to exploit the data from PDTB, we have supplemented our grammar with the dependency specification for constituents. Thus the output of the analysis can be presented in the form of pure dependency tree. At the same time, we unify classes of derivation trees that correspond to one dependency structure. We then define a canonical form of the derivation to select one representative of the class that is used for assigning the edge probabilities.

The dependency structures for all possible analyses are stored in the form of packed dependency graph. An example of the graph for the sentence Petr jde na trh s volem (literally: *Peter goes to the market with an ox.*) looks like

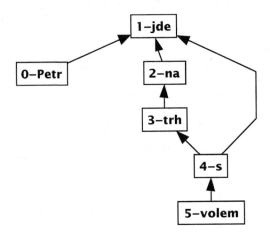

The packed dependency graph enables us to recover all the possible standard dependency trees with some additional information gathered during the analysis. The example graph represents two dependency trees only. However, in the case of more complex sentences, especially those with complicated noun phrases, the saving is much higher.

4   Conclusions

The implemented system has already approved that it does not end in its experimental stage. One of the many possible exploitations of the syntactic parser is its incorporation into the project of the proposed algorithm for translating natural language sentences into constructions of transparent intensional logic (Normal Translation Algorithm) [9].

The packed dependency graph should also be supplemented with the possibility to impose edge incompatibilities when the incorporated trees contain forbidden combinations of dependencies. This procedure will be based on checking the valency frames of the given verb.

References

1. Pollard, G. and Sag, I.: *Head-Driven Phrase Structure Grammar*, University of Chicago Press, 1994.
2. Neidle, C.: Lexical-Functional Grammar, *Encyclopedia of Language and Linguistics*, vol. 3, pp. 2147–2153, Pergamon Press, Oxford, 1994.
3. Schabes, Y., Abeille, A. and Joshi, A., K.: Parsing strategies with 'lexicalized' grammars: Application to tree adjoining grammars, In *Proceedings of the 12th COLING*, pp. 578–583, Budapest, Hungary, 1988.
4. Smrž, P. and Horák, A.: Implementation of Efficient and Portable Parser for Czech, In *Proceedings of TSD '99*, pp. 105–108, Springer-Verlag, Berlin, 1999.
5. Manning, C., D. and Schütze, H.: *Foundations of Statistical Natural Language Processing*, MIT Press, Cambridge, Massachusetts, 1999.
6. Tomita, M.: *Efficient Parsing for Natural Languages: A Fast Algorithm for Practical Systems*, Kluwer Academic Publishers, 1986.
7. Moore, R., C.: Improved Left-Corner Chart Parsing for Large Context-Free Grammars, In *Proceedings of the 6th IWPT*, pp. 171–182, Trento, Italy, 2000.
8. Hajič, J.: Building a Syntactically Annotated Corpus: The Prague Dependency Treebank, In *Issues of Valency and Meaning*, pp. 106–132, Karolinum, Prague, 1998.
9. Smrž, P. and Horák, A.: Determining Type of TIL Construction with Verb Valency Analyser, In *Proceedings of SOFSEM '98*, pp. 429–436, Springer-Verlag, Berlin, 1998.

Aggregation and Contextual Reference in Automatically Generated Instructions

Geert-Jan M. Kruijff and Ivana Kruijff-Korbayová*

Institute of Formal and Applied Linguistics (ÚFAL)
Faculty of Mathematics and Physics, Charles University, Prague, Czech Republic
gj@ufal.mff.cuni.cz, korbay@ufal.mff.cuni.cz

Abstract. We describe an implemented approach to text and sentence planning in a system for automatic generation of instruction texts. The approach aims at planning good quality texts through maximising coherence and cohesion.

1 Planning Textual Coherence and Cohesion

The quality of *any* text is for an important part determined by its *coherence* and *cohesion*. Informally, a coherent text makes sense and is intelligible for a reader, while a cohesive text is economic and sticks together. Figure 1 shows three short instruction texts which convey the same content, but differ in coherence and cohesion: (1) illustrates a coherent but minimally cohesive version, characterised by many repetitions; (2) illustrates cohesive but rather incoherent versions, where incoherence is due to inappropriate pronominalisation; finally, (3) illustrates coherent as well as cohesive versions.

Both coherence and cohesion are a matter of degree. A good quality text can be characterised by exhibiting maximal coherence and maximal cohesion at the same time. We consider (3i) less cohesive than (3ii), because the latter version has a smoother thematic progression, and consequently allows pronominalisation in the last sentence. Precise and general quantification of coherence and cohesion is, however, rather difficult.

The principal means to increase text cohesion are *aggregation* and *contextual reference*. Aggregation involves expressing multiple pieces of content in a compact way using linguistic expressions of higher complexity, e.g. one complex sentence rather several simplex ones, or complex nominal groups involving disjunction or conjunction. Contextual reference means using contextually suitable forms of abbreviated reference to entities which either have already been mentioned or are related to already mentioned entities by some inferable relation.

We employ the working hypothesis that the *goal* of aggregation and contextual reference is *increasing text cohesion*, while *not decreasing text coherence*. We discuss how to make this goal more precise, in order to be able to employ it in a multilingual system for automatic generation of instructions [7,6].

---

* The work reported here was carried out in the context of the AGILE project, supported by the European Commission within the COPERNICUS programme, grant No. PL961104. We would like to thank John Bateman for an extensive discussion.

P. Sojka, I. Kopeček, and K. Pala (Eds.): TSD 2000, LNAI 1902, pp. 87–92, 2000.

(1) *Coherent but minimally cohesive*
> Draw a line segment:
>> First specify the start point of the line segment.
>> Then specify the end point of the line segment.
> Draw an arc segment:
>> First switch to the ARC mode. Enter a.
>> Then snap the arc to the end point of the line segment:
>>> Enter endp. Select the line segment.
>> Finally, specify the end point of the arc segment.

(2) *Cohesive but rather incoherent*
> To draw a line segment specify the start point and end point of the line segment.
> Draw an arc segment:
>> First switch to the ARC mode by entering a.
>>> i. Then in order to snap it to the end point of the line segment,
>>>   enter endp and select it.
>>> ii. Then snap the arc segment to the end point of the line segment
>>>   by entering endp and selecting it.
>> Finally specify { the end point of the arc segment | its endpoint }.

(3) *Coherent and cohesive*
> Draw a line segment by specifying its start point and end point.
> Draw an arc segment.
>> First switch to the ARC mode by entering a.
>>> i. Then enter endp and select the line segment
>>>   in order to snap the arc segment to the end point of the line segment.
>>> ii. Then snap the arc segment to the end point of the line one
>>>   by entering endp and select the line segment.
>> Finally specify the end point of the arc segment.

Fig. 1. Differences in coherence and cohesion in instruction texts

The planning of aggregation and contextual reference starts from considering how the content is structured and how its pieces are related. This leads to the question where the planning of aggregation and contextual reference should be placed relative to the reference architecture for NLG systems [8]. This architecture consists of a set of modules, set in a sequence. First comes the specification of the content that is to be realized by the text. Given that content, a *text planner* creates a *text plan* (TP) that organises the content into such a structure that it becomes possible to realize the content in a linear fashion. Subsequently, a *sentence planner* interprets the TP, and generates sentence plans (SPs) that specify how to realize bits of content identified by the TP by (possibly complex) sentences. Finally, these SPs are fed sequentially into a *lexico-grammar* that generates the individual sentences, the sequence of which makes up the text realizing the content that was served at the beginning.

To deal with the issues of aggregation and contextual reference, we propose to work with a two-stage process. First, aggregation and contextual reference *as a means to increase cohesion* are planned within **text planning**, because of their effect on establishing a thematic progression, which concerns larger text units than a single sentence. Thematic progression consequently influences ordering – primarily, "new" information is to be ordered towards the end of the sentence.[1] Second, aggregation and contextual reference *as a linguistic form of expression* are planned at the level of **sentence planning**. There, on the basis of the TP we specify or constrain the form used to realize the content. These constraints are still, as far as possible, relatively language-independent, except where it concerns language-specific realization of particular concepts (cf. the discussion in [6]). As a consequence, particular aspects of cohesion are left to the individual lexico-grammars. For example, some decisions that lead to increased cohesion are a matter of linguistic realization. Notably, this concerns the "deletion"[2] of material which would otherwise result in repetition. The conditions for deletion are language-specific, and deletion can be restricted by particular syntactic contexts. Therefore, we conceive of deletion as a lexico-grammatical realization issue, and not one of sentence planning.

Abstractly put, a contextually appropriate content realization should take the form of a *minimally complex, and maximally informative (or maximally individuating) expression*. For aggregation, this means realization by a suitable complex expression. With regard to clause complexes, a decision needs to be made, for example, between different types of semantic relations (e.g., Purpose vs. Means), between ways of realizing these and of realizing the relata themselves (e.g. as hypotactic clause complex or as a clause and a nominalisation).

For contextual reference, maximal informativity means that, ideally, an expression should refer unambiguously. At the same time, minimal complexity requires a form as simple as possible. The choice of the exact linguistic form depends on the presence of "competitors" in the context. For example, in the context established in (3), there is a mode, a line segment and an arc segment. In order to determine a particular segment in a possible sequel, one would utter either 'the line segment' or 'the arc segment'. In another sequel where attention was already centered on segments, one could refer by the more cohesive expressions 'the line one' or 'the arc one'. Moreover, to refer to a highly activated entity, for instance the most recently mentioned segment, one can use a pronoun.

Below we elaborate on these ideas, discussing how they have been implemented in a multilingual system for automated text generation [7,6]. We focus on the module responsible for text- and sentence-planning, an earlier version of which we discussed in for example [3].

2 Text and Sentence Planning in AGILE

Our text and sentence planning module (TSM) is capable of planning a plethora of text types as found in software manuals, and one or more styles within each text type. In this paper, we only consider the text type of *full procedural instructions*, on which we

---

[1] The tag "new" is not entirely accurate, even though it is often used: information can be either new in the sense of *adding* information, or it can be new in the sense of *modifying* information that had already been available in the context. Cf. the discussion of handling word order in AGILE in [5].

[2] Cf. the literature on phenomena like *deletion, ellipsis, gapping, stripping, etc.*

illustrate the TSM's capabilities in planning different types of aggregation and contextual reference to enhance coherence and cohesion.[3]

In order for a reader to easily understand how to accomplish the task to which the instructions pertain, the text needs to reflect in a perspicuous fashion the hierarchical organisation of the task at hand as well as the sequence of steps to be carried out. The hierarchical organisation of the tasks is reflected straightforwardly by the hierarchical organisation of the text, or by the hypotactic and paratactic relationships between clauses within clause complexes. The former is an issue of layout, while the latter is a part and parcel of aggregation. Below, we broadly consider three different classes of aggregation: discourse aggregation (rhetorical relations like Purpose or Means), syntactic aggregation (conjunction or disjunction), and explicit sequence marking.

The main characteristic of the cooperation between the phases of text planning and sentence planning in the AGILE TSM is that the TP contains *all* the decisions how to relate the realizations of various bits of content. The sentence planner only *interprets* these decisions, as reflected in the TP, and creates SPs that state how to realize these relations.

Discourse aggregation. In the task-oriented setting of AGILE, discourse aggregation is formulated as handling the relation between two tasks where one of them corresponds to a goal, and the other is a step within a method accomplishing or contributing to accomplishing the goal. Prototypically, such content configuration yields the RST relations of Purpose and Manner.

We regard the distinction between these two relations in terms of the difference between "enablement" and "generation" between processes [2]. Generation holds between two processes a and b if the performance of a automatically brings about the occurrence of b. Enablement holds between a and b if the execution of a brings about a set of conditions that are necessary, but not necessarily sufficient for the subsequent performance of b. In our TPs, enablement is modelled by Purpose, and generation by Manner. The distinction is made on the basis of the underlying concepts. As a simplification, we treat simple physical actions as generating and higher level processes as enabling.

Syntactic aggregation. Syntactic aggregation also takes place between tasks, but in this case not between hierarchically related tasks, but rather between sequentially related ones or between alternatives accomplishing the same goal. As steps in a PROCEDURE-LIST constitute a sequence, they can be related through conjunction with or without additional explicit sequence marking, whereas methods in a METHOD-LIST are alternatives, and therefore can be listed in a disjunction. In both cases, impose complexity constraints on the tasks that can be related through either conjunction or disjunction.

Figure 2 shows a section of a TP which specifies aggregation of tasks. It contains one RST-purpose relation, and one conjunction. Each relation-node indicates that the left-daughter task and the task dominated by the immediate non-terminal node below the relation node are to be aggregated.

---

[3] The other text types the TSM is capable of planning are summaries/"cheat sheets", functional descriptions, tables of content, and overviews.

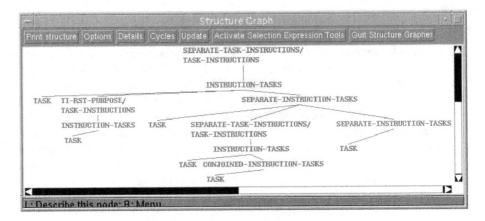

Fig. 2. Text plan showing conjunction and RST-purpose

In addition to relations like RST-purpose and RST-manner, or conjunction and disjunction, we also plan sequence realization. The straightforward way of reflecting the order of steps is by the corresponding ordering of sentences in the output. However, when the content is complex, more elaborate structuring of the generated text becomes needed as a means to facilitate a reader's orientation. We employ the following repertoire of sequence realization styles:

Running text sequence: *unmarked* (continuous paragraph) or *linguistically marked* (continuous paragraph including overt sequence discourse markers).

List sequences: *unmarked* (bullet list), *numbered* (numbered list) or *linguistically marked* (bullet list including overt sequence discourse markers).

Sequence discourse markers are expressions like 'first', 'further', 'finally', 'now', 'then', etc. (and their Bulgarian, Czech and Russian counterparts).

Sentence planning. Each of the leaves in the TP (like the tasks, the Task-Title, and the Side-effect in Figure 2) is linked to a bit of content in the content specification. For more discussion, see [3,6].

The sentence planner then performs its job as follows. It begins by traversing the TP, and creating SPs specifying how the content of each leaf should be realized as a single clause. While recursively traversing the TP depth-first manner, the sentence planner leaves *traces* that indicate whether the sentence planner has encountered any nonterminal node specifying a particular type of relation (e.g., conjunction). Once the sentence planner has created SPs for all the leaves, the recursion is reversed, and all the SPs are collected into a large sequence of SPs. It is at this point of "collecting the SPs" that the traces are being processed. When the sentence planner encounters a trace, then we add to the sequence of plans a *complex* sentence plan specifying the two clauses *and* their relation *as a clause complex*, and not the sentence plans for the individual clauses themselves.

Thus, the sentence planner only *interprets* the TP —it does not make any independent decisions about how to relate clauses. As we have already seen, this places all the responsibility for planning such relations with the text planner. This is an important point, for this means that we can effectively write *text grammars* just like we write lexico-grammars; only, in the case of text grammars we specify how to generate texts, not individual sentences. Together with the fact that the existing sentence planner can easily be extended to cover any type of relation distinguished by the text planner, we obtain a perspicuous and principled way in which we can plan and realize textual coherence and cohesion.

A final word should be said about contextual reference and information structure. The space-limits of the current paper do not permit us to elaborate much on the approach we take (but see [5]). In a nutshell, when processing the TP we build a discourse model that keeps track of what bits of content have already been used (i.e. introduced in the discourse). Whenever such content is re-used, the sentence planner specifies it as *contextually bound* [9]. Subsequently, the uses this information to generate contextually appropriate word order, as discussed in [5] and inspired by [9]. In the future, we hope to extend this approach adopting the proposals discussed in [1].

References

1. J. A. Bateman. 1999. Using aggregation for selecting content when generating referring expressions. In *Proceedings of the 37th Annual Meeting of the Association for Computational Linguistics*, pages 127–134, Maryland, United States of America.
2. J. Delin, T. Hartley and D. Scott. 1996. Towards a contrastive pragmatics: syntactic choice in English and French instructions. In *Language Sciences* 18 (3–4): 897–931.
3. G.J.M. Kruijff and I. Kruijff-Korbayová. 1999. Text structuring in a multilingual system for generation of instructions. In [4].
4. Václav Matoušek, Pavel Mautner, Jana Ocelíková and Petr Sojka (Eds.) *Proceedings of Text, Speech and Dialogue '99*, Czech Republic. Springer Verlag.
5. I. Kruijff-Korbayová and G.J.M. Kruijff. 1999. Handling Word Order in a Multilingual System for Generation of Instructions. In [4].
6. G.J.M. Kruijff et al. 2000. Multilinguality in a text generation system for three Slavic languages. In *Proceedings COLING 2000*.
7. I. Kruijff-Korbayová. 1998. Generation of instructions in a multilingual environment. In Petr Sojka, Václav Matoušek, Karel Pala, and Ivan Kopeček (Eds.), *Text, Speech and Dialogue (Proceedings TSD '98)*, Brno, Czech Republic, September.
8. E. Reiter and R. Dale. 2000. *Building Natural-Language Generation Systems*. Cambridge University Press, Cambridge, England.
9. P. Sgall, E. Hajičová and J. Panevová. 1986. *The Meaning of the Sentence in Its Semantic and Pragmatic Aspects*. D. Reidel Publishing Company, Dordrecht, Boston, London.

Information Retrieval by Means
of Word Sense Disambiguation

Luis Alfonso Ureña[1], José María Gómez Hidalgo[2], and Manuel de Buenaga[2]

[1] Dpto. de Informática, Universidad de Jaén
Avda. Madrid 35, 23071 Jaén, Spain,
laurena@ujaen.es,
[2] Dpto. de Inteligencia Artificial, Universidad Europea – CEES
Villaviciosa de Odón, 28670 Madrid, Spain,
jmgomez@dinar.uem.es, buenaga@dinar.uem.es

Abstract. The increasing problem of information overload can be reduced by the improvement of information access tasks like Information Retrieval. Relevance Feedback plays a key role in this task, and is typically based only on the information extracted from documents judged by the user for a given query. We propose to make use of a thesaurus to complement this information to improve RF. This must be done by means of a Word Sense Disambiguation process that correctly identifies the suitable information from the thesaurus WORDNET. The results of our experiments show that the utilisation of a thesaurus requires Word Sense Disambiguation, and that with this process, Relevance Feedback is substantially improved.

1 Introduction

Information access methods must be improved to overcome the information overload that most professionals face nowadays. Information access tasks, like Information Retrieval (IR), help the users to access a great amount of text they found in the Internet and their organisations. For instance, about 90% of the information in corporations exists in the form of text [8].

In a typical IR environment, users perform a series of iterative searches refining the query after each search. Many IR systems can automatically refine the user's query by making use of a set of documents that have been shown to the user, and that he or she has marked as relevant or not relevant. This Relevance Feedback (RF) process usually improves the quality of the search results.

The RF process is usually based only on the use of documents retrieved by the system and judged by the user. This information can be complemented with other information extracted from additional resources like *thesauri*. In this work, we explore the utilisation of the lexical database WORDNET to complement documents' information for RF.

Our experiments demonstrate that the use of WORDNET can improve RF results when a Word Sense Disambiguation (WSD) process is applied. The raw data obtained from WORDNET must be refined by a sense identification process for them to be

P. Sojka, I. Kopeček, and K. Pala (Eds.): TSD 2000, LNAI 1902, pp. 93–98, 2000.

effective. For automatically disambiguating query terms, more information than the query itself is required, and provided in the form of the documents judged by the user in a RF setting. We have applied a WSD algorithm based on the integration of resources that enables us to use WORDNET for RF.

The results of our experiments show that: firstly, using WORDNET without WSD to complement documents' information decreases RF performance; and secondly, using WSD applied to WORDNET information substantially improves RF based on the information of documents.

This paper is organised as follows. First we describe the RF approach used in this work. After that, the use of WORDNET and WSD for RF is presented. Next, we describe our experiments and results. Finally, the conclusions of our work are shown.

2   Relevance Feedback by Query Expansion

In most retrieval situations, it is customary to conduct searches iteratively as a sequence of partial search operations, which allows the results of earlier searches to be used to improve the output of later searches. One possibility consists of asking the user the relevance of certain documents retrieved in earlier search operations, and using these assessments to construct improved query formulations. This process, known as Relevance Feedback, has been shown experimentally to improve retrieval effectiveness greatly [11].

The most popular model for Information Retrieval is the Vector Space Model (VSM). In this framework, it has been demonstrated that the *Ide dec-hi* RF method was the best performing one [10]. This method is based on expanding the original query with terms from retrieved documents, using all the ones considered relevant by the user, and the first non-relevant document.

When evaluating RF effectiveness, it is preferable to employ the residual collection method. For a given query, the first n documents retrieved are examined to assess relevance. Then, the query formulation is improved using those documents, and a new search using the new query is performed over the document collection, excluding the first n documents retrieved for the previous query. This way, we can avoid the unfair and unrealistic situation in which already seen documents can be retrieved again, biasing the results to be much better than the original ones.

3   Using Word Sense Disambiguation in Relevance Feedback

The Query Expansion process described earlier is based only on the use of the documents retrieved. Nevertheless, other resources like *thesauri* can be used to complement the information contained in documents [11]. An example of advanced thesaurus is the lexical database WORDNET [6], which has been successfully employed in other classifications tasks like Text Categorisation [2]. In RF, and for every word sense in a query, a set of synonyms can be extracted from WORDNET and used to complement the documents' information obtained from the previous query.

Unfortunately, the incorporation of many heterogeneous words can impact negatively on the RF performance. This is caused by the great number of senses that a word can have. We would not like to retrieve documents concerning "river" when we perform a query like "bank" to know about financial interests. We require a WSD process to identify the correct sense of the words occurring in the query in order to effectively use a thesaurus. This is just an example of a Natural Language Processing task where WSD can improve the performance of the system, among others like Text Categorisation [2], Cross-Language Information Retrieval [3], Information Extraction, or Machine Translation [5].

The lexical database WORDNET has been used in IR before, but for it to be useful is essential to apply WSD [14]. In a general IR setting, the information of the query words is not enough to identify word senses, but in RF we can take advantage of the retrieved documents as an additional context to perform an effective WSD process.

In the latest years, many WSD approaches have been proposed, which can be classified according to the knowledge sources they make use of. Some approaches are based on the utilisation of some kind of lexicon or lexical database [16]. Other people make use of unlabelled [9] or semantically labelled [1] text corpora as a training collection. Finally, recent works propose the combination of several knowledge sources like lexical databases, text corpora, heuristics, collocations, etc. for WSD [15]. We follow the latter approach, combining the utilisation of the lexical database WORDNET, and the semantically-tagged text corpus SEMCOR [7] as described in [13].

The main idea of our WSD method is taking advantage of WORDNET information as an initial base for refining the representation of word senses through a learning algorithm. For instance, the Rocchio and the Widrow-Hoff learning algorithms admit the definition of an initial representation of classes to be learned. A set of WORDNET synonyms are extracted and used as initial representation of each word sense. Then, the learning algorithm is applied taking as input a collection of labelled data (SEMCOR) to refine the initial representation of word senses, obtaining better results in final tagging of new words than the use of any of the resources alone [13]. The senses of new words (the query words) can be identified using the context of documents where they occur, that happen to be the retrieved documents in the previous query.

As a concluding remark, we can observe that the utilisation of WSD in other Natural Language Processing tasks like RF is a natural and interesting way of evaluating WSD algorithms. WSD can hardly be considered an independent task, and WSD techniques should be compared in the framework of the task where WSD is being applied. Then, a WSD approach is better than others when the task where it is applied in, is improved by that approach more than by others. This indirect evaluation must complement the direct, standalone evaluation of WSD approaches.

4   Evaluation and Discussion of Results

For the experiments developed in this paper, we have employed the IR system Smart [11]. This system is a well known standard that implements the RF option described earlier in this paper. The number n of documents considered in the RF process is 15. Additionally, a set of 5,000 documents has been extracted from the Wall Street Journal corpus in the IR test collection TREC, widely used in IR system evaluation [4]. We have also randomly selected a set of 50 queries (topics) among the first hundred, each one with at least one relevant document in the subset selected from the Wall Street Journal corpus.

The thesaurus employed in this work is the lexical database WORDNET [6]. Among the several lexical and concept relations in WORDNET, we have used only the synonymy relation.

The VSM employed promotes a recall/precision based evaluation. Recall is defined as the number of relevant documents retrieved by the system over the number of relevant documents in the collection. Precision is defined as the number of relevant documents retrieved by the system over the number of documents retrieved. These metrics are calculated by a special module of Smart. Precision is calculated at the eleven levels of recall 0.0, 0.1, 0.2, ... , 1.0, and averaged over them. Also the average over the three levels 0.2, 0.5 and 0.8 is calculated.

Table 1. Precision averaged over the 11 standard levels of recall, and over the three levels 0.2, 0.5 and 0.8, for the initial run and the different queries constructed by the RF process.

Level	Original Query		Expanded Query	Expanded+WSD Query
	initial run	*feedback*	*feedback*	*feedback*
11-pt average:	0.1094	0.1853	0.1693	0.2088
% change:		69.4	54.75	84.73
3-pt average:	0.1106	0.1894	0.1719	0.2176
% change:		71.20	55.42	96.74

The results of our experiments are presented in Table 1 and Figure 1. The Table 1 shows the precision averages over the eleven and three recall levels for: the original query; the RF process based only on documents; the RF process based on documents and thesaurus without disambiguation; and the RF process based on documents and thesaurus with disambiguation. The Figure 1 shows the four approaches in a typical recall/precision graph obtained from the precision at the eleven recall levels.

The experiments results presented in Table 1 and Figure 1 show that:

- Using a thesaurus to complement the information of documents in a RF process usually performs worse than using only the documents. The average precision shows a drop of 15% and 25%. This is caused by the ambiguities in the query words and the high number of senses, and the great number of synonyms extracted from WORDNET.
- Using a thesaurus and a WSD algorithm to complement the documents information leads to a substantial improvement in the performance. The average precision exhibits an improvement of 15% and 25%. The reasons for this are the accuracy of the WSD algorithm and the restriction of words obtained from the thesaurus to those strictly needed.

The set of words extracted from the retrieved documents for the query expansion process is complemented by a set of precise and informative words obtained from the thesaurus, increasing the amount and quality of information available for constructing the new query.

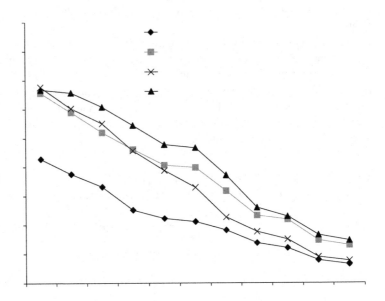

Fig. 1. Recall/precision graph for the initial run and the different queries expanded with documents, and synonyms with and without WSD.

These results also show that the disambiguation method employed in this work is as effective as to be of practical use. A direct evaluation was performed and reported elsewhere [12], showing that the WSD was very effective. These indirect results complement the direct ones.

5   Conclusions

In this paper, we have presented an approach that integrates the use of documents and thesaurus information for Relevance Feedback. The process is based on the utilisation of a Word Sense Disambiguation algorithm that effectively takes advantage of the information extracted from the lexical database WORDNET for Relevance Feedback. The results of our experiments show that making use of WORDNET improves Relevance Feedback only when performing a Word Sense Disambiguation process.

As a conclusion, we present an advance in the RF task that helps to alleviate the information overload problem. Also, we outline an evaluation model for WSD approaches based on the evaluation of the task they are applied in.

References

1. R. Bruce and W. Janyce. Word sense disambiguation using decomposable models. In *Proceedings of 33rd Annual Meeting of the Association for Computational Linguistics*, 1994.
2. M. Buenaga, J.M. Gómez, and B. Díaz. Using WORDNET to complement training information in text categorization. In *Proceedings of Second International Conference on Recent Advances in Natural Language Processing (RANLP)*, 1997.
3. G. Grefenstette. *Cross-Language Information Retrieval.* Ed. by G. Grefenstette Kluwer Academic Publishers, 1998.
4. D. Harman. Overview of the fourth Text Retrieval Conference (TREC-4). In *Proceedings of the Fourth Text Retrieval Conference*, 1996.
5. A. Kilgarriff. What is word sense disambiguation good for? In *Proceedings of Natural Language Processing Pacific Rim Symposium*, 1997.
6. G. Miller. WORDNET: A lexical database for English. *Communications of the ACM*, 38(11), 1995.
7. G. Miller, C. Leacock, T. Randee, and R. Bunker. A semantic concordance. In *Proceedings of the 3rd DARPA Workshop on Human Language Technology*, 1993.
8. Oracle. Managing text with Oracle8(TM) ConText Cartridge. In *An Oracle Technical White Paper*, 1997.
9. P. Pedersen and R. Bruce. Distinguishing word senses in untagged text. In *Proceedings of the Second Conference on Empirical Methods in Natural Language Processing*, 1997.
10. G. Salton and C. Buckley. Improving retrieval performance by relevance feedback. *Journal of the American Society for Information Science*, 41(4):288–297, 1990.
11. G. Salton and M.J. McGill. *Introduction to Modern Information Retrieval.* McGraw-Hill, 1983.
12. L.A. Ureña, M. Buenaga, M. García, and J.M. Gómez. Integrating and evaluating WSD in the adaptation of a lexical database in text categorization task. In *Proceedings of the First Workshop on Text, Speech, Dialogue TSD '98*, 1998.
13. L.A. Ureña, M. de Buenaga, and J.M. Gómez. Integrating linguistic resources in TC through WSD. *Computers and the Humanities*, 2000. In press.
14. E. Voorhees. Using WORDNET to disambiguate word senses for text retrieval. In *Proceedings of SIGIR '93*, 1993.
15. Y. Wilks and M. Stevenson. Word sense disambiguation using optimised combinations of knowledge sources. In *Proceedings of COLING-ACL*, 1998.
16. L. Xiaobin and S. Spakowicz. WORDNET-based algorithm for word sense disambiguation. In *Proceedings of the Fourteenth International Joint Conference on Artificial Intelligence*, 1995.

Statistical Parameterisation of Text Corpora

Gregory Y. Martynenko and Tatiana Y. Sherstinova

Department of Phonetics, St. Petersburg State University,
Universitetskaya nab. 11, Saint-Petersburg, Russia
gymart@ts4306.spb.edu

Abstract. Statistical parameters, usually used for diagnostic procedures, in many cases cannot be considered to be consistent ones from the statistical point of view, being strongly dependent on sample size. It leads to considerable devaluation of diagnostic results. This paper concerns the problem of consistency verification of parameters in the initial (pre-classification) stage of research. A complete list of parameters, which may be useful for description of text lexicostatistical structure, was determined. Each of these parameters was exposed to the justifiability test. In the result, a number of consistent parameters have been selected, which represent a description tool for the system characteristics of any text and corpora. Having rapid speed of convergence to the limit values, they may effectively perform classification procedures on text data of the arbitrary size. The proposed model of approximation makes it possible as well to forecast the values of all parameters for any sample size.

1 Consistency of Text Statistic Parameters

In the multitude of statistical-classificational linguistic tasks (e.g., taxonomic, typological, attributional, etc.), the central position is occupied by a diagnostic task, which may be solved in two ways. The first approach implies that a "collection" of parameters supposed to be useful for classification procedures is formed, and thereafter from the whole multitude of parameters the actually essential ones (from the point of view of concrete task and corpora) are selected by means of multidimensional analysis procedures [1]. Such method has proved its high efficiency, especially in case of successful selection of the teaching population.

The second approach is based on traditional philological conceptions about the language structure and genre/stylistic differentiation of texts. In this case, the main systematic/structural mechanisms of language functioning and its genre/stylistic types (correlation between parataxis and hypotaxis, preposition and postposition, compactness and distantness, static and dynamics) are taken into account, and further the concrete symptomatic attributes associated with these system characteristics are being determined [2].

However, not depending on general method, the parameters that are usually used for diagnostic procedures in many cases cannot be considered as consistent ones from the statistical point of view (i.e. they strongly depend on sample size). It leads to considerable devaluation of the diagnostic results because they are inevitably obtained on texts and corpora of different sizes.

P. Sojka, I. Kopeček, and K. Pala (Eds.): TSD 2000, LNAI 1902, pp. 99–102, 2000.

2   Research Material

The problem of convergence of text lingua/stylistic parameters to some limit values (that is their consistency) is being investigated on the material of the Computer Anthology of Russian Short Stories of the XX-th century, which is created by the Department of Mathematical and Computational Linguistics of St. Petersburg University and on the material of other corpora created in Russia and European countries.

Anthology of Russian Short Stories represents a text database consisting of about 2500 text samples (approximately 10 millions of word units). The corpus is divided into a number of "chronological cuts" (chronological periods), which merit special microanthologies to be created for them. In chronological periods, we tried to present the maximum quantity of writers, active in the given literary epoch. For the outstanding writers (such as Anton Chekhov, Igor Bunin, Andrey Kuprin, Maxim Gorky, Fiodor Sologub, Andrey Platonov, Michael Zoshchenko and some others), the author's anthologies are created. The system of frequency dictionaries is being formed for the whole corpora, for each chronological period, and for individual prominent writers. The principles of dictionary structurisation depend in each case on a number of parameters (in particular, see [1]).

3   Methods of Data Order in Frequency Dictionaries

Any frequency dictionary represents a lexicographic composition, any article of which contains the name of lexical unit and accompanying it statistical data of different kind (e.g., absolute frequency of the lexeme in concern, its frequency rank, quantity of lexical units with the identical frequency, etc.). Analysing information accumulated in frequency dictionaries, it is possible to build statistical distributions, whose concrete types are determined by the fact, what particular information is functioning as dependent and independent parameters. The main distributions are the following: polynomial, rank, and spectral ones. In polynomial distribution, the role of independent parameter plays the varying name of lexical units, whereas its frequency functions as dependent parameter. In rank distribution, independent parameter is represented by frequency rank of the lexical unit, while dependent one – by its frequency (in this distribution parameter "name" simply disappears). In spectral distribution, the frequency of lexical unit serves as an independent parameter, and the quantity of lexical units with the identical frequency functions as a dependent one.

4   Types of Scales and Corresponding Parameters

Mathematical statistics distinguishes different scales (quantitative, ordinal, nominal) and has developed a number of data processing methods, which are applicable just for the appropriate scale. The most promoted system of techniques has been elaborated for the quantitative parameters. Basing to the considerable extent on the theory of moments, it implies an advanced system of mean and variance values, characteristics of distribution forms, etc., and effectively uses as well a system of ordinal statistics (mode, median, quartile, etc.).

We discussed in previous paragraph that the central distributions used in processing of frequency dictionaries are rank, spectral, and polynomial ones. Though rank and spectral distributions have the outward appearance of quantitative scales, they are characterised by an extremely great variance of parameters in both rank and frequency scales. This fact induces some researchers to doubt the possibility to apply here the theory of moments (because of their prone to infinity), and therefore to suggest instead some other characteristics, not depending on the sample size. What concerns polynomial distribution, it cannot apply here the theory of moments theoretically as its variance is of quality nature.

5   Statistic Parameters and Consistency Test

Analysis of the recent scientific works and the results of our own investigations allowed us to determine a rather complete list of parameters, which may be used for description of text lexicostatistical structure. Each of these parameters was exposed to the consistency test. Table 1 presents the list of parameters subdivided into three groups according to the type of scale.

Table 1. List of parameters used for description of text lexicostatistical structure

Nominal scale	Quantitative (frequency) scale	Ordinal (rank) scale
Mode (Mo)	Mean frequency ($\bar{f}$)	Rank mean frequency ($\bar{r}$) (differentiation coefficient)
Dictionary size (N)	Geometric mean frequency ($\bar{f}_g$)	Rank variance coefficient (V_r)
Maximal frequency ($f_{\max}$)	Frequency variance coefficient (V_f)	Rank median (Me) (equilibrium measure)
Entropy (E)	Frequency median (Me_f)	Rank golden section (G_r)
Maximal entropy ($E_{\max}$)	Golden section (G_f)	Rank mean deviation (d_r)
Order coefficient $\frac{E}{E_{\max}}$	Diversity coefficient (S)	Variation coefficient on d_r (V_r)
Analytics measurement (A)		Coefficient of concentration $\left(\frac{\bar{f}_r}{N}\right)$
		Logarithmic concentration coefficient $\left(k = \frac{\log \bar{r}}{\log N}\right)$

Methodology for consistency test has been elaborated using the method of least squares with a number of principle modifications, caused by the complicated character of parameters dependence on the sample size [2]. In our hypothesis test, the null hypothesis was stated as "all parameters converge to their limit values" (alternative hypothesis – "all parameters increase or decrease without limits"). For approximation of experimental data, the Weibull function has been used for increasing dependencies, and the inverse of the Weibull function – for decreasing ones.

6 Conclusion

Our main results are the following:

1. Theoretically all the parameters have either upper or lower limits. This means that in principle they are statistically consistent. However, for the most of parameters actual consistency is achieved only in the very big sample sizes, which are hardly attainable in ordinary linguistic tasks.
2. The most consistent parameters turned out to be (in decreasing order): order coefficient $\left(\frac{E}{E_{\max}}\right)$, equilibrium measure ($Me_r$), logarithmic concentration coefficient $\left(k = \frac{\log \bar{r}}{\log N}\right)$, diversity coefficient (a number of words whose absolute frequency equals to "1" – S), differentiation coefficient ($\bar{r}$). These parameters along with some other ones represent a description tool for the system characteristics of any text and corpora. Moreover, their rapid speed of convergence to the limit values allows to effectively perform classification procedures on text data of the arbitrary size.
3. The proposed model of approximation makes it possible to forecast the values of all parameters for any sample size.

References

1. Marusenko M.A: Attribution of anonymous and pseudonymous literary works by means of pattern recognition theory. Leningrad. Leningrad State University, 1990.
2. Martynenko G.Y.: Fundamentals of Stylometrics. Leningrad. Leningrad State University, 1988.
3. Frequency Dictionary of Chekhov's Short Stories: Ed. Martynenko G.Y. Collected by A.O.Grebennikov. St. Petersburg, 1998.
4. Khajtun S.D.: Scientific measurement. Present Conditions and Perspectives. Moscow. "Nauka", 1983.
5. Shrejder Y.A., Sharov A.A.: Systems and Models. Moscow. "Radio i sviaz", 1982.

An Efficient Algorithm for Japanese Sentence Compaction Based on Phrase Importance and Inter-Phrase Dependency

Rei Oguro[1], Kazuhiko Ozeki[1], Yujie Zhang[2], and Kazuyuki Takagi[1]

[1] The University of Electro-Communications, Chofu, Tokyo 182-8585, Japan
[2] ATR Spoken Language Translation Research Laboratories,
Seika-cho, Kyoto 619-0288, Japan
rei@ice.uec.ac.jp, ozeki@ice.uec.ac.jp, takagi@ice.uec.ac.jp,
yujie.zhang@slt.atr.co.jp

Abstract. This paper describes an efficient algorithm for Japanese sentence compaction. First, a measure of grammatical goodness of phrase sequences is defined on the basis of a Japanese dependency grammar. Also a measure of topical importance of phrase sequences is given. Then the problem of sentence compaction is formulated as an optimisation problem of selecting a subsequence of phrases from the original sentence that maximises the sum of the grammatical goodness and the topical importance. A recurrence equation is derived by using the principle of dynamic programming, which is then translated into an algorithm to solve the problem. The algorithm is of polynomial-time with respect to the original sentence length. Finally, an example of sentence compaction is presented.

1 Introduction

With the rapid increase of electronic publications, text summarisation is becoming an important technical area in recent years [1]. Most widely used methods for text summarisation are based on the idea of extracting important sentences from the whole text according to some criterion. However, in some applications such as on-line generation of TV closed-captions, it is sometimes necessary to shorten each sentence as it comes in. Requirements for such sentence compaction are:

1) Shortened sentences retain the original information as much as possible.
2) Shortened sentences are grammatically correct and natural.
3) The compaction rate is adjustable to meet the specification of the summarisation system.
4) The computational load is small, and the computation can proceed without having to wait for the end of the input sentence.

Several methods for Japanese sentence compaction have been proposed [2,3,4,5]. None of them, however, satisfies all the requirements above. In this paper, the sentence compaction problem is formulated as an optimisation problem of selecting a subsequence of phrases from the original sentence that maximises the sum of grammatical goodness and topical importance. The grammatical goodness is defined

P. Sojka, I. Kopeček, and K. Pala (Eds.): TSD 2000, LNAI 1902, pp. 103–108, 2000.
© Springer-Verlag Berlin Heidelberg 2000

on the basis of a Japanese dependency grammar. Then a recurrence equation is derived by using the principle of dynamic programming. This equation is easily translated into an algorithm, which is expected to satisfy all of the requirements 1) - 4). Finally, an example is presented to demonstrate how a sentence is shortened depending on the specified length.

2   Problem Formulation

Let $w_0 w_1 \cdots w_{M-1}$ be a Japanese sentence represented as a sequence of phrases, where a phrase is a syntactic unit called "bunsetsu" in Japanese, consisting of a content word with or without being followed by a string of function morphemes such as particles and auxiliary verbs. The problem of sentence compaction here is to select a "good" subsequence of phrases from the original sentence. In order to formulate this problem, a measure of goodness of a phrase sequence must be defined. The structure of a Japanese sentence can be viewed from a dependency grammatical point; it can be described by specifying which phrase modifies which phrase in a wide sense. Thus, a dependency structure on a subsequence $w_{k_0} w_{k_1} \cdots w_{k_{l-1}}$ of the original sentence can be represented by a mapping

$$c : \{k_0, k_1, \ldots, k_{l-2}\} \longrightarrow \{k_1, k_2, \ldots, k_{l-1}\} \tag{1}$$

such that $w_{c(m)}$ is the phrase modified by w_m $(m \in \{k_0, k_1, \ldots, k_{l-2}\})$. For a normal Japanese sentence, this mapping must satisfy

a) $m < c(m)$ $(m \in \{k_0, k_1, \ldots, k_{l-2}\})$,
b) if $m < n$ then $c(n) \le c(m)$ $(m, n \in \{k_0, k_1, \ldots, k_{l-2}\})$.

The condition a) comes from the fact that modification always occurs from left to right in Japanese. The condition b) requires that two pairs of phrases in modification relation do not cross with each other.

Let $p(m, n)$ be a function that represents the strength of inter-phrase dependency between w_m and w_n, or the degree of validity for w_m to modify w_n. Then the grammatical goodness of the phrase sequence $w_{k_0} w_{k_1} \cdots w_{k_{l-1}}$ can be measured by $\max_c \sum_{i=0}^{l-2} p(k_i, c(k_i))$, where c runs over all the dependency structures on the phrase sequence. Let $q(m)$ be another function to represent the topical importance of w_m. Then the topical importance of the phrase sequence can be measured by $\sum_{i=0}^{l-1} q(k_i)$. The total goodness of the phrase sequence $w_{k_0} w_{k_1} \cdots w_{k_{l-1}}$ is defined as the sum of the grammatical goodness and the topical importance:

$$g(k_0, k_1, \ldots, k_{l-1}) \triangleq \begin{cases} q(k_0), & \text{if } l = 1; \\ \max_c \sum_{i=0}^{l-2} p(k_i, c(k_i)) + \sum_{i=0}^{l-1} q(k_i), & \text{otherwise.} \end{cases} \tag{2}$$

Now the problem of sentence compaction is formulated as follows:

Problem   For a given sentence $w_0 w_1 \cdots w_{M-1}$ represented as a sequence of phrases, find its subsequence $w_{k_0} w_{k_1} \cdots w_{k_{N-1}}$ of a specified length N that maximises the function $g(k_0, k_1, \ldots, k_{N-1})$.

3   Recurrence Equation

To solve the problem above, its partial solutions and the relationship among them are considered. Let $f(m, n, l)$ be the maximum value of $g(k_0, k_1, \ldots, k_{l-1})$ over all the subsequences of phrases of length l, starting with w_m and ending with w_n $(1 \le l \le n - m + 1)$:

$$f(m, n, l) \triangleq \max_{m=k_0 < k_1 < \ldots < k_{l-1}=n} g(k_0, k_1, \ldots, k_{l-1}) \tag{3}$$

Then it is shown that $f(m, n, l)$ satisfies the following recurrence equation:

1. for $m = n$ (only $l = 1$ is allowed):

$$f(m, n, l) = q(m) \tag{4}$$

2. for $m < n$ $(2 \le l \le n - m + 1)$:
   (a) for $l = 2$:
$$f(m, n, l) = f(m, m, 1) + f(n, n, 1) + p(m, n) \tag{5}$$

   (b) for $l = 3$:

$$f(m, n, l) = \max \begin{cases} f(m, m, 1) + \max_{m < m' < n}\{f(m', n, 2)\} + p(m, n); \\ \\ \max_{m < n' < n}\{f(m, n', 2) + p(n', n)\} + f(n, n, 1) \end{cases} \tag{6}$$

   (c) for $l \ge 4$:

$$f(m, n, l)$$
$$= \max \begin{cases} f(m, m, 1) + \max_{m < m' \le n-l+2}\{f(m', n, l-1)\} + p(m, n); \\ \\ \max_{2 \le l' \le l-2,\ m+l'-1 \le n' < m' \le n-l+l'+1} \\ \qquad \{f(m, n', l') + f(m', n, l-l') + p(n', n)\}; \\ \\ \max_{m+l-2 \le n' < n}\{f(m, n', l-1) + p(n', n)\} + f(n, n, 1) \end{cases} \tag{7}$$

This recurrence equation can be proved by noting that maximisation of $g(k_0, k_1, \ldots, k_{l-1})$ with respect to $(k_0, k_1, \ldots, k_{l-1})$ subject to $m = k_0 < k_1 < \ldots < k_{l-1} = n$ is equivalent to maximisation of $g(k_0, k_1, \ldots, k_{l-1})$ with respect to $(l', m', n', k_0, k_1, \ldots, k_{l'-1}, k_{l'}, k_{l'+1}, \ldots, k_{l-1})$ subject to $1 \le l' \le l - 1$, $m \le n' < m' \le n$, $m = k_0 < k_1 < \ldots < k_{l'-1} = n'$, $m' = k_{l'} < k_{l'+1} < \ldots < k_{l-1} = n$.

4   Algorithm

4.1   Tabular Computation

The above recurrence equation can be directly translated into an algorithm as shown in Figure 1. Because there is a large freedom in the order of computation, this is one

```
for n := 0 to M − 1 do
  begin
    for m := n downto 0 do
      begin if (m = n) then f(m, m, 1) := q(m);
        else
          begin
            for l := 2 to n − m + 1 do
              begin
                if (l = 2) then f(m, n, l) := Eq.(5);
                else if (l = 3) then f(m, n, l) := Eq.(6);
                else f(m, n, l) := Eq.(7);
              end;
          end;
      end;
  end;
```

Fig. 1. Algorithm for recursive computation of $f(m, n, l)$

of many versions of the translation that yield the same result. Actual computation is carried out by using a table to store the computed value of $f(m, n, l)$, which is looked up in later computation steps.

The time-complexity of this algorithm is of $O(M^6)$, where M is the length of the original sentence. Although $O(M^6)$ might seem to be large, there is no computational difficulty for practical values of M. In fact, the algorithm, coded in C, completes the computation for $M = 40$ within 1 sec on UltraSPARC-IIi (270MHz).

4.2   Back-Trace

In order to recover the optimum phrase sequence, it is necessary to keep the record of the values of variables, for back-pointers, that attain the maximum in the recurrence equation. Three tables are used for the purpose: $bp[m, n, l].lp$, $bp[m, n, l].np$, and $bp[m, n, l].mp$. In the middle case of Eq.(7), for example, the back-pointers are set as $bp[m, n, l].lp := l'$, $bp[m, n, l].np := n'$, and $bp[m, n, l].mp := m'$, where l', n', and m' are the values of those variables that attain the maximum. The back-trace proceeds in the following way. First, the optimum starting phrase and ending phrase are sought for a specified length N:

$$(m_0, n_0) := \text{argmax}_{m,n} f(m, n, N). \tag{8}$$

Starting with (m_0, n_0) as the initial value, the function in Figure 2 performs a back-trace to give the final solution

$$solution := out(m_0, n_0, N). \tag{9}$$

5   Example of Sentence Compaction

An example of sentence compaction is presented in Table 1 to show how a sentence is shortened according to the specified length. The value of $q(m)$ was defined based on

```
function out(m, n, l): char string
    begin
        if (m = n) then out :="wm";
        else
        begin
            l' := bp[m, n, l].lp;
            n' := bp[m, n, l].np;
            m' := bp[m, n, l].mp;
            out := out(m, n', l') ⊕ out(m', n, l − l');
        end;
    end.
```

Fig. 2. Back-trace function. The sign $\oplus$ denotes concatenation of two character strings.

the part-of-speech of the content word in w_m. The value of $p(m, n)$ was defined on the basis of the morphological information about w_m and w_n, and also the inter-phrase distance between w_m and w_n in the original sentence [6]. As is seen in Table 1, all the shortened sentences are natural and make sense, retaining important information in the original sentence to the extent the length is allowed.

Original Sentence ($M = 9$): mata[1] (*also*) sodeya[2] (*sleeve and*) sodekuchi[3] (*end of sleeve*) pokettoguchinadoga[4] (*opening of pocket*) aburayogorede[5] (*by oil dirt*) henshokuwo[6] (*discolor*) okosu[7] (*be caused*) kotomo[8] (*cases*) arimasu[9] (*happen*).

(*Also some cases may happen that the sleeves, the end of sleeves, and the opening of pockets are discoloured by oil dirt.*)

Table 1. Example of sentence compaction. Phrases are represented by their numbers in the original sentence. N denotes the specified length of the shortened sentence.

Length N	Shortened Sentence
8	(2) (3) (4) (5) (6) (7) (8) (9)
7	(2) (3) (4) (6) (7) (8) (9)
6	(2) (3) (4) (6) (7) (8)
5	(2) (3) (4) (6) (7)
4	(3) (4) (6) (7)
3	(6) (7) (8)
2	(6) (7)

6   Concluding Remarks

The Japanese sentence compaction problem was formulated as an optimisation problem, and an efficient algorithm was derived. Because the computation proceeds input-synchronously, it is suited for on-line sentence compaction. The algorithm can also output the dependency structure (parse tree) of a shortened sentence in a manner similar to the one described in [7].

The values of $q(m)$ and $p(m,n)$ adopted in the example are only tentative. Therefore our future work includes:

1) Establishing a method to give the appropriate values of $q(m)$ and $p(m,n)$.
2) Finding an optimal weighting balance between the topical importance and the grammatical goodness.
3) Carrying out a large scale evaluation on this method.

References

1. Okumura, M., Nanba, H.: Automated text summarisation: A survey. Journal of Natural Language Processing **6**(6)(1999) 1–26.
2. Wakao, T., Ehara, T., Shirai, K.: Summarization methods used for captions in TV news programs. Technical Report of Information Processing Society of Japan, 97-NL-122-13 (1997) 83–89.
3. Katoh, N., Uratani, N.: A new approach to acquiring linguistic knowledge for locally summarizing Japanese news sentences. Journal of Natural Language Processing **6**(7) (1999) 73–92.
4. Hori, C., Furui, S.: Automatic speech summarization based on word significance and linguistic likelihood. Technical Report of Information Processing Society of Japan, 99-SLP-29-18 (1999) 103–108.
5. Mikami, M., Masuyama, S., Nakagawa, S.: A summarization method by reducing redundancy of each sentence for making captions of newscasting. Journal of Natural Language Processing **6**(6) (1999) 65–81.
6. Zhang, Y., Ozeki, K.: Dependency analysis of Japanese sentences using the statistical property of dependency distance between phrases. Journal of Natural Language Processing **4**(2) (1997) 3–19.
7. Ozeki, K.: A multi-stage decision algorithm to select optimum bunsetsu sequences based on degree of kakariuke-dependency. IEICE Transactions **J70-D**(3) (1987) 601–609.

Word Senses and Semantic Representations
Can We Have Both?*

Karel Pala

NLP Laboratory, Faculty of Informatics, Masaryk University Brno
Botanická 68a, 602 00 Brno, Czech Republic
pala@fi.muni.cz

Abstract. In this paper, we offer one possible way to bridge the gap existing between the lexical and logical semantic analysis of natural language expressions. We look for a link that would allow us to perform a more adequate and integrated semantic analysis of natural language expressions. The solution is to combine the descriptions of lexical units as they are developed within the area of lexical semantics (e.g. WordNet) with logical analysis of sentence meanings worked out within the Transparent Intensional Logic framework.

The data structures based on both approaches may take the form of richer dictionary entries that together would form a dictionary of the new type – a Lexico-Logical Dictionary (LLD).

1 Introduction

Present approaches to semantic analysis in the NLP field typically follow two directions which do not seem to be very well integrated. The first direction can be briefly characterised as *lexicalist* and it concentrates primarily on exploration of the word senses or senses of selected word collocations (phrases). A good survey of the techniques used in this direction (with regard to the word disambiguation) can be found in [4].

The second direction may be labelled as *logical* and it pays attention mostly to the techniques that enable us to describe formally sentence meanings and build what is usually characterised as *semantic representations* of the sentences. Here, various logical formalisms are employed, particularly, first order logic (FOPL) is the most frequently used one. A good example of this approach can be found in [1]. There have been earlier attempts to explore word meanings within the Montague Grammar framework [2] where attention has been paid to the issues on how word meanings, as they are treated within generative semantics by means of decomposition analysis, can be integrated into Universal Grammar. Dowty's approach is theoretically stimulating in several ways, mainly it shows how things can be done, however, if one is looking for more applicable results that could be used in experimental NLP systems, he or she will probably not be satisfied. Though some relevant theoretical problems are addressed in [2], in a sense his

---

* This research has been partially supported by the Czech Ministry of Education under the grant VS97028.

analysis appears to be rather narrow because he pays attention only to English, which due to its poor morphology does not allow one to see some of the phenomena in the full extent. Take, e.g. verbal aspect – it is not a grammatical category in English (as it is the case in Czech or Russian), or the derivational morphology and lexical rules as discussed by Dowty certainly cannot be regarded general enough. Also, the version of the componential analysis dealt with by Dowty (and by generative semanticists) is interesting only from the theoretical point of view and according to our knowledge it has not been immediately used in building any existing dictionary. Further, it will become obvious that among logical approaches we rather prefer not to use Universal Grammar but TIL formalism (see below) which, in our opinion, is suited better for the task.

2   Lexicalist View – Word Senses

In this area, the attention is essentially concentrated on obtaining plausible descriptions of the word senses or the senses of word collocations. Standardly, they are studied within the field of lexical semantics (lexicology) and the result of this effort is the information about senses of the individual lexical units as it can be found in various dictionaries. The descriptions of the word senses may take a different form depending on the type and purpose of a dictionary – starting from the classical dictionaries using definitions based on genus proximum and distinguishers, and ending, e.g., with the machine lexical databases like WordNet, where the sense descriptions are based on the synsets, Top Ontology (yielding a selected set of semantic labels (features)) plus hypero/hyponymy hierarchy.

In the following, we will refer to WordNet-like dictionaries since they can be regarded as good representatives of the description that employs extensively the semantic relations between words. As the developers of Czech WordNet, which has been built within EuroWordNet-2 project [10], we also have the positive experience with them.

Thus, within EuroWordNet-1,2 framework [13], each lexical unit is treated as a *synset* corresponding to the respective word sense. Therefore, it can be seen that each lexical unit due to its position in the respective hypero/hyponymical tree and the links given by it can be associated with a set of semantic features that can be regarded as a characterisation (or description) of its sense. These data now can be obtained automatically by the Polaris database tool developed within EuroWordNet-1,2. Moreover, in this framework, it is now possible to exploit what is called *Internal Language Relations (ILR)* which link together lexical units according to the semantic relations having the nature of the semantic cases (agent, patient, instrument, etc.).

The presented approach deals preferably with word senses or senses of collocations but as far as we know, in this approach there is no complete way on how to build representations of sentence meanings or, in other words, their *semantic representations (SR)*. Thus, the issues of reference are not addressed here.

3   Logical View – Sentence Meanings

Logical analysis of sentence meanings, as in [6] or [2], offers techniques for building SR of the sentences. Typically, this can be done by means of a selected logical formalism such as first order logic (FOPL, [1]) or one of the intensional logic calculi – we will prefer here *Transparent Intensional Logic (TIL)* by [12] and [6] since it does not suffer from the shortcomings which are typical of FOPL. In these formalisms, the individual semantic representations may take form of logical formulae as we know them from FOPL or from Lambda Calculus if Transparent Intensional Logic is chosen.

These formulae follow the compositional principle and they yield a description of sentence meaning (its reference) in terms of the entities like extensions (in FOP) or extensions and intensions (TIL). This means that sentence like

(1) *John loves his computer.*

can be represented as

(1a) $\lambda w \lambda t$ (**lov**$_{wt}$ (**J**, (**comp**$_{wt}$))).

Thus, in TIL we get a formula which represents a proposition stating that there is a relation-in-intension between two individuals. It should be added that TIL exploits the ramified theory of types, therefore its expressive power in comparison with FOPL appears to fulfill better the requirements that arise in realistic NLP systems.

In our NLP Laboratory, we work on *Normal Translation Algorithm* that takes (Czech) input sentences and as its output and produces their semantic representations in the form of Lambda formulae and their corresponding semantic trees [3].

However, in this kind of analysis, which is necessary for building reasonable knowledge representations and making inferences from them, there is something missing as well. It is obvious that we lack here the idiosyncratic lexical information that can be associated with word senses occurring in the sentence like (1) and that is certainly used in semantic analysis of (1) when it is performed by humans. Thus, we know that the expression *his computer* in (1) denotes an individual object (having logical type `iota`, which is the type of individual) but there is no way to associate this information with the fact that typically a computer *is a machine able to process information*. This kind of fact can be obtained from the respective knowledge representation, however, as we have tried to show above, at present it can be automatically retrieved from a lexical database of the WordNet type: thus we are led to a reasonable conclusion: it makes sense to attempt to combine the two mentioned ways of semantic analysis and try to integrate them.

4   The Link – Lexico-Logical Dictionary (LLD)

A possible solution that would allow us to intertwine both the lexical and logical analysis of NL expressions is, in our opinion, to build a data structure that can be implemented as a dictionary of the new type. It can comprise in its entries both the lexical information about lexical units (e.g. as they are now in WordNet) and the information about the log-ical types that can be associated with natural language expressions. It can be shown [11] that if we treat verbs as logical predicates, we can assign the respective logical types to them (mostly intensions). For example, in the TIL framework many verbs denote relation-in-intension between two individuals: thus the verb *to love* from (1) above can be associated with the following logical type:

(1b) $(o\iota\iota)_{\tau\omega}$.

The verbs denoting properties of individuals (typically intransitives), e.g. *to read* as in

(2) *Our son reads well.*

can be associated with the following logical type:

(2a) $(o\iota)_{\tau\omega}$.

To give another example, take the verbs denoting propositional attitudes such as *believe*, *know*, and *think*. They can be associated with the logical type

(3) $o(\iota, o_{\tau\omega})_{\tau\omega}$

constructions of order n.

Our preliminary analysis also shows that some regular relations can be found between semantic classes of verbs [5] and the corresponding logical types, for example, the verbs denoting relation-in-intension between two individuals will certainly constitute well defined classes (transitives) whereas the verbs expressing property of an individual will clearly constitute another collection of typical verb classes (intransitives). The idea then is to explore the semantic classes of (Czech) verbs and try to find the correspondencies between them and the logical types as they are defined within TIL.

In this respect, we also have to pay an attention to the valency frames which at the first place have to be distributed according to the individual verb senses they belong to and only then the relations to the corresponding logical types can be looked for. The problem, however, is where to find the relations between the valency frames and word senses of the respective verbs (at least for Czech). One may hope that the explicit information of this sort might perhaps be found in some (really good) dictionaries but unfortunately this is not the case with the Czech ones. Thus, we face the task of building data structures for verbal lexical units that would contain the valency frames distributed according to their respective word senses, e.g. in the following form for the four senses of Czech verb *spát (sleep)*:

spát:1 i.

valency frame: : *dobře, tvrdě (well, hard)*
WordNet semantic features: BE ASLEEP, REST
logical type: $(o\iota)_{\tau\omega}$ (property of individuals).

spát:2 i.

valency frame: : *v hotelu (in the hotel)*
WordNet semantic features: LODGE + RESIDE + OCCUPY A POSITION
logical type: $(o\iota\iota)_{\tau\omega}$ (relation-in-intension between individuals)

spát:3 i.

valency frame:
WordNet semantic features: COPULATE + MAKE CONTACT + CONNECT TOGETHER
logical type: $(o\iota\iota)_{\tau\omega}$ (relation-in-intension between individuals)

spát:4

valency frame: : *v hrobě, tiše (in the grave, quietly*
WordNet semantic features: BE IN A STATE + BE AT REST + BE DEAD
logical type: $(o\iota)_{\tau\omega}$ (property of individuals).

The work on building this kind of data structures has already started and the first examples can be found both in Czech WordNet and other Czech lexical resources that are being prepared in NLP Laboratory at the Faculty of Informatics, Masaryk University. The starting list of Czech verbs with their valency frames now contains about 15 000 items [9] but they are related to the respective senses yet.

Analogous interesting relations seem to hold between the senses of nouns, their valency frames and the logical types and their semantic features as yielded by their positions in the hypero/hyponymical trees in WordNet. As it can be seen from the examples of the verb entries presented above, the noun (as well as adjective and adverb) entries comprising both the respective lexical and logical information can be built in a similar fashion. Take, e.g. an entry for the lexical unit *hlava (head)*:

hlava:1

valency frame: : *hlava člověka (man's head)*
WordNet semantic features: BODY PART + PART OF A NATURAL OBJECT + ENTITY
logical type: ι (an individual) or $(o\iota)_{\tau\omega}$.

hlava:2

valency frame: : *hlava na počítače (a brain in computers)*
WordNet semantic features: COGNITION + KNOWLEDGE + PSYCHOLOGICAL FEATURE
logical type: $(o\iota)_{\tau\omega}$ (property of individuals).

hlava:3

valency frame: : *hlava oddělení (head of the section)*
WordNet semantic features: INDIVIDUAL + BEING + ENTITY + CAUSAL AGENCY
logical type: $(o\iota)_{\tau\omega}$ (property of individuals) or $\iota_{\tau\omega}$ (individual role).

hlava:4

valency frame: : *hlava kola (head of the wheel)*
WordNet semantic features: PART + PHYS.OBJECT + ENTITY
logical type: $(o\iota)_{\tau\omega}$ (property of individuals).

hlava:5

valency frame: : *hlava v Bibli (chapter in the Bible*
WordNet semantic features: SECTION + WRITING + COMMUNICATION
logical type: $(o\iota)_{\tau\omega}$ (property of individuals).

hlava:6

valency frame: : *hlava na desetikoruně (heads on the ten crown coin*
WordNet semantic features: SIDE + SURFACE + ARTEFACT + PHYS.OBJECT + ENTITY
logical type: $(o\iota)_{\tau\omega}$ (property of individuals).

Note that several logical types can be associated with a given noun but which type will be selected depends on the local context in which the noun can take place. In our view, it would be necessary to work not only with single nouns but with the typical collocations like *head of the department* as well.

5   Conclusions

In the presented contribution, we payed our attention to the gap existing presently between the present approaches to the lexical and logical semantic analysis of natural language expressions. We are trying to find a link that would allow us to perform a more integrated semantic analysis of NL expressions.

In our opinion, it is necessary to combine the descriptions of the lexical units as they are developed within the area of lexical semantics with the logical analysis of sentence meanings as worked out within TIL framework. The data structures that are based on both approaches may take, as we tried to show, the form of the richer dictionary entries that together would form a dictionary of the new type – a Lexico-Logical Dictionary (LLD).

References

1. Allen, J., Natural Language Understanding, Benjamin/Cummings, Redwood City, CA, 1995.
2. Dowty, D., R., Word Meaning and Montague Grammar, Kluwer, Dordrecht, Second edition, 1991, esp. p. 27–36.
3. Hadacz, L., Semantic Inference in Human-Machine Communication, Proceedings of Text, Speech, Dialogue '99 Conference, Springer Verlag, p. 353–356, MarienBad, 1999.
4. Ide, N., Véronis, J., Word Sense Disambiguation: The State of Art, Computational Linguistics, vol. 24, No. 1, March 1998, pp. 1–40.
5. Levin, B., English Verb Classes and Alternations, The University of Chicago Press, 1993.
6. Materna, P., Concepts and Objects, Acta Philosophica Fennica, vol. 63, Helsinki, 1998.
7. Pala, K., O sémantických reprezentacích (On Semantic Representations), SP FFBU (Proceedings of Faculty of Arts, Brno University), A 32, pp. 24–35, Brno, 1984.
8. Pala, K., Rychlý, P., Smrž, P., DESAM – An Annotated Corpus for Czech, Proceedings of SOFSEM '98, Springer, 1998.
9. Pala, K., Ševeček, P., Valence českých sloves (Valency Frames of Czech Verbs), SP FFBU (Proceedings of Faculty of Arts, Masaryk University), A 45, pp. 41–54, Brno, 1997.
10. Pala, K., Ševeček, P., Česká lexikální databáze typu WordNet (Czech Lexical Database of WordNet Type), SP FFBU (Proceedings of Faculty of Arts, Masaryk University), A 47, pp. 51–64, Brno, 1999.
11. Podlezlová-Koželouhová, B., Sémanticky orientovaný generativní českých sloves nepřechodných (Semantically Oriented Generative Description of the Czech Intransitive Verbs), Diploma Thesis, Faculty of Arts, Masaryk University, Brno, 1974.
12. Tichý, P., The Foundations of Frege's Logic, De Gruyter, 1988.
13. Vossen, P., et al., Set of Common Base Concepts in EuroWordNet-2, Final Report, 2D001, Amsterdam, October 1998.

Automatic Tagging of Compound Verb Groups in Czech Corpora[*]

Eva Žáčková, Luboš Popelínský, and Miloslav Nepil

NLP Laboratory, Faculty of Informatics, Masaryk University
Botanická 68, CZ-602 00 Brno, Czech Republic
glum@fi.muni.cz, popel@fi.muni.cz, nepil@fi.muni.cz

Abstract. In Czech corpora, compound verb groups are usually tagged in a word-by-word manner. As a consequence, some of the morphological tags of particular components of the verb group loose their original meaning. We present an improved method for automatic synthesis of verb rules. These rules describe all compound verb groups that are frequent in Czech. Using these rules, we can find compound verb groups in unannotated texts with high accuracy. The system for tagging compound verb groups in an annotated corpus that exploits the verb rules is described.

Keywords: compound verb groups, corpora, morphosyntactic tagging, inductive logic programming

1 Compound Verb Groups

Recognition and analysis of the predicate in a sentence is fundamental for the meaning of the sentence and its further (semantic) analysis. In more than half of Czech sentences, a predicate contains a compound verb group.

E.g. in the sentence *Mrzí mě, že jsem o té konferenci nevěděla, byla bych se jí zúčastnila.* (literal translation: *I am sorry that I did not know about the conference, I would have participated in it.*), there are three verb groups:

<vg> *Mrzí* </vg> *mě, že* <vg> *jsem o té konferenci nevěděla* </vg>, <vg> *byla bych se jí zúčastnila.* </vg>

I <vg> *am sorry* </vg> *that I* <vg> *did not know* </vg> *about the conference,*
I <vg> *would have participated* </vg> *in it.*

Verb groups are often split into more parts with so-called gap words. In the second verb group, the gap words are *o té konferenci* (*about the conference*). In annotated Czech corpora, including DESAM [2], compound verb groups are usually tagged in a word-by-word manner. As a consequence, some of the morphological tags of particular components of the verb group loose their original meaning. In the above sentence, the

---

[*] This research has been partially supported by the Czech Ministry of Education under the grant VS97028.

P. Sojka, I. Kopeček, and K. Pala (Eds.): TSD 2000, LNAI 1902, pp. 115–120, 2000.

word *jsem* is tagged as a verb in present tense, but the whole verb group to which it belongs – *jsem nevěděla (I did not know)* – is in past tense. Similar situation appears in *byla bych se jí zúčastnila (I would have participated in it)* where *zúčastnila* is tagged as past tense while it is just a part of past conditional.

We consider a compound verb group to be a list of cohesive verbs and maybe reflexive pronouns *se, si*. Such a group is obviously compound of auxiliary and full-meaning verbs, e.g. *budu se smát* where *budu* is an auxiliary verb (like *will* in English), *se* is the reflexive pronoun and *smát* means *to laugh*. As word-by-word tagging of verb groups is confusing, it is useful to find and assign a new tag to the whole group. This tag should contain information about the beginning and the end of the group and about the particular components of the verb group. It must also contain information about relevant grammatical categories that characterise the verb group as a whole. Without finding all parts of a compound verb group and without tagging the whole group (what is necessary dependent on other parts of the compound verb group), it is impossible to continue with any kind of semantic analysis.

In [5], a proposal of the method for automatic finding of compound verb groups in the corpus DESAM is introduced. We describe here an improved method that results in definite clause grammar rules – called verb rules – which contain information about all components of a particular verb group and about their tags. We describe also some improvements that allow us to increase the accuracy of verb group recognition.

2   Learning Verb Rules

The process of learning verb rules [5] is split into three steps: finding verb chunks (i.e. finding boundaries of simplex sentences in compound or in complex sentences, and elimination of gap words), generalisation of the chunk and verb rule synthesis.

2.1   Verb Chunks

The observed properties of a verb group are the following: its components are either verbs or reflexive pronoun *se (si)*; a verb group cannot cross the boundary of a sentence; and between two components of the verb group, there can be a gap consisting of an arbitrary number of non-verb words or even a whole sentence.

In the first step, the boundaries of all simplex sentences are found. Then each gap is replaced by tag gap. The method exploits only the lemma of each word (nominative singular for nouns, adjectives, pronouns and numerals, infinitive for verbs) and its tag. We will demonstrate the whole process using the third simplex sentence of the clause mentioned in the first section – *byla bych se jí zúčastnila (I would have participated in it)*:

```
být/k5eApFnStMmPaI by/k5eAp1nStPmCaI se/k3xXnSc4
on/k3xPgFnSc2p3 zúčastnit/k5eApFnStMmPaP
```

After substitution of gaps, we obtain:

```
být/k5eApFnStMmPaI by/k5eAp1nStPmCaI se/k3xXnSc4
gap
zúčastnit/k5eApFnStMmPaP
```

2.2 Generalisation

The lemmata and the tags are now being generalised. Three generalisation operations are employed: elimination of (some) lemmata, generalisation of grammatical categories and finding grammatical agreement constraints.

Elimination of lemmata. All lemmata except forms of auxiliary verb *být (to be)* (*být, by, aby, kdyby*) are rejected. Lemmata of modal verbs and verbs with similar behaviour are replaced by tag modal. These verbs have been found in the list of more than 15 000 verb valencies [3]. In our example, it is the verb *zúčastnit* that is removed.

```
být/k5eApFnStMmPaI by/k5eAp1nStPmCaI k3xXnSc4
gap k5eApFnStMmPaP
```

Generalisation of grammatical categories. By exploiting linguistic knowledge, we can observe that some grammatical categories are not important for verb group description. These categories may also be removed. Very often it is negation (e), or aspect (a). For some verbs, even person (p) can be removed (see below). Values of those grammatical categories have been replaced by ? in our example.

```
být/k5e?pFnStMmPa? by/k5e?p?nStPmCa? k3xXnSc?
gap k5e?pFnStMmPa?
```

Finding grammatical agreement constraints. Another situation appears when two or more values of some category are related. In the simplest case, they have to be the same – e.g. the value of attribute person (p) in the first and the last word of our example. More complicated is the relation among the values of attribute number (n). They should be the same except when a polite way of addressing occurs, e.g. in *byl byste se jí zúčastnil (you would have participated in it)*. Thus, we have to check whether the values are the same or the conditions of a polite way of addressing are satisfied. For this purpose, we add the predicate check_num() that ensures agreement in the grammatical category number and we obtain:

```
být/k5e?p_n_tMmPa? by/k5e?p?n_tPmCa? k3xXnSc?
gap k5e?p_n_tMmPa? check_num(n)
```

2.3 DCG Rules Synthesis

Finally, the verb rule is constructed by rewriting the result of the generalisation phase.

```
verb_group(vg(Be,Cond,Se,Verb), Gaps) -->
  be(Be,_,P,N,tM,mP,_),                  % být/k5e?p_n_tMmPa?
  cond(Cond,_,_,Ncond,tP,mC,_),          % by/k5e?p?n_tPmCa?
   check_num(N,Ncond,Cond,Vy),
  reflex_pron(Se,xX,_,_),                % k3xXnSc?
  gap([],Gaps),                          % gap
  k5(Verb,_,_,P,N,tM,mP,_).              % k5e?p_n_tMmPa?
```

The meanings of non-terminals used in the rule are the following: be() represents auxiliary verb *být*, cond() represents various forms of conditionals *by, aby, kdyby*, reflex_pron() stands for the reflexive pronoun *se (si)*, gap() is a special predicate for the manipulation with gaps, and k5() stands for an arbitrary non-auxiliary verb. The particular values of some arguments of non-terminals represent required properties. Simple cases of grammatical agreement are treated through binding of variables. More complicated situations are solved by employing constraints like the predicate check_num().

The method has been implemented in Perl. 126 definite clause grammar rules were constructed from the annotated corpus which describe all verb groups that are frequent in Czech. Although the method described displays quite good accuracy on the test set (the correct verb rule has been correctly assigned to 92.3% verb groups), it has some drawbacks. In about 13% of complex sentences, some of the compound verb groups were not correctly recognised. It was observed that almost 46% of errors were caused by incorrect lemma selection.

3   Fixing Misclassification Errors

To fix the most frequent error – incorrectly recognised lemma of a word in the verb group – we combined two approaches. Rules that recognised a word-lemma couple of a very small frequency in the corpus (actually those that did not appear there) were supposed to be incorrect. The second approach, which exploits inductive logic programming (ILP) techniques, reads the context of the lemma-ambiguous word and results in disambiguation rules [4].

For testing, we randomly chose the set of 600 examples including compound or complex sentences. 251 sentences contained only one verb. The results obtained are in Table 1. The first line contains the number of examples used. The following line shows the results for the original method. Then the rules with the word-lemma couple of a very small frequency have been discarded; the accuracy is in the third line. The last line contains the percentage of correct rules after the lemma disambiguation was employed. The column '> 1 verb' concerns the sentences where at least two verbs appeared. The last column displays accuracy for all sentences.

Table 1. Fixing

	number of correct rules(%)	
	> 1 verb	all
number of examples	349	600
original method	86.8	92.3
– non-frequent lemmata	91.1	94.8
+ lemma dis. employed	92.8	95.8

4   Tagging Verb Groups

We now describe a method for compound verb group tagging in morphologically annotated corpora. We decided to use SGML-like notation for tagging because it allows an easy incorporation of the new tags into the DESAM corpus. The beginning and the end of the whole verb group and beginnings and ends of its particular components are marked. For the sentence *byla bych se jí zúčastnila (I would have participated in it)*, we receive:

```
<vg tag="eApFnStPmCaPr1v0" fmverb="zúčastnit">
  <vgp>byla</vgp>
  <vgp>bych</vgp>
  <vgp>se</vgp>
  jí
  <vgp>zúčastnila</vgp>
</vg>
```

where `<vg>` `</vg>` point out the beginning and the end of the verb group, whereas `<vgp>` `</vgp>` mark components (parts) of the verb group. The assigned tag – i.e. values of significant morphologic categories – of the whole group is included as a value of attribute called `tag` in the starting mark of the group. Value of the attribute `fmverb` is the full-meaning verb; this information can be exploited, e.g., for searching and processing of the verb valencies afterwards. The value of the attribute `tag` is computed automatically from the verb rule that describes the compound verb group.

We are also able to detect other properties of compound verb groups. In the above example, the new category `r` is introduced. It indicates that the group is reflexive (`r1`) or not (`r0`). The category `v` enables us to mark whether the group is in the form of polite way of addressing (`v1`) or not (`v0`). The differences of the `tag` values can be observed comparing the previous and the following example. For the sentence *nebyl byste se jí zúčastnil (you would not have participated in it)*, we receive:

```
<vg tag="eNpMnStPmCaPr1v1" fmverb="zúčastnit">
  <vgp>nebyl</vgp>
  <vgp>byste</vgp>
  <vgp>se</vgp>
  jí
  <vgp>zúčastnil</vgp>
</vg>
```

The set of attributes can also be enriched, e.g., with the number of components. We also plan to include into the attributes of `<vg>` a compound verb group type. It will enable us to find the groups of the same type but with different word order or the number of components.

5   Conclusion

Let us notice that sometimes compound verb groups are defined in a less general way. In contrast to it, we also include into the groups some verbs which are in fact infinitive participants of verb valencies. However, we are able to detect such cases and recognise the "pure" verb groups afterwards. We believe that for some kind of shallow semantic analysis – e.g. in dialogue systems – our approach is more convenient. We are also able to recognise the form of polite way of addressing a person (which has no equivalent in English, but similar phenomenon appears, e.g., in French or German). We extend the tag of a verb group with this information, because it is quite important for understanding the sentence. E.g. in *šel jste (vous êtes allé)*, the word *jste* should be counted as singular although it is always tagged as plural.

Another approach that deals with the recognition and morphological tagging of compound verb groups in Czech appeared in [1]. Basic compound verb groups in Czech like active present, passive past tense, present conditional etc., are defined in terms of grammatical categories used in the DESAM corpus. Two drawbacks of this approach can be observed. First, verb groups may only be compounds of a reflexive pronoun, verbs *to be* and not more than one full-meaning verb. Second, the gap between two words of the particular group cannot be longer than three words. The verb rules defined here are less general then the basic verb groups [1]. Actually verb rules make partition of them. Thus, we can tag all the basic verb groups without the limitations mentioned above.

References

1. K. Osolsobě. Morphological Tagging of Compound Verb Forms in Czech Corpus. Studia Minora Facultatis Philosophicae Universitatis Brunensis Brno, 1999.
2. K. Pala, P. Rychlý, and P. Smrž. DESAM – Annotated Corpus for Czech. In *Plášil F., Jeffery K.G. (Eds.): Proceedings of SOFSEM '97, Milovy, Czech Republic. LNCS 1338*, Springer, 1997, pp. 60–69.
3. K. Pala and P. Ševeček. Valencies of Czech Verbs. Studia Minora Facultatis Philosophicae Universitatis Brunensis, A45, 1997.
4. T. Pavelek and L. Popelínský. Mining Lemma Disambiguation Rules from Czech Corpora. In *Principles of Knowledge Discovery in Databases: Proceedings of PKDD '99 Conference, LNAI 1704*, Springer, 1999, pp. 498–503.
5. E. Žáčková and K. Pala. Corpus-Based Rules for Czech Verb Discontinuous Constituents. In *Text, Speech and Dialogue: Proceedings of TSD '99 Workshop, LNAI 1692*, Springer, 1999, pp. 325–328.

Sensitive Words and Their Application to Chinese Processing

Fuji Ren[1] and Jian-Yun Nie[2]

[1] Faculty of Information Sciences, Hiroshima City University, Japan
ren@its.hiroshima-cu.ac.jp
[2] Department of Computer Science and Operation Research, University of Montreal, Canada
nie@iro.umontreal.ca

Abstract. Sensitive words are the compound words whose syntactic category is different from those of their components. According to the segmentation, a sensitive word may play different roles, leading to significantly different syntactic structures. If a syntactic analysis fails for a Chinese sentence, instead of examining each segmentation alternative in turn, sensitive words should be first examined in order to change the syntactic structure of the sentence. This will lead to a higher efficiency. Our examination of a machine-readable dictionary shows that there are a great number of such words. This shows that sensitive word is a widespread phenomenon in Chinese.

1   Introduction

Sensitive words refer to those Chinese compound words whose syntactic category is different from those of their components. For example, the string "*jiang lai*" may be segmented as a single word or as two words. In the first case, it is an adverb, meaning "in the future". In the second case, it becomes a sequence of an auxiliary verb and a verb, meaning "will come". The segmentation of sensitive words is critical in the determination of the syntactic structure of the whole sentence. However, this problem has been neglected in the past. People usually segment Chinese words using a longest-matching algorithm, which segment the above string systematically to a single word. Even if a backtracking strategy is used, the second segmentation will be suggested far later, after several other segmentation results have been examined. In this paper, we argue that sensitive words should not be dealt with in the same way as other segmentation ambiguities. They represent a possible breaking point that may change significantly the syntactic structure of the sentence. Therefore, if a segmentation result does not lead to a success in syntactic analysis, the sensitive words should be first checked. This may greatly improve the efficiency of Chinese analysis.

In this paper, we will first describe the problem of sensitive words in more detail, and their impact in Chinese segmentation. Then we will carry out a survey on a machine-readable dictionary. Our analysis shows that there are a great number of sensitive words in this dictionary. Some compositions are particularly productive in sensitive words. This shows clearly that sensitive word is not an isolated, but widely spread phenomenon in Chinese. A correct processing is necessary.

P. Sojka, I. Kopeček, and K. Pala (Eds.): TSD 2000, LNAI 1902, pp. 121–126, 2000.

2   Chinese Segmentation and Sensitive Word

There have been two main groups of approaches to Chinese segmentation: dictionary-based approach [1,4,5,8] and statistical approach [2,3,7]. We will only describe the first approach here. The second approach usually leads to similar results.

Dictionary-based approaches operate according to a very simple concept: a correct segmentation result should consist of legitimate words – the words stored in a dictionary or derivable from some rules. In general, however, several legitimate word sequences may be obtained from a Chinese sentence. The longest matching algorithm is then used to select the word sequence that contains the longest (or equivalently, the fewest) words. For example, the sentence "*ji qi fan yi bu zhun que*" (Machine translation is not accurate) may be segmented, among others, in the following ways:

> *ji qi fan yi / bu / zhun que* (machine translation, not, accurate = MT is not accurate)
> *ji qi / fan yi / bu / zhun que* (machine, translate, not, accurate ˜ MT is not accurate)
> *ji qi fan yi / bu / zhun / que* (machine translation, not, allow/accurate, indeed)

Among these possible solutions, the longest-matching algorithm will choose the first one. In most cases, the longest-matching method can choose the correct solution. Its accuracy is typically around 90% [6]. However, if the sentence is slightly changed to "*ji qi fan yi wen zhang bu zhun que*" (Using machines to translate articles is not accurate), then the algorithm will choose the following wrong segmentation:

> *ji qi fan yi / wen zhang / bu / zhun que* (machine translation, article, not, accurate)

The correct segmentation should separate "*ji qi fan yi*" into two words. These examples illustrate the impact of segmentation to the whole Chinese analysis.

The problem of segmentation is its ambiguities. Many Chinese words containing at least two characters can be decomposed into simpler words (in modern Chinese). However, most such decompositions do not change radically the syntactic categories. Typically, a compound noun, if decomposed into Noun + Noun structure, would not change significantly the syntactic structure of the sentence. On the other hand, a decomposition may lead to two words with very different categories. For example, "*jiang lai*" (in the future – an adverb), if decomposed into "*jiang / lai*" (will, come – a auxiliary + verb sequence) would make a big difference in sentence's structure. It is this case that sensitive words are involved.

Among the compound words of the last case, we still distinguish two different cases:

1. Once decomposed, the words are unusual, or they cannot appear together;
2. The component words are usual words, and can follow each other in normal Chinese sentences[1].

We only consider the words in the second case to be sensitive words. The string "*zhun que*" (accurate) is an example of the first case. "*zhun*" (accurate/permit) and "*que*"

---

[1] We use "normal sentences" because one can always imagine some very peculiar sentences for many word sequences. However, these sequences do not occur in normal texts.

(indeed) separately are also words. However, they do not appear together in modern Chinese. This is not a sensitive word. On the other hand, it is easy to find cases where "*jiang lai*"(in the future) should be separated into "*jiang / lai*" (will, come). Therefore, it is a sensitive word.

Now, why sensitive words are interesting to study? Usually, Chinese processing follows the following pattern: one starts with the best segmentation result, if the subsequent analysis fails, we restart with the second best segmentation result, and so on. In this pattern, the quality of a segmentation result is solely based on word length. In fact, many segmentation ambiguities only affect word length, but not their meaning and the syntactic structure of the sentence. Taking such an alternative would not help at all the subsequent analysis if the first failed. Therefore, it is better to take an alternative that will lead to a significant change in sentence structure. This is the role of sensitive words: when a first analysis with the best segmentation result fails, we should first try to break down sensitive words involved. In this way, we can expect to arrive at the correct analysis result more quickly.

This approach is perfectly compatible with the common practice in MT to group words into long phrases. The advantage of grouping words into phrases is its high efficiency: if an expression may be unambiguously recognised, it is useless to analyse its composition and it can be translated directly as a whole. Therefore, in many machine-readable dictionaries (in particular, for Chinese), long phrases are also included. Then how many words are sensitive words in such a dictionary? This is the question we will examine in the next section by analysing an online Chinese dictionary.

3   Analysis of Sensitive Words in a Machine-Readable Dictionary

The machine-readable Chinese dictionary we analyse here contains 87 599 words (phrases). This is a dictionary used by a segmentation program, and manually checked by a Chinese linguist. The aim of the analysis is to show the extent to which sensitive words are spread in Chinese.

The meaning of the symbols we will use is given in Table 1.

In many cases, compound words (phrases) are constructed from simpler words according to some rules. The following rules are commonly used:

NC + NC ⟶ NC	(*gong si + zhi yuan* = employee of a company)
NC + V ⟶ V	(*ren gong + fan zhi* = artificially breed)
NC + V ⟶ NC	(*ji qi + zhe tu* = drawing by machine)
VTR + NC ⟶ NC	(*jing + kou* = import)
VTR + NC ⟶ VINT	(*buo + zhong* = weed)
V + V ⟶ V	(*bian + yin* = edit and print)

Sensitive words are mainly due to the fact that a Chinese word (especially single-character word) may play different roles. For example, "*ba men*" (guard the door) corresponds to the rule V + NC ⟶ VINT. However, "*ba*" is can also be a preposition that introduces the object in the structure "*ba* Something Verb", meaning "to Verb Something". The string "*ba men*" can also be considered as a sequence of "ba Something"

Table 1. Symbols and their meaning

Symbol	Meaning	Example
ADJ	adjective	*nei* (inside)
ADV	adverb	*yi hou* (after)
CONJ	conjunction	*he* (and)
NC	common noun	*ji qi* (machine)
PREP	preposition	*bi* (in comparison with)
QUAN-CL	quantity +classifier	*ji ge* (several)
VAUX	auxiliary verb	*neng* (can)
VINT	intransitive verb	*xue xi* (study)
VTR	transitive verb	*guan li* (manage)
V	VINT or VTR	

as in "*ta ba men da kai*" (he opens the door = he *ba* door open). Therefore, "*a men*" is a sensitive word. In our examination of the MRD, we intuitively determined a set of compositions that are the most propitious for sensitive words according to Chinese grammar. These compositions are shown in Table 2, together with some examples that show normal situations where the word should be broken down.

Table 3 shows the number of sensitive words that we determined manually from a machine-readable dictionary for each word composition. The criteria used are those stated earlier, namely, 1) the component words may play significantly different roles from their compound in reasonable circumstances. 12 357 possible sensitive words have been identified according to the compositions from 87 600 words in the dictionary. Among them, 764 are actual sensitive words. The numbers shown in Table 3 are higher because some words fall into several categories. The proportion of sensitive words is surprisingly high. It is near 1% of all the items in our dictionary. In addition, a high proportion of sensitive words are very common words, as we can see in the examples in Table 2.

We can further observe the high percentage of sensitive words for the NC+VAUX composition (38.4%). The main reason is that most words ending with *hui* (association) and *neng* (energy) may also be separated into two words, and once separated, *hui* and *neng* are usually interpreted as auxiliary verbs (*jiang* – will, *neng* – can).

Most sensitive words involve nouns (NC). The highest numbers of sensitive words are obtained from NC+VTR and ADV+NC compositions. In addition, the percentages of sensitive words of these compositions are relatively high.

From these observations, it becomes clear that we cannot consider the items in a dictionary as inseparable. It is important to make distinction between sensitive and non-sensitive words.

4   Conclusions and Future Work

In this paper, we described a new concept – sensitive word – in the Chinese language. We first described how sensitive words may affect Chinese segmentation. The purpose of distinguishing sensitive words from non-sensitive words is to increase the efficiency of Chinese analysis and MT. We argue that if a segmentation solution fails to produce

Table 2. Some compositions of sensitive words and examples

Composition	Example word	Example sentence
ADV + NC	*hou men* (back door // after door)	*ta / jin lai / hou / men / hai / kai / zhe* I / enter / after / door / still / open = The door remained open after I came in
ADV + QUAN-CL	*hao ji ge* (several // well, several)	*an dun / hao / ji ge,* ... settle / well / several / person / after, = after settling down several people,
ADV + VAUX	*quan neng* (all-round // all, can)	*ta men / quan / neng / jing / da xue* they / all / can / enter / university = They can all go to university
ADV + VINT	*cai neng* (capability) // then, do)	*ni / tong yi / le / ta / cai / neng / zuo* you /agree / already / this / condition / he / then / do = He accepts only if you agree with this condition
PREP + NC	*ba men* (guard the door // to, door)	*ta / ba / men / da kai* he / to / door / close = He closed the door
PREP + V	*cong lai* (ever // since, come)	*cong / lai / zhe li / yi hou* ... from / come / here / after ... = since coming here ...
VAUX + PREP	*xiang dao* (think about // think, to)	*wo / xiang / dao / na er / qu* I / think / to /there / go = I want to go there

Table 3. Statistics of sensitive words in the dictionary

Composition	nb. words with the pattern	nb. sensitive words (percentage)
ADV + ADV	401	10 (2.5%)
ADV + NC	2230	103 (4.6%)
ADV + PREP	294	9 (3.1%)
ADV + QUAN-CL	9	4 (44.4%)
ADV + VAUX	148	3 (2.0%)
ADV + VINT	1265	20 (1.6%)
ADV + VTR	1155	87 (7.5%)
CONJ + NC	131	14 (10.7%)
CONJ + VTR	94	24 (25.5%)
NC + PREP	628	45 (7.2%)
NC + VAUX	249	95 (38.2%)
NC + VTR	3994	252 (6.3%)
PREP + NC	748	39 (5.2%)
PREP + V	453	15 (3.3%)
VAUX + PREP	96	5 (5.2%)
VAUX + VTR	363	19 (5.2%)
VTR + NC	5976	57 (1.0%)

a translation, it is useless to try to break non-sensitive words into their components. On the other hand, sensitive words may be broken down, and this usually leads to a new syntactic structure for the whole sentence. Thus we have higher chance to reach at the correct interpretation of the sentence.

In order to see the scale of sensitive words in Chinese, we examined a machine-readable Chinese dictionary. The number of sensitive words found is surprisingly high.

We found 12 357 words which correspond to the composition patterns we determined among 87 600 words in the dictionary. Among them, 764 are actual sensitive words. In other words, about 0.9% of dictionary items are sensitive words. This shows that sensitive words are widely spread in Chinese. It is worth doing more intensive study in the future.

This paper only concerns the phenomenon of sensitive word and its percentage in a MRD. We will continue our study by analysing the proportion of sensitive words in Chinese text. This will also give another useful indication on how each composition is productive in sensitive words.

References

1. Chang, J.-S., Chen, C.-D. and Chen, S.-D. Chinese word segmentation through constraint satisfaction and statistical optimisation. ROCLING-IV, Taiwan, 1991, pp. 147–165.
2. Chiang, T.-H., Chang, J.-S., Lin, M.-Y. and Su, K.-Y. Statistical models for segmentation and unknown word resolution. 5th R.O.C. Computational Linguistics Conference, 1992, pp. 123–146.
3. Dunning, T., Accurate Methods for the Statistics of Surprise and Coincidence. Computational Linguistics, vol. 19, 1993, pp. 61–74.
4. Li, B.-Y., Lien, S., Sun, C.-F. and Sun, M.-S. A maximal matching automatic Chinese word segmentation algorithm using corpus tagging for ambiguity resolution. R.O.C. Computational Linguistics Conference, Taiwan, 1991, pp. 135–146.
5. Liang, N. Y. and Zhen, Y.-B. A Chinese word segmentation model and a Chinese word segmentation system PC-CWSS. COLIPS, 1(1), 1991, pp. 51–55.
6. Liu, K.Y. Estimation report of Chinese word segmentation, Chinese Computer World, vol. 584, no. 12, 1996, pp. 187–189.
7. Sproat, R. and Shih, C. A statistical method for finding word boundaries in Chinese text. Computer Processing of Chinese and Oriental Languages, 4(4), 1991, pp. 336–351.
8. Yeh, C.-L. and Lee, H.-J. Rule-based word identification for Mandarin Chinese sentences – A unification approach. Computer processing of Chinese and Oriental Languages, 5(2), 1991, pp. 97–118.

Testing a Word Analysis System for Reliable and Sense-Conveying Hyphenation and Other Applications*

Martin Schönhacker* and Gabriele Kodydek

Institute of Computer Graphics, Algorithms and Data Structures Group,
Vienna University of Technology, Favoritenstraße 9–11/186, A–1040 Vienna, Austria
*currently: Franklin & Marshall College, Lancaster, PA 17604–3003, USA
m_schoenhack@acad.fandm.edu, schoenhacker@apm.tuwien.ac.at,
kodydek@apm.tuwien.ac.at
www.apm.tuwien.ac.at/

Abstract. In this article, we present a test environment for a word analysis system that is used for reliable and sense-conveying hyphenation of German words. A crucial task is the hyphenation of compound words, a huge set of those can readily be formed from existing words. Due to this fact, testing and checking all existing words for correct hyphenation is infeasible. Therefore we have developed special test methods for large text files which filter the few problematic cases from the complete set of analysed words. These methods include detecting unknown or ambiguous words, comparing the output of different versions of the word analysis system, and choosing dubious words according to other special criteria. The test system is also suited for testing other applications that are based on word analysis, such as full text search.

1   Introduction

We propose methods for testing a word analysis system for reliable and sense-conveying hyphenation of German words. A particular goal of the presented test environment was to enable especially the comparison of the results of different versions of such a word analysis system.

In Section 2, we will give a short description of the hyphenation method SiSiSi (the German acronym for "Sichere Sinnentsprechende Silbentrennung"). In Section 3, we will describe the test system. The results of empirical tests follow in Section 4. Finally, we conclude by describing the possibilities to incorporate other applications into the presented test environment in Section 5.

2   SiSiSi: Reliable and Sense-Conveying Hyphenation

The SiSiSi method provides reliable and sense-conveying hyphenation of German words [1], see also [3]. Since the most difficult problem in this context is the hyphenation

---

* This project was in part supported by *Hochschuljubiläumsstiftung der Stadt Wien* under the grant number H-75/99.

P. Sojka, I. Kopeček, and K. Pala (Eds.): TSD 2000, LNAI 1902, pp. 127–132, 2000.

of (long) compound words, the application is based on word analysis: Compound words are split into single words, which are in turn decomposed into atomic parts (= atoms) according to the rules for word formation in German. With respect to their use in word synthesis, atoms can coarsely be classified into prefixes, stems, and suffixes. In practice, it turns out to be advisable to use a more detailed classification of atoms, which in particular allows for a limitation of the sets of permissible suffixes for certain classes of words [6,7]. The word analysis system consists of two basic building blocks: the atom table, which contains all the atomic components of words, and a recursive decomposition algorithm, which actually performs the word analysis and splits words into atoms according to grammar rules. After analysis, hyphenations between consecutive single words and between prefixes and stems have already been identified. Thereafter, an algorithm based on the sequence of consonants and vowels is used to find any hyphens in the identified stem-suffix parts and in polysyllabic prefixes such as *unter* (under).

The result of hyphenation for every given input word is a set of hyphenation variants for that word. Points of hyphenation between single words of a compound are marked as major hyphenation points ("Haupttrennstellen", displayed as "="), those within single words as minor hyphenation points ("Nebentrennstellen", represented by "-"). Some minor hyphenation points such as those following closely after a major hyphenation point are marked by "_" because it is less advisable to use these hyphens for end-of-line divisions. The word *Wort=zer_le-gungs=ver_fah-ren* (word decomposition method) gives a good example for the usage of the different types of hyphens.

Different variants of hyphenation for a particular word often result from the fact that there are several grammatically correct decompositions for that word, although not all of them are necessarily meaningful, e.g. *Per-so-nal=man_gel* (manpower shortage) and *Per-son=alm=an_gel* (formed from the components "person", "mountain pasture", and "fishing rod"), where the latter obviously does not make much sense. Only hyphens contained in all hyphenation variants are considered to be reliable and are used in the final result.

3   Test System

A considerable amount of testing is needed to ensure that no correctly spelled word will receive an incorrect hyphenation, and orthographically and grammatically illegal words will be recognised as such. As SiSiSi looks for all allowed decompositions of a word, the following holds: if the atom table contains all atomic components of the German language and the implemented word formation rules do not exclude any correct word formation, then for any correctly spelled word none of the found *reliable hyphenation points* (i.e. occurring in all decompositions) is wrong. This immediately results from the fact that the set of found decompositions contains the correct decomposition.

Ideally, any existing word should be tested and checked for. However, the possibility to form an infinite number of new compound words make this approach infeasible. Therefore, selective tests are used which present to the user only words matching certain filter criteria.

A test system has been implemented which tests word analysis and hyphenation. The system incorporates three different versions of SiSiSi. Two of these versions use a very

Hyphenation vectors:
- `+ wach=stu_ben` vector for the meaning "police offices"
- `+ wachs=tu_ben` vector for the meaning "tubes of wax"
- `= wachstu_ben` combined vector, containing only reliable hyphenation points

Sequence of atoms:
- `+ wach·stube·n`
- `+ wachs·tube·n`

Sequence of attributes (when using simple grammar rules as in UrSi):
- `+ wach=stuben` which corresponds to:
- `+ S...=S....E` stem *wach* + stem *stube* + suffix *n*
- `+ wachs=tuben` which corresponds to:
- `+ S....=S...E` stem *wachs* + stem *tube* + suffix *n*

Fig. 1. Example for the various representations of a result

detailed classification of atoms and a grammar derived from German word formation rules. The first one (denoted ReSi) adheres to the new rules, which have come into effect in 1998 as a result of the reform of German orthography; the other one (HelSi) adheres to the old rules which continue to be in effect until 2005. For purposes of comparison, a primitive version (UrSi) using an extremely simple word grammar according to the old rules for German orthography has also been included; however, this version allows a considerable number of meaningless compounds, such as attaching the same suffix repeatedly to a stem.

The test system presented here allows for easy testing of hyphenation based on word analysis. Both isolated words and entire text files in various formats (that is with different representations of the German umlauts ä, ö, ü and other special characters such as ß or é) can be tested. The results for hyphenating a given word are being presented in a structured format on screen, and can also be logged to an output file. On screen different views are used in order to get an insight into the functionality of the algorithm.

As an example, we use the compound word *wachstuben*. It can be formed in two different ways that are both legal and meaningful, but render different ways of hyphenation: either from the words *wach* (to watch) and *stuben* (rooms), meaning "police office", or from *wachs* (wax) and *tuben* (tubes). Notice that *stuben* is formed using the stem *stube* plus a plural suffix *n*; *tuben* is formed analogously. The views for this example are given in Figure 1.

The view called *hyphenation vectors* shows all distinct ways for hyphenating the word plus the so-called combined hyphenation vector at the bottom, which is the result of combining all hyphenation variants. It contains only the reliable hyphenation points for the given word, which are those hyphens that occur in all variants. A second view called *sequence of atoms* shows all the constituents of each distinct decomposition, separated by a dot. The most details are presented in the view called *sequence of attributes*, which shows for each decomposition all atoms along with their respective function.

3.1 Special Methods

The test system allows for immediate comparison of the results of all three versions of SiSiSi, as well as for intense testing of any of them.

Filtering *unknown words* from the large amount of analysed words in the test file is probably the most obvious way of finding problematic words. We call a word *unknown*, if the system is not able to find a legal decomposition for it and therefore cannot provide proper hyphenation for it. Mostly such a word is not spelled correctly. Otherwise an error of our system (an incorrect rule or a missing atom) has been found. As a third possibility, the tested word might be a biographical or geographical name, an abbreviation, or an uncommon (possibly foreign) word.

Additionally, the test environment contains a function for detecting all *ambiguous words*, that is all words which have at least two distinct hyphenation vectors because they can be broken up in more than one way. Undesired ambiguities, such as in the case where one of the decompositions is absolutely meaningless, can be eliminated by adding the desired compound word (without suffixes) with an appropriate major hyphenation point to the atom table since atomic parts are not further decomposed by the algorithm.

When comparing two or all three of the versions, the output contains all words for which the considered variants do not find identical hyphenation vectors. The comparison of ReSi and HelSi is mainly used to detect words that were affected by the reform of the German orthography, whereas HelSi and UrSi are compared to examine the impact of the more sophisticated classification of atoms and grammar rules.

The rules of orthography permit the usage of hyphens within a compound word in order to disambiguate it or to increase its readability, such as in *Wach–Stube* (police office) or *Tee–Ei* (tea ball). The test system accepts an input word with such hyphens (–) between its constituent single words or with indicators for optional hyphenation points (˜) and only provides those hyphenation variants which comply with these predefined hyphens. This feature allows using correctly hyphenated words as input for checking whether the correct hyphenation variant is found by SiSiSi. It is therefore useful for identifying words for which SiSiSi provides no or only incorrect hyphenation, e.g. due to missing atoms.

The test system includes a function for restricting the length of the words to be analysed to any interval. For example, the number of test cases can be reduced by ignoring words with a length less than four letters, since it is rather unlikely that wrong hyphenations for such short words are produced (according to the old rules they remain undivided; according to the new rules a hyphen can be set after a single initial vowel in polysyllabic words with at least three letters, but we mark this as an undesirable hyphenation point).

For the two versions based on detailed grammar rules (i.e. ReSi and HelSi), more selective tests using elaborate filter criteria have been implemented. These criteria have been chosen with care to exhibit the few potential problem cases. For instance, it is possible to select words which contain atoms with varied functionality and can therefore be problematic (e.g. *ende* can be used as a stem or as a suffix: *Spiel=en_de* (the end of the game) as well as *Spie-len-de* (players).

Two filter criteria allow the specification of a set of composition rules and derivation rules respectively in order to examine the validity and area of application of these rules for word composition and derivation. Another criterion allows filtering words which contain atoms of specific atom classes. This is useful for examining words which contain atoms of specified stem or suffix classes. Furthermore, a filter can be used to discard words which only contain a single atom since these words are either monosyllabic and therefore not hyphenated at all, or they are hyphenated according to the consonants-vowel-rules. Therefore no problems are expected for such words.

A considerable amount of testing conducted using this test system played a vital role in improving the word analysis system, e.g. by uncovering stem classification errors or missing stems (often naturalized foreign-language words), which could subsequently be corrected. The next section shows a short extract from the empirical tests we conducted using the presented test system.

4   Experimental Results

For our tests, we have tried to find large text files that cover all stems and preferably all types of word forms of the German language. Unfortunately, most dictionaries were not available to us in an appropriate form for our test runs or they did not contain a sufficient variety of word forms.

We used a test file with more than 209,000 different word forms (available via `http://www.sibiller.de/anagramme/`) to look for unknown words using HelSi. Initially, 12.5% of the words were unknown. These words were further examined and used for updating the atom table. Note that the test file contains a large number of inflected word forms, derivations, and compound words. Therefore by adding a single atom, a large number of unknown words could be eliminated. Among the unknown words were biographical and geographical names and a number of word forms using these stems. The number of words reported as unknown is slightly biased due to some misspelled or abbreviated words in the test file, which our system correctly failed to recognize.

Furthermore, we have compared the ReSi and HelSi versions using a list provided in [5] (also available online via `http://www.duden.de/`) which contains words and phrases which are affected by the reform of German orthography. From this list, two test files of about 2,000 words each were created with respect to the new and old orthography. The comparison showed the expected differences: ReSi and HelSi both correctly analysed the words according to the corresponding spelling rules and recognised words spelled according to the respective other orthography rules. Furthermore, the results correctly pointed out words with letter combinations such as *st* and *ck* to which different hyphenation rules apply.

We plan to perform further tests using another set of test files that was created by exporting word forms from the Morphy morphological analyser [4].

5   Outlook

Other applications based on word analysis can easily be incorporated into the test system, and can then also be tested as described. One example is sense-conveying full text search, which uses the word analysis algorithm to return a set of atoms which determine the meaning of a given input word [2]. The meaning is determined by the components of compound words and by prefixes and stems in simple words. For example, the word *Textverarbeitungssysteme* (text processing systems) contains {*text, verarbeitung, system; verarbeit*} (text, processing, system; process) as meaningful components. If there are several variants for forming a word from atoms, the meaning of that word may turn out to be indeterminable without context. The result will then contain several sets of atoms which provide meaning, e.g. *Baumast* → {*baum, ast*} (tree, branch), {*bau, mast*} (build, mast). For sense-conveying full text search, testing is necessary to detect words that cannot be broken up into their meaningful atoms in the correct manner. A function which returns the atoms providing meaning has already been included in the test system for all three versions. There are further plans to incorporate similar functions for spell checking, as well as for checking the proper capitalisation of words, as all nouns are being capitalised in German.

References

1. Barth, W., Nirschl, H.: Sichere sinnentsprechende Silbentrennung für die deutsche Sprache. Angewandte Informatik 4, 1985, pp. 152–159.
2. Barth, W.: Volltextsuche mit sinnentsprechender Wortzerlegung. Wirtschaftsinformatik, vol. 32, no. 5, 1990, pp. 467–471.
3. Kodydek, G.: A Word Analysis System for German Hyphenation, Full Text Search, and Spell Checking, with Regard to the Latest Reform of German Orthography. Proc. of the Third Int. Workshop on Text, Speech and Dialogue, Brno, Czech Republic, 2000.
4. Lezius, W., Rapp, R., Wettler, M.: A Freely Available Morphological Analyzer, Disambiguator, and Context Sensitive Lemmatizer for German. In: Proceedings of the COLING-ACL 1998, Montreal, Canada, 1998.
5. Sitta, H., Gallmann, P.: Duden, Informationen zur neuen deutschen Rechtschreibung, ed. Dudenredaktion, Dudenverlag, Mannheim, 1996.
6. Steiner, H.: Automatische Silbentrennung durch Wortbildungsanalyse. Ph.D. thesis, Institute of Computer Graphics, Vienna University of Technology, 1995.
7. Steiner, H., Barth, W.: Sichere sinnentsprechende Silbentrennung mit Berücksichtigung der deutschen Wortbildungsgrammatik. Tagungsband Konvens'94, ed. H. Trost, Vienna, 1994, pp. 330–340.

The Challenge of Parallel Text Processing

Milena Slavcheva

Institute for German Language
R5, 6-13, D-68161 Mannheim, Germany
Bulgarian Academy of Sciences
CLPII, LMD, 25 A, Acad. G. Bonchev St., 1113 Sofia, Bulgaria
milena@lml.bas.bg

Abstract. The paper presents the technology of building a large German-French parallel corpus consisting of official documents of the European Union and Switzerland, and private and public organisations in France and Germany. The texts are morphosyntactically annotated, aligned at the sentence level and marked up in conformance with the TEI guidelines for standardised representation. The multi-level alignment method is applied; its precision is improved due to the correlation with the constraints of the classical alignment method of Gale and Church. The alignment information is encoded externally to the parallel text documents. The process of creating the corpus is an interesting algorithm of applying a number of software tools and adjusting intermediate production results.

1   Introduction

Parallel texts are a basic resource for data-driven multilingual research in the domain of Human Language Technology. The first and underlying step to terminology and translation studies is the compilation of a text corpus according to the most up-to-date requirements in the field. This paper presents the technology of building a large German-French parallel corpus of proposed size of 30 million words (15 million words per language). At present, the algorithm of production has been tested on 2 million words (1 million words per language). The bilingual corpus consists of official documents of the European Union and Switzerland, and private and public organisations in France and Germany. The parallel German and French texts of the corpus are morphosyntactically annotated, aligned at the sentence level and marked up in conformance with the TEI guidelines [1] for creating text documents in a standardised format.

2   The Input and Output of the Parallel Text Processing

The initial input to the processing are texts in html or pdf format, downloaded from the WWW and converted into plain text format. The result of the conversion are text files where the structure of texts, essential for their automatic processing, is preserved to a varying extent. Paragraphs are the anchor structural units regarding the alignment procedure and the software tools used in the production chain.

P. Sojka, I. Kopeček, and K. Pala (Eds.): TSD 2000, LNAI 1902, pp. 133–138, 2000.

Depending on the specific features of their layout and the extent to which their structure is violated, the text files are preprocessed automatically and also manually, so that their quality is improved. The preprocessing is accelerated by the "visibility" of the actual paragraph structure, since many of the texts are treaties, laws and administrative documentation containing much numbering and having conventional structure. At the same time, the texts are problematic due to their administrative style: they contain numerous lists of items that have to be delimited in proper text portions having the form of sentences or paragraphs. A serious problem is the specific punctuation in the German and French versions or the lack of punctuation marks in the text portions containing lists of items. The proper structuring of the texts has to be defined in such a way that it ensure the successful operation of the software tools that perform the markup assignment and the alignment. The solution is to split the list items and similar structural units into separate paragraphs. The delimiting of paragraphs interacts specifically with the tokenising of sentences regarding the list items and the necessity to achieve parallel structuring of the corresponding German and French texts. The greater number of paragraph units, and, respectively, the smaller number of sentences within paragraphs improves the precision of the alignment process. We take the liberty to assign logical structure to the texts which enhances the automatic procedures, since there is a full change of the representation mode when compared to the multi-media visualisation of the texts in the WWW environment.

The final output of the processing are legal TEI documents consisting of two parts: 1) a header providing the metatextual information, and 2) a text body consisting of encoded basic structural units (paragraphs) and basic linguistic units (sentences and words with attached morphosyntactic tags and lemmas). The paragraphs and sentences are uniquely identified within the text. Figure 1 provides an example of a final German text document and its parallel French counterpart.

The alignment between corresponding segments in the bilingual parallel text documents is on the sentence level. Its encoding is externalised and is in the form of a separate document file where a link group element combines link elements indicating the correspondence of textual segments in the German and French parallel documents. Figure 2 represents the encoding of the alignment information.

The particular format of the standardised representation was defined by the following factors: the structural peculiarities of the texts, the software tools available, the rich linguistic information encoded in the texts, the large amount of textual data, and the possibility for further elaboration and processing of the parallel corpus.

The markup scheme was defined so that those tags are assigned to the text structural units which are minimally required by MLAlign [2] – the program we use for aligning and for encoding the alignment information. It is also defined so that the tags can be assigned automatically using the programs available. The elements required by MLAlign are divisions, paragraphs and sentences supplied by the *id* attribute which identifies them uniquely within the standardised document. Each text represents one single division so that the requirements of the aligning program are fulfilled without further elaboration of the division structure. In defining the sentence boundaries and assigning the corresponding tags, accomplished automatically by MARK-ALISTeR [3], the well known problem between linguistic plausibility and formal convenience necessary for the automatic processing arises. In fact, the sentence delimiters are used for defining

Source text (German)

```
<p id="d1p3">
<s id="d1p3s3">
<w ana="CARD">1</w>
<c ana="PUN">.</c>
<w ana="ADJD" lemma="gestuetzt">gestuetzt</w>
<w ana="APPR" lemma="auf">auf</w>
<w ana="ART" lemma="d">die</w>
<w ana="NN" lemma="unknown">Schlussfolgerungen</w>
...
</s>
</p>
```

Target text (French)

```
<p id="d1p3">
<s id="d1p3s3">
<w ana="ADJ:num">1</w><c ana="PON:sep">.</c>
<w ana="VER:pper" lemma="voir">vu</w>
<w ana="DET:def" lemma="le">les</w>
<w ana="NOM" lemma="conclusion">conclusions</w>
<w ana="PRE" lemma="sur">sur</w>
...
</s>
</p>
```

Fig. 1. Parallel German and French TEI conformant documents

```
<linkGrp type="alignment" source="/110104tagdere.txt"
crdate="empty" targOrder="Y" targType="seg" targFunc="null null"
target="/110104tagfrre.txt" domains="b1 b1"
evaluate="all">
<xptr from="ID (d1p1s1)" id="x1"/>
<xptr from="ID (d1p2s2)" id="x2"/>
<xptr from="ID (d1p3s3)" id="x3"/>
...
<link targets="d1p1s1 x1"/>
<link targets="d1p2s2 x2"/>
<link targets="d1p3s3 x3"/>
...
</linkGrp>
```

Fig. 2. Alignment encoding

suitable portions of text which are rather sentence-like chunks enhancing the correct operation of the aligning tools. At the paragraph level, there is no other differentiation of structural elements than the paragraph.

The German and French documents also contain the appropriate TEI markup for the morphosyntactic annotation attached to each word token in the texts. The morphosyntactic tags and the lemmas are values of the respective *ana* and *lemma* attributes specifying all word and punctuation elements in the texts.

3   The Alignment Method and the Documentation of the Textual Data

The multi-level alignment method [2] is applied; it is based on the logical structure of texts represented in a hierarchy of elements. The idea is to make use of the information present in texts that are already marked up and to obtain alignment results at levels of different depth in the structural hierarchy of texts (e.g., division, paragraph or sentence level). This hierarchical alignment algorithm is meant to cope with cases where the source and target texts may not have been encoded in a strictly parallel way at the intermediate levels (e.g., paragraphs) between the root element (i.e., division) and the leaves (i.e., sentences), and it allows the recombination of elements at a given level, even if they belong to two different units at the upper level [2]. The method is designed for application to independently created SGML or XML encoded text documents where the encoding scheme may vary.

The MLAlign program [2] is the software application of the multi-level alignment method which we use to align the sentence level segments in the parallel German and French texts. The input to the program are TEI conformant text documents, and the output is a link-group file with pointers to the aligned segments (i.e., sentences) in the parallel texts. Thus the alignment information is encoded externally to the text documents. This particular strategy of encoding and storing different types of information in different documents corresponds to the idea of general use and multiple reuse of standardised linguistic resources.

Although, as pointed above, the hierarchical alignment method is designed to produce correct alignments at a given level (primarily at the sentence level) in case there are discrepancies in the parallel structure at a higher level (usually the paragraph level), in reality the precision rate of the alignment operation is highly correlated to the quality of the encoding in the input text documents. In the case of the parallel text processing described in this paper, the quality of the performance of MLAlign is highly improved by the following factors: 1) the German and French TEI encoded text documents are produced simultaneously and have uniform standardised representation; 2) correlation is established with the constraints of the classical alignment method of Gale and Church [4].

In the initial steps of the production chain, the sentence tokeniser and the paragraph and sentence boundaries marker in the German and French texts is MARK-ALISTeR [3], a software system for alignment. It is based on the Gale and Church statistical method for sentence alignment whose high rate of precision relies on the equal number of paragraphs in the parallel texts. MARK-ALISTeR provides a friendly editing environment for the preprocessing of the source and target texts so that the parallel structure necessary for accomplishing the sentence alignment is obtained.

The two alignment programs have a different design, hence the different input, intermediate and final output, and different utilities for obtaining the desired results.

In the production chain of textual resources described in this paper, the advantages of the two approaches to the alignment process and to the representation of the alignment results are utilised and combined in an efficient way.

4   The Technology of Attaining the Desired Final Result

The process of creating the corpus is an interesting algorithm of applying a number of software tools, obtaining intermediate products and adjusting the output of a given "milestone" program so that it becomes the appropriate input to the "milestone" program coming next in the production chain. The operating peculiarities of the programs determine the order of their application so that the production chain is the most optimal and economical one.

After the initial preprocessing of the texts as described in Section 2, the texts enter MARK-ALISTeR, a system for marking, aligning and searching translation equivalents. The editing facilities of the preprocessing mode of the system are used for obtaining strict parallel paragraph structure where necessary. The program acts as a sentence boundaries delimiter of the two parallel texts. The precision of the sentence delimiting is decreased by the frequent occurrence of specific abbreviations in the German and French texts due to their administrative style (e.g, the German z.B.). The program editor provides for correction of the automatically defined sentence boundaries. A valuable function of MARK-ALISTeR is the assignment of TEI markup to the paragraph and sentence units and the option of saving the two marked texts separately as an intermediate result. The output to the aligning proper function of the system is a bitext with no markup assigned which contains sequences of alignments on the sentence level. This output is stored as a result, but the production chain continues with the further processing of the files which are the output of the program marking operation.

The files in question are the input to the IMS TreeTagger [5] developed for German, French and English. It assigns a morphosyntactic tag and a lemma to each word-level token in the German and French texts.

The output files from the TreeTagger are automatically cleaned up and converted into TEI conformant format by a specially developed program. The division, paragraph and sentence elements are assigned unique identifiers. The result is shown in Figure 1. A header is attached to each text document according to the requirements of the TEI guidelines.

The TEI conformant parallel text documents are then processed by the MLAlign program, and the link-group file encoding the alignment information is generated (Figure 2) which consists of three parts: 1) external pointers to the segments of the target text that will be aligned; 2) links between the units of textual segments to be aligned that consist of more than one text unit; 3) links between aligned segments in the source and target texts. The alignment representation scheme is XML conformant.

5   Conclusion

The data-driven linguistic investigations require textual data of large quantity whose production is tedious and time-consuming, and very often at the expense of quality.

The technology of producing the large bilingual parallel corpus described in this paper provides a reasonable degree of quality of the textual data.

Acknowledgement

The author is indebted to Elena Paskaleva, Martin Wynne, Alexander Genchev, Tomaz Erjavec, Helmut Schmid and Laurent Romary for the invaluable help.

References

1. Sperberg-McQueen, C. M., Burnard, L. (Eds.): Guidelines for Electronic Text Encoding and Interchange. Text Encoding Initiative. Chicago and Oxford (1994).
2. Romary, L., Bonhomme, P.: Parallel Alignment of Structured Documents. In: Jean Veronis (Ed.): Parallel Text Processing. Kluwer Academic Publisher (to appear).
3. Paskaleva, E., Mihov, S.: Second Language Acquisition from Aligned Corpora. In: Proceedings of the International Conference "Language Technology and Language Teaching", Groningen (1997).
4. Gale, W., Church, K.: A Program for Aligning Sentences in Bilingual Corpora. In: Computational Linguistics 19(1), (1993) 75–102.
5. Schmid, H.: Probabilistic Part-of-Speech Tagging Using Decision Trees. In: Proceedings of International Conference on New Methods in Language Processing, Manchester, UK (1994).

Selected Types of Pg-Ambiguity:
Processing Based on Analysis by Reduction*

Markéta Straňáková

Faculty of Mathematics and Physics, Charles University, Prague, Czech Republic
marketa.stranakova@ufal.mff.cuni.cz

Abstract. A need for the detection of ambiguous prepositional groups (Pg's) is discussed in the paper. Criteria for automatic Pg-disambiguation are presented, with special accent on word order patterns and verbonominal collocations, the main source of non-projective constructions caused by non-congruent Pg-modifiers of nouns. Usefulness of the proposed criteria and their ordering within an analysis by reduction is introduced.

1   Description of the Problem

Based on the stratificational, dependency-oriented Functional Generative Description of Czech (FGD), four types of ambiguity can be distinguished according to the level of language description containing units which introduce the possibility of two (or more) readings of a sentence.

With prepositional groups (Pg's), the ambiguity defined as an asymmetric relation between the level of surface structure and the adjacent morphemic level is frequent, i.e. the situation when two or more possible functions on the level of the surface representation of the sentence are expressed by the same morphemic form (cf. morphemic ambiguity in the terms defined in [4]). In phrase structure oriented formalisms, the corresponding problem is known as PP-attachment, see [1].

From a strictly syntactic point of view, a Pg can modify (depend on) a verb, a noun or an adjective (typically deverbal) in the sentence, as in the following example.

Example (1): V období, kdy prudce poklesl zájem na domácím trhu, dokázala továrna část výroby exportovat. (PDT, bmd03zua.fs ♯4, shortened)
[at - time - when - sharply - fell - demand - on - domestic - market - managed - factory - part - (of) production - (to) export]
(At the time when the demand on the domestic market sharply fell, the factory managed to export part of its production.)
Analysing the Pg *na domácím trhu* [on (the) domestic market], the valency frame of the noun *zájem* [demand] is important.

zájem . . .   Act (Gen/Adj$_{pos}$) Pat (*na*+Loc/*o*+Acc)
Thus, the Pg *na domácím trhu* [on (the) domestic market] can be treated either (a) as a

---

* The research reported on this paper has been supported by the grant VS 96/151.

free modifier (Locative) belonging to the verb *poklesnout* [to fall], or
(b) as an attribute of the noun *zájem* [demand] - either as (ba) a valency modifier (Patient)
or (bb) a free modifier (Locative). (The valency slot of Pat with *zájem* [demand] is
occupied by a General Participant in cases (a) and (bb).)

In general, a sentence with a Pg that can be analysed as a modifier belonging to
any of two (or more) distinct sentence members can have two (or even more) different
meanings (as in (a) and (ba)) – hence the need for criteria that allow for the detection of
occurrences of ambiguous Pg's.

The appropriate (human) analysis of a sentence is based on a wide range of syntactic,
but also semantic and even pragmatic, knowledge. We try to detect the types of input
information the automatic procedure can take into account and to determine the criteria
both for the detection of Pg-ambiguity and for Pg-disambiguation.

Prague Dependency Treebank (PDT) serves as a basic source of data for Czech.

2   Proposal of the Criteria

We presuppose the existence of a lexicon with detailed information containing complete
valency frames for verbs, nouns and also adjectives. The verbonominal collocations
must be also kept in the lexicon with their valencies. Optionally, the semantic features
of nouns and verbs can be used if they are available. The procedure proposed operates
on data provided by full morphological analysis.

2.1   Word Order Patterns (WOP's)

The surface word order serves as the basic purely grammatical clue to the Pg-ambiguity
detection. Typically, Pg satisfies word order constraints, which have been embodied in
WOP's.

Basic unambiguous WOP's.
  – V immediately followed by Pg (such V is the Pg governor);
  – Pg at the very beginning of a clause (V is the prototypical Pg governor);
  – Adj and Pg are separated by any verb form (V is the Pg governor).
These WOP's are relevant for Pg's in prototypical positions. The analysis of
prolific non-projective constructions caused by non-congruent Pg-modifier of noun
is discussed in the subsection 2.2.

Basic suspicious WOP's.
  – a sequence of N's at the beginning of a clause followed by Pg;
  – a sequence of V, N and Pg (in this order);
  – Pg between N and V (from the left to the right);
  – Pg between V and Adj (V - Pg - Adj - N) or Pg being followed by an adjective,
    a noun and a verb (in this order) (Pg - Adj - N - V).
There can be strings of nouns instead of a single N in all of these word order patterns
(all of them either without a preposition or in a prepositional case).

WOP's with a preferable reading.
  – N being followed by a congruent Adj and Pg (in this order) (then Pg is preferably
    treated as belonging to such Adj);

  - Pg between N and a congruent Adj (then Pg is preferably treated as belonging
    to such Adj).

There are some regular exceptions to these rules, as the specific contrastive position
of Adj or collocations characteristic for scientific terminology.

2.2 Verbonominal Collocations

A verbonominal collocation can be described as a collocation of a noun and a verb
(often with very general meaning) where the noun part has a valency slot filled in by Pg.
With verbonominal collocations, the word order constraints may be violated and thus
the WOP's defined in subsection 2.1 cannot be taken into account.

Two types of verbonominal collocations can be distinguished; both of them must be
kept in the lexicon (among the entries of the noun item).

  - A verbonominal collocation consists of a verb with very general meaning and of
    a noun with valency requirements (type (1), *mít šanci/peníze na co* [to have a
    chance/money for st.], *podat stížnost na koho/co* [to submit (a) complain of sb./st.]).
  - Both a noun and a verb constituting a verbonominal collocation have valency slots
    requiring the examined Pg (type (2), *klást nároky na koho/co* [to make demands on
    sb./st.]).

From the purely syntactic point of view there are two systematic possibilities how
to analyse such collocations – the Pg can be treated either as an attributive nominal
modifier or/and as a verbal modifier, which either is registered in a valency frame, or is
its optional free modifier. In agreement with the valency requirements, we propose the
following solution.

Solution. Concerning Pg-disambiguation two issues must be solved:
  - If only the nominal part of the verbonominal collocation has a valency slot
    requiring the examined Pg (type (1)) then the Pg is analysed as an adnominal
    modifier (in agreement with the valency requirements of the noun). The word
    order constraints must be relaxed, non-projective constructions may arise (see
    below).
  - For type (2), where both the name and the verb constituting the verbonominal
    collocation require valency Pg-modifier, WOP's are applied. Two structures are
    preserved whenever it is possible (the one treating Pg as an adnominal modifier
    and the other with Pg as a verbal modifier).

*Example (2): Finanční prostředky na nákup technického vybavení a učebnic poskytly
... (PDT, bm122zua.fs ♯21)*
[financial – means/sources – for purchase – (of) technical – equipment – and – textbooks –
provided]
(Financial sources for technical equipment and textbooks were provided by ...)
The verb *poskytnout* [to provide] constitutes a verbonominal collocation together with
the noun *prostředek* [means], type (1):
    prostředek ... Aim (*na*+Acc, *pro*+Acc, *k*+Gen)
According to the solution proposed the structure with the noun chosen as the Pg governor
is preserved (the other one, with the Pg as free verbal modifier (also Aim), is excluded).

In such constructions, the Pg modifies the whole verbonominal collocation and cannot be seen as a purely nominal modifier; this is supported by the changes in syntactic structure of such groups in case of adjectival derivation:

poskytnout (prostředky (na něco)) → prostředky (poskytnuté (na něco))
[to provide means for st.]   [means/sources provided for st.]
The Pg is treated as a nominal modifier in the verbonominal collocation. The other syntactic structure is relevant for the construction with a deverbal adjective: *poskytnutý* (pl *poskytnuté*) [provided] is a congruent attribute following its governing noun *prostředky* [means]; thus, according to the WOP, the Pg *na něco* [for st.] is preferably treated as a modifier of the adjective.

Description of non-projective constructions. The dependency tree is projective if all nodes (n_i) - lying between a governor node (n_g) and a node (n_d) depending on n_g - depend (directly or indirectly) on this governor node (n_g). Otherwise it is non-projective. (The formal definition of projectivity and non-projectivity can be found e.g. in [3].)

Observations. (valid for verbonominal collocations, type (1))
  – A valency modifier of a noun expressed by Pg can precede its noun governor in the surface structure of a sentence. (Analysing such a Pg modifier WOP's cannot be applied).
  – A valency modifier of a noun expressed by Pg and its noun governor can be 'separated' by the verb form, we can get a non-projective structure on the level of surface representation (WOP's cannot be taken into account).
  – Free modifiers of a noun expressed by Pg's must follow their governor on the surface level – the WOP's are applied.

Example (3): Na uveřejnění odpovědi má podle něho právo každá fyzická nebo právnická osoba . . . (PDT, bmd23zua.fs ♯46, modified))
[on – publication – (of) reaction – has – according to – him – right – every – person – or – legal – entity]
(According to him, every person or legal entity has the right of publication of reaction . . .)
The noun *právo* [right] constitutes a verbonominal collocation, type (1) together with the verb *mít* [to have].
      právo . . . Pat (Gen/*na*+Acc/*k*+Dat/infinitive)
The Pg *na uveřejnění (odpovědi)* [of publication (of reaction)] meets the valency requirement of the noun *právo* [right] resulting in a non-projective construction.

3   Arrangement of the Criteria

An **analysis by reduction** (RA) is a general method that can naturally underlie any automatic parsing procedure.

The analysis by reduction consists of stepwise simplification of an extended sentence so that its syntactic correctness is preserved. In each stage the simplification is realized by deleting one word of a sentence and possibly rewriting other words. This process is non-deterministic, in each stage any of the mutually independent words can be deleted.

In the next paragraphs we propose the partial use of RA for the detection of Pg-governors. (For the particular description of the criteria used see [6].)

Routine. In every possible stage of analysis in which Pg is reduced all criteria under consideration are applied.

Step 1. The word order pattern of the simplified sentence is specified.

Step 2. All valency requirements of autosemantic verbs, nouns and adjectives are examined. With respect to word order limits (as they are embodied in WOP) every suitable valency slot is filled in by the tested Pg. If some verbonominal collocation, type (1) is detected then the valency requirements are satisfied regardless of the relevant word order limitations. Possible new structures are evaluated according to the reliability of valency frames.

Step 3. The information following from the word order pattern of the simplified sentence is applied. All possible dependencies are marked. New structures are of lower preference than the ones described in the preceding point.

Step 4. Optionally, semantically based criteria can be applied serving for the evaluation of existing structures.

Step 5. The formal criteria are checked with regard to the original sentence. If any new structure violates these criteria then it is excluded from further analysis.

Step 6. If at least one new structure satisfies the formal criteria then Pg is deleted. Otherwise this branch of analysis is excluded because it does not preserve the condition of correctness.

Example (4): Rodiny mají nárok na příspěvek. (PDT, bl103zu.fs, shortened)
[Families have (a) claim to (an) allowance.]
(a) If the verbonominal collocation *mít nárok* [to have (a) claim], type (1) is taken into account the reduction of the Pg *na příspěvek* [to allowance] starts in two stages (see Figure 1, bold arrows). According to the solution proposed above the dependency pair *nárok na příspěvek* [claim to allowance] is created (in agreement with the valency requirement of the noun).
(b) If the verbonominal collocations are not considered the analysis *mít na příspěvek* is also allowed. The reduction of Pg then starts in further two stages (see Figure 1, dotted arrows). The two analyses satisfy the condition on preserving syntactic correctness, both are successful. However, the second structure *mít na příspěvek* accidentally has another meaning than the original sentence has. Its meaning is connected with a frozen collocation *mít na něco (prostředky/peníze/ ...)* [to have the wherewithal's for fee]. The source of this coincidence lies in the lexical entries, therefore it cannot be covered by general rules.

4   Conclusions

We have tried to illustrate the usefulness of criteria for detection of Pg-ambiguity based on word order patterns and valency requirements of nouns and adjectives. Special interest has been devoted to verbonominal collocations and to their contribution to analysis of

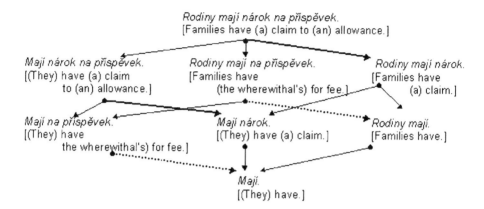

Fig. 1. The possible stages during RA

non-projective constructions. The last section has been focussed on the analysis by reduction. The mechanism of this type of analysis has been illustrated and the treatment of the proposed criteria has been discussed.

References

1. Allen, J.: Natural Language Understanding. The Benjamin/Cummings Publishing Company, 1987.
2. Holan, T., Kuboň, V., Oliva, K., Plátek, M.: On Complexity of Word Order. Special Issue TAL on Dependency Grammars (to appear).
3. Marcus, S.: Sur la notion de projectivité. In: Zeitschr. für math. Logic und Grundlagen d. Math. XI, 1965, pp. 181–192.
4. Panevová, J.: K otázkám homonymie a neutralizace ve stavbě věty. Jazykovedné štúdie **16**, 1981, pp. 85–89.
5. Sgall, P., Hajičová, E., Panevová, J.: The Meaning of the Sentence in Its Semantic and Pragmatic Aspects. Dordrecht:Reidel and Prague:Academia, 1986.
6. Straňáková, M.: Selected Types of Pg-Ambiguity. PBML **72**, 1999, pp. 29–58.

Cohesive Generation of Syntactically Simplified Newspaper Text

Yvonne Canning, John Tait, Jackie Archibald, and Ros Crawley

School of Computing, Engineering & Technology
University of Sunderland
St. Peter's Campus, Sunderland, UK
yvonne.canning@sunderland.ac.uk

Abstract. This paper describes SYSTAR (SYntactic Simplification of Text for Aphasic Readers), the PSet module which splits compound sentences, activises seven agentive passive clause types, and resolves and replaces eight frequently occurring anaphoric pronouns. We describe our techniques and strategies, report on the results obtained after evaluation of a corpus of 100 newspaper articles downloaded from the website of a daily provincial, and briefly report on experimental studies with aphasic participants.

1   Introduction

In this paper we will describe SYSTAR (SYntactic Simplification of Text for Aphasic Readers), a system which we believe demonstrates that general text simplification which retains the meaning and coherence of original text is feasible. SYSTAR is part of PSet (Practical Simplification of English Text)[1], a system which lexically and syntactically simplifies newspaper text for aphasic readers [6].

Aphasia is an acquired language impairment which may follow brain damage caused by, for example, head injury or stroke. Those affected were previously normal language-users and intellect is not affected. Research has shown that certain constructions may be difficult for aphasic readers to comprehend [11]. For instance, passive clauses can be problematic [5], though world knowledge may enable interpretation of semantically non-reversible clauses; the resolution of anaphors can be difficult [7]; and the complexity of sentences is increased by multiple verbs and their functional argument structures [3]. Accordingly, SYSTAR splits compound sentences, activises some passive clauses, and resolves and replaces eight anaphoric pronouns. SYSTAR's training and test data were articles taken from a local newspaper's website.

2   Cohesion

SYSTAR takes as input text which has been analysed as follows: i) a tagger [9] assigns part of speech (POS) to each word; ii) verbs and nouns are morphologically analysed;

---

[1] PSet is a 3-year project funded by UK Engineering & Physical Sciences Research Council (Grant No: GR/L50105).

iii) the sentence is parsed [2], e.g., (S (NP ("A" AT1) ("cat" NN1)) (VP ("have+s" VHZ) (VPPAS ("be+en" VBN) ("attack+ed" VVN) (PP ("by" II) (NP ("a" AT1) ("dog" NN1)))))). VPPAS is the Verb Phrase PASsive marker.

SYSTAR splits compound sentences which can mean that what were within-sentence anaphora cross sentence boundaries, frequently resulting in sentences that begin with anaphoric pronouns. Splitting of sentences also entails the removal of conjunctions, which are sometimes used to facilitate text "flow". Activisation of passive clauses, i.e. change of voice, entails the rearrangement of clauses within a sentence. When these sorts of changes are made to text, it is essential that the cohesion of the original text is maintained to ensure that interpretation of the discourse is not disrupted [10]. Also, as Quirk et al. [13] caution "a shift of meaning may accompany shift of voice".

SYSTAR maintains cohesion by:

- Ensuring anaphoric expressions are replaced by the most recent noun phrase (NP).
- Ensuring resolved anaphors are not replaced if the original NP appears previously within the sentence, to avoid ambiguous replacements.
- Replacing original sentence-opening anaphors with NPs to maintain text style.
- Preserving the tense, mood and aspect of passive verb phrases (VPs).

3 Text Patterns and Simplifications

SYSTAR's simplification module utilises production rules, the left hand (LH) of which is a simplifiable text pattern; i.e. an ordered description of the significant markers of the input sentence parse. Unification pattern matching takes place, during which the input sentence is matched against the LH. The right hand (RH) of each rule is a simplified text pattern, an ordered description of the variables corresponding to the required transformed output parse tree; after unification bound tree fragments are substituted into a copy of the RH. Sentences are recursively re-applied to each rule until there is no unification and all rules have been applied, ensuring that multiple instances of a text pattern are correctly processed.

3.1 Passive Clause Patterns

Within SYSTAR, only agentive passives can be activised. Thus, the preposition phrase marker (PP) and preposition ("by" II) are matched and the subsequent NP is checked to ensure, that it is not a temporal expression, e.g. "by September". [13] define six passive verb clause types: present tense (is attacked); past tense (was attacked); modal auxiliary verb (should be attacked); perfective aspect (have been attacked); progressive aspect (was being attacked); modal + perfective (may have been attacked). To these should be added the habitual contrast (used to be attacked). Currently there are three VPPAS rules and these cover the above seven clause types. All text preceding the passive phrase is bound (?a) and the final NP of that text, which will be the object of the activised version, is removed and bound to a new variable (?x). Any text following the passive phrase is bound separately (?e) to ensure surrounding text is not affected. Figure 1 shows the modal parse tree, consisting of two verb groups: modal and primary auxiliary-and-lexical. However, perfective, progressive and modal + perfective clauses also unify with

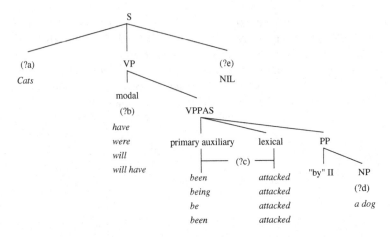

Fig. 1. General Modal Passive Pattern

Table 1. Modal Passive Clause Sub-patterns

(? b) Modal		(? c)		Clause Type	Output Forms
		Aux	Lexical		
has/have/etc.		VBN	VVN	Perfective	Modal depends on agent no.
		been	attacked		Lexical unchanged.
were/is/etc.		VBG	VVN	Progressive	Modal depends on agent no.
		being	attacked		-ing form of lexical.
will/can/etc.		VBO	VVN	Modal	Modal unchanged.
		be	attacked		Base form of lexical.
would/can/etc.	VHO	VBN	VVN	Modal+Perfective	Modal unchanged.
	have	been	attacked		Lexical unchanged

this tree and analysis of verbs within bindings is required to determine the clause type and correct output. Table 1 shows the modal sub-patterns.

4   Anaphora Resolution and Replacement

An analysis of pronoun usage in newspaper articles was reported in [4]. As a result of this analysis it was decided that eight frequently occurring coreferring anaphors (singular "he", "she", "him" and "her"; plural "they"; singular possessives "his" and "her"; plural possessive "their") would be resolved and replaced. The anaphora resolution algorithm is based on CogNIAC [1]. Each NP is given an ID number and is input to an entity tool which assigns properties according to phrase-marker, POS-tag or word. Properties are Gender, Number and EntityType. EntityTypes are: Company, Organisation, Person and Items, where "Items" are other plural NPs which can be referred to by "they" or "their", such as "the roads". The entity tool is an array whose cells hold multiple entries. For instance, the top 88 British surnames, according to 1996 UK electoral rolls, appear within one cell. There are three fields in the array, holding: the location of the indicator, the indicator itself, and the properties associated with it. Indicators are ranked so for instance honorifics such as "Princess" are ranked above names such as "Mary", to allow for anomalies such as "Princess Michael of Kent". Once a pronoun is detected, all possible antecedents are recalled. We resolve according to coreference restrictions and recency only, and this currently returns 85% precision. After resolution the chosen antecedent's ID is attached to the pronoun (4 "he" PPSH1), and during replacement the corresponding NP is substituted.

5   Evaluation

To evaluate the system an initial corpus consisting of 100 newspaper articles was created. The numbers of compound sentences, passive clauses and anaphors are given in Table 2. From a total of 405 passive clauses only 60 were activisable; the rest were either agentless or were incorrectly parsed. From a total of twenty compounds, two were incorrectly parsed. We believe twenty is an untypically low figure for this sort of text, but were unable to investigate this further in the current round of evaluations. The remainder of this section presents our results.

5.1   Anaphora Resolution

Preliminary results of anaphora resolution show recall of 81.5% with precision of 85%, where recall is the percentage of correctly resolved anaphors from the total to be resolved, and precision is the percentage of correctly resolved anaphors from the total resolved. This result is likely to improve as the entity tool's coverage is increased. Plural anaphors are problematic; at present 50% are incorrectly resolved. If plurals are not included we achieve 88% recall and 92% precision.

6   Compound Sentence Simplification

All compound sentences were correctly unified; only one, with an example of NP ellipsis, gave ungrammatical output: "He is a football fanatic and won with the phrase ... " became "He is a football fanatic. Won with the phrase ... ". This will be solved by the insertion of the previous subject (He) and will be implemented in a future version of the system.

6.1   Passive Clause Activisation

Approximately 70% of activised clauses are grammatically acceptable. The following example demonstrates how meaning can be changed. The passive's subject (he) is part of a relative clause but the entire clause is bound. The original sentence was: "The convicted football hooligan who claims he is being harassed by the police has launched a formal complaint." SYSTAR's current libellous output is: "Police are harassing the convicted football hooligan who claims he has launched a formal complaint".

Table 2. 100-Article Corpus Statistics

Total Words:							69,000
Compound Sentences							18
Activisable VPPAS Clauses							60
Clause Types	Past:	26	Habitual Contrast:	2	Progressive:	4 Present: 3	
	Modal:	11	Modal + Perfective:	2	Perfective:	12 (1 negative)	
Anaphoric Pronouns							655
Pronoun Types	He:	192	She:	76	Him:	19 Her: 5	
	His:	138	Possessive Her:	48	They:	83 Their: 94	

6.2 Experimental Study

A recent pilot experiment [8] measured six aphasic participants' reading time and comprehension of sentence pairs holding cross-sentence anaphors compared to similar sentences with anaphors replaced by original NPs. Results showed that replacement shortened reading time for five out of the six participants and enabled everyone to correctly answer all questions.

7   Future Work and Conclusion

We believe SYSTAR has already demonstrated the feasibility of text simplification retaining (in general) meaning and cohesion, despite using only limited linguistic data and no world knowledge. Of course current performance falls short of what is required for a practical application but we have identified ways forward with all problems. Future work to be done includes the following:

- Further rules are required to improve precision of anaphora resolution
- Grammatical relations (subject and object) will be included in the next version of the parser to aid replacement of elided NPs and improve anaphora resolution

Section 5 pointed out some limitations of our current work. However, all aphasic participants commented on the usefulness and effectiveness of simplified text [8] and the simplifications may be useful to others such as deaf readers [12]. The fact that our approach focusses on linguistic knowledge indicates that it should be comparatively easily applicable to other domains and applications.

References

1. Baldwin, B. CogNIAC: high precision coreference with limited knowledge and linguistic resources. In *Proceedings of the ACL/EACL'97 Workshop on Operational Factors in Practical, Robust Anaphora Resolution*, 1997.
2. Briscoe, E. and Carroll, J. Developing and evaluating a probabilistic LR parser of part-of-speech and punctuation labels. In *Proceedings of the ACL/SIGPARSE 4th International Workshop on Parsing Techniques*, Prague, 1995.

3. Byng, S. Sentence processing deficits: Theory and therapy. *Cognitive Neuropsychology*, 5(6), 1988.

4. Canning, Y. and Tait, J. Syntactic simplification of newspaper text for aphasic readers. In *Customised Information Delivery Workshop, SIGIR 99*, Berkeley, California, 1999.

5. Caplan, D. and Futter, C. Assignment of thematic roles by an agrammatic aphasic patient. *Brain and Language*, 27:117–135, 1986.

6. Carroll, J., Minnen, G., Canning, Y., Devlin, S., and Tait, J. Practical Simplification of English Newspaper Text to assist aphasic readers. In *AAAI-98 Workshop on Integrating Artificial Intelligence and Assistive Technology*, Madison, Wisconsin, 1998.

7. Caspari, I., Parkinson, S. R., LaPointe, L. L., and Katz, R. C. Working memory and aphasia. *Brain and Cognition*, 37:205–223, 1998. Academic Press.

8. Devlin, S. and Canning, Y. Automatic text simplification for readers with aphasia. In *The British Aphasiology Society Biennial International Conference*, City University, London, 1999. Platform Presentation.

9. Elworthy, D. Does baum-welch re-estimation help taggers? In *Proceedings of the 4th ACL conference on Applied Natural Language Processing*, pages 53–58, 1994.

10. Halliday, M. A. K. and Hasan, R. *Cohesion in English*. Number 9 in English Language Series. Longman, 1976.

11. Lesser, R. *Linguistic Investigations of Aphasia*. Edward Arnold, 1978.

12. Quigley, S. P. and Paul, P. V. *Language and deafness*. Singular Publishing Group, Inc, San Diego, CA, 2nd edition, 1994.

13. Quirk, R., Greenbaum, S., Leech, G., and Svartvik, J. *A Grammar of Contemporary English*. Longman Group Limited, 1972.

TEA: A Text Analysis Tool
for the Intelligent Text Document Filtering

Jan Žižka[1], Aleš Bourek[2], and Luděk Frey[1]

[1] Department of Information Technologies
Faculty of Informatics, Masaryk University in Brno
Botanická 68a, 602 00 Brno, Czech Republic
zizka@informatics.muni.cz, xfrey@informatics.muni.cz
[2] Department of Biophysics
Faculty of Medicine, Masaryk University in Brno
Joštova 10, 662 43 Brno, Czech Republic
bourek@med.muni.cz

Abstract. This paper describes results achieved with a text-document classification tool TEA (TExt Analyzer) based on the naïve Bayes algorithm. TEA provides also a set of additional functions, which can assist users at fine-tuning the text classifiers and improving the classification accuracy, mainly through modifications of dictionaries generated during the training phase. Experiments, described in the paper, aimed at supporting work with medical unstructured text documents downloaded from the Internet. Good and stable results (around 97% of the classification accuracy) were achieved for selecting documents in a certain area of interest among a large number of documents from different areas.

1 Introduction

Nowadays, computer users can access incredibly large volumes of text documents via networks from databases and the Internet. Traditional retrieval methods, based on key words, typically provide, as a response, too many documents that are not actually relevant. Screening out uninteresting documents is usually a time-consuming and tedious work. Contemporary overview of selected Machine Learning tools to Information Retrieval can be found in [5]. Automated selection of interesting documents helps users to concentrate on their primary tasks. In the case of pure-text documents, an intelligent filter is entirely dependent on the word contents. The following sections describe a text analysis tool TEA, which is based on the naïve Bayes classifier and the task of which is to assist its users in training and using an effective text-document classifier.

2 The TEA Structure

TEA [2] consists of the following three parts: (1) the naïve Bayes classifier, (2) the training algorithm, and (3) supporting functions that enable users to work with word

P. Sojka, I. Kopeček, and K. Pala (Eds.): TSD 2000, LNAI 1902, pp. 151–156, 2000.

frequency dictionaries, to fine-tune the process of learning and classification, and to perform selected text analyses.

As the basic classification algorithm, TEA uses the naïve Bayes probabilistic classifier based on principles described in [6]. TEA learns from user-labeled sets of training examples. An example is a text document. Since the task of the classifier is to predict if a new, previously unseen example belongs to a group of interesting or uninteresting documents, two document classes are used: the *positive* class includes interesting documents while the *negative* class contains the rest. Each example is represented as a sequence of individual words (tokens). In the TEA system, a word is a string of characters delimited by white space. Before processing, all upper-case letters are converted into their lower-case equivalents. Strings longer than 15 characters are truncated.

The naïve Bayes classifier makes word independence assumptions which substantially reduce the number of parameters. Even if these assumptions are not generally correct, in practice it works well, see [1] or [4]. Let w_i stands for an i-th word in the dictionary containing all distinct words from the entire set of training examples. The degree to which a text document belongs to a certain class $c_j \in C = \{c_1, c_2, \ldots, c_{|C|}\}$, where $|C|$ is the number of classes, is given by the value $E(c_j)$:

$$E(c_j) = P(c_j) \prod_{i=1}^{n} P(w_i|c_j) \,, \tag{1}$$

$$P(c_j) = \frac{N_{docs_j}}{N_{docs}} \,, \tag{2}$$

where $E(c_j)$ is the estimate how much a new classified document is expected to be a member of c_j, $P(c_j)$ is an *a priori* probability that a document belongs to the class c_j, N_{docs_j} is the number of documents in the class c_j, N_{docs} is the total number of documents in all classes, $P(w_i|c_j)$ is the relative frequency (*a posteriori* probability) of w_i in the class c_j, and n is a number of words in the classified document. To avoid the problem with different number of interesting and uninteresting documents, it is useful to implement the m-estimate method for computations of terms $P(w_i|c_j)$:

$$P(w_i|c_j) = \frac{n_i^{(j)} + 1}{N_j + N_d} \,, \tag{3}$$

where $n_i^{(j)}$ is the occurrence number of the i-th word w_i in the class c_j, N_d is the total number of distinct words, and N_j is the number of distinct words in the class c_j (see [3]).

TEA's training process (see Table 1) assumes the existence of two classes of documents: one for positive (interesting, relevant) examples and one for negative (uninteresting, irrelevant) examples. The training is equivalent to setting up all the parameters that are needed for the classification process. Also, it is possible to retrain the classifier any time later when more examples are available. After training the naïve Bayes classifier, the user can utilize it to predict a class for new documents. The classification algorithm is straightforward (see Table 2).

Table 1. Algorithm 1: The training procedure

---

1. For the entire set of N_{docs} training documents, store all the pairs *(a distinct word, its frequency)* into the dictionary.
2. For both possible classifications $c_j \in \{interesting, \ uninteresting\}$, and for all documents in the training set, find out N_{docs_j}, compute $P(c_j)$ and $P(w_i|c_j), i = 1, \ldots, N_d$.

Table 2. Algorithm 2: The classification procedure

---

1. Within a new document, separate individual words w_i and find out their total number, n.
2. Compute the membership degree of the new document in each of the two classes c_j:

$$M_j = P(c_j) \prod_{i=1}^{n} P(w_i|c_j) \ . \tag{4}$$

3. Find out which class corresponds to the $\max(M_1, M_2)$, and assign it to the document.

In addition to the basic naïve Bayes method, TEA includes various functions that support the users' work with dictionaries that create the basis for the classifier. The dictionaries are built during the training process and contain words and their frequencies for the negative and positive examples. TEA's functions enable the users to customize classifiers to a high degree, depending on their area of interest; moreover, different users can share the same collection of text documents from different points of view. Another important task, which TEA supports, is the preprocessing of the raw text data obtained as the results of the users' queries. Unfortunately, the space available for describing the TEA system does not allow to provide full details; however, some essential TEA's functions are obvious from the following section, which describes experiments with medical text documents.

3   Results of Experiments

The experiments with training and classification were carried out to reveal possible strong and weak aspects of the naïve Bayes algorithm applied to real-world data obtained from the Internet. Particularly, extensive tests focused on pure-text documents – medical articles downloaded from MEDLINE using the conventional method based on sets of key words. Data obtained by this procedure typically contain many irrelevant and uninteresting documents, therefore the user cannot avoid some kind of postprocessing to get the needed information.

The results, described in this paper, were obtained using three series of tests. In all the cases, the classification of training examples was done manually by an expert in the field of interest. The first group of experiments aimed at finding documents relevant to the 'assisted reproduction'. Here, the set of interesting documents consisted of 701 articles while the uninteresting documents included topics such as 'contraception' (434 articles), 'gynecological endocrinology' (417) and 'computers in medicine' (258). Altogether, the set of uninteresting documents consisted of 1,109 articles from three different medical areas.

The goal of the second group of experiments was to find out how the classifier can assess which new documents are or are not interesting for the given user (provided that the same user classified training examples) in just one area of interest – in this case, 'assisted reproduction'. The user marked 299 articles as interesting and 402 as uninteresting (together, 701 documents).

As the second group of experiments provided rather unstable results, the third group was carried out. In this case, the number of interesting documents was decreased by the random selection so that it was the same as the number of uninteresting documents, i.e., 299.

Each test series was performed four times and consisted of eight-fold cross-validation. Thus, each test was carried out 32 times. The total result was obtained as the average from the partial results. Generally, the classification was influenced by several factors that increased the difficulty of learning and decreased the classification accuracy. First, the documents contained a large number (12,631) of different word forms. Second, there were too many irrelevant attributes (words) which did not contribute to the classification at all, e.g., conjunctions, auxiliary verbs, etc. Third, the documents contained several kinds of noise: wrong classifications performed by the human expert, misspelled words, abbreviations having the form of a word, and so like. Some of the tests attempted to eliminate the influence of these factors.

3.1   Original Document Contents

The results of experiments with the naïve Bayes algorithm applied to the original data without any change of the word contents are shown in Table 3. In the column *Original*, the classification accuracy (always given in percentage) is shown for the original set of text documents. This set included 24 of 701 misclassified examples (i.e., examples which were incorrectly classified as uninteresting). After reclassification, the overall accuracy increased as indicates the column *Reclassified*. The fourth column, *Balanced*, shows the results obtained after balancing the number of interesting (299) and uninteresting (402) examples. Because of the decreased number of uninteresting examples (from 402 to 299), the accuracy slightly decreased, too. However, balancing the number of positive and negative examples resulted in the decreased standard deviation values, i.e., more stable results. Finally, the column *All Areas* shows the results of experiments that attempted to select interesting articles from one specific area ('assisted reproduction') among all topics mentioned above. Obviously, this was the strongest feature of the naïve Bayes algorithm. Here was the task of the classifier much easier because the interesting articles differed much more from the rest of the data unlike the other cases where the task was to find interesting documents just within one specific area. This was also the reason why the human expert originally misclassified some of the positive examples.

Table 3. The results of experiments with the original document contents. The numbers show the classification accuracy in percentage.

Original	Reclassified	All Areas	Balanced
68.0 ± 11.55	73.1 ± 11.54	94.3 ± 5.69	72.7 ± 8.04

3.2   Modified Document Contents

The main results are summarized in Table 4. The goal of this group of experiments was to find out how the classification accuracy and the stability of results could be improved by modifying the document contents using the tools included in TEA. From all the experiments, Table 4 shows the best results achieved. Essentially, the tests were divided into the three categories according to the method of selecting interesting articles: (1) within one area of interest – see the column *One Area*; (2) within documents with balanced number of positive and negative examples – see the column *Balanced*; and (3) within all medical areas covered by the documents – see the column *All Areas*. In addition, the document contents was gradually modified by: (1) removing the most common English words (100, 200, 300), including numbers (one, two, three, . . .); (2) removing words with low occurrences (from 1 to 6) in the training set; (3) removing words with low rate between the positive and negative examples (if a certain word occurs with (almost) the same – high or low – number in both classes, then its contribution to the classification can be neglected); (4) considering 'unknown' words, e.g., words in a foreign language – sometimes those words can contribute to a more accurate classification, so the user of TEA can assign different weights to such words; and (5) reducing the number of different word forms by using only their stem.

Table 4. The summarized results of experiments with the classification of medical text documents. The numbers show the classification accuracy in percentage.

	One Area	Balanced	All Areas
w/out the first 100 most common English words	73.6 ± 11.95	73.1 ± 8.09	95.4 ± 4.78
w/out words occurring less than twice	73.1 ± 12.38	72.6 ± 8.20	95.6 ± 4.57
w/out words having the low occurrence rate	70.1 ± 20.67	72.1 ± 10.51	97.1 ± 1.98
weighted unknown words	73.5 ± 8.34	71.9 ± 11.73	96.1 ± 3.95
using only the stem of words	71.1 ± 18.01	73.1 ± 9.63	95.4 ± 3.97

4   Conclusions

The naïve Bayes algorithm is an efficient tool for the document classification. The best results can be expected in the cases when the task is to select articles within a certain area of interest from a large number of different-topic documents. Once the articles are selected, the accuracy of a further, finer classification within a given area decreases. This paper suggests a tool which can, to a certain degree, improve results of the basic naïve Bayes algorithm by increasing or decreasing the influence of several text-document attributes. The experiments revealed that the classification accuracy can be improved mainly by removing irrelevant attributes such as the first 100 most common words, words occurring in the documents less than twice or three times, and removing words which occur in interesting and uninteresting documents with (almost) the same ratio. These conclusions are not too surprising and are in keeping with other experiments carried out in the area of text-document retrieval. Tools like TEA can assist at the process of fine-tuning text document classifiers for individual users because the optimal setting is usually a difficult task.

The experiments with the real-world text documents also revealed that possibly the biggest disadvantage is the fact that the training needs both positive and negative examples. While it is relatively easy to find positive examples, it is practically impossible to find all negative examples as their number is usually too high. Thus, the task of training strongly depends on creating a well-representative, balanced set of examples, which is, in practice, often impossible.

References

1. Domingos, P., Pazzani, M.: Beyond Independence: Conditions for the Optimality of the Simple Bayesian Classifier. Proceedings of the 13th International Conference on Machine Learning ICML '96 (1996), 105–112.
2. Frey, L.: Automatic Filtration of Text Documents by Machine Learning Methods. Master Thesis, Faculty of Informatics, Masaryk University in Brno (2000). In Czech.
3. Joachims, T.: A Probabilistic Analysis of the Rocchio Algorithm with TFIDF for Text Categorization. Proceedings of the 14th International Conference on Machine Learning ICML '97 (1997), 143–151.
4. Lewis, D.D.: Naïve (Bayes) at Forty: The Independence Assumption in Information Retrieval. Proceedings of the 10th European Conference on Machine Learning ECML '98. Springer Verlag Berlin Heidelberg New York (1998), 4–15.
5. Special Issue of Machine Learning Journal on Information Retrieval. Machine Learning Journal, Vol. 39, No. 2/3, May/June, 2000. Kluwer Academic Publishers (2000).
6. Mitchell, T.M.: Machine Learning. McGraw-Hill, New York (1997).

Competing Patterns for Language Engineering
Methods to Handle and Store Empirical Data*

Petr Sojka

NLP Laboratory, Faculty of Informatics, Masaryk University in Brno
Botanická 68a, 602 00 Brno, Czech Republic
sojka@informatics.muni.cz

Abstract. In this paper we describe a method of effective handling of linguistic data by means of *covering and inhibiting patterns* – patterns that "compete" each other. A methodology of developing such patterns is outlined. Applications in the areas of morphology, hyphenation and part-of-speech tagging are shown. This pattern-driven approach to language engineering allows the combination of linguist expertise with the data learned from corpora – layering of knowledge. Searching for information in pattern database (dictionary problem) is blindingly fast – linear with respect to the length of searching word as with other finite-state approaches.

1 Introduction

There is a need to store empirical language data in almost all areas on natural language engineering (LE). Finite-state methods [21,13,16,17,10] have found their revival in the last decade. The theory of finite-state automata (FSA) and transducers (FST) is a well developed part of theoretical computer science (for an overview, see e.g. [6,2]). As the finite-state machines (FSM) needed tend to grow with increased demand for quality of language processing, more attention is being given to the efficiency of the handling of FSM [18,3]. The size of some FSM used in natural language processing exceeds ten millions states (e.g. weighted finite automata and transducers for speech recognition). Practical need to reduce the size of these data structures without losing their expressiveness and excellent time complexity of operations on them is driving new research activities – trend of experimental Computer Science is seen. Several FSM-based software tools [19,23,28,7] have already been implemented for LE.

In this paper we explore a method of FSM decomposition that allows a significant size reduction of FSM – the idea of storing empirical data using *competing patterns*. The data structure *trie* and pattern technique have been developed by Liang [14] for hyphenation algorithm in TeX [11, Appendix H]. We defined several kinds of patterns and our extensive experiments showed that the method is applicable in several areas of language engineering. *Bootstrapping* and *stratification* techniques allow us to speed up

---

* This research has been partially supported by the Czech Ministry of Education under the Grant VS97028 and by the Grant CEZ:J07/98:143300003.

P. Sojka, I. Kopeček, and K. Pala (Eds.): TSD 2000, LNAI 1902, pp. 157–162, 2000.

development of such machines – space savings and time of development savings are enormous.

This paper is organized as follows. In Section 2, we give basic definitions and short overview of known results. Section 3 discusses pattern development methodology. Section 4 describes in detail applications in the area of Czech morphology. An overview of results for hyphenation and compound word division is given in Section 5. Possible applications like part-of-speech (POS) tagging are described in Section 6.

2   Patterns

We start by formally introducing different kinds of patterns and basic notions (for a detailed discussion and examples, see e.g. [2,8]).

Definition 1   (pattern). *Let's have two disjoint alphabets Σ (the alphabet of* terminals*) and V (the alphabet of* variables*). Patterns are words over monoid $\langle \Sigma \cup V, \cdot, \varepsilon \rangle$. Patterns consisting of terminals only called* terminal patterns*. The language $L(\alpha)$ defined by pattern α consists of all words obtained from α by leaving the terminals unchanged and substituting a terminal word for each variable v. The substitution in our case has to be* uniform*: different occurences of v are replaced by the same terminal word. If the substitution replaces variables always by* nonempty *word, such language L_{NE} is non-erasing, and such pattern is called* NE-pattern*. Similarly, we define* erasing *language L_E as a language generated by* E-pattern *such that substitution of variable v by empty word ε is allowed.*

As an example of E-pattern may serve pattern $SVOMPT$ for English sentences where the variables denote Subject, Verb, Object, Mood, Place, Time. An obvious useful task is to infer a pattern common to all input words in a given sample by the process of *inductive inference*. It has been shown in [8] that *inclusion problem* is undecidable for both erasing and non-erasing pattern languages. It is easy to show that decidability of *equivalence problem* for non-erasing languages is trivial. The decidability status of the equivalence problem for E-patterns remains open. These results show that trying to infer language description in the form of set of patterns (or the whole grammar) automatically is very hard task. It has been shown that decomposition of the problem by using *local grammars* [5] or building cascades of FSM [7] is a tractable, but very time-consuming task. Methods for the induction of patterns (from corpora) are needed.

Definition 2   (classifying pattern). *Let $\langle A, \leq \rangle$ be a partially ordered system, $\leq$ be a* lattice order *(every finite non-empty subset of A has lower and upper bound). Let . be a distinguished symbol in $\Sigma' = \Sigma \cup \{.\}$ that denotes the beginning and the end of word –* begin of word marker *and* end of word marker*. Classifying patterns are the words over $\Sigma' \cup V \cup A$ such that dot symbol is allowed at the beginning or end of patterns.*

Terminal patterns are "context-free", they apply anywhere in the classified word – dot symbol in a pattern specifies pattern at the beginning and end of word. Classifying patterns allow us to build *tagging hierarchies* on patterns.

Definition 3   (word classification, competing word patterns). *Let P be a set of patterns over $\Sigma' \cup V \cup A$ (competing patterns, pattern base). Let $w = w_1 w_2 \ldots w_n$ be a word to*

```
      h y p h e n a t i o n
11            1n a
11                    1t i o
12            n2a t
12                    2i o
12          h e2n
13  .h y3p h
14          h e n a4
15          h e n5a t
      .h0y3p0h0e2n5a4t2i0o0n.
      h y-p h e n-a t i o n
```

In this example $\langle A, \leq \rangle$ is $\mathbb{N}$ (natural numbers). There are 5 pattern levels $-11 \ldots 15$. Patterns in odd levels are *covering*, in an even levels *inhibiting*. Winner pattern is .h0y3p0h0e2n5a4t2i0o0n. Pattern h e n5a t wins over n2a t, thus hyphenation is possible.

Fig. 1. Competing patterns and pattern levels

classify with P. Classification classify$(w, P) = a_0 w_1 a_1 w_1 \ldots w_n a_n$ of w with respect to P is computed from pattern base P by competition. All patterns whose projection to Σ match substring of w are collected. a_i is supremum of all values between characters w_i and w_{i+1} in matched patterns. classify(w, P) is also called winning pattern.

An example of competing patterns is shown in Figure 1. Competing patterns extend the power of FST somewhat like adding the complement operator with respect to A. Ideally, instead of storing full FST, we make patterns that embody the same information in even more compact manner. Collecting patterns matching given word can be done in linear time, using trie data structure for pattern storage.

3   Methodology

Pattern Generation Size-optimised full-coverage pattern generation for a given word-list is an NP-complete task. However, there are several pattern generation strategies that allow the choice between size-optimal or coverage-optimal patterns [27] with `patgen` program [15]. A generation process can be parametrised by several parameters whose tuning strategies are beyond the scope of this paper; see [27,24] for details. Parameters could be tuned so that virtually all hyphenation points are covered, leading to about 99.9 % efficiency, and size is not far from optimum. Further investigation and research is necessary to find sufficient conditions for finding optimal results.

Stratification Technique As word-lists from which patterns are generated are rather big (5,000,000 for Czech morphology or hyphenation, even more for other tasks as POS tagging), they may be stratified. Stratification means that from 'equivalent' words only one or small number of representants are chosen for the pattern generation process.

Bootstrapping Technique Developing patterns is usually an iterative process. One starts with hand-written patterns, uses them on input word-list, sees the results, makes the correction, generates new patterns, etc. This technique proved to speed up pattern development process by the order of magnitude. We usually do not start from scratch, but use some previously collected knowledge (e.g. word-list).

4   Application to Czech Morphology

For the information extraction, information retrieval systems, indexing and similar
tasks we need information on many kinds of sub-word divisions: dividing a word into
atoms (cutting of prefixes, compound words recognition etc.) [12]. We have created
several competing pattern sets using the word database of Czech morphological analyser
ajka [22]. We have taken a word-list of 564974 Czech words (6.6 MB) with marked
prefix segmentation and added 51816 similar ones (starting with the same letters, but
morphologically different). We were able to build patterns that were able to perform
prefix segmentation on 99.9% of words of our input word-list and 98% of words in our
test set.

In comparison to naïve storage of word segmentation, there is several order of
magnitude higher compression ratio. Even compared to storage of FSM using suffix
compression in a trie, patterns compacted in trie data structure gives about tenfold of
space reduction, still with linear access time.

5   Application to Hyphenation and Compound Words

We have used the pattern technique to cover Czech and German hyphenation points
and compound word borders. From a Czech word-list (372562 words, approx. 4 MB),
we were able to create 8239 patterns (40 KB) that cover 99.63% hyphenation points.
From a German word-list (368152 words, 5 MB), we were able to create 4702 patterns
(25.2 KB) that cover 98.37% hyphenation points.

To cover compound word hyphenation was more difficult, as longer patterns are
needed. With slightly different parameters of pattern generation, we were able to
create patterns for German compound words with 8825 patterns (70.2 KB) with 95.28%
coverage. Higher coverage is at the expense of pattern size growth.

For details of hyphenation pattern generation for compound words in Czech and
German using patgen, see [27,24,25].

6   Outline of an Application to Part-of-Speech Tagging

Two mainstream approaches are being used for the POS task: *linguistic*, based on hand-
coded linguistic rules (constraint grammars) [9,20] and *machine learning* (statistical,
transformation-based) approaches, based on learning the language model from corpora.
Their combination is probably what is needed – the 'built-in' linguistic knowledge should
be communicated to and take preference over e.g. statistical knowledge acquired during
learning. We hope that ordered and competing patterns will be a viable unifying carrier
of information that will allow combination of both approaches.

Finite-state cascaded methods have already been applied to the POS task [1]. Let
us outline one possible approach. Given sentence $w_1\ w_2\ \ldots\ w_n$, an ambiguous tagger
gives various possible tags: $p_{11}\ \ldots\ p_{1a_1}$ for the first word, $p_{21}\ \ldots\ p_{2a_2}$ for the second,
etc. Writing output as $(p_{11}\ \ldots\ p_{1a_1})(p_{11}\ \ldots\ p_{2a_2})\ \ldots\ (p_{n1}\ \ldots\ p_{na_n})$, the task is to
choose the right POS p_{ij} for every w_i. Taking tag set from Brown corpus (the Brown
University Standard Corpus of Present-day American English) [4] for the sentence "The
representative put chairs on the table.", we get the output

```
. AT ( NN - JJ )    ( NN  VBD - ) ( NNS - VBZ ) IN AT  NN   .
  The representative put          chairs          on the table .
```

Hyphenation markers immediately after POS tag show good solutions for training. Such 'word-lists' (for each sentence from training corpus we get one 'hyphenated word') are used by `patgen` for disambiguation patterns generation. Sentence borders are explicitly coded. This or similar notation can be used for both formulation of ambiguous tagging decision strategies of variable context length by linguists. In comparison to classical constraint grammars, our experience shows that obligation to write only rules which are true in any context is very hard and only a few linguists are able to do so. Having pattern/rule levels/hierarchy helps to develop disambiguation strategies more easily and quickly. Generalisation for patterns over tree hierarchies is worked on.

7 Conclusion

We have shown effective methods for empirical language data storage and handling by means of competing patterns. Our *pattern-driven approach to language engineering* has been tested in several areas – hyphenation and morphology using prototype solution – programs `patgen` and TEX and their algorithms and data structures were used. Search in the pattern database is blindingly fast (linear with respect to the text length). Optimal pattern generation has non-polynomial time complexity, but sub-optimal solutions can be hand-tuned to meet the requirements. It remains to show that this approach is applicable and useful in areas as phonology, syllabification, speech segmentation, word sense or semantic disambiguation and speech processing. We believe that pattern-driven approach will be explored in NLP systems for various classification tasks soon.

Acknowledgement The author would like to thank reviewers for their suggestions to improve wording of the paper, and Radek Sedláček for providing a prefixed word-list for experiments described in Section 4.

References

1. Steven Paul Abney. Part-of-Speech Tagging and Partial Parsing. pages 118–136, Dordrecht, 1997. Kluwer Academic Publishers Group.
2. J. Richard Büchi. *Towards a Theory of Formal Expressions.* Springer-Verlag, New York, U.S.A, 1989.
3. Cezar Câmpeanu, Nicolae Sânteau, and Sheng Yu.   Minimal cover-automata for finite languages. In Jean-Marc Champarnaud, Denis Maurel, and Djelloul Ziadi, editors, *Lecture Notes in Computer Science 1660*, pages 43–56, Berlin, Heidelberg, 1998. Springer-Verlag.
4. Nelson W. Francis and Henry Kučera. *Frequency Analysis of English Usage: Lexicon and Grammar.* Houghton Mifflin, 1982.
5. Maurice Gross. The Construction of Local Grammars. [21], pages 329–354.
6. Jozef Gruska. *Foundations of Computing.* International Thomson Computer Press, 1997.
7. Jerry R. Hobbs, Douglas Appelt, John Bear, David Israel, Megumi Kameyama, Mark Stickel, and Mabry Tyson. FASTUS: A Cascaded Finite-State Transducer for Extracting Information from Natural-Language Text. [21], pages 383–406.

8. Tao Jiang, Arto Salomaa, Kai Salomaa, and Sheng Yu. Decision problems for patterns. *Journal of Computer and Systems Sciences*, 50(1):53–63, 1995.
9. Fred Karlsson, A. Voutilainen, J. Heikkilä, and A. Antilla. *Constraint Grammar: A Language-Independent System for Parsing Unrestricted Text*. Mouton de Gruyter, Berlin, 1995.
10. Lauri Karttunen, Jean-Pierre Chanod, Gregory Grefenstette, and Anne Schiller. Regular Expressions for Language Engineering. *Natural Language Engineering*, 2(4):305–328, 1996.
11. Donald E. Knuth. *The TEXbook*, volume A of *Computers and Typesetting*. Addison-Wesley, Reading, MA, USA, 1986.
12. Gabriele Kodydek. A Word Analysis System for German Hyphenation, Full Text Search, and Spell Checking, with Regard to the Latest Reform of German Orthography. In Sojka et al. [26], pages 51–56.
13. András Kornai. *Extended Finite State Models of Language*. Cambridge University Press, 1999.
14. Franklin M. Liang. *Word Hy-phen-a-tion by Com-put-er*. Ph.D. Thesis, Department of Computer Science, Stanford University, August 1983.
15. Franklin M. Liang and Peter Breitenlohner. PATtern GENeration program for the TEX82 hyphenator. Electronic documentation of PATGEN program version 2.3 from web2c distribution on CTAN, 1999.
16. Mehryar Mohri. On some applications of finite-state automata theory to natural language processing. *Natural Language Engineering*, 2(1):61–80, 1996.
17. Mehryar Mohri. Finite-State Transducers in Language and Speech Processing. *Computational Linguistics*, 23(2):269–311, 1997.
18. Mehryar Mohri. Minimization algorithms for sequential transducers. *Theoretical Computer Science*, 234:177–201, 2000.
19. Mehryar Mohri, Fernando C.N. Pereira, and Michael D. Riley. FSM Library – General-purpose finite-state machine software tools, 1998. http://www.research.att.com/sw/tools/fsm/.
20. Karel Oliva, Milena Hnátková, Vladimír Petkevič, and Paven Květoň. The Linguistic Basis of a Rule-Based Tagger of Czech. In Sojka et al. [26], pages 3–8.
21. Emmanuel Roche and Yves Schabes. *Finite-State Language Processing*. MIT Press, 1997.
22. Radek Sedláček. Morphological Analyzer of Czech (in Czech). Master's thesis, Faculty of Informatics, April 1999.
23. Max Silberztein. INTEX: an FST toolbox. *Theoretical Computer Science*, 234:33–46, 2000.
24. Petr Sojka. Notes on Compound Word Hyphenation in TEX. *TUGboat*, 16(3):290–297, 1995.
25. Petr Sojka. Hyphenation on Demand. *TUGboat*, 20(3):241–247, 1999.
26. Petr Sojka, Ivan Kopeček, and Karel Pala, editors. *Proceedings of the Third Workshop on Text, Speech and Dialogue — TSD 2000*, LNAI 1902, Brno, Czech Republic, Sep 2000. Springer-Verlag.
27. Petr Sojka and Pavel Ševeček. Hyphenation in TEX – Quo Vadis? *TUGboat*, 16(3):280–289, 1995.
28. Bruce W. Watson. Implementing and using finite automata toolkits. [13], pages 19–36.

Recognition and Labelling of Prosodic Events in Slovenian Speech

France Mihelič[1], Jerneja Gros[1], Elmar Nöth[2], and Volker Warnke[2]

[1] University of Ljubljana, Faculty of Electrical Engineering,
Tržaška 25, SI-1000 Ljubljana, Slovenia
mihelicf@fe.uni-lj.si, nejka@fe.uni-lj.si,
http://luz.fe.uni-lj.si
[2] Universität Erlangen-Nürnberg,
Martensstrasse 3, 91058 Erlangen, BRD
noeth@informatik.uni-erlangen.de, warnke@informatik.uni-erlangen.de

Abstract. The paper describes prosodic annotation procedures of the GOPOLIS Slovenian speech data database and methods for automatic classification of different prosodic events. Several statistical parameters concerning duration and loudness of words, syllables and allophones were computed for the Slovenian language, for the first time on such a large amount of speech data. The evaluation of the annotated data showed a close match between automatically determined syntactic-prosodic boundary marker positions and those obtained by a rule-based approach.

1 Introduction

Research and development in the field of spoken language technology encouraged and supported by the European Community resulted in many experimental and also commercially available systems for speech recognition, understanding, synthesis and dialogue for different European languages [1].

Noticeable progress in this field in the recent years was also made for one of the minor European languages, Slovenian. As a result of our own investigations and our collaboration with foreign partners, a multilingual dialogue system was developed [3]. Slovenian speech recognition, understanding and synthesis systems are the most important achievements of the research group in Slovenia [4].

The usage of prosodic parameters in speech recognition and understanding and quality prosody modelling in speech synthesis resulted in large improvements in the performance of these systems [5,6,7]. At present, not much work has been done in this field for the Slovenian language. The research group at the University of Erlangen-Nürenberg has some important research results in the field of prosodic analysis for the German language [5,9,8] and also some experience with prosody processing for other languages [10]. In a combined effort of the Slovenian and the German research groups, procedures for automatic prosodic parameter measurement and evaluation were tested on Slovenian speech material. We tried to recognise prosodic events and evaluate them statistically.

P. Sojka, I. Kopeček, and K. Pala (Eds.): TSD 2000, LNAI 1902, pp. 165–170, 2000.

2   Selection of Prosodic Events

Syntactic-prosodic boundaries along the lines of [5], annotated for transliterations of read speech and acoustic-prosodic boundaries and word accents labelled via acoustic perceptual sessions were chosen for the initial experiments.

Table 1. Syntactic-prosodic boundary labels

–   : clause boundaries
–   : constituent boundaries likely to be marked prosodically
–   : boundaries that syntactically belong to the normal constituent boundaries probably not
      marked prosodically because they are "close" to a   boundary
–   : every other word boundary

We performed automatic labelling with syntactic-prosodic boundaries of the Slovenian GOPOLIS speech corpus (50 speakers, 8,645 utterances, 5,077 different corpus sentences) according to [8, pp. 140–144]. In the labelling procedure, we distinguished between 4 types of boundaries as listed in Table 1. Here is an example of labelled text[1]:

Ali   imate   kakšno letalo   čez tri tedne?
(Is there a flight in three weeks?)

Acoustic-prosodic boundaries and word accent labels were defined as in VERB-MOBIL [8]. They are described in Tables 2 and 3.

Table 2. Acoustic-prosodic boundary labels

–   : prosodic clause boundary
–   : prosodic phrase boundary
–   : irregular boundary, usually hesitation lengthening
–   : every other word boundary

Table 3. Word accent labels

–   : the most prominent (primary) accent within a prosodic clause
–   : all other accented words are marked as carrying secondary accent
–   : unaccented words

Here is a labelled sample sentence[2]:
Lahko ponovite   odgovor   ,   prosim   ?
(Can you repeat the answer, please?)

---

[1] M0 labels qare not indicated in the example
[2] The default classes B0 and   labels are not indicated in the example.

3   Data Preparation

The experiments on prosodic events classification we wanted to perform required some specific data preparation. Speech signals of read Slovenian texts from the GOPOLIS speech corpus [11] were used for 'the experiments. The GOPOLIS pronunciation dictionary was extended with stress and syllable markers. Special categories denoting *silence, non-word, consonants* and *syllable-root* were added. A special format for representing word graphs was used.

The segmentation of the speech signals was performed automatically using the ISADORA net [12]. An important feature of the Isadora net environment is the automatic detection of silence segments not indicated in the transliteration.

The text corpus of the GOPOLIS database has been created automatically using a context-free grammar consisting of 189 sentence templates [15]. The sentence templates cover the most frequent dialogue situations occurring at airline timetable information retrieval.

In order to obtain a version of the GOPOLIS database annotated with boundary information,   and   labels were inserted into the sentence templates. Then the sentence generation process was repeated.

The   markers were generally set according to rhythmic constraints.   markers – as described above – were set, if an   boundary was too close to the beginning or end of the utterance or too close to an   boundary, i.e. they were also set according to rhythmic constraints.   markers were placed between main/subordinate clauses and around embedded clauses.

Acoustic-prosodic boundaries and word accent labels were marked manually by perception tests using visualisation of speech signals and listening. In total, 1000 signals (6 speakers) were labelled, representing 12% of the whole GOPOLIS speech corpus. The annotation was conducted by the first author; intralabeller consistency has not yet been evaluated.

4   Features Selection and Pattern Classification

Classification using only prosodic feature sets describing duration segmental characteristics on the word level, speaking rate, energy and pitch was performed. Pitch periods were computed for the entire GOPOLIS database based on the inverse filtering algorithm [9]. Various statistical parameters previously determined on the training set were used in the duration and energy normalisation procedures [9, pp. 165–182]. All 95 features forming "the best word features set" according to experiments performed on German speech [9, page 258] were computed for the Slovenian speech data.

Energy and pitch features are based on the short-term energy and F0 contour, respectively. Some of the features that are used to describe a pitch contour are shown in Figure 1. Additionally, we use the mean and the median as features [2].

Neural nets were used for classification. The SNNS software [13] was used for neural net modelling. Several net configurations and initialisations were tested in the experiments.

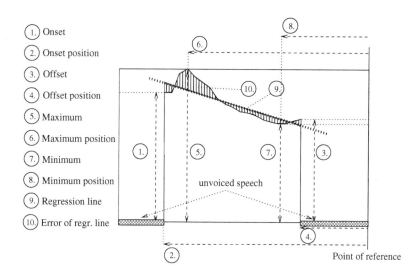

Fig. 1. Example of features used to describe a pitch contour

5   Recognition Results

Four classification schemes with different clustering for the syntactic-prosodic boundaries were tested. The results indicating overall recognition rate and classwise computed recognition rate are displayed in Table 4. 5 female and 5 male speakers were selected for the test set while the remaining 40 speakers were used in the training set.

The classification of   markers versus other categories and classification into three classes (   ) are the most important for further use in semantic parsing of recognised word strings [6]. By comparing the obtained results to the results obtained on the ERBA corpus [14] (82%, 72%), the results on Slovenian speech data are even slightly better. This indicates at least the correctness of the automatic procedure for boundary labelling and also the appropriate feature selection and classification procedure for the Slovenian language.

Table 4. Recognition results for different classification schemes for syntactic-prosodic boundaries. App. 40000 labels were used in the training set, 8400 in the test set, label   at the end of the utterance was not included in the tests.

Classification schemes	Recognition overall	Recognition classwise
	74.1%	77.5%
	80.7%	80.3%
	87.3%	87.7%
	87.5%	87.6%

Due to the lack of manually labelled data[3], the results of the experiments on acoustic-prosodic boundary classification and word accent classification are not so reliable. They might be significantly improved using a larger training set. The results are displayed in Table 5. Two turns of classification experiments were performed. Both times 5 speakers were used for training and 1 speaker for testing.

Table 5. Recognition results for different classification schemes for acoustic-prosodic boundaries and word accent labels. Approx. 4500 labels were used in the training set and 840 labels in the test set for acoustic-prosodic boundaries; the label   at the end of the utterance was not included in the tests. Approx. 5000 labels in the training set and 1000 labels in the test set for the word accent labels.

Speaker	Classification schemes	Recogn. overall	Recogn. classwise
01M		73.9%	79.8%
03M		66.8%	67.2%
01M		64.1%	62.5%
03M		72.5%	69.9%

6   Conclusion

Useful knowledge on prosodic events for the Slovenian speech was gained as an intermediate results of the described experiments. Pitch periods for the complete GOPOLIS speech database were computed and they can be used as a reference for further investigations. Several statistical parameters concerning duration and loudness of words, syllables and allophones were computed for the Slovenian language, for the first time on such a large speech database.

The obtained research results encourage us to continue the co-operation of both partner groups. Data collection and annotation as well as development of semantic parsers, using prosodic information as additional input, will be the next steps of our research. The computed prosodic parameters will also be applied in the prosody prediction process for Slovenian text-to-speech synthesis.

Acknowledgement

France Mihelič thanks the DAAD for its support enabling his study visit in Erlangen from May to July 1999, during which most of the presented work was done. Special thanks go to F. Gallwitz and J. Buckow who helped organising the experiments in Erlangen and to S. Dobrišek and J. Žibert from the University of Ljubljana for their support.

---

[3] Only approx. 12% of all GOPOLIS corpus was manually labelled.

References

1. Andersen, P.: Language Technology and Multilinguality – The European Dimension. Invited Lecture, Proceedings of the Conference Language Technologies for the Slovene Language, Eds. T. Erjavec, J. Gros, Ljubljana, 1998, pp. 9–13.
2. Buckow, J., V. Warnke, R. Huber, A. Batliner, E. Nöth, H. Niemann: Fast and Robust Features for Prosodic Classification. Proc. Text, Speech and Dialogue, Lecture Notes in Artificial Intelligence 1692, Marienbad, 1999, pp. 193–198.
3. Aretoulaki, M, S. Harbeck, F. Gallwitz, E. Nöth, H. Niemann, J. Ivanecky, I. Ipšić, N. Pavešić, V. Matoušek: SQEL: A Multilingual and Multifunctional Dialogue System. Proc. Int. Conf. on Spoken Language Processing, 1998, pp. 855–858.
4. Ipšić, I, F. Mihelič, S. Dobrišek, J. Gros, N. Pavešić: A Slovenian Spoken Dialog System for Air Flight Inquires. Proceedings of the Eurospeech '99, Budapest, Hungary, 1999, pp. 2659–2662.
5. Batliner, A., R. Kompe, A. Kießling, M. Mast, H. Niemann, and E. Nöth: M = Syntax + Prosody: A syntactic-prosodic labelling scheme for large spontaneous speech databases. Speech Communication, **25**, 1998, pp. 193–222.
6. Boros, M., J. Haas, V. Warnke, E. Nöth, and H. Niemann: How Statistics and Prosody can guide a Chunky Parser. Proc. of the AIII Workshop on Artificial Intelligence in Industry, Stará Lesná, Slovakia, 1998, pp. 388–398.
7. Gros, J., F. Mihelič, N. Pavešić: Speech Quality Evaluation in Slovenian TTS. First International Conference on Language Resources and Evaluation, Eds. A. Rubio, N. Gallardo, R. Castro, A. Tejada, Vol. I, Granada, Spain, 1998, pp. 651–654.
8. Kompe, R.: Prosody in Speech Understanding Systems. Springer-Verlag Berlin Heidelberg, Lecture Notes in Artificial Intelligence 1307, 1997.
9. Kießling A.: Extraktion und Klassifikation prosodischer Merkmale in der automatischen Sprachverarbeitung. Schaker Verlag, 1997.
10. Haas, J., V. Warnke, H. Niemann, M. Cettolo, A. Corazza, D. Falavigna, G. Lazzari: Semantic Boundaries in Multiple Languages. Proceedings of the Eurospeech '99, Vol. I, Budapest, Hungary, 1999, pp. 535–538.
11. Dobrišek, S., J. Gros, F. Mihelič, N. Pavešić: Recording and Labelling of the GOPOLIS Slovenian Speech Database. First International Conference on Language Resources and Evaluation, edits. A. Rubio, N. Gallardo, R. Castro, A. Tejada, Vol. II, Granada, Spain, 1998, pp. 1089–1096.
12. Schukat-Talamazzini, E.G.: Automatische Spracherkennung – Grundlagen, statistische Modelle und effiziente Algorithmen. Vieweg, Braunschweig, 1995.
13. Stuttgart Neural Network Simulator. http://www-ra.informatik.uni-tuebingen.de/SNNS, 1999.
14. Bakenecker, G., U. Block, A. Batliner, R. Kompe, E. Nöth, P. Regel-Brietzmann: Improving Parsing by Incorporating 'Prosodic Clause Boundaries' into a Grammar. Proc. Int. Conf. on Spoken Language Processing, Vol. 3, Yokohama, 1994, pp. 1115–1118.
15. Gros, J., F. Mihelič, N. Pavešić: Sentence hypothesisation using Ng-gram models. Proceedings of the Eurospeech '95, Vol. 3, Madrid, 1995, pp. 1759–1762.

Rules for Automatic Grapheme-to-Allophone Transcription in Slovene

Jerneja Gros, France Mihelič, Simon Dobrišek, Tomaž Erjavec, and Mario Žganec

University of Ljubljana, Faculty 16 Electrical Engineering,
Tržaška 25, SI-1000 Ljubljana, Slovenia
nejka@fe.uni-lj.si, http://luz.fe.uni-lj.si

Abstract. The domain of spoken language technologies ranges from speech input and output systems to complex understanding and generation systems, including multi-modal systems of widely differing complexity (such as automatic dictation machines) and multilingual systems (for example, automatic dialogue and translation systems). The definition of standards and evaluation methodologies for such systems involves the specification and development of highly specific spoken language corpus and lexicon resources, and measurement and evaluation tools [5]. This paper presents the MobiLuz spoken resources of the Slovene language, which will be made freely available for research purposes in speech technology and linguistics.

1 Introduction

The domain of spoken language technologies ranges from speech input and output systems to complex understanding and generation systems, including multi-modal systems of widely differing complexity (such as automatic dictation machines) and multilingual systems (for example, automatic dialogue and translation systems). The definition of standards and evaluation methodologies for such systems involves the specification and development of highly specific spoken language corpus and lexicon resources, and measurement and evaluation tools.

In the beginning, standards for these areas have been derived from the consensus within the spoken language community previously established in a number of European and national projects, with reference to important initiatives in the US and Japan. Primary among these have been the SAM projects (centred on component technology assessment and corpus creation), SQALE (for large vocabulary systems assessment) and both SUNDIAL and SUNSTAR (for multi-modal systems.)

Past and present projects with significant outputs in the domain of assessment and resources include ARS, RELATOR, ONOMASTICA and SPEECHDAT, as well as major national projects and programs of research such as VERBMOBIL in Germany. This has led to an initial documentation of existing practice which was relatively comprehensive but in many respects heterogeneous and widely dispersed. The lack of generic technologies and resources and the wide diversity of formats and specifications has hindered the effective reutilisation of existing resources. In 1993, the EAGLES

P. Sojka, I. Kopeček, and K. Pala (Eds.): TSD 2000, LNAI 1902, pp. 171–176, 2000.

(Expert Advisory Group on Language Engineering Standards) initiative was launched within the framework of the CEU's DGXIII Linguistic Research and Engineering (LRE) Programme, to accelerate the provision of standards for developing, exploiting and evaluating large-scale language resources. A special working group has been set up for this purpose, named the Spoken Language Working Group (SLWG). The project resulted in the publication of comprehensive guidelines documenting existing working practices in Europe and guidelines for spoken language resource creation and description [5].

2   Slovene Speech Corpora

For the Slovene language, several attempts in speech data collection were made in the past, resulting in various speech corpora: SNABI [12,13], LUZ diphones [8], GOPOLIS [4] and SPEECHDAT-Slovene [14], distributed by ELRA.

The collected speech data mainly represented the domain of intended applications and are not available for distribution, except for the Slovenian SpeechDat(II) FDB-1000 corpus containing phonetically rich sentences. The corpus consists of read and spontaneous speech and was recorded through an ISDN card (1.000 speakers). A phonetic lexicon with canonical transcriptions in SAMPA is also provided. However, due to its high cost (20.000 EUR), the Slovene SPEECHDAT corpus can hardly be used for research or even development purposes. We therefore decided to create a collection of various Slovene speech data, freely available for research purposes in speech technology and linguistics. Such speech resources are essential for building multi-lingual speech recognition and text-to-speech synthesis applications.

The idea is in the process of being finalised within the MobiLuz project funded by the Slovene Ministry of Science and Technology and the Slovene mobile telephone operator Mobitel d.d.

The MobiLuz project collects and integrates resources of several previous project, e.g. the EU Copernicus SQEL and MULTEXT-East and will provide three main deliverables:

1. MobiLuz Slovene speech corpus,
2. MobiLuz Slovene speech corpus annotations and lexicon and
3. MobiLuz speech tools.

The next three sections detail our work on these deliverables.

3   MobiLuz Slovene Speech Corpus

The MobiLuz Slovene speech corpus includes various collections of speech data pronounced by multiple speakers, either as read speech or spontaneous speech. In particular, the corpus consists of the following components:

- a fully updated and revised version of the 50 speaker GOPOLIS corpus of air travel inquiries,
- isolated spoken commands (digits, common control commands etc.) and
- recordings of live dialogues.

3.1   Gopolis

The GOPOLIS corpus is a large multi-speaker speech database, derived from real situation dialogues concerning airline timetable information services. It was used as the Slovenian speech database within the SQEL project (Copernicus COP-94 contract No. 01634) for building a multi-lingual speech recognition and understanding dialogue system [11], capable of passing information over the telephone line to a client in one of four European languages – German, Czech, Slovak and Slovenian. The name of the database has been derived from "GOvorjena POizvedovanja o Letalskih Informacijah v Slovenskem jeziku", meaning "Spoken Flight Information Queries in the Slovene Language".

The sentence corpus was drawn from listening to recordings of real situation dialogues between anonymous clients' inquiries and telephone operators at the Adria Airways information centre (15 hrs of speech stored on audiotapes).

The selected 300 typical sentences were compiled into the form of rewrite rules to obtain a generative sentence pattern grammar [7]. Using this grammar, we produced 22,500 different sentences for short introductory inquiries, long inquiries and short confirmations. 5,077 of them were selected to form the final sentence corpus.

Each of the total of 50 speakers (25 female and 25 male) read about 100 randomly selected unique corpus sentences and 71 sentences of welcome greetings, introductory phrases, short affirmations and farewell greetings, common to all of the speakers. Each session has a list of attributes with speaker and recording session descriptors.

3.2   Isolated Commands

A set of isolated commands spoken by various speakers has also been recorded. Included are the most common commands used in telecommunication applications and commands for navigating windows applications.

3.3   Recording Conditions

The recording sessions were performed in a normal laboratory acoustic environment. Additional noise, such as background speech or slamming doors was avoided. The utterances were acquired by a close talking microphone and simultaneously by telephone. Thus an additional analysis of both audio devices was enabled.

A set of recording environment programs was developed for the HP 9000 workstation platform. The user interface program built for recording communicates with two audio servers over the network, displays and saves the acquired signals and displays the sentences that a speaker should utter. So the acoustic realizations are in form of read continuous speech. The program is also equipped with loudness detection and an acoustic messaging system. It takes care of the correct maximum loudness level, begin and end pauses and synchronises the acquired telephone and microphone speech signals.

The audio servers use the HP 9000/735 common audio hardware components and the additional Gradient Technology DeskLab hardware with a full telephone interface (DeskLab is a data acquisition and play device, which communicates via SCSI with a workstation). The speaker has to press a space bar key to signal the start of the recording session and then again to finish it. The program requires at least half a second of silence at the beginning and at the end of the utterance. A sampling rate of 16 kHz for both microphone and telephone signals and a 16-bit data format with MSB-LSB byte order was chosen.

4   Corpus Annotations and Lexica

The GOPOLIS corpus is encoded in accordance with TEI recommendations [15], in particular, the base tagset for Transcriptions of Speech, the additional tagsets for Simple Analytic Mechanisms and Language Corpora, and some local modifications. The corpus contains the TEI header, giving the File, Encoding and Profile descriptions. Here general information about the corpus, including speaker descriptions is given. The body of the corpus consists of the 5,077 sentences (utterances), each marked with an ID and references to its speakers.

The utterances are segmented into words and punctuation marks, and each word is given in its orthographic form, as well as in the automatically derived phonetic transcription. Furthermore, the words were automatically tagged for their lemma and morphosyntactic description. Some sample data will contain also prosodic annotations.

Two lexica accompany the corpus: a pronunciation dictionary and a word-form lexicon with the morphosyntactic descriptions.

4.1   Transcription and Tagging

The phonetic transcriptions in the corpus are based on the Slovene MRPA set [2,17] containing machine-readable phonetic symbols equivalent to the Slovene IPA symbols [16].

The morphosyntactic descriptions and lexicon are based on the MULTEXT-East (Slovene) tagset and lexicon [3,10]. The lexicon contains lemmas, their full inflectional paradigms and the morphosyntactic descriptions of the wordforms [6]. The descriptions have a feature-structure like format and encode informations such as part-of-speech, number, case, etc. These descriptions and lexicon are then used to automatically tag and lemmatise the corpus. The tagger used is TnT [1], which had been trained on the Slovene MULTEXT-East corpus.

4.2   Speech Segmentation and Alignment

The automatic segmentation is performed using the DTW based approach described in [4] where the speech material is automatically segmented and labelled using dynamic time warping alignment of a natural utterance with a synthesised speech signal. The synthesis of speech signals was achieved by simply concatenating labelled diphone speech signals using a simplified TD-PSOLA technique. The diphone inventory used was borrowed from the Slovenian text-to-speech system S5 [9]. The diphone inventory consists of a set of segmented and labelled diphone speech signals. Every diphone in the inventory is segmented into two separated phones and voiced phones were additionally marked with pitch period markers.

According to the phonetic transcription of the natural speech signal, a sequence of concatenated diphone speech signals was generated. A conventional DTW alignment of the utterance with the synthesised speech signal was performed with two sequences of feature vectors derived from both speech signals. This method has the advantage that we do not need labelled reference speech signals since we know the phone boundaries of the synthetic speech signal.

5   Speech Tools

The MobiLuz speech corpus will be accompanied by the Sigmark software developed in cooperation with Masterpoint, a user-friendly program interface which allows manual editing, viewing and marker corrections of speech signals on various levels (phone, word and phrase levels).

Markers can also be copied from one level to the other which proves to be very useful for synchronising marker sets on different levels.

6   Conclusion

The MobiLuz project is aiming to set up an infrastructure of Slovene spoken resources necessary for building various multi-lingual speech recognition and synthesis applications. For example, the GOPOLIS speech corpus, which will become available in the scope of MobiLuz, has already been successfully used for training of the HMM-based speech recognition engine in the multilingual automatic dialogue system SQEL [11].

Acknowledgements

The development of MobiLuz speech corpus was supported by the Slovene mobile telephony operator Mobitel d.d. and grant of the Slovene Ministry of Science and Technology. The development of the resources contained in the corpus have also been supported by the EU Copernicus projects SQEL and MULTEXT-East.

References

1. Brants, T. (2000): TnT – A Statistical Part-of-Speech Tagger. Proceedings of the ANLP-NAACL, in print, Seattle.
2. Dobrišek S., Kačič Z., Gros J., Horvat B. and Mihelič F., (1996): An Initiative for Standardisation of Phonetic Transcription of Slovenian Speech, Proceedings of the Fifth Electrotechnical and Computer Science Conference ERK'96, pp. 247–250, Portorož, Slovenia, 1996.
3. Dimitrova, L., Erjavec, T. Ide, N. Kaalep, H.J., Petkevič, V. and Tufis, D. (1998): Multext-East: Parallel and Comparable Corpora and Lexicons for Six Central and Eastern European Languages. COLING-ACL '98 Proceedings, pp. 315–319.
4. Dobrišek S., Gros J., Mihelič F. and Pavešić N. (1998): Recording and Labelling of the GOPOLIS Slovenian Speech Database, Proceedings of the First International Conference on Language Resources and Evaluation, pp. 1089–1096. Granada, Spain.

5. EAGLES Handbook (1997): Handbook of Standards and Resources for Spoken Language Systems. Editors D. Gibbon, Roger Moore and Richard Winski. Berlin: Mouton de Gruyter.
6. Erjavec T. (1998): The MULTEXT-East Slovene Lexicon. Proceedings of the ERK'98 Conference, Portorož, Slovenia, pp. 189–192.
7. Gros J., Mihelič F. and Pavešić N., (1995): Sentence Hypothesisation Using Ng-Gram Models, In Proceedings of the the Fourth European Conference On Speech Communication and Technology, pp. 1759–1762, Madrid, Spain.
8. Gros J., Ipšić I., Mihelič F. and Pavešić N. (1996): Segmentation and labelling of Slovenian diphone inventories, COLING '96, pp. 298–303, Copenhagen, Denmark.
9. Gros, J., Pavešić, N. and Mihelič, F. (1997): Text-to-speech synthesis: a complete system for the Slovenian language. Journal of Computing and Information Technology. 5(1). pp. 11–19.
10. Ide, N., Tufis, D. and Erjavec, T. (1998): Development and Assessment of Common Lexical Specifications for Six Central and Eastern European Languages. Proceedings of the First International Conference on Language Resources and Evaluation, LREC'98, Granada, pp. 233–240.
11. Ipšić I., Mihelič F., Dobrišek S., Gros J. and Pavešić N. (1998): An overview of the spoken queries in European languages: the Slovenian spoken dialogue system. Proceedings of the scientific conference Artificial Intelligence in Industry from Theory to Practice and 3rd SQEL Workshop on Multi-Lingual Information Retrieval Dialogues, High Tatras, Slovakia, pp. 431–438.
12. Kačič Z. and Horvat B. and Derlič R. (1994): Zasnova baze izgovorjav slovenskega jezika SNABI. Proceedings of the ERK '94. Portorož, Slovenia.
13. Kačič Z. and Horvat B. (1998): Izgradnja infrastrukture, potrebne za razvoj govorne tehnologije za slovenski jezik. Proceedings of the Conference on Language Technologies for the Slovene Language. Ljubljana. pp. 100–104.
14. Kaiser J. and Kačič Z. (1998): Development of Slovenian SpeechDat Database. Proceedings of the Workshop On Speech Database Development for Central and Eastern European Languages, Granada, Spain, 1998.
15. Sperberg-McQueen, C.M., and Burnard, L., eds. (1994): Guidelines for Electronic Text Encoding and Interchange. Chicago and Oxford.
16. Šuštaršič R., Komar S. and Petek B. (1998): Slovene IPA Symbols, Illustrations of the IPA.
17. Zemljak M., Kačič Z., Dobrišek S. and Gros J. (2000): A Machine-readable Phonetic Transcription of the Slovene Speech, in preparation.

An Adaptive and Fast Speech Detection Algorithm

Dragos Burileanu[1], Lucian Pascalin[1], Corneliu Burileanu[1], and Mihai Puchiu[2]

[1] "Politehnica" University of Bucharest, Faculty of Electronics and Telecommunications
Blvd. Iuliu Maniu 1-3, Sect. 6, Bucharest 77202, Romania
bdragos@mESsnet.pub.ro, lucianp@mESsnet.pub.ro, cburileanu@mESsnet.pub.ro
[2] Graphco Technologies Inc. Romanian Office
Calea Floreasca 91-111, Sect. 1, Bucharest 714011, Romania
mpuchiu@graphcotech.ro

Abstract. The detection of speech from silence (actually background noise) is essential in many speech-processing systems. In real-field applications, the correct determination of voice segments highly improves the overall system accuracy and minimises the total computation time. This paper[1] presents a novel robust and reliable speech detection algorithm to be used in a speaker recognition system. The paper first introduces some basic concepts on speech activity detection and reviews the techniques currently used in speech detection tasks. Then, the proposed speech/non-speech detection algorithm is described and experimental results are discussed. Conclusions about the algorithm performances are finally presented.

1 Introduction

The problem of separating the speech segments of an utterance from the background noise is called *speech detection* (or *endpoint detection*, or even *voice activity detection*). This is very important in many areas of speech signal processing: speech and speaker recognition, speech compression and transmission. A proper location of regions of speech (sometimes together with pause removal), not only reduces the amount of processing, but also increases the accuracy of the speech processing system.

Speech detection is an old and known problem; however, it has not been completely answered until today. The major difficulty of the speech detection task deals with the variability of the speech and background noise patterns. The noise and voice inconsistency often leads to the inaccurate detection of the speech endpoints, by cutting phonemes or passing non-speech events to the speech processing system.

Another important problem is the absence of an accurate method of checking the correctness of a speech detection algorithm, or for comparing two or more candidate methods. The location of the speech endpoints in the presence of high-level noise becomes a complex task even for experienced phoneticians. The commonly used manual method consists of a rough approximation, followed by a more precise endpoint location with acoustical and visual assistance.

The methods used in speech detection can be classified into two general categories, according to their basic principles:

---

[1] This work was sponsored by Graphco Technologies Inc., Newtown, Pennsylvania, USA.

- *explicit methods*, that detect the endpoints independently of the subsequent processes; the main techniques are *energy-based, pattern recognition-based*, or use *Hidden Markov Models* or *neural networks* to explicitly determine the endpoints [1,3,5,6];
- *implicit methods*, that use the application itself to detect the endpoints; this approach assumes that the endpoint detection is an implicit part of the speech processing system and is developed along with the application [7].

All these techniques may work well enough for high signal to noise (SNR) ratios, but most of them are not really adaptive and degrade their performances as the noise signal increases. Furthermore, the techniques based on training have difficulties in finding features that are discriminatory between unvoiced speech and silence and also can fail when the environment noise does not match the training or when human artefacts and background voice corrupt the speech.

Many speech detectors developed for real-field applications (such as those used in noisy office, factory, moving cars or airplane cockpit environments) additionally use *speech enhancement techniques* [4]. Without any doubt, these hybrid methods perform better, but they usually need a priori knowledge of the noise statistics and are rather time consuming, leading to slow system response.

2   Description of the Speech Detection Algorithm

The proposed algorithm is based on short-term parameter estimation. It relies on two classical measures of speech, one with meaning of magnitude and the other with meaning of frequency: E_x – the *pseudoenergy* of the input signal, and ZCR – the *zero-crossing rate*, calculated over all samples of a signal frame [2,5,6]; we found that a frame-length of 15 ms is a good choice for accurate detection.

The procedure of speech detection and silence elimination for a recorded utterance consists in four steps:

I. Pre-processing. Because the ZCR is highly susceptible to 50/60 Hz hum, very low frequency noise, DC offset, etc., the waveform is first high-pass filtered. The filter is used only for energy and ZCR computing and does not affect the input signal.

II. Speech boundaries rough estimation. Two energy thresholds, T_1 and T_2, are calculated over all M frames of the input signal, based on three typical values of the speech signal and according to the following equations:

$$En\_\max = \max E_x(i) \ , \quad i = 1, 2, \ldots, M \tag{1}$$

$$En\_\min = \min E_x(i) \ , \quad i = 1, 2, \ldots, M \tag{2}$$

$$T_1 = En\_\min \left(1 + 2 \log_{10} \frac{En\_\max}{En\_\min}\right) \tag{3}$$

$$SL = \frac{\sum_i E_x(i)}{\sum_i 1} \ , \text{ where } i \text{ is the index for all frames having } E_x > T_1 \tag{4}$$

$$T_2 = T_1 + 0.25 \ (SL - T_1) \tag{5}$$

In the previous equations, En_max is the peak energy value of the input speech signal, En_min is the minimum energy value (typically the silence or background noise minimum level), and SL is the average level of the signal above T_1.

The speech boundaries are approximately estimated based on the following energy criteria:

1. When energy exceeds T_1 and subsequently exceeds T_2, the crossing point with T_1 level is declared a 'preliminary startpoint' (PS).
2. When energy falls below T_2 and then falls below T_1, the crossing point with T_1 level is declared a 'preliminary endpoint' (PE). The region between the PS and the PE will be further called 'word'.
3. A short isolated 'word' is a 'noise spike'; it is marked as unnecessary and it will be rejected in the silence removal procedure.

III. Speech boundaries fine adjustment. After a first guess of the 'word' boundaries based on energy criteria, possible unvoiced regions near the 'word' (and belonging to the 'word') will be also considered as "speech", according to ZCR-based methods. Only after this step, one obtains the real start-endpoints of the declared 'voice segments'.

The ZCR parameter has generally a different behaviour in speech regions than in the silence (background noise) ones. However, because of its rapid variations, we found that it is rather difficult to correctly determine this behaviour; therefore, our algorithm uses an additional parameter: a *smoothed ZCR* ($SZCR$), that uses the three left and right neighbour values of the ZCR and describes the overall trend of the ZCR. It has a clean curve and roughly indicates the endpoints location; ZCR will be used to accurately refine the found points. To distinguish consonants from silence, we also calculate a *medium ZCR* (ZCR_{med}) and two variation areas for ZCR (denoted D_1 and ranging between ZCR_{low} and ZCR_{high}) and SZCR (denoted D_2 and ranging between $SZCR_{low}$ and $SZCR_{high}$).

After computing these values, an unvoiced speech segment is added to the 'word' using the following criteria:

4. A region near to a 'word', for which $SZCR$ leaves D_2 area just closed to the 'word', belongs to the 'word' until the $SZCR$ curve re-enters into D_2 area.
5. A region near to a 'word', having $SZCR$ outside the D_2 area and not complying with rule no. 4, belongs to the 'word' until the $SZCR$ curve enters into D_2 area.
6. After the new boundary of the 'word' is established (using rules no. 4 or 5), it is refined back until the ZCR curve is in the same side of the D_1 area like the $SZCR$ curve.
7. A long region that is added to the 'word' using rules no. 4 / 5 and 6 is truncated if it is the left region of the 1st 'word' in the utterance or the right region of the last 'word'. This rule helps to remove the deep breath at the beginning or at the end of an utterance.

IV. Silence elimination. All frames that are not detected as 'voice segments' by steps **II** and **III** are considered as 'silence' and removed from the given utterance.

3   Experimental Studies

To evaluate the accuracy of our algorithm and its robustness to various acquisition conditions, we performed a great number of experiments: optically and acoustically assisted tests on various commercial databases (YOHO, TIMIT, CTIMIT, NTIMIT, HTIMIT, FFMTIMIT) and tests using a specific recognition system.

Qualitative tests were done on hundreds of recorded utterances from the above-mentioned databases. We verified the endpoint detection in distinct conditions: high and low SNR, typical background noises, different microphones and transmission channels; silence removed utterances were optically checked and listened and finally compared with the original utterances. The conclusion was that the algorithm accurately detects the speech boundaries and copes with many different acquisition conditions; the few errors are mainly related to high noise energy or limited bandwidth transmission and telephone line attenuation. Figures 1 to 4 show the overall speech detection procedure applied on a same phrase ("Don't ask me to carry an oily rag like that"), uttered by the same speaker, in four databases: TIMIT (clean speech), CTIMIT (cellular telephone speech in various noise conditions), NTIMIT (standard telephone speech), and HTIMIT (different telephone handsets used); white zones indicate speech regions and grey zones indicate the rejected 'silence' regions.

We also completed a quantitative test: a precise comparison of automatically and manually labelled endpoints on 300 sentences from the YOHO database. The time distances between the 1,740 manually defined endpoints and the endpoints detected by our algorithm were measured. Assuming an acceptable distance of one frame (15 ms) between a real and an estimated endpoint, the resulted algorithm accuracy was better than 98%.

Finally, we performed a group of tests using a speaker verification system and four subsets of the YOHO database (26 speakers, each with 24 enrolment phrases and 40 verification phrases). The tests were accomplished on the original files that contain silence and then on the processed files (with silence removed by our algorithm); a basic parameter representing *the Equal Error Rate* (EER) was calculated. The results indicated that using the proposed algorithm an average EER improvement of 2.67% (absolute value) is obtained.

4   Conclusions

Our main purpose was to develop and test a robust speech detection algorithm for a speaker recognition system having the following distinctive features:

- the possibility of use in any speaker recognition system and therefore independent of the recognition algorithm;
- the adaptability on the background noise level;
- an accuracy "as high as possible" of the detected speech boundaries; this means to include all significant acoustic events within the detected speech segments (and then to eliminate the non-speech regions of an utterance);
- the possibility of detecting and rejecting some typical background noises: isolated short external noises (including human artefacts), or very low frequency noise (for example 50/60 Hz hum);

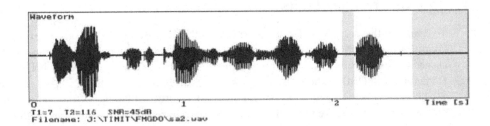

Fig. 1. TIMIT sentence

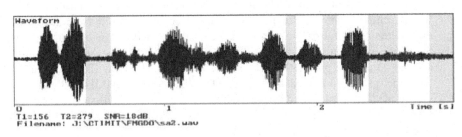

Fig. 2. CTIMIT sentence

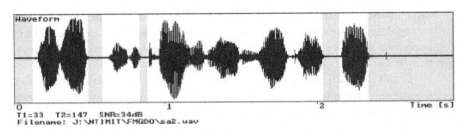

Fig. 3. NTIMIT sentence

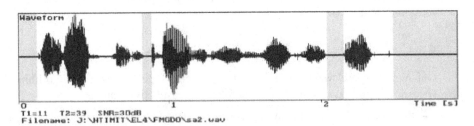

Fig. 4. HTIMIT-EL4 sentence

– a reasonable complexity and consequently operation in real-time on a previously acquired utterance.

Considering these fundamental requirements, we designed and implemented a novel *explicit energy-based speech detection algorithm*. Tested on many of the available databases and also using a particular speaker recognition program, it proved to be an accurate, adaptive and fast speech detection algorithm. As it was mentioned, the algorithm was designed for an off-line processing; nevertheless, it could be easily changed for an on-line version, with only a few minor modifications.

References

1. Cohn, R. P.: Robust Voiced/Unvoiced Speech Classification Using a Neural Net. Proceedings of ICASSP '91, vol. 1, Paper S7.6 (1991).
2. Draganescu, M., Stefan G., Burileanu C.: Electronica functionala. Ed. Tehnica, Bucharest (1991), 443–480.
3. Herrera, A., Ramos A, Yamasaki K.: Speech Detection in High Noise Condition. Proceedings of ICSPAT '96, Boston, vol. 2 (1996), 1774–1778.
4. Le Bouquin Jeannes, R., Faucon G.: Voice Activity Detector Based on the Averaged Magnitude Squared Coherence. Proceedings of ICSPAT '95, Boston, vol. 2 (1995), 1964–1968.
5. Rabiner, L. R., Sambur M. R.: An Algorithm for Determining the Endpoints of Isolated Utterances. The Bell System Technical Journal, vol. 54 (1975), 297–315.
6. Tolba, H., O'Shaughnessy D.: Voiced-Unvoiced Classification Using the First Mel Frequency Cepstral Coefficient. Proceedings of ICSP '97, Seoul, vol. 1 (1997), 137–142.
7. Tucker, G. B., Spanias A. S., Loizou P. C.: A HMM-Based Endpoint Detector for Computer Communication Application. Proceedings of ICSPAT '95, Boston, vol. 2 (1995), 1969–1973.

Optimal Pitch Path Tracking
for More Reliable Pitch Detection*

Petr Motlíček and Jan Černocký

Brno Univ. of Technology, Inst. of Radioelectronics,
motlicek@urel.fee.vutbr.cz, cernocky@urel.fee.vutbr.cz

Abstract. This paper presents an application of one method for improving
fundamental frequency detection from a speech. The method is based on searching
the best pitch paths over one or more words. It uses the idea that the fundamental
frequency of a speaker cannot change sharply in a short time so that the pitch
should not vary rapidly over one (or a few) words. This technique is created for
improving pitch detection. It cannot detect the pitch itself, but it uses some pitch
detectors. We compare some of them here and we try to determine which is the
most suitable one for our method.

1   Introduction

The word pitch (in the context of speech processing), as defined operationally by
psychoacousticians, is the frequency of pure tone that is matched by the listener to a more
complex (usually periodic) signal. This is a subjective definition. When we speak of a
"pitch detector", we usually refer to a device that measures the fundamental frequency
of an incoming signal; this is an objective definition. Pitch detection and fundamental
frequency estimation are often used interchangeably. The pitch detection is not such an
easy task. We have a lot of difficulties, which we can encounter [1]:

- Sub-harmonics of fundamental frequency often appear that are sub-multiples of the
  "true" frequency.
- Fundamental frequency changes with time, often with each glottal period.
- In many cases when strong sub-harmonics are present, the most reasonable objective
  pitch estimate is clearly at odds with the auditory percept.
- It is difficult to distinguish periodic background noise from breathy voiced speech.
- The dynamic range of the voice fundamental frequency is large. The pitch of some
  male voices can be as low as 50 Hz, whereas the pitch of children's voice can be as
  high as 600 Hz.

These different kinds of behaviour make pitch detection difficult.

In the literature, a lot of techniques for pitch detection can be found. Among
the essential ones, we can count autocorrelation function (ACF) [4]. Instead of ACF,

---

* This work is supported by the Ministry of Education, Youth and Sports of the Czech Republic –
project No. VS97060, and by the Research programme of Brno University of Technology "Research of electronic communication systems and technologies", No. CEZ:J22/98:262200011.

P. Sojka, I. Kopeček, and K. Pala (Eds.): TSD 2000, LNAI 1902, pp. 183–188, 2000.

normalised cross correlation function (NCCF) can be used [2]. NCCF is often able to estimate the pitch better than an ordinary ACF. Another method uses linear prediction LPC and the fundamental frequency is estimated from its error signal. In these techniques, the pitch can be found using long-term prediction (LTP). Cepstral pitch detection is popular as well. Here the pitch is estimated from the cepstral train [3,5].

Using only one of the pitch detectors mentioned above, we almost never get good pitch estimation. We find out that these techniques often have problems with recognition of voiced and unvoiced parts of speech. Moreover, they often detect wrong values of pitch in speech (some higher harmonics or sub-harmonics), even though the fundamental frequency is still approximately unvarying. Therefore some other techniques are applied in order to remove these drawbacks. One of the often used methods is the oversampling of input signal (usually 6 times). Another one is the median filtering of obtained pitch sequence. Finally, one of the ways that can improve pitch estimation is the optimal pitch path detection.

2   Pitch Detector Experiments

All methods that can work as pitch detectors were used in the experiments. We determined their ability to detect the pitch on about twenty Czech words (two speakers). On the whole, it can be said that the best pitch estimation is obtained using NCCF. It gives the biggest probability that we find out the "true" pitch. One example is given in Figure 1. NCCF, ACF, cepstrum and ACF of LPC-error signal are shown for one frame of input speech signal. The correct value of lag for this frame is around 90 samples. As it is shown in Figure 1, the best estimation of "true" pitch is obtained using NCCF, because of the biggest peak with respect to other peaks of its function. The other detectors failed to estimate the "true" pitch (caused by sub-harmonics of input signal).

2.1   Techniques for Improving Pitch Estimation

As mentioned before, we are not able to achieve good pitch estimation using uniquely pitch detectors. Therefore some other techniques that can improve this estimation are used. These techniques are applied at the sequence of lags (one lag refers to one frame of speech signal). The first possibility is the median filtering of lags' sequence. By this filter we can remove some wrong estimation of pitch in frames. It can also repair some wrong determination of one or a few voiced or unvoiced frames in lags' sequence. Some problems can be caused by a small sampling frequency of speech signal. Thus, an oversampling of the input signal (mostly 6 times) can bring better pitch estimation.

We have found out that estimating of voiced or unvoiced frame is not so problematic. Problems are mostly caused by sub-harmonics of the "true" fundamental frequency in signal that are obtained after using some pitch detectors. These drawbacks cannot be removed by previous methods. When ACF is computed (or other previously mentioned functions) we often find out that the interesting interval contains two, three, or sometimes more peaks, caused by sub-harmonics of the pitch. Thus, if only one maximum of ACF is looked for, some sub-harmonics of fundamental frequency could be determined instead of the "true" pitch, because it can have a larger value than the real fundamental frequency.

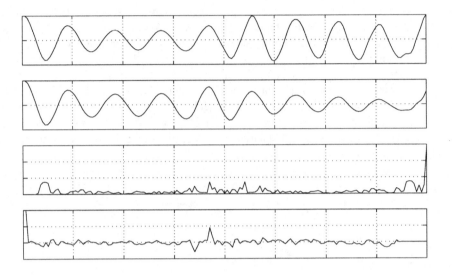

Fig. 1. Pitch detectors and their output functions of 117th frame of input speech signal (two Czech words "létající prase")

These drawbacks can be eliminated by using a method which looks for optimal pitch path in lags' sequence.

2.2   Optimal Pitch Path Detector

This detector looks for the suitable paths of lags in the input signal of n frames. First of all, a matrix **A** is given. This matrix contains a parameterisation (ACF, NCCF, ...) for each frame in one row (so that it has n rows). In each row, 4 peaks are found and their positions are recorded in matrix **M** (n times 4). The corresponding values are stored in matrix **V** (n times 4). Next, the unvoiced frames are detected: each element of **M** is taken and we determine if the following or the previous row of **M** contains a similar value (in any column). Therefore, if for the i-th frame any of $m_{i,k}$ satisfies:

$$m_{i,k} \in m_{i-1,m} \pm const, \qquad \forall i,k, \qquad m \in [1,4] \tag{1}$$

or

$$m_{i,k} \in m_{i+1,m} \pm const, \qquad \forall i,k, \qquad m \in [1,4], \tag{2}$$

where $const$ is a constant, the i-th frame is declared voiced, otherwise it is unvoiced.

The next step is to seek all paths in *voiced portions* of matrix **M**. A path is determined by its mean lag value stored in vector **b**. This vector is initialised to empty. When processing new row of **M**, its entries are compared to elements of **b**. If an entry $m_{i,k}$ lies closed enough to an element b_i, it is clustered to b_i and b_i is updated using:

$$b_{i(new)} = \frac{b_{i(old)} + m_{i,k}}{2}. \tag{3}$$

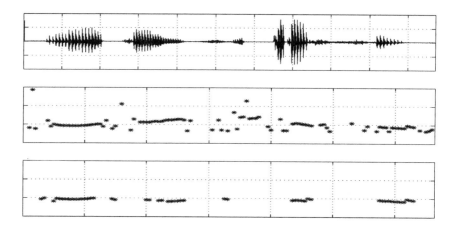

Fig. 2. Estimation of fundamental frequency of two Czech words "létající prase"
Upper panel: Input signal (10781 samples, 8 kHz, 133 frames)
Middle panel: Pitch estimation using only NCCF
Lower panel: Estimation using optimal pitch path technique (appliedon NCCF)

If not, a new entry in **b** is created: $\mathbf{b} = [\mathbf{b}\; m_{i,k}]$. It is obvious that the length of **b** is not a priori known. A vector **c** associated to **b** contains a sum of respective maximal values from the matrix **V**. This vector therefore contains a "quality measurement" of pitch paths. At the end of a voiced portion, values of **c** are normalised by path lengths and the optimal mean lag b_d is determined:

$$d = \arg\max_i(\mathbf{c}), \qquad i \in [1, m], \tag{4}$$

where m is the number of candidate paths. The optimal path associated with b_d is extracted from **M**. Finally, a simple energy detector marks the "unvoiced" frames where the energy falls below a pre-determined threshold.

The estimation of fundamental frequency of speech using optimal pitch path detection in comparison with raw NCCF, can be seen in Figure 2. This method is likely to recognise voiced and unvoiced parts of speech successfully.

3   Evaluation of Results

Optimal pitch path detection was tested on a reference database from OGIvox[1] (Center for Spoken Language Understanding) that include simultaneous speech and electroglottograph (EGG) data. The OGIvox database contains a directory with signal files and a directory with "pitch ticks" (obtained by EGG) associated to these signal

[1] Thanks to Mike Bacon (OGI, Portland, Oregon) for the permission to use it.

files. We have created a script that processes one thousand signal and EGG files from OGIvox.

First, the real pitch is computed from the "ticks" for each frame of signal files, whereas the pitch is determined as a time period between the two closest "ticks". However, it could happen that a frame contains only one, or more than two "pitch ticks". Therefore, we compute the pitch using "ticks" not only from the current frame, but also by using two "ticks" from two neighbouring frames. Then time periods are determined and the mean value represents the pitch of this frame.

Second, the pitch was computed by using optimal pitch path detection for all files and the results were statistically compared:

- The error of the detection of voiced frames in comparison with OGIvox (1,000 signal files) is 22.5%.
- The error of pitch detection in voiced frames is 9.6%.

Comparison of the results for one OGIvox signal file is shown in Figure 3.

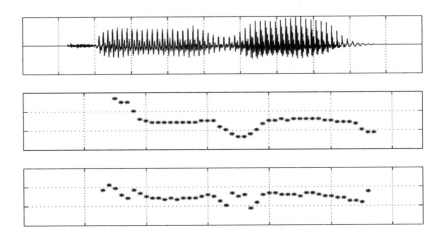

Fig. 3. Estimation of fundamental frequency F0 on signal file from OGIvox database:
Upper panel: Input signal (10880 samples, 16 kHz, 67 frames)
Middle panel: "Real" pitch computed from EGG
Lower panel: Estimation using optimal pitch path technique (applied on NCCF)

4   Conclusions

We have tested several methods for improving pitch detection. In general, the optimal pitch path detection gives the best results. The biggest problems in pitch detection are caused by higher harmonics or sub-harmonics of the fundamental frequency. Only optimal pitch path detection of all mentioned techniques is able to find out the "true" fundamental frequency in speech signal. This method works with short sections of speech signal (a few words), thus it is able to recognise the change of pitch of a speaker not immediately, but after processing of one section of speech signal. The disadvantage of this technique is its high complexity in comparison with other methods. The best pitch detector, which can be used with the optimal pitch path technique, is based on NCCF.

Optimal Pitch Path Detection was tested on OGIvox database (pitch provided by EGG). Determining "true" pitch in voiced frames was very good (error 9.6% for computing over 1,000 signal files of speech). In detection of voicing, the error was 22.5%. However, a very simple detector of energy was used in the test, a more sophisticated detector should improve this figure.

References

1. B. Gold and N. Morgan. *Speech and Audio Signal Processing*, pages 214–227 and 415–430, New York, 1999.
2. D. Talkin. A Robust Algorithm for Pitch Tracking (RAPT). In Kleijn, W. B. and Paliwal, K. K. (Eds.), *Speech Coding and Synthesis*. New York: Elseviever, 1995.
3. B. P. Bogart, M. J. R. Healy, and J. W. Tukey, The frequency analysis of time series for echoes: Cepstrum, pseudo-autocovariance, cross-cepstrum and shape tracking, in *Symphosium on Time Series Analysis* (M. Rosenblatt, Ed.), (New York), pp. 209–243, John Wiley and Sons, 1963.
4. L. R. Rabiner, On the use of autocorrelation analysis for pitch detection, *IEEE Trans. Acoust., Speech, Signal Processing*, vol. ASSP-25, pp. 24–33, February 1977.
5. J. Černocký. *Speech Processing Using Automatically Derived Segmental Units*, Ph.D. Thesis, ESIEE, France, 1998.

FlexVoice: A Parametric Approach to High-Quality Speech Synthesis

György Balogh, Ervin Dobler, Tamás Grőbler, Béla Smodics, and Csaba Szepesvári

Mindmaker Ltd., Budapest, Hungary
bogyom@mindmaker.hu, dobler@mindmaker.hu, grobler@mindmaker.hu,
sbela@mindmaker.hu, szepes@mindmaker.hu http://www.flexvoice.com

Abstract. FlexVoice, an integrated text-to-speech (TTS) system is presented
in this paper. Its most distinctive feature is its low memory and CPU load
while preserving the high quality of leading TTS systems. FlexVoice uses a
hybrid approach that combines diphone concatenation with LPC-based parametric
synthesis. Major improvements of speech quality are achieved by the careful
design of each module at all synthesis levels (such as selection of training data for
the various machine learning methods and that of the basic synthesis units for the
parametric synthesiser). FlexVoice currently supports US English with two male
and two female voices.

1 Introduction

The general idea of developing FlexVoice was to build a TTS system that has significantly
lower memory and CPU time requirements than nowadays' high-quality text-to-
speech systems, while preserving their intelligibility and naturalness. Time-domain
concatenative synthesis has been judged recently as the method that can achieve the
highest quality [1]. Time-domain methods, however, have some serious shortcomings,
such as limited ability to modify pitch and duration values of segments, which leads to
either a quality drop or huge segment inventories. FlexVoice uses concatenative synthesis
from a parametric approach. This method has advantages over time-domain methods like
easy prosody matching, smaller database, low computational load and large-scale voice
manipulations.

2 General Structure

FlexVoice is a concatenative, diphone-based LPC synthesis system. It is a hybrid system
in the sense that it concatenates fundamental units but segment concatenation takes
place in a parametric space instead of the conventional wave space. This hybrid property
ensures the small size and good quality of FlexVoice. FlexVoice has a modular structure.
Modules perform diverse tasks but each module can be categorised as either language-
dependent or language-independent. Language-independent modules can be re-used in
languages other than English without modification.

P. Sojka, I. Kopeček, and K. Pala (Eds.): TSD 2000, LNAI 1902, pp. 189–194, 2000.

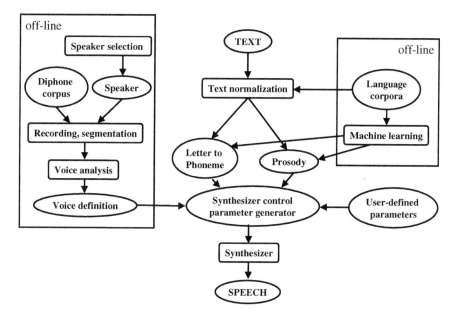

Fig. 1. Flow chart of the FlexVoice TTS system

3   Low-Level Modules and Procedures

Low-level modules are those that produce the final wave output from a sequence of phoneme, pitch, and duration values. All low-level modules are language-independent except the design procedure of the diphone corpus.

3.1   Speaker Selection

Speaker selection is a crucial point because all of the following steps may suffer from an inappropriate selection. Not only the voice properties but also the linguistic abilities of the speaker are rigorously examined. Though speaker selection is strongly subjective, there are some guidelines which should be followed. The speaker should:

– be a native speaker of the language (US English)
– have a "standard" dialect that is acceptable for the language community
– be able to articulate clearly and naturally at the same time
– have a pleasant voice when synthesised

Though these constraints are not easy to fulfil, they do not necessarily guarantee good results. A preliminary subjective listening test was constructed to select speakers from seven female and six male voices. For the test, a sentence was constructed that contained all phoneme types. The necessary diphones to synthesise the sentence were recorded from each speaker (approximately 50 diphones per speaker). A diphone is recorded as part of a sample word, and no sample word was allowed to be the same as in the test sentence. The test sentence was then synthesised in all speakers' voices, using both natural and synthetic prosody. Subjective evaluation was carried out by ten subjects to evaluate the quality of the synthesised voices.

3.2 Diphone Corpus

Extra care must be taken when designing the diphone database. This is even more true because all diphones are represented with a single word (or phrase) that is recorded only once. The phone alphabet used in FlexVoice contains 56 sounds. This is the adapted version of the SAMPA English system to US English, plus allophonic variations such as aspirated stops, syllabic consonants, diphthongs, etc. are included. Taking into account that some phone pairs are excluded by allophonic rules, all possible diphones have been looked for. The total number of diphones used in FlexVoice is about 2200. The remaining 900 diphones are theoretically possible but hardly ever appear in English speech.

3.3 Recording and Segmentation

Evidently, recording strongly influences the quality of synthesised speech. The analysis algorithms in FlexVoice turned out to be robust against noise and pitch fluctuations. Nevertheless, high quality studio recording cannot be omitted. Care must be taken to ensure that an appropriate dynamic range is used, the recording loudness is kept constant and side effects like pops and chirps are filtered out. Recording the whole diphone corpus takes approximately 5 hours.

After recording is done, the diphone positions should be marked in the corpus words. No automatic algorithm has been found which performed the segmentation task with the desired accuracy, segmentation is thus done semiautomatically: a specific tool has been developed to display the spectra and waveform of corpus words, helping the expert place the diphone markers. Three markers are used to mark a diphone, the first is inside the first phone, the second is at the border of the two phones, the third is inside the second phone. The exact positions of the first and last markers inside the phones are determined by the phonetic properties of the given sound to ensure smooth concatenation during synthesis, still considerable expertise is needed to place the markers correctly. Segmentation of a whole diphone corpus takes approx. 10 man-days.

3.4 Voice Analysis

Voice analysis is a process that creates a speaker-definition file from the segmented corpus. The model used in FlexVoice is a source-filter model. The goal of voice analysis is to separate the filter part from the source, to determine the filter parameters (spectral analysis), and to determine the amplitudes of the harmonic and noise parts of the source (source estimation).

Spectral Analysis The filter model of FlexVoice is an autoregressive (AR) model. The parameters of the all-pole filter are determined with the Levinson-Durbin algorithm. Experiments have shown no significant impact of pitch synchronous analysis, therefore

Gauss-windows with constant window shift (6 ms) are used. The order of the all-pole filter is 20, and an additional normalisation factor is computed for every filter. Filter normalisation is a critical issue because the loudness values of different diphones coming from different sample words must be equalised. The pitch-dependence of the normalisation factor is ignored; filter normalisation can thus be an off-line process. The estimation of the normalisation factor is done by measuring the energy of the synthesised wave.

Loudness The loudness values of different diphones coming from different corpus words may differ but these diphones should be concatenated smoothly during synthesis. FlexVoice specifies a loudness target value for each phoneme and diphones are equalised so that the loudness value at the beginning of the diphone equals the target value of the first phoneme while the loudness value at the end equals the target value of the second phoneme. Since filters are normalised, loudness equalisation can be performed by modifying the source amplitudes only.

Source Estimation Source estimation determines the amplitudes of the harmonic and the noise sources. Since the overall loudness is determined by loudness equalisation, the only task is to determine the harmonic/noise ratio. Some phoneme-specific constraints are also added to eliminate recording and estimation errors.

3.5   Synthesiser Control Parameter Generator

The task of this module is to create a series of synthesiser control parameters from the phoneme string given by high-level modules. This is done by concatenating analysed diphones. Smoothing is performed at diphone boundaries. Source amplitudes are interpolated linearly while filter coefficients are converted to area parameter space, interpolated linearly, then converted back.

3.6   Synthesiser

The synthesiser is a modified version of the Klatt synthesiser [2]. The main differences are that FlexVoice uses linear filters instead of resonators, and uses a single filter (the vocal tract in [2], omitting the parallel tract). There are two sources for filter input: a harmonic (voicing) and a noise source, both normalised to have unit energy density. The voicing source is based on the one in [2] but can optionally be supplemented with a coloured noise component. The noise source emits Gaussian white noise.

4   High-Level Modules

The input of the high-level part is ASCII text, the output is a string of phoneme, duration and pitch values. The high-level part uses a multi-level data structure to represent the different linguistic, phonetic and prosodic information. Every high level module uses this data structure for both input and output. FlexVoice uses various machine-learning techniques as well as rule-based technologies for completing the high-level tasks. The main modules are described in this chapter in order of execution.

4.1 Text Normalisation

FlexVoice uses a modified bottom-up chart-parser to solve the text normalisation problem. A tokeniser analyses the input text and finds the word boundaries. The frequently used patterns are placed in a grammar that is applied on the output of the tokeniser. The parser may give multiple results with a given probability, therefore further analysis is required to select the best solution. After a pattern is recognised, FlexVoice creates tokens representing parts that should be converted into words. There is a dictionary containing patterns that describe how to create words from tokens. This dictionary contains further instructions in order to help the extraction process. Each keyword can have different possible results called variants depending on context, style, or the speaker. The dictionary also contains dialect information to enable FlexVoice to differentiate between British and US English. With this technology, FlexVoice can handle the vast majority of text normalisation problems.

4.2 Part-of-Speech Tagger

FlexVoice uses a Part-of-Speech (POS) tagger as the first step of linguistic analysis. The tagger is a simple n-gram language model which was trained on an untagged text corpus.

4.3 Word Prominence Computation

FlexVoice assigns a discrete-valued word prominence information for each word. The prominence class is computed from the POS tags using a table created by human experts.

4.4 Letter-to-Phoneme Conversion

FlexVoice uses a machine-learning approach for the letter-to-phoneme conversion. For training, a pronunciation dictionary is used that contains approximately 60,000 words with their American English phonetic transcriptions and word stress information. The phoneme and grapheme strings are aligned with a probabilistic model which uses a phoneme-to-letter transition matrix created by human experts to limit the search space. A C4.5 decision tree algorithm is used to predict the phoneme and stress information using features like context and history. The generalisation performance of the model is 70% on word level and 93% on phoneme level. FlexVoice uses an editable pronunciation and POS-tag dictionary. Every word is looked up in this dictionary first, the decision tree is used only if the word is not found. The dictionary is also used for resolving the homograph ambiguity. Finally, there are some hand-driven rules for context-dependent word pronunciations such as "the" before consonants/vowels.

4.5 Prosody Models

The whole prosody generation module is based on neural networks. Four separate multi-layer perceptron models were trained with a variant of the backpropagation algorithm on a large annotated corpus: one for intonational phrase boundary prediction, one for phoneme duration prediction, and two for pitch contour prediction.

Phrase Boundaries FlexVoice splits sentences into intonational phrases that are separated with pauses in human speech. The neural network predicts a probability value for every word pair being a phrase boundary using features such as POS tags of the word context and punctuation information. For the yes/no decision for a word pair being a phrase boundary, a threshold is used on the network output. The analog output of the network is used to determine the duration of the intonational pause. The duration of the pause depends linearly on the output of the neural network.

Duration The neural network for duration predicts the z-score of the duration for every phoneme using features such as phonetic context and phrase break information. The generalisation performance of the model is 0.59 (correlation coefficient) measured in the z-score space.

Pitch Contour Two separate neural networks are used for the pitch contour prediction. One for declarative sentences and one for questions. The networks predict a normalised pitch value for each phoneme using features such as phonetic context and POS information of the word context.

5   Conclusions

Subjective listening tests have shown that FlexVoice can produce high-quality synthesised speech that compares favourably with competing products, using only a fraction of resources of a nowadays' average PC. The current version, in its unoptimised state, uses 2 MB RAM per base voice and about 15 percent of CPU time of a PIII 450 MHz processor. In addition, a significant number of different manipulated voices can be derived from a base voice. Future improvements include, among others, the development of an automatic segmentation tool and improvement of the voicing source model.

References

1. Dutoit, T.: An Introduction to Text-To-Speech Synthesis. Kluwer Acad. Publ., Dordrecht (1997).
2. Klatt, D.H., Klatt, L.C.: Analysis, Synthesis, and Perception of Voice Quality Variations among Female and Male Talkers. J. Acoust. Soc. Am. **87** (1990) 820–857.

The Continuous and Discontinuous Styles in Czech TTS

Tomáš Duběda[1] and Jiří Hanika[2]

[1] Charles University, Prague, Faculty of Arts, Nám. J. Palacha 2, 116 38 Praha 1
dubeda@ff.cuni.cz
[2] Charles University, Prague, Faculty of Mathematics and Physics,
Malostranské nám. 25, 118 00 Praha 1
geo@cuni.cz, http://epos.ure.cas.cz/

Abstract. In this paper, a partial prosodic analysis of two sets of speech styles in Czech is described. Four styles have been chosen as representatives of discontinuous styles (Address, Spelling, Headings, Dates and Prices); three styles are representing continuous styles (Weather Forecast, Sport News, News). Based on this analysis, the prosody of the selected speech styles has been simulated using the Epos [3] speech system.

1 Introduction

At present, the text-to-speech conversion as such is already a well-solved problem. Working speech synthesisers are available for hundreds of languages and many complete TTS systems have reached the commercial applicability stage, at least for major languages. Only few of them, however, produce a natural output, partly because the subjective requirements for naturalness in the speech community are less benevolent than they were ten years ago. Worse still, many applications of TTS are, from a grammatic point of view, very eccentric and there are little or no detailed descriptions of human speaker behaviour under such conditions. Given a text in a Latin-type writing system, the open problems reside almost exclusively in the prosody domain.

It is well known that not every aspect of usual human behaviour is suitable for simulation in TTS. For example, the Czech word stress, which is partly intensity-based, has been found very tricky to implement automatically in the same way, because some occurrences are frequently misinterpreted as a semantic emphasis or even emotional speech by listeners. On the other hand, a pure pitch-based approach led to correct and relatively natural results. That's why building a description for a given speech style is an iterative process. If too close an imitation fails, reasons and alternative ways have to be looked for. Our research has been verified using the Epos speech system [3], which has been originally designed exactly for the task of testing hypotheses in prosody modelling in TTS, and whose standard prosody has been configured to use the prosody modelling strategy described in [5].

P. Sojka, I. Kopeček, and K. Pala (Eds.): TSD 2000, LNAI 1902, pp. 195–200, 2000.
© Springer-Verlag Berlin Heidelberg 2000

2   The Styles of Speech

We have chosen the term "speech styles" to designate different types of situations in which speech synthesis is used, as well as the associated speech behaviour of human speakers. Thus, the term does not correspond to a classical, linguistic definition: in this article, the speech styles are characterised by the type of text, its syntax, conveyed information, interactivity and similar factors. As most factors contributing to a speech style are completely text-based, a TTS system has to focus on the prosody modelling to perform well in a given speech style.

In many cases, a non-specific speech synthesiser is primarily designed for continuous, fully grammatical speech (sequence of sentences with their transphrastic relations), e.g. a news article. However, to meet the demands of everyday life, many applications have to cope with tasks that differ from such non-specific text, the task being a sequence of phone numbers, short answers and alerts (Yes, No, Continue, Repeat) or anything else. To study the prosody of these language productions, we used a corpus of natural speech recordings made by the participants of the COST 258 project. The corpus includes 13 languages spoken by 17 speakers. For each language, a set of 15 short texts had been recorded, ranging from a proper name spelling to an interactive database query. For Czech, one male speaker (a rather grave voice) was recorded.

Our aim was to detect relevant prosodic cues that mark the chosen speech styles difference, to quantify them, and to incorporate their models into the non-specific prosody module as described above. Our starting point was necessarily the above mentioned set of prosodic rules for Czech, and we also tried to use standard facilities of this rule set in all cases that option seemed adequate. The modelling was based on data that came from the analysis of a single speaker, which means that it emulates *his* speech behaviour rather than "average" Czech speech behaviour. We consider this approach to be well-founded, since the speaker's prosody is fully acceptable. The phonetic analysis was performed using the SpeechStudio software by Petr Horák.

3   Continuous and Discontinuous Styles

The language (performance) can be seen as a continuum of texts ranging from the most central (i.e. fully grammatical) spoken texts to the periphery of language, and so do speech styles. The core of a natural language is associated with prosodic features which have often been subjected to a phonetic analysis. On the other hand, many, if not most, speech-enabled systems focus on a very different application domain: dialogue systems with limited or formalised output, screen readers for blind users, or speech interfaces of monitoring systems. The speech styles employed by human speakers in such circumstances are often termed discontinuous, because the prosodic utterance typical for such speech style is shorter than a sentence, and, from the grammatical point of view, is thus incomplete. On the other hand, the more classical speech styles differ only slightly in the repertoire of prosodic devices applied, because the structural differences of texts found there are minor as well. In fact, a "standard" [5] prosodic analysis for the language in question suits continuous styles well, and that's why a standard text-to-speech processor handles these styles acceptably. Discontinuous styles show three important features:

1. Their application domain tends to be specialised and narrow, which makes them easily formalised, while less linear,
2. As the syntactic rules are relaxed within a discontinuous style, the phrases are very short and redundancy is suppressed; that is particularly unfortunate, as numerals, proper names and other sensitive texts are likely to occur in some of these styles.
3. Staying at the periphery of language, they differ from each other considerably.

For these reasons, the analysis of a continuous speech style is a very different task from that of a discontinuous speech style.

4   Discontinuous Styles

A superficial auditive comparison of the recorded speech sequence and its synthetic imitation in the automatic TTS synthesis designed primarily for continuous texts was used to determine the prosodic features upon which the model should be based: terminal/non-terminal F0 contours, insertion of pauses, F0 declination and timing. Some other proposed features were rejected, as their significance in the recorded speech sequence was unclear. Four styles in this category have been studied: "Address", "Headings", "Dates and Prices" and "Spelling".

Some of the styles in question have a rigid structure (e.g. a name – address – phone number sequence generated by a database), but show no 'real' syntax and mostly lack any punctuation at the input. It is thus necessary to insert additional punctuation marks into the synthesised speech sequences in order to obtain a suitable prosody reflecting the 'pseudo-syntax' of the utterance.

The insertion of a comma implies a non-terminal contour, the insertion of a stop implies a terminal contour. According to our auditive evaluation, the insertion of punctuation marks is sufficient to generate satisfactory intonation contours. The automatic duration increase and intonation decrease at the end of prosodic boundaries (which is a quasi universal prosodic feature in Czech) seems to be sufficient too.

The insertion of commas and stops also implies the presence of pauses. For numerals, a clear and slow realization is required, because the information is very compact and there is no redundancy in the utterance.

Thus, the sequence first name – last name – street – block – zip code – city – phone number in the "address" style was split with additional punctuation marks that imply the corresponding pause and intonation contour generation rules as follows:

(database output)

```
Josef Novák
Národní třída 16
110 00 Praha 1
21 63 89 15
```

(prosody modelling; other TTS transformations not shown)

```
Josef Novák, [pause 480 ms/rising contour] Národní třída 16,
[pause 480 ms/rising contour] 110 00, [pause 480 ms/rising
contour] Praha 1. [pause 640 ms/falling contour] 21,
[p. 480 ms/rising] 63, [p. 480 ms/rising] 89,
[p. 480 ms/rising] 15. [p. 480 ms/falling]
```

The "spelling" style requires special treatment for F0 declination (gradual pitch descent through the sentence). Unlike the declination used with continuous speech, the spelling declination is much more abrupt.

5   The Continuous Styles

Three representative styles with a high frequency have been chosen out of the spectrum of continuous speech styles defined by the COST 258 project: non-specific news report (N), weather forecast (WF) and sport news report (SN). It has been said above that continuous styles, staying in the centre of the language system, show less variation and can be generated by the non-specific prosodic module more satisfactorily than discontinuous styles. In fact, the observed differences are often very subtle, and the degree of acceptability for the three styles is rather high, even if only the non-specific prosody modelling is employed.

We focused on the following properties:

– Speech and articulation rate
– Length of prosodic units (stress unit and intonation unit)
– Pauses
– Timing of final clauses
– F0 contours in final position

The units of prosodic segmentation that our synthesis operates with are stress unit (SU, a chain of syllables with an initial stress, mostly comprising of at most one semantic word and zero or more grammatical words), and intonational unit (IU, a chain of stress units terminated by a phonological F0 contour, corresponding mostly to an inter-punctuation stretch or clause). Let us note at this place, that our hierarchy of linguistic units such as clause or sentence is also methodologically based on the TTS application, i.e. the usual punctuation and transformational rules are used to delimit such units. This attitude is a special case of using the standard facilities of our base rule set where possible; for our texts however – and for almost all of Czech in general – the "graphical" units coincide with their prosody description counterparts, i.e. there happens to be no discrepancy between the two points of view.

The average articulation rate (syllable count divided by articulation time, i. e. without pauses) is about 5.23 syll/s and doesn't depend on the speech style chosen significantly. (This is however not always true locally; special attention must be paid to clause-final stress units.)

The length of sentences and intonation units (IU, inter-punctuation stretch of stress units) is as follows:

The N text shows very long sentences and intonation units; the other two texts comprise of more clauses, especially the SN text, which is the most dynamic and expressive one. This observation has no direct effect on our TTS prosody modelling, while it gives some insight into the differences observed among the texts. It is also possible to employ the style difference – if any – in treating certain punctuation-less constructions as clause terminators in some cases, for example, but such heuristics are hard to propose, test and evaluate.

Table 1. Lengths of prosodic units

Text	N	WF	SN
Average sentence length (syll.)	61.6	27.3	19.9
Average IU length (syll.)	23.2	11.3	12.2

The average length of a stress unit is about 2.73 syllables for all the three styles, i.e. the basic characteristics of the texts are comparable.

Table 2. Pauses

Text	N	WF	SN
Total number of pauses	10	17	16
Frequency of pauses (syllables/pause)	18.5	11.3	9.9
Average pause duration (ms)	552.9	684.1	522.9
No-punctuation pause average duration (ms)	146.0	88.0	425.0
Average duration of a pause after a comma	357.0	357.0	235.0
Average duration of a pause after a stop	1652.0	1329.0	958.0

The frequency of pauses increases in the order *SN-WF-N* and it is inversely proportional to the length of a suprasegmental unit for physiological reasons. Spontaneous pauses (pauses corresponding to no punctuation mark or any other clause terminator, which leaves 16% of all the pauses) are to be ignored at the present stage, because no complex syntactic analysis is performed by Epos. Therefore, pauses can be safely inserted almost exclusively at clause-marking or sentence-marking punctuation. The values in the "Average duration of a pause after a comma" and "Average duration of a pause after a stop" rows were directly inserted into the corresponding prosodic rules.

The timing was studied only in terms of clause-final lengthening:

Table 3. Clause-final lengthening

Text	N	WF	SN
Average syllable duration of a clause-final SU (ms)	196	253	223
Average syllable duration of a sentence-final SU (ms)	186	179	182
Clause-final / sentence-final SU syllable duration ratio	1.05	1.41	1.23

The table shows that the clause-final lengthening increases in the *WF-SN-N* order.

Observe that sentence-final stress units are actually shorter than clause-final ones in general. This unexpected phenomenon is indicative of information-dense speech styles such as weather forecasts, where phrasing and speech are both particularly important.

There, a pause indicates a sentence-level break, while an overall slowdown, *including the pause*, marks a clause-level break. That way, lengthening proper is not a phrasing marker in presence of a pause and can safely be somewhat suppressed. This effect is obviously not critically dependent on average sentence length. As far, as the *SN* style is concerned, a limitation of our corpus may come into play: a real-life *SN* production may be much less planned and syntactically coherent, and pausing and phrasing is likely to behave differently.

Modelling of such style-dependent differences is straightforward.

References

1. Dohalská, M., Duběda, T.: Experiments with Duration and Intensity Variation in Czech Text-to-Speech. Proceedings of the 6th Czech-German Workshop on Speech Processing, Prague, September 1996.
2. Dohalská, M., Duběda, T., Mejvaldová, J.: Speech Styles in Synthetic Czech. oral presentation, COST 258 Executive Committee meeting, Budapest, September 1999.
3. Hanika, J., Horák, P.: Epos – A New Approach to the Speech Synthesis. Proceedings of the First Workshop on Text, Speech, Dialogue – TSD'98, Brno, Czech Republic, September 1998, pp. 51–54.
4. Hanika, J., Horák, P.: Dependences and Independences of Text-to-Speech. Hans-Walter Wodarz (Ed.): Forum Phoneticum 69, Frankfurt a. M., to appear.
5. Palková, Z., Ptáček, M.: Prosodic Issues in Czech: An Application in TTS. Proceedings of the XIIIth International Congress of Phonetic Sciences, Stockholm 1995, Vol. 4, pp. 380–383.

Automatic Speech Segmentation
with the Application of the Czech TTS System

Petr Horák and Betty Hesounová

Institute of Radio Engineering and Electronics,
Academy of Sciences of the Czech Republic, Prague
Chaberská 57, 182 51 Praha 8, Czech Republic
horak@ure.cas.cz, betty@ure.cas.cz

Abstract. This article presents automatic phonetic segmentation of natural speech based on the use of a speech synthesiser and dynamic time warping (DTW) algorithm. The speech synthesiser is used to create a synthetic reference speech pattern with phonetic segmentation information (phonemes, diphones, syllables, intonation units, etc.). The reference synthetic speech pattern is then used in the alignment process. The main motivation for this work lay in the lack of usable segmentation tools for Czech, especially for the creation of prosodically labelled databases. The segmentation system has been developed for Czech and it uses the Czech TTS system.

1 Introduction

The automatic phonetic speech segmentation is an important tool for many fields of speech research. It can be used for creation of large prosodically labelled databases for research of natural prosody generation (e.g. by neural nets), for automatic creation of new speech synthesis inventories, and, last but not least, for the purposes of speech recognition. There are many freely available prosodically labelled natural speech corpora for world languages (i.e. English, French or German), but none for Czech. The new automatic segmentation system should simplify the creation of new corpora. The idea of using speech synthesis for automatic segmentation is not new. Automatic segmentation for French is thoroughly described by F. Malfrère and T. Dutoit in [1]. The developed algorithm is based on the idea of [2] by the same authors and improved by G. Strecha in [3] and [4]. Most reports on automatic segmentation are based on using the Hidden Markov Models for TTS alignment. The alignment is basically performed by a trained recognition system. Such recognition systems are typically trained on phoneme models, that is, they acquire some knowledge of the spectral features of phonemes on the basis of many realizations of each phoneme in various phonetic contexts and pronounced by various speakers.

2 Speech Synthesis

The Epos speech system [5,6] is used for creating phonetically labelled synthetic speech. The 8 kHz LPC speech synthesis based on concatenation of 441 Czech and Slovak

P. Sojka, I. Kopeček, and K. Pala (Eds.): TSD 2000, LNAI 1902, pp. 201–206, 2000.

diphones and vowel bodies is used in Epos for this purpose [7,8]. The missing information about boundaries between sounds in each diphone was added for this purpose. The Epos with the modified male voice LPC inventory is capable of producing synthetic speech, together with the information about diphones, sounds, syllables and intonation units (similar to words), from written text. The described speech system is illustrated in Figure 1.

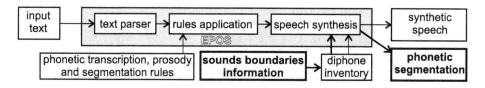

Fig. 1. Enhanced speech synthesis Epos (the bold parts were added).

3   Segmentation

The segmentation algorithm uses separate sentences, therefore a text has to be separated into sentences before the segmentation. The first step of the segmentation consists in the extraction of relevant features from both the reference and the natural speech signals. Both signals are processed frame by frame in each sentence. Six sets of parameters have been used to characterise each speech frame. The first set of parameters defines the representation of the local speech spectral envelope – the cepstral coefficients c_i obtained from linear prediction analysis of the frame [9].

$$c_0 = \ln \sqrt{\alpha}, \tag{1}$$

$$c_n = -a_n - \frac{1}{n} \sum_{k=1}^{n-1} (n-k)c_{n-k}a_k, \quad \text{for } n > 0, \tag{2}$$

where α is linear prediction gain coefficient, $a_0 = 1$ and $a_k = 0$ for $k > M$, M is order of linear prediction analysis. The delta cepstral coefficients Δc_i form the second set of coefficients.

$$\Delta c_0(i) = c_0(i), \tag{3}$$

$$\Delta c_n(i) = c_n(i) - c_n(i-1), \tag{4}$$

where $c_j(i)$ is j^{th} cepstral coefficient of ith frame. The third and fourth sets of parameters are formed by the short time energy and its first difference [10].

$$E(i) = \sum_{m=-\infty}^{\infty} (x(m)w(i.N.(1-\mu)-m))^2, \tag{5}$$

$$\Delta E(i) = E(i) - E(i-1), \tag{6}$$

where x is the speech signal, i is number of the frame, N is frame length, m is frame overlapping and M is order of linear prediction analysis, $w(a) = 1$ if $0 \leq a < N$, $w(a) = 0$ otherwise.

Finally, the zero-crossing rate and the delta zero-crossing rate coefficients are added to the first four sets of coefficients.

$$Z(i) = \sum_{m=-\infty}^{\infty} f(x(m)x(m-1))w(i.N.(1-\mu)-m), \qquad (7)$$

$$\Delta Z(i) = Z(i) - Z(i-1), \qquad (8)$$

where x is the speech signal, i is number of the frame, N is frame length, m is frame overlapping, $w(a) = 1$ if $0 \leq a < N$, $w(a) = 0$ otherwise, $f(a) = 1$ if $a < k_z (k_z < 0)$, $f(a) = 0$ otherwise.

All of the six parameters sets are normalised into the interval $\langle -1, 1 \rangle$. The block diagram of the phonetic segmentation process is shown in Figure 2.

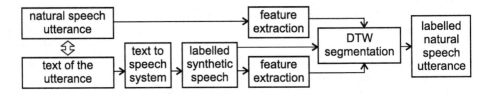

Fig. 2. Phonetic segmentation process

The second step of the process is the segmentation itself. It is realized with a classical dynamic time warping algorithm with accumulated distance matrix **D**.

$$\mathbf{D} = \begin{pmatrix} D(1,J) & D(2,J) & \cdots & D(I,J) \\ D & D & \cdots & D \\ \vdots & \vdots & D(i,j) & \vdots \\ D(1,2) & D(2,2) & \cdots & D(I,2) \\ D(1,1) & D(2,1) & \cdots & D(I,1) \end{pmatrix} \qquad (9)$$

where I is number of frames of the first signal and J is number of frames of the second signal. This DTW algorithm uses symmetric form of warping function weighting coefficients [11]. The weighting coefficients are described in Figure 3. In the beginning the marginal elements of the distance matrix are initialised (see Equations 10 and 12). Other elements of the distance matrix are computed by the Equation 13 [11].

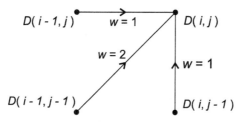

Fig. 3. Weighting coefficients w for symmetric form

$$D(1,1) = d(x(1), y(1)) \tag{10}$$
$$D(i,1) = D(i-1,1) + d(x(i), y(1)) \quad i = 1 \ldots I \tag{11}$$
$$D(1,j) = D(1, j-1) + d(x(1), y(j)) \quad j = 1 \ldots J \tag{12}$$
$$D(i,j) = MIN \left(\begin{array}{c} D(i-1,j) + d(x(i), y(j)) \\ D(i-1, j-1) + d(x(i), y(j)) \\ D(i, j-1) + d(x(i), y(j)) \end{array} \right) \tag{13}$$

where $d(x(i), y(j))$ is distance between the ith frame of the first signal and the jth of the second signal (see Equation 14), $MIN(x)$ is the minimum function. The distance $d(x, y)$ is a weighted combination of a cepstral distance, an energy distance and a zero-crossing rate distance used to compare a frame from the natural speech signal x and a frame from the synthetic reference signal y.

$$d(x,y) = \alpha_0 \sum_{i=0}^{n_{cep}} (c_i(x) - c_i(y))^2 + \beta \sum_{i=0}^{n_{cep}} (\Delta c_i(x) - \Delta c_i(y))^2 +$$
$$+ \gamma (E(x) - E(y))^2 + \delta (\Delta E(x) - \Delta E(y))^2 + \tag{14}$$
$$+ \varphi (Z(x) - Z(y))^2 + \eta (\Delta Z(x) - \Delta Z(y))^2$$

An optimisation phase over the different parameters used in the distance has led to the following values: frames of 20 ms with a $n = 0.7$ (14 ms) overlap, linear predictive analysis order $M = 8$, $\alpha = 1.5$; $\beta = 1.25$; $\gamma = 1.5$; $\delta = 1$; $\varphi = 1$; $\eta = 1.5$, zero-crossing rate constant $k_z = -20000$.

The next section shows the results of the first experiments performed with our segmentation system.

4   Results

The system presented in the previous section has been preliminary tested and evaluated with one male and one female Czech native speaker. Each speaker pronounced 72 sentences consisting of 3994 phonemes. The automatic segmentation results were compared with manual segmentation of the same data. For the purpose of comparison, Czech sounds were divided into 10 groups according to the manner of articulation and un/voicedness.

The segmentation errors were computed for the beginnings of phonemes and for their lengths. The errors were divided into 7 categories according to their absolute value in milliseconds. The automatic segmentation results were in most cases better for the female voice although the male speech synthesis voice was used.

The difference between average lengths of manual and automatic labelling was smallest in the group of vowels. Very good results were obtained also in the class of unvoiced explosives, probably owing to their distinct spectrum. Fricatives were, on the other hand, automatically labelled with a marked deviation. The reason might be that initial and final parts of fricatives, as opposed to explosives, are into a greater extent realized on the bordering speech sounds, especially vowels. Considerable differences were found in the group of nasals. This was probably caused by the fact that it is often difficult to distinguish the spectrum of nasals from that of other sonorants.

The automatic segmentation algorithm is very robust. In cases when the natural speech utterance and synthetic speech utterance are not the same, the algorithm skips unequal parts and continues on corresponding parts of speech signals.

5   Applications

The main application of the Czech speech segmentation system is the creation of prosodically labelled speech databases which are needed for further research on prosody modelling, especially for the training of neural nets for the automatic pitch contour generation or for the LPC analysis and synthesis of pitch contours performed in our lab [12].

Another application is the use of automatic segmentation for accelerating the creation of new voices for existing speech synthesisers on the basis of a first set of synthesis units [13]. The phonetic segmentation of speech signals into syllables, sounds (corresponding to phonemes) and intonation units is useful for speech prosody processing while phonetic segmentation to diphones and sounds is helpful for creation of new speech inventories. The research in field of Czech phoneme duration motivated by [14] and [15] was started with the use of the above described automatic speech segmentation.

6   Conclusions

The preliminary evaluation of the automatic segmentation algorithm shows that the accuracy of the automatic segmentation is sufficient for creating prosodically labelled speech corpora and for prosody transplantation, but it is not convenient for a new TTS inventory creation. However, the automatic segmentation algorithm can be used for a new TTS inventory creation supplemented with a manual or semiautomatic adjustment. New speech corpora from several speakers have been recorded. We are working now on the manual labelling of these speech corpora for a better evaluation of the presented system. We plan to use the described automatic segmentation system for creation of a new 16 kHz diphone inventory which could be used for 16 kHz automatic segmentation algorithm. We also plan to extend the new diphone inventory by CC diphones and by two Czech consonants missing in the current 8 kHz diphone inventory (velar "n" and unvoiced "ř").

Acknowledgements

This work was supported by the grant No 102/96/K087 "Theory and Application of Speech Communication in Czech" of the Grant Agency of the Czech Republic and by the Czech Ministry of Education, Youth and Physical Training supply for the COST 258 project.

Special thanks to Guntram Strecha from TU Dresden for his effort on automatic segmentation during his stay in our lab.

References

1. F. Malfrère, T. Dutoit: Speech Synthesis for Text-To-Speech Alignment and Prosodic Feature Extraction. Proc. ISCAS '97, Hong-Kong, pp. 2637–2640.
2. F. Malfrère, T. Dutoit: High-Quality Speech Synthesis for Phonetic Speech Segmentation. In: Proc. EuroSpeech '97, Rhodes, Greece, pp. 2631–2634.
3. G. Strecha: Automatic Segmentation of Speech Signal. Pre-diploma stay final report, IREE Academy of Sciences, Czech Republic, 1999 (in German).
4. J. Tučková, G. Strecha: Automatic Labelling of Natural Speech by Comparison with Synthetic Speech. In: Proc. the 4th Int. Workshop on Electronics, Control, Measurement and Signals ECMS '99, Liberec, Czech Republic, May 31–June 1, 1999, pp. 156–159.
5. J. Hanika, P. Horák: Epos – A New Approach to the Speech Synthesis. In: Proceedings of the First Workshop on Text, Speech, Dialogue – TSD'98, Brno, Czech Republic, September 23–26, 1998, pp. 51–54.
6. J. Hanika, P. Horák: The Epos Speech System: User Documentation ver. 2.4.42. Available on the web page http://epos.ure.cas.cz/epos.html.
7. M. Ptáček, R. Vích, E. Víchová: Czech Text-to-Speech Synthesis by Concatenation of Parametric Units. In: Proc. URSI ISSSE'92, Paris, France, pp. 230–232.
8. R. Vích: Pitch Synchronous Linear Predictive Czech and Slovak Text-to-Speech Synthesis. In: Proc. of the 15th Intern. Congress on Acoustics ICA'95, Trondheim, Norway, 1995, Vol. III, pp. 181–184.
9. J. D. Markel, A. H. Gray jr.: Linear Prediction of Speech. Springer-Verlag, Berlin Heidelberg, New York, 1976.
10. L. R. Rabiner, R. W. Schafer: Digital Processing of Speech Signals. Bell Laboratories, Incorporated, 1978.
11. H. Sakoe, S. Chiba: Dynamic Programming Algorithm Optimization for Spoken Word Recognition. In: IEEE Trans. on Acoustics, Speech and Signal Proc., Vol. ASSP-26, 1978, pp. 43–49.
12. P. Horák: The LPC Analysis and Synthesis of F0 Contour. In: Proceedings of the First Workshop on Text, Speech, Dialogue – TSD'98, Brno, Czech Republic, September 23–26, 1998, pp. 219–222.
13. T. Portele, K.-H. Stöber, H. Meyer, W. Hess: Generation of Multiple Synthesis Inventories by a Bootstrapping Procedure. In: Proc ICSLP '96, 1996, pp. 2392–2395.
14. K. Bartkova, C. Sorin: A Model of Segmental Duration for Speech Synthesis in French. In: Speech Communications 6, Elsevier Science Publishers B.V., North-Holland, 1987, pp. 245–260.
15. Klatt, D. H.: Linguistic Use of Segmental Duration in English: Acoustic and Perceptual Evidence. In: J. Acoust. Soc. Am., Vol. 51, pp. 1270–1278.

Speaker Identification Using Autoregressive Hidden Markov Models and Adaptive Vector Quantisation

Eugeny E. Bovbel, Igor E. Kheidorov, and Michael E. Kotlyar

Dept. of Radiophysics, Belarussian State University
F. Scoriny, 4, 220050, Minsk, Belarus
Tel, fax: (0172) 770-890
ikheidorov@poboxes.com

Abstract. Wide-frequency spectral analysis, autoregressive hidden Markov models (ARHMM) and self-organising neural networks (SOM) have been used for high accuracy speaker features modelling. The initial ARHMM parameters estimation based on Kalman filter is proposed. The five-keyword speaker identification system has been built and tested. The experiments show that this approach provides high accuracy of speaker identification even if the same words are pronounced by different speakers.

1 Introduction

By its nature, speech signal has two aspects. Firstly, it is highly dependent on physical parameters of vocal tract. Secondly, the speech is produced under neural control of the human, so that it is affected by the person-specific characteristics such as accent, pronunciation, speed, timbre, etc. It gives us the possibility to use these features for speaker identification.

We model the person-specific characteristics taking into consideration the speech signal parameters interrelation between close frames. This approach provides us with the useful information about pronunciation mode. From this viewpoint, statistical methods based on autoregressive HMMs are very attractive, because the standard HMM does not care about temporary close observations interrelation, which makes valued information about acoustical structure of the phoneme loose.

2 Autoregressive Hidden Markov Models

The speech utterance can be modelled by the sequence of the discrete stationary states with immediate transitions between them. Let $\overline{O} = (O_1, O_2, \dots, O_N)$ be the observation vector sequence for the given utterance, and $\overline{q} = (q_1, q_2, \dots, q_N)$ be the appropriate HMM states sequence. $O_n = (x_{n,1}, x_{n,2}, \dots, x_{n,K})$ is the n-th K-dimensional observation vector. For each state q, it is necessary to define distribution of observation vectors $b_q(O)$. We assume that the vector sequence $\overline{O}$ components conform

P. Sojka, I. Kopeček, and K. Pala (Eds.): TSD 2000, LNAI 1902, pp. 207–210, 2000.

the P-order autoregressive model:

$$x_{n,k} = -\sum_{i=1}^{P} a_{k,i} x_{n-i,k} + \epsilon_k \tag{1}$$

where ϵ_k are independent zero-mean Gaussian random values with dispersion σ^2; $a_{k,i}$ are autoregression coefficients (linear prediction coefficients) for k-th component of observation vector.

With this assumption for each state q, we can estimate observation vector components distribution as following:

$$b_q(x_{n,k}|x_{n-1,k}, x_{n-2,k}, \dots, x_{n-P,k}) =$$
$$= \frac{1}{\sqrt{2\pi\sigma_q^2}} \exp\left(-\frac{1}{2\sigma_q^2}(x_{n,k} + \sum_{i=1}^{P} a_{k,i,q} x_{n-i,k})^2\right) \tag{2}$$

Thus, the autoregressive hidden Markov model is a model of a twice stochastic process: the model state sequence is first-order Markov process, and the observation vectors sequence is a random process too and is modelled by P-order autoregression.

3   Initial Estimation of ARHMM Parameters

We have used Kalman filter to estimate initial autoregression parameters for ARHMM. Consider linear system. States of the system in moment t and in moment $t-1$ are constrained by the system equation:

$$q_t = F q_{t-1} + N_t \tag{3}$$

where F is a linear operator, N represents system noise.

Let q_t be a linear system state in moment t. At every moment t, we perform measuring of system output y_t, which is a function of system state:

$$y_t = H q_t + G_t \tag{4}$$

where H is a measuring operator, G_t is measuring noise. If we suppose $q_t = (a_1, a_2, \dots, a_P)$, $y_t = x_{t,k}$, we can rewrite (3) and (4) as the following:

$$q_t = q_{t-1} + N_t \tag{5}$$

$$y_t = H_t q_t + G_t \tag{6}$$

$$H_t = -diag(y_{t-1}, y_{t-2}, \dots, y_{t-P}) \tag{7}$$

Using Kalman algorithm, if y_t sequence is given, we can estimate system parameters q. The detailed description of Kalman filter can be found in [6].

4   Experiment

Five belarussian words spoken by 5 speakers have been sampled at 44 kHz rate in different environmental conditions during 3 months. 130 samples per word per dictor have been taken, 3250 samples in total. Samples have been separated in two nonintersecting sets: the training and the testing one. Mel-cepstrum and delta-cepstrum have been used as observation vectors. Separated SOM-codebooks and mixed discrete-continuous ARHMMs have been built for cepstrums and delta-cepstrums. Probabilities given by corresponding cepstr- and delta-cepstr ARHMMS were multiplied. Two codebooks (for cepstrums and delta-cepstrums) were trained on all vectors made from the training set. Then, ARHMM pairs have been trained on the training set – one ARHMM pair per word per dictor, 25 model pairs in total.

First series of experiments have been carried out to determine the optimal codebook size (see Figure 1).

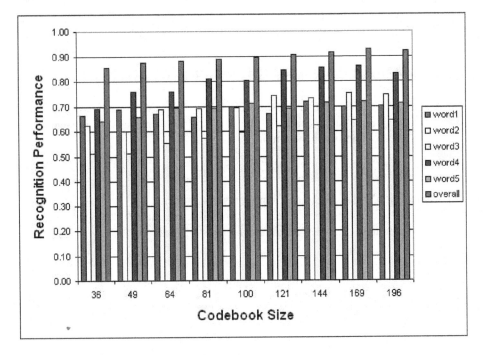

Fig. 1. Optimal codebook size

The training set consisted of 5 samples per word per speaker, remaining samples were used for testing. As we can notice, optimal codebook size is about 139, which is rather high when compared with that in usual word-recognition tasks.

Second series of experiments was designed to estimate our speaker recognition system's overall performance (see Figure 2).

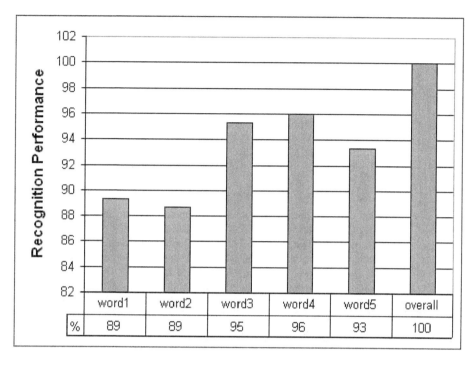

Fig. 2. Speaker recognition system's overall performance

Training set consisted of 30 samples per word per speaker, remaining samples were used for testing. As we can see, overall recognition performance, when every speaker pronounces the sequence of the same 5 words, is close to 100%.

References

1. D.A. Reynolds, Speaker identification and verification using Gaussian mixture speaker models, Speech Communication, 17(1–2), pp. 91–108, 1995.
2. H.A. Bourlard and N. Morgan Connectionist Speech recognition: A Hybrid Approach. Kluwer Academic Publishers, Boston M.A., 1994.
3. B.H. Juang, L.R. Rabiner, Mixture autoregressive hidden Markov models for speech signals, IEEE Trans. ASSP-33, pp. 1404–1412, 1985.
4. E.I. Bovbel, I.E. Kheidorov, P.P. Tkachova, The analysis of speaker individual features based on autoregressive hidden Markov models, Proc. of EUROSPEECH '99, vol. 3, pp. 1191–1194, September 5–9, 1999, Budapest, Hungary.
5. T. Kohonen, The self-organizing map, Proceedings of IEEE, vol. 78, 1990. pp. 1464–1480.
6. Youji Iiguni, A real-time learning algorithm for a multilayered neural network based on the extended Kalman filter, IEEE Transactions on Signal Processing, vol. 40, April 1992, pp. 959–966.

Morpheme Based Language Models for Speech Recognition of Czech[*]

William Byrne[1], Jan Hajič[1,2], Pavel Ircing[3], Pavel Krbec[1,2], and Josef Psutka[3]

[1] Johns Hopkins University, Baltimore MD, USA
[2] Charles University, Prague, Czech Republic
[3] University of West Bohemia in Pilsen, Czech Republic

Abstract. In our paper we propose new technique for language modelling of highly inflectional languages such as Czech, Russian an other Slavic languages. Our aim is to alleviate main problem encountered in these languages, which is enormous vocabulary growth caused by great number of different word forms derived from one word (lemma). We reduced the size of the vocabulary by decomposing words into stems and endings and storing these sub-word units (morphemes) in the vocabulary separately. Then we trained morpheme based language model on the decomposed corpus. This paper reports perplexities, OOV rates and some speech recognition results obtained with new language model.

1   Introduction

In this paper we propose new approach to language modelling which would be suitable for highly inflectional languages such as Czech, Russian and other Slavic languages. When we try to build large vocabulary speech recognition system for these languages, we encounter one major problem – excessive vocabulary growth caused by great number of different word forms derived from one word (lemma). Since state-of-the-art speech recognition engines are capable of handling vocabularies whose size is somewhere in the range from 20 K to 60 K words, we have to restrict the vocabulary and therefore we obtain very high OOV (Out Of Vocabulary) rate.

Inflectional change of the word mostly affects word ending, whereas stem remains constant and moreover the number of different endings is relatively very small (approximately 700). So it seems to be a good idea to decompose words into stems and endings and to treat these units (let's call them morphemes) separately as if they were independent words.

Our paper presents both characteristics of such morpheme based language models (perplexities, OOV rates) and results of speech recognition experiments performed with these models.

* This work was supported by the projects KONTAKT No. ME293, No. VS97159 and No. VS96151 of the Ministry of Education in Czech Republic and by NSF Grants No. IIS-9810517 and No. IIS-9820687.

P. Sojka, I. Kopeček, and K. Pala (Eds.): TSD 2000, LNAI 1902, pp. 211–216, 2000.

2 Czech Speech and Text Corpora, Baseline System

2.1 CZBN Broadcast News Corpus

CZech language Broadcast News (CZBN) corpus was collected for acoustic training. Satellite transmissions of Voice of America broadcasts were recorded by the Linguistic Data Consortium (LDC) and transcribed at the University of West Bohemia according to protocols recommended by LDC for use in Broadcast News LVR evaluation. The recordings span the period February 8 through May 31, 1999. The corpus consists of 62 recordings of 30 minute news broadcasts yielding in total over 20 hours of broadcast material. Portions of the shows containing music, speech in music, or other non-speech material are marked, but speech found during those periods is not transcribed. Therefore corpus yields approximately 19:30 minutes of transcribed material from each 30 minute broadcast.

2.2 Text Corpus

For language modelling purposes, we collected texts from newspapers Lidové Noviny [5] spanning the period 1991 through 1995. Corpus contains approximately 33 million tokens (650 K distinct words). Text data had to go through several preprocessing stages in order to obtain clear and unambiguous data.

2.3 Baseline System

Acoustic training and speech recognition experiments were conducted on the CZBN corpus using HTK, the hidden Markov model toolkit [6]. The recognition system is based on a continuous density HMMs trained on approximately 18 hours of speech. The speech features parameterisation employed in training and test are mel-frequency cepstra, including both delta and delta-delta sub-features; cepstral mean subtraction is applied to all features on a per utterance basis. Triphone state clustering was carried out using broad acoustic phonetic classes similar to those used for English.

Baseline bigram language model was trained on Lidové Noviny corpus using CMU-Cambridge Statistical Modelling Toolkit [3]. As the vocabulary for this language model, we used 20 K most frequent words from the corpus. Witten Bell discounting was applied. Baseline results are shown in the Table 1.

Table 1. Baseline results

Vocabulary size	OOV-Rate on the test set	Test set perplexity	Word Accuracy
20 036	15.18%	584.34	47.89%

3   Morpheme Based Language Models

3.1   Word Decomposition

As we already mention, major cause of enormous vocabulary growth is the highly inflected nature of Czech language. Therefore we decomposed text corpus and 20 K language model vocabulary into stems and endings (morphemes) using Czech Morphological Analyser [4]. Stems and endings were marked with different marks (stems with '+' sign and endings with '−' sign) in order to allow them to be conjoined back after the recognition. Endings of zero length were discarded since they are not necessary for reconstruction of the original words. Examples of the decomposition are given in Table 2.

Table 2. Example of decomposition into stem and ending

Word	Decomposition	Translation
biskup	biskup+	the bishop
biskupa	biskup+ −a	(for the) bishop
biskupovi	biskup+ −ovi	(about the) bishop
biskupem	biskup+ −em	(with the) bishop
jet	je+ −t	to go
jedu	jed+ −u	I go
jedeš	jed+ −eš	you go (singular)
jede	jed+ −e	he goes
jedeme	jed+ −eme	we go
jedete	jed+ −ete	you go (plural)
jedou	jed+ −ou	they go

We obtained quite interesting results. As can be seen in Table 3, size of the vocabulary was reduced by 52%. Moreover endings observed in 20 K cover endings from the test set almost completely. Even the word OOV-rate dropped by 19%, because now some words which were originally unknown (and therefore constituted an OOV) can be composed of known stem and known ending.

Table 3. Comparison of the word vocabulary and the morpheme vocabulary

	Vocabulary size	OOV-Rate on the test set
Word vocabulary	20 036	15.18%
Morpheme vocabulary	9 621	12.46%
– stems	9 258	12.32%
– endings	363	0.20%

3.2   Basic Morpheme Based Language Model

In our first morpheme based language model morphemes were treated as if they were independent words. No distinction between stems and endings was made. Bigram language model was trained on decomposed corpus using decomposed vocabulary. Witten Bell discounting was applied as in the word language model training. Results for this language model are shown in Table 4.

Test set perplexity of this language model is much lower than the perplexity of the baseline model, but there is a catch in this. One has to bear in mind that the perplexity depends on the number of tokens in the test set in the sense that higher number of tokens makes the perplexity lower. In our basic morpheme based model morphemes were consider to be separate words and therefore number of tokens in the test set increased in comparison with word based model. So although in the morpheme based experiment the test set was generated by the language model with lower probability, perplexity quite considerably decreased. However, word accuracy is a fair measure of quality of the language model and we achieve excellent improvement with our new language model – over 37%.

This result is in contradiction with the results obtained by other authors who tried to use word decomposition for language modelling of highly inflectional languages [2]. Their word accuracy decreased when they used morpheme based model. There can be several causes of such contradictory results. First of all, paper [2] deals with Serbo-Croatian. Although both Czech and Serbo-Croatian belong to the Slavic language family, they are of course not identical. Second reason could be that we used decomposition which better represents the nature of the language. And finally, improvement could be task-dependent, because CZBN corpus has some characteristics different from other Czech speech corpora. For example it contains high number of foreign words, since Voice of America news report mainly on international issues.

Table 4. Results for basic morpheme based language model

Vocabulary size	OOV-Rate on the test set	Test set perplexity	Word Accuracy
9621	12.46%	161.15	65.96%

Possible flaw of this morpheme based language model emerges if we look more closely at the probabilities assigned to the particular morphemes. Prediction of the ith word ending e_i is based on the knowledge of the corresponding stem s_i, because language model assigns the probability $P(e_i|s_i)$ to the ending e_i. Such dependency is strong, because particular stem can be followed by relatively small set of endings.

On the other hand prediction of the stem s_i depends on the preceding ending e_{i-1}, probability assigned to such stem is $P(s_i|e_{i-1})$. In this case the dependency is very weak, because the ending bears information about grammatical properties of the word (such as case of the noun, person of the verb etc.), not information about the word itself. So bigrams are in fact reduced to unigrams. Therefore our morpheme based language model should be modified.

3.3   Modified Morpheme Based Language Model

As we argued in the previous section, prediction of the stem s_i shouldn't be based on the knowledge of the preceding ending e_{i-1}. Common sense hints us to use the dependency on the previous stem s_{i-1}, i.e. the language model should assign the probability $P(s_i|s_{i-1})$ to stem s_i. Since the word stem gives us the major part of the information about the word (in most cases almost the same information as the lemma), quality of such dependency should be comparable to word bigrams.

Prediction of the ending is more complicated. Firstly, ending e_i should depend on the corresponding stem s_i (see previous section). In addition, the Czech language makes extensive use of agreement. It means that for example a noun and its adjectival or pronominal attribute must agree in gender, number and case. Since these morphological categories often affect word ending, prediction of the ending e_i should also be based on preceding ending e_{i-1}.

Let's now write down our modified language model more formally. Model assigns the probability:

$$P(s_i|s_{i-1})$$

to the stem s_i and the probability:

$$\xi \cdot P(e_i|s_i) + (1 - \xi) \cdot P(e_i|e_{i-1})$$

to the ending e_i, where ξ is the parameter in the range $0 \leq \xi \leq 1$.

Text corpus had to be modified before training of this new morpheme based language model. Now we have to incorporate also endings of zero length, into the corpus as well as into the language model vocabulary. Perplexity results for various ξ are given in Table 5. Low values of the perplexity are due to the fact that number of tokens in the test set further increased because of endings of zero length, which were not present in the previous language model. However, it should be mentioned that modified morpheme based language model with the parameter $\xi = 0.0$ generated the test set with higher probability than basic morpheme based model and we could consider this model to be the best of all morpheme based models.

Table 5. Comparison of the test set perplexity for various ξ

ξ	Test set perplexity
0.0	40.13
0.25	48.07
0.5	57.59
0.75	68.98
1.0	82.64

As can be seen in the Table 5, model with the parameter $\xi = 0.0$ has the lowest perplexity. So the knowledge of the preceding ending e_{i-1} probably doesn't give us much information about the ending e_i. Looking into the test set, one discovers a possible source of this problem. Endings of zero length constitute almost a half of all endings (48%) in the test set and such percentage holds for training corpus as well. Therefore one could expect that endings of zero length are followed by other endings more or less with the same frequency. So there is no chance to get strong dependencies between the endings in the language model.

In order to obtain fair comparison between basic and modified morpheme based language model, speech recognition experiments have to be performed. That would involve some kind of lattice re-scoring and HTK toolkit isn't very well suited to handle such large lattices. However, results of the experiment performed on the task with 600 word vocabulary were promising.

4   Conclusion

In this paper we introduced new language models based on morphemes. Using these models we manage to significantly reduce the size of the language model vocabulary, OOV rate and even to greatly improve word accuracy. In our future work we should test our techniques on large test sets from various domains to prove their robustness. Furthermore we have to perform speech recognition experiments using modified morpheme based language model described in Section 3.3.

References

1. W. Byrne et al.: Large Vocabulary Speech Recognition for Read and Broadcast Czech. In: Proceedings of TSD '99. 1999.
2. P. Geutner, M. Finke, P. Scheytt: Adaptive Vocabularies for Transcribing Multilingual Broadcast News. ICASSP. 1998.
3. P. Clarkson, R. Rosenfeld: The CMU-Cambridge Statistical Language Modelling Toolkit.
4. J. Hajič: Computational Morphology of Czech. Karolinum Press, Charles University. Prague. In prep.
5. http://www.lidovenoviny.cz
6. S. Young et al.: The HTK Book. Entropic Inc. 1999.

A Large Czech Vocabulary Recognition System for Real-Time Applications

Jan Nouza

Technical University of Liberec, Department of Electronics and Signal Processing,
Hálkova 5, 461 17 Liberec, Czech Republic
jan.nouza@vslib.cz

Abstract. In this paper, we propose two methods for speeding up discrete-utterance recognition in vocabularies with hundreds to several thousands of words. We show that acceptable results as well as short response time can be achieved if the words are represented by concatenated monophone models (multi-mixture HMMs). In such case, the computation load of the classic Viterbi procedure can be reduced significantly if a proper caching scheme is used. In several experiments done with test vocabularies containing hundreds and thousands of Czech words, we demonstrate that the recognition procedures can be speeded up by a factor of 50 to 100 without a loss of accuracy. The method is well suited for voice controlled systems with a large branching factor and low syntax, i.e. in voice portals, telephone directory assistance, etc.

1 Introduction

Automated voice-operated services, mainly those allowing access over telephone, become more and more popular [1]. As an example, we can mention system InfoCity developed at our university that has been in public use since March 1999 and recently it registers about 50 to 100 calls per day. The system offers information about culture, sport, transport and commerce in Liberec in the form of a simple dialogue between a caller and the computer [2]. Up to now the speech input to the system was limited to a small vocabulary with tens to hundreds of words. For many commercially interesting applications, like a telephone directory assistance, automatic call routing, time-table inquiries, etc., larger vocabularies with several thousands entries are necessary.

These services to be practically applicable need a speech recognition module that proves a high accuracy and fast response. On the other side, they need not to be designed necessarily for continuous speech processing. They often take input in the form of short answers, either isolated words or phrases. A typical example is an automated telephone directory inquiry service. A caller is asked to specify the surname of the wanted person, his/her first name, the city name and the street name. At each step the recognition system must search within a large vocabulary, which may or may not be partly constrained by the context following from the previous step.

In this paper, we propose methods for speeding up classification from large lists of candidates in an isolated-word recognition task and we test them for the Czech language.

P. Sojka, I. Kopeček, and K. Pala (Eds.): TSD 2000, LNAI 1902, pp. 217–222, 2000.

2   Speech Databases for Training and Testing

A speech recognition system that is to be flexible must operate with an inventory of sub-word units. In our case these units are phonemes. To train their statistic models, we had to design, record and annotate a large corpus of spoken Czech. For testing purposes, we prepared several databases that try to address practical tasks.

2.1   A Database for Training Czech Sub-word Units

There are several strategies to make a good training database. One, described in [3], takes an available corpus of spoken utterances and attempts to select those fulfilling some statistical criteria. We used another approach proposed in [4]. A special set of 80 sentences was constructed in the way that each Czech phoneme was represented by a sufficient number of samples. The goal was to cover all biphones occurring in Czech and thus create a chance for training triphones by a merging or cloning method [5,6].

The 80-sentence set covers all 41 single phonemes defined in [7]. The less frequent phonemes have at least 16 occurrences while the vowels, for example, occur in several hundred variants. The set covers almost 99% Czech biphones and about 3500 different triphones. Up to now the sentences have been recorded by some 35 people, some provided multiple recordings. The database contains almost 10 hours of speech signal that has been segmented and labelled at the phoneme level [8].

2.2   Testing Databases

For evaluating new methods and testing potentially interesting applications, we have prepared and collected several databases. Their features are summarised in Table 1.

Table 1. Databases of Czech words used for testing

Database name	Vocabulary size	# Phonemes per word (average)	Confusability
Names	360	6.3	high
Surnames	800	7.5	middle
City names	5 346	8.7	middle
Voc10K	10 000	6.9	high

The first set includes all Christian names in the Czech calendar, the second is a selection of surnames from the Liberec telephone directory, the third contains all local (city and village) names in the Czech Republic and the last consists of the most frequent 10 thousand words in an 80 Mword newspaper corpus. Each database has its specific features. For example, the Names set includes quite a lot of minimal pairs or groups, like *Jan-Jana, Daniel-Daniela, Alena-Ilona-Elena-Helena, Miroslav-Miloslav-Jaroslav*. In the City name set, there are both very short and very long items, like *Aš* vs. *Blatnice_pod_Svatým_Antonínkem*. The Voc10K set often contains several morphological forms of the same word, from which some cannot be distinguished on acoustic level, e.g. *volal-volala-volali-volaly-volalo*.

Each database consists of 1000 test words recorded by 10 speakers through a standard front-end employed in our recognition engine. Hence, each recorded item passed through the same endpoint and parameterisation procedure like in a live test.

3   Methods for Efficient Word Recognition

The phonemes in our system are represented by three-state hidden Markov models (HMMs) with left-to-right structure and no skips, as shown in Figure 1. Output pdfs are multi-mixture gaussians defined in the 18-dimensional space of parameters derived from LP cepstrum. A word (or phrase) model is created by concatenating appropriate phoneme models. Monophones or triphones can be employed alternatively, as it is depicted in Figure 1.

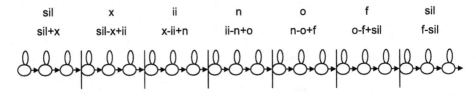

Fig. 1. A model of Czech word Chýnov created by concatenating monophone or triphone three-state HMMs

After training models of different type and size and testing them on the Name set, we got results that are summarised in Table 2. We can see that the score obtained with 16-mixture monophones is almost comparable with that of the triphones of the same size. However, the recognition time (measured on a PC 600 MHz) for the best models is too long (about 8 s for a word). A considerable reduction of the computation load is necessary if we want to employ the models in practical applications.

Table 2. Recognition results obtained for the Name set and different models

Model type	Recognition score [%]	Average recognition time per word [ms]
Monophones – 4 mixtures	87.1	2570
Monophones – 8 mixtures	88.2	4960
Monophones – 16 mixtures	91.5	8350
Triphones – 16 mixtures	91.9	8400

3.1   Reducing State Likelihood Computations

Anybody who implemented an HMM recogniser knows that most computation time is spent by calculating state output probabilities. If a signal represented by F frames is to be matched to M word models, each having (in average) N states, the total number of evaluations of multi-dimensional multi-mixture gaussian functions is equal to the product $F \times M \times N$. For typical values, it may lead to $100 \times 1000 \times 20 = 2M$ gaussian evaluations needed for the classification of a word. This large number can be reduced by adopting various schemes based on the beam search strategy. However, these schemes carry a potential danger of loss of accuracy, which may happen, particularly, in case when word endpoints are not determined correctly.

Our approach is based on reducing the number of likelihood calculations by caching the already computed values and reusing them if the frame is matched to the same state. The frequency of repeated calculations for the same frame-state pair is very high for monophones, because there are only 41×3 different states in a Czech system. Moreover, the cache hit rate increases with increasing the vocabulary. For illustration, if the caching scheme is used for the recognition within the Voc10k vocabulary, 99.94% of the likelihood values can be fetched from the cache. Obviously, this rate is much lower for triphones, where there are several thousands of different states. The impact of the caching scheme on the computation time is demonstrated in Table 3.

3.2   Eliminating Computations for Same Word Sub-strings

Another savings in the matching (Viterbi) algorithm can be achieved if we realize that some words in the vocabulary share same sub-strings of phonemes, especially at initial parts. If the models of these words enter the matching procedure one after another, some of the accumulated likelihood values computed for the previous model can be reused for the next model. This is shown in Figure 2.

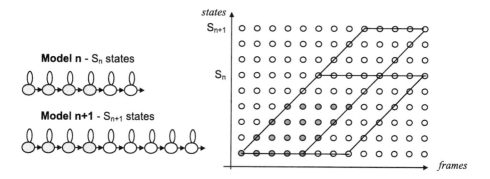

Fig. 2. An example of two models sharing the first 4 states. In the frame-state space there are points (filled by gray colour) whose accumulated likelihood values computed for model n can be reused for model $n + 1$. The demarcation lines delimit the Viterbi search space for each model.

Utilising this fact and organising the vocabulary in the way that the neighbouring words enable the highest possible reduction factor, we can save another significant portion of the computation load. When organising the vocabulary, we may use the alphabetic order but also we must take into account the length of the neighbouring words (more precisely, the number of states of the corresponding models). The impact of this secondary cache scheme is demonstrated in Table 3.

Table 3. Recognition times achieved with the Names set for the original and the optimised computation schemes. The values represent average classification times per word. The C1 method is that described in Section 3.1, the C2 is the combination of the two caching methods mentioned in this chapter.

Model type	Original time [ms]	C1 method time [ms]	C2 method time [ms]
Monophones – 4 mixtures	2570	160	90
Monophones – 8 mixtures	4960	190	110
Monophones – 16 mixtures	8350	250	160
Triphones – 16 mixtures	8400	2450	1780

4   Practical Experiments

In the previous text, we showed that it is possible to reduce the computation load of isolated-word recognition without a loss of accuracy. The reduction is considerable, in particular, for the system based on monophones. For triphones, the caching scheme has only a small effect. Hence, a triphone-based system must rely on other paradigms (e.g. the already mentioned beam search) that are sub-optimal and may introduce some additional errors.

We have implemented the methods into a word recognition system. Recently it operates with 16-mixture monophone models, that provide the same scores as the triphone ones, but in time 10 to 50 times shorter. The results from experiments with different test databases are summarised in Table 4. The recognition rate was significantly lower for the Voc10K database. This is because it contains many groups of words that can be distinguished only in a context.

Table 4. Recognition results from experiments with different test databases

Database type	Recognition score [%]	Recognition time per word [ms]
Names	91.5	160
Surnames	89.4	350
City names	87.1	1120
Voc10K	75.8	1260

5   Conclusions

Two methods are proposed for speeding up recognition of words or utterances spoken in an isolated way. A considerable reduction of classification time is achieved, in particular, for a monophone-based system. In the recognition test with a 5 Kword vocabulary (the

City Names), the reduction factor was higher than 100, while the score was still at an acceptable level for a practical task. It should be mentioned that the test data came from live recordings and therefore the reported results correspond with those obtained in on-line tests performed under computer room conditions.

Recently the recognition module based on the monophone models (adapted for telephone signals) have been built in the automated information system InfoCity. In spite of the lower signal quality, the system runs with average recognition rate about 90%.

Acknowledgements

The research reported in this paper was supported by the Grant Agency of the Czech Republic (grant no. 102/96/KO87), by the Czech Ministry of Education, through research goal project MSM 242200001 and by project Kontakt no. ME293.

References

1. Proc. of Workshop Voice Operated Telecom Services (Do they have a bright future?). Ghent, May 2000.
2. Nouza J., Holada M.: A Voice-Operated Multi-Domain Telephone Information System. Proc. of 25th Int. Conference on Acoustics, Speech and Signal Processing (ICASSP2000), Istanbul, June 2000 (to appear).
3. Radová V., Vopálka P.: Methods of Sentences Selection for Read-Speech Corpus Design. Proceedings of the 1st Workshop on Text, Speech and Dialogue, Plzeň 1999, pp. 165–170.
4. Hájek D.: A Continuous Speech Recognition System. MSc thesis (in Czech). Technical University of Liberec, May 1998.
5. Hájek D., Nouza J.: A Quasi-Triphone Model Created by Merging Context-Specific Phone Models. In Studientexte zur Sprachkommunikation, Heft 14 (Elektronische Sprachsignalverarbeitung), Cottbus 1997, pp. 85–92.
6. Ming J., O'Boyle O., Owens M., Smith F.J.: A Bayesian Approach for Building Triphone Models for Continuous Speech Recognition. IEEE Trans. Speech and Audio Processing, vol. 7, no. 6, 1999, pp. 678–684.
7. Nouza J., Psutka J., Uhlíř J.: Phonetic Alphabet for Speech Recognition of Czech. Radioengineering, vol. 6, no. 4, Dec 1997, pp. 16–20.
8. Nouza J., Myslivec M.: Creating and Annotating Speech Database for Continuous Speech Recognition. Proc. of 4th ECMS Workshop, Liberec, May 1999, pp. 147–151.

Building a New Czech Text-to-Speech System Using Triphone-Based Speech Units*

Jindřich Matoušek

University of West Bohemia, Department of Cybernetics,
Univerzitní 8, 306 14 Plzeň, Czech Republic
Tel.: +420 19 7491 150, Fax: +420 19 279050
jmatouse@kky.zcu.cz

Abstract. This paper presents ARTIC, a brand-new Czech text-to-speech (TTS) system. ARTIC (Artificial Talker in Czech) is a concatenation-based system which consists of three main, and relatively independent, components: speech segment database (SSD), text analyser and speech synthesiser. A statistical approach to speech segment database construction is used. Text processing module includes the phonetic transcription of written text and the conversion to synthetic units. Speech processing is performed using a PSOLA algorithm.

1   Introduction

In this paper, we describe ARTIC (Artificial Talker in Czech), a brand-new Czech TTS system. The system is concatenation-based (see Figure 1), so speech segment database must be constructed before the synthesis itself. In contrast to many working systems today, we use triphone-based speech units. Statistical approach is employed to find these units from natural speech corpus and to select the appropriate representatives to be used during speech synthesis.

The aim of a TTS system is to generate speech at the output of the system from the arbitrary input text. The first task is then to process the input text and to convert it to the sequence of units which are then used in the speech synthesis stage. This process is called text processing.

The last task of a TTS system is to generate speech. Since concatenation-based approach to speech synthesis is used in our system, a method how to concatenate units smoothly is proposed and described.

The paper is organised as follows. Section 2 describes the SSD construction process from more detailed point of view. In Section 3 text processing is depicted. Section 4 then concerns the speech processing. Finally, Section 5 contains the conclusion and outlines our future work.

---

* This work was supported by the project No. VS97159 and No. MSM23520004 of the Ministry of Education of Czech Republic.

P. Sojka, I. Kopeček, and K. Pala (Eds.): TSD 2000, LNAI 1902, pp. 223–228, 2000.

2   Speech Segment Database

Hidden Markov Models (HMMs) are used as a statistic tool for an automatic speech corpus segmentation [1]. The main advantage of this approach is that labour-intensive and time-consuming manual work is reduced to minimum. Moreover, comparing to traditionally used diphones, more precise speech units – triphones – can be employed. Triphone HMMs are then trained on the basis of the speech corpus.

2.1   Speech Corpus

In our system we use a large single-speaker continuous-read-speech corpus (SC). SC comprises about 90 minutes of naturally read speech recorded from four radio tales. The speech was sampled with 44 kHz and quantised into 16 bits. Then it was listened to, divided into utterances and annotated. For the purposes of HMM training (see Section 2.2), each utterance was resampled with 16 kHz, Hamming windowed with 25 ms and pitch-asynchronously parameterised using 39 mel frequency cepstral coefficients (including energy, delta and acceleration coefficients). To be able to perform a PSOLA algorithm, each utterance was also a subject of a pitch-mark detection algorithm, which computed the positions of pitch-marks (i.e. moments of glottal closures) in the speech signal. As the last step, each utterance was transcribed automatically using Czech phonetic transcription rules (see Section 3.1).

2.2   Automatic Segmentation of a Speech Corpus

The automatic segmentation of the speech corpus was performed in a similar way as in [2]. Three state left-to-right HMMs with no skips and with 6 ms frame rate were used to model triphones. Starting from 45 Czech phones, 8,540 cross-word triphone models

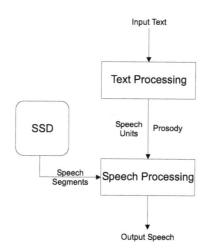

Fig. 1. Simplified scheme of our concatenation-based TTS system

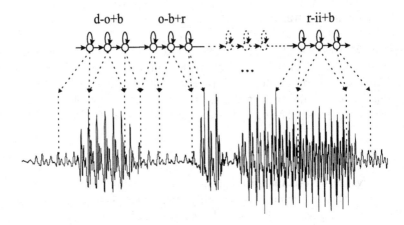

Fig. 2. Example of automatic speech segmentation into clustered states

(which were seen in the SC) were trained using the HTK system [6]. These models consist of 25,617 generally different states. Ideally, all possible Czech triphones should occur often enough in SC to be modelled reasonably by HMMs. Taking into account a great number of triphones (91,125 theoretically possible), it is practically impossible to create such a SC. Hence, described SC, which is thought to be sufficiently representative, is used and an efficient algorithm is employed to cluster acoustically similar sub-phone units (so called clustered states [1] – i.e. units that correspond to states of a triphone HMM) using binary decision trees [4]. Thanks to this technique, triphone HMMs are more robust and moreover, triphones not present in the SC can be made up of appropriate clustered states. After clustering, the number of triphones increased to 16,176. These triphones (so called tied triphones) cover all possible speech context and shared only 7,742 clustered states (see Table 1). The clustered states represent the basic speech units of our TTS system. Finally, triphone HMMs are used to automatically segment the SC into these units (see Figure 2). As a result, time labels of each speech unit are added to the SC.

Table 1. Number of triphones and states before and after tree-based state clustering

Units	Before Clustering	After Clustering
Triphones	8,540	16,176
States	25,617	7,742

2.3 Speech Segment Selection

After segmenting, there are multiple instances of each speech unit in the SC. In our system, each speech unit is represented by a single speech segment. Simple segment selection algorithm (similar to [1]) is adopted to choose suitable segments. For the later use both too short and low-energy instances are undesirable. Hence, statistics about each speech unit duration and energy were computed over all instances of given speech unit. Then, instances with duration or energy lesser than corresponding median values (and some threshold) are not selected. From resulting instances, segment with maximum HMM score imposed by the Viterbi search is chosen as a representative and is stored to the SSD. Median values were used rather than mean values, because using mean values in some cases (when only few instances were present for particular speech unit in the SC and one of them has duration or energy much more greater than the others) led to selecting an incorrect segment and to synthesising the speech unit with incorrect duration or energy (see Section 4).

3   Text Processing

Text is the only input of the TTS system. Hence, text should be processed thoroughly to obtain important knowledge about what to synthesise. Text analyser is an important part of a TTS system, because it tells the synthesiser which speech units to use and how to modify them. Firstly, input text should be pre-processed, i.e. some operations must be performed to transcribe digits, abbreviations, etc. This is not the case of our system in the time of writing this paper, as we suppose that only "clean" text can appear at the input of our TTS system. Then, ideally, the "clean" text should be subject of syntactic, semantic, morphological, and contextual analysis to get important phonetic and prosodic information. Since our system generates monotonous speech so far, no prosody analysis is required except of simple pause detection analysis. So the key task of text analyser consists of converting input text to the sequence of clustered states – the basic speech units needed by the synthesiser. This process requires phonetic transcription (letter-to-phone conversion) to be done (see Section 3.1 for more details). Finally, it is no problem to convert the sequence of phones to a sequence of triphones and then to a sequence of clustered states using the decision trees. Example of text processing is shown in Table 2.

3.1   Automatic Phonetic Transcription

Since Czech is a "phonetic language" both with a high degree of inflection (there are many forms for a single word, e.g. noun) and with a high degree of derivation (usage of prefixes and suffixes), it is useful to apply phonetic transcription rules in the form (1) to generate a sequence of phones from a sequence of letters [7]. Letter sequence A with both left context C and right context D is transcribed as phone sequence B.

$$A \rightarrow B/C_- D \,. \tag{1}$$

The next rule is an example of a typical Czech phonetic rule, which transcribes nasal letter n to phone [ň]. Right context is formed by letters $ě$, i, or $í$, left context is ignored.

$$n \rightarrow ň/_- \langle ě, i, í \rangle \,. \tag{2}$$

In our system we currently use a set of about 50 transcription rules. For less inflectional languages (e.g. English) different, dictionary-based approach to phonetic transcription

Table 2. Example of text-processing

Text:	Myslím, tedy jsem.
Pauses:	Myslím [P] tedy jsem
Phones:	pau mislím pau tedi sem pau
Triphones:	pau pau-m+i m-i+s i-s+l s-l+í l-í+m í-m+pau pau pau-t+e t-e+d e-d+i d-i+s i-s+e s-e+m e-m+pau pau
Tied Triphones:	pau pau-m+i m-i+s i-s+l s-l+í l-í+m í-m+pau pau pau-t+e t-e+d ee-d+ii d-i+s i-s+e s-e+m e-m+pau pau
Clustered states:	pau_2_1 pau_4_1 m_2_4 m_3_3 m_4_66 i_2_54 i_3_168 i_4_89 s_2_107 s_3_112 s_4_42 l_2_43 l_3_104 l_4_94 í_2_35 í_3_113 í_4_108 m_2_80 m_3_113 m_4_5 pau_2_1 pau_4_1 t_2_18 t_3_10 t_4_39 e_2_71 e_3_122 e_4_112 d_2_44 d_3_34 d_4_36 i_2_77 i_3_107 i_4_82 s_2_109 s_3_89 s_4_70 e_2_113 e_3_35 e_4_173 m_2_68 m_3_1 15 m_4_6 pau_2_1 pau_4_1

is almost always used. In this conception "phonetic dictionary", which contains phonetic transcription of all words, is employed. In our system, this approach is also used to transcribe non-Czech words like foreign names, etc. Our dictionary of exceptions currently consists of about 620 stem-like forms.

4   Speech Processing

Speech synthesiser takes care of speech processing and forms the core of the TTS system. Concatenation-based synthesiser prosodically modifies speech segments stored in the SSD and then concatenates them according to sequence of speech units delivered by the text analyser. A PSOLA technique was selected to perform the concatenation and to change both the fundamental frequency (F_0) and the duration of speech units to desired values. Time-domain version of this algorithm (i.e. TD-PSOLA) has been incorporated into the system so far [5], because it is easy to implement and gives high-quality speech, so it is very suitable to use in the first version of our system.

The positions of pitch-marks play the key role in PSOLA algorithm. As mentioned in Section 2.1, pitch-mark detection algorithm was used to determine the positions in voiced speech. In unvoiced speech, there is no vocal cords activity and hence no pitch-mark positions are found. To be able to change the duration of unvoiced parts of speech, "pitch-marks" are uniformly distributed in unvoiced speech regions. Each pitch-mark defines a short-term signal, which is centered on the current pitch-mark position and Hanning windowed. The size of the short-term signal is defined either by the previous or the next pitch-mark position. Fundamental frequency of speech units to concatenate is then modified by changing the distance between short-term signals centered on adjacent pitch-mark positions. Monotonous F_0 is used for the present. Duration of speech units is changed by inserting or deleting short-term signals, preserving the desired F_0. The requested duration of every speech unit is set to its median value computed over all instances of the speech unit in SC (see Section 2.3). Moreover, energy of each speech unit is scaled to have its median value.

5 Conclusion and Future Work

Described TTS system aims to generate intelligibly and naturally sounding speech. To achieve this, a very precise, automatically built triphone-based Czech SSD and a PSOLA technique are used. Although the very first fully functional version of our system has been implemented so far, the first output samples are very hopeful and promising.

There are a lot of things to improve in all three major parts of the system, of course. As for SSD, we will focus to pitch-synchronous HMM training and will make some experiments with model topology. Text processing should be also enhanced to pre-process text and to detect prosodic features (i.e. F_0 contour and duration distribution). Of course, speech processing needs to be improved too. Our aim is to implement a PSOLA algorithm in parametric-domain to enable controlling spectral properties of resulting speech (as proposed, e.g., in [3]).

References

1. Donovan R.E., Woodland P.C.: A Hidden Markov-Model-Based Trainable Speech Synthesizer. Computer Speech and Language, 13., 1999, pp. 223–241.
2. Matoušek J.: Speech Synthesis Using HMM-Based Acoustic Unit Inventory. Proceedings of Eurospeech '99. Budapest, 1999, pp. 2323–2326.
3. Matoušek J., Psutka J., and Tychlt Z.: Statistical Approach to the Automatic Synthesis of Czech Speech. In Proceedings of TSD '99, edited by Matoušek, V., Mautner P., Ocelíková, J., Sojka P., Mariánské Lázně, 1999, pp. 376–379.
4. Young S.: Tree-Based State Tying for High Accuracy Acoustic Modelling. Proceedings of the ARPA Workshop on Human Language Technology. Plainsboro, New Jersey, 1994, pp. 307–312.
5. Moulines E., Verhelst W.: Time-Domain and Frequency-Domain Techniques for Prosodic Modification of Speech; In: Speech Coding and Synthesis, edited by Kleijn W.B., Paliwal K.K. Elsevier, 1995, pp. 519–555.
6. Young S. et al.: The HTK Book. Entropic Inc., 1999.
7. Psutka J.: Communication With Computer by Speech (in Czech). Academia, Prague, 1995.

Acoustic and Perceptual Properties of Syllables in Continuous Speech as a Function of Speaking Rate

Hisao Kuwabara and Michinori Nakamura

Teikyo University of Science and Technology
Uenohara, Kitatsuru-gun, Yamanashi, 409-0193, Japan
Kuwabara@ntu.ac.jp

Abstract. Fifteen short sentences spoken by four male speakers have been used as the test material. Each speaker has been asked to pronounce the sentences with three different rates: fast, normal, and slow. For perceptual experiment, two kinds of segmentations have been made: 1) one-syllable segmentation and 2) two-syllable segmentation. In the one-syllable segmentation, individual CV-syllables have been taken out from their contexts and presented to listeners. In the two-syllable segmentation, every consecutive two syllables have been isolated from the running speech, and the listeners have to identify each of the two syllables. In the first experiment, the results reveal that individual syllables do not have enough phonetic information to be correctly identified especially for the fast speech. The average identification of syllables for the fast speech is 35% and even vowels are identified less than 60%. In the second experiment, however, syllable identifications rose to a certain extent: for the fast speech, 54% for the first syllable and 73% for the second syllable. For the normal speech, they were 50% and 88%, respectively and for the slow speech, they were 56% and 90% respectively.

1   Introduction

Speech technologies have been developed a great deal recently and speech signals can be processed more precisely than ever before in such areas as speech recognition and synthesis. Keeping this technological background in mind, this study has been conducted as a basic research in order to provide an acoustic data for these speech technologies.

Japanese language basically consists of a series of consonant-vowel syllables (CV-syllables). Unlike English or other languages, each syllable corresponds exactly to one Japanese alphabet which is called "Kana". As it is well known, each syllable in a continuous speech does not carry enough phonetic information to be correctly identified by itself, but rather spread over adjacent phonemes due mainly to co-articulation effects [1,2]. There are some attempt to recover these reduced ambiguous phonemes [3,4]. These perceptual evidences must be attributed to such acoustic properties of each phoneme as shortening its duration, reduction of pitch and formant frequencies. Our recent studies [5,6] show that the speaking rate affects very much on the acoustic values of phonemes in continuous speech, such as duration and formant frequencies, which are partly included again in this paper.

P. Sojka, I. Kopeček, and K. Pala (Eds.): TSD 2000, LNAI 1902, pp. 229–236, 2000.

This paper deals mainly with the perceptual properties of individual CV-syllables and vowels when they are taken out of their phonetic environment. Comparisons are also being made between the perceptual results and the acoustic values of individual syllables.

2   Speech Material

The speech material that has been used in this experiment is the same as in [5,6], which consists of fifteen short sentences uttered by four male adult speakers. As it is mentioned in the literature, they were asked to read the sentences three times with different speaking rate: normal speed which is referred to as "n-speech" in this paper, fast rate (also referred to as "f-speech") and slow rate ("s-speech"). There is a rhythm when it comes to speak a Japanese sentence. The rhythm, which is sometimes called syllable-timed, is based on the mora which roughly corresponds to a Japanese letter or CV-syllable. The number of morae per minute defines the speaking rate. Generally, normal speaking rate (n-speech) falls into a speed from 300 to 400 morae per minute but it considerably differs from speaker to speaker, especially between the young and the old. No special guidance and equipment have been used to control the speed in pronouncing the n-speech, f-speech and s-speech. For the f-speech, individual speakers were asked to pronounce the sentences twice as fast as the n-speech that they usually utter in daily conversation. For the s-speech, they were also asked to pronounce half as slow as the n-speech. For each speed, speech data were actually measured later on for speakers individually.

3   Perceptual Experiment

This experiment is designed to investigate on how each CV-syllable or vowel will be perceived by human listeners when it is isolated from its phonetic environment. Thus, each CV-syllable or vowel must be electrically cut off from the stream of speech. It is obvious that the co-articulation effect will certainly depend on the rate of speaking. The purpose of this experiment is to find out how large the effect will be in terms of phoneme identification for every speaking rate.

3.1   Test Material

There are 291 morae in the fifteen sentences. Among the four speakers' utterance, one speaker's speech is used this time since the main purpose of this experiment is to compare the perceptual difference of individual syllables between speaking rate. The remaining three speakers speech is left for further investigation into finding difference among speakers.

There is no clear-cut definition on how to divide syllables in a running speech unless a silent interval exists between two successive syllables. It is almost impossible to draw a line between two syllables if the speech wave of two successive syllables continues without silence. Thus, we have decided to separate these syllables by audition with the help of a speech-wave editor on a computer. The beginning and the end of a syllable are defined as follows. At first, a piece of speech wave which roughly corresponds to three syllables with the syllable in question in the middle is selected on the computer screen. Then, the starting point of the speech wave is cut off step-by-step until the entire preceding syllable is not audible. This defines the beginning of the syllable in question. Next, the start point of the syllable is fixed and similarly, the end point is cut off step-by-step until the successive syllable becomes not audible, which defines the end of the middle syllable. It is somewhat complicated and time consuming. In this way, a total of 873 (291 × 3) test materials have been obtained for perceptual experiment.

3.2 Hearing Test

1-Syllable Segmentation. For each speaking rate, the 291 speech material are randomised and presented to listeners over a loudspeaker in a sound-proof chamber. Six listeners, including the author, participated in the hearing test and they were asked to identify each piece of speech sound as one of the Japanese syllables or vowels. Listeners' response data were grouped in the following three ways:

- Syllable identification: whether the entire CV-syllable was correctly identified or not.
- Consonant identification: whether the consonant part was correctly identified or nor.
- Vowel identification: whether the vowel part was correctly identified or not.

For the single vowels in the sentences, consonant perception was not counted and the syllable identification was counted only if it was perceived as a single vowel. If a stimulus /a/ was identified as /pa/, for example, the syllable identification is regarded as incorrect but the vowel identification is correct. The syllable identification will be correct only when it is perceived as /a/.

2-Syllable Segmentation. Every consecutive two syllables were taken out from the continuous speech and also randomly presented to listeners. Each speech piece, therefore, consists of two successive syllables and the listeners were required to identify each of the two syllables. Identification scores for the first syllable and for the second syllable were pooled and calculated separately.

3.3 The Results

1-Syllable Segmentation.

Syllable Identification. Table 1 shows the average percent of identification in the three categories. Identification of individual syllables is very poor, as low as 35%, for the f-speech. Even the vowel part has been identified less than 60%. It has increased to 59% for the n-speech indicating that the individual syllables in the n-speech do not have enough phonetic information to be correctly identified. However, it goes up to as high as 86% for the s-speech and almost perfect identification has been achieved.

Figure 1 shows a graphic illustration of the average identification of CV-syllables isolated from their phonetic environment for every speaking rate. Identification score

Table 1. Percentage of average identification score for CV-syllables, consonant and vowel parts

	fast	normal	slow
syllable	35	59	86
consonant	31	58	87
vowel	59	86	91

seems to increase almost linearly as the rate becomes slow. No drastic jump in identification can be observed from fast to normal or from normal to slow, but essentially, little coarticulation effect is taking place in the slow speech. This might be a speaker dependent phenomenon and further investigation will be needed.

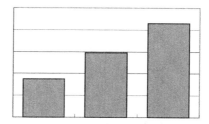

Fig. 1. Average identification for CV-syllables taken out from their phonetic environments for each speaking rate

Average Consonant and Vowel Identification. Figure 2 represents the average identification scores for consonant and vowel parts for every speaking rate. Relatively high scores for vowel part for every speaking rate can be seen from the figure but it is still less than 60% for the fast speech. Consonant, on the other hand, is extremely low for the fast speech and also for the normal speech while it goes almost as high as the vowel part for the slow speech. In other words, slow speech has almost no co-articulation effect in terms of phonetic information to be identified by humans for at least this speaker. An interesting fact is that the fast and normal speech have a common feature that the identification differences between consonant and vowel parts are exactly the same (28%), though their absolute values of individual parts are different.

Vowel part is identified more than 80% for both normal and slow speech while it is less that 60% for the fast speech. This contrasts to the consonant score which increases almost linearly from fast to slow, 27% increase from fast to normal and 29% increase from normal to slow. Another interesting fact is that the scores of vowels for the fast speech and consonant for the normal speech is almost the same. No immediate implication and explanation are given here towards this fact.

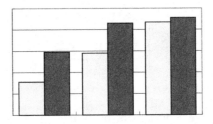

Fig. 2. Average identification scores for consonant part (left bar) and vowel part (right bar) in each CV-syllable

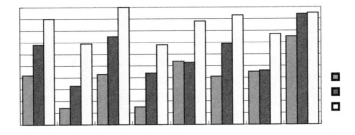

Fig. 3. Average identification for every consonant category. bars on the left hand side, middle, and the right hand side on each category represent scores for the fast, normal, and *slow* speech, respectively.

Average Identification for Consonant Category. Let's look more closely at the results with every consonant category. Figure 3 stands for the result which is compiled according to every manner of articulation. They are voiceless plosives, voiced plosives, affricates, voiceless fricatives, voiced fricatives, nasals, liquids, and semi-vowels. As a whole, semi-vowel has the highest score for all speaking rate. If we focus our attention on the fast speech, it can be observed that the least identification scores are voiced plosives and voiceless fricatives. Almost all voiceless fricative samples are perceived as an affricate which indicates that there is an artifact of cutting off the very beginning of the noise release for each fricative samples. Voiced plosive samples, on the other hand, are found to be confused within the same consonant category and /d/ samples are very often perceived as /r/ sound. Generally, identification goes up as the speaking rate goes down and, for slow speech, around 80% or higher scores are seen to be achieved. An interesting fact is that the identification of the voiced fricatives and liquid consonants for the fast and normal speech show almost the same score. No relevant explanation for this can be found yet.

For voiceless/voiced plosives and affricates, a significant increase in identification is observed either from fast to normal or from normal to slow. This probably reflects the fact that duration of consonants increases as the speaking rate decreases.

For each speaking rate, voiced plosives show the lowest score of identification while semi-vowels exhibit the highest score with an exception of affricates for the slow speech (100%).

Identification for Individual Consonants. Let's look at the response data more closely for each consonant. Figure 4 represents the result for 19 individual consonants that have appeared in the test material. For each consonant, the top bar stands for the result for the fast speech, second bar for the normal speech and the bottom bar for the slow speech.

It clearly shows that the lowest score is observed for the voiced plosive /g/ for all speaking rate. /g/ is very often perceived as a single vowel and one of another plosives. On the other hand, the highest score for all speaking rate is obtained for semi-vowel /w/. Semi-vowel /y/ shows almost as high scores as the /w/ sound but a little lower for the slow speech. Voiceless fricative /sh/ has the least percentage for the fast speech. Almost all /sh/ samples were perceived as /ch/ especially in the fast speech because of artifact. A strange phenomenon is that a voiced fricative /z/ changes its score between fast and normal, i.e. score for the fast speech exceed significantly that for the normal speech. One reason for this is the way of speaking of this speaker. This speaker often pronounces the /s/ sound as the /z/ sound in the fast speech but not in the normal and slow speech.

There is an interesting contrast if we compare scores between bilabial and alveolar consonants, such as /p/ vs /t/, /b/ vs /d/ and /m/ vs /n/. It is observed that the alveolar consonants are always higher than the bilabial ones.

2-Syllable Segmentation. Every two consecutive syllables were taken from their context and presented to listeners. The listeners were asked to identify both of the two syllables for every speech stimulus. Identification scores for the first and for the second syllables were obtained separately. Figure 5 represents the result of average syllable identification. It is interesting to note that the score for the 1st syllables do not vary very much across the three speaking rates. The scores for the 2nd syllables are far greater than those for the 1st syllables.

4 Conclusions

A perceptual experiment has been performed in order to investigate how individual CV-syllables, which are the basic constituent of the Japanese spoken language, carry phonetic information and how they differ when the speaking rate changes. Individual CV-syllables are taken out from their phonetic environments for three different speaking rates, fast, normal and slow and presented to listeners for identification. It has been found that individual syllables carry very little phonetic information for the fast speech (35%),

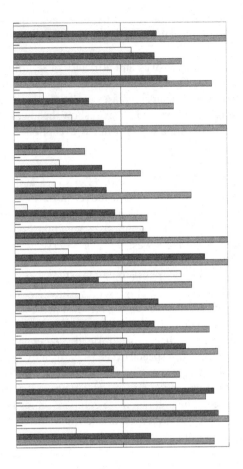

Fig. 4. Identification of individual consonants for the *fast* (upper bar), *normal* (middle bar) and for the *slow* (bottom bar) speech

fairly low for normal speech (59%) and high for the slow speech (86%). The CV-syllable identification is determined almost entirely by consonant perception.

Identification for consonant and vowel parts in a CV-syllables are collected separately. It has been found that the consonant identification increases with almost the same ratio as the speaking rate goes down. However, the identification of the vowel part shows quite different pattern. It significantly increases from fast to normal but little from normal to slow. For slow speech, consonant perception, and hence syllable perception, shows very high identification score. This experiment is done only for one speaker, and the results will include those which may reflect speaker's individuality. Further investigations will be needed to offset this sort of speakers variability.

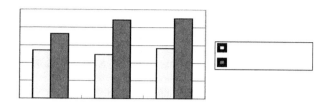

Fig. 5. Percentage of average syllable identification for the 1st and 2nd syllables in each speech stimulus

References

1. Fujimura, O., and Ochiai, K: Vowel identification and phonetic contexts, J. Acoust. Soc. Am., vol. 35, 1963, pp. 1889.
2. Kuwabara, H.: Perception of CV-syllables isolated from Japanese connected speech, *Language and Speech*, vol. 25, 1982, pp. 175–183.
3. Lindblom, B.E.F, and Studdert-Kennedy, M.: On the role of formant transitions in vowel recognition, J. Acoust. Soc. Am., vol. 42, 1967, pp. 830–843.
4. Kuwabara, H.: An approach to normalization of co-articulation effects for vowels in connected speech, J. Acoust. Soc. Am., vol. 77, 1985, pp. 686–694.
5. Kuwabara, H.: Acoustic properties of phonemes in continuous speech for different speaking rate, Proc. of ICSLP, 1996, pp. 2435–2438.
6. Kuwabara, H.: Acoustic and perceptual properties of phonemes in continuous speech as a function of speaking rate, Proc. of EuroSpeech, 1997, pp. 1003–1006.

NL-Processor and Linguistic Knowledge Base in a Speech Recognition System

Michael G. Malkovsky and Alexey V. Subbotin

Moscow State University, Computational Mathematics and Cybernetics Department,
119899, Vorobjovy Gory, Moscow, Russia
malk@cs.msu.su, lesha@isd.srcc.msu.su

Abstract. The linguistic methods providing grammatical and lexical control of the acoustic recognition results are described. The Parser (NL-Processor) uses original local grammar, ATN-type grammar, and comprehensive computer dictionaries (Linguistic Knowledge Base – LKB). To choose the best of the plausible strings, a special meta-level is introduced that deals with the multi-criterion choice problem. An important feature of the techniques employed is that the best string does not necessarily have to be a grammatical one. The original approach to lexical n-grams dictionary correction is described too. Later this approach was generalised and now it is considered as a base of the new computer-aided technology of the LKB construction. The main component of this approach is the METAMODEL, based on UML and fuzzy mathematics. Both human and computer should participate in LKB construction process: human contributes to this process his intelligence and language intuition, computer – his speed, memory and computational capabilities.

The paper describes linguistic methods providing grammatical and lexical control of the acoustic and phonetic recognition results. These methods were elaborated for American English by the Moscow State University team (Agreement between ACCENT, Inc., a California corporation, and Computational Mathematics and Cybernetics, Department of the Moscow State University). The project scope was the development of the speaker-independent recognition system for translating an input speech signal to text. The commercial software product was not developed, but the experts' positive assessment of the approach and its potentiality was the motivation of the United States Patent registration (E. Komissarchik, et al. "Knowledge-based speech recognition system and methods having frame length computed based upon estimated pitch period of vocalic intervals", No. 5,799,276).

The goal of our team was the improvement of the acoustic and phonetic recognition accuracy by taking into account grammatical and semantic information. The model of the American English and the Linguistic Knowledge Base (LKB) and NL-processor (Parser) were developed. This work was done in the cooperation with the linguists. Model includes 28 main grammatical classes and about 300 grammatical grades of words.

The LKB used in the analysis process includes grammatical dictionaries, corpora of lexical bigrams (the pairs of words provided by statistical information), corpora of admissible and inadmissible sequences of syntactic classes, a grammar table, and a dependency co-occurrence dictionary. The grammatical dictionaries employed are: the

P. Sojka, I. Kopeček, and K. Pala (Eds.): TSD 2000, LNAI 1902, pp. 237–242, 2000.

grammatical dictionary of separate words, the grammatical dictionary of phrasal verbs (e.g. "get away", "get around to"), the grammatical dictionary of collocations (e.g. "on end", "as ever", "Microsoft Word"), the grammatical dictionary of the so-called "segments", i.e. sequences of words merged into one phonetic word (e.g. "isn't", "it's" for "it is" or "it has").

Entries in any of the grammatical dictionaries contain the symbols of syntactic classes assigned to the entry units (Noun, Verb, Conjunction, etc.), more particular grammatical features of these units (Number, Person, Transitivity, etc.), their semantic features (Human, PhysObject, InfoObject, etc.), and a frequency tag.

The Parser takes as an input the results of acoustic and phonetic recognition – so called "word garland" with one or more (for homophones "it's" – "its", "boys – boy's – boys'" or for quasi-homophones "boys – poise") word choices specified for each word of the utterance pronounced. Any word choice has a so-called "penalty" – a numerical estimation of the acoustic and phonetic recognition accuracy. The Parser processed grammatical and lexical properties of the words in a garland ("I have read/red this book" – "I have this red/read book") in order to transform a garland into a set of word strings as tentative representations of the utterance and to form a complex plausibility estimate for each of these strings. The grammatical and lexical properties considered are: the grammatical features of words and collocations; the grammatical structure of each string as a whole and/or of the phrases that the string might contain; the grammatical "events" found to be present in the strings (such as ellipsis, anaphora, deviant forms, lack of agreement, etc.); the frequency of words, collocations, and lexical pairs.

The general scheme of the parsing envisages two levels of processing: local grammatical analysis providing preliminary filtering of the word garlands along with their transformation into word strings; global grammatical analysis grading these strings by their preferability and choosing the ones that are more plausible as representations of the utterance.

Local grammatical analysis of the word garland associates grammatical features with the candidate word choices in the garland using triplet table to reject those of the candidate strings, which are considered to be absolutely inadmissible, and to weigh the remaining strings. The output of the local grammatical analysis is a set of word strings; each string individually ranked and weighted based on locally applied grammatical rules.

In the local grammatical analysis step, the admissible and inadmissible sequences of syntactic classes are used which describe local syntactic relations. The corpora of such sequences include a table of admissible triplets, each triplet provided in them with certain grammatical features to be used in the analysis, and a table of inadmissible quadruplets, the so-called "anti-quadruplets". Each line in the triplet table includes a triplet of syntactic classes (e.g. Verb – SubordinateConjunction – Noun), an operator (so-called "demon") that checks the admissibility of this triplet, the triplet frequency tag, and its Grammatical-events marker.

Global grammatical analysis which follows the local one takes as its input the candidate word strings produced by the local analysis, and establishes the non-local syntactical relations structure of each string using the grammar table and the dependency co-occurrence dictionary. The grammar table constitutes a table-like representation of a formal ATN-type (augmented recursive transition network) grammar which determines grammatical compatibility of distantly located parts of the sentence and finds all admissible variants of the sentence's syntactic structure. It deals with the descriptions of structural phrases possible in a sentence and a set of operators providing access to the dependency co-occurrence dictionary. The dependency co-occurrence dictionary contains entries both for lexical and for various types of grammatical items, specifying for each of such items its predictions for the structural elements (dependents and/or governors) that may be co-occurred with the corresponding text item in a sentence.

The syntactical relations structure associated with a word string in the course of its global analysis is used as a basis for the grammatical descriptor of the string, this descriptor comprising information on the properties of its structure as a whole, as well as of the structure of the phrases it might contain. The grammatical descriptor is used to verify certain non-local contextual requirements, as well as to weigh the plausibility of the word string as a representation of the input utterance.

The meta-level uses the results of all the previous steps of processing the input utterance to choose the best of the candidate word strings for its representation. It has to deal with a multi-criterion choice problem, the criteria involved being of three types: criteria resulting from the phonetic/acoustic weighting of various word choices; criteria based on the results of the local grammatical analysis of the word garlands; and criteria based on the grammatical descriptors of the candidate word strings constructed by the global analysis. An important asset of the meta-level procedures is that the best string chosen does not necessarily have to be a full and grammatical sentence. The Parser can accept both non-sentential strings, like newspaper headings, and ungrammatical expressions (to be often found in spontaneous speech).

The meta-level procedures are described by means of production rules representing statements that can be illustrated by the following one: "If the given choice for word N violates sentence grammaticality requirement of type 7 (i.e. a noun phrase after a copula does not have a determiner in it), but this choice is characterised by the acoustic and phonetic steps as absolutely reliable, then this choice is considered to be correct notwithstanding the violation mentioned." The set of such production rules may be changed at will, so that the system can be tuned in to recognise different speech styles: on the one hand, it can be made to accept only strictly grammatical sentences, on the other, the meta-level rules may be added to make acceptable various types of ungrammatical structures.

At the conclusion of the grammatical analysis step, it is expected that in most cases all words of the sentence will be defined with a confidence level exceeding a predetermined threshold value. This sentence will therefore be presented to the user as the correct spelling of the input utterance.

The main features of the methods described are:

- the utterance recognition results are controlled primarily with the help of the grammatical, rather than lexical restrictions (this makes the Parser independent of the domain of the input utterances);
- the grammatical analysis is applied to word garlands, i.e., to more complex objects than word strings;
- the grammatical analysis techniques envisage two levels of processing: local and global (this permits more accurate control of recognition results);

- local grammatical analysis provides very fast preliminary filtering of the word garlands and their transformation into word strings, using tables of triplets and quadruplets of syntactic classes;

- global grammatical analysis grades the resulting word strings by their preferability and specifies the ones that are more plausible as representations of the input utterance, using an ATN-type grammar and a dependency co-occurrence dictionary arranged within an object-oriented paradigm (this makes possible to introduce not only grammatical, but also semantic control of the recognition results);

- to choose the best of the plausible strings, a special meta-level is introduced that deals with the multi-criterion choice problem (this provides an improvement over the existing techniques in that the best string does not necessarily have to be a grammatical one).

Linguistic module (LKB and Parser) helps to improve the accuracy of acoustic and phonetic recognition from 94–95% to 95–97%.

The original approach to lexical n-grams corpora correction is described too in the paper. In particular, we have proceeded further research of methods for improvement of lexical bigrams processing issues. New methods of the bigrams corpora correction were developed for speech recognition system, when the project mentioned was closed. These methods resulted in additional improvement (1–2%) of recognition accuracy.

The bigrams are very powerful recognition improvement facility, but we can't ignore the problem of the corpora representativity. As bigrams are gathered on some text corpus, they are very suitable to be used in recognition of the text from this corpus. However, for the texts from another domain, they don't work so well.

There are two ways to improve the situation. The first one is to use more representative text corpus. The second one is to try to fill the bigrams corpora (dictionary). Choosing the second approach, we have developed several methods of bigram dictionary improvement such as "paradigm filling", "transformations", "clusterization". The main idea of all these methods – it is necessary to analyse the current dictionary and to find what bigrams can/should be added. This analysis is based on the statistical principles, because bigram dictionary is used statistically. The main rule of thumb is the following: "It's not a trouble to add some incorrect bigrams if you add with them much more correct ones." For example, if we insert a new set of bigrams into the dictionary, some are correct and some are incorrect, the heuristic of adding is good if it adds more correct bigrams, than incorrect ones.

The main rule of the "paradigm filling" method is the following. Let one of the morphological forms WF1 of some word Wrd is in the bigram (WF1 W), contained in the dictionary. WF is a form of some other word. In this case we can add into the dictionary the bigrams (WF2 W), (WF3 W), ... , where WF2, WF3, ... – the other forms of Wrd. For example, if in the dictionary we have a bigram "brown dog", then we can add a bigram "brown dogs". For this method the heuristics in a form of productions were developed, which describe conditions and process for this method.

The principle of the "transformations" is the transformation of entire bigram, which represents some consistent word combination. For example, the bigram "dog runs" can be transformed into "running dog". Rules for this kind of transformation are described by productions too and contain conditions when such transformations are possible. These rules are based on transformational grammar of American English.

The main idea of "clusterization" is to find a cluster of the "similar" words ("similar" in the sense that, they may participate in the common lexical contexts). For example, if we decide that, the days of the week are in one cluster, and in the dictionary there are bigrams "on Monday", "Sunday morning", "Saturday evening", we may add the following bigrams "on Sunday", ... , "on Saturday", "Monday morning", ... , "Saturday morning", "Sunday evening", ... , "Friday evening". If clusters are fixed, this method may be described by productions too.

The safest method is the "paradigm filling". It adds very little incorrect bigrams – only ones which contains words having non-full paradigm. The "transformations" method is more dangerous, because syntactic rules that it's based on have much more exceptions than morphological ones. The "clusterization" should be used carefully involving human control over the clusters, which are the base for dictionary correction, because this method uses semantic level information. This method is applicable to small, consistent and evidential clusters.

Later, the main idea of this approach – a combination of statistical and knowledge-based methods – was generalised. Now we consider it as a base of the new computer-aided technology of the LKB construction. The basic principles of this technology are the following:

- computer contributes in the process its capabilities to handle routine work, find patterns and regularities in data;
- human expert controls the process and contribute his or her intelligence and language intuition;
- for every LKB construction project unique method is required, but this method can be built as a combination of the existing proved methods;
- a lot of experiments should be conducted to find right combination of methods (statistical methods vs. linguistics-based ones, automatic methods vs. semi-automatic or manual, corpus-based methods of knowledge acquisition).

However, there are some problems in implementation of this approach:

1. There exist a lot of different linguistic models, which result in different LKB construction methods. These methods may contain useful heuristics, but they cannot be used and even more combined due to the differences in the basic models.
2. Some methods have programming implementations but they cannot be used directly, as they are based on different technologies, programming languages, data formats, etc.

Thus, the following approach to the implementation of the proposed technology was chosen:

1. To build METAMODEL which is a modelling facility permitting the mapping of different LKB models, algorithms and heuristics into the common formalism. This METAMODEL should be based on international standards and its building, analysis and mapping should be supported by industrial technology.

2. To build LKB construction system which implements this METAMODEL and facilitates the experiments with different combination of the methods. This system should be based on standard technologies.

The METAMODEL was build as Unified Modelling Language extension. This language is standardised in Object Management Group and is de-facto a standard for object modelling languages. We build our METAMODEL as "UML profile" – standard way to extent UML metamodel. We extend the UML modelling facilities with fuzzy mathematics which permits the representation of non-precise linguistic information and Petri nets formalism – for rigorious description of the distributed algorithms.

For LKB construction system, the architecture was developed which is based on CORBA (as the most powerful for the present distributed object-oriented standard technology). The architecture includes such components:

- Data Access Servers, which incapsulates data sources and represent common interface based on fuzzy semantic net abstraction;
- Processor Components, which can be deployed on Data Access Servers or Application Servers and implement different processing algorithms;
- Workflow Server, which permits to describe distributed processes of data analysis in declarative form and to experiment with combination of the data sources and algorithms;
- other components, such as repository servers, user interfaces, system level services.

The mapping from the METAMODEL to this architecture was developed which permits to map models to the implementation in the LKB system. The mapping process can be automated with the UML CASE tool.

Russian Phonetic Variability and Connected Speech Transcription

Vladimir I. Kuznetsov and Tatiana Y. Sherstinova

Department of Phonetics, St. Petersburg State University,
Universitetskaya nab. 11, St. Petersburg, Russia
paul@phonet.lang.pu.ru, tanya@ts4306.spb.edu

Abstract. The study of pronunciation variability is an important phonetic task, which has many applications (in speech synthesis and recognition systems, language teaching, forensic phonetics, etc.), and well-known variability of Russian speech deserves special investigations. Generally, one may distinguish geographical, functional, social and national variability of pronunciation. At the same time any type of pronunciation is characterised by its own internal variability. It concerns as well the standard speech. Database of contemporary Russian speech variability is currently being created in the Laboratory of the Experimental Phonetics of St. Petersburg University in order to investigate pronunciation variance of different speech types. The database of sound material is formed by recordings of the Phonetically Representative Texts pronounced by 1) standard Russian speakers, 2) regional Russian speakers, 3) speakers from the former USSR republics to which Russian is a second language, and 4) foreigners from European, Asian and American countries. Along with the sound database, an expert linguistic system is being created, which allows analysis and investigation of particular speech samples, types and corresponding parameters. An important role here plays the system of speech transcription, which should adequately reflect the actual variability.

1   Introduction

Natural continuous speech of any language is known to be a complex phenomenon depending on great amount of factors. "Weak" articulation of Russian (in contrast to many other languages) and the abundance of Russian grammar structure usually cause considerable modifications and simplifications in continuous speech sound sequences when compared with that of the ideal (full-style) speech. The variety of phonemes pronouncing turns out to be extremely high, and therefore complicating (sometimes even making impossible) their identification. The problem becomes more complicated when we analyse non-standard speech: that of regional Russian speakers, speakers from the former USSR republics (to whom Russian is a second language), and foreigners. The study of pronunciation variability is an important phonetic task, which has many applications (in speech synthesis and recognition systems, language teaching, forensic phonetics, etc.).

P. Sojka, I. Kopeček, and K. Pala (Eds.): TSD 2000, LNAI 1902, pp. 243–247, 2000.

2 Research Methodology

The "distance" of any natural pronunciation from its "ideal" variant in any phonetic aspect (both segmental and prosodic) may be statistically evaluated. The smallest distance may be observed in standard speech, the distance will increase for colloquial standard speech, regional and dialect speech, and Russian speech by foreigners. We see our task to elaborate the procedures of speech estimation based on its comparison with the ideal pronunciation rules: first, on the material of standard speech, and then regional and dialect speech.

The following method of speech estimation (which is now realizing in the segmental (transcriptional) aspect) is proposed. It is planned to analyse the real transcription of database segments (allophones, groups of allophones and syllables) together with conditions of their realization (e.g., stress, phonemic identity, syntagmatic position, context). All sound realizations may be divided then into the following groups: 1) regular, which regularly coincide with ideal transcription (always or in determined cases); 2) irregular, which may vary from ideal; 3) "inadequate", which practically never coincide with ideal; 4) personally specific, characterising the particular speaker. For each group, the sets of rules (conditions) should be defined, and the variation series for each parameter may be built. Generalisation of the obtained material will produce the empirical model of Russian speech.

Analysing non-standard (regional, dialect, etc.) speech variety makes it possible to determine the boundary values of estimation parameters that divide the pronunciation into "right" (standard) and "wrong" (non-standard). Only in this stage of research, language pronunciation norm may be actually estimated and the adequate model of Russian speech may be created.

The described method may be used as well for evaluation of speech in other aspects, including prosody and temporal dynamics.

3 Standard Speech Variability

3.1 Sound Material

Research material is represented by the recordings of the Phonetically Representative Text (PRT), which is one of the central components of the Phonetic Fund of Russian Language. PRT was specially composed so that it comprises 200 most frequent syllables of Russian. Moreover, 95% of its vocabulary consists of high-frequent Russian words occurring in different phrase positions. The various statistic parameters of the PRT (in particular, syllable representation, distribution of rhythmic structures, average length of words, frequency of stressed and unstressed words, consonant coefficient, etc.) coincide with the data obtained by processing of the multitude of Russian texts [1,2]. The recordings of PRT seem to be the best material for such kind of research because: 1) they represent the models of Russian pronunciation for the concrete speakers, and 2) textual identity of recordings justifies and simplifies the comparison procedures.

The speakers with standard pronunciation have been selected for the recordings of the PRT. The material has been recorded in specially equipped sound-treated chamber. The speakers read out the text, with which they had been acquainted beforehand.

3.2   Data Analysis

The pronouncing of phoneme segments has been analysed using auditory and acoustic methods: researchers-auditors, experts of the phonetic analysis, have been listening to the vowels both in context (syllable) and separated off the context. At their disposal, there were the sonograms and oscillograms, and the broad context was known. In the result of complex analysis of each sound (phoneme), experts have determined their so-called "real" phonetic transcription [3]. The information on the actual pronouncing in the recordings of the PRT was presented in the relational database [4], which allowed to evaluate quality variation of the given speech samples. The detailed description is being made for each segment of the database. It comprises in particular the "real" transcription, "ideal" phonemic and phonetic transcriptions, attributes of the sound, duration of the signal segments, acoustic features, phonetic and paralinguistic comments.

3.3   Conclusions

The processing of connected speech revealed high variety of Russian phonemes (especially vowels) pronouncing [3,4,6]. In fact, standard speakers may pronounce, instead of theoretically predicted (or "near") vowels, a variety of different sounds, even surprisingly unlike the prescribed ones. On the other hand, individual speakers may show an inclination to the use in speech of some or other particular sounds either generally or in concrete cases. All these differences are not usually noticeable by the Russians (all analysed recordings are being perceived as just "standard", without any distinctive features) and may be revealed only by means of computer analysis [7]. Generally, strong phrase position (under syntagmatic, logical or emphatic stress) assists pronouncing striving to an ideal one (both phonetically and phonemically). Weak phrase position, on the contrary, causes considerable modifications of the phonemes up to their complete falling out. In the result, a number of vowels lose their own relevant features and even gain the characteristics of some other phonemes.

4   Connected Speech Transcription

While processing and analysing standard speech data, we have noticed that there exist essential differences between actual data and traditional transcribing tools. We have discussed this phenomenon in our recent works [4,6]. As vowels turned out to be much more variable when compared with consonants, most "problems" of transcription related to them. First, each vowel phoneme has individual number of allophones which may not coincide with the theoretically predicted ones. Then, one and the same segment (from both acoustic and perceptive points of view) may represent allophones of different phonemes, whereas different segments may represent the same phoneme. Another important factor which may modify their pronouncing is prosodic position of sounds. It is very important that the development of transcribing tools destined for connected speech processing, speech synthesis and recognition systems should take into account these results of experimental phonetic speech analysis.

5   Regional Speech Variability

5.1   Sound Material

Russian speech has been a subject of a many-years research program of the Department of Phonetics of St. Petersburg State University. A special phonetically representative text has been created, which allows analysis of regional pronunciation peculiarities. In the result of a serial of expeditions, a big collection of audio recordings of this text from the different regions of Russia and the former USSR republics has been formed [8]. Detailed phonetic transcription was made for all recordings. Summary regional peculiarities are presented in the special tables of phonetic parameters [9].

5.2   Data Analysis

From all the multitude of recordings, the most "representative" ones reflecting 20 regional variants of Russian speech are selected. For the primary analysis, it is planned to investigate both "good"-Russian and "poor"-Russian recordings for each regional/national region. The selected recording are segmented into syllables, words, syntagmes, and phrases. This segmentation will be further used for the access to the regional peculiarities in the database. Tables of phonetic parameters reflecting summary regional peculiarities are being organised as a relational database, which should allow one to conduct parameter search on request. Each pronunciation peculiarity (phonetic parameter) will have references to the correspondent sound samples. The expert database should allow the following: 1) on request of particular regional pronunciation the user may see the orthographic and transcriptional texts, to listen to it, and see the tables of the relevant parameters and linguistic comments; 2) on request of phonetic parameter, to find regional variants with such peculiarities and to listen and review the other database samples. The reduced version of this database is planned to be presented in the Internet.

6   Conclusion

Variability models of real speech should be necessarily taken into account for optimisation of many speech technologies and products. The obtained algorithms and statistical data may also be interesting for theoretical phonetics and linguistic studies, for teaching of Russian, and especially for phonetic interference studies and forensic phonetics.

Acknowledgements

This work is supported by the Russian Foundation for Humanitarian Research: project N 99-04-12015b "Regional Variants of the Russian Speech in the Internet".

References

1. Bondarko L.V., Stepanova S.B. Text Module "Phonetically Representative Text". In: Bulletin of the Phonetic Fund of Russian Language. Bochum-Leningrad, N 4, 1992, pp. 132–134.
2. Bondarko L.V., Zinder L.R., Stern A.S. Statistic Characteristics of Russian Speech. In: Hearing and Speech in Norm and Pathology. Leningrad, 1977.
3. Kuznetsov V.I. Vowels in Russian Speech. St. Petersburg State University, 1997.
4. Kuznetsov V.I. and Sherstinova T.Y. Phonetic Transcription for the Systems of Speech Synthesis and Recognition. In: Proceedings of the International Workshop "Text, Speech and Dialog" TSD '98. Brno, Czech Republic, 22–26 September 1998, pp. 263–267.
5. Sherstinova T.Y. Database FON2 of Russian Normative Speech. In: Proceedings of the Second International Workshop "Speech and computer" SPECOM '97. Cluj-Napoka, Romania, 27–30 October 1997, pp. 81–84.
6. Sherstinova T.Y. Russian Phonemes and Allophones in Continuous Speech: for Speech Synthesis and Recognition Systems. In: Proceedings of the Second International Workshop "Speech and computer" SPECOM '98. St. Petersburg, 26–29 October 1998, pp. 269–274.
7. Sherstinova T.Y. Speech Evaluation in Russian Phonetic Database. In: Proceedings of the First International Conference on Language Resources and Evaluation. Granada, Spain, 28–30 May 1998.
8. Interference of the Sound Systems. St. Petersburg State University, 1984.
9. Scientific Reports "Peculiarities of Russian Language Functioning in the Dialect and National Regions of the USSR (sound aspect)". Leningrad State University. Department of Phonetics. 1975–1986.

Database Processing
for Spanish Text-to-Speech Synthesis

J. Gómez-Mena, M. Cardo, J.L. Madrid, and C. Prades

E.T.S.I.T.-U.P.M., Ciudad Universitaria, 28040 Madrid, Spain
mena@gtd.ssr.upm.es

Abstract. In this paper we will present the method we have used to collect a large database using live recording of a radio transmission and of an announcer. Our selection method uses phonetic and prosodic context information and frequency domain measurements in a search algorithm based on minimising two cost functions: the concatenation cost between adjacent speech units and the distance between the selected unit and a previously calculated target segment. For each basic unit, on average, we have collected around 100 similar units in different phonetic and prosodic contexts. To segment the basic units, we have used our highly accurate speech recognition system described in [1]. This collection of units has been used in our TTS system giving marked improvement in naturalness. With this new system, we hope to help people with disabilities that need to listen or speak using artificial speech.

1   Introduction

Speech synthesis today is a mature technology in terms of intelligibility, but in naturalness it has yet some severe shortcomings to overcome. The use of the text to speech system by people with speaking disabilities is our major goal. Its lack of naturalness has hindered its practical applications, because of the perception of "machine voice" by the listeners.

The synthesis techniques that currently present the best quality are data-based techniques, in which the synthesised voice is made by means of concatenating different pre-recorded voice segments, called "synthesis units". Some transformation is applied to these concatenated units; we use the TD-PSOLA (Time Domain Pitch Synchronous OverLap-Add) method [2].

Our approach consists in improving the quality and size of the voice segment database. In previous versions of our TTS system, only one token of each synthesis unit was stored. This implies that most of the time, the time domain and spectral characteristics of the synthesised unit will differ from the features of the stored voice segment. This segment would have to go through heavy signal processing, thus suffering from distortion and the loss of some subtle but important phonetic and prosodic information.

The main difficulty with this approach is the very high cost of the collection and adaptation of the voice segments. The huge size of the new database made the manual methodology we had used before infeasible, so we had to develop automatic procedures to obtain and segment the synthesis units.

P. Sojka, I. Kopeček, and K. Pala (Eds.): TSD 2000, LNAI 1902, pp. 248–252, 2000.

2   Database Collection

To improve the overall quality of synthesised speech, reducing distortion upon voice segments, we decided to increase the number of tokens of each voice segment contained in the database. Each token would have been uttered in a different phonetic and prosodic context, so the modifications made by the synthesis program in order to adapt the segment's features to the synthesised prosody would be much smaller, leading to a less noticeable distortion.

We planned to include in the database about 100 tokens of each synthesis unit. Since we use 780 different units, the database size grew to almost 80,000 voice segments that made the manual selection, segmentation and inclusion of each segment in the database infeasible.

2.1   Automatic Data Acquisition

Instead of working with a speaker, we chose to follow another approach: the recording of a live FM radio program. We could achieve a fairly good signal quality using a high-end receiver plus a data acquisition card that digitised the analog broadband audio signal; the quality was almost as good as we could have achieved in our sound laboratory. The sound samples were stored in a hard disk, allowing further processing.

This method let us capture a lot of information, pronounced in a state-of-the-art studio by a professional speaker. The huge range of prosodic situations recorded was important for our purposes of recording voice in different contexts, and probably better than what could be obtained by hand-crafting such an enormous number of phrases for a speaker.

After recording, the voice segments must be segmented and the pitch must be marked, in order to be used in the TD-PSOLA synthesis method. This would have been a cumbersome task, but for the automatic segmentation application, we developed it base on a speech recognition system.

2.2   Automatic Segmentation

Our research group has developed a Flexible Vocabulary Speech Recognition System based on semi-continuous HMM (Hidden Markov Models) [1]. These are statistical state models used for pattern recognition that provide a natural and highly reliable way of recognising speech, which is characterised as a parametric random process. This recognition system must be trained with a known utterance; it segments the input speech, generating the model network. We have used the training feature to automatically segment the recorded speaker's speech. Figure 1 shows the process.

As our system is still under development, some manual corrections of the segmentation results had to be made on no more than 5% of the recorded utterances.

3   Database Construction

Before including a segment in the speech database, it must endure some transformations: power normalisation, a segmentation analysis in which segments that do not comply with

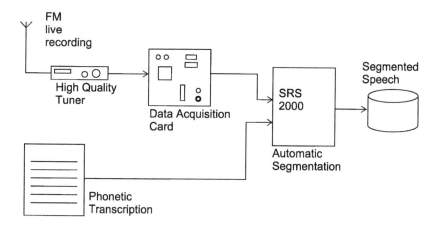

Fig. 1. Database collection

some minimal requirements can be rejected, and the calculation of some parameters which will be useful at synthesis time.

Each token of every synthesis unit will be stored with some auxiliary information, so as to be able to identify and to differentiate the context in which it was recorded, and to allow the computation of a *distance* to other synthesis units [3].

The following features are computed and stored for each token:

Phonetic context: information about the allophones preceding and following each segment.

Prosodic context: fundamental frequency, duration, logarithmic power and the first cepstral coefficients. The cepstrum is a measurement of the spectral envelope; it frees us from the everlasting difficult computation of formants. They are computed on two windows, at the beginning and at the end of each segment.

When including a new token in the database, these features are measured and then compared to the other tokens belonging to the same synthesis units; thus allowing us to select for inclusion only the different enough tokens which cover the widest possible decision space [4]. A segment will be added to the database only if it broadens the choice of different contexts at synthesis time.

4   Speech Synthesis

A new method for the selection of units at synthesis time was implemented. It is based on a function minimisation algorithm; this function is the sum of two cost functions:

- The *target cost*, an estimation of the difference between a predicted target unit t_i, and each of the tokens of this unit stored in the database.
- The *concatenation cost*, an estimation of the quality of the join between two consecutive units u_{i-1} and u_i.

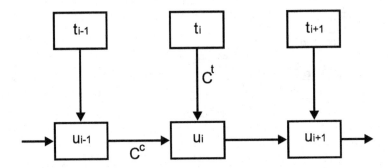

Fig. 2. Costs for unit selection

The target cost is computed as a weighted distance, using the following features: phonetic context, duration, power and pitch. When computing the concatenation cost, our goal is to minimise the acoustic distortion, so to calculate the distance between the units at both sides of the join, we chose to use the pitch difference and the cepstral distance (the Euclidean distance of the cepstral coefficients, which has proven to be a good measurement of acoustic distortion).

Special care had to be taken in the selection and optimisation of a good set of weighing coefficients for both target and concatenation costs; an automatic tuning method comparing the mean Euclidean cepstral distance between vectors from selected units and target segments, known as the special test case of synthesising natural speech utterances from the speaker of the source database. This method is computationally expensive but produces much better speech than hand tuned weights.

Both the database and the selection procedure were implemented with the purpose of transferring the most of the computational load to the process of building the database itself, thus freeing the synthesis program, which can be run in any low-end personal computer.

5   Results

The method that we have described here undertook some preliminary testing, showing a promising improvement in the naturalness of the synthesised sentences.

Due to time constraints, we still have not tested the described system completely. We are planning to write a thorough testing procedure in which a large number of listeners will be exposed to voice synthesised from different speakers resembling different genders, ages and social background.

The conclusion that we draw from the few experiments made is that having in the database so many speech samples extracted from a broad spectrum of phonetic and prosodic contexts enables us to find a near optimal candidate at synthesis time, minimising the extent of the signal-processing transformations and thus reducing the acoustic distortion in the synthesised speech.

6 Discussion and Future Work

Any improvement on the quality and naturalness of our system will increase its applications in the realm of aids for the speaking-impaired people, because synthetic speech will be more readily acceptable by any listener. This can increase social acceptance for people with disabilities.

The architecture of our system was intended to allow easy modification or substitution of any software module. Thus, improvements in the HMM-based speech recogniser or in the synthesis algorithm can be quickly ported to our system, improving its overall quality or performance. Future work will aim to improve the prosody generation module, because in this work we have not yet used very complex models. It should be time to include the latest theories of energy, duration and pitch modelling, with which we could achieve dramatic improvements, especially in long sentences.

References

1. SRS-2000: A Speech Recognition System, Internal Report, Escuela Técnica Superior de Ingenieros de Telecomunicación, Universidad Politécnica de Madrid, 1999.
2. Eric Moulines and Francis Charpentier.: "Pitch-synchronous waveform processing techniques for text-to-speech synthesis using diphones". Speech Communication, 1990, vol. 9, pp. 453–467.
3. Alan W. Black and Nick Campbell: "Optimising selection of units from speech databases for concatenative synthesis". Proceedings of Eurospeech '95, Madrid, 1995, vol. 1, pp. 581–584.
4. W.J. Wang, N. Campbell et al.: "Tree-based unit selection for English speech synthesis". Proceedings of the International Conference on Acoustics, Speech and Signal Processing, Minneapolis, 1993, vol. 2, pp. 191–194.

Topic-Sensitive Language Modelling

Mirjam Sepesy Maučec and Zdravko Kačič

University of Maribor, Smetanova 17, SI-2000 Maribor, Slovenia

Abstract. The paper proposes a new framework to construct topic-sensitive language models for large vocabulary speech recognition. Identifying a domain of discourse, a model appropriate for the current domain can be built. In our experiments, the target domain was represented with a piece of text. By using appropriate features, sub-corpus of a large collection of training text was extracted. Our feature selection process was especially suited to languages where words are formed by many different inflectional affixatation. All words with the same meaning (but different grammatical form) were collected in one cluster and represented as one feature. We used the heuristic word weighting classifier $TFIDF$ (term frequency / inverse document frequency) to further shrink the feature vector. Final language model was built by interpolation of topic specific models and a general model. Experiments have been done by using English and Slovenian corpus.

1 Introduction

In this article we address the problem of constructing language models for large vocabulary speech recognition. N-gram language models have proved to be surprisingly powerful [1] and easy to implement. Trigram models are most commonly used. Through the growing availability of textual data in electronic form, N-gram models have sought some improvements in reducing the problem of sparseness. Unfortunately, they do possess several drawbacks. N-gram techniques are unable to model long range dependencies. They lack any ability to exploit the linguistic nuances between domains.

If we could effectively identify the domain of discourse, a model appropriate for the current domain could be used. In this case, language models adapted to particular task need to be built.

In our experiments we were looking for methods of topic adaptation in unrestricted domains. We do not assume that a document belongs to only one of a number of disjoint topic sets. Every document, story or conversation is seen as a unique and hitherto unseen combination of several elemental topics.

2 Topic Adaptation

By using all training text in language model probabilities calculation, we get the model of general language.

P. Sojka, I. Kopeček, and K. Pala (Eds.): TSD 2000, LNAI 1902, pp. 253–258, 2000.

The goal of the adaptation is to lower the language model perplexity by providing a higher probability of words and word-sequences which are characteristic of the domain of discourse [2]. Being able to cluster training documents into topic-specific clusters, topical models can be built.

Initially, we made an experiment where we measured the perplexity of test samples, for which the topics were known in advance.

10 topics (A, B, ... , J) were randomly selected from the broadcast news corpus (1996 Hub-4 experiment). The stories in the corpus are annotated with keywords. By using them, clusters of stories with the same keyword were created. For all of the 10 selected topics, single-topic language models were built by using merely the text in their cluster. Among all of the single-topic models, the perplexity of the correct model was always the smallest.

We wanted to design models which:

– are able to predict general language and
– deliver a degree of topic specialisation.

Combined language models were created by interpolating topic models (TOP) and a general model (GEN):

$$P_{COM}(w) = \lambda P_{TOP}(w) + (1 - \lambda)P_{GEN}(w). \tag{1}$$

P_{TOP} denotes the probability given by the topic model, P_{GEN} the probability given by the general model and P_{COM} the probability given by a combined model.

Table 1. Perplexities of topic models, the general model and combined models computed on test samples of known topic.

model	test sample									
	A	B	C	D	E	F	G	H	I	J
GEN	157	58	281	63	210	142	324	143	47	222
TOP	247	146	241	91	205	174	263	145	148	229
COM	80	50	125	54	99	80	130	81	44	100

The results (see Table 1) show that the perplexities given solely by the topic models are the worst. The volume of text available to create a topic model is only a fraction of that available for general model. This leads to the data sparseness problem. The combined model gave the best results for all topic test samples.

3   Topic Representation

It is unlikely that sufficient training material will exist to create a good model of a predefined topic. In most cases, we have only a sample from the target environment. From the large amount of text, we want to extract documents which are semantically most similar.

Documents and clusters are represented as a set of words, named features $d_i = [w_1, w_2, \ldots, w_m]$. In contrast to n-gram modelling, word order is ignored, which is of course in line with the semantic nature of the approach. It has been argued that maximum performance is often not achieved by using all available features, but using a good subset of those only. We have done experiments to show that it makes sense to group features into clusters. We want to group all words with the same meaning (but different grammatical form) in one cluster and represent them as one feature.

3.1   Fuzzy Clustering

We propose a novel approach for feature selection based on soft comparison of words. The usual way of learning on text defines a feature for each word that occurred in the training documents. This can result in some hundred of thousands of features. Having no additional knowledge source (lexicon) for this task, we define a membership function (μ_C), which associates to each word ($w \in \vartheta$) a number representing the grade of membership of this word in a cluster of words with the same meaning ($c \in C$). C denotes a set of clusters. Cluster c is defined as fuzzy set $\tilde{c}$:

$$\tilde{c} = \{ (w, \mu_C) \mid w \in \vartheta \}. \tag{2}$$

Each cluster defines its own fuzzy set. We want to collect all inflection forms of a lemma in one cluster automatically.

The words were compared by using a fuzzy comparison function (μ_ϑ). Each word w defines its own fuzzy set $\tilde{w}$:

$$\tilde{w} = \{ (w, \mu_\vartheta) \mid w \in \vartheta \}. \tag{3}$$

The function sees the word as a sequence of characters. It returns value 1 if words are the same and 0 for extremely different words. In other cases it returns the value between 0 and 1. The comparison function is created by using fuzzy rules, which provide a natural way of dealing with partial matching. The rules are expressed as fuzzy implications, which use linguistic variables to express similarity (similar, very similar, not very similar, quite similar, ...). We have made experiments with three different similarity functions. The first was constructed by using language independent rules. The rule compares parts of words (sequences of one, two, three, ... characters) and implies the degree of similarity. For example:

$$\textit{tree character sequences of words are the same} \Rightarrow \textit{words are quite similar} \tag{4}$$

The second similarity function was adapted to English language. For example, the parts of words like co-, ex-, non-, pre-, re-, ... were treated as prefixes and parts like -ed, -able, -ing, ... as suffixes of words with the same meaning. For example:

$$\textit{words differ in the suffix -s} \Rightarrow \textit{words are the same} \tag{5}$$

This kind of rules are expressed as crisp implications.

The third similarity function was adapted to the highly inflected Slovenian language and has the greatest number of rules.

Having similarity values for word pairs, we created a cluster hierarchy by using single link agglomerative clustering. Similarity values of the words can be represented as a weighted, undirected graph where nodes of the graph represent the words and the weight of an edge represents the similarity of words connected by the edge. To save space, we kept only the edges with weights greater then a prespecified threshold. The result of the single link hierarchy are locally coherent clusters. To avoid a chaining effect (and consequently elongated clusters) we modified the merging criterion. Clusters were made one at the time. A word was added to the cluster if its average similarity with all words in cluster was the largest among all the words not yet clustered. We started building a new cluster as soon as the largest similarity value did not exceed a prespecified threshold. This approach has still a running time of $O(N^2)$ and space requirement of $O(N)$. As an example, there are some randomly selected clusters of English language presented (see Table 2).

Table 2. Example of English clusters

Cluster No.	words in cluster
21	aadmirable admirable admirably admira admirally admire admired admirer admires admir admirers admiring admiration
3263	bbecause becau becaue beca bec
6457	chinasports sports sport sporto sporty sported sporter sportin sporting sportscar sportsman sportsmen sportcoat sportless
6645	cilnton clnton cinton tonton
7269	conferenced conferences conferencing teleconference teleconferenced teleconferences teleconferencing videoconferences
17199	iraq iraqi iraqis iraqs iraqian iraqui

3.2 Feature Vector Shrinking

Each cluster defines one feature. The number of clusters represents a feature vector length. We have further shrunk the vectors by a feature scoring measure $TFIDF$ (term frequency / inverse document frequency), defined as:

$$TFIDF(w_i, d) = TF(w_i, d) \cdot (\log(|D|) - \log(DF(w_i)) + 1). \tag{6}$$

$TF(w_i, d)$ is the number of times word w_i occurs in topic corpora d. $|D|$ denotes the total number of topic corpora. $DF(w_i)$ is the number of topic corpora in which the word w_i occurs at least once.

4 Topic Classification

Once we have the topic corpora ($\overrightarrow{d}$) and test documents ($\overrightarrow{t}$) represented as vectors of features, we used topic detection to determine the most similar topic clusters to a new piece of text. We used the *TFIDF* classifier:

$$H_{\mathrm{arg\,max}\,TFIDF} = \arg \max_{d \in D} \frac{\vec{t} \cdot \vec{d}}{\|\vec{t}\| \cdot \|\vec{d}\|}. \tag{7}$$

5 Language Model Interpolation

After selecting k most similar topics, individual trigram language models for each topic were built and interpolated together with the general model to produce a new language score [3].

$$P_{NEW}(w) = \sum_{j=1}^{k} \lambda_k P_{TOP_k}(w) + (1 - \sum_{j=1}^{k} \lambda_k) P_{GEN}(w). \tag{8}$$

6 Experiments

In our experiments, we were using the broadcast news corpus (1996 CSR Hub-4 Language Model for English language) and newspaper news corpus (Večer for Slovenian language) due to their semantic richness.

All language models were trigram models with the vocabulary of 64,000 most frequent words.

The English broadcast news corpus was organised into topic-specific clusters of documents based on manually-assigned keywords. We were experimenting with topic clusters that have at least 300 articles. 244 clusters satisfied this constraint. For a new piece of text we want to model, 10 most similar topics were extracted. Ranking all the topics by similarity value from 1 to 244, the correct topic cluster was always between the top 10 clusters (see Table 3). Language models built from each of the top 10 topic clusters were interpolated with a general language model. By using the language independent similarity function, we achieved a 10% perplexity reduction. By using to English language adapted similarity function, the perplexity reduction was slightly better (14%) (see Table 3). PP NEW denotes the perplexity of a new language model and topics selected by adapted similarity function.

Table 3. Rank of correct topic, perplexity of a new model and improvement of a new model in comparison with the combined model

	test sample									
	A	B	C	D	E	F	G	H	I	J
rank of correct topic	1	8	6	9	8	4	3	8	7	3
PP NEW	69	52	110	53	91	71	112	79	45	89
Improvement [%]	14	-4	12	2	8	11	14	2	-2	11

Unfortunately, the Slovenian newspaper corpus is not yet annotated with keywords. Clustering was done automatically. At the beginning each document defined its own cluster. We merged clusters iteratively by using the *TFIDF* classifier until we have got less then 100 of them. Three test samples were manually created. All of them consist of 5 documents similar in topic. For every sample, 10 most similar clusters were extracted. Language models were built in the same way as in the previous experiment with English corpus. By using the language independent similarity function, we have got a 15% perplexity reduction. By using to Slovenian language adapted similarity function, the perplexity reduction was up to 30% (see Table 4).

Table 4. Perplexity of a general and new model and improvement of the new model in comparison with the general model

	test sample		
	X	Y	Z
PP GEN	230	154	220
PP NEW	161	115	189
Improvement [%]	30	25	14

7   Conclusion

In our experiments we have shown that topic adaptation does result in decrease in perplexity. Adapted models can exploit the localisation of information within a topic domain. To train a language model, it does not make sense to use only a small portion of the topic specialised text. Large volumes of unrestricted text should be used to keep the characteristics of language in general.

References

1. Jelinek F.: Statistical Methods for Speech Recognition. MIT Press (1997).
2. Donnelly P. G., Smith F. J., Sicilia E., Ming J.: Language Modelling with Hierarchical Domains. Proc. Eurospeech (1999).
3. Seymore K., Rosenfeld R.: Using Story Topics for Language Model Adaptation. Proc. Eurospeech (1997).

Design of Speech Recognition Engine*

Luděk Müller, Josef Psutka, and Luboš Šmídl

University of West Bohemia, Department of Cybernetics,
Univerzitní 22, 306 14 Plzeň, Czech Republic
muller@kky.zcu.cz, psutka@kky.zcu.cz, smidl5@kky.zcu.cz

Abstract. This paper concerns a speaker independent recognition engine of Czech continuous speech designed for Czech telephone applications and describes the recognition module as an important component of a telephone dialogue system being designed and constructed at the Department of Cybernetics, the University of West Bohemia. The recognition is based on a statistical approach. The left-to-right three-state HMMs with an output probability density function expressed as multivariate Gaussian mixture are used to model triphones as basic units in acoustic modelling and stochastic regular grammars are implemented to reduce a task perplexity. A real time recognition process is supported by a very computation cost reduction approach estimating log-likelihood scores of Gaussian mixtures and also by a beam pruning used during Viterbi decoding. The present paper concerns the main part of the engine – a speaker independent recognition engine for continuous Czech speech.

1 Introduction

This paper concerns the speaker independent recognition of Czech continuous speech for the telephone application and describes a recognition module designed for this purpose at the University of West Bohemia. The task of this module is to recognise and transcribe continuous Czech telephone speech to a word sequence restricted by a stochastic regular grammar. The paper is structured as follows. A short review of the dialogue system is given in Section 2. Section 3 describes the speech recognition engine, which is based on a statistical approach. The statistical approach means that the recognition module incorporates front-end, acoustic model, language model and decoding block providing the search for the best word sequence matching the incoming acoustic signal with respect to the grammar. The acoustic model is depicted in Section 3.1. The remaining parts of the article deal with the individual subsystems of the speech recognition engine. How the telephone signal is captured and preprocessed in front-end is briefly given in Section 3.2. Section 3.3 deals with the block that evaluates HMM's output probability density functions. The grammar implementation is presented in Section 3.4. Finally, the results and conclusions are given in Section 4.

* The work was partially supported by the Ministry of Education of the Czech Republic, project no. MSM235200004, and by the Grant Agency of the Czech Republic, project no. 102/96/K087.

2   Dialogue System

At the Department of Cybernetic an endeavour has recently been exerted to develop a laboratory applicable telephone dialogue system. The dialogue system consists of three main parts – a speech engine, dialogue manager, and dialog application. The dialogue application is a task-oriented module keeping knowledge on a lexicon, dialogue structure, etc., and the dialogue manager controls a communication between users and the system. To date, the speech engine contains only a speech recognition module; a speech synthesis module will be added to the engine in the near future. The digitisation of an input analog telephone signal and/or a generation of a synthesised speech signal are provided by a telephone interface board. Figure 1 illustrates the used system architecture.

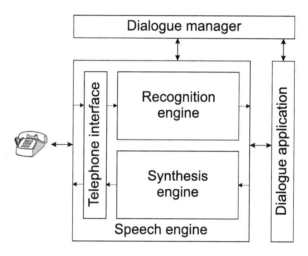

Fig. 1. Telephone dialogue system

3   Speech Recognition Engine

The core of the speech recognition engine is implemented in C++ and designed as platform independent. The platform specific implementation layer has been built for an implementation on MS Windows NT/95/98/2000. Our goal was to design a very fast recognition module without decreasing recognition accuracy suitable for telephone dialogue applications and for embedded systems. Several instances of the designed speech recognition engine can operate on one PC in real time. Furthermore, each engine module can be implemented as a set of several tasks (see Figure 2), each of them running as an individual process on a computer.

The speech recognition engine is based on a statistical approach. The task of this module is to recognise and transcribe continuous Czech telephone speech to a word sequence restricted by a stochastic regular grammar. The recognition module

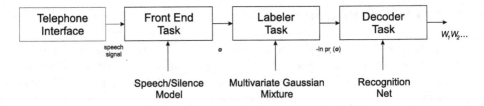

Fig. 2. Speech recognition engine

incorporates front-end, acoustic model, language model (represented by a stochastic regular grammar) and decoding block, that provides search for the best word sequence which matches the incoming acoustic signal with respect to the grammar.

The speech recognition engine can run in two different modes – ContinuousSpeak mode or SentenceSpeak mode. If the engine is running in the SentenceSpeak mode, all tasks are working continuously until a signal of the end of an utterance is generated by the application and sent to the engine. Then the decoder gives a result. If the engine is running in the ContinuousSpeak mode, the decoder gives a result immediately after a silence of predefined length is detected by the silence detector. Both of the speak modes are illustrated in Figure 3.

3.1   Acoustic Modelling

The basic speech unit of our system is a triphone. A triphone is a phone situated between two specific phones. Each individual triphone is represented by an HMM with a continuous output probability density function assigned to each state. Each density

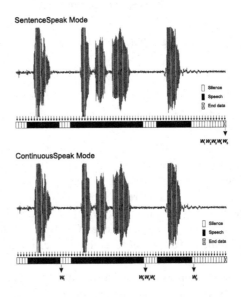

Fig. 3. SentenceSpeak mode vs. ContinuousSpeak mode

in our model is given by a mixture of multivariate Gaussians where each Gaussian has a diagonal covariance matrix. The number of mixtures for each model was obtained experimentally. At present, we use 8 mixtures for each state of each model in our system.

As the number of Czech triphones is too large, phonetic decision trees were used to tie states of Czech triphones. This gives us a more robust estimate of HMM parameters. That is because all the data associated with each individual state can be pooled and after tying, several states can share the same output probability distribution. For each state of each phone, an individual phonetic tree was constructed and the states were clustered. Initially, all states of a specific phone state position were associated with the root node of the tree. Depending on each answer attached to each tree node, the pool of states was split into two parts and this process of splitting continued until the states had reached to leaf nodes. All states in the same leaf node were then tied.

3.2   Front-End Task

The digitisation of an input analog telephone signal and/or a generation of a synthesised speech signal are provided by a telephone interface board. In the current implementation, the DIALOGIC D/21D board is used. Via this board, the telephone system is able to operate up to 2 telephone lines. This is reached through the capability of the system to run several speech recognition engines simultaneously.

Since the DIALOGIC D/21D is only a half-duplex board (at one moment we can either capture or play the signal), we had to implement a function allowing a fast start of recording after a playing has been performed.

The aim of the front-end processor is to convert a continuous speech signal to a sequence of feature vectors. The parameterisation process used in our system is based on the Mel-Frequency Cepstral Coefficients (MFCCs). The pre-emphasised acoustic waveform (by applying the first-order high frequency amplification and the pre-emphasis coefficient of 0.97) is segmented into 25 millisecond frames every 10 ms. Hamming window is applied to each frame and MFCCs are computed to generate final acoustic vectors. We use a filterbank with 26 triangular filters, 13 MFCCs including the 0th coefficient. The 13 delta and 13 delta delta MFCCs are computed and appended to the static MFCCs of each speech frame.

The front-end includes a silence detector technique based on an energy of an acoustic signal. If the feature vector has been labelled as silence, then the labeller task does not compute the likelihood score and the decoder task is waiting for speech data.

3.3   Labeller Task

There are 1822 different tied states, each of them represented in the space of dimension 39 (13 MFCCs + 13 delta + 13 delta delta) by the mixture of 8 Gaussian distributions in our telephone dialog system. During the decoding, for an input vector o in each frame (every 10 ms it is necessary to compute), a large number of log-likelihood score (LLSs)

$$- \ln pr_j(o) = - \ln \left[\sum_{i=1}^{8} c_{ji} N(o, \mu_{ji}, \Sigma_{ji}) \right] , \tag{1}$$

where c_{ji} is the weight of the i-th component in the j-th mixture, $N(., \mu, \Sigma)$ is a multivariate Gaussian distribution with mean vector μ and covariance matrix Σ, and $j = 1, \dots, 1822$. To compute all 1822 LLSs, it entails nearly 1 million operations of multiplication, 0.5 million operations of addition, 1 thousand calculations of the exp function, and 1.5 thousand calculations of the log function.

Let us mention that in the case of simple recognition tasks with a small vocabulary, it is necessary to compute in each frame period only several tens of LLSs. This means that the labeller can be run in the "on demand" mode – the decoder asks the labeller for the computation of only several particular LLSs. In the case of more complicated tasks with middle or large vocabulary, it is necessary to compute during each frame period several hundreds (maybe all of the 1822) LLSs. To implement a real time speech recogniser with a small computation cost, it is important to reduce or simplify the large number of calculations.

We solve this problem by applying a quite new technique, which makes it possible to establish relatively exactly (in the original space of dimension 39) the first 50 or 100 best (most probable) LLSs. The proposed technique uses efficiently relevant statistical properties of the Gaussian mixture densities by combining them with the so-called "a priory hit" technique and the kNN method. This approach allows more than 90% computation cost reduction without any substantial decrease of the recognition accuracy.

3.4   Decoder Task

The decoder uses a crossword context dependent HMM state network, which is generated by a Net generator. The input of the Net generator is a text grammar format represented by an extended BNF that respects the VoiceXML description. The whole net consists of one or more connected grammars. Grammars can be connected together in run-time. A considerable part of the net is generated before the decoder starts but every part of the net can be generated on demand in run-time. The decoder uses a Viterbi search technique with an efficient beam pruning.

The decoder contains a rejection technique to reject incoming utterances that do not match any word sequence defined by the grammars. It is required that the speech recognition engine must not select any sentence from the set of sentences defined by the grammar and should inform the dialogue manager that no sentence matches the input utterance.

Furthermore, the decoder task can run in a key-phrase spotting mode too. The same Viterbi search technique is used. We must only enlarge the HMM decoding net. The recursive mumble models are added at the beginning and at the ending of the net or are put into the net in order to capture and absorb non-key-phrase parts inside the sentence.

4   Results and Conclusion

To evaluate the performance and reliability of our engine, the following experiments were provided. The 100 utterances (sentences) were randomly chosen from the telephone speech corpus [3] from an economic area. The vocabulary size of the corpus was 475 words. The first test was performed with a zerogram model. The second one used a bigram language model [2]. Both models were implemented as a static regular grammar. For evaluating the recognition results, we used two standard measures: Correctness (Co) and Accuracy (Ac) which are defined as

$$Co = (N - D - S)/N \times 100\% = H/N \times 100\%, \tag{2}$$

$$Ac = (N - D - S - I)/N \times 100\% = (H - I)/N \times 100\%, \tag{3}$$

where N is the total number of events (i.e. words) in the reference transcription, S is the number of substitution errors, D is the number of deletion errors, I is the number of insertion errors and $H = (N - D - S)$. The results of several recognition experiments are summarised in Table 1.

Table 1. Identification results

Model	Co	Ac	H	N	D	S	I
0-gram	82.13	76.87	1108	1349	79	162	71
2-gram	96.44	94.29	1301	1349	21	27	29

References

1. Müller, L., Psutka J.: The Speaker Independent Recognition Module for the Czech Telephony Dialogue System, ICSPAT '99, Orlando, USA, (1999).
2. Jelinek, F.: Statistical Methods for Speech Recognition, MIT Press, Cambridge, (1997).
3. Radová, V., Psutka J., Šmídl L., Vopálka P., Jurčíček F.: Czech Speech Corpus for Development of Speech Recognition Systems. In Proceedings of the Workshop on Developing language resources for minority languages, Athens 2000.

Combining Multi-band and Frequency-Filtering Techniques for Speech Recognition in Noisy Environments

Peter Jančovič, Ji Ming, Philip Hanna, Darryl Stewart, and Jack Smith

School of Computer Science, The Queen's University of Belfast
Belfast BT7 1NN, Northern Ireland, UK
Tel: +44 1232 274072, Fax: +44 1232 666520
p.jancovic@qub.ac.uk

Abstract. While current speech recognisers give acceptable performance in carefully controlled environments, their performance degrades rapidly when they are applied in more realistic situations. Generally, the environmental noise may be classified into two classes: the wide-band noise and narrow band noise. While the multi-band model has been shown to be capable of dealing with speech corrupted by narrow-band noise, it is ineffective for wide-band noise. In this paper, we suggest a combination of the frequency-filtering technique with the probabilistic union model in the multi-band approach. The new system has been tested on the TIDIGITS database, corrupted by white noise, noise collected from a railway station, and narrow-band noise, respectively. The results have shown that this approach is capable of dealing with noise of narrow-band or wide-band characteristics, assuming no knowledge about the noisy environment.

1 Introduction

For speech recognition, the most common feature representation of a frame is the logarithm filter-bank energy (logFBE). However, this parameterisation is highly correlated, what does not fit the assumptions in Hidden Markov Models (HMM) using diagonal covariance matrices. Thus, a linear transformation is needed to decrease the correlation. In the full-band approach, usually, the Discrete Cosine Transform (DCT) is applied to the frequency dimension over the entire logFBE feature vector, leading to the cepstral representation. However, in the case of narrow-band noise, which affects only some local frequency regions, this transformation will cause the noise to be spread across all the feature components. This is not desirable. In order to avoid this spreading, the entire logFBE feature vector can be split into several sub-vectors, each representing the feature of a sub-band and subsequently, by applying individual DCT within each sub-vector the correlation can be decreased. This is the typical parameterisation used in the multi-band approach.

Recently, an alternative way to de-correlate the logFBE features has been studied in [4,5]. In this method filtering is applied to the frequency dimension of each logFBE feature vector. When this method is used in the full-band approach, this yields better

P. Sojka, I. Kopeček, and K. Pala (Eds.): TSD 2000, LNAI 1902, pp. 265–270, 2000.

results than using the DCT technique for wide-band noisy speech recognition. Another advantage of the frequency filtering technique is that it usually employs FIR filters of a length of 2 or 3 samples. This means that after performing frequency filtering (FF) a narrow-band noise will not be spread over entire feature vector as was usually encountered in the DCT approach.

In this paper, we investigate the employment of the feature vectors obtained after FF in a multi-band speech recognition system. For the combination of sub-bands the probabilistic union model was used [3]. The paper is organised as follows: in the next section, the frequency filtering technique and its employment in the multi-band approach is described. In Section 3, the probabilistic union model is explained and the results of the experiments are shown in Section 4.

2   Frequency Filtering Parameterisation Employed in Multi-band Approach

The frequency filtering technique, studied in [4,5], was defined as a filtering operation performed on the frequency dimension of a logFBE feature vector. It can be seen as a liftering operation of cepstral parameters, but performed in the spectral domain. The frequency filters are designed to equalise the variance of the cepstral coefficients. In this work, we use the FIR frequency filter proposed in [4], which has a transfer function given bellow

$$H(z) = z - z^{-1} \tag{1}$$

The frequency characteristic of this filter is depicted in Figure 1, which shows that this filter corresponds to an emphasising of the cepstral coefficients with the middle indices.

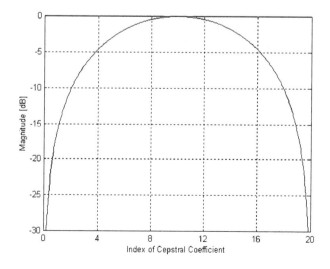

Fig. 1. Frequency characteristic of filter (1)

As the impulse response of (1) is $h(k) = \{1, 0, -1\}$, the filtering operation consists of a subtraction of the two logFBEs of the bands adjacent to the current one. This means that if the speech signal is corrupted by narrow-band noise that affects i components of the logFBE vector, after performing the frequency filtering only $i + 2$ components of the vector will be affected. Because of such a small spread effect of the noise this filtering approach is particularly suitable for being used in the multi-band system. Each feature vector is split into several sub-vectors – each corresponding to a specific sub-band.

3 Probabilistic Union Model

In the multi-band approach an important problem is to find an optimal strategy for combining the sub-bands. One possible way to solve this problem was recently introduced in [3], i.e. the probabilistic union model, where the sub-band combination is base on the union of random events.

If we assume a system with N sub-band feature streams $o = (o_1, o_2, \dots, o_N)$, where o_n represents the feature stream from the n'th sub-band, in traditional HMM the overall likelihood is computed using the "and" operator (i.e. as product) of the individual likelihoods:

$$p(o) = p(o_1 \wedge o_2 \wedge \cdots \wedge o_N) = p(o_1) \cdot p(o_2) \cdots p(o_N) \qquad (2)$$

When some sub-bands are corrupted by noise, applying "and" operator may destroy the ability of the model to discriminate between correct and incorrect word classes. We can alternatively assume that, in a given feature streams $o = (o_1, o_2, \dots, o_N)$, the useful features that characterise the speech utterance may be any of the o_n's, $n = 1, \dots, N$. This can be expressed, based on the disjunction (i.e. inclusive "or") operator $\vee$, as

$$o_\vee = o_1 \vee o_2 \vee \cdots \vee o_N \qquad (3)$$

where $o_\vee$ is a combined observation based on $\vee$. In [3] a disadvantage of (3) was observed, i.e. it effectively averages the ability to discriminate between correct and incorrect words. Thus, a combination of the "and", "or" operators between the sub-bands has been suggested.

Specifically, if the noise occupies M-bands (M<N), then there exist (N-M) bands of clean speech. These can be combined with the "and" operator to accumulate their discriminative information. The "or" operator is taken over all possible (N-M) out of N combinations and we obtain a model

$$o_\vee = \bigvee_{n_1 n_2 \cdots n_{N-M}} (o_{n_1} \wedge o_{n_2} \wedge \cdots \wedge o_{n_{N-M}}) \qquad (4)$$

which is called the Union Model with order M. Implementing the union model in a conventional HMM means only a modification in the calculation of the observation probability during the decoding stage. This can be approximated as [3]

$$p(o|\lambda) = p(o_\vee|\lambda) = \sum_{\forall (n_1 n_2 \cdots n_{N-M})} p(o_{n_1}) \cdot p(o_{n_2}) \cdots p(o_{n_{N-M}}) \qquad (5)$$

A union model with $order = 0$ and $order = N - 1$ corresponds to the product and sum combination of the sub-bands, respectively. Moreover, it is important to note that in the particular case of frequency filtered parameterisation $order = 0$ means de facto the full-band approach.

4   Experiments

The above described frequency filtering technique has been combined with the probabilistic union model in the multi-band approach. The experiments have been carried out using TIDIGITS speaker-independent database consisting of 11 words ('one', 'two', ... , 'nine', 'oh', 'zero'). The models were trained on clean speech and applied to both clean and noisy speech recognition.

In the front-end preemphasis was used and the input signal was divided into 30 ms long, Hamming windowed frames obtained every 10 ms. For comparison, the experiments were carried out with the frequency filtered (FF) parameterisation as well as the typical multi-band parameterisation (defined below) and the full-band (FB) parameterisation. In the case of full-band and the FF, a filter-bank analysis with 20 Mel-scaled filters was used to achieve logFBE feature vector for each frame. In the full-band parameterisation, DCT was applied on this vector to achieve mfcc-parameters (the c_0 was excluded). In the case of FF, the logFBE feature vector was frequency filtered by using the filter defined in (1) and split into 5 sub-vectors corresponding to 5 sub-bands, each of a length of 4 components. This constitutes 5 streams. For the typical multi-band approach a filter bank analysis with 35 Mel-scaled filters was used; the logFBE vector was divided into 5 sub-bands (each consisting of 7 components); within each sub-band, the DCT was performed and the first 4 DCT coefficients composed the sub-band feature vector. We again have 5 streams. In order to include dynamic spectral information, delta parameters were computed in both cases and formed the next 5 streams. The probabilities of these 10 streams were merged at the frame level using the probabilistic union model. In the full-band approach the delta parameters was simply added to the static parameters. A 12-state HMM is estimated for each word, with the first and the last states being tied among all the vocabulary words to account for the silence part of the utterances.

Firstly, tests were performed for clean speech recognition. Based on (4), for each model with N sub-bands, recognition can be performed with different model orders (i.e. M) from 0 to $N - 1$. Table 1 presents the recognition results obtained by using the typical multi-band and the frequency filtered parameterisation for clean speech. If the order in union model is low the typical approach achieves slightly better results. However, a very interesting point is the robustness of these two approaches to the order of the union model. For the typical approach as the order increases the recognition score decreases, and for $order = 6$ and higher the performance degradation is rapid. On contrary, the FF approach shows a very robust performance towards the order variation and keeps the rate around 97%.

Next, experiments in the presence of stationary narrow-band noise and wide-band noise were conducted. The narrow-band noise, added to the speech, is generated by passing the Gaussian white noise through a band-pass filter. We fix the bandwidth of the noise at 100 Hz and vary the central frequency of the noise. For wide-band

Table 1. Recognition results of the multi-band system for clean TIDIGITs achieved by the FF and the typical multi-band approach

Multi-band method	Order of Union Model									
	0	1	2	3	4	5	6	7	8	9
FF	98.4	97.6	97.4	97.2	97.2	97.0	96.9	97.0	97.1	97.1
Typical	99.2	99.4	99.4	99.3	99.0	98.6	96.7	92.7	82.7	65.8
Full-band (FB): static+delta / delta	98.0 / 95.4									

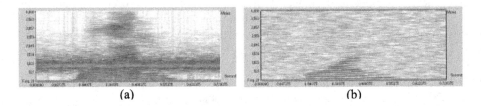

(a)   (b)

Fig. 2. Spectrograms of an utterance, "one", corrupted by stationary narrow-band noise with central frequency at 900 Hz (a), and white noise (b)

noise corruption, white, railway station and pub noises were added to the clean speech utterances, respectively. Figure 2 shows an example of the noisy speech.

The recognition results for wide-band noise and narrow-band noise are presented in Table 2 and Table 3, respectively. From Table 2 it can be seen that in the case of wide-band noise, the FF approach achieved in all cases the best results for $order = 0$ and highly outperformed the typical multi-band parameterisation. Results in Table 3 show that both approaches achieved similar results for narrow-band noise corruption and the high order robustness with the FF approach is observed.

Table 2. Recognition results of the multi-band system in wide-band noise (SNR=10dB) for the FF approach / the typical multi-band approach

Order of Union Model	White	Railway station	Pub
0	76.2 / 12.4	93.3 / 45.7	71.1 / 38.5
1	55.7 / 15.3	88.0 / 44.0	57.3 / 40.4
2	50.7 / 20.7	85.4 / 32.8	58.6 / 41.8
3	47.1 / 18.8	82.6 / 22.5	55.1 / 37.0
4	44.7 / 18.4	81.2 / 19.5	54.5 / 30.6
5	43.5 / 37.9	79.3 / 74.3	53.6 / 67.1
6	42.7 / 23.6	78.2 / 59.4	53.1 / 57.9
FB: static+delta / delta	33.2 / 64.8	91.8 / 83.9	59.4 / 72.9

Table 3. Recognition results of the multi-band system in stationary narrow-band noise (SNR=0dB) for the FF approach / the typical multi-band approach

Order of Union Model	Noise central frequency (Hz)			
	900	1200	1800	2400
0	9.1 / 22.2	9.5 / 21.6	16.1 / 35.5	9.7 / 23.2
1	9.2 / 53.6	11.2 / 63.1	36.7 / 45.6	26.8 / 22.2
2	52.5 / 73.1	45.8 / 64.4	79.4 / 42.5	88.7 / 54.2
3	85.3 / 78.9	88.9 / 69.7	83.5 / 44.5	89.7 / 50.9
4	84.4 / 84.8	86.9 / 78.2	85.7 / 56.7	89.9 / 57.2
5	84.0 / 84.9	85.2 / 86.4	85.2 / 85.3	90.7 / 85.0
6	84.0 / 74.7	84.4 / 75.5	85.0 / 72.3	90.7 / 73.2
7	83.7 / 61.4	83.7 / 60.7	84.9 / 57.6	90.0 / 59.8
8	83.5 / 41.3	83.6 / 40.3	84.6 / 36.7	90.0 / 39.5
9	82.9 / 19.0	83.5 / 20.0	84.5 / 19.1	90.0 / 21.0
FB: static+delta / delta	16.0 / 79.7	15.3 / 81.9	16.5 / 78.0	18.3 / 81.9

5   Summary

An employment of frequency filtering parameterisation and the probabilistic union model in a multi-band approach has been described in this paper. As a consequence of the properties of the frequency filtering (FF) and the union model, this technique has a considerable potential to cope with additive noise with no knowledge about the noise characteristics (e.g. bandwidth). The experiments with FF parameterisation have shown similar results as typical multi-band parameterisation in narrow-band noise corruption, and the results for wide-band noisy speech have shown a significant improvement. Moreover, high robustness on the order of the union model was observed for the FF approach. However, for various noise environments the best order of the union model can differ. This will be explored in the future.

This work was supported by UK EPSRC grant GR/M93734.

References

1. Tibrewala, S., Hermansky, H., *Sub-band Based Recognition of Noisy Speech*, Proc. ICASSP '97, Munich, Germany, 1997, pp. 1255–1258.
2. Bourlard, H., *Non-Stationary Multi-Channel (Multi-Stream) Processing Towards Robust and Adaptive ASR*, Proceedings of Robust Methods for Speech Recognition in Adverse Conditions, Tampere, Finland, 1999, pp. 1–10.
3. Ming, J., Smith, J., *Union: A New Approach for Combining Sub-band Observations for Noisy Speech Recognition*, Proceedings of Robust Methods for Speech Recognition in Adverse Conditions, Tampere, Finland, 1999, pp. 175–178.
4. Nadeu, C., Hernando, J., Gorricho, M., *On the Decorrelation of the Filter-Bank Energies in Speech Recognition*, Proc. Eurospeech '95, pp. 1381–1384.
5. Macho, D., Nadeu, C.: *On the Interaction between Time and Frequency Filtering of Speech Parameters for Robust Speech Recognition*, Proc. ICSLP '98, pp. 1487–1490.

Allophone- and Suballophone-Based Speech Synthesis System for Russian

Pavel Skrelin

Department of Phonetics, St. Petersburg State University
Universitetskaya nab. 11, Saint-Petersburg, Russia
paul@phonet.lang.pu.ru

Abstract. The speech synthesis system developed at the Department of Phonetics of St. Petersburg University combines the advantages of two methods of concatenative speech synthesis – diphone- and allophone- based ones. In a new synthesis, we use physical realizations of allophones for the formation of the consonant inventory. The physical realizations of allophones are chosen with regard to their right phonetic context. In formation of the vowel set, we used the method which combines allophone and diphone based synthesis principles: the database contains halves of vowel allophones (from the physical beginning of the allophone up to its middle and from the middle of the allophone up to its right physical boundary).

1   Introduction

The diphone-based system developed at the Department of Phonetics uses about 3000 units, the allophone-based system uses about 3300 physical realizations of allophones, but this quantity can be reduced by 30% without affecting the quality of the synthesised speech [3,4]. The formation of sound units inventory requires considerable time and effort for speaker recording and material segmentation. This makes the introduction of new speakers' voices into the system very problematic, as this procedure is also labourious and time-consuming. The reduction of the number of basic units makes it possible to reduce time and effort in including new voices into the synthesis system. The inventory of sound units in the newly developed speech synthesis system, which combines principles of allophone- and diphone- based systems, does not exceed 800; thus the time required for the formation of the database is reduced 4 times.

2   Principles of Sound Unit Set Formation

A new speech synthesis system for Russian is based on allophone synthesis principles, e.g. on the using sound units, corresponding to the realizations of allophones in their natural physical limits. The difference of this system from the one developed earlier [3] consists in the following: in the process of the sound stream formation vowel allophones are constructed from vowel halves. The physical boundaries of vowel-halves (half-diphones or half-allophones) are chosen in such a way as to minimise spectral smoothing

P. Sojka, I. Kopeček, and K. Pala (Eds.): TSD 2000, LNAI 1902, pp. 271–276, 2000.

at the junction of formants and harmonics. Ideally the boundaries between vowel-halves are put in the middle of the vowel stationary part.

Thus, the inventory of sound units for speech synthesis includes:

1. Consonant allophones in their physical boundaries. For voiced consonants, 3 allophones for each phoneme are required depending on the characteristics of the right context (before an unrounded vowel, before a rounded vowel, before a consonant). For voiceless consonants, 5 allophones for each phoneme are required, depending on the characteristics of the right context (before an unrounded vowel, before a rounded vowel, before a voiceless consonant, a sonant and a pause). Sonants require 5 allophones each also depending on the properties of the right context (before an unrounded or a rounded vowel, before a voiced, voiceless consonant or a sonant, and before a pause). 11 allophones are required for /r/, considering its articulatory and acoustical properties and depending on its left and right phonetic contexts (between vowels, after a vowel before a voiceless consonant, after a vowel before a voiced consonant or a sonant, after a vowel before a pause, after a pause before a vowel, after a pause before a voiceless consonant, after a pause before a voiced consonant or a sonant, after a consonant before a vowel, after a consonant before a voiceless consonant, after a consonant before a voiced consonant or a sonant, after a consonant before a pause). It should be noted that for sonants, a sound unit corresponding to the realization of an allophone often performs a purely symbolic function, as its physical beginning may form part of the vowel allophone preceding it, while its end may be included in the vowel allophone following it [4].
2. Left vowel halves, which preserve physical characteristics determined by the left context. For the list of left contexts taken into account see [4].
3. Right vowel halves which preserve physical characteristics determined by the right context. Compared to the list of right contexts described in [4], the vowels before /r/ are added to the set.

At present the system uses 173 consonant allophones and 576 halves of vowel allophones. This number can be increased if we include fragments of theoretically possible, but exceptionally rare vowel allophones (for example, unstressed /o/) or consonants. Thus the whole number of sound units for synthesis will not exceed 800. It should be stated that the synthesis principle employed in the new system can be called allophonic only conventionally, as the structure of the sound units used is more complicated: some vowel allophones (and, consequently, their halves) include fragments of the preceding and following consonants; the beginning or end of the consonant allophone can be included in the vowel allophones; some of such consonants can be present in the database for the principle of the synthetic sound stream formation to be supported. For example, a post-stressed [j] is a 2 bytes signal of zero amplitude.

3   Vowel Segmentation

The quality (naturalness) of sound of the constructed allophone depends on how accurately the boundaries between vowel halves are determined. In order to facilitate manual segmentation a procedure of mounting a signal on the bases of two fragments was included into EDS for Windows ver. 1.032 (a program for digital treatment of speech signals developed at St.-Petersburg State University of Telecommunication). This procedure allows the audio control of the mounting process and visual control of acoustic properties in the junction of two parts of the constructed signal in time and frequency domains. The segmentation process consists of three steps. The aim of the first step is to determine the physical beginning of second (right) vowel halves: for one (left) half-vowel taken from the most neutral left context (for example, after bilabials for rounded vowels or after velars for /a/), all second (right) halves are chosen (acoustic properties of right halves depend on the right context). The boundary place is chosen in such a way that physical positions of formants and harmonics were similar and corresponding to formant and harmonic values at the end of the used left half-vowel. Similarly, at the second step for one right half-vowel taken from the most neutral right context all left half-vowels are chosen. At the third step the remaining boundaries (between allophones) are determined. Segmentation made, the program allows listening to all variants of constructed vowel allophones. This procedure is used for determination of boundaries between vowels.

After segmentation the resulting vowel halves are normalised in amplitude and pitch is labelled. Pitch labelling is automatic, but the possibility of manual correction of inaccurately determined boundaries between Fo periods is provided. In the process of half-vowel set formation for speech synthesis we obtained an important theoretical and practical results. We found that the position of a stationary part of the vowel [e] doesn't depend on softness of the left context. It means that the set of all necessary allophones can be formed with right vowel halves taken from vowels in hard left context only. These vowel halves can be used for constructing vowel allophones both in hard left context and in soft left context. A similar situation is found for the right vowel halves of [u], but their usage is restricted to unstressed vowels. It should be noted, that in diphone set formation for diphone synthesis system we have used two basic allophones for each vowel (in stressed and unstressed positions): one taken from the soft left context, the other taken from hard left context [1].

4   Modification of Physical Parameters of Allophones

4.1   Spectral Smoothing in Allophone Forming

A possible lack of coordination in formants and harmonics positions at the junction of vowel halves in allophone formation requires the use of a special procedure of spectral parameters smoothing at the boundaries of vowel halves. The application of traditional spectral smoothing algorithms can result in distortion of individual characteristics of speaker's voice and in lowering of the naturalness of synthesised speech [4]. We tried to avoid it by maximally precise choice of vowel halves from the point of view of spectral parameters at their boundaries. As a result, the effect of spectral smoothing is minimal and does not cause changes of individual characteristics of the speaker's voice. What is more, when the smoothing mode is off, it does not lead to perceptible change of the synthetic voice quality. This fact demonstrates a high quality of the segmentation made. However, as the possibility of difference in formants and harmonics positions at the half-vowels junctions exists, the necessity for smoothing remains. This procedure can become more required when using automatic means of sub-allophones extraction.

For spectral smoothing, the procedure of audiomorphing [6] is used, but in calculations of initial and target spectra we use FFT instead of LPC which results in better sound quality. Some distortions in generated F0 periods are prevented by Hanning window treatment in time domain. This procedure is working in real-time mode.

4.2   Modification of Fundamental Frequency

In developing new speech synthesis system, we decided not to use traditional F0 modification means in time domain. The new algorithm of F0 modification consists of three steps.

1. Pitch-synchronous spectra of initial signal are calculated. Then for each F0 period a signal presenting the sum of n F0 harmonics is generated (harmonics amplitudes is calculated on the initial spectrum basis). After that a new signal is pitch-synchronously subtracted from the initial one. This procedure results in residual signal without the initial F0 and harmonics.
2. A new signal is generated on the basis of calculated synthetic background: it presents the sum of n harmonics of target F0. Amplitude values are calculated on the basis of spectra obtained in the first step.
3. Synthetic background is added to residual signal weighed in time domain.

To obtain a real-time mode operation of this algorithm, a part of calculations is implemented beforehand and the calculated results are saved in a special database. Some data can be manually modified if necessary. Probably in the future by modification of this data values, the individual characteristics of a speaker's voice could be modified in the required direction. On the other hand, as the database contains the generalised data on formants and harmonics positions in allophones this information can be used for speech recognition tasks (knowledge-based, of course).

4.3   Duration Modification and Amplitude Smoothing

The allophone duration is done in the same mode as in our previous system [3]. After all kinds of signal treatment, the amplitude smoothing at the boundaries of physical realizations of allophones is performed. To obtain it, the amplitude of the last n F0 periods of an allophone is gradually driven to the amplitude value of the first F0 period of the following allophone. As a basis for calculations of the energy of the first F0 period of the following allophone and n F0 periods, energy values of preceding allophones are linearly interpolated to that value. Naturally if the allophone is followed by a pause or a voiceless plosive, its amplitude is gradually driven to zero. This procedure is used only for vowels, voiced consonants and sonants, and it is working in real-time mode.

5   Text Processing

Text processing means (stress marking, grapheme-to-phoneme conversion, intonation transcription etc.) were developed for our allophone-based speech synthesis system [5].

However, in the last four years these means were improved to a great extent: the lexicon content was modernised and its volume optimised, the deepness of context analysis was increased, new pre-processing means were developed. For the time being, the lexicon contains about 110 000 lexems giving more than 2 400 000 word-forms, about 800 000 of this quantity are proper names forms.

The lexicon structure was modified, too. For fulfilling some tasks of the project "Segmentation of Continuous Speech as a Model of Language System Levels Interaction" (RFBR grant 98-06-80431), the transcription variants of some word-forms were introduced in the dictionary in addition to quasi-transcription of word-forms, the pronunciation of which requires special rules. These transcription variants reflect more frequent deviations form the pronunciation standard. Such supplement allows modelling of non-standard, but widespread, pronunciation of frequent lexems. The use of the adaptive transcriber for grapheme-to-phoneme conversion [2] makes it possible to obtain the same result without adding special pronunciation variants to the dictionary. However, the automatic transcription cannot be limited to certain word-forms, as in this case all the word-forms in the text will obtain non-standard characteristics. On the other hand, the adaptive transcriber can easily provide different pronunciation variants to all lexemes in the dictionary; it allows the use of such dictionary for speech recognition tasks.

6   Conclusion

The described speech synthesis system for Russian showed good characteristics of intelligibility of synthesised speech and a higher level of its naturalness compared to the previous allophone-based system. Naturally this higher level of naturalness is due not to the new technology of allophone construction from two vowel halves, but to new methods of artificial modification of physical parameters of the sound stream. A much smaller number of sound units required for speech synthesis facilitates to a great extent the task of forming a basic set of sound units when new voices are added to the synthesis system. New methods of manipulation of spectral parameters of allophones now used for fundamental frequency modification can be used for obtaining new voices on the bases of one sound units set by artificial creation of the required characteristics in the spectra of sound units.

A new dictionary containing standard and different non-standard pronunciation variants of word-forms together with the database of formants and harmonics positions in the allophones set can be used in knowledge-based speech recognition systems.

References

1. Bondarko L.V., Kuznetsov V.I., Skrelin P.A. (1997) Zvukovaja sistema russkogo jazyka v svete zadach kompil'ativnogo sinteza. In: Bulleten' foneticheskogo fonda russkogo jazyka, N 6, St-Petersburg-Bochum, 60–84.
2. Shalonova K. (1997) Flexible Transcriber for Russian Continuous Speech. In: Proc. of SPECOM'97. Cluj-Napoca, 171–174.
3. Skrelin P. (1999) Allophone-Based Concatenative Speech Synthesis System for Russian. In: Proc. of the TSD '99 (Plzen), LNCS 1692, 156–159.

4. Skrelin P. (1997) Concatenative Russian Speech Synthesis: Sound Database Formation Principles. In: Proc. of the SPECOM '97, Cluj-Napoka, 157–160.
5. Skrelin P. (1996) The Linguistic Software of the Concatenation Synthesis Systems for Russian Speech. In: Proc. of the SPECOM '96, St.-Petersburg, 165–166.
6. Slaney M., Covell M., Lassiter B. (1996) Automatic Audio Morphing. In: Proc. of the 1996 International Conference on Acoustics, Speech and Signal Processing, Atlanta.

Diphone-Based Unit Selection
for Catalan Text-to-Speech Synthesis

Roger Guaus i Térmens and Ignasi Iriondo Sanz

Secció de Tecnologies de la Parla, Dept. de Comunicacions i Teoria del Senyal
Enginyeria Arquitectura La Salle, Universitat Ramon Llull
Pg. Bonanova 8, 08026 Barcelona, Catalunya
rguaus@salleURL.edu, iriondo@salleURL.edu
http://www.salleURL.edu

Abstract. This paper describes a Unit Selection system based on diphones that was developed by the Speech Technology Group of the Enginyeria Arquitectura La Salle School, Universitat Ramon Llull. This system works with a PSOLA synthesiser for Catalan language which is used in an Oral Synthesised Message Editor (EMOVS) and Windows applications developed using Microsoft SAPI. Some common questions about Unit Selection are formulated in order to find solutions and achieve a better segmental speech quality.

1   Introduction

Latest investigations in our Speech Technology Group have been focussed in Catalan language text-to-speech conversion based on unit concatenation (i.e. diphones and triphones).

Catalan is the native language of Catalonia, the Valencian Country and the Balearic Islands (central east and north east part of the Iberian Peninsula), which is spoken by more than 6 million people. Nevertheless, these are bilingual areas where Spanish is also spoken, and, in fact, it is the dominant language for communication (news, TV, radio, ...) in the region. Thus Catalan is a minority language under Spanish influence. Like other languages, Catalan has several varieties (Central, North-occidental, Valencian, Balearic and others) that are spoken in different areas of the territory. We have focussed our studies in the Central variety which is spoken near the city of Barcelona.

1.1   Previous Studies

Unit concatenation has been the focus of our work during the last years. It is well known that the segmental quality of synthetic speech is limited by the number of joins that can be encountered in an utterance. In order to resolve these join mismatches and to improve the segmental quality of the speech, different systems based on different ways of coupling diphones were developed, [1,2,3]. The synthetic speech obtained with these systems had good intelligibility but it was not natural enough to be used in most applications (e.g. broadcast news, ...). Some experiences based on phone unit selection [4,5,6] were

P. Sojka, I. Kopeček, and K. Pala (Eds.): TSD 2000, LNAI 1902, pp. 277–282, 2000.

developed to improve the generated speech quality but since poor quality was achieved, new systems based on half phone unit selection [7] came into consideration.

We propose an approach for adapting a text-to-speech system based on diphone and triphone concatenation architecture (using a Catalan pre-designed database) to a unit selection structure. Therefore, there is a basic difference between a traditional diphone- (i.e. half-phone-) based traditional system of unit selection [7] and ours: we chose to use diphones and triphones as basic units, as opposed to half phones (or half diphones).

2   Unit Selection Based on Diphones

While a phone-based unit selection system has about 37 basic units for Catalan language, a unit selection system based on diphones has to consider all possible combinations among phones (i.e. more than 1200 units[1]).

Since the basic units in the present method are diphones and triphones, this approach will provide, at least, the same speech quality than a diphone- and triphone-based synthesis system (without using unit selection). To increase the segmental quality of the generated speech using unit selection, more units have to be added to the basic corpus. Thus, a unit selection database for diphones has to be divided into two halves. The first half contains only one version of each unit and it has to be designed for each language. The second half is created by adding a large set of texts. Different versions of the units described in the first half of the database are extracted from these texts.

2.1   The Designed Part of the Database

This half of the database is specially designed for Catalan language and it consists of 895 diphones and 312 triphones (1207 units on the whole). This total amount of units ensures all possible combinations of phones and they are enough to create any utterance in Catalan.

Since not all the possible combinations among phones are allowed (i.e. aleatory combinations), the phonetic transcription module should only generate pairs included on these 1207 units. Other non-pronounceable combinations are not allowed. This is not a hard objective in Catalan, since a phonetic transcription module can be implemented with a limited set of rules and a few exceptions (Catalan phonetic transcription is more difficult than Spanish but easier than English). Notice that phone-based and half-phone- based systems permit all possible combinations between phones because the phone pairs are not defined. This could generate combinations among phones that could not be actually pronounced.

This already-designed database is the same one used for a simple diphone concatenation system (without using unit selection) previously developed for Catalan and described in [3].

2.2   Non-designed Part of the Database

This half of the database is generated by means of a large set of non-designed texts in order to ensure the availability of different versions of each unit defined in the first part of

---

[1] Let us mention 'units' as a synonymous of 'diphones and triphones'.

the database. Therefore, in order to generate this half of the database, the system searches the units described in the first part and includes the new version on the non-designed database. Usually, different versions of a unit are characterised by the prosody (pitch, duration, energy, etc.) and the articulation context.

An important difference between this system and a phone-based one is that, in the former, mid-phone joins are allowed, while in the latter only boundary joins were permitted.

3   Database Evaluation: Super-unit Mean Length Parameter

Some questions usually arise when unit selection systems have to be designed: How do units interact in a unit selection database [8]? How does speech quality improve in front of database size increase? How large the database has to be? How does the database style influence the segmental speech quality?

In order to answer these questions, we have defined a new parameter to estimate the segmental quality of the speech. Let L_{su} (Super-Unit Length) be the number of units consecutively chosen from the database to generate a synthesised utterance. These consecutively chosen units constitute a super-unit. Then, a super-unit contains at least one unit.

The segmental quality of the speech is directly related to the mean length of the chosen super-units. Thus, let us define $\bar{L}_{su}$ (Mean Super-Unit Length) as

$$\bar{L}_{su} = \frac{1}{N_{su}} \sum_{i=1}^{N_{su}} L_{su}(i) = \frac{N_u}{N_{su}} \tag{1}$$

where N_u is the number of units and N_{su} is the number of super-units, both in the generated utterance.

Let us generate the Catalan utterance 'Un hivern plàcid' ('A quiet winter'). Table 1 shows the units and super-units that are chosen by the system[2]:

Table 1. Unit selection example for a Catalan utterance

Text	*Un hivern plàcid*
Transcription	[uniBERmplasit]
Units	[un] [ni] [iB] [BE] [ERm] [mp] [pla] [as] [si] [it]
Super-units	[un] [niBERm] [mp] [plas] [sit]

To generate the desired phrase, ten units are selected from the already-designed half of the database. Then the unit selection process searches in the non-designed database the longest units that match with the input transcription. In this case, five super-units are

---

[2] SAMPA notation is used.

found in the process output. It can be easily seen that, for example, $L_{su}([niBERm]) = 4$ (this super-unit is composed by 4 units). If we apply equation (1), it can be seen that, in this case, $\bar{L}_{su} = 2$.

$\bar{L}_{su}$ increases when super-units are longer (and then the number of super-units decreases) and the super-unit length depends on different parameters such as database size, database style vs. target style correlation and database utterance mean length ($\bar{L}_{DB}$).

4   Experiment

A mixed database divided into two parts is used. The already-designed half of the database is extracted from a previous text-to-speech converter for Catalan language. This Catalan corpus consists on 1207 units (including diphones and triphones).

In order to evaluate the style influence, two different non-designed databases have been created. Politics-style and Society-style non-designed databases containing 86,000 units each have been extracted from the Catalan newspaper AVUI [9].

On the other hand, three different style test texts (politics, society and literature) have been chosen from books and newspapers to test politics-style and society-style databases. These three different texts allow us to evaluate the style influence on the database and they are large enough to ensure that the value of $\bar{L}_{su}$ for one of the databases will not change when more test text is added (i.e. to ensure reliable statistics).

For evaluating the behaviour of $\bar{L}_{su}$ in front of database size variation, the value of $\bar{L}_{su}$ has been measured using a database from 2,000 to 86,000 units in steps of 2,000 units. This process has been performed 6 times (two database styles against three test text styles). The value of $\bar{L}_{su}$ is calculated as explained before (see Section 3) using a Viterbi search algorithm.

5   Results

The results of $\bar{L}_{su}$ are obtained depending on database size. In Figure 1, it can be seen that the obtained curve works as a permanent convex growing function. Therefore, it can be said that an increase in the size of a small database is fairly more noticeable than the same increase in a larger database.

Figure 1 shows curves which are generated by checking the politics-style database against the politics-style test text and the society-style database against the society-style test text. The behaviour of $\bar{L}_{su}$ is similar in both cases.

The interaction between different test text styles and database styles is shown in Figure 2. The best result of $\bar{L}_{su}$ for the politics-style database is obtained when the politics-style test text is applied. Society-style test text has a lower result than the policy-style one. Literature-style test text has the worst result because it includes a large amount of unusual words.

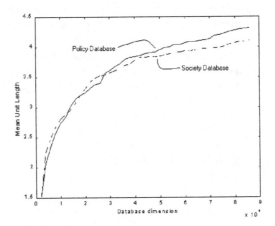

Fig. 1. Super-unit mean length vs. database dimension

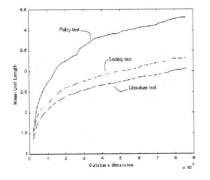
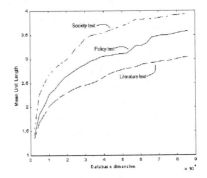

Fig. 2. Super-unit mean length database size vs. of politics-style and society-style database respectively, using three different test text styles

6   Conclusions

As it can be seen in the curves, about 45,000 units for the size of a database is an acceptable value in order to obtain a $\bar{L}_{su}$ close to 4 units per super-unit. A larger database would generate a high computation load without achieving any clear improvement.

Database style is an important parameter which determines the final value of $\bar{L}_{su}$. Notice that the difference between politics and society styles in Figure 2 is around 0.5 units per super-unit. Unlike what could be expected, when database size is increased, the influence of the style remains equally strong.

Which is the relation between $\bar{L}_{su}$ and the segmental speech quality? Since $\bar{L}_{su}$ is a mean value, generated speech can have a signal portion without transitions (consecutive units from the database) and another signal portion with unit transitions (units separated from the database). This produces quality variations, so that global quality is not uniform.

The main disadvantage of this system lies in the fact that it depends on a designed database, so that new voices are difficult to create because more than 1,200 units have to be specially recorded. However, this already-designed part of the database does not add design costs.

On the other hand, the text extracted from Catalan newspapers contains foreign words, specially from Spanish, that are transcribed as if they were Catalan although they should be pronounced in the original language. In this respect, it might be convenient to consider the use of text sources other than the mentioned ones.

We hope that all of these ideas help to achieve a high quality text-to-speech synthesiser in Catalan language.

References

1. Guaus, R., Oliver, J., Moure, H., Iriondo, I., Martí J.: Síntesis de voz por concatenación de unidades: Mejoras en la calidad segmental. Tecniacústica 98, Lisboa (1998) 123–125.
2. Guaus, R. Oliver, J., Gudayol, F., Martí, J.: Síntesis de voz utilizando difonemas: Uniones entre vocales. SEPLN 97, Madrid (1997) 234–456.
3. Guaus, R.: Implementació i millores d'un sistema de síntesi de veu d'alta qualitat utilitzant PSOLA. Projecte final de Carrera, ETSETB, Universitat Politècnica de Catalunya, Barcelona (1999).
4. Black, A.W.: Optimizing Selection of Units from Speech Databases for Concatenative Synthesis. Eurospeech '95, Madrid (1995).
5. Conkie, A.: Robust Unit Selection System for Speech Synthesis Joint Meeting of ASA, EAA and DAGA, Berlin (March 1999).
6. Beutnagel, M., Conkie, A., Schoeter, J., Stylianou, Y., Sydral, A.: The AT&T Next-Gen TTS System. Joint Meeting of ASA, EAA and DAGA, Berlin (March 1999).
7. Beutnagel, M., Conkie, A., Sydral, K.: Diphone Synthesis using Unit Selection. 3rd ESCA/COCOSDA Workshop on speech synthesis. Jenolan Caves, Austalia (November 1998).
8. Beutnagel, M., Conkie: Interaction of Units in a Unit Selection Database. EUROSPEECH '99, Budapest, Hungary (September 1999).
9. Avui Catalan newspaper URL: http://www.avui.com.

Analysis of Information in Speech
and Its Application in Speech Recognition

Sachin S. Kajarekar[1] and Hynek Hermansky[1,2]

[1] Oregon Graduate Institute of Science and Technology,
Beaverton, OR, USA.
sachin@ece.ogi.edu, hynek@ece.ogi.edu
`http://www.asp.ece.ogi.edu/index.html`
[2] International Computer Science Institute, Berkeley, CA, USA.

Abstract. Previous work analyzed the information in speech using analysis of variance (ANOVA). ANOVA assumes that sources of information (phone, speaker, and channel) are univariate gaussian. The sources of information, however, are not unimodal gaussian. Phones in speech recognition, e.g., are generally modeled using a multi-state, multi-mixture model. Therefore, this work extends ANOVA by assuming phones with 3 state, single mixture distribution and 5 state, single mixture distribution. This multi-state model was obtained by extracting variability due to position within phone from the error term in ANOVA. Further, linear discriminant analysis (LDA) is used to design discriminant features that better represent both the phone-induced variability and the position-within-phone variability. These features perform significantly better than conventional discriminant features obtained from 1-state phone model on continuous digit recognition task.

1   Introduction

Speech signal and features extracted from the signal contain various sources of information. For speech and speaker recognition, phone, speaker, and communication channel (henceforth referred as channel) are the most important sources. Previous work [2,3] analyzed information in speech using analysis of variance (ANOVA) [8]. The contribution of phone, speaker and channel was estimated in spectral and temporal domains.

As explained in Section 2, ANOVA assumes that sources have unimodal gaussian distribution[1]. Sources of information in speech, however, are more complex, e.g., phones are typically modeled using a multi-state, multi-mixture model. In this paper, therefore, we extend ANOVA to measure phone information assuming such multi-state gaussian distribution. We show that sources can be recombined into useful and harmful sources. Thus, e.g. for speaker independent automatic recognition of speech (ASR), phone information represents the useful information and all other sources contribute harmful information. This relates ANOVA to our work on discriminant features (e.g., FIR RASTA

---

[1]   Information is proportional to variance if sources have gaussian distribution [7].

P. Sojka, I. Kopeček, and K. Pala (Eds.): TSD 2000, LNAI 1902, pp. 283–288, 2000.

filters in temporal domain [1] and discriminant bases in spectral domain [5]) using linear discriminant analysis (LDA). We show that improvement in the estimate of phone information could lead to more robust features.

The paper is organized as follows. In Section 2, we give a brief overview of ANOVA and extend it for multi-state sources. This is followed by a short description of LDA. In Section 3, experimental setup is described and in Section 4, we present results of ANOVA and LDA. We conclude with summary of our work in Section 5.

2   ANOVA and LDA

2.1   ANOVA

ANOVA assumes that sources have unimodal gaussian distributions. From given data, sources are segregated as follows. First, mean and variance of each source is estimated and any observation X_{ijkl} is expressed as a linear combination of means of sources – phone (i), speaker (j), channel (k), their interactions and an error term

$$X_{ijk} = \bar{X}_{....} + \bar{X}_{i...} + \bar{X}_{.j..} + \bar{X}_{..k.} + \bar{X}_{ij..} + \bar{X}_{.jk.} + \bar{X}_{i.k.} + \bar{X}_{ijk.} + \epsilon_{ijkl}, \quad (1)$$

where $\bar{X}$ represents the mean of the source or source interaction. Then the decomposition of total information (Σ_{total}) follows from the above definition as

$$\Sigma_{total} = \Sigma_i + \Sigma_j + \Sigma_k + \Sigma_{ij} + \Sigma_{jk} + \Sigma_{ik} + \Sigma_{error}. \quad (2)$$

For speech recognition, we are interested only in the phone information. Thus, we can rewrite the above equation as

$$\Sigma_{total} = \Sigma_p + \tilde{\Sigma}_{error}$$
$$= \frac{1}{a} \sum_{i=1}^{a} (\bar{X}_{i...} - \bar{X}_{....})^2 + \frac{1}{abcd} \sum_{i=1}^{a} \sum_{j=1}^{b} \sum_{k=1}^{c} \sum_{l=1}^{d} (X_{ijkl} - \bar{X}_{i...})^2. \quad (3)$$

So far, we assumed a single-state model for phone. For multiple-state phone model, the above equation becomes

$$\Sigma_{total} = \frac{1}{aS} \sum_{i-1}^{a} \sum_{s=1}^{S} (\bar{X}_{i...}^s - \bar{X}_{....})^2 + \frac{1}{abcdS} \sum_{i-1}^{a} \sum_{j=1}^{b} \sum_{k=1}^{c} \sum_{l=1}^{d} (X_{ijkl}^s - \bar{X}_{i...}^s)^2 \quad (4)$$

where S =number of states. In the above equation, first term is rewritten as

$$\frac{1}{aS} \sum_{i=1}^{a} \sum_{s=1}^{S} (\bar{X}_{i...}^s - \bar{X}_{....})^2 = \frac{1}{aS} \sum_{i=1}^{a} \sum_{s=1}^{S} (\bar{X}_{i...}^s - \bar{X}_{i...})^2 + \frac{1}{a} \sum_{i=1}^{a} (\bar{X}_{i...} - \bar{X}_{....})^2. \quad (5)$$

This shows that the phone information (assuming a multiple state model) is the sum of the phone information with a single-state model (second term) and the average position within-phone information (first term).

2.2   LDA

Given that features represent phone classes, LDA [6] is used to select directions that represent the maximum useful (across-class, Σ_a) information while suppressing harmful (within-class, Σ_w) information. We refer to these directions as linear discriminants. For speech recognition, phone information is the useful information and other sources represent the harmful information. Therefore, $\Sigma_a = \Sigma_p$ and $\Sigma_w = \tilde{\Sigma}_{error}$. The discriminant directions (E) are obtained from these matrices as

$$E = eig(\Sigma_{error}^{-1} * \Sigma_p). \tag{6}$$

Discriminant features $(\tilde{X})$ are obtained by projecting original features (X) on discriminant directions (E), i.e., $\tilde{X} = XE$.

3   Experimental Setup

OGI Stories [4] database was analyzed with ANOVA. The database contains about 3 hours of phonetically hand-labeled conversational speech. That represents 210 speakers, speaking for about 50 sec each, through different telephone channels. A set of most frequently occurring 38 phonemes from this database was used in this study.

15 critical band spectra, calculated using 25 ms Hamming window at 100 Hz, were used as features in the spectral analysis. For the temporal analysis, each band was analyzed independently. A 101 dimensional feature vectors [1] were used which were labeled by phonemes in their center.

Discriminant were derived independently in spectral and temporal domains using features described above. Spectral discriminants were referred as spectral bases [5] and temporal discriminants were referred as FIR RASTA filters [1]. Discriminants were also derived from sequential optimization in frequency and time domains as follows. First, spectral discriminant bases were derived. The critical band spectra were projected on 8 spectral discriminants to form new 8 dimensional feature vectors. Temporal discriminants were designed separately for temporal streams of these 8 features. These temporal streams were filtered using first 3 temporal discriminants from each stream to obtain $8 * 3 = 24$ features.

The discriminant features were evaluated on the continuous-digit recognition task. Digits were modeled using 23 context independent monophone classes that were trained using 5-state, 3-mixture HMM. The baseline system used 24 features – 8 cepstral coefficients and their derivatives (Δs) and double derivatives ($\Delta\Delta$s)in time. Temporal means were removed from features in each file (cepstral mean normalization). Spectral LDA (sLDA) system used 8 spectral discriminant features + 8 Δs + 8 $\Delta\Delta$s with mean normalization. Temporal LDA (tLDA) system used 45 temporal discriminant features. For system using joint discriminants (sLDA+tLDA), it was empirically observed that temporal discriminants from first stream of spectral discriminants were less noisy than those obtained from subsequent spectral streams. We compared 1) the system with features derived using identical discriminants (derived from the first stream) for all 8 streams to 2) the system with features derived using different temporal discriminants for each stream. Significantly better performance was obtained using the system with identical discriminants. Results of such a system are reported in this paper.

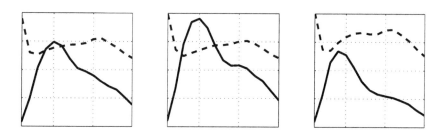

Fig. 1. Spectral Domain: The diagonal of across-class covariance (denoted by solid line) and with-class covariance (denoted by dotted-line) for 3 states. Note the higher phone information in the center state.

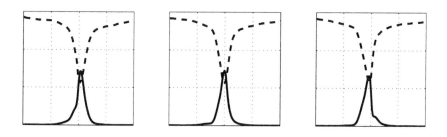

Fig. 2. Temporal Domain: The diagonal of across-class covariance (denoted by solid line) and with-class covariance (denoted by dotted-line) for 3 states. Note the anti-symmetry in the covariances for states 1 and 3.

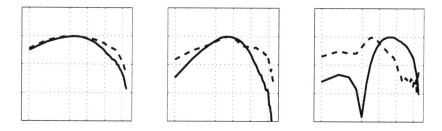

Fig. 3. Frequency response of temporal discriminants: Discriminants using 1-state phone model (demoted by dotted-line) and discriminants using 3-state phone model (denoted by solid line).

4   Results

The Σ_p and $\tilde{\Sigma}_{error}$ for 3-state phone model are shown in Figures 1 and 2 for spectral and temporal domains respectively. In spectral domain, discriminant information $(trace(\Sigma_{error}^{-1} * \Sigma_p))$ is highest in the center state. This is expected as the center state represents the most stable part of the phone. In temporal domain, covariances for states 1 and 3 are asymmetric with respect to $t = 0$ due to the fact that these state are shifted in time with respect to the center state. Using these covariances, we derived the spectral and temporal discriminants (refer to Section 2). Spectral discriminants using multi-state phone model were similar to those derived from 1-state phone model[2]. They also performed similar to discriminants derived from 1-state phone model. Temporal discriminants using multi-state phone model, however, were different from those those derived from 1-state phone model. They also performed better than discriminants from 1-state phone model. In both domains, discriminants derived from 5-state phone model were similar to discriminants derived from 3-state phone model in the structure and performance.

We further investigated sequential optimization of time-frequency domains using LDA (refer to Section 3). The recognition results using these discriminants (sLDA+tLDA) were better than baseline features (WER=6.4%), and discriminants obtained independently from spectral (sLDA) and temporal (tLDA) domains. The performance was further improved to 5.5% using discriminants derived from 3-state phone model. These improvements are significant at $\alpha = 0.05$.

5   Conclusions

In this work, we showed that results from ANOVA can be used to derive discriminant features for ASR. This was done by first grouping sources into useful and harmful sources. Then LDA was used to obtain discriminant features. In our previous work on ANOVA and LDA, the phone was assumed to have unimodal gaussian distribution. The phone model used for recognition, however, is more complex. In this paper, we improved the estimate of phone information using multi-state phone model in ANOVA. The discriminant features using this extension were found to significantly outperform both conventional features and discriminant features obtained from the 1-state phone model.

References

1. S. van Vuuren and H. Hermansky: Data-driven design of RASTA-like filters. Proc. of EUROSPEECH, Greece (1997) 409–412.
2. Sachin S. Kajarekar, N. Malayath and H. Hermansky: Analysis of Sources of Variability in Speech. Proc. of EUROSPEECH, Budapest (1999) 343–346.
3. Sachin S. Kajarekar, N. Malayath and H. Hermansky: Analysis of Speaker and Channel Variability in Speech. Proc. of ASRU, Colorado (1999).

---

[2] Interested reader can refer to [5] for a more detail discussion.

4. R. Cole and M. Noel and T. Lander: Telephone speech corpus development at CSLU. Proc. ICSLP, (1994).
5. H. Hermansky and N. Malayath: Spectral basis functions from discriminant analysis Proc. of ICSLP, Sydney, (1998).
6. K. Fukunaga: Statistical Pattern Recognition, 2nd ed., Academic Press, San Diego (1998).
7. Thomas M. Cover and Joy A. Thomas: Elements of Information Theory, John Wiley & Sons, Inc (1991).
8. Robert V. Hogg and Elliot A. Tannis: Statistical Analysis and Inference, 5th ed., Prentice Hall (1997).

What Textual Relationships Demand Phonetic Focus?
A Corpus Study of Italics in Swedish Children's Books

Sofia Gustafson-Čapková and Jennifer Spenader

Computational Linguistics, Department of Linguistics
Stockholm University, 106 91 Stockholm, Sweden
sofia@ling.su.se, jennifer@ling.su.se

Abstract. This study examines the textual relationships involved in the use of italics which is considered by the researchers to be the author's way of textually signalling what in speech would be realized with phonetic prominence. Four Swedish children's stories were studied. Each instance of italics usage was analysed. Italics usage seemed to fall into two categories, CONTRAST or EMPHASIS, and phonetic focus seems to be the most appropriate way for the author to signal this. In order to interpret the examples, it was necessary to take the beliefs of the individual characters and the common ground into consideration. The authors argue that processing some examples involved accommodating a contrast set and that this process often characterised cases of EMPHASIS.

1 Introduction

Italics is often a textual marker for words and expressions that the author intends to be processed as phonetic focus in spoken form. What relationship do italicised expressions have with their context, and how does italics affect the interpretation of the message? Are there relationships that are more dependent on prosodic correlates than others, to the degree that they are best expressed in text with italics rather than with syntactic transformations that would have had a comparable focussing effect? Is it possible to develop reliable, objective definitions of these relations so that they can be consistently identified? In order to answer these questions a corpus study if Swedish children's literature was conducted.

2 Background

Reading Swedish text aloud, it becomes clear that italicised items are given phonetic prominence. Other researchers have also pointed out this connection between italics and phonetic prominence [1]. Phonetic prominence is expressed by pitch accent, e.g. a marked change in the level of fundamental frequency (F_0) and vowel lengthening. Pitch accent placement is one device for marking the conceptual saliency of part of an intonation group and hence of the sentence [1].

Many different characterisations of conceptual saliency have been proposed. In a framework of New and Old information as described by Cruttenden [1], Old information

P. Sojka, I. Kopeček, and K. Pala (Eds.): TSD 2000, LNAI 1902, pp. 289–294, 2000.

will fall outside the focus, and therefore cannot be given pitch accent. Gundel [2] has described the same phenomenon, but in slightly different words. Semantic focus, which she categorises as New information, is said to be expressed with phonetic prominence [2].

Contrast is also a term associated with conceptual salience, though most intonationists find it difficult to give a clear definition of the concept. [1] gives an informal definition, arguing that focussing Old information gives rise to a contrastive interpretation, which in turn involves comparison within a limited set.

There is thus a connection between phonetic prominence and conceptual salience. However, the pitch accent associated with semantic focus is a property of every sentence. Italics is special in that it signals a phonetic prominence which is stronger than default pitch accent. The concepts expressed with italics could in turn be assumed to be conceptually more salient than average semantic focus.

What relations then give rise to the need to mark this strong conceptual salience in text or speech? Rooth [8] points out that varying the placement of focus gives a different interpretation to the whole message, and thus can affect the interpretation of the entire discourse. This means that, for the clarity of communication in a speech synthesis system, it is of great importance to assign phonetic prominence appropriately. One way to better understand what relations motivate extraordinary prominence is to study italicised words in context.

3   Method

All italicised expressions in four Swedish children's stories ([3,4,5,6]) were excerpted. 102 examples in all were found. Each italicised expression was analysed in context, and in relation to other examples, and an attempt was made to sort into similar usage. After working with the first text, a working definition of EMPHASIS and CONTRAST was made and applied to the other books. All texts were categorised twice by both authors with a time lapse of at least one week in order to control for consistency of classification. Before the second categorisation, the definitions were further revised.

4   Results

Various irrelevant instances of italics usage were discarded (13).[1] These examples were judged by the researchers not to mark phonetic focus in speech. This resulted in 89 examples, all contained within quoted speech, either a character speaking to himself or to others. The books contain narratives as well as dialogues, private monologues, and what could be called public monologues (e.g. the character is speaking to him- or herself but other characters are present). Throughout the books, the author only comments minimally on the characters' state-of-mind. This information is instead communicated mainly through dialogues and monologues. Additionally, the setting is described.

The examples could be categorised into two groups, CONTRAST, 46 examples, EMPHASIS, 40 examples. 3 examples seemed ambiguous and were left unclassified.

---

[1] These examples included a letter within the text, examples of shouting where the entire text was in italics and a case where italics marked waltz-timing.

CONTRAST:

There is a relationship between a concept presented earlier in the discourse and the italicised concept. The contrasted concept may be explicit or implicit.

Note that the mere existence of a possible contrastive element in the world is not sufficient. It must be present, explicitly or implicitly, in the preceding text so that it can truly be considered to have been part of the common ground of the characters in the story (to the extent that this can be ascertained from the text).

Example 1. CONTRAST-EXPLICIT [6, page 26]
SWE Är ni inte glada? *Jag* är hemskt glad och och lättad.
ENG Aren't you happy? *I* am terribly happy and relieved.

Here, the contrast is explicit ("ni" vs. "jag"), even to the extent that the two contrasted concepts are both characters involved in the current discourse, making identification easy.

Example 2. CONTRAST-IMPLICIT [5, page 68]
SWE Det måste vara sant, tänkte mumintrollet upprörd. Jag *är* släkt med honom.
ENG It must be true, thought Moomin upset. I *am* related to him.

In the several pages leading up to this line, Moomin has been reluctant to believe that he is a distant relative of a certain troll. He is presented with evidence that convinces him that he is related, and the relationship signalled by the italics is the contrast between being related and not being related. In order to understand this example we must know what beliefs Moomin holds, as revealed to the reader earlier in the story.

EMPHASIS:

Signals that the reader's (or the listening character's) attention should be focussed on the concept itself and italics (or phonetic focus) helps bring this concept to the foreground.

In the next example, Snusmumriken wants to focus Sniff's attention on the buried treasure, rather than on his sea sickness, and he does this clearly with phonetic focus.

Example 3. EMPHASIS [3, page 100]
SWE Jag kräks! skrek Sniff.
Hör du Sniff, sa Snusmumriken.
Det är mycket möjligt att det finns *sjunkna skatter* på havsbotten.
ENG "I am going to vomit!" screamed Sniff.
"Listen here Sniff", said Snusmumriken. "It is quite possible that there is *buried treasure* on the ocean bottom."

In the example below, danger is already present as a concept in the context and phonetic focus is used to direct our attention to the aspect of the degree of danger.

Example 4. EMPHASIS: [3, page 4]
SWE Hur farlig? frågade Mumintrollet.
Jag skulle närmast säga *enormt* farlig, svarade det lilla djuret Sniff allvarsamt.
ENG "How dangerous?" asked Moomin.
'I would say *enormously* dangerous", answered the little creature Sniff seriously.

5 Discussion

Developing a reliable definition for the different functions of italics is difficult, in part because the two categories seem to be at two ends of a continuum. Cases of EMPHASIS can often be seen as implicit CONTRAST. Whenever a concept is brought to the foreground, i.e. emphasised, it necessarily becomes contrasted with those discourse items not emphasised. Still, this natural effect is insufficient to be considered CONTRAST as we have defined it above. CONTRAST demands that a contrasted concept or contrast set be present in the common ground *before* the utterance containing the italicised expression occurs. A complication arises in that once a sentence with the italicised element is "spoken" by the character, the common ground of the listening participants is incremented with the information introduced by the sentence with the italicised element. Examine the italicised word with subscript 2 in the example below.

Example 5. EMPHASIS (subscript 2) [5, page 78].
SWE (Mumin:) En hemul har kommit hit ... Han tänker bo i ett snöhus och just nu *badar*$_1$ han i floden.
Aj, en *sån*$_2$ slags hemul, sa Too-ticki allvarligt.
ENG (Moomin:) "A hemul has just come here ... He's going to live in a snow house and right now he is *bathing*$_1$ in the river!"
"Oh, one of *those*$_2$ hemuls", said Too-ticki seriously.
(Lit: "A such kind hemul")

This example cannot be classified as CONTRAST according to our definition because previous to Too-ticki's statement there is nothing that invokes a contrast set having to do with different categories of hemuls. However, as soon as Too-ticki's statement is made, we understand that she believes that there are different types of hemuls. Note that from Too-ticki's perspective, her utterance is contrastive with a context set within her individual belief, but our definitions are meant to be interpreted from the point of view of an objective listener, and it therefore must be considered EMPHASIS.

To understand Too-ticki's statement Moomin needs to have a concept of different types of hemuls. We believe Moomin will accommodate this new concept, by creating a contrast set against which he can evaluate Too-ticki's statement. Accommodation as a process for discourse understanding among cooperative participants was first introduced by Lewis [7]. It involves a cooperative listener incorporating propositions or concepts necessary to understand the message of the speaker. Too-ticki's belief in the existence of different categories of hemuls is retrievable from her statement. Our definition of EMPHASIS then becomes CONTRAST without a previously introduced contrast set, or with a rather underspecified contrast set. Problem examples were often those where there was a very vague or implicit contrast set, and where whether or not accommodation took place would depend on the reader's processing strategy, or understanding of the situation. Indeed, what we understood of an utterance is surely slightly different than what the discourse participants (who in our data are fictional characters) understood, or were meant to understand.

For some examples, an analysis of EMPHASIS as accommodated CONTRAST was hard to apply. These were cases where it was difficult to pinpoint a plausible hypothetical contrast set, and the concept seems merely to have been foregrounded. Reexamine Ex. 5, looking this time at the italicised word marked with subscript 1. "Bathing" is classified as EMPHASIS but it could be considered CONTRAST with, for example, abnormal things to do in winter, abnormal things that hemul's do compared with other creatures, etc. All of these possible contrast sets are vaguely present in the preceding text, but whether or not it can be considered CONTRAST seems to depend on who interprets the utterance.

In summary, in order to correctly categorise, understand and eventually perhaps identify the textual relationships of CONTRAST and EMPHASIS we need to keep track of two things: 1) the beliefs of the individual characters, 2) those beliefs which are part of the common ground (to the extent that we can identify this by examining the text). Additionally, we must have a working definition of what types of concepts can be contrasted.

What textual relationships demand phonetic focus? The simple answer is CONTRAST and EMPHASIS. Prosody is one of the most basic ways of focussing the listener's attention. But in addition to prosody there are other lexical and syntactic means of showing CONTRAST[2] and EMPHASIS[3]; why did the author find these examples so special that she felt that forced phonetic prominence was required? One drawback of our method is that we chose only to examine examples with italics, which means we cannot say how frequent these relationships are among the other speech examples in the text. However, if CONTRAST is infrequent in the other dialogue examples, then we could conclude that cases of CONTRAST and EMPHASIS that are syntactically and lexically unmarked demand phonetic focus.

The examples studied also had a tendency to be emotionally-loaded. For example, common to most of the examples of monologues (9 private, 2 public) was the use of contrast with belief revision (in 8 of the examples), e.g. when as speaker changed his/her mind about an earlier personal belief this contrastive meaning was often marked with italics. Many of the examples also involved a speaker presenting a personal belief, or an attitude towards a concept, to the other characters; this belief was not part of the common ground. Both of these tendencies in the examples studied suggest that individual belief revision, as well as belief sharing, are special types of information introduction that need to be marked to be correctly understood, and that phonetic focus best signals this.

6   Conclusions

Italics usage seems to be a textual tool intentionally chosen by the author to force a certain interpretation by controlling the prosodic realization of the sentence in question. Examples could be divided into two categories, CONTRAST and EMPHASIS, but these were not unambiguously distinct but rather formed a continuum. Interpretation of both these categories seems to require examining the statement with a contrast set as background, and we believe understanding involves either identifying an earlier contrast set or accommodating a contrast set. Other findings included the tendency of belief revision and belief or attitude expressions to contain italics. This suggests that focussing

---

[2] E.g. "A . . . but B . . . ", or "Despite A, B", though many of these constructions also carry set prosodic patterns.

[3] E.g. topicalisation and in text through punctuation such as "!"

in these circumstances may be most naturally expressed in speech through phonetic focus, rather than by other linguistic devices.

For an application, such as speech synthesis, it is important to assign phonetic prominence to the right items, so that the listener will make the preferred interpretation. If listeners do accommodate contrast sets, overgeneration of phonetic focus could mislead the listener into accommodating a contrasting element, even in cases where contrast was not intended. This would increase processing demands on listeners and could result in misinterpretation of the message.

References

1. Cruttenden, A.: Intonation. Cambridge University Press, Cambridge, UK. (1986).
2. Gundel, J.: On Different Kinds of Focus. In: Bosch, J., and Van der Sandt, R. (Eds.): Focus and Natural Language Processing, vol. 3, Discourse. IBM Working Papers of the Institute for Logic and Linguistics, 8. (1994).
3. Jansson, T.: Kometen kommer. AWE/Gebers (1946).
4. Jansson, T.: Farlig midsommar. AWE/Gebers (1952).
5. Jansson, T.: Trollvinter. AWE/Gebers (1957).
6. Jansson, T.: Det osynliga barnet. AWE/Gebers (1962).
7. Lewis, David: Scorekeeping in a Language Game, Journal of Philosophical Logic, 8, (1979) 339–359.
8. Rooth, M.: The Handbook of Contemporary Semantic Theory. Lappin, S. (ed), Blackwell Publishers (1996).

Speaker Identification
Using Kalman Cepstral Coefficients[*]

Zdeněk Švenda and Vlasta Radová

University of West Bohemia, Department of Cybernetics,
Univerzitní 22, 306 14 Plzeň, Czech Republic
svendaz@kky.zcu.cz, radova@kky.zcu.cz

Abstract. In this paper an approach to speaker identification based on an estimation of parameters of a linear speech-production model is presented. The estimation is based on the discrete Kalman estimator. It is generally supposed that the vocal tract can be modelled by a system with constant parameters over short intervals. Taking this assumption into account, we can derive a special form of the discrete Kalman estimator for the model of speech production. The parameters of the vocal tract model obtained by the above mentioned Kalman estimation are then used to compute a new type of cepstral coefficients which we call Kalman cepstral coefficients (KCCs). These coefficients were used in text-independent speaker identification experiments based on discrete vector quantisation. Achieved results were then compared with results obtained by using the LPC-derived cepstral coefficients (LPCCs). The experiments were performed in a closed group of 591 speakers (312 male, 279 female).

1 Introduction

There are many methods for signal processing. A set of methods assumes that a combination of glottal cords, vocal tract and radiation can be modelled by a simple system with a known single all-pole transfer function which has unknown parameters. The parameters of such model have to be then estimated. For this purpose, either a very popular method of linear predictive coding [2,3] or methods based on a Kalman estimator [1] can be used. Another set of signal processing methods analyse signal in frequency domain, for example using a filterbank. In this way, energy in particular frequency band can be obtained. Mel-frequency cepstral coefficients can be derived from this energy [4].

2 Model of Speech Production

The speech waveform is an acoustic pressure wave that originates from voluntary physiological movements of anatomical structures such as the vocal cords, vocal tract,

---

[*] The work was supported by the Ministry of Education of the Czech Republic, project no. MSM235200004, and by the Grant Agency of the Czech Republic, project no. 102/96/K087.

P. Sojka, I. Kopeček, and K. Pala (Eds.): TSD 2000, LNAI 1902, pp. 295–300, 2000.

nasal cavity, tongue and lips. Human speech production can be modelled by a linear filter where the glottal cords, vocal tract, and radiation are individually modelled as linear filters [2,3]. The input of the total filter is either a quasi-periodic impulse sequence for voiced sounds or a random noise sequence for unvoiced sounds, with a gain factor G set to control the intensity of the excitation. The glottal cords can be modelled by second-order low-pass filter $G(z)$. The vocal tract model $V(z)$ can be described as all-pole model, where each pole of this model corresponds to a formant or resonance frequency of the sound. The radiation model $R(z)$ describes the air pressure at the lips and can be reasonably approximated by a first-order backward difference. Combining the glottal pulse, vocal tract, and radiation yields a single all-pole transfer function given by

$$H(z) = G(z) V(z) R(z) = \frac{G}{1 + \sum\limits_{i=1}^{Q} a_i z^{-i}} , \qquad (1)$$

where a_i are unknown parameters of model. With this transfer function, we get a difference equation for synthesising the speech samples $y(k)$ as

$$y(k) = -\sum_{i=1}^{Q} a_i y(k-i) + Gu(k) , \qquad (2)$$

where $u(k)$ is the input of the filter.

It can be noted that $y(k)$ is predicted as a linear combination of the previous Q samples. Therefore, the speech production model is often called the *linear prediction* (LP) model, or the *autoregressive model*.

3   Feature Extraction

The feature extraction can be divided into two steps. First, a set of predictors coefficients has to be obtained, and then this set has to be transformed into feature vector.

In practice, the predictor coefficients $\{a_i\}$ describing the autoregressive model must be computed from the speech signal. Since speech is a time-varying signal and the vocal-tract configuration changes over time, an accurate set of predictor coefficients is adaptively determined over short intervals (10–30 ms) called frames, during that time-invariance is assumed. The gain G is usually ignored to allow the parameterisations to be independent of the signal intensity [2,3].

3.1   Linear Predictive Coding

One of the standard methods for predictor coefficients calculation is the *autocorrelation* method. The predictor coefficients can be obtained by solving the equation

$$\boldsymbol{R}\boldsymbol{a} = \boldsymbol{r} , \qquad (3)$$

where $\boldsymbol{R}$ is Toeplitz autocorrelation matrix, $\boldsymbol{a}$ is vector of predictor coefficients, and $\boldsymbol{r}$ is a vector of autocorrelation coefficients. It is assumed that the speech samples are identically zero outside the frame of interest. A computationally efficient algorithm known as the Levinson-Durbin recursion can be used to solve this equation [3].

3.2   The Discrete Kalman Estimator

In the state, space a system can be generally described by equation system

$$x_{k+1} = A_k x_k + B_k y_k + \Gamma_k \xi_{k+1} \,,$$
$$y_{k+1} = C_k x_k + D_k y_k + \Delta_k \xi_{k+1} \,, \tag{4}$$

where x_k is an internal immeasurable part of state, y_k is an external measurable part of state, A_k, B_k, C_k and D_k are matrices describing relations among vectors x_k, y_k, x_{k+1} and y_{k+1}, the term $\Gamma_k \xi_{k+1}$ represents system errors and the term $\Delta_k \xi_{k+1}$ represents an additive noise in the observation process (ξ_{k+1} is the white noise).

In an arbitrary step k, the state of the system is not known exactly. The estimate of actual state is given by normal distributions

$$\begin{bmatrix} x_{k+1} \\ y_{k+1} \end{bmatrix} \sim N \left\{ \begin{bmatrix} \widehat{x}_{k+1} \\ \widehat{y}_{k+1} \end{bmatrix}, \begin{bmatrix} A_k P_k A_k^T + \Gamma_k \Gamma_k^T & A_k P_k C_k^T + \Gamma_k \Delta_k^T \\ C_k P_k A_k^T + \Delta_k \Gamma_k^T & C_k P_k C_k^T + \Delta_k \Delta_k^T \end{bmatrix} \right\}, \tag{5}$$

where $\widehat{x}_k$ and $\widehat{y}_k$ are the estimates of x_k and y_k in step k. On the assumption that the vector of unknown parameters x is random with known mean μ_0 and covariance P_0 and independent on the random distribution of initial state s_0, the optimal estimate of the vector of parameters μ_k can be obtained by recursive algorithm

$$K_{k+1} = \left(A_k P_k C_k^T + \Gamma_k \Delta_k^T \right) \left(C_k P_k C_k^T + \Delta_k \Delta_k^T \right)^{-1} \,,$$
$$\mu_{k+1} = A_k \mu_k + B_k y_k + K_{k+1} \left(y_{k+1} - C_k \mu_k - D_k y_k \right) \,, \tag{6}$$
$$P_{k+1} = \left(A_k P_k A_k^T + \Gamma_k \Gamma_k^T \right) - K_{k+1} \left(C_k P_k A_k^T + \Delta_k \Gamma_k^T \right) \,,$$

with initial conditions μ_0 and P_0. K_k represents so called Kalman gain, μ_k the best a posteriori estimate and P_k the covariance of estimate dependent on observation.

3.3   A Special Form of the Discrete Kalman Estimator for the Model of Speech Production

The linear model of speech production (2) is a system with time-invariant parameters over short interval (see above). It means that the transition matrix A_k is the identity over this interval and the matrices B_k and Γ_k are zero. It can be seen from (2), that matrix D_k is zero as well. Taking this assumptions into account the linear model of speech production in state representation can be described by the equation system

$$x_{k+1} = x_k = x \,,$$
$$y(k) = C(y_k) x + \Delta_k \xi_{k+1} \,, \tag{7}$$

where $x = [a_1, a_2, \dots, a_Q]^T$, $y_k = [y(k-1), y(k-2), \dots, y(k-Q)]^T$ and $C(y_k) = [-y_k]^T$. If we take into account forms of the matrices A_k, B_k, C_k, D_k and Γ_k, we can derive a special form of Kalman estimator (6) for the linear model of speech production

$$K_{k+1} = -P_k y_k \left(y_k^T P_k y_k + \Delta_k^2 \right)^{-1} \,,$$
$$\mu_{k+1} = \left(I + K_{k+1} y_k^T \right) \mu_k + K_{k+1} y(k+1) \,, \tag{8}$$
$$P_{k+1} = \left(I + K_{k+1} y_k^T \right) P_k \,,$$

where I represents the identical matrix.

3.4   Cepstrum

In many speaker identification applications, the predictor coefficients are transformed into feature vectors consisting of so-called *LPC-derived cepstral coefficients* (LPCCs). A recursive relation between the LPC-derived cepstral coefficients and the predictor coefficients is given as [2,3]

$$c\left(k\right) = -a_k - \sum_{i=1}^{k-1}\left(\frac{i}{k}\right)c\left(i\right)a_{k-i}\ . \tag{9}$$

We used this formula for computation of so-called *Kalman cepstral coefficients* (KCCs) from the predictor coefficients produced by the Kalman estimator (described in Section 3.2).

4   Experiments

All experiments described in this section were performed following this initial condition: $P_0 = 5\,000\,000\,I$ (I is the identical matrix) and $\mu_0 = [0,\dots,0]^T$.

4.1   Reconstructed Spectrum

The predictor coefficients $\{a_i\}$ allows the computation of the signal spectrum. Using the substitution $z = e^{j\omega}$ in transfer function (1), we obtain $|H\left(j\omega\right)|$ that represents the spectral envelope of the speech. In Figure 1, the reconstructed spectra (dashed line), the predictor coefficients $\{a_i\}$ were estimated by the algorithm (8), and spectra evaluated by Fourier transformation (solid line) are compared.

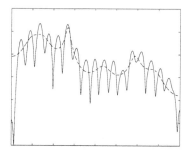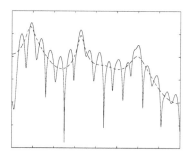

Fig. 1. Spectrum of the vowel a (left) and e (right) spoken by a female speaker

4.2   Speaker Identification

Database. The database consisted of speech signal obtained from 591 speakers (312 male, 279 female). Every speaker spoke a different set of short Czech sentences and isolated words during one session. The speech signal was transferred through a telephone channel, sampled at the 8 kHz sampling rate and stored in a μ-law 8 bit format. Before further processing, the 8 bit μ-law digitalised samples were finally converted to linear 16 bit PCM samples. About 40 s of obtained speech were regarded as training data for each speaker and were used to form a reference model. The remaining speech data (on average 30 s per speaker) were used for identification tests.

Feature Extraction. The speech signal was windowed by a 16 ms Hamming window (128 samples) and not pre-emphasised. For each 16 ms segment, a feature vector of 12th order of either LPCCs or KCCs was formed. The feature vectors were then mean normalised even though it is not necessary because the training and testing condition were the same. Segments of silence were removed from the speech data before the feature extraction using an adaptive energy threshold speech/silence detector.

Vector Quantisation. The vector quantisation is an approach used for reduction of an extensive data set. The data set $X = \{x_i | i = 1, \ldots, N\}$, where N is the number of vectors in the set X, is mapped onto a finite set of M ($M \ll N$) codebook vectors $W = \{w_i | i = 1, \ldots, M\}$. Each vector is assigned to the nearest codebook vector. In the result, every codebook is composed of centroid vectors (means) representing nonoverlapping regions in the feature space. Every codebook obtained in this way is included in the reference database. During an identification phase each sequence of input vectors of an unknown speaker is quantised using K codebooks corresponding to K different speakers. The unknown speaker is then identified as the reference speaker with the minimum average distortion. This method of speaker identification is described in more detail in [4].

Experimental Results. In our experiments, we formed codebooks of either 80 or 320 vectors. The experimental results are summarised in Table 1.

Table 1. Identification results

Codebook size 80			Codebook size 320		
Coefficients	# correct	Correct [%]	Coefficients	# correct	Correct [%]
LPCCs	578	97.80	LPCCs	582	98.48
KCCs	576	97.46	KCCs	582	98.48

As the table shows, in the case with the codebook of 80 vectors, better results were obtained when the LPCCs were used, but the difference is almost insignificant. In the second case, using the codebook of 320 vectors, the results are absolutely identical.

5   Conclusion

Results of our experiments show that the predictor coefficients calculation based on discrete Kalman estimator can be usable in speech processing. It can be usable for the reconstruction of signal spectra (see Section 4.1) as well as for speaker identification application (see Section 4.2). The handicap of this algorithm is its very high time consuming.

References

1. Mack G. A., Jain V. K.: A Compensated-Kalman Speech Parameter Estimator. IEEE Signal Processing Magazine (1985).
2. Mammone R. J., Zhang X., Ramachandran R. P.: Robust Speaker Recognition. IEEE Signal Processing Magazine (1996).
3. Psutka J.: Communication with Computer by Speech. Academia, Prague (1995) (in Czech).
4. Radová V., Švenda Z.: An Approach to Speaker Recognition Based on Vector Quantization. First International Conference on Advanced Engineering Design, Prague (1999).

Belarussian Speech Recognition
Using Genetic Algorithms

Eugene I. Bovbel and Dzmitry V. Tsishkou

Radiophysics Department, Belarussian State University
F. Skoryna Av. 4, 220050, Minsk, Belarus
tishkovdv@mail.com

Abstract. One of the factors complicating activity with speech signals is its large degree of acoustic variability. To decrease influence of acoustic variability of speech signals, it is offered to use genetic algorithms in speech processing systems. We constructed a program model which implements the technology of speech recognition using genetic algorithms. We made experiments on our program model with a database of separated Belarussian words and achieve optimal results.

1 Introduction

The essential successes on a way of construction of devices which are capable of perceiving speech are recently reached. First of all, this success is connected with the development and intrusion of statistical methods for speech recognition [1,2]. Statistical methods, founded on HMM [3,4], are widely used for solving practical problems. For example, recognition of phonemes, insulated words and continuous speech, identification and verification of the speaker, diagnosis of diseases along a talking path. The flexible and potent mathematical vehicle of HMM [4,5] allows an easy use of effective simulation of variability of a speech signal. One of the factors which makes the activity with speech signals comlicated is its large degree of acoustic variability. This is conditioned by a series of causes. The first is that the speech of each individual is determined by physical properties of a talking path, such as the length of a voice channel, size of a larynx, etc. The second, i.e. the generating of speech [2], is impossible without a verification of compliance with organs of speech, features of which are determined on the learning process of a concrete person and represent a dialect or regional accent. The third is, and it is known, that the availability of irregularity of a voice channel is mirrored in features of speech of the person. For a decreasing influence of acoustic variability [1,2,3] of speech signals, it is offered to use genetic algorithms in speech processing systems.

The philosophies which were fundamentals of genetic algorithms, were formulated in activities of Mendel, the abbot of a monastery in the city of Brno (Czech Republic). Now under the term *genetic algorithms* – not one model hides, because of the broad enough class of computing algorithms [6] that it contains, sometimes it is not enough to find similarity with each other. It is necessary to note that genetic algorithms have a series of properties, which make them rather attractive for speech signals processing. To these properties, it is possible to relate:

P. Sojka, I. Kopeček, and K. Pala (Eds.): TSD 2000, LNAI 1902, pp. 301–306, 2000.

- The genetic algorithms are based on principles of population genetics and are very friendly for simulating not only acoustic variability, but also non-steady signals, to which, the speech signal concerns also.
- The genetic algorithms tend to find global or strong local optima of a given function in their search domain.
- The genetic algorithms can optimise multimodal and discontinuous functions without the need for any gradient information whatsoever.

2   Genetic Algorithms

Let separate voice expression be shown by a sequence of acoustic vectors: $O = \{O_t | t = 1, \dots, T\}$. The vector of observation O_t which is usually used for recognition of words looks like: $O_t = \{X_n | n = 1, \dots, N\}$, where X_n are some coefficients, usually they are customary cepster and deltacepster coefficients [4,5]. The genetic algorithm usually uses representation of this vector in the form of a chromosome: $M = \{g_i | i = 1, \dots, N\}$, where each parameter X_n is described by a gene g_i. Each gene g_i consists of alleles, which are selected from the final alphabet. It is necessary to have a function $f(X)$, which estimates as far as the combination of parameters presented by the vector X_n.

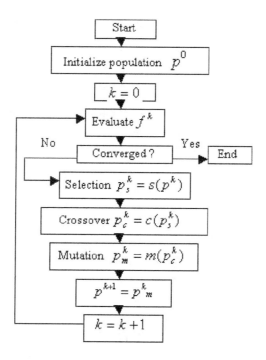

Fig. 1. The diagram of activity of genetic algorithm

Criteria of an estimation of X_n is maximisation of $f(X_n)$. The genetic algorithm works with a set of chromosomes. The set of chromosomes is called a population and is meant: $P = \{M_l | l = 1, 2, \ldots, L\}$, where L is the size of a population.

The procedure of transition from one population to other performs series of applications of the genetic operators:

- Selection, which implements the genetic algorithm analog of fitness-based survival.
- Crossover, which hybridises surviving designs to produce better designs.
- Mutation, which randomly perturbs designs to ensure lasting population diversity

This process is fully described in [6]. The activity of genetic algorithm on the diagram guesses availability of the criteria of a convergence. As the given criteria, we will use an estimation of change of an average fitness on all population [6]. In cases when the given criteria varies insufficiently essentially during some number of breeds, it is possible to speak about the completion of the genetic algorithm's work.

3   Hidden Evolution Method

While constructing systems of speech recognition, it is necessary to utilise the expressed algorithms at a stage of processing and analysis for coercion of input data in the form, which will provide the stable characteristics and will allow the reduction of influence of some variable parameters. One of the algorithms, which will be utilised in the system of speech recognition, is the method of hidden evolution. We have developed this method, as the procedure of analysis of the arrays of decimal numbers, and therefore it is an algorithm independent of a context. Any map can be represented as a sequence of pairs of decimal numbers. Let's consider this sequence from the point of view of fundamental bases of genetic algorithms. Let a pair of numbers represent number m of the unique representatives, which have survived as a result of the evolution, of the generation number m. Also, a pair of numbers number $m + 1$ represents the unique representatives, which have survived as a result of evolution, of the generation number $m + 1$. Let's assume that the pair of numbers m is the ancestors of a pair of numbers number $m + 1$, within the framework of accuracy with which we can install it. Being grounded on accessible information, the method of the hidden evolution reconstructs the evolutionary process, which is hidden from us, and saves its parameters in the compact form, which has received a title a matrix of evolution. As well as the genetic algorithm, method of the hidden evolution follows from one generation to another, but thus the amount of generations is uniquely determined by parameters of the map and algorithm. The stage of reconstruction for each generation has an identical scheme, in which all possible processes of crossover and mutation are simulated and the data on the process for which connection between generations are saved is closest to the actual data. We have utilised value of the operator one-point crossover and two values of operators one-point mutation, as values of indexes of two units on string and on columns accordingly for addition to value of the given unit of unity on each generation. The data on the process of reconstruction are brought in a matrix of evolution, as additive values. After that, the matrix of evolution passes normalisation.

Fig. 2. Evolution Matrixes

4   Pre-classification Stage

During the implementation of the speech recognition system with the usage of genetic algorithms, we use some stages of analysis and processing of the map. One of them is the pre-classification stage. This stage is intended for the implementation of the procedure to optimize clusterisation – middle classes are more remote from each other, and the objects inside classes concentrate more strongly to middles classes in the space of signs. Here, we solve a problem of the decrease of the bridging clusters and, therefore, the complexity of a problem of recognition is reduced. We implemented the given procedure being grounded on methods of transition from characters of one alphabet to characters of another. A set of possible implementations of the given method allows the encoding of all possible methods of transition at the fixed alphabets under the particular scheme and to utilise genetic algorithm for implementation of the procedure of optimisation of clusterisation. Other essential advantage of the given approach consists of a reduction of an amount of characters of the alphabet and the implementation of the procedure of pre-classifications. We save the unique information about each object and we reduce the memory size necessary for its storage. We obtain a standard unit as an average on all accessible units of matrixes of evolution with equivalent indexes. As outcome of work of the procedure of conversion from the infinite alphabet of characters in the binary alphabet of characters on all accessible indexes, we obtain a binary vector. As for the binary alphabet and templates of dimension $n \times n$ exists $2^{n \times n}$ different variants of the function of conversion F, we use genetic algorithm for searching the best value of units of the function of conversion. A measure of correspondence of the optimum solution is the distance between binary vectors.

5   Speech Recognition Using Genetic Algorithms

We use conditionally-independently properties of the object as streams. The procedure of learning and recognition passes on each stream irrespective of remaining streams and further integral analysis of outcomes follows. In the multistream speech recognition system, we have used the concept of frames as the scheme for creating streams of the maiden level. As a result of the preliminary analysis of an original vector of observations (containing 12 cepsters and 12 delta-cepsters at each discrete time position), we broke it into the 2d frames. At a restricted information quantity, because of a digital signature, way to escalate the quantity of streams is to use frames with overlap. The optimum selection of a ratio of the sizes of overlap and frame allows to speak about a maximum approaching

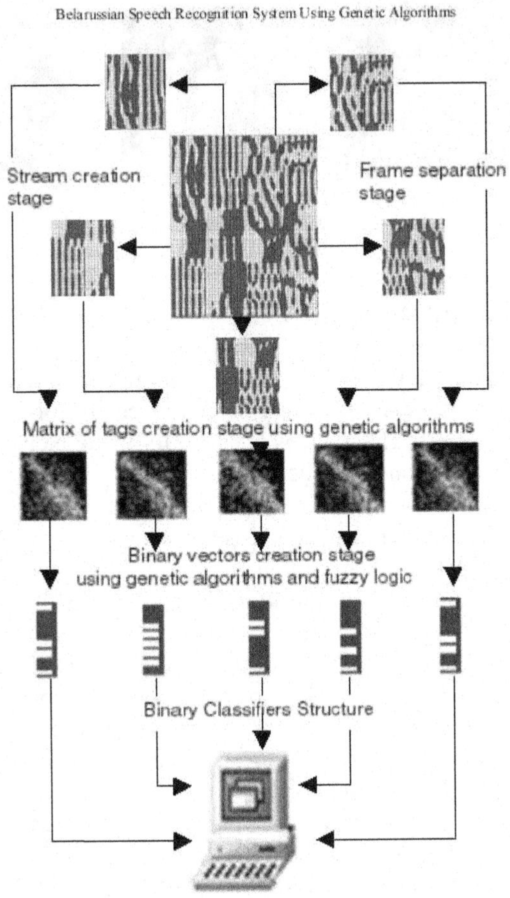

Fig. 3. Belarussian speech recognition system using genetic algorithms, where vector of observations is shown in the 2d bottom view projection.

of streams to independent tags. The output data confirmed by the analysis of comparative parameters multistream simulators and hardware systems of speech recognition, which we have elaborated. Each frame serves input data for the conforming stream after the normalisation stage based on an asymmetry measure. For conversion of the frame to a matrix of tags, we have used a method of hidden evolution. We have elaborated the given method for speech analysis. The method of hidden evolution will use the basic concepts of population genetics [6] and analyse the frame as a set chromosome. Outcome of the analysis is the preservation of unique characteristics for each frame in the compact form by the way matrixes of tags of the size 8×8. After that a matrix of tags to become with input dates for the subsequent stage of classification. Further with the help of the coded bank of filters and fuzzy logic, we translate a matrix of tags of each stream to a binary vector of size 64. Using genetic algorithm, which is specially adapted for the given operation, we optimise the scheme of conversion on a grade level so that the binary vectors of one class become closer to each other and further from the quoters of diverse classes. The binary vectors are used as input dates of each stream. We use binary classifiers as structure, which stores the indispensable information for the identification process and quantity of computing resources on some orders smaller than for more composite discriminatory analysis's demands.

6   Experimental Setup

For realization of experiment, the database was built. 20 Belarussian words were recorded for 50 times by ten speakers with a sampling rate of 44100 Hz. A 30 ms Hamming window with the size of frame 10 ms was used for segmentation. For each record of the database, a vector of the observation consisting of 12 cepstral and 12 delta-cepstral coefficients were constructed. Next we implement genetic algorithms technique for speech signals recognition system. Ten speech signal records (from different speakers) of each word were used for training and forty for testing. We get the following experimental results after testing all words from the database:

- Amount of memory to store information about each record is 64 bit.
- The system does not need to rebuilt itself so as to add new word record.
- The computation time required to add each record to genetic algorithms speech recognition system's structure is 3 sec.
- Computational time for recognising each record is less than 0.1 sec.
- The recognition rate under the conditions listed above (on the same database used for training and recognition) is 100%.

All tests were made on a Pentium2-400 class workstation.

References

1. Jelinek F. Распознавание непрерывнои реци статистицескими методами. ТИИЭР, 1976, vol. 64 No. 4, pp. 131–161, (in Russian).
2. Lawrence Robber and Biing-Hawing Jung. Fundamentals of Speech Recognition. PTR Prentice-Hall Inc, Englewood Cliff, 1993.
3. Hero, A. Bourland and Nelson Morgan. Connectionist Speech Recognition: A Hybrid Approach. Kluwer Academic Publishers, Boston MA, 1994.
4. E.I. Bovbel, P.P. Tkachova, and I.E. Kheidorov. The usage of hidden Markov models based on autoregressive principles for isolated word recognition. Proc. of. SPIE 13th Annual Intern. Symposium AeroSense, vol. 3720, April 5–9, 1999, Orlando, Florida, USA.
5. E.I. Bovbel, P.P. Tkachova, and I.E. Kheidorov. The analysis of speaker individual features based on autoregressive hidden Markov models. Proc. of Eurospeech'99, Budapest, Hungary, September 22–26, 1999.
6. E. Michielssen, Y. Rahmat-Samii and D.S. Weile. Electromagnetic systems design using genetic algorithms. Modern Radio Science. Oxford University Press. pp. 91–123.

A Discriminative Segmental Speech Model
and Its Application to Hungarian Number Recognition

László Tóth, András Kocsor, and Kornél Kovács

Research Group on Artificial Intelligence of the Hungarian Academy of Sciences and of the
University of Szeged
H-6720 Szeged, Aradi vértanúk tere 1., Hungary
tothl@inf.u-szeged.hu, kocsor@inf.u-szeged.hu, coree@inf.u-szeged.hu

Abstract. This paper presents a stochastic segmental speech recogniser that models the a posteriori probabilities directly. The main issues concerning the system are segmental phoneme classification, utterance-level aggregation and the pruning of the search space. For phoneme classification, artificial neural networks and support vector machines are applied. Phonemic segmentation and utterance-level aggregation is performed with the aid of anti-phoneme modelling. At the phoneme level, the system convincingly outperforms the HMM system trained on the same corpus, while at the word level it attains the performance of the HMM system trained without embedded training.

1   Introduction

The currently most popular stochastic approach to automatic speech recognition statistically models the joint distribution $P(W, A)$ of the acoustic observations A and the possible transcriptions W. During recognition, an incoming signal is identified as the transcription with the maximum a posteriori probability, so the result is

$$W^* = \arg \max_W P(W|A) = \arg \max_W P(A|W)P(W), \tag{1}$$

where the latter, decomposed form is derived using Bayes' formula. We will call those models that use this decomposed form and work with $P(A|W)$ "generative".

We know about very few systems that model $P(W|A)$ directly. Some authors refer to these as "recognition" [6], or "perception" [5] (vs. "production") models. Owing to the lack of a commonly accepted name, we will call these models "discriminative", in accordance with general pattern recognition terminology. Since this may be misleading (generative models can be trained discriminatively as well), we should stress here that we use this naming for the *models* and not necessarily for their *training technique*.

This paper describes a segment-based recogniser built on discriminatively trained segmental classifiers. Section 2 discusses the segmental framework in general. Section 3 then describes the phoneme classifier and related issues, while Section 4 presents our results. The paper closes with concluding remarks and planned future developments.

P. Sojka, I. Kopeček, and K. Pala (Eds.): TSD 2000, LNAI 1902, pp. 307–313, 2000.

2   Segment-Based Recognition

In the following, we suppose that a speech signal A is given as a series of frame-based observation vectors $A = a_1 a_2 \ldots a_T$, while the possible transcriptions W are given as series of phonemic labels $W = w_1 w_2 \ldots w_n$. We will model the conditional probability $P(W|A)$ in a decomposed form, as we want to keep our system general enough for continuous speech recognition as well. In our framework, $P(W|A)$ is decomposed as

$$P(W|A) = \prod_i P(w_i|A) = \prod_i P(w_i|A_i), \qquad (2)$$

where the first equation covers the assumption that the phonemes are independent (we presume phonetic correlation to be modelled by an independent language model), and the second equation reflects the assumption that the identity of a particular phoneme w_i depends only on a particular segment $A_i = a_j a_{j+1} a_{j+t}$. The phonemic probabilities $P(w_i|A_i)$ can then be trained on a manually segmented and labelled corpus. The learning algorithms that are used to model $P(w_i|A_i)$ will be called the "phoneme classifier", which will be discussed in the next section.

Equation (2) implicitly assumes that we know the phonetic segmentation of the signal. However, since automatic segmentation cannot be done reliably, we have to evaluate many possible segmentations S during recognition. This means that we work with $P(W, S|A)$ from which S has to be finally removed by marginalisation. Formally,

$$P(W|A) = \sum_S P(W, S|A) = \sum_S P(W|S, A)P(S|A) \approx \max_S P(W|S, A)P(S|A).$$
$$\qquad (3)$$

For a given S, $P(W|S, A)$ can be calculated using equation (2). The more problematic issue is with $P(S|A)$. From a practical viewpoint, it gives a weighting of the phoneme models that normalises the different segmentation paths. One might try a heuristic "aggregation function" to combine the classifier outputs, but a bad strategy could lead to errors like the preference of short or long words. The most popular solution for avoiding the problems associated with $P(S|A)$ is to run a frame-based (e.g. HMM) recogniser, and re-score only the N best paths by the segmental phoneme models [11]. We, however, wanted to model $P(S|A)$ with discriminative classifiers, for which we trained segmental probabilities $P(s_i|A_i)$. In this two-class training, the phonemes of the manually labelled corpus acted as positive examples for the class "phoneme", while (quasi-)randomly cut pieces of the database served as examples of the "anti-phoneme", whose class thus covers any segment that is a part of or a composite of some phonemic segments. One motivation for approximating $P(S|A)$ from the phoneme/anti-phoneme probabilities was that it made it possible to train $P(s_i|A_i)$ and $P(w_i|A_i)$ on the same features. This allowed us to unite the two classifiers into one, which considerably decreased the computational costs.

The simplest way to approximate $P(S|A)$ from the values $P(s_i|A_i)$ is

$$P(S|A) = \prod_{s_i \in S} P(s_i|A_i). \qquad (4)$$

Unfortunately, this formula does not guarantee proper normalisation between different segmentations. For this, all segments should be considered, like in

$$P(S|A) = \prod_{s_i \in S} P(s_i|A_i) \prod_{s_j \in \overline{S}} (1 - P(s_j|A_j)), \tag{5}$$

where $\overline{S}$ denotes the set of *all other* segments that occur in *any* other segmentation. However, the space of all segments is prohibitively large. Thus, we approximated the second product in (5) by considering only those elements of $\overline{S}$ that are "near-misses" of the elements of S. More precisely, for a given segment $s \in S$, we utilised the anti-phoneme probability of the two nearest segments in $\overline{S}$ that overlap either boundaries of s. To get the best performance, these probabilities had to be raised to empirically chosen powers (indicating that these values represent also those segments not utilised explicitly).

As the third important issue concerning segmental recognition, we stress that the approximation of the sum with the best segmentation in (3) turns the summation into a search problem. In contrast to an HMM system where the probabilities belonging to different state sequences can be evaluated efficiently by dynamic programming, in segmental models the probability of a segment cannot be simply composed from the probabilities of "sub-segments" (i.e. frames), but need a call to the classifier. Thus, for an acceptable execution speed, the effective pruning of the space of possible segmentations is crucial. Our system performs a depth-first search to find the best segmentation of an utterance. When a leaf is reached in the search space, its probability value serves as a threshold to avoid traversing less promising segmentation paths. In this way, on the average, the system can find the N best segmentations quite efficiently.

Finally, the number of possible segmentations can be reduced drastically by the application of a signal processing algorithm that segments the utterance based on local changes in the spectrum. When choosing the parameters for such an algorithm, one should bear in mind that insertion errors only increase the search space, but deletion errors have the risk of completely misrecognizing the utterance in question.

3   Discriminative Phoneme Classification

3.1   Segmental Features

Although there are many sophisticated segmental models offered in the literature [1], we used a simple technique similar to that of the SUMMIT system [3]. At the frame level, the speech signals were represented by their critical-band log-energies, and the averages of the 24 critical-band log-energies of the segment thirds (divided in a 1-2-1 ratio) were used as segmental features for phoneme classification. The advantage of this method is that it needs only trifling additional calculations following the computation of the frame-based features. Moreover, it returns the same number of segmental features independent of the segment length, which was a prerequisite for the classifiers used.

Apart from phoneme classification, we also needed features that discriminate phonemes from anti-phonemes. We used the variances of the features along the segments to filter out candidates that contain boundaries inside them, and the derivatives of the features at the boundaries to remove candidates with improbable start and end-points. These segmental features were calculated only on 4 wide frequency bands, as it proved sufficient.

A special segmental feature is the duration of the phoneme. We consider it especially important for languages like Hungarian where phonemic duration can play a discriminative role. As our preliminary experiments found duration to be useful indeed, it was employed as a segmental feature in all our experiments. Thus, including duration, 77 features altogether were used to represent the segments.

3.2   Feature Space Transformations

A special problem with discriminative segmental models is that since the observations are from a continuous space, contextual variability cannot simply be addressed by triphone models, as is usual with generative modelling. Furthermore, since the number of features increases the computational cost of most classifiers non-linearly, it should be kept as low as possible. For these reasons, we attach great importance to feature space transformation methods. These methods may aid classification performance and can also reduce the dimensionality of the data. Linear discriminant analysis (LDA), principal component analysis (PCA) and independent component analysis (ICA) are the traditional (linear) transformation techniques [2,8]. Recently the non-linear version of these linear transformations have become a popular research topic in statistical learning theory. We performed experiments applying the so-called "Kernel non-linearisation idea" [10,8] on LDA. Rather than going into mathematical details, we demonstrate the effect of this transformation on two artificially generated data sets, both consisting of two classes. Figure 1 shows that in both cases the otherwise interweaving classes become separable by one straight line after the transformation (the sets were encircled only for the ease of visualisation).

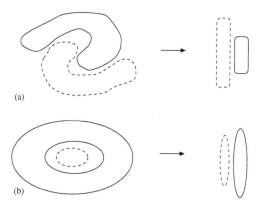

Fig. 1. The effect of Kernel-LDA on two point sets, both consisting of two classes

3.3   Classifiers

It is known that artificial neural networks (ANN), under proper conditions, can be used to approximate a posteriori probabilities [7]. In a previous study [4], we also found ANNs to be the best for phoneme classification. In the experiments below, "ANN" means three-layer MLPs trained with back-propagation. The number of hidden neurons was 150 in the phoneme classification, and 50 in the phoneme/anti-phoneme classification tests.

For the classification task, we also experimented with a promising new technique called support vector machines (SVM). Owing to the lack of space, we refer the interested reader to Vapnik [10] for an overview on SVM. In all the experiments with SVM, a second-order polynomial kernel function was applied.

4   Experimental Results

We evaluated our system on a small corpus, where the training set consisted of 20, while the test set of 6 talkers pronouncing 52–52 Hungarian numbers. The recordings were of reasonably good quality, sampled and quantised at 22050 Hz, 16-bit. The whole database was manually segmented and labelled. Due to the restricted domain, the corpus contained only 28 different phonemic labels.

For a comparison, an HMM system was also trained on the same corpus using monophone models (the corpus is too small to train triphones). The description of the HMM recogniser can be found in Szarvas [9].

4.1   Phoneme-Level Results

Table 1 shows the segmental classification errors. In the case of the phoneme classification (28 classes), we have a comparative result from the HMM which shows that the segmental discriminative models give significantly better results. In addition, one can notice that the classifiers attained the same performance after LDA and K-LDA, in spite of the transformations considerably reducing the number of features. Similar observations hold for the phoneme plus anti-phoneme (29 classes) and phoneme/anti-phoneme classification tasks (in the latter case no transformation was applied, as there were only two classes).

Table 1. Segmental classification error rates

		No transf. (77 feat.)	LDA (27 feat.)	K-LDA (27 feat.)
28 phone- mes	HMM	9.34%	—	—
	ANN	7.78%	7.81%	5.79%
	SVM	5.81%	5.12%	4.59%
28 ph. + antiph.	ANN	6.78%	6.87%	6.54%
	SVM	7.90%	6.14%	5.89%
phoneme/ antiph.	ANN	6.92%	—	—
	SVM	5.10%	—	—

4.2   Word-Level Results

Table 2 shows the error rates on the word level (all experiments were performed with ANN classifiers). The first column shows the error rate when the recogniser examined all possible segments that can be composed from 5-frame chunks of the signal. The result is comparable with the performance of the HMM (without embedded training), but the runtime was over an order of magnitude worse.

The result in the second column was attained when the recogniser used only the segments found by an algorithm that looked for local changes in the spectrum. On average, this algorithm cut a phoneme into only 1.84 pieces. Runtime with this search space reduction was close to real-time, but unfortunately the error rate became more than double. Visual inspection showed that almost all new errors were caused by deletion errors in the automatic segmentation.

Finally, we ran an experiment substituting the manual segmentation in place of the automatic segmentation mentioned above. Surprisingly, we got worse results than with the 5-frame "fake-segmentation", which indicates that the manual segmentation in many cases does not coincide with the boundaries suggested by the acoustic features. From this, we concluded that a version of the expectation-maximisation algorithm (that is iterative "recognise-and-retrain" loops) could significantly improve the system's performance. The fact that the HMM performed much better with embedded training than with training on the manual segmentation also reinforces this assumption.

Table 2. Word error rates

Segmental Model			HMM	
5-frame segm.	Autom. segm.	Manual segm.	No embed. tr.	Embedded tr.
1.28%	3.20%	1.92%	1.60%	0.32%

5   Conclusion

From our results (and the similar ones found in the literature), we conclude that although segmental models can quite easily outperform HMM on the phoneme level, this gain can be easily lost on the utterance level. In our case, it means that a better aggregation strategy, that is a better approximation of $P(S|A)$ must be found – preferably one that can be trained discriminatively at the utterance level. Also, to reach acceptable execution speed, we have to look for some better pruning methods, since the spectrally-based segmentation algorithm proved unreliable, and doing a full search (using the 5-frame fake segments) is very slow. Implementation of an iterative training algorithm also promises much improvement. Finally, so far we used only a fixed vocabulary, thus an interesting question is the integration with a probabilistic language model, which quite probably needs some different technique than in the case of an HMM system.

References

1. Fukada, T., Sagisaka, Y. and Paliwal, K. K., Model Parameter Estimation for Mixture Density Polynomial Segment Models, *Proc. of ICASSP '97,* pp. 1403–1406, Munich, Germany, 1997.
2. Fukunaga, K., *Statistical Pattern Recognition,* New York: Academic Press, 1989.
3. Halberstadt, A. K., Heterogeneous Measurements and Multiple Classifiers for Speech Recognition, *Ph.D. Thesis, Dep. Electrical Engineering and Computer Science, MIT,* 1998.
4. Kocsor, A., Tóth, L., Kuba, A. Jr., Kovács, K., Jelasity, M., Gyimóthy, T. and Csirik, J., A Comparative Study of Several Feature Transformation and Learning Methods for Phoneme Classification, accepted for publication in the *International Journal of Speech Technology.*
5. Mariani, J., Gauvain, J. L., Lamel, L., Comments on "Towards increasing speech recognition error rates" by H. Bourlard, H. Hermansky, and N. Morgan, *Speech Communication,* 18 (1996), pp. 249–252.
6. Morgan, N., Bourlard, H., Greenberg, S., Hermansky, H., Stochastic Perceptual Auditory-Event-Based Models for Speech Recognition, *Proc. of ICSLP '94,* pp. 1943–1946, 1994.
7. Richard, M. D. and Lippmann, R. P., Neural network classifiers estimate Bayesian a posteriori probabilities, *Neural Computation,* 3(4):461:483, 1991.
8. Schölkopf, B., Smola, A. and Müller, K. -R., Nonlinear Component Analysis as a Kernel Eigenvalue Problem, *Neural Computation,* Vol. 10(5), 1998.
9. Szarvas, M., Mihajlik, P., Fegyó, T. and Tatai, P., Automatic Recognition of Hungarian: Theory and Practice, accepted for publication in the *International Journal of Speech Technology.*
10. Vapnik, V. N., *Statistical Learning Theory,* John Wiley & Sons Inc., 1998.
11. Zavaliagkos, G., Zhao, J., Schwartz, R. and Makhoul, J., A Hybrid Segmental Neural Net/Hidden Markov Model System for Continuous Speech Recognition, *IEEE Trans. Speech and Audio Proc.,* Vol. 2, No. 1, Part II, January 1994.

Comparison of Frequency Bands
in Closed Set Speaker Identification Performance

Özgür Devrim Orman[1] and Levent Arslan[2]

[1] TÜBİTAK
Ulusal Elektronik ve Kriptoloji Araştırma Enstitüsü, Gebze, 41470 Kocaeli
oorman@mam.gov.tr
[2] Boğaziçi Üniversitesi
Elektrik-Elektronik Mühendisliği Bölümü, Bebek, 80815 İstanbul
arslanle@boun.edu.tr

Abstract. Lots of words can be said about the importance of speaker identification for people, but no word might be as meaningfull as the imagination of a life without having any speaker identification ability. For example, if we cannot identify people from their voices, without having any additional information it is impossible for us to decide on whom we are talking to on telephone. Of course, this ability seems so simple for us, but computer-based implementations are still far from human abilities. Furthermore, any speaker identification system on computers cannot be designed as an optimum solution. It is known that there is no optimum feature set definition for speaker identification systems. In this work, we study speaker identification performance dependency on the choice of frequency bands.

1 Introduction

Speaker identification process can be subdivided into three phases: i) Transformation of training set speaker records to feature vectors database, ii) Training of the system using these data, and iii) Identification performance test. In the first phase, we can use various methods to generate feature sets, such as LPC cepstrum [1] or mel-cepstrum [2] representations. The process in the second phase depends on the choice of identification method. In this phase we can use Vector Quantisation [3], Gaussian Mixture Models (GMM) [4], Hidden Markov Models [5] or various types of Neural Network architectures such as Radial Basis Function Networks [6,7]. The theoretical details of GMM method are given in Section 2. In the last phase, speaker identification performance of the system is tested using test feature vectors database.

Selection of feature vector parameters has been studied in previous works [1,8,9]. In Sambur's paper [8], important characteristics of various acoustic features are analysed. These acoustic features are vowels, nasals, strident consonants, fundamental frequency, and timing measurements. Moreover, to determine the overall feature ranking, he uses a "knock out" procedure that determines the least important feature parameter at each step using error performance criteria. In Atal's work [1], acoustic parameters in speaker identification are classified in eight different groups. These groups are: intensity, pitch, short-time spectrum, predictor coefficients, formant frequencies and bandwidths, nasal coarticulation, spectral correlations, timing and speaking rate. On the other hand, In O'Shaughnessy's work [9], acoustic features are subdivided into two groups, inherent features and learned ones. F-ratio is accepted as a good measure of the amount of speaker identification information that is carried by any analysed feature.

Our approach to the feature selection problem differs in many ways from the previous works, i.e. those that we have mentioned. In order to analyse the speaker identification performance dependency on a frequency band, we use training and test sets which are composed of including only the filtered power spectrum values in the analysis frequency range. Apart from that, in this work we propose new performance measures which are vector and speaker ranking. The experimental results on speaker identification performance dependency on frequency bands and the methodology are given in Section 3. The results of this work are discussed in Section 4.

2   GMM Based Speaker Identification System

The main idea behind this method is to model the statistical behaviour of a speaker's acoustic characteristics by using a mixture of multidimensional Gaussian distributions. Properties of these multidimensional Gaussians, such as mean vectors and covariance matrices, are calculated using Expectation Maximisation (EM) algorithm. In this method, each speaker is represented by K multidimensional Gaussians. Parameter set of the ith speaker is represented as follows.

$$\lambda_i = \{p_j, \underline{\mu}_j, \Sigma_j\} \quad j = 1, \dots, K \tag{1}$$

$\underline{\mu}_j$: Mean vector of jth Gaussian,

Σ_j: Covariance matrix of jth Gaussian,

p_j: Probability of jth Gaussian.

Conditional probability of observation of the test vector $\underline{\mu}$ in terms of the ith speaker's parameter set is calculated as given below.

$$p\left(\underline{x}/\lambda_i\right) = \sum_{j=1}^{K} p_j b_j(\underline{x}) \tag{2}$$

$$b_j(\underline{x}) = \frac{1}{\sqrt{(2\pi)^M |\Sigma_j|}} \exp\left\{ -\frac{1}{2} \left(\underline{x} - \underline{\mu}_j\right) \frac{1}{\Sigma_j} \left(\underline{x} - \underline{\mu}_j\right)^T \right\} \tag{3}$$

EM algorithm can be formulated as follows.

$$p\left(r/\underline{x}_{i,j,T}\right) = \frac{p_r b_r(\underline{x}_{i,j,T})}{\sum_{k=1}^{K} p_k b_k(\underline{x}_{i,j,T}} \quad r = 1, \dots, K \tag{4}$$

$$\mu_k = \frac{\sum_{j=1}^{D} p(k/\underline{x}_{i,j,T}, \lambda_i)\underline{x}_{i,j,T}}{\sum_{j=1}^{D} p(k/\underline{x}i, j, T, \lambda_i)} \tag{5}$$

$$\rho_k^2 = \frac{\sum_{j=1}^{D} p(k/\underline{x}_{i,j,T}, \lambda_i)\underline{x}_{i,j,T}^2}{\sum_{j=1}^{D} p(k/\underline{x}i, j, T, \lambda_i)} \tag{6}$$

$$p_k = \frac{1}{D} \sum_{j=1}^{D} p(k/\underline{x}_{i,j,T}, \lambda_i) \tag{7}$$

In these formulas, $\underline{x}_{i,j,T}$ represents the ith speaker's j^{th} training future vector. This optimisation procedure is ended, if the calculated likelihood value does not increase more than a predefined threshold between consecutive iterations.

Identification test of any speaker, who is in the set, includes two phases. In the first phase, likelihood value of subject speaker's test set is calculated for each candidate speaker. The second phase includes assignment of speaker who has the highest likelihood ratio, to the subject speaker's identity. Suppose that H represents the assigned speaker and X_S represents the whole set of test vectors of the subject speaker, we can formulate this decision process as

$$H = \arg\max_{1 \le i \le l} \Pr(\lambda_i/X_S) \tag{8}$$

Using Bayes rule, we can rewrite $\Pr(\lambda_i/X_S)$ as in (9).

$$\Pr(\lambda_i/X_S) = \frac{p(X_S/\lambda_i)\Pr(\lambda_i)}{p(X_S)} \tag{9}$$

Assuming the probability of each speaker is equal and $p(X_S)$ value is the same for each speaker, we can simplify (9) to (10).

$$H = \arg\max_{1 \le i \le I} p(X_S/\lambda_i) \tag{10}$$

3   Speaker Identification Performance Analysis

Speaker identification system requires both training and test vector sets for speaker identification process. In order to test the speaker identification performance on a discrete frequency band, the training and test sets are generated including only the filtered power spectrum values in analysis frequency range. It is also observed that, these frequency bands must not be shorter than 500 Hz. In the experiments, we use TIMIT speech corpus [10] that has eight different dialect regions of American English. TIMIT already includes voice active regions in utterances, so in this work we do not need to use a voice activity detection mechanism. The speaker sets we used are restricted to only the records of speakers in the fifth dialect region; this approach cancels the effect of dialect region difference in speaker identification performance. Moreover, we work on three speaker sets. First set includes only male speakers, second set includes only female speakers, and third set includes both male and female speakers. The number of speakers in all these sets is equal to twenty-four. Performance analysis in the same gender also eliminates the information carried by gender difference that is valuable for speaker identification. We generate the training set using the unique utterances from all speakers' records, these files have "sa" prefixes, and the files with "si" prefix are used in the test set. Furthermore, the phonetic dominance problem in training is cancelled by using these unique utterances.

In the experiments, speech records are segmented in 20 ms frames and the duration between adjacent frames is kept at 10 ms. Each frame is weighted using Hamming window and transformed to frequency domain using DFT, then the power spectrum of a frame is calculated using these coefficients. The power spectrum coefficients are passed through a filter bank that is composed of uniform triangular filters. Training and test files for each frequency band are generated using the filtered power spectrum. The training phase is the same as given in Section 2. On the other hand, speaker identification performance is measured according to two criteria: vector ranking and speaker ranking.

In *vector ranking*, we compare the statistical likelihood values of each test vector in terms of candidate speakers, and then we assign a rational number between 0 and 1 to the identification performance of the correct speaker. The mean value of all speakers' performance values is calculated and assigned as a final measure of speaker identification performance value for this frequency interval. On the other hand, in *speaker ranking*, we compare the statistical likelihood values of each speaker's test set in terms of candidate speakers, then we do the same numerical assignment as in the previous method that we have explained. Also, the final measure of speaker identification performance value at this frequency interval according to the speaker ranking is obtained by calculating the average of all speaker's performance values. After we calculate the performance on each frequency band, we can visualise how the speaker identification performance varies along the whole frequency axis. These results are also examined comparing with calculated F-ratio [1] values at each frequency band. Also, F-ratio for this case is the ratio of inter-speaker variance to intra-speaker variance at that frequency band, and it is interesting to note that there is a correlation between calculated F-ratio values and vector ranking results.

4   Conclusion

Observations in this work give us a new perspective about the importance of frequency bands in speaker identification systems. Although mel-scale is used in speaker identification systems generally, it is possible to define a new scale using the results of this work. In addition to that, we have already developed a new filter bank according the results of this work, it is called "speaker sensitive frequency scale filter bank" (SSFSF). In the speaker identification test including 462 speakers of TIMIT corpus, the system with SSFSF gives better identification results as compared with the system including mel-scale filter bank. Furthermore, the following work that we focus on is a subjective test to compare our observations and human auditory system responses.

References

1. Atal, B.S., "Automatic recognition of speakers from their voices", Proc. IEEE, vol. 64, pp. 460–474, 1976.
2. Davis, S.B. and Mermelstein, P., "Comparison of parametric representations for monosyllabic word recognition in continuously spoken sentences", IEEE Trans. Acoust. Speech, Signal Processing, vol. ASSP-28, pp. 357–366, 1980.
3. Rosenberg, A.E., and Soong, F.K., "Evaluation of a vector quantisation talker recognition system in text independent and text dependent modes", Computer Speech and Language, vol. 22, pp. 143–157, 1987.
4. Reynolds, D.A., Rose, R.C., "Robust text-independent speaker identification using Gaussian mixture speaker models", IEEE Trans. Speech and Audio Processing, vol. 3, pp. 72–83, 1995.
5. Tishby, N.Z., "On the application of mixture AR hidden Markov models to text independent speaker recognition", IEEE Trans. Signal Processing, vol. 39, pp. 563–570, 1991.
6. Oglesby, J. and Mason, J., "Radial basis function networks for speaker recognition", in Proc. ICASSP, May 1991, pp. 393–396.
7. Orman, Ö.D., Arslan L., "A comparative study on closed set speaker identification using RBF network and modular networks", Accepted for presentation in TAINN 2000.
8. Sambur, M. R., "Selection of Acoustic Features for Speaker Identification", IEEE Trans. Acoust. Speech, Signal Processing, vol. ASSP-23, pp. 176–182, 1975.
9. O'Shaughnessy, D. "Speaker Recognition", IEEE ASSP Magazine, pp. 4–17, October 1986.
10. "Getting started with darpa TIMIT CD-ROM: an acoustic phonetic continuous speech database", National Institute of Standarts and Technology (NIST), Gaithersburg, MD (prototype as of Dec. 1988).

Recording and Annotation of the Czech Speech Corpus

Vlasta Radová and Josef Psutka

University of West Bohemia, Department of Cybernetics,
Univerzitní 22, 306 14 Plzeň, Czech Republic
radova@kky.zcu.cz, psutka@kky.zcu.cz

Abstract. The paper reassumes our papers presented at the previous TSD workshops [2,3] and concerns the Czech speech corpus which is being developed at the Department of Cybernetics, University of West Bohemia in Pilsen. It describes procedures of corpus recording and annotation.

1 Introduction

The Czech speech corpus described in this paper is being developed at the Department of Cybernetics at the University of West Bohemia in Pilsen since 1998. The purpose of the corpus is to provide enough speech data for training of Czech continuous speech recognition systems. Our goal is to collect the corpus containing speech of at least 100 speakers, each of them is asked to read a set of 150 sentences. The texts to be read are selected from 3 Czech newspapers and have to satisfy several requirements that were specified in [3].

For the recording of the corpus, a special program was developed which allows to record each utterance by two different microphones simultaneously. The function as well as the interface of the recording program are described in Section 2.

Before the utterances can be used for training of a speech recognition system, they have to be annotated. The annotation is a process during which the speech data are divided into segments and various non-speech events (like lip smack, throat clear, etc.) and various kinds of noise (e.g. chair squeak, door slam) are indicated in the utterances. In our corpus, the segments are defined as such parts of the utterance that contain either a whole sentence or some of the specified non-speech events. Since the non-speech events can be either isolated (which means no speech co-occurs with such an event) or they can co-occur with the speech, several types of descriptors were used to mark the place where the events occurred in the speech. The process of the corpus annotation is described in Section 3.

2 Recording of the Corpus

The corpus is recorded in an office room where no person but the speaker is present during the recording. However, there is some noise from neighbouring offices in the recording room.

P. Sojka, I. Kopeček, and K. Pala (Eds.): TSD 2000, LNAI 1902, pp. 319–323, 2000.
© Springer-Verlag Berlin Heidelberg 2000

In order to record the corpus, we developed a special recording program *Vlny*. It allows the corpus to be recorded sentence by sentence. Each sentence is recorded by two microphones simultaneously. One of the microphones is a close-talking microphone yielding utterances of a very high quality. The other one is a desk microphone which records utterances with a common office noise. Such an arrangement enables to yield two identical utterances that differs only in the amount of noise that they contain.

At the beginning of the recording session, each speaker obtains some instructions. The instructions provide a general introduction to the project and a description of the task. The speakers are asked to read each sentence through before they utter and record it. They are also instructed to speak naturally and clearly in their usual accent at normal loudness. Each speaker is given a short demonstration on how to operate the recording program.

The actual recording process consists of several steps, each co-ordinated by clicking on screen buttons. A typical window that appears after a sentence is recorded is given in Figure 1. At the top of the window there is the sentence that has just been read. Below it there are two windows, each of them contains a figure of the signal from a microphone. The left window is for the close-talking microphone, the right window is for the desk microphone. The speaker has the possibility to check that the recording from any microphone is satisfactory by clicking on the corresponding *Play* button. Below the signal window there is also a scale window for each microphone. It shows the level of the signal at the input to the computer. The optimal level is approximately 50% and it should be adjusted by a supervisor during the demonstration phase, using a pre-amplifier for each microphone separately. During the actual recording, it is not allowed to change the settings of the pre-amplifiers any more. However, when the level of the signal in any microphone decreases below 10% or increases above 90%, the speaker is asked by the program to read the sentence once more in a more or less loud voice respectively. Similarly, when either the silence between clicking on the *Start* button and the beginning of the utterance, or the silence between the end of an utterance and clicking on the *Stop*

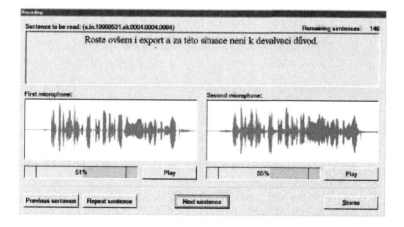

Fig. 1. A typical window of the recording program *Vlny*

button is shorter than 0.5 s, the speaker is asked to repeat the sentence once more. In addition to this, the speaker has a possibility to repeat the sentence on the base of his/her own decision by clicking on the *Repeat sentence* button. The *Previous sentence* button gives a chance to the speakers to go back to the previous sentence, the *Next sentence* button moves the speaker to the next sentence. The actual recording of a sentence is controlled by the *Start* and *Stop* buttons that appear after the *Next sentence* button is pressed.

3 Annotation of the Corpus

During the annotation process, each utterance is transcribed in the form of how it was really pronounced. This means that it contains with mispronunciation, unintelligible pronunciation, various non-speech events and various kinds of noise, if they occurred during the utterance. The rules that we use for the annotation of the corpus are as follows:

- Non-speech events and noises are indicated by a descriptor enclosed in square brackets. The descriptors contain only capitalised alphabetic characters and underscores and are drawn from the list in Table 1.

Table 1. List of the descriptors of non-speech events and kinds of noise

AH	LOUD_BREATH
COUGH	PAPER_RUSTLE
DOOR_SLAM	SIGH
GRUNT	TONGUE_CLICK
LIP_SMACK	UNINTELLIGIBLE
MM	MOUSE_CLICK
PHONE_RING	MIKE_OVERLOAD
THROAT_CLEAR	REMOTE_ENGINE
UH	NOISE
UM	KNOCK_ON_MIC
CHAIR_SQUEAK	MUSIC
CROSS_TALK	BACKGROUND_MUSIC
ER	SIGNAL_MISSING
LAUGHTER	SILENCE

- The descriptor is placed at the point at which the non-speech event occurred.
  E.g.: *Sdělil to ministr školství [THROAT_CLEAR] Jan Sokol.*
- If a non-speech event overlaps a spoken lexical item, the descriptor is placed close to the item that co-occurred with and the character "<" or ">" is appended to the descriptor depending on whether the description is placed right or left of the co-occurring lexical item.
  E.g.: *Akcie Komerční banky [CHAIR_SQUEAK>] poměrně zřetelně oslabily.*
  Or: *Akcie Komerční banky poměrně [<CHAIR_SQUEAK] zřetelně oslabily.*
  Both alternatives are equivalent and mean that a chair squeaked during the pronouncing of the word *poměrně*.

- If a non-speech event overlaps with more than one lexical item, the character "/" is appended to the descriptor and the descriptor is then used like brackets bounding the lexical items.

  E.g.: *Nabídka [NOISE/] udržela ceny ustálené. [/NOISE]*

- If the waveform is truncated (e.g. due to a recording error by the system), the symbol "~" is used to mark the incompletely spoken sentence:

  E.g.: *Společnost bude z rozhodnutí vlády nejprve* ~

- Mispronounced but intelligible words are bounded with the mark "*". For example, if the prompt was *Předsedové stran se domluvili* and the speaker has read *Předsedové stran se domlouvili*, the utterance is transcribed as *Předsedové stran se *domlouvili**.

- Unintelligible words are replaced by the non-speech event [UNINTELLIGIBLE].

For annotation of all utterances we use *Transcriber*, a very useful tool for segmenting, labelling and transcribing speech [1]. It was developed in France and is freely available at http://www.etca.fr/CTA/gip/Projets/Transcriber/. A typical window of this tool is given in Figure 2. The upper part of the window is basically a text editor which allows the user to type the transcription of the utterances. In addition to this, the speaker of the utterance can also be specified here. At the bottom part of the window the speech signal is depicted.

4   Conclusion

This paper deals with the Czech speech corpus that is being developed at the Department of Cybernetics of the University of West Bohemia in Pilsen. It reassumes our papers

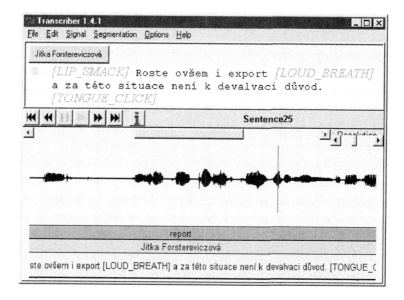

Fig. 2. A typical window of the *Transcriber*

presented at previous TSD workshops, where some questions about the corpus design were discussed [2] and algorithms for sentences selection [3] were described. The presented paper concerns with two problems – utterances recording and corpus annotation.

Acknowledgements

The work was supported by the Ministry of Education of the Czech Republic, project no. VS97159, and by the Grant Agency of the Czech Republic, project no. 102/96/K087.

References

1. Barras C. et al.: Transcriber: a Free Tool for Segmenting, Labelling and Transcribing Speech. In: First International Conference on Language Resources and Evaluation (LREC), 1998.
2. Radová, V.: Design of the Czech Speech Corpus for Speech Recognition Applications with a Large Vocabulary. In: Sojka, P., Matoušek, V., Pala, K., Kopeček, I. (eds.): Text, Speech, Dialogue. Proc. of the First Workshop on Text, Speech, Dialogue. Brno, Czech Republic, 1998, pp. 299–304.
3. Radová, V., Vopálka, P.: Methods of Sentences Selection for Read-Speech Corpus Design. In: Matoušek, V. et al. (eds.): Text, Speech and Dialogue. Proc. of the Second Workshop on Text, Speech, Dialogue. Springer-Verlag, Berlin Heidelberg, 1999, pp. 165–170.

A Text Based Talking Face

Léon J.M. Rothkrantz and Ania Wojdel

Delft University of Technology, Knowledge Based Systems
Zuidplantsoen 4, 2628 BZ Delft, The Netherlands
Phone +312787504, Fax +312787141
L.J.M.Rothkrantz@cs.tudelft.nl

Abstract. Facial expressions and speech are means to convey information. They can be used to reinforce speech or even complementary to speech. The main goal of our research is to investigate how facial expressions can be associated to text-based speech in an automated way. As a first step we studied how people attach *smileys* to text in chat sessions and facial expressions to text balloons in cartoons. We developed an expert system with a set of rules that describe dependencies between text and facial expressions. The specific facial expressions are stored in a nonverbal dictionary and we developed a search engine for that dictionary. Finally we present a tool to generate 3D facial animations.

1   Introduction

Human communication is based on verbal and nonverbal behaviour. It is commonly assumed that natural language is used to communicate objective information to other people and nonverbal behaviour is used to convey subjective and affective information. Speech has a verbal and a nonverbal aspect. It is more appropriate to speak about the denotative and connotative aspect of multi-modal communication. The denotative aspect is based on the grammar and the denotative aspect is based on the rules of communication.

In [1] P. Ekman introduced the concepts emblems and emotional emblems. The last ones are expressed by employing parts of the corresponding affect they refer to, while the first ones are used to replace and repeat verbal elements. Most of the time both are intentional, deliberate actions used to communicate. In general, they are produced consciously and are driven by the semantics of the utterance. They are conventionalised. Since they are discourse driven, the user enters their appearance. What is needed is a library of possible emblems. Efron gave a large list of them [2] and Ekman proposes a set of words, which have a corresponding emblem. Nevertheless the user can build his/her own emblem and add them to the library [3].

In this paper, we mainly investigate which facial expressions people show while reading a text. This knowledge can be used to create a text-based talking face. This talking face can be used as an affective user-friendly communicative human computer interface. Human computer-interaction is mainly based on text/picture and mouse, keyboard and screen input/output. However, one of the most user-friendly interface is a talking face.

P. Sojka, I. Kopeček, and K. Pala (Eds.): TSD 2000, LNAI 1902, pp. 327–332, 2000.
© Springer-Verlag Berlin Heidelberg 2000

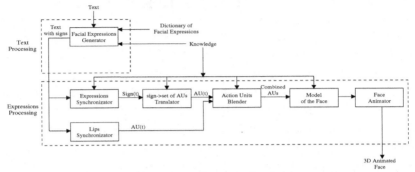

Fig. 1. Design of the system for generating facial expressions

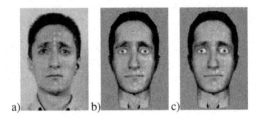

Fig. 2. Activation of AU1 – (a) original photo, (b) manually adapted model, (c) parametrised deformation of the model

2   Animated 3D Faces

The whole idea of the system for generating facial animation is based on a "facial script language". In 1970, P. Ekman and F.W. Friesen [4] developed an universal Facial Action Coding System (FACS) based on Action Units (AUs), where each facial expression can be described as a combination of AUs. Since most of all we want to represent real human behaviour, not only artistic imagination, we decided to base facial movements on AUs as defined by Ekman. This means that we want to design and to develop a script language of facial expressions, where basic variables are Action Units. We consider AUs as words in a "normal" language. When we have AUs as characters, we can define words of our script language: facial expressions. Facial expressions, the same as words in a "normal" language have their own syntax and semantics. We discuss this in more detail in Section 3.

In order to have a full definition of the language, we also need to define a grammar of the script language. That means we have to define rules of how facial expressions can be combined together. Grammatical rules will be implemented in different modules of the system in such a way that they will support the user while creating animation.

Our design of the system for facial animation is as follows: it has a modular structure, where each module is dedicated to a given task and each module has his own knowledge about dependencies between facial expressions for its level. The schematic design of the system is presented in Figure 1. We developed a first prototype of a synthetic 3D face showing facial expressions. The facial expressions can be generated by activating the

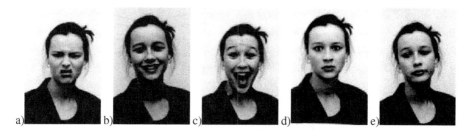

Fig. 3. Examples of different facial expressions – (a) disgust (b) happiness (c) weirdness (d) fear (e) sadness

corresponding AUs. In Figure 2 we give an example. More details about the underling model for facial animation is given in [5].

3   Nonverbal Dictionary

In a common dictionary of some language, words are presented in alphabetic order. We can find the spelling of the words, sometimes the phoneme presentation, the meanings in different contexts and rules of transformations of the words. Usually a dictionary will be used to check up the spelling of words or to find different meanings of words. Our nonverbal dictionary will have the same functionality. We developed a prototype of dictionary with 200 nonverbal words.

Nonverbal dictionary is composed of nonverbal words, i.e. facial expressions. Every facial expression can be described in terms of Action Units (AUs). We use these AUs and their intensity as the spelling components. Thus the nonverbal alphabet is the set of AUs in numerical order AU1 to AU43 and in order of intensity. We associate with every expression one characteristic verbal label, namely the name of the emblem. The facial expressions displayed in Figure 3 are labelled as disgust, happiness, weirdness, fear and sadness. We give different meanings of the corresponding expression in different contexts.

Finally we give a geometric description of facial expressions. The characteristic shape of the eyes, mouth, eyebrows, the appearance of wrinkles, and the colour, light-intensity of different parts of the skin characterise every facial expression. To have a uniform description of this geometric features, we use a fixed list of items and every expression is scored according to this list (i.e. eyeballs in a central, upward, downward, left, right position). Some features are scored on an ordinal 3-points scale corresponding to the intensity.

4   Search Modalities

We implemented different search modalities and we discuss them in more details.

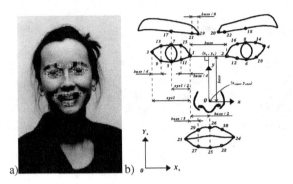

Fig. 4. Facial characteristic points – (a) on a real face (b) on a generic model

Pictures:

The most natural way to find the meaning of a given facial expression is to look it up in the dictionary and try to find the best pattern match. We automated this procedure and designed and implemented a system named ISFER for the automatic recognition of facial expressions. From a picture of a facial expression, we extract the position of some characteristic facial points (see Figure 4). We feed the coordinates of those points into a fuzzy rule expert system [6]. The output of the system is a list of activated AUs and their intensity. With use of the activated AUs, we can look up the corresponding facial expression in our dictionary. If the facial expression is out of the vocabulary, we find the best similar expression using S*-algorithm.

Line Drawings:

It is well known that schematic drawings of facial expressions can convey emotional meanings very well. If we want to look up a facial expression and there is no picture available, the user can generate a line drawing of the corresponding facial expression. To support the user, we designed a special tool to generate facial expressions. With the use of sliders, we can change the shape of the mouth, eyes and eyebrows. Next, the user can ask for the N best matching faces from the nonverbal dictionary.

Genetic Algorithm (GA):

If the user has a specific facial expression in his mind, he can look it up using a tool based on GA. The system comes up with four facial expressions as representatives of 4 clusters covering the whole nonverbal dictionary. The user selects the best fitting picture. Based on this user feedback, the system comes up with another 4 pictures and again the user is requested the best fitting one. The system uses GA to select appropriate representative facial expressions and the user feedback is used as fitness function.

5   Text Generated Emotions

During on-line chatting, *emoticons/smileys* can be attached to a text. These *smileys* are composed of "keyboard characters". There are software tools available, which transform these characters to corresponding pictures/line drawings of facial expressions. We use these symbols to generate appropriate 3D animated faces as background or next to the text. In an experiment, we asked 28 postgraduate students from the Department of Computer Science to take part in 5 chat-sessions. To support the user, we designed a nonverbal keyboard with 50 characteristic facial expressions as buttons. These buttons are available in a window and can be added to the text by simple clicking of the mouse. Students were requested to chat with fellow students and use the *emoticons* as much as possible. It was even allowed to send *emoticons* without any text.

All the chat sessions were recorded in a logfile. The question is whether it is possible to generate the *smileys* automatically. To put it in another way: *is it possible to define knowledge rules, which associate smileys with a text in an automated way?* From the corpus of the logged chat-sessions, we extracted more than 300 production rules. Some examples are displayed in Table 1. With these rules we developed an expert system which generates the *emoticons* in an automated way. The input of the system is one line of text. We developed a robust chart parser to parse and to extract the relevant features from the text. It proved that chatters use simple language. Unfortunately, the text doesn't satisfy the rules of the Dutch grammars. Chatters use their own words and their own grammar.

However, to associate the right *emoticon*, it is important to know if the chatter is speaking about his emotions or the emotions of other people. Further, it is important to know that he is stating that he wants to convey a specific emotions or that he does not want to convey a specific emotion.

Chatting is a way of interaction. A single utterance is related to the utterance of the last speaker. We found out that chatters adapt to some role playing. They can play different roles depending of the context, their moods, etc. In case of ambiguity, a safe heuristic is to reflect the emotions of the last speaker.

It proved that in case the *emoticon* was not related to emotional features in the text (punctuators, special words, and onomatopoeia) we couldn't generate them in an automated way. In that case the affective/emotion is not enclosed in the text. We need information from the context and the history of the dialogue or information with respect to the prosody or intonation of spoken language related to that text.

However, in case *emoticons* are used to stress some text features with an emotional loading, we were able to generate *emoticons* in an automated way, that is to say we generate "default options" or common used options. In many cases, there are many options possible. However, not every option has the same user appreciation.

Table 1. Examples of *emoticons*

Punctuation		Emblems		Emotions		Onomatopoeia	
?	:-Q	wink	;-)	happy	:-)	Oops	;-*
!	:-o	woman	>-	laughing	:-D	Ha ha	;-D
, ;	':-|	unclear	:-$	excited	8-)	Hmmm	:-I
.	:-|	Lincoln	=|:-)=	sad	:-(	Hi hi	:->>

6   Text Generated Facial Expressions

In many cartoons, we have a lot of facial expressions. Some of these facial expressions are closely related to text balloons. We assume that there is a high correlation between the text in the balloon and the corresponding facial expression. In some cartoons, this is stressed by underlining some words. To test this hypothesis, we removed the facial expressions in the picures of a cartoon magazine. We presented the facial expressions on a different sheets. In an experiment, students were requested to select the most appropriate facial expression related to a text balloon. To be sure that no context information was used, we mixed the text balloons in a random way. Again we found that facial expressions were selected on the basis of emotional features related to the text.

7   Conclusion

In this paper we described a general model for a talking face. A prototype for facial animation is described. The main problem was how to choose appropriate facial expressions reading a text or listening to speech. As a first step, we created a nonverbal dictionary with facial expressions and special designed search facilities. Emoticons were used as a facial expression script language. In an experiment, students were requested to add emoticons to their text in chat-sessions and to add facial expressions to predefined text balloons from cartoons. We were able to define some rules and heuristics how to associate facial expressions to text. It was possible to associate facial expressions to specific keywords in an automated way. However, in general, there are many choices of facial expressions. The appropriateness of the choice depends on features which are not included in the text such as prosody and context. In the near future, we will investigate how to associate facial expressions with spoken text, i.e. text with prosodic information used in speech synthesis.

References

1. P. Ekman, Movements with precise meanings. *Journal of Communication, 26*, pp. 14–26, 1976.
2. D. Efron, *Gesture, Race and Culture*, The Hague, Mouton & Company, 1972.
3. C.Pelachaud, N.I. Badler, and M.Steedman, Generating facial expressions for speech, *Cognitive Science*, vol 20, no. 1, pp. 1–46, 1996.
4. P. Ekman and W.F. Friesen, *Unmasking the Face*. Englewood Cliffs, New Jersey, USA: Prentice-Hall, Inc., 1975.
5. A. Wojdel and L.J.M. Rothkrantz, A Performance Based Parametric Model for Facial Animation, to be published in *Proceedings of IEEE International Conference on Multimedia and Expo*, New York City, NY, USA, August 2000.
6. M. Pantic and L.J.M. Rothkrantz, Expert system for automatic analysis of facial expressions, to appear in *Image and Vision*, 2000.

Dialogue Control in the Alparon System

Léon J.M. Rothkrantz, Robert J. van Vark, Alexandra Peters, and Niels A. Andeweg

Knowledge Based System Group, Delft University of Technology,
Zuidplantsoen 4, 2628 BZ Delft, The Netherlands
L.J.M.Rothkrantz@cs.tudelft.nl, R.J.vanVark@cs.tudelft.nl

Abstract. The main topic of this paper is on modelling a human operator in the dialogue manager of the Alparon system. First, a corpus of 200 human-human dialogues have been analysed by applying an approach surpassing a finite state automation approach. The corpus analysis resulted in a set of common strategies applied by professional human operators in similar situations. Secondly, a prototype system has been built based on the Alparon dialogue manager. This has been done by translating the strategies into knowledge rules and heuristics as these are used by the dialogue control modules in the Alparon dialogue manager.

1 Introduction

Dialogue management is the key factor in automated speech processing systems for information retrieval and transaction services for it can overcome the shortcomings of a one-shot approach. In a one-shot approach, the user specifies his requirements to the system in one turn. Then, the system tries to understand the user's requirements using the information provided in this turn and the system gives an appropriate response, also in one turn. If this approach fails, the user has to start again from scratch. In a one-shot approach one cannot speak of a dialogue-like interaction as there is simply an iteration of actions followed by reactions.

To behave in a more user-friendly fashion, the system has to be able to cope with a wide variety of phenomena like speech recognition errors, misunderstandings, partial specification of user requirements, conflicting requirements, etc. To cope with these phenomena, the system engages in a dialogue with the user using information collected in previous turns to improve the current interpretation of the user's requirements. Therefore dialogue management is an essential element for a user-friendly automated speech processing system.

Researchers at the Delft University of Technology have developed a natural language system aimed at information retrieval and transaction services. The focus of the Alparon system is on dialogue management, especially for speech-enabled applications. Other components of the automated speech processing system, like a speech recogniser, parser and speech generation, are only incorporated to make a complete test bed for testing dialogue strategies. The goal of the Alparon project is to investigate the application of human-human strategies in human-computer dialogues.

This paper describes an approach to model a human operator using the dialogue manager of the Alparon system. This paper especially focusses on retrieving the user's

P. Sojka, I. Kopeček, and K. Pala (Eds.): TSD 2000, LNAI 1902, pp. 333–338, 2000.
© Springer-Verlag Berlin Heidelberg 2000

requirements and not on presenting the information itself. Modelling the information of presentation has been presented earlier by researchers of the Delft University of Technology (see [1]). First, applicable human-human strategies have to be analysed. This was done by analysing a corpus of over 200 human-human dialogues between customers requiring travel information and professional operators. The analysis of this corpus is described in Section 2. Secondly, the human-human strategies have to be translated to knowledge rules and heuristics as they are applied in the dialogue control components of the Alparon dialogue manager. A description of the Alparon prototype modelling a human operator can be found in Section 3. The final section presents conclusions and future work.

2   Computational Dialogue Management

One way to design an effective, efficient and user-friendly dialogue manager is to apply a corpus-based approach. In such an approach, a corpus of human-human dialogues is studied to derive applicable strategies. In the Alparon project, a corpus was available consisting of 5,000 recorded and annotated human-human dialogues on timetable information in public transport. A selection of 500 was coded using the Alparon coding scheme [2]. This coding scheme applies dialogue acts to code the influence of an utterance to the dialogue context.

A dialogue can be represented as a tree. Every layer in the tree represents a turn in the dialogue and the nodes correspond to individual dialogue acts. As many dialogue acts can be found in a dialogue, the tree grows exponentially as the dialogue progresses. Applying such methods would call for a huge corpus.

Therefore, another way of representing the dialogue discourse was needed. In this paper, a dialogue is considered from the operator's point of view. This corresponds to the dialogue manager's point of view as the the operator will be modelled in the Alparon system. A computational model of the operator combines thoughts about the hypotheses, the client's intentions and the prompt choices. The model is constructed using goal-directed principles. The operator bases his/her behaviour on a comparison of a representation of the goal-state and the current state. The operator can use the planning strategy means-end analysis. Means-end analysis requires a measure of distance between the current state and the goal-state. The next step is then chosen based on an evaluation of how much this step will reduce the distance to the goal state. A useful reaction of the operator provides new information, reduces the uncertainty or provides clearness, whereas an inappropriate reaction takes extra time or causes confusion.

As such, the quality of an operator's prompt is defined by the extent the prompt will get the dialogue nearer to the goal, being defined as providing the information the client desires. One way to assess the quality of the prompts is by applying an evaluation function that provides a score for each prompt. At each step the prompt with the highest score is chosen. It is possible to think several steps ahead and combine the weights that belong to these steps. This way all the possible paths through a dialogue are scored and the path with the highest score can be chosen. Thinking several steps ahead is effective in finding the best path through a dialogue. The shortest path without detours produces the most efficient dialogue but it is questionable whether the client appreciates such

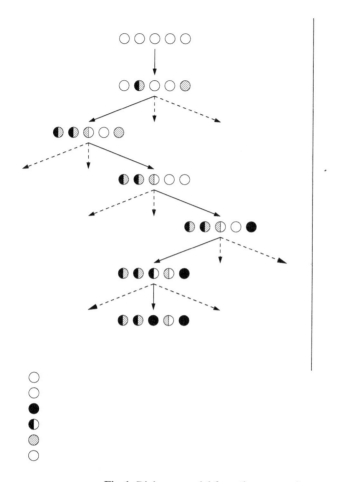

Fig. 1. Dialogue model from the operator's perspective

a dialogue. The factors that influence the professional operator in deciding on which prompt to choose have to be combined in these weights.

In Figure 1 the operator's mental state during a dialogue is displayed. The operator's thoughts are illustrated in the picture by using slots, represented by five circles. The goal is to fill the slots. All slots are empty at the beginning of the dialogue. Every state represents the operator's thoughts at that time. A new state is displayed after an operators prompt and the client's reaction to it. The next state indicates if there are differences in the operator's thoughts about the slots as compared to the previous state. At every state there are different ways to continue the dialogue. This is indicated in the figure by multiple arrows on a level. Using an optimal strategy implies that in the next state a maximal slot-filling is achieved. This slot-filling is done by reducing uncertainty about the slots or asking for new information.

Dialogue graphs were constructed for 200 dialogues selected from the Alparon corpus. In a one-step approach those prompts were selected providing a maximal filling of the slots. In about half of the cases it was possible to generate knowledge rules and heuristics how to select the appropriate prompt. In the other cases the history has to be taken into account or a multiple step approach, or the client took the freedom to take the initiative or could not provide the information. Some examples of heuristics derived using this strategy, are:

- if there is a (non-empty) subset of open slots and a (non-empty) subset of filled slots, ask for information covering as much of the open slots as possible;
- if one slot in the current state is not completely filled, immediately ask for the missing information to solve the ambiguity concerning the slot;
- if the subset of not complete filled slots contains more than one slot, handle the individual slots one after the other;
- as long as new information can be provided, assumptions of the operator are not verified;

It should be stressed that in the current application the operator needs information from the client to define a query for a database. This might cause the operator's behaviour to be rather slot-oriented, as was found for the current domain. There is a tendency from the operator to formulate open questions. In case of automated speech-driven systems there is a tendency to generate closed questions to prevent misunderstanding. In the next section, an approach is presented which compromises both extreme viewpoints.

3   The Alparon Natural Language System

The Alparon natural language system focusses on applying human-human strategies in dialogue management for information and transaction services. The Alparon dialogue manager consists of several modules (see Figure 2). This modular design was chosen to create a flexible and extensible system. When implementing information services, the dialogue manager should be able to interpret the user's utterance in the context of the ongoing dialogue. This interpretation is then used to generate a response to the user's utterance. Information on the current state of the dialogue and domain knowledge can be used to perform these tasks.

The main topic of this paper is on using human operator strategies to implement the dialogue control mechanism in the Alparon dialogue manager. This mechanism is to reason out a system response after the user's utterance is interpreted. These responses are the system's only means of influencing the user and thus controlling the dialogue. An approach surpassing a finite-state automation approach should be applied.

In the original design of the Alparon system, the task of generating system responses was placed with the response generation module and the control board. All the processing necessary to generate the system response should be done by the response generation module. This would include processing the user's turn on a dialogue level, since the context-updating module only takes care of the user's turn on an information level. In the actual design for dialogue control as described in this paper, another module was added, the dialogue updating module, to determine the consequences of the user's turn on a dialogue level.

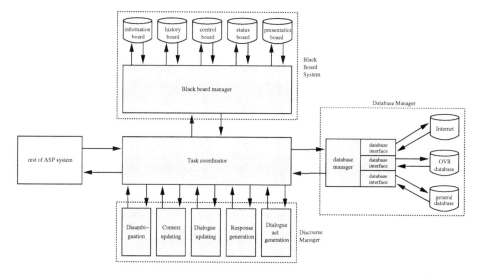

Fig. 2. Alparon dialogue manager overview

The dialogue updating module is charged with updating of goalstack according to the state of the dialogue in each turn. The goalstack is used to structure the goals that define what must be achieved during the dialogue. In information retrieval dialogues the dialogue structure highly resembles the task structure. So a plan based approach is used in which the goals embody the plan to accomplish the task and subtasks in such a dialogue. When disambiguation and context updating modules have interpreted the user's turn and extracted the factual information from it, the dialogue updating module processes the consequences of the new information and the user's turn on a dialogue level. The goalstack is updated to reflect this new situation.

The task of the response generation module is to generate the actual system response. Given the goals that still have to be achieved, the response generation module places communicative actions linked to those goals and selects communicative actions to be combined in a system response. The communicative actions are linked to goals and they are designed to help achieve the goals.

The control board is used to store the goal structure and the communicative actions, both the possible ones and the ones selected for the system response. This goal structure and the communicative actions implement the rules and strategies extracted by our corpus analysis. Other information related to dialogue control is also placed on blackboards, e.g. conflicts in the system beliefs of the dialogue. All the information used for dialogue control is present on the blackboards.

4   Conclusions

In this paper, we presented a prototype of a dialogue management system. The dialogue control strategies implement a human operator applying rules and strategies extracted from a corpus of human-human dialogues. In the research environment of the Alparon system, dialogue control is designed as a generic framework. Within this framework various rulesets can be defined to specify the behaviour of dialogue control. By changing these rulesets, various approaches to dialogue control can be implemented and refined. The rulesets specify one engine, consisting of all components for dialogue control. As a result, the actual strategy for dialogue control is defined by these rulesets.

References

1. M.M.M. Rats, R.J. van Vark, and J.P.M. de Vreught. Corpus-based information presentation for a spoken public transport information system. In *ACL/EACL Workshop on Interactive Spoken Dialog Systems: Bringing Speech and NLP Together in Real Applications*, pp. 106–113, 1997.
2. R.J. van Vark, J.P.M. de Vreught, and L.J.M. Rothkrantz. Classification of public transport information dialogues using an information based coding scheme. *Dialogue Processing in Spoken Language Systems, Lecture Notes in Artificial Intelligence (1236)*, pp. 55–69, 1997.

ISIS: Interaction through Speech
with Information Systems

Afzal Ballim, Jean-Cédric Chappelier, Martin Rajman, and Vincenzo Pallotta

Computer Science Department, Swiss Federal Institute of Technology (EPFL), Lausanne

Abstract. This paper presents the result of an experimental system aimed at performing a robust semantic analysis of analysed speech input in the area of information system access. The goal of this experiment was to investigate the effectiveness of such a system in a pipelined architecture, where no control is possible over the morpho-syntactic analysis which precedes the semantic analysis and query formation.

1 Introduction

The general applicative framework of the ISIS project[1] [10] was to design an information system NLP interface for automated telephone-based phone-book inquiry. The objective of the project was to define an architecture to improve speech recognition results by integrating higher level linguistic knowledge. The availability of a large collection of annotated telephone calls for querying the Swiss phone-book database (i.e. the Swiss French PolyPhone corpus [11]) allowed us to propose and evaluate a very first functional prototype of software architecture for vocal access to database through phone.

The processing of the corpus data is performed at various linguistic levels by pipelined modules, where each module takes as input the output of the preceding module. The main goal of this architecture is to understand how far it is possible to go without using any kind of feedback and interactions among different linguistic modules. The proposed architecture for the functional prototype contained 3 modules:

- a speech recognition (SR) system [2], taking speech signals as input and providing N-best sequences in the compact form of a lattice;
- a stochastic syntactic analyser (i.e. parser) extracting the k-best analysis [8];
- a semantic module in charge of filling the frames required to query the database [5].

The present paper describes first the parsing module and then the semantic module.

2 Syntactic Analysis

The forest of syntactic trees produced by this phase have been used to achieve two different goals:

---

[1] ISIS project started on April 1998 and finished on April 1999. It was funded and overseen by SwissCom; the partners were EPFL, ISSCO (Institute Dalle Molle, University of Geneva) and IDIAP (Institute Dalle Molle, Martigny).

P. Sojka, I. Kopeček, and K. Pala (Eds.): TSD 2000, LNAI 1902, pp. 339–344, 2000.
© Springer-Verlag Berlin Heidelberg 2000

1. the k-best analyses are used to disambiguate speech recogniser hypothesis as, due to the lack of a good language model for the application (lots of proper nouns), the lattices obtained from the SR module were of low quality: almost none of them contained a single syntactically correct sentence;
2. syntactic parses served as supplementary input for the robust semantic analysis which aims at producing query frames for the information system.

Resources. Low-level processing (morphological analysis and tagging) was performed by ISSCO using tools developed in the European Linguistics Engineering project MULTEXT. For syntactic analysis, ISSCO developed a Feature Unification Grammar (FUG) based on a small sample of the Polyphone data.

The FUG was translated into a equivalent Context-Free Grammar (CFG) necessary for parsing the lattices coming out of the SR module. The reasons for translating the FUG in a CFG were: (1) to be able to directly parse the lattices coming out of the speech-recognition module, without listing their whole content explicitly; (2) to have a very fast parsing module and (3) to be able to do robust partial analysis in the (very frequent) case of no complete parsing at the sentence level.

Some may argue that context-free models are not very realistic from a linguistic perspective and that higher-level descriptions[2] should be used instead. Others may argue that context-free models are not realistic for real-time speech recognition since they may lead to important overheads in computational cost for real-world applications.

For real-world applications, only methods with low algorithmic complexity can be considered. Such a constraint imposes severe limitations on the sophistication of the linguistic models that can be used, and most often, only Finite-State models, which allow efficient parsing (linear time), can be considered. However, lower-level language models such as Finite-State Automata do not provide the analysed sentence with useful syntactic structure that may be necessary for the subsequent processing modules (e.g. semantic).

We argue that CFG have both advantages to be efficient enough for implementation in real-time speech recognition applications and to incorporate at least some linguistic descriptions.

We are nonetheless well aware of the fact that the writing of a grammar (mandatory for applications that require good performances) cannot reasonably be made within a context-free formalism. In our opinion, CF formalism is rather to be considered as a kind of "machine code" for syntactic descriptions, provided that some translation mechanisms from higher level description formalisms are available.

The original FUG grammar had 94 rules. We implemented an optimised CFG translation leading to 28,253 context-free rules with 6,648 non-terminals (whereas the CF backbone of the FUG grammar had 25 main categories). The lexicon had 6,962 words and 174 Part-of-Speech tags.

Experimental Results. We experimentally addressed the two questions: (1) Does the pipelined coupling of a CFG parser to the SR module significantly improve the recognition? (2) Is the parsing feasible in a reasonable time?

---

[2] HPSG for instance

The first preliminary experiments we made were, for both aspects, promising [9]. Experiments were carried out for several different parameter settings of the speech recogniser[3]. On the average over all the experiments, in 35% of the cases the coupling with a SCFG strictly improved the results and in 67% of the cases it did at least as well as without SCFG. Furthermore, when restricted to the two parameter sets for which the speech-recogniser produced its best results, the former results improved to 50% and 80% respectively.

It is worth emphasising that, using our computationally efficient parser [8], the overhead in time due to the adjunction of a CFG parser is negligible with respect to the speech recognition time.

3   Robust Semantic Analysis

In theory, a complete dialogue management system requires total semantic understanding of the input. However, it is still very difficult to get any useful semantic representation from free dialogue, even for a limited domain as here considered. A different approach considers that a dialogue management can be achieved by a light parsing of the texts. This method needs neither a full semantic understanding of the language nor a deep investigation in the meaning and senses of the words. It is merely based on the knowledge of certain *cue-phrases* able to describe a shallow semantic structure of the text. These cue-phrases or terms should be relevant enough to give a coherent semantic separation of the different parts[4]. Nonetheless, the set of terms must not be rigid to avoid boolean results, but there must be a set of semantically similar terms with a degree of confidence for each. This would generate hypothetic semantic descriptions. In fact, these terms which correspond to semantic fields, are able to isolate texts parts. In case of a failure in obtaining a full and precise semantic description, a minimum description would indeed be derived. Therefore in all cases only relevant parts would undergo the understanding process. While the semantic analysis will in general reduce the degree of ambiguity found after syntactic analysis, there remains the possibility that it might *increase* some degree of ambiguity due to the presence of coherent senses of words with the same syntactic category (e.g., the word "Geneva" can refer to either the canton or the city). A simple notion of context can be useful to fill by default those slots for which we have no explicit information. For instance, it is possible to fill automatically the *locality* slot using information about the caller's prefix number in case of he does not explicitly specify any locality. We assume that his request actually refers to the same locality denoted by the above prefix number. For doing this type of hierarchical reasoning, we exploit the meta-programming capabilities of logic programming and we used a meta-interpreter which allows multiple inheritance among logical theories [7].

Robust Definite Clause Grammars. Left-corner Head-driven Island Parser [4,14] (LHIP) is a system which performs robust analysis of its input, using a grammar defined in an extended form of the Definite Clause Grammar (DCGs) formalism used

---

[3] Several values for the "acoustic factor" were tested.

[4] A similar approach has been proposed by Grefenstette [12].

for implementation of parsers in Prolog. The chief modifications to the standard Prolog 'grammar rule' format are of two types: one or more right-hand side (RHS) items may be marked as 'heads', and one or more RHS items may be marked as 'ignorable'. LHIP employs a different control strategy from that used by Prolog DCGs, in order to allow it to cope with ungrammatical or unforeseen input. A number of tools are provided for producing analyses of input by the grammar with certain constraints. For example, to find the set of analyses that provide maximal coverage over the input, to find the subset of the maximal coverage set that have minimum spans, and to find the analyses that have maximal thresholds.

We introduced weights into LHIP rules with the main goal of inducing a partial order over the generated hypotheses. The following schema illustrates how to build a simple weighted rule in a compositional fashion where the resulting weight is computed from the sub-constituents using the minimum operator. Weights are real numbers in the interval $[0, 1]$.

```
cat(cat(Hyp),Weight) ~~> sub_cat1(H1,W1), ...,sub_catn(Hn,Wn),
    {app_list([H1,...,Hn],Hyp), min_list([W1,...,Wn],Weight)}.
```

This strategy is not the only possible since the LHIP formalism allows a greater flexibility. Without entering into formal details we can observe that if we strictly follow the above schema and we impose a cover threshold of 1 we are dealing with *fuzzy DCG grammars* [13,3]. We actually extend this class of grammars with a notion of *fuzzy-robustness* where weights are used to compute confidence factors for the membership of islands to categories[5]. We actually extend this class of grammars with a notion of *fuzzy-robustness* where weights are used to compute confidence factors for the membership of islands to categories[5].

In our case study we try to integrate the above principles in order to effectively compute hypotheses for the query generation task. The weighted LHIP rules are designed considering two kind of knowledge: *domain knowledge* is exploited to provide quantitative support (or confidence factor) to our rules. *Linguistic knowledge* is used for determining constraints in order to prune the hypotheses space. We are concerned with lexical knowledge when we need to specify lexical LHIP rules which represent the building blocks of our parsing system.

As pointed out in [6], lexical knowledge plays an important role in Information Extraction since it can contribute in guiding the analysis process at various linguistic level. In our case, we are concerned with lexical knowledge when we need to specify lexical LHIP rules which represent the building blocks of our parsing system. *Semantic markers* are domain-dependent word patterns and must be defined for a given corpus. They identify *cue-words* serving both as *separators* among logical subparts of the same sentence and as *introducers* of *semantic constituents*. The generation of frame filling hypotheses is performed by rules that specify the orders of chunks interleaved by semantic markers (e.g. separators and introducers), compose weights and filter hypotheses by using domain knowledge. The grammar should also provide a mean to provide an empty constituent when all possible hypothesis rules have failed.

---

[5] Development of this notion is currently under investigation and not yet formalised.

4 Conclusions

From a very superficial observation of the human language understanding process, it appears clear that no deep competence of the underlying structure of the spoken language is required in order to be able to process acceptably distorted utterances. On the other hand, the more experienced is the speaker, the more probable is a successful understanding of that distorted input. How can this kind of fault-tolerant behaviour be reproduced in an artificial system by means of computational techniques? Several answers have been proposed to this question and many systems implemented so far, but no one of them is capable of dealing with robustness as a whole. The use of domain knowledge has turned out to be crucial since our particular goal is to process a queries without any request of clarification from the system. Due to the inaccuracy and ambiguity generated by previous phases of analysis, we need to select the best hypotheses and often recover information lost during that selection.

Although robustness can be considered as being applied at either a syntactic or semantic level, we believe it is generally at the semantic level that it is most effective. This robust analysis needs a model of the domain in which the system operates, and a way of linking this model to the lexicon used by the other components. It specifies semantic constraints that apply in the world and which allow us, for instance, to rule out incoherent requests. Taking the assumption that the information system being queried is relatively close in form to a relational database, the goal of the interpretative process is to furnish a query to the information system that can be viewed in the form of a frame with certain fields completed, the function of the querying engine being to fill in the empty fields.

We can conclude that robustness in dialogue is crucial when the artificial system takes part in the interaction since inability or low performance in processing utterances will cause unacceptable degradation of the overall system. As pointed out in [1], it is better to have a dialogue system that tries to guess a specific interpretation in case of ambiguity rather than ask the user for a clarification. If this first commitment results later to be a mistake, a robust behaviour will be able to interpret subsequent corrections as repair procedures to be issued in order to get the intended interpretation.

References

1. J.F. Allen, B. Miller, E. Ringger, and T. Sikorski. A robust system for natural spoken dialogue. In *Proc. 34th Meeting of the Assoc. for Computational Linguistics*. Association of Computational Linguistics, June 1996.
2. J.M. Andersen, G. Caloz, and H. Bourlard. Swisscom "advanced vocal interfaces services" project. Technical Report COM-97-06, IDIAP, Martigny, December 1997.
3. Peter. R.J. Asveld. Towards robustness in parsing – fuzzifying context-free language recognition. In J. Dassow, G. Rozemberg, and A. Salomaa, editors, *Developments in Language Theory II – At the Crossroad of Mathematics*, Computer Science and Biology, pages 443–453. World Scientific, Singapore, 1996.
4. A. Ballim and G. Russell. LHIP: Extended DCGs for Configurable Robust Parsing. In *Proceedings of the 15th International Conference on Computational Linguistics*, pages 501–507, Kyoto, Japan, 1994. ACL.

5. Afzal Ballim and Vincenzo Pallotta. Robust parsing techniques for semantic analysis of natural language queries. In Rodolfo Del Monte, editor, *Proceedings of VEXTAL99 conference*, November 1999. to appear.

6. R. Basili and Pazienza M.T. Lexical acquisition and information extraction. In Pazienza M.T., editor, *Information Extraction – A multidisciplinary approach to an emerging information technology*, volume 1299 of *LNAI*, pages 44–72. Springer Verlag, 1997.

7. A. Brogi and F. Turini. Meta-logic for program composition: Semantic issues. In K.R. Apt and F. Turini, editors, *Meta-Logics and Logic Programming*. The MIT Press, 1995.

8. J.-C. Chappelier and M. Rajman. A generalised cyk algorithm for parsing stochastic cfg. In *1st Workshop on Tabulation in Parsing and Deduction (TAPD98)*, pages 133–137, Paris, April 2–3, 1998.

9. J.-C. Chappelier, M. Rajman, R. Aragues, and A. Rozenknop. Lattice parsing for speech recognition. In *Proc. of 6ème conférence sur le Traitement Automatique du Langage Naturel (TALN '99)*, pages 95–104, July 1999.

10. J-C. Chappelier, M. Rajman, P. Bouillon, S. Armstrong, V. Pallotta, and A Ballim. ISIS project: final report. Technical report, Computer Science Department – Swiss Federal Institute of Technology, September 1999.

11. G. Chollet, J.-L. Chochard, A. Constantinescu, C. Jaboulet, and Ph. Langlais. Swiss french polyphone and polyvar: Telephone speech database to model inter- and intra-speaker variability. Technical Report RR-96-01, IDIAP, Martigny, April 1996.

12. G. Grefenstette. Light parsing as finite-state filtering. In Kornai A., editor, *Proceedings of the ECAI 96 Workshop on Extended Finite State Models of Language*, pages 20–25, 1996.

13. E.T. Lee and L.A. Zadeh. Note on fuzzy languages. *Information Science*, 1:421–434, 1969.

14. C. Lieske and A. Ballim. Rethinking natural language processing with prolog. In *Proceedings of Practical Applications of Prolog and Practical Applications of Constraint Technology (PAPPACTS 98)*, London, UK, 1998. Practical Application Company.

Centering-Based Anaphora Resolution
in Danish Dialogues[*]

Costanza Navarretta

Center for Language Technology
Njalsgade 80, 2300 Copenhagen S - DK
Tel. +(45) 35 32 90 65, Fax. +(45) 35 32 90 89
costanza@cst.ku.dk

Abstract. In this paper, we present the results of applying two different centring algorithms [1,9] to Danish discourses. Then we describe how we have adapted the algorithm for resolving anaphora referring to both individual NPs and discourse deictics presented in [3] so that it covers Danish discourse deictics. The modified algorithm has been manually tested on Danish dialogues and the obtained results have been evaluated.

1   Introduction

Resolving anaphors is an important task in many NLP applications. Most of the current anaphora resolution algorithms only deal with coreference between anaphors and individual NPs in written texts. In particular, algorithms based on centring theory [4] have been studied and tested extensively in many languages, but not for Danish. Recently centring has also been applied to dialogues, i.e. [2] and [3]. Eckert and Strube [3], in particular, present an algorithm, henceforth the ES99-algorithm, for the resolution of anaphors in English dialogues. The ES99-algorithm which applies to both anaphors referring to individual NPs and discourse deictics is based on rules for discriminating among individual NPs and discourse deictics, mainly determined by the syntactic constructions in which the anaphors occur. After having tested whether centring works on Danish texts, we have adapted the rules of the ES99-algorithm to Danish and applied the modified algorithm to Danish dialogues.

This paper is organised as follows. In Section 2, we briefly describe two centring algorithms, the BFP-algorithm [1] and the S98-algorithm [9] and we present the results of their application on Danish texts. In Section 3, we outline the ES99-algorithm. In Section 4, we briefly present the Danish discourse deictics found in the two dialogue corpora Bysoc and SL[1] and we describe the modified ES99-algorithm accounting for Danish data. Finally in Section 5, we evaluate the results obtained by manually testing the ES99-algorithm on the SL dialogues.

---

[*] The research described has partially been funded by the Staging project which is funded by the Danish Research Councils.

[1] Both corpora have been collected by researchers at the Department of General and Applied Linguistics at the University of Copenhagen.

P. Sojka, I. Kopeček, and K. Pala (Eds.): TSD 2000, LNAI 1902, pp. 345–350, 2000.
© Springer-Verlag Berlin Heidelberg 2000

2   Centering and Danish Data

The centring theory fits into Grosz and Sidner's model of discourse structure [5], according to which a discourse is composed of discourse segments which exhibit *global coherence*. A discourse segment is composed of a sequence of utterances which exhibit *local coherence*. The latter phenomenon is accounted for by the centring theory. The basic assumption behind centring is that some entities in an utterance are more central than others and this fact influences the use of referring expressions. The entities which link an utterance U_n to the others in the same discourse segment are called the *centres* of that utterance. Each utterance is assigned a set of *forward-looking centres*, C_f, and, with the exception of the initial utterance of the segment, a *backward-looking center*, C_b. The C_b of an utterance U_n connects with one of the *forward-looking centres* of the preceding utterance U_{n-1}, while the *forward-looking centres* exclusively depend on the expressions in U_n. The *forward-looking centres* are partially ordered to reflect relative prominence. In the BFP-algorithm, *forward-looking centres* are ranked according to the obliqueness of the grammatical relations of the subcategorised functions of the main verb (subject > object > object2 > complements > adjuncts). The first element in the C_f list is called the preferred centre, $C_p(U_n)$. In BFP, four types of transition relations across pairs of utterances, *continue, retain, shifting-1, shifting*, are identified. The discriminating elements between the transitions are given in Table 1 [1, p. 157].

Table 1. Transition States

	$C_b(U_n) = C_b(U_{n-1})$ OR no $C_b(U_{n-1})$	$C_b(U_n) \neq C_b(U_{n-1})$
$C_b(U_n) = C_p(U_n)$	*continue*	*shifting-1*
$c_b(U_n) \neq c_p(U_n)$	*retain*	*shifting*

The following two rules constrain centre realization in BFP:

Rule 1: If any element of $C_f(U_{n-1})$ is realized by a pronoun in U_n, then $C_b(U_n)$ must also be realized by a pronoun

Rule 2: The centre transitions have the following ranking:
continue > retain > shifting-1 > shifting

The BFP-algorithm consists of three steps:

1. **construct** the proposed anchors for an utterance and possible *Cb-Cf* combinations
2. **filter** by i.e. contra-indices, sortal predicates, centring rules and constraints
3. **rank** by transition orderings.

The S98-algorithm [9] treats both intrasentential and intersentential anaphors. In S98, the functions of the *backward-looking centre* and the *transitions* in the centring theory are replaced by the order of elements in a list of salient discourse entities, the **S-list**. The ranking criteria for the elements in the S-list are based on [7] and [8], where discourse entities are classified into *hearer-old* (OLD), *mediated* (MED) and *hearer-new* (NEW). The two tuples (x, utt_x, pos_x) and (y, utt_y, pos_y) in the S-list indicate that the entity x is evoked in utterance utt_x at position pos_x and that y is evoked in the utterance utt_y at position pos_y respectively. Given that utt_x and utt_y refer to U_n or U_{n-1}, the following ranking constraints on the S-list entities are valid [9, p. 1253]:[2]

1. if $x \in$ OLD and $y \in$ MED, then $x \prec y$
   if $x \in$ OLD and $y \in$ NEW, then $x \prec y$
   if $x \in$ MED and $y \in$ NEW, then $x \prec y$
2. if $x,y \in$ OLD or $x,y \in$ MED or $x,y \in$ NEW,
   then if $utt_x > utt_y$ then $x \prec y$
   if $utt_x = utt_y$ and $pos_x < pos_y$ then $x \prec y$

Strube's algorithm for anaphora resolution consists in testing a referring expression against the elements in the S-list from left to right until the test succeeds. The S-list is then updated so that new elements are inserted according to the S-list ranking criteria. When the analysis of an utterance is finished all the entities which were not realized in the utterance are removed from the S-list.

We have applied the two algorithms to randomly chosen chapters of a pc-manual (10,715 words) and newspaper articles (9,914 words). In the test discourse segments were paragraphs and utterances were clauses. Following [9] we have extended the BFP-algorithm to cover complex clauses following the strategy described in [6].[3] We manually marked expletives and discourse deictics.

The success rate for the BFP-algorithm was 72.5% while the S98-algorithm had a success rate of 91.67%. The difference between the results obtained with the two algorithms is mainly due to the fact that the BFP-algorithm does not account for intrasentential anaphors. The cases where both algorithms failed in resolving pronominal anaphora comprise complex plural antecedents (coordinated and split ones), generic use of the neuter pronoun *det* (it), plural pronouns without antecedents, ambiguity of antecedents. Although the results obtained in tests applied to different kinds of discourse in different languages cannot be compared, the results obtained in our test are similar to those obtained in other languages (i.e. [9,10]). This indicates that centring also works for Danish.

3   The ES99-Algorithm

In the ES99-algorithm the types of anaphora identified are individual anaphors, discourse deictics, inferable-evoked anaphors and vague anaphors. Predicates that are preferably associated with abstract objects are marked as **i-incompatible** (*I) while predicates that

---

[2] We mark ranking precedence with $\prec$.

[3] Kameyama treats tensed clauses as independent utterances, while untensed clauses are treated as part of the main clause. Tensed clauses comprise reported speech, which is not accessible to the superordinate level, non-report complements and relative clauses which are accessible to the superordinate level, but less salient. The remaining types are processed at the same level as the main clause.

are preferably associated with individual objects are marked as **a-incompatible** (*A).
As an example, we quote the *I predicates given in [3, p. 40]:

- Equating constructions where a pronominal referent is equated with an abstract
  object, e.g., *x is making it easy, x is a suggestion.*
- Copula constructions whose adjectives can only be applied to abstract entities, e.g.,
  x is true, x is false, x is correct, x is right, x isn't right.
- Arguments of verbs describing propositional attitude which only take S'-comple-
  ments, e.g., *assume.*
- Object of *do.*
- Predicate or anaphoric referent is "a reason", e.g., *x is because I like her, x is why
  he's late.*

Individual anaphors are resolved with the S98-algorithm, while abstract objects are
treated in a so called A-list. The A-list is filled when discourse deictics occur and elements
remain in the list only for one dialogue act (I, Initiation).[4] A context ranking procedure
describes the order in which the parts of the linguistic contexts are accessed.

4   The Modified Algorithm

We have adapted the ES99-algorithm so that it covers Danish data identified in our
dialogue corpora. The focus in our description is on discourse deictics. In Danish the
most used discourse deictic is *det* which corresponds to both *it* and *that*.[5] *Dette* (this) is
another discourse deictic, but it is mainly used in written language and did not occur at
all in our dialogues.

When used as discourse deictic *det* can refer to an infinitive or a finite clause, as it
is the case in the following examples:

(1)   a.   *At ryge er farligt og det er også dyrt*
           (Smoking is dangerous and it is also expensive)
      b.   *Jeg skal måle dit blodtryk.*
           (I have to measure your blood pressure.)
           Hvorfor det? (Why (that)?)

Det refers to a verb phrase when it is used as the object complement with *have* (have),
modal verbs and with the verb *gøre* (do).

(2)   a.   *Jeg faldt, men det gjorde hun ikke*
           (I fell, but she did not)

Det refers to a clause in constructions with verbs such as *tro* (think), *sige* (say), *vide*
(know):

---

[4] In [3] grounded acts are used as domain for the resolution algorithm instead of clauses. We
have followed the same discourse model.

[5] The pronoun *det* usually co-refers with (from now on we simply write *refers to*) nominals in
neuter gender. It is also used as expletive. *Det* is also the neuter definite article (the) and the
demonstrative adjective (that).

(3)   *Han lyver.* (He is lying)
       Det tror jeg ikke (I do not think so)

Det can also refer to more clauses, or to something that can be vaguely inferred from the previous discourse. On the basis of the deictics in the Danish dialogues we have defined the following types of ***I** predicate for Danish:

– constructions where a pronoun is equated. with an abstract object, e.g., *x gør det svært* (x is making it difficult)
– copula constructions with adjectives which can only be applied to abstract entities, such as *x er sandt* (x is true)
– arguments of verbs indicating propositional attitudes which take S'-complements, such as *tro* (believe), *antage* (assume)
– arguments of verbs such as *sige* (say) and *vide* (know)
– object of *gøre* (do)
– object of *have* (have) if the verb was not used as a main verb in the previous clause
– object of modal verbs
– predicate or anaphoric referent is a reason, such as *x er fordi* . . .   (x is because)

Our ***A** predicates are the following:

– constructions where a pronominal referent is equated with a concrete individual referent, such as *x er en legemsdel* (x is a body part)
– copula constructions with adjectives which can only be applied to concrete entities, such as *x er dyr* (x is expensive), *x er rød* (x is red)
– arguments of verbs describing physical contact/stimulation, e.g., *slå x* (hit x), *spise x* (eat x)

5   Evaluation and Conclusion

We have applied the modified ES99-algorithm to randomly chosen SL dialogues (9,728 words). It must be noted that we only used one annotator in our test, while in the test reported in [3] there were two annotators. The precision and recall of the modified algorithm on our dialogues were of 64.7% and 70.4%, respectively. These results are similar to those reported in [3]. Most of the wrongly resolved anaphors are due to the fact that the algorithm cannot distinguish between discourse deictics and vague anaphors. Some errors are due to missing information on nominals referring to abstract objects, some depended on the chosen discourse model.

In conclusion, both centring algorithms and the ES99-algorithm seem to perform as well for Danish as for English. Future work consists in testing the algorithms on more types of dialogue, identifying more discriminating predicates and adding more lexical and domain knowledge to the modified ES99-algorithm.

References

1. Brennan, S. F., Friedman, M. W. and Pollard, C. J.: A Centering Approach to Pronouns. In *Proceedings of the ACL-87*. Stanford University,California, USA (1987) 155–162.
2. Byron, D., Stent, A.: A Preliminary Model of Centering in Dialog. In *Proceedings of the ACL-98*. Université de Montréal, Quebec, Canada (1998) vol II, 1475–1477.
3. Eckert, M., Strube, M.: Resolving Discourse Deictic Anaphora in Dialogues. In *Proceedings of the EACL-99*. (1999) 37–44.
4. Grosz, B., Joshi, A. K. and Weinstein, S.: Centering:A Framework for Modeling the Local Coherence of Discourse. *Computational Linguistics*. **21(2)** (1995) 203–225.
5. Grosz, B. J., Sidner, C. L.: Attention, Intentions, and the Structure of Discourse. *Computational Linguistics*. **12(3)** (1986) 175–284.
6. Kameyama, M.: Intrasentential centering: A case study. In Walker, M., Joshi, A., and Prince, E. (Eds.) *Centering Theory in Discourse*. Oxford University Press, Oxford, U.K. (1998) 89–112.
7. Prince, E. F.: Toward a taxonomy of given-new information. In Cole, P., (Ed.), *Radical Pragmatics*. Academic Press (1981) 223–255.
8. Prince, E. F.: The ZPG Letter: Subjects, definiteness, and Information-status. In Mann, W., Thompson, S. A., (Ed.), *Discourse Description. Diverse Linguistic Analyses of a Fund-Raising Text.*. John Benjamins (1992) 295–325.
9. Strube, M.: Never look back: An alternative to centering. In *Proceedings of the ACL-98*, Université de Montréal, Quebec, Canada (1998) vol II, 1251–1257.
10. Tetreault, J.R.: Analysis of Syntax-Based Pronoun Resolution Methods. In *Proceedings of the 37th ACL*. Maryland, USA (1999) 602–605. 1999.

Some Improvements on the IRST Mixed Initiative Dialogue Technology

Cristina Barbero, Daniele Falavigna, Roberto Gretter,
Marco Orlandi, and Emanuele Pianta

ITC-irst, 38050 Povo, Trento, Italy,
barbero@itc.it, falavi@itc.it, gretter@itc.it, orlandi@itc.it, pianta@itc.it,
http://www.itc.it/

Abstract. The paper describes the ITC-irst approach for handling spoken dialogue interactions over the telephone network. Barge-in and utterance verification capabilities are going to be introduced into the developed software architecture. Some research activities that should enable accessing information in a new large applicative domain (i.e. the tourism domain) have been started. Objectives of the research are: language model adaptation and efficient information presentation, using a mixed representation approach.

1   Introduction

Recently, ITC-irst has developed a software architecture for information access in restricted domains [1]. The architecture is formed by some modules, namely: telephone driver, dialogue engine, automatic speech recognition, speech synthesiser, database access, graphical interface, scheduler and language generation.

Some of the functions performed by the above modules can be invoked through an Application Programming Interface (API) consisting of classes developed in either the *Java* or *C++* programming languages.

To demonstrate the effectiveness of the technology, a spoken dialogue prototype for train timetable inquiry has been developed. In this case, the task consists in understanding only few concepts (i.e. departure/arrival dates and cities). Since the performance obtained on this task resulted quite satisfactory [1], a new prototype, working on a much larger domain, has been recently developed. This latter one allows accessing information contained in a tourism database provided by the "Azienda Provinciale del Turismo" (APT) del Trentino, an organisation that coordinates the activities of most of local operators in "Trentino Alto-Adige" (North of Italy).

2   Mixed Initiative Dialogue Strategy

The basic idea underlying the dialogue engine lies in the definition of a set of "contexts", containing "concepts" associated to subgrammars. Therefore, a direct relation between concepts and grammars, activated during the various steps of the interaction, has to be established.

P. Sojka, I. Kopeček, and K. Pala (Eds.): TSD 2000, LNAI 1902, pp. 351–356, 2000.

Our approach for language modelling makes use of recursive transition networks [2]. These are finite-state networks whose arcs allow linking other grammars in a recursive way. The resulting language is context free. Since the decoding step of a speech utterance can backtrack both the grammars and the words along the best path of the language graph, the recognised string consists of a mix of words and structured information, i.e. it can be seen as a parse tree. Therefore semantic tags are included in the recognised string as reported below:

```
''I want to go in an (TYPE( hotel )TYPE) (STARS( 3 stars)STARS) in
(LOCALITY( levico )LOCALITY)''.
```

In the string above, the tag TYPE represents the type of accommodation requested by the caller (hotel, hostel, camping, etc.), the tag LOCALITY is the name of the place the caller wants to stay.

The development of the understanding part of the system basically consists in designing a set of grammars. Each basic concept has associated one or more grammars, which strictly model the concept itself. In this way, the system developer has the complete control of both the concepts and the ways users are allowed to refer to them. On the other hand, hand-modelling the parts of the sentence which do not carry useful information for the task (e.g. "I want to go in an" in the sentence above) is a time consuming and tedious activity. For this type of task, stochastic language models are more effective.

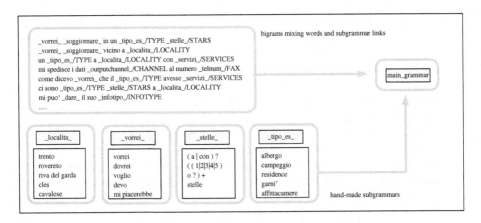

Fig. 1. Grammars used for speech recognition

In our approach, we mix the two formalisms: at the top level, a bigram grammar is activated, which is initially trained on a small set of hand-written sentences representing (in the designer's intention) what the users will say. These sentences mix words and links to other grammars (see Figure 1). As the first prototype is used to collect more and more interactions, their transcriptions can be easily added to the initial training set to build a more realistic bigram model.

The dialogue engine has to interpret the description of an application, which is both declarative (for what concerns contexts and concepts) and procedural (for the definition of the actions that must be executed in some dialogue states, for instance, the preparation of a database query). Each concept has associated a set of features, that specify how it will be used during the user interaction. For instance, it can be associated to a label, to a grammar, possibly to a procedure for some text processing, to some vocal prompts and to some other information.

2.1   New System Capabilities

Recently, the barge-in capability has been introduced into the prototype system. It is realized using the echo cancellation function of the telephone board: the start-end-point detection algorithm has been adapted to cope with the echo cancelled signal. Some work is going to be done in order to establish some criteria for echo cancellation activation (active only during some phases of the interaction, from the beginning of the voice prompt or after a time interval from the beginning of the prompt itself, etc.).

Some preliminary work, concerning word verification, has been carried out using an approach similar to the one described in [3]. With this approach, confidence measures can be evaluated for each part (e.g. a single word or sequences of words) of the recognised string. In this way, the confirmation phase of the information provided by the user will often be avoided, thus rendering faster and less annoying interaction. Some preliminary results will be reported in Section 4.

Finally, to improve flexibility and portability of ITC-irst speech technology an Application Programming Interface has been recently developed for requiring services (recognition, transcription, wave source, grammar compiling, etc.) to a server. The API defines a cross-platform software interface and consists of a set of *Java classes* providing methods for enabling speech recognition functions within Java applications. The Java platform offers: portability, powerful and compact environment, network aware and security. In the same way, Java classes for handling spoken dialogue applications, according to the previously described dialogue strategy, have been added to the API. This makes the introduction of spoken dialogue functionalities within existing or new systems or services easier, especially in the ones that would be used through Internet. In particular, some financial services are going to be designed in collaboration with companies working in the field of call centre products. A version of the API that uses *C++ classes* is also available.

3   Tourism Information Prototype

The database of APT of Trentino includes information on accommodation, structures and services, localities, events, sport, leisure time, art and culture, natural resorts, local products, holiday offers and packages, transportation. At present, we have defined and are testing a dialogue model for asking some general information about accommodation (e.g. type, category, position, services, address, etc.) and localities (e.g. altitude, description, transportation, etc.).

The user is completely free in the choice of the information to ask, both in the order the requests are made and in the linguistic expressions be used. To efficiently cope with this task, the system must be capable of updating the language models, for handling the dialogue, with the large and variable data set containing the required information. This process must be simple, so as to allow easy updating and using of the data collected during user's interactions. Note that all the names of localities and receptive structures of Trentino are included in the system. In the future, we plan to deal with other kinds of information contained in the database (like prices of accommodation and events).

An important issue raised by the new domain is the flexibility in the presentation of the requested information. In the train timetable domain the system could give its answers using a restricted pool of fixed templates, whereas presenting information in the tourism domain turns out to be a more complex task. In fact, tourism information is vast, rich and needs to be organised in a coherent discourse structure. Therefore, we make use of a more powerful generation component based on Mixed Representations, which is a generalisation of template-based generation. This approach allows selecting, for each application domain, the best trade-off between efficiency and linguistic sophistication [4].

In the following, some more details about the Mixed Representation approach are given. A clear distinction is generally made between deep natural language generation (based on conceptual models of language, and usually rated as flexible but inefficient) and template-based approaches (based on combination of fixed strings, efficient but not flexible), see [5]. In the last few years, templates have been used also within deep generation architectures, in order to improve efficiency ([6,7]). All these attempts to integrate templates within deep generation architectures can be characterised as using Mixed Representations. In the adopted approach [4], we use precompiled generation knowledge whenever possible, while retaining the possibility of using a full-fledged deep generation approach when strictly necessary. For instance, let's consider the sentence *[subject] si trova a [N] metri sul livello del mare* ("[subject] is situated at [N] meters above sea level"). The Mixed Representation approach allows restricting the use of flexible generation techniques only to the [subject] of the sentence (that could be, for example, *l'albergo a 3 stelle con sauna*, "the 3-stars hotel with sauna", or *il campeggio Bellavista*, "the camping Bellavista").

To implement the Mixed Representations approach, we use the Hyper Template Planning Language (HTPL): see [4] for a detailed description of the formalism and its interpretation mechanisms. The linguistic representation levels that can be mixed in an HTPL expression range from message representation to fixed strings. As an example, let's consider the following message: the hotel "Bellavista" has been selected during the dialogue, and the user asks for its altitude. Let's suppose the sentence *L'hotel Bellavista si trova a 1000 metri sul livello del mare* ("The Bellavista hotel is situated at 1000 meters above sea level") has to be generated. The module that plans the answer can use one of the following three templates:

1. `{message(give-information+altitude+hotel(hotel-name=X, altitude=Y))}`
2. `{message({hotel}, [hotel-name=X]),``si trova'',message(attribute, {altitude=Y])}`
3. `{``L'hotel'',X,``si trova'',``a'',Y,``metri sul livello del mare''}`

The first representation is abstract and flexible, but requires a lot of computation to be realized. On the contrary, the third representation is "ad hoc", but computationally efficient. At each time, the planner can choose the most suitable representation.

4   Experiments and Results

Some experiments have been carried out in order to assess the performance of the utterance verification approach. A database, formed by about 2000 speech files, has been used as a test set. Each file contains an utterance of either a name of a person or of an Italian city. All of the files have been collected through the public telephone network.

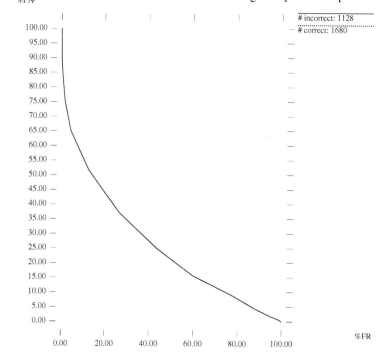

Fig. 2. Receiving Operating Curve of the word verification test. # correct and # incorrect represent the numbers of the correctly and incorrectly recognised words respectively.

The vocabulary of the test database consists of about 1000 words, while the grammar used for recognition is formed by a loop of about 12000 words, including the words in the test set itself. In the experiments, the threshold that controls the beam width during the decoding step has been set to a value that allows to obtain a word accuracy of about 50%. In this way, the number of the correctly recognised words is similar to the number of the incorrectly recognised ones. Then, confidence measures have been evaluated for each recognised word by summing the confidence scores of each hypothesised phoneme of the word itself (see [3]). To normalise the phone scores, a single state Hidden Markov Model, whose output probability is represented by a mixture of 100 Gaussians, has been appropriately trained. Finally, a word verification test has been carried out by evaluating the False Rejection (%FR) rate and the False Acceptance (%FA) rate obtained with different values of the acceptance/rejection threshold (i.e. the verification threshold). The relation between %FR and %FA is shown in Figure 2.

At present, the prototype system for accessing tourism information is used to collect interactions with some users. For this purpose a set of tasks has been defined: each caller is given two or three tasks. Up to now about 100 dialogues have been acquired, 34 of them have been controlled. Table 1 summarises the state of the acquisition.

Table 1. *Dialogue acquisitions for accessing tourism information*

Info obtained	(Yes) 21	(Partially) 4	(No) 9			
#Turns	(1–5) 1	(6–10) 14	(11–15) 8	(16–20) 2	(21–25) 5	(> 25) 4
System	(1) 2	(2) 2	(3) 14	(4) 8	(5) 8	

First row of the table indicates if the given task was completely (Yes), partially or at all (No) accomplished. Note that 21, out of 34, dialogues were considered to be successful.

Second row of the table reports the distribution of dialogues according to their corresponding number of turns. Several callers have interacted with a number of turns ranging between 6 and 10.

Third row of the table reports the dialogue distribution according to a subjective score (1:bad, 5:good) given by the authors. The score takes into account the overall performance of the system, i.e. it is a combination of speech recognition accuracy and dialogue effectiveness.

References

1. D. Falavigna, R. Gretter: Flexible Mixed Initiative Dialogue Over the Telephone Network. *Proc. of International Workshop on Automatic Speech Recognition and Understanding*, Keystone, Colorado, December 1999.
2. F. Brugnara, M. Federico: Dynamic Language Models for Interactive Speech Analysis. *Proc. of Eurospeech*, pp. 1827–1830, Rhodes, Greece, 1997.
3. R. A. Sukkar, C. H. Lee: Vocabulary Independent Discriminative Utterance Verification for Nonkeyword Rejection in Subword Based Speech Recognition. *IEEE Trans. on Speech and Audio Processing*, Vol. 4, no. 6, pp. 420–429, November, 1966.
4. E. Pianta, L. Tovena: Mixing representation levels: The hybrid approach to automatic text generation. *Proc. of AISB '99 Workshop on Reference Architectures and Data Standards for NLP*, Edinburgh, pp. 8–13, April 1999.
5. E. Reiter: NLG vs Templates. *Proc. of Fifth European Workshop on Natural Language Generation*, Leiden, 1995.
6. N. Cancedda, G. Kamstrup, E. Pianta, E. Pietrosanti: SAX: Generating Hypertext from SADT Models. *Proc. of Third Workshop on Applications of Natural Language to Information Systems*, Vancouver, 1997.
7. S. Busemann, H. Horacek: A Flexible Shallow Approach to Text Generation. *Proc. of Ninth International Natural Language Generation Workshop*, Niagara Falls, 1998.

Dictionary-Based Method for Coherence Maintenance in Man-Machine Dialogue with Indirect Antecedents and Ellipses[*]

Alexander Gelbukh, Grigori Sidorov, and Igor A. Bolshakov

Natural Language Laboratory, Centre for Computing Research (CIC),
National Polytechnic Institute (IPN), Av. Juan de Dios Batiz, s/n, esq. Mendizabal,
Zacatenco, C.P. 07738, Mexico D.F., Mexico.
gelbukh@cic.ipn.mx, sidorov@cic.ipn.mx, igor@cic.ipn.mx

Abstract. Resolution of referential ambiguity is one of the most challenging problems of natural language processing. Especially frequently it is faced within dialogues. We present a heuristic algorithm for detection of the indirect antecedents for dialogue phrases based on the use of a dictionary of prototypic scenarios associated with each headword as well as of a thesaurus of the standard type. The conditions for filtration of the candidates for the antecedent are presented. We also present a similar algorithm for reconstruction of elliptical phrases of a special kind using a combinatory dictionary.

1 Introduction

The problem of usual (direct) anaphora resolution in a wide range of NLP tasks – from language understanding to statistics, translation, and abstracting – have been the area of active research in recent years [4,7,13,17]. The prevailing approaches to resolution of direct anaphora are nowadays an integrated and an alternative ones [19,20,21]. The former approach is based on the integration of different kinds of knowledge like syntactic, semantic, and discourse, see also [1,9], while the latter uses statistical information, neural networks or the principles of reasoning with uncertainty. For ellipsis resolution, there is also a tendency to use integrated information [14]. On the other hand, there are attempts to exclude some types of knowledge from algorithms [18]. At the same time, the idea to create methods using only dictionaries like WordNet is on the agenda [15]. In this paper, we try to exploit the ideas connected with dictionary-based approaches.

Indirect anaphora has drawn less attention than the direct one. The investigation was mainly focussed on its various theoretical aspects rather than on practical algorithms of resolution [16,25]. For example, in [8] and [12], a givenness hierarchy is proposed. A proposal similar to our approach can be found in [23]. The authors note that "this kind of reference (indirect anaphora) has not been thoroughly studied in natural language processing, but is important for coherence resolution, language understanding, and machine translation.". The method they suggest is based on a dictionary of examples

---

[*] Work done under partial support of CONACyT, REDII-CONACyT, and CGEPI-IPN, Mexico.

of the form "*X* of *Y*" extracted from a text corpus. This dictionary plays the role analogous to that of our scenario dictionary, while the latter is much richer in the semantic and syntactic types of relations; also we build our dictionary on the basis of existing dictionaries of various types rather than extract it from a corpus.

Dialogue is also actively investigated, though not in relation with the anaphoric phenomena. As an example of a recent research in dialogue, see [3].

In this paper, we describe a dictionary-based method of restoration of indirect anaphoric and elliptical links in application to the dialogues where the phenomena in question are much more frequent [27,10]. In the first part of the paper, we discuss the problem of indirect anaphoric antecedents, and in the second part, we discuss a modification of our algorithm to be applied to ellipsis. We formulate necessary conditions for the detection of the presence of the phenomenon (anaphora or ellipsis, correspondingly); then we discuss the structure of the dictionary used by the algorithm; finally, the algorithm is described.

For simplicity, we consider the micro-dialogues, containing the phrase of one of the participants (the computer) and the answer of the other (the human), like

Example 1. "*There is a PS/2 computer in the store.*"
"*Is the motherboard from Intel?*"
Example 2. "*There is a printer in the store.*"
"*Narrow?*"
Example 3. "*The user found an error in the program.*"
"*Really fatal?*"

Example 1 demonstrates the case of the indirect anaphora. The problem is in the interpretation of the definite clause in the second utterance of the first dialogue. Usually, the definite clause refers to some entity already introduced in the common view of the participants of the communication (in this case implicitly). Examples 2 and 3 illustrate the cases of the elliptical construction where the omitted word was introduced into the dialogue in the previous utterance(s), and the purpose of the utterance is to clarify or add a detail to a previous one. Thus, we leave aside the cases where the omitted word was introduced, say, by the extralinguistic situation (say, both participants see a strange man; "*Drunk*," says one of them) or by the pragmatics of the communication.

2   Indirect Antecedents in Dialogue

Let us call the entities implicitly or potentially introduced by a word a *prototypic scenario* of this word. For example, the scenario for the word *house* includes *kitchen*, *roof*, *windows*, *district*, *place*, *owner*, etc. We suggest that the indirect anaphoric relation holds between a word and an element of the prototypic scenario of another word previously appeared in the text; such an implicitly introduced element does not have its own surface representation in the text.

We call the words that are equivalent for our algorithms *compatible*. Thus, synonyms, derivatives, hyperonyms, hyponyms, and metaphors of a word can be compatible with it.

Let us denote the potential antecedent x, the anaphor y, and the scenario of a word w, $S(w)$. Denoting the compatibility relation between the words w and u as $w \sim u$, we can formulate the following condition:

Condition 1. Indirect anaphoric relation between x and y is possible only if any of the following conditions holds:

$\exists w \in S(x)$ such that $y \sim w$, or

$\exists w \in S(y)$ such that $x \sim w$, or

$\exists w \in S(x)$ and $\exists u \in S(y)$ such that $u \sim w$.

The algorithm for detecting anaphoric links between the utterances in the dialogue works as follows. It analyses the current utterance word by word. If a word is introduced with a definite article or a demonstrative pronoun, then it is a potential anaphor, and the algorithm tries to find a plausible antecedent for it. It looks for the possible candidates first within the same utterance and then in the previous utterance(s); from right to left. The candidates are a priori scored the score the lower the score the greater the distance; the algorithm stops when an antecedent with high score is found or the scores become too little, see Figure 1.

Namely, let *distance* be the distance between the possible antecedent and the potential anaphor. Currently, we use the linear distance. In a more sophisticated version of the algorithm, the syntactic distance (the number of constituents between the two words) or some combination of the two measures can be used.

Let *probability-of-variant$_n$* be the a priori probability associated with the corresponding parts 1, 2, and 3 of Condition 1. This probability is a statistical characteristic of the given language (or sublanguage) that characterises the frequency of the use of the corresponding constructions.

Let *threshold* be the maximum allowed value which depends on *distance* and *probability-of-variant$_n$*. It is used to determine the stop condition of algorithm.

Determining the exact values of these parameters goes beyond the scope of this paper; in our experiments, we used the following approximate values found empirically: *threshold* = 0.05, *probability-of-variant$_1$* = 1, *probability-of-variant$_2$* = 0.75, and *probability-of-variant$_3$* = 0.4.

To check the possibility of an indirect antecedent, a prototypic scenario dictionary is used. In our experiments, we used a dictionary compiled from several sources, Currently the dictionary contains about 1,000 entries, and the scenarios contain in total about 40,000 words.

3   Ellipsis in Dialogue

For the purposes of the coherence maintenance in the dialogue with ellipsis it is appropriate to view the interpretation as establishing a link (similar to a syntactic one) between the corresponding words across the utterances. For instance, in Example 3 the link holds between the words *fatal* and *error*:

$$user \xleftarrow{subj} found \xrightarrow{obj} error \xrightarrow{attr} fatal$$

Let us call such a link *elliptical relation*, the word *fatal* being the source of the relation and the word *error* being its target.

---

repeat for each definite noun x of the utterance, from left to right

    repeat for each word y, from right to left, from the last word of the previous utterance

    $distance$ = the distance between x and y

    if $\exists\, n$ such that part n of Condition 1 holds for x and y **then**

        the variant y of the antecedent for x is temporarily stored,

        its weight w =$probability\text{-}of\text{-}variant_n \times (1/distance)$

    if $(max\{probability\text{-}of\text{-}variant_i\} \times (1/distance) < threshold)$ **then**

        break the loop and go to next x

        else pass to the next word y to the left

    end

    The variant y (if any) with the best weight w is chosen and sent to the output.

end

Fig. 1. The algorithm for finding antecedent(s)

To restore the elliptical relations in the dialogue, we use the same idea as for the indirect anaphoric relations. Namely, we try to find a highly probable target for such a relation and in this way detect the very presence of the relation.

We call the words that potentially, with high probability can form a word combination *combinable*, and denote this as $u \lhd w$. Here u is the governor and w is the dependent: *error* $\lhd$ *fatal* is true since the syntactic combination *fatal* $\longleftarrow$ *error* is highly probable; however, *fatal* $\lhd$ *error* is not true since *fatal* $\longrightarrow$ *error* is impossible. Also *program* $\lhd$ *fatal* is not true since normally *fatal program* is not a combination that can be normally expected in the text. Note that this is a lexical property of the corresponding words, specified in the dictionary, rather than the syntactic relation in a specific context.

Condition 2. Elliptical relation between x and y is possible only if $x \lhd y$.

If the lexical information is not available for a specific word, a relaxed condition using only the parts of speech POS (x) and POS (y) can be used, with less reliability of the positive result:

Condition 3. Elliptical relation between x and y is possible only if POS $(x) \lhd$ POS (y).

Since we treat the type of the ellipsis under consideration as a potential insertion of a word into the target utterance, the Condition 3 can be generalised as follows (though such a generalised condition is much more expensive computationally to test):

Condition 4. Elliptical relation between x and y is possible only if the utterance containing the target (x) remains syntactically correct when the source (y) is added to it and syntactically connected to x.

The algorithm for detecting potential antecedents is very similar to the one for detecting the indirect antecedents. Namely, for each case of structural incompleteness, the hypothesis of possible elliptical link is checked by trying, word by word, the candidates in the previous utterance and verifying Conditions 2 to 4. Since Condition 3 is less computationally expensive, it is tried first; then Condition 2. The process stops when a plausible antecedent is found or when the distance from the end of the previous utterance becomes too large.

To check Condition 2, a dictionary of word combinations is used. For each headword, the dictionary lists the words that can syntactically combine with it, together with the necessary prepositions (or grammatical cases). In addition to the mere fact of combinability, the dictionary can specify a quantitative measure of the probability (frequency) of the combination in the texts.

In our experiments, we use the CrossLexica dictionary [2] in its part of word combinations. The Russian version of this dictionary contains more than 500,000 word combinations; the English version is under construction.

As in the case of the indirect anaphora, some lexical relations – such as synonyms, hyponyms, etc. – are transparent for syntactical combinability.

References

1. Azzam, S., K. Humphreys, R. Gaizauskas: Evaluating a Focus-Based Approach to Anaphora Resolution. Proc. of COLING-ACL'98, 1998, pp. 74–78.
2. Bolshakov, I.A., A.F. Gelbukh: A Very Large Database of Collocations and Semantic Links. NLDB '2000: 5th International Conference on Applications of Natural Language to Information Systems, Versailles, France, June 28–30, 2000. Lecture Notes in Computer Science, Springer.
3. Carberry, S., Lambert, L.: A process model for recognizing communicative acts and modelling negotiation subdialogues. Comp. Ling., **25** (1), 1999: 1–54.
4. Carter, D.: Interpreting anaphora in natural language texts. Ellis Horwood, Chichester, 1987.
5. Cassidy, P.: An Investigation of the Semantic Relations in the Roget's Thesaurus: Preliminary results,
   `http://www.cs.cmu.edu/afs/cs/project/ai-repository/ai/new/FSN_DOC.ASC`,
   1996.
6. Chierchia, G.: Dynamics of Meaning: Anaphora, Presupposition, and the Theory of Grammar. University of Chicago Press, 1995.
7. Cornish, F.: Anaphora, Discourse, and Understanding: Evidence from English and French. Oxford University Press, 1999.
8. Erku, F., J. K. Gundel: The pragmatics of indirect anaphors. In J. Verschueren and M. Bertuccelli-Papi (Eds.), The pragmatic perspective: Selected papers from the 1985 International Pragmatics Conference. John Benjamins, Amsterdam, 1987. pp. 533–545.
9. Ferrandez, A., M. Palomar, L. Moreno: Anaphor resolution in unrestricted text with partial parsing. Coling-98, 1998, pp. 385–391.
10. Gelbukh, A., Sidorov, G.: On Indirect Anaphora Resolution. Proc. PACLING-99, Pacific Association for Computational Linguistics, University of Waterloo, Waterloo, Ontario, Canada, August 25-28, 1999, pp. 181–190.
11. Gelbukh, A., G. Sidorov, A. Guzmán-Arenas: Use of a Weighted Topic Hierarchy for Document Classification. In: Text, Speech and Dialogue, Lecture Notes in Artificial Intelligence 1692, Springer, 1999.
12. Gundel, J., N. Hedberg, R. Zacharski: Givenness, Implicature and Demonstrative Expressions in English Discourse. Proc. of 25th meeting of Chicago Linguistic Society, Part II (Parasession on Language in Context). Chicago, 1988. pp. 89–103.
13. Fretheim, T, J. K. Gundel (eds.): Reference and referent accessibility. John Benjamins, Amsterdam, 1996.
14. Hahn, U., M. Strube, K. Markert. Bridging textual ellipses. Proc. of the 16th International Conference on Computational Linguistics, 1996. pp. 496–501.

15. Hirst, G., D. St-Onge: Lexical chains as representations of context for the detection and correction of malapropisms. In: Christiane Fellbaum (editor), WordNet: An electronic lexical database and some of its applications, Cambridge, MA: The MIT Press, 1998.
16. Indirect Anaphora Workshop. Lancaster University, Lancaster, 1996.
17. Kameyama, M.: Recognizing Referential Links: an Information Extraction Perspective. Proc. of ACL '97/EACL '97 workshop on Operational factors in practical, robust anaphora resolution. Madrid, 1997.
18. Kennedy, C., B. Boguraev. Anaphora for Everyone: Pronominal Anaphor Resolution without a Parser. Coling-96, 1996.
19. Mitkov, R.: Pronoun Resolution: the Practical Alternative. In: S. Botley and T. McEmery (eds), Discourse Anaphora and Anaphor Resolution, Univ. College London Press, 1997.
20. Mitkov, R.: Factors in Anaphora Resolution: They are not the Only Things that Matter. A Case Study Based on Two Different Approaches. Proc. of the ACL'97/EACL'97 workshop on Operational factors in practical, robust anaphora resolution. Madrid, 1997.
21. Mitkov, R.: An Integrated Model for Anaphora Resolution. Coling-94, 1994, pp. 1170–1176.
22. Morris, J., Hirst, G.: Lexical cohesion, the thesaurus, and the structure of text. Computational linguistics, **17(1)**, March 1991, 21–48.
23. Murata, M., H. Isahara, M. Nagao: Resolution of Indirect Anaphora in Japanese Sentences Using Examples "X no Y (Y of X)." ACL'99 Workshop on Coreference and Its Applications, Maryland, USA, June 22, 1999.
24. Partee, B., P. Sgall (Eds.): Discourse and Meaning. Papers in Honour of Eva Hajičova. Benjamins, Amsterdam/Philadelphia, 1996.
25. Sanford, A. J., S. C. Garrod, A. Lucas, R. Henderson: Pronouns without explicit antecedents? Journal of Semantics, 1983, 2: 303–318.
26. Sidorov, G., A. Gelbukh: Demonstrative pronouns as markers of indirect anaphora. Proc. 2nd International Conference on Cognitive Science and 16th Annual Meeting of the Japanese Cognitive Science Society Joint Conference (ICCS/JCSS99), July 27–30, 1999, Tokyo, Japan, pp. 418–423.
27. Sidorov, G., A. Gelbukh: A method of detection and resolution of hidden anaphora (in Russian, abstract in English). Proc. Annual International Conf. on Applied Linguistics Dialogue-99, May 30–June 5, 1999, Moscow, Russia. pp. 288–297.
28. Ward, G., B. Birner: Definiteness and the English existential. Language, 1994, **71**: 722–742.
29. Coling-ACL'98 Workshop "Usage of WordNet in Natural Language Processing Systems." August 16, 1998, Université de Montréal, Montréal, Canada.

Reconstructing Conversational Games in an Obligation-Driven Dialogue Model

Jörn Kreutel

SAIL LABS S.L., Roger de Llúria, 50
E-08009 Barcelona, Spain
jkreutel@sail-labs.es

Abstract. Departing from a dialogue model that uses DISCOURSE OBLIGATIONS as basic expressive means we will propose a set of inference rules that assign intentional structures to sequences of dialogue moves. We then can demonstrate that from our point of view CONVERSATIONAL GAMES can be seen as macro-structures which are decomposable into smaller functional units where the coherence between the latter is explained in terms of obligations.

1 Introduction

In the course of the last decade, research in dialogue modelling has come to pay increasing attention to the language-specific aspects of dialogue. This tendency, which has resulted in dialogue being dealt with as a phenomenon of the use of natural language in a social context rather than as just a particular case of rational agency, is underlined by the use of DISCOURSE OBLIGATIONS as expressive means that allow the modelling of the actions of dialogue participants (DPs) in an explanatorily more adequate way than mere intention-based approaches (see [12,5]).

It is in the context of obligation driven models for dialogue that a concept of INFORMATION STATE (IS) has been developed which has proved to be of considerable influence in dialogue related research (see [9,13]). Our aim here is to sketch the outlines of a very simple model of IS using discourse obligations, which adheres to the formalisation principles proposed by the TRINDI workgroup that stresses the idea of dialogue being describable in terms of INFORMATION STATE UPDATES (see [13]). We will propose a set of inference rules for the dialogue model outlined by Kreutel & Matheson in [5] which operate on ISs and assign an intentional structure to a sequence of dialogue moves. This way we can show that a 'bottom-up' approach to dialogue modelling yields results at the descriptive level that are equivalent to the ones proposed in intention based explanations while proving to be superior as far as its explanatory power is concerned. In particular, we will show how the structuring aspect of CONVERSATIONAL GAMES can be reconstructed in terms of obligations.

Thus we intend to provide arguments for the strong attractiveness a model using information states and discourse obligations as expressive means has for dialogue related research in the academic field as well as in the area of practically applied language technology.

P. Sojka, I. Kopeček, and K. Pala (Eds.): TSD 2000, LNAI 1902, pp. 363–368, 2000.
© Springer-Verlag Berlin Heidelberg 2000

2   Information States and Intentional Structure

Kreutel & Matheson [5] assume a very basic notion of IS which includes just the DIALOGUE HISTORY (DH) as a sequence of moves, and a representation of the DPs' obligations (OBL). The dialogue acts used are a subset of those proposed by Poesio & Traum [9], where the acts are sub-classified into CORE SPEECH ACTS (assert, ask, accept, etc.) and ARGUMENTATION ACTS (answer, info_request, etc.). This classification captures the idea that any speech act may appear in a wider discourse context, where argumentation acts characterise the context-dependent actions of core speech acts. Obligations are represented as stacks of address and answer elements.

The updating of information states is done based on the notion of INFORMATION STATE UPDATE SCENARIOS. Update scenarios are meant to specify certain 'constellations' of IS, corresponding to situations like the turnholder's replying to an assertion, to a question, or to an assertion that is meant as an answer to a question. Each scenario can be defined based on the information in IS, i.e. on the overall structure of the DPs' obligations and the history of the dialogue.

The intentional structure INT is built up by means of inference rules given the information in DH. Departing from the idea that dialogue acts dispose of an 'expressive' function, which is to convey the mental state of the speaker (see [11]), we assume that from the occurrence of certain dialogue acts in DH, the DPs can infer each other's intentions and the way they are related and managed:

- Formally, we represent INT as a quadruple $< I, \gg, sat, drop >$, where I is the set of the DPs' intentions, $\gg$ is the two-place relation of *immediate dominance* in I, which is defined on the base of the *dominance* relation proposed by Grosz & Sidner [4], and sat and $drop$ are 1-place relations in I that correspond to the sets of satisfied and dropped intentions, respectively.
- After each move, I is updated according to inference rules that associate dialogue acts with intentions, e.g. $i_a : shared\_belief(p)$ and $i_b : resolved(q)$ with an assertion of a that p and a question of b whether q, respectively. In the same way, we infer $i_a : resolved(q)$ from a's performance of an answer or an info_request argumentation act.
- sat, on the other hand, is determined by inferring contents of intentions from dialogue acts, e.g. $shared\_belief(p)$ from the acceptance of an assertion that p or $resolved(q)$ from the acceptance of an assertion as an answer to a question whether q. An intention is said to be satisfied iff its content occurs in DH.
- Finally, for updating $\gg$, we attach a new intention as immediately dominated by the last intention which has neither been satisfied nor dropped.

Given these rules, we assume the structure below as the representation of an ordinary question-answer sequence:

(1)   A[1]: Did Helen come to the Party?
        B[2]: No.
        A[3]: Ok.

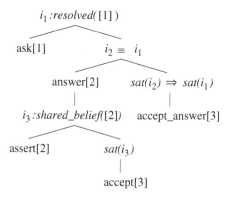

As the tree shows, we assume that the intentions associated with dialogue acts reformulate the idea that an askee adopts an asker's desire for information when answering a question (see [2]): i_1 and i_2 are identical with respect to their content, but individualised over the two DPs. The tree also captures the notion that the intention i_3 associated with the assertion in [2], which is offered as an answer to the question, is *dominated* by the askee's intention that the question should be resolved, and thus significantly differs from a discourse-initial assertion due to its context. As i_1 and i_2 have the same content, satisfaction of the latter by A's acceptance of B's answer automatically means satisfaction of i_1.[1]

Having thus outlined how the model proposed by Kreutel & Matheson [5] can be extended to allow for an account of the intentional structure of dialogue, the following section will discuss the advantages of the obligation-driven model as opposed to the notion of conversational games.

3   Reconstructing Conversational Games

The notion of conversational games has proved to be very useful in dialogue modelling from the descriptive (see [3,1]) as well as from the computational (see [7,8]) point of view. However, in terms of explanatory power the games approach runs into similar difficulties as the ones pointed out by Traum & Allen in [12] for intention-based approaches to dialogue in that capturing uncooperative actions is at best very awkward *within* the concept of a game. We argue that our own approach reconstructs the structural aspects of the games model and extends the coverage to include some data for which an approach using games is arguably too rigid.

Following a proposal by Eklundh [3] to associate conversational games with intentions – or 'discourse segment purposes' in Grosz & Sidner's terms (see [4]) – we could associate the games question-answer, answer and assert with i_1, i_2 and i_3 in (1), respectively, thus labelling the discourse segments that correspond to the intentions in our model with types of games. So far, then, on a descriptive level our treatment of

---

[1] See [5] for the motivation to analyse the evaluation of an assertion that is meant as an answer to a question as a two-fold process involving the dialogue acts accept and accept_answer in example (1).

INT coincides with the basic structural mechanisms of the games model. However the latter has problems in providing a satisfactory explanation of sequences of moves that deviate significantly from the 'canonical' structure of a game, but which nevertheless can be seen as very common in human interaction. For instance:

(2)   A[1]: Did Helen come to the Party?
       B[2]: Did Jack come?
       A[3]: Yes.
       B[4]: Ok.
       B[5]: Then Helen didn't come.
       A[6]: Ok.

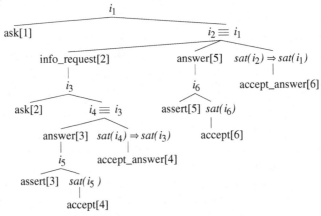

In terms of dialogue processing, either by humans or machines, the idea of a conversational game allows a distinction of the moves that follow the initial one in terms of 'preferred' or 'dispreferred' moves (see [6,3,7]) and assumes an increased processing effort for all the cases which are considered to be dispreferred. According to this point of view, for question-answer games an assertion which provides an answer will always be considered the preferred follow-up move to a question.

The possibility of the askee replying to a question with a question, as in (2), which can be considered a reasonably common case in information-oriented interaction (see INSERTION SEQUENCES in [6]), will thus have to be treated as an exception along with requests for clarification or utterances that express the askee's inability or unwillingness to answer. Apart from the fact that the latter falls completely outside the scope of the games model (if one does not assume the contradictory notion of an 'uncooperativity game'), this way of prioritising the range of possible follow-up moves in a dialogue must be seen as too strict. The obligation-driven approach, on the other hand, simply assumes that a question obliges the askee to provide an answer which resolves the question, and thus a situation where an askee replies with a question ultimately in order to provide an answer can be seen as just an alternative to the 'canonical' case.

However, in spite of their explanatory weakness, conversational games have proved to be of great use in speech and language technology and can still be seen as one of the leading notions in dialogue related research. In particular, the possibility of modelling games as recursive transition networks (see for instance [7]), and thus of determining significant 'states' of a game, has made the games model an attractive candidate for dialogue systems which make use of probabilistic heuristics to influence the behaviour of, for example, modules for speech and speech act recognition (see [14,10]). However, as we have pointed out above, our model defines a set of update scenarios as the framework for determining or interpreting the DPs' actual actions. In terms of scenarios, the ordinary question-answer sequence in example (1) can be analysed as follows:

(3)   A[1]: Did Helen come to the Party?
          REPLY_QUESTION
       B[2]: No.
          REPLY_ANSWER ⊃ REPLY_ASSERT
       A[3]: Ok.

While B's move in [2] takes place in the context of a scenario in which B has to answer a question, [2] itself results in an information state in which DP_1 (A) is obliged to address [2] and DP_2 (B) is obliged to answer [1]. This constellation of the DPs' obligations characterises a scenario in which DP_1's actions can be interpreted as expressing his evaluation of the answer provided by DP_2 and is identical to the situation after A's move [5] in the more complex example below:

(4)   A[1]: Helen did not come to the Party.
       B[2]: How do you know that?
       A[3]: Her car wasn't there.
       B[4]: Ok. But she could have come by bicycle.
       A[5]: I stayed there until 4am and she didn't show up.
       B[6]: Ok.

With our model assuming the classification of information states in terms of update scenarios as part of the expressive means, we propose an alternative to the games approach also in terms of the model's capacity to feed back heuristic analyses to other modules in a dialogue system – in the same way that a games-based account allows follow-up moves to be ranked. Therefore, for each scenario, probabilities can be assigned to each admissible subsequent action, thus allowing for the interpretation of ambiguous or 'noisy' responses. This way we are able to introduce a notion of prioritisation, which we have argued is problematic for the games approach in explanatory terms, at a higher level in our model. It should be noted that we have not undertaken such an analysis; however, it seems clear that the scenario-based account can be used to provide the same formal properties as conversational games, and hence similar predictive power can be assumed.

4   Conclusion

Beginning with a dialogue model which uses discourse obligations as basic means to predict the actions of participants in a dialogue, we have proposed a set of inference rules which operate on the information in the dialogue history to determine a representation of the DPs' intentions. We have shown that the structures generated by our rules can be reinterpreted in terms of the notion of conversational games.

We have suggested that the obligation-based approach is able to reconstruct games structures at the descriptive level and also to flexibly integrate probabilities as developed in the games framework. In addition to this, however, taking into account the equivalence between 'states' in a games model and 'scenarios' on the one hand, and the definition of scenarios in terms of the DPs' obligations on the other, we claim that conversational games should be seen as structures that emerge from the DPs' acting according to the obligations imposed on them rather than as primitives in the theory of dialogue modelling.

References

1. Carletta, J., Isard, A., Isard, S., Kowtko, J., Doherty-Sneddon, G., Anderson, A.: HCRC Dialogue Structure Coding Manual. Research Paper 82, Human Communication Research Centre, University of Edinburgh (1996).
2. Cohen, P.R., Levesque H.J.: Performatives in a Rationally-based Speech Act Theory. In: Proceedings of the 28th Annual Meeting of the Association for Computational Linguistics, University of Pittsburgh, Pittsburgh, Pa. (1990).
3. Eklundh, K.S.: The Notion of Language Game: A Natural Unit of Dialogue and Discourse. University of Linköping, Department of Communication Studies (1983).
4. Grosz, B.J., Sidner, C.L.: Attention, Intentions, and the Structure of Discourse. In: Computational Linguistics 12(3) (1986) 175–204.
5. Kreutel, J., Matheson, C.: Modelling Questions and Assertions in Dialogue Using Obligations. In: Proceedings of Amstelogue 99, University of Amsterdam (1999).
6. Levinson, S.C.: Pragmatics. Cambridge University Press, Cambridge (1983).
7. Lewin, I.: The Autoroute Dialogue Demonstrator: Reconfigurable Architectures for Spoken Dialogue Understanding. Technical report, prepared by SRI International Cambridge Computer Science Research Centre for the UK Defence Evaluation and Research Agency, Malvern (1998).
8. Pulman, S.: The TRINDI Project: Some Preliminary Themes. In: Proceedings of the Twente Workshop on Language Technology (1998).
9. Poesio, M., Traum, D.: Towards an Axiomatisation of Dialogue Acts. In: Proceedings of the Twente Workshop on Language Technology (1998).
10. Poesio, M., Mikheev, A.: The Predictive Power of Game Structure in Dialogue Act Recognition: Experimental Results Using Maximum Entropy Estimation. In: Proceedings of ICSLP-98 (1998).
11. Sadock, J.: Comments on Vanderveken and on Cohen and Levesque. In: Cohen, P., Morgan, J., Pollack, M. (eds.): Intentions in Communication. MIT Press, Cambridge/MA (1990).
12. Traum, D., Allen, J.: Discourse Obligations in Dialogue Processing. In: Proceedings of the 32nd Annual meeting of the Association for Computational Linguistics (1994).
13. Traum, D., Bos, J., Cooper, R., Larsson, S., Lewin, I., Matheson, C., Poesio, M.: A Model for Dialogue Moves and Information State Revision. TRINDI Deliverable D2.1 (1999).
14. Wright, H., Poesio, M., Isard, S.: Using High Level Dialogue Information for Dialogue Act Recognition Using Prosodic Features. In: Proceedings of the ESCA Workshop on Prosody and Dialogue, Eindhoven (1999).

Prosody Prediction
from Tree-Like Structure Similarities

Laurent Blin[1] and Mike Edgington[2]

[1] IRISA-ENSSAT, F-22305 Lannion, France
blin@enssat.fr
[2] Speech Technology and Research Lab, SRI International,
Menlo Park, CA-94025, USA
mde@speech.sri.com

Abstract. We present ongoing work on prosody prediction for speech synthesis. This approach considers sentences as tree-like structures and decides on the prosody from a corpus of such structures using machine learning techniques. The prediction is achieved from the prosody of the closest sentence of the corpus through tree similarity measurements in a nearest neighbour context. We introduce a syntactic structure and a performance structure representation, the tree similarity metrics considered, and then we discuss the prediction method. Experiments are currently under process to qualify this approach.

1 Introduction

Producing a natural prosody remains a problem in speech synthesis. Several automatic prediction methods have already been tried for this topic, including decision trees [1], neural networks [2], and HMMs [3]. We are introducing a new prediction scheme. The original aspect of our approach is to consider sentences as tree-like structures and to decide on the prosody from a corpus of such structures. The prediction is achieved from the prosody of the closest sentence of the corpus through tree similarity measurements using the nearest neighbour algorithm. We think that reasoning on a whole structure rather than on local features of a sentence should better reflect the many relations influencing the prosody. This approach is an attempt to achieve such a goal.

The data used in this work is a part of the Boston University Radio (WBUR) News Corpus [4]. The prosodic information consists of ToBI labelling of accents and breaks [5]. The syntactic and part-of-speech informations were obtained from the part of the corpus processed in the Penn Treebank project [6].

We firstly describe the tree structures defined for this work, then present the tree metrics that we are using, and finally discuss how they are manipulated to achieve the prosody prediction.

2 Tree Structures

So far we have considered two types of structures in this work: a simple syntactic structure and a performance structure [7]. The comparison of their use should be helpful

P. Sojka, I. Kopeček, and K. Pala (Eds.): TSD 2000, LNAI 1902, pp. 369–374, 2000.
© Springer-Verlag Berlin Heidelberg 2000

for providing some interesting knowledge about the usefulness or the limitations of the different elements of information included in each structure.

2.1 Syntactic Structure

The syntactic structure considered is built exclusively from the syntactic parsing of the given sentences. Three main levels can be viewed in this structure:

- a syntactic level, representing the syntactic parsing of the sentence, which can be identified as the backbone of the structure, and which can extend over several depth levels in the tree; each node is coding one syntactic label;
- the words of the sentence, with their part-of-speech tagging;
- the syllable description of the words; each node at the previous level has as many sons as syllables it is composed of.

Figure 1 shows the syntactic structure for the sentence: "Hennessy will be a hard act to follow" extracted from the corpus. For clarity aspects, the syllable level has been omitted.

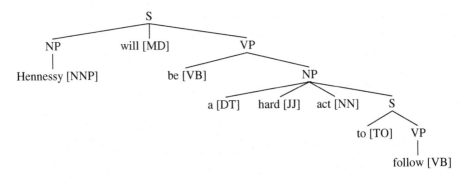

Fig. 1. Syntactic structure for the sentence: "Hennessy will be a hard act to follow". (Syntactic labels: *S*: simple declarative clause, *NP*: noun phrase, *VP*: verb phrase; Part-of-speech labels: *NNP*: proper noun, *MD*: modal, *VB*: verb in base form, *DT*: determiner, *JJ*: adjective, *NN*: singular noun, *TO*: special label for "to")

2.2 Performance Structure

The performance structure used in our approach is a combination of syntactic and phonological informations. It can be divided in two main parts:

- the upper part of the structure is a binary tree in which each node represents a break between the two parts of the sentence contained into the subtrees of the node. This binary structure defines a hierarchy: the closer to the root the node is, the more salient (or stronger) the break is.
- the lower part represents the phonological phrases into which the whole sentence is divided by the binary structure. The subtree for each phonological phrase can be divided in three depth levels:

- a first one to label the phrase with a syntactic category (the main one);
- a second level for the words of the phrase; a simplification has been performed by joining them into phonological words: they are composed of one content word and of the surrounding function words (4 content words categories are considered: nouns, adjectives, verbs and adverbs);
- a last level to represent the syllables of each phonological word of the previous level.

No break is supposed to occur inside such a phonological phrase.

Figure 2 shows a possible performance structure for the same example: "Hennessy will be a hard act to follow." The syllable level is also not represented.

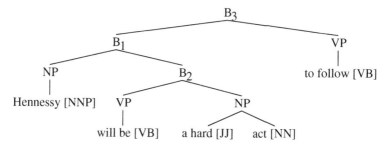

Fig. 2. Performance structure for the sentence "Hennessy will be a hard act to follow". The meanings of the syntactic and part-of-speech labels are identical to those in Figure 1. B_1, B_2 and B_3 are break-related nodes.

2.3 Discussion

The syntactic structure follows the labels and parsing employed in the corpus description. Its construction presents no difficulty, for any sentence inside or outside the corpus.

However, a problem occurs with the performance structure. As exposed above, this structure contains not only syntactic and part-of-speech information but also prosodic information with the break values. Building this structure for the sentences in the corpus can be done since the real prosodic values are available. Nevertheless, the aim of this work is to predict the prosody, so these data are not available in practice for a new sentence. Therefore, to achieve a prediction using this structure representation, we firstly need to predict the location and the salience of the breaks in a given sentence. The chosen method, defined by Bachenko and Fitzpatrick [8], provides rules to infer a default phrasing for a sentence. Basically, it firstly divides a sentence into phonological words and phrases (the lower parts of our structure), and then establishes the salience of the breaks between the phrases, using simple considerations about the length of the phonological phrases (defining the hierarchy of the upper binary part of our structure). Since this process furnishes an estimation of the phrasing, we will have to quantify its effects.

3   Tree Metrics

Once the tree structures have been defined, we need to determine the tools to manipulate them to predict the prosody. We have considered several similarity metrics to calculate the "distance" between two tree structures. These metrics are inspired from the Wagner and Fisher's editing distance [9].

3.1   Principles

In an analogous way to this well known string editing distance, it is necessary to introduce a small set of elementary transformation operators between two trees: the insertion of a node, the deletion of a node, and the substitution of a node by another one. It is then possible to determine a set of specific operation sequences that transform any given tree into another one. Specifying costs for each elementary operation (possibly a function of the node values) allows the evaluation of a whole transformation cost by adding the operation costs in the sequence. Therefore the tree distance can be defined as the cost of the sequence minimising this sum.

3.2   Considered Metrics

Many metrics can be defined from this principle. The differences come from the application conditions which can be set on the operators. In our experiments, three such tree metrics are tested. They all preserve the order of the leaves of the trees, an essential condition in our application.

The first one, defined by Selkow [10], allows only substitutions between nodes at the same depth level in the trees. Moreover, the insertion or deletion of a node involves respectively the insertion or deletion of the whole subtree depending of the node. These strict conditions should be able to locate very close structures.

The two other ones, defined by Taï [11] and Zhang [12], allow the substitutions of nodes whatever their locations are inside the structures. They also allow the insertion or deletion of lonely nodes inside the structures. Compared to [10], these less rigorous stipulations should not only retrieve the very close structures, but also other ones which wouldn't have been found by the previous metric.

3.3   Operation Costs

As exposed in the algorithm principles in Section 3.1, a tree is "close" to another one because of the definition of the operator costs. From this consideration, and from the definition of the tree structures in this work, these costs have been set to achieve two goals:

- to allow the only comparison of nodes of the same structural nature (break-related nodes together, syllable-related nodes together ...);
- to represent the linguistic "similarity" between comparable nodes or subtrees (to set that an adjective may be "closer" to a noun than to a determiner ...).

These operation costs are currently manually set. To decide on the scale of values to affect is not an easy task, and it needs some human expertise. One possibility would be to further automate the process, using machine learning techniques to set these values.

4   Prosody Prediction

Now that the tree representations and the metrics have been defined, they can be used to predict the prosody of a sentence. The simple method that we are currently using is the nearest neighbour algorithm: given a new sentence, the principle is to find the closest match among the corpus of sentences of known prosody, and then to use its prosody to infer the one of the new sentence.

From the tree metric algorithms manipulated, it is possible to retrieve the relationships which led to the final distance value: the parts of the trees which were inserted or deleted, and the ones which were substituted or unchanged. This mapping between the nodes of the two structures also links the words of the represented sentences. It then gives a simple way to know where to apply the prosody of one sentence onto the other one.

Unfortunately, this process may not be as easy. The ideal mapping would be that each word of the new sentence has a corresponding word in the closest sentence (preserving the order of the words). Hopelessly, the two sentences may not be as closed as desired, and some words may have been inserted or deleted. To decide on the prosody for these words is a problem. We are currently developing a new technique based on analogy to complete this method. As exposed above, the distance provides a mapping between the two structures. We would like to find in the corpus one or more couples of sentences sharing the same tree transformation. The understanding of the impact of this transformation on the prosody should allow us to apply a similar modification onto the initial couple.

5   First Results

So far we have run experiments to find the closest match of held-out corpus sentences using the syntactic structure, and the performance structure for each of the distance metrics. We are using both the "actual" and estimated performance structures to quantify the effects of this estimation. Cross-validation tests have been chosen to validate our method.

The experiments are not all complete, but an initial analysis of the results doesn't seem to show many differences between the tree metrics considered. We believe that this is due to the small size of the corpus we are using. With only around 300 sentences, most structures are very different, so the majority of pairwise comparisons should be very distant. We are currently running experiments where the tree structures are generated at the phrase level. This strategy implies to adapt the tree metrics to take into consideration the location of the phrases in the sentences (two similar structures should be privileged if they have the same location in their respective sentences).

6   Conclusion

We have presented a new prosody prediction method. Its original aspect is to consider sentences as tree-like structures. To predict the prosody of a sentence, we are using tree similarity metrics to find the closest match in a corpus of such structures, and then its prosody is used to infer the one of the first sentence. Further experiments are needed to validate this approach.

A development of our method would be the introduction of focus labels. In a dialogue context, some extra information can refine the intonation. With the tree structures that we are using, it is easy to introduce special markers upon the nodes of the structure. According to their locations, they can indicate some focus either on a word, on a phrase or on a whole sentence. With the adaptation of the tree metrics, the prediction process is kept unchanged.

References

1. Ross, K.: Modelling of intonation for speech synthesis, Ph.D. Thesis, College of Engineering, Boston University, 1995.
2. Traber, C.: F0 generation with a database of natural F0 patterns and with a neural network, Talking machines: theories, models and designs, 1992, pp. 287–304.
3. Jensen, U., Moore, R.K., Dalsgaard, P., Lindberg, B.: Modelling intonation contours at the phrase level using continuous density hidden Markov models, Computer Speech and Language, vol. 8, 1994, pp. 247–260.
4. Ostendorf, M., Price, P.J., Shattuck-Hufnagel, S.: The Boston University Radio News Corpus, Technical Report ECS-95-001, Boston University, 1995.
5. Silverman, K., Beckman, M.E., Pitrelli, J., Ostendorf, M., Wightman, C.W., Price, P.J., Pierrehumbert, J.B., Hirschberg, J.: TOBI: A standard for labelling English Prosody, Int. Conf. on Spoken Language Processing, vol. 2, 1992, pp. 867–870.
6. Marcus, M.P., Santorini, B., Marcinkiewicz, M.A.: Building a large annotated corpus of English: the Penn Treebank, Comp. Linguistics, vol. 19, 1993.
7. Gee, J.P., Grosjean, F.: Performance structures: a psycholinguistic and linguistic appraisal, Cognitive Psychology, vol. 15, 1983.
8. Bachenko, J., Fitzpatrick, E.: A computational grammar of discourse-neutral prosodic phrasing in English, Comp. Linguistics, vol. 16, N. 3, 1990, pp. 155–170.
9. Wagner, R.A., Fisher, M.J.: The string-to-string correction problem, Journal of the Association for Computing Machinery, vol. 21, N. 1, 1974, pp. 168–173.
10. Selkow, S.M., The tree-to-tree editing problem, Information Processing Letters, vol. 6, N. 6, 1977, pp. 184–186.
11. Taï, K.C., The tree-to-tree correction problem, Journal of the Association for Computing Machinery, vol. 26, N. 3, 1979, pp. 422–433.
12. Zhang, K., Algorithms for the constrained editing distance between ordered labelled trees and related problems, Pattern Recognition, vol. 28, N. 3, 1995, pp. 463–474.

A Speaker Authentication Module in TelCorreo

Leandro Rodríguez Liñares[1] and Carmen García Mateo[2]

[1] E.T.S.E. Informática, Campus As Lagoas
32004 – Ourense, Spain
leandro@tsc.uvigo.es
[2] E.T.S.E. Telecomunicación, Campus Universitario de Vigo
36200 – Vigo (Pontevedra), Spain
carmen@tsc.uvigo.es

Abstract. Our experiments in Speaker Recognition showed that the combination of Speaker Verification and Utterance Verification techniques is an efficient way of improving the performance of a Speaker Authentication System.
This technique is now implemented in the speaker authentication module of TelCorreo, an e-mail client that allows Internet users to read their e-mail using speech through the telephone.

1   Introduction

TelCorreo [1,2] is a real-world application designed to give its users the ability to access their electronic mailbox and handle their electronic messages through a simple telephone call. It can be viewed as a bilingual (Spanish/Galician) e-mail client application which interacts with the user through a speech interface.

Traditionally, the security of systems like TelCorreo relied on the use of some private code or password. Given the fact that it has been designed as a dialogue system, the basic technology it uses allowed us to implement a voice-based user authentication module.

At present, there are very few speaker recognition systems to be deployed in real-world applications. The performance achieved by most of the techniques proposed in the literature dramatically drops for out-of-lab conditions. Scanning the literature, we can find two generic approaches for designing a speaker authentication system:

- Verifying the actual content of the speech as a mean of verifying the speaker identity. We call these systems "Utterance verifiers" [3].
- Verifying the speaker voice by itself as a way of verifying the identity. This approach is by nature speech content independent. We call these systems "Speaker verifiers" [4], and although these systems are not speech recognisers, they usually share with speech recognisers most of their technology, namely, most of them are based on a HMM (Hidden Markov Model) formulation with a front-end based on cepstral analysis.

Our experiments in Speaker Recognition showed that the combination of Speaker Verification and Utterance Verification techniques is an efficient way of improving

P. Sojka, I. Kopeček, and K. Pala (Eds.): TSD 2000, LNAI 1902, pp. 375–380, 2000.

the performance of a Speaker Authentication System. In [5] and [6], several ways of combining such systems are explored using our database called "TelVoice".

Among the explored combination techniques, the neural network combination outperforms the others due to its ability to learn the optimal operation point from the data. However, the real-world implementation of this scheme is only possible when a certain amount of experimental data has been collected.

For TelCorreo, we decided to use what we called the "restrictive criterion". This is equivalent to demand that both tests have to be passed simultaneously to accept the speaker.

The rest of this paper is structured as follows. Section 2 explains the module design from the users' point of view, while Section 3 presents TelCorreoDB: an experimental frame adequate for testing the speaker authentication technology used in TelCorreo. Section 4 presents the implementation details. Finally, some conclusions are included.

2   Speaker Authentication Module Design

In this section, the speaker authentication module is presented from the user's point of view. When the user access to the system, he/she is asked to input the personal identification number using the telephone keypad. From this moment, the goal of the speaker authentication module is to decide if the speaker is actually who he/she claims to be.

The first thing the system does is to verify if the voice speaker authentication option is activated or not for this presumed speaker:

1. If not, the user is asked to input his personal user's password using the telephone keypad. If the password is correct, the rest of the call is managed by the system's kernel.
2. If the option is activated, there are two possible situations:
   (a) If the user has trained an acoustic model previously, he is asked to pronounce the personal user's password. These utterance is used by the speaker authentication module to determine if the accessing attempt has to be accepted or not.
   (b) If there is no model for this user, he is asked to introduce the personal user's password with the telephone keypad. After the password is verified, the system asks if the user wants to train his model or not in this moment. If he does, the user is asked to repeat a set of phrases for training a model that will be used in the following accessing attempts. If the user does not want to train a model in this moment, the control of the call is passed to the system's kernel.

3   TelCorreoDB

When transferring technology from laboratory to the real-world, an important point is how to test and adjust the systems before their field deployment. This process must be made in conditions close to the ones the system is going to have to deal with in the real-world.

With this purpose in mind, we recorded TelCorreoDB: a database designed as an experimental frame adequate for testing the speaker authentication technology used in TelCorreo. TelCorreoDB includes voice of 15 speakers recorded in the same conditions in which these speakers would access through the speaker authentication module. Each speaker recorded one training session, which consists of 8 fixed phrases up to a total of approximately 50 seconds and three test sessions, each one with a pronunciation of the personal user's password.

We used TelCorreoDB for the following tasks:

1. Testing the components of the speaker authentication module: parametrisation, training, users' information maintenance . . .
2. Estimating thresholds for the speaker verification sub-module.
3. Training the world model.

4 Implementation Details

4.1 Front-End Block

The modules should share technology as much as possible due to computational reasons. This includes a front-end block that performs the parametrisation of the input utterance. The used parametrisation consists of the energy and 12 mel-cepstra coefficients with their first and second derivatives. This makes a total of 39 parameters per vector.

4.2 Utterance Verification Sub-module

The Utterance Verifier in TelCorreo is the same speech recogniser used for the dialogue management. As the accessing codes consist of four digits, a simple grammar that allows all the possible combination is used. In [1], it is stated that TelCorreo is a bilingual system that can be used in Spanish or Galician indistinctly. Thus, the grammar must allow the presence of digits in both languages. The output of the utterance verifier consists in the sequence of five recognised digits.

4.3 Speaker Verification Sub-module

We decided to use 16-mixtures covariance-tied GMM's (Gaussian Mixture Models), which are a special case of continuous HMM's where the number of states is one. This type of model has proved to be effective for modelling the speaker identity in text-independent speaker recognition applications [4].

In a speaker verification problem, the goal is to determine whether a person is who he or she claims to be. The most straightforward approximation would be to use the log-likelihood of the sequence of parameters given the supposed speaker's model $\log(P(\mathbf{O}/\lambda_k))$. This is what it is called *unnormalised log-likelihood score*. The speaker is accepted when the unnormalised score $S_{\mathrm{unnor}}(\mathbf{O}, k)$ is above a certain threshold τ_k:

$$S_{\mathrm{unnor}}(\mathbf{O}, k) = \log(P(\mathbf{O}/\lambda_k)) \geq \tau_k$$

In [4], it is stated that to avoid taking the verification decision on a relative score dependent on non-speaker utterance variations some normalisation procedure must be used. This normalisation alleviates effects like voice quality or speaker's vocal tract variations. One possible solution to these problems is to use another probability $P(\mathbf{O}/\widehat{\lambda_k})$ as a normalisation factor to calculate the a normalised score:

$$S_{\mathrm{nor}}(\mathbf{O}, k) = \frac{\log(P(\mathbf{O}/\lambda_k))}{\log(P(\mathbf{O}/\widehat{\lambda_k}))} \geq \tau_k$$

$\widehat{\lambda_k}$ is called the *antimodel* and represents the universe of possible speakers but the presumed one. There are typically two strategies to build it up: to train a world model shared by all the speakers or to use a set of speaker-dependent models called cohort or background models. It is normally accepted that the use of cohort models give better performance than using a world model.

When transferring technology from laboratory conditions to real-world applications, several restrictions must be applied. This is particularly true in the Speaker Verification Sub-module, where the data available to training or estimation procedures is limited. Thus, we have applied several restrictions:

- The number of registered users in TelCorreo is not constant. Then, the use of cohort models for normalisation purposes is not practical, as each new registration would imply to recalculate the cohorts for each registered speaker. We decided to use a *world model*, trained using TelCorreoDB. This model consists of a variance-tied 48-mixtures GMM.
- As previously stated, a set of thresholds must be estimated in order to decide if a utterance belongs to a user or not. Theoretically, there are two possibilities: to use one threshold shared by all the speakers or to use speaker-dependent thresholds. The latter option give better results in laboratory conditions. However, threshold estimation needs to be performed in the conditions where the verification process is going to be performed, and in a real world system this is not a practical approach. Then, shared threshold must be used, and these thresholds are a priori calculated using TelCorreoDB.

4.4 Sub-modules Combination

In summary, the system has to decide if a utterance belongs to a speaker or not. This decision has to be made based on a string of recognised digits and an acoustic score calculated by the Speaker Verification Sub-module.

It was previously said that we decided to use the "restrictive criterion", that is, to demand that both tests have to be passed simultaneously to accept the speaker. To take into account variations of channel or voice quality that would degrade the verification performance, a two-level verification is performed based on the use of two thresholds in the Speaker Verification Sub-module. We call these thresholds τ_{low} and τ_{high}, where $\tau_{low} < \tau_{high}$.

The verification procedure is as follows. First, the recognised sequence of digits is studied. This can lead the system to three distinct situations:

1. If the sequence of digits is totally correct, $S_{\text{nor}}(\mathbf{O}, k)$ is compared with τ_{low}. If $S_{\text{nor}}(\mathbf{O}, k) > \tau_{low}$ the speaker is accepted, otherwise is rejected.
2. If there is only one error in the sequence of digits, $S_{\text{nor}}(\mathbf{O}, k)$ is compared with τ_{high}. As before, if $S_{\text{nor}}(\mathbf{O}, k) > \tau_{high}$ the speaker is accepted, otherwise is rejected. By one error in the sequence of digits we mean one substitution, one insertion or one deletion.
3. If there is more than one error in the sequence of digits the accessing attempt is rejected.

This can be expressed as follows:

$$\left. \begin{array}{l} N_{errors} = 0 \\ S_{\text{nor}}(\mathbf{O}, k) > \tau_{low} \end{array} \right\} \Rightarrow Accepted$$

$$\left. \begin{array}{l} N_{errors} = 1 \\ S_{\text{nor}}(\mathbf{O}, k) > \tau_{high} \end{array} \right\} \Rightarrow Accepted$$

$$Otherwise \quad \Rightarrow Rejected$$

The estimation of thresholds τ_{low} and τ_{high} is performed using TelCorreoDB. One ROC (Receiver Operating Characteristic) is built representing the false acceptance rate percentage (%FA) versus the false rejection rate percentage (%FR) when the value of the threshold is varied. We decided to use τ_{low} and τ_{high} as shown in Table 1. It can be argued that the used database is rather small and that these results may have low statistical significance. However, these thresholds are a first estimation and will probably have to be modified.

Table 1. Estimated values for thresholds τ_{low} and τ_{high}

	Value	%FA	%FR
τ_{low}	-1	≈ 5	≈ 10
τ_{high}	-0.5	≈ 3	≈ 18

5   Conclusions and Further Work

TelCorreo is a bilingual e-mail client over the telephone line that integrates state-of-the-art speech technology [1]. One of the main and novel components of TelCorreo is the User Authentication Module which is described in depth.

TelCorreo is still under development. A few days before writing this article, TelCorreo was deployed in real-world with real users. The real-world working of the system will raise new issues that will have to be solved. Examples of such issues are the refinement of the thresholds or the adaptation of the users' models.

References

1. L. Rodríguez-Liñares et al.: TelCorreo: A bilingual e-mail client over the telephone. In this Proceedings of TSD 2000.
2. In `http://www.gts.tsc.uvigo.es/telcorreo` a description of TelCorreo can be found.
3. Q. Li et al.: Verbal Information Verification. EuroSpeech '97, Rhodes, Greece, 1997.
4. D. Reynolds: Comparison of Background Normalization Methods for Text-Independent Speaker Verification. Speech Communication, Vol. 2, pp. 963–966, 1997.
5. L. Rodríguez-Liñares: Estudio y Mejora de Sistemas de Reconocimiento de Locutores mediante el Uso de Información Verbal y Acústica en un Nuevo Marco Experimental. Ph.D. Thesis, Universidade de Vigo, Spain, 1999. `http://www.tsc.uvigo.es/~leandro/archivos/Tesis.ps.gz`.
6. L. Rodríguez-Liñares and C. García-Mateo: A Novel Technique for the Combination of Utterance and Speaker Verification Systems in a Text-dependent Speaker Verification Task. ICSLP '98, Sydney, Australia, 1998.

TelCorreo: A Bilingual E-mail Client over the Telephone

Leandro Rodríguez Liñares[1], Antonio Cardenal López[2],
Carmen García Mateo[2], David Pérez-Piñar López[2],
Eduardo Rodríguez Banga[2], and Xabier Fernández Salgado[2]

[1] E.T.S.E. Informática, Campus As Lagoas
32004 – Ourense, Spain
leandro@tsc.uvigo.es
[2] E.T.S.E. Telecomunicación, Campus Universitario de Vigo
36200 – Vigo (Pontevedra), Spain
cardenal@tsc.uvigo.es, carmen@tsc.uvigo.es, dperez@tsc.uvigo.es, erbanga@tsc.uvigo.es,
xsalgado@tsc.uvigo.es

Abstract. In this paper we present TelCorreo [1]: an e-mail client that allows the Galician Internet users to read their e-mail messages from locations where there is no web-connected computer available. This task is performed using speech through the telephone, and the system uses speech technology developed in Galician, including a speech recognition system and a text-to-speech converter.

1 Introduction

Over the last years, the internet is getting more and more important in everybody's lives. Services like e-mail are becoming essential ways of communication and, each day, more and more people need to have permanent access to these services. An important issue in all kinds of communication involving computers is the language. Major languages like English, Spanish or German are nowadays of common use in communication services and many systems and applications are deployed or under development. However, in minor languages an important effort is needed in order to deploy communication technology products.

"Galego" or Galician is one of the four official languages in Spain. It is mainly spoken in Galicia (northwest part of Spain) and approximately 7% of the Spanish population would like to use this language for any kind of communication including, of course, those involving computers. This leads to the need of developing communication technology products in Galician [2].

The technology used in TelCorreo was initially developed for the Galician language. However, the linguistic reality of this country is that of a bilingual area, and this fact led us to the development of bilingual applications capable of operating in Spanish and Galician indistinctly. An important advantage in the development of such applications is the linguistic and phonetic similarity between both languages.

The next section of this paper describes the main features of TelCorreo. Its modules are described deeper in Section 3, while Section 4 presents some conclusions and open questions in the implementation of the system.

P. Sojka, I. Kopeček, and K. Pala (Eds.): TSD 2000, LNAI 1902, pp. 381–386, 2000.
© Springer-Verlag Berlin Heidelberg 2000

2   System Overview

TelCorreo is a bilingual (Spanish and Galician) e-mail client application implemented on a PC computer. Services offered by TelCorreo are well-known functions present in all traditional graphical mail clients. Among other functions, we can enumerate:

- The user is informed about the number and category of messages in his mailbox.
- The system reads the mail headers (subject, sender, date) and its contents.
- Attachments are identified.
- The user can reply or forward a message.

TelCorreo integrates all the resources needed to give a voice service through the telephone line. It is well known that individual modules work reasonably well for their purposes: speech recognition, speech synthesis, mail processing ... Integrating all these tools in a fully functional real-life application gives us the opportunity to test and evaluate each component working on real situations and interfacing its results with the system. Overall performance measures can be taken, and influence of each module in performance and usability can be studied, shredding light over key aspects and problems to solve for each system resource.

The long-term goal of TelCorreo is to get a fully functional real-life application with natural language dialogue interaction through the telephone. Conversational speech offers an attractive alternative to keypad input for telephone-based interaction. It is familiar, requires minimal physical effort for the user, and leaves hands and eyes free. Since physical space presents no constraint for a speech system, the number of commands is virtually unlimited.

Exclusive speech access is, however, dangerous in telephone-based applications. Line quality variations, error-prone speech recognisers and other real-life situations lead to problems for service usage and dissatisfaction for the user. As a result, the system was designed with two simultaneous interfaces: the user can handle TelCorreo with his voice or with the telephone keypad.

The dialogue between the user and the system is based on a flexible menu-driven structure (as described below). Actions and options can be selected through voice or keypad commands. The speech interface gives support for two languages: Galician and Spanish.

TelCorreo can be viewed, therefore, as a mixed-initiative menu-driven dialogue system. The system takes the initiative to identify the user during the login process and to get and read the mail headers from the mailbox. The user can interrupt these actions for querying the server for some information or asking to end the session.

3   Basic Structure

TelCorreo is designed as a highly modular application, developed mainly in the C/C++ language. The software is organised in different modules around a kernel which drives and coordinates their activity and interaction. Figure 1 shows this basic structure.

In the following, a short description of TelCorreo modules is included.

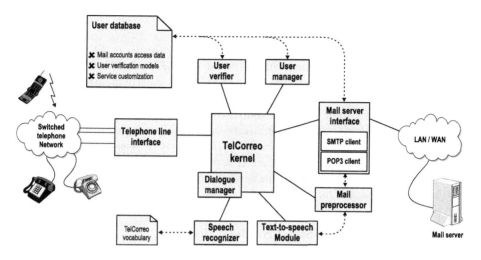

Fig. 1. TelCorreo basic structure

3.1 Application Kernel

This kernel is in charge of two main tasks:

- To centralise the application control.
- To specify an interface with the rest of the modules while maintaining independency between them.

The modules are viewed by the kernel as software services [3].

Actions performed by these software services may be, for example, reading the headers, authenticating the user or giving help to the user. The transition between states can be triggered by the user or by events concerning the messages or the system state.

An important point is that the system allows the user to interrupt the reading of the messages or headers in any moment thus forcing a transition.

The application kernel holds a close relation with the dialog manager, which is in charge of the interaction with the user. The dialogue manager is, however, independent from the kernel.

3.2 Telephone Line Interface

TelCorreo uses a hardware card from TEIMA and its software control environment HITO [4] to transmit and receive information through the telephone line. The access and control of this software is encapsulated in the line interface module, which communicates exclusively with the kernel.

TelCorreo takes advantage of some key features of this hardware. Specially important is its capability to detect voice activity in the line and to interrupt other services. Messages or actions may be interrupted by the user. This capability highly improves the ergonomy of the system.

3.3 Speech Recognition Module

In this moment, the recognition engine used by TelCorreo is the continuous speech phonetic recogniser provided with HITO and with the line interface hardware.

TelCorreo speech interface is based on keywords, each of them meaning something the user can do. The interface between the recogniser and the dialogue manager includes a very simple semantic parser that translates the word identifiers found by the recogniser to meaning identifiers that TelCorreo can deal with. This simple parser makes TelCorreo bilingual: the user can speak to the system in Galician or Spanish indiscriminately.

TelCorreo is under development. One of the modules where more efforts are being spent is the speech recogniser. The newly developed speech recogniser described in [5] will be integrated in the next months.

3.4 Bilingual Text-to-Speech Synthesis Module

TelCorreo uses our Galician text-to-speech conversion system, called Cotovía [6]. It is based on overlapped concatenation of waveform segments. This system is included in TelCorreo as a DLL developed using C programming language. It generates telephone-band (4 kHz) masculine and feminine voice. The pitch and articulation rate are parameters that can be also configured by the user.

The Text-to-Speech module is completely independent from TelCorreo, and for this reason integrates all the functions needed by a stand-alone synthesiser (specially text preprocessing).

3.5 E-mail Server Communication Module

TelCorreo needs to communicate with the mail server that holds users mailboxes in order to retrieve the messages. The POP3 client in the mail server interface module gives this functionality. It is programmed in Perl and highly integrated with the mail preprocessor. An additional feature of the module is that voice attachments may be opened and read to the user.

In order to support sending answers to certain messages through the telephone interface, a SMTP client is also included. It builds the answers and handles also voice attachments, which can be sent with short voice messages.

3.6 Message Preprocessing Module

Electronic mail gives people the opportunity to communicate almost instantly. As a consequence, it is very common to find ill-formed phrases, punctuation errors, unknown words or abbreviations, etc. To solve this problem, it is necessary to use a message preprocessor that formats the text which will be sent to the synthesiser. This module was developed in PERL programming language. It processes the whole e-mail message (headers included) and it performs the following tasks:

1. Extraction of the e-mail constituents.
2. Language identification. This is performed by a voting system on language-specific word appearances. The detected languages are Spanish, Galician and English. English parts are not read, but only detected.
3. Spanish and Galician specific characters processing and/or correction.
4. Headers extraction in multi-part messages.
5. Extraction of information in headers like "Content-Transfer-Encoding", "Content-type" and "Filename".
6. Typification of the body of the message: text; enriched text; image, audio or video file, etc.
7. "Quoted printable" decodification.
8. Cite elimination.
9. Detection and/or elimination of smilies.
10. Elimination of non-alfanumeric characters.

3.7 Dialogue Manager

This module is responsible of handling the user telephone interface. It offers all the actions and options of the telephone mail service, and includes functions to detect and correct dialog errors. This dialogue manager is structured as a sequence of basic dialogue units called *menu elements*, which are executed sequentially in an order imposed by the menu configuration and the user dialog actions and queries.

The set of menu elements are handled by a finite-state machine which supports different levels of execution. Each state is meant for a different general requirement of the dialogue. For example, a typical menu element has an introductory state in which reads a message to the user (giving him information about the dialog situation, for example).

This stiff structure was made more flexible by means of defining what we call *direct execution elements* and *implicit confirmation elements*. Basically, they hide the options to the user and conduct their actions with more naturality, while maintaining the general structure and the interface with the speech recogniser and the semantic analyser.

3.8 Speaker Authentication Module

Traditionally, the security of systems like TelCorreo relied on the use of some private code or password. Since TelCorreo has been designed as a dialogue system, its basic technology makes possible the implementation of a voice-based user authentication module. This module is explained in depth in [7].

4 Conclusions and Further Work

TelCorreo is still under development. A few days before writing this article, TelCorreo was deployed in real-world with real users. However, it is too soon to reliably evaluate the problems and questions that will have to be solved to get an acceptable degree of system usability and user satisfaction.

For more information on field trial results, please consult [1].

References

1. In http://www.gts.tsc.uvigo.es/telcorreo a description of TelCorreo can be found.
2. C. García-Mateo and M. González-González: An overview of the existing language resources for Galician. LREC: First International Conference on Language Resources and Evaluation – Workshop on Language Resources for European Minority Languages, Granada, Spain, (1998).
3. Relano, José and Tapias, Daniel and Villar, Juan M. and Gancedo, María and Hernández, Luis: Flexible Mixed-Initiative Dialogue for Telephone Services. EuroSpeech '99, Vol. 3, pages 1179–1182 (1999).
4. TEIMA Audiotex: Sistema Operativo HITO: Manual del Programador. Madrid, Spain (1998).
5. Cardenal López, Antonio and García Mateo, Carmen: Practical Considerations for the Development of a Real-time State-of-art Large-vocabulary Continuous Speech Recogniser. Submitted for publication in ISCA ITRW ASR Workshop to be held in Paris, (2000).
6. Fernández Salgado, Xavier and Rodríguez Banga, Eduardo: Segmental Duration Modelling in a Text-to-Speech System for the Galician Language, EuroSpeech '99, Budapest, Hungary (1999).
7. L. Rodríguez-Liñares and C. García-Mateo: A speaker authentication module in TelCorreo. TSD 2000.

A Syntactical Model of Prosody as an Aid to Spoken Dialogue Systems in Italian Language

Enzo Mumolo

Dipartimento di Elettrotecnica, Elettronica ed Informatica
Universita' di Trieste, Via Valerio 10, 34127 Trieste, Italy
mumolo@univ.trieste.it   http://smartlab.univ.trieste.it

Abstract. An algorithm for modelling and generating prosody, based on a syntactical analysis, is described in this paper. The model provides a common framework for including prosody in spoken dialogue systems. The algorithm has been used to develop a system for natural language interaction with a mobile robot.

1   Introduction

In some applications, there is the need to develop a system that can engage in a collaborative spoken dialogue with human operators using natural language. Using the syntactical model of prosody described in this paper, an algorithm is proposed which gives a contribution for solving this problem. In fact, using this algorithm, a system for performing a vocal dialogue with a mobile robot [1] is under way and quite good preliminary results have been achieved, as it will be shown in the paper. The mobile robot was integrated with a word spotting engine and a TTS synthetiser. Simple vocal commands, inserted in a natural language sentence, can be given to the robot. Furthermore, it can answer using vocal messages.

The key idea of this model is to provide a syntactical description of a prosodic profile by a number of simple elementary curves. With respect to other contributions in the field [7,6], in our case the curves are not described by an analytic function; rather, the curves are directly extracted from spoken utterances. Moreover, our definition of elementary curves is different. In other approaches [5], the linguistically relevant modulations of the fundamental frequency are interpreted into pre-defined configurations of stylised 'pitch movements', derived with a perceptual approach [8]. Finally, the algorithm described here provides a common framework for synthesis and recognition applications using natural language.

Generally speaking, a sentence can be segmented into clauses which are roughly related to the principal, secondary and final meaning of the utterance. Our model is based upon the identification of the clauses in a spoken utterance and on the determination of parameters related to prosody; furthermore, the stress points within the sentence are de-emphasised, for getting rid of the events which are not related to the intonation itself. For the sake of simplicity, prosody has been characterised using only fundamental frequency; clearly the algorithm can be easily extended to other parameters.

P. Sojka, I. Kopeček, and K. Pala (Eds.): TSD 2000, LNAI 1902, pp. 387–392, 2000.

The declarative sentences have been modelled with the following elementary curves: Principal Initial Profile (PI), Principal Non Initial Profile (PNI), Secondary Initial Profile (SI), Secondary Non Initial Profile (SNI) and Final Profile (FI); while for interrogative sentences, Principal Initial Profile (PIN), Secondary Non Initial Profiles (SNIN) and Final Profiles (FPIN) have been used. On the basis of these segments, the syntactical model of declarative sentences can be described as:

$$(PI)(SNI)^*(FP)|(SI)(SNI)^*(PNI)(SNI)^*(FP).$$

Interrogative sentences have been simply modelled as $(PIN)(SNIN)^*(FPIN)$.

It is worth noting that the model for declarative sentences is more complex than that for interrogative sentences, due to some system constraints.

2   Estimation of Basic Prosodic Groups

The estimation of the BPGs starts by using an initial set of spoken utterances in which the breath groups, i.e. the point where a speaker usually interrupts to breath, are taken into account.

A breath group has been considered as a clause and hence it is the basis to derive the BPGs. If the breath group can be grammatically described as (noun, verb, noun), it is called Principal, otherwise it is called Secondary.

Ten utterances are acquired, manually segmented into breath groups and labelled into BPGs using an interactive tool. The estimation of the fundamental frequency is performed using the eSRPD algorithm [3]. To simplify subsequent processing, the pitch has been interpolated using a Lagrange interpolator in order to obtain a continuous profile. Thus, a set of approximated BPGs is obtained; for each BPG, at least two versions are obtained from the ten utterances. The elementary profiles with the same label are averaged together using a Dynamic Programming Algorithm (DPA) in order to filter out stress, microprosodic and idyosincratic events of the spoken utterance. The BPGs obtained so far are the initial seeds of a subsequent iterative refinement procedure. Another set of ten utterances is used for the refinement. Some utterances are in the form $(PI)(SNI)(FP)$ and $(SI)(PNI)(FP)$ for declarative sentences; similarly for the interrogative sentences. Some finite-state syntaxes are built accordingly and a forced recognition is performed using One Stage DPA where the templates are the seeds obtained as described above and the unknown pattern is the f_0 profile of the utterances of the refinement set. If the number of seeds is K and the number of f_0 points in an utterance is N, the algorithm is described as:

Step 1 $D(1,j,k) = \sum_{n=1}^{j} d(1,n,k), k = 1,\ldots,K$
Step 2 2a) For $i = 2,\ldots,N$ do steps 2b $\rightarrow$ 2e
    2b) For $k = 1,\ldots,K$ do steps 2c $\rightarrow$ 2e
    2c) $D(i,1,k) = d(i,1,k) + \min\{D(i-1,1,k), D(i-1,J(k^*),k^*),$
    $k^* = 1,\ldots,K\}$
    2d) For $j = 2,\ldots,J(K)$ do step 2e
    2e) $D(i,j,k) = d(i,j,k) + \min\{D(i-1,j,k), D(i-1,j-1,k), D(i,j-1,k)\}$
Step 3 Backtracking with syntactical constraints

This way, the utterances are BPG-segmented according to the DPA optimisation criteria, thus giving a new set of BPG starting from the initial seeds. This procedure is repeated for all the utterances.

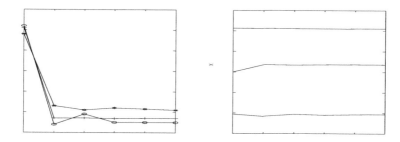

Fig. 1. Convergence of refinement procedure for declarative sentences – left panel: One Stage DPA score versus iteration number for the three BPGs; right panel: segmentation points of the three BPG versus iteration number

As a new set of BPG is obtained, the new elementary profiles and the previous ones – the reference templates – are DPA averaged if they have the same label; the weights assigned to the new and previous BPGs are 0.9 and 0.1 respectively. The procedure is iterated until convergence is reached. It can be observed that, at each iteration, both the endpoints and the actual values adapt to the correct values. Convergence is indicated by the decreasing behaviour of the DPA score. Some representative results are shown in Figure 1 for a declarative sentence.

3   On the Use of the Syntactical Model to Help Recognising Commands Spoken Using Natural Language

There are several possible uses of our model of prosody in a recognition system. The simplest one is to determine if the spoken sentence is a declarative or an interrogative one, and to use this information together with a keyword recognition system. This way, a keyword can be interpreted as being part of an interrogative clause or of a declaration. For example, the word 'localisation' can be used in a sentence like 'can you perform localisation of my position?' or 'give me all the localisation information!'; if the keyword recognition system says that the word 'localisation' is present in the input phrase (which was uttered in natural language), by identifying the prosodic model we can perform two completely different tasks. By the way, this can be a real dialogue with the robot.

4   Automatic Segmentation of the Input Text into BPGs with a Syntactical Approach

In this section, we describe the identification of the BPGs from an input text. The general linguistic framework for the pre-processing and syntactical analysis phases has been derived from the work of [2].

4.1   Pre-processing of the Input Text

Consider the sets of symbols defined in the following.

Definition 1 *Let us define a set of symbols as* $T_1 = \{gv, gn, gnv, gp, gpv, ga, gav, fr, frv, fs, fsv\}$ *where "g" stands for group, "n" for nominal, "v" stands for verbal, "p" for prepositional, "a" for adjunt, "f" for phrase, "r" for relative and "s" stands for secondary. Define moreover* $T_2 = \{\langle . \rangle, \langle , \rangle, \langle : \rangle\}$ *and* $N_2 = \{\langle PF0 \rangle, \langle PF10 \rangle, \langle PF20 \rangle, \langle PF30 \rangle, \langle PF40 \rangle, \langle PF50 \rangle, \langle PF60 \rangle, \langle PF70 \rangle, \langle PF80 \rangle\}$.

The output of the pre-processing module is a sequence of elements of the set T_1. First, a lexical analysis (LA) of the input text is performed. The purpose of the LA is to give the following stages the suitable information on each word of the input text. The lexical analyser can be built at different levels of complexity but, at least, its output should include the word's grammatical category. Moreover, in case of lexical ambiguities, the LA should furnish all the possible categories. According to [2], we developed an LA composed by a dictionary and an automata. The dictionary contains all the lexicon, using a morphemic approach, while the automata's task is to make a morphological analysis of the input text and to give, as output, the grammatical categories. The dictionary is structured as a graph, which is analysed with a depth-first strategy. The automata is, as a matter of fact, an Augmented Transition Network (ATN) [4]. The next step of the pre-processing phase concerns the stress assignment. Clearly, stress assignment is fundamental for the correct generation and modelling of the prosody. According to [2], the stress is obtained with a list of rules together with a number of exceptions. The list is searched and as soon as a suitable rule is found, the algorithm returns.

4.2   Syntactical Analysis

The goal of the syntactical analysis is to determine high-level suprasegmental character-istics of the sentence, such as the "breath groups" and the prosodic profiles. Moreover, the syntactical information are fundamental to solve ambiguities, or homographs. The input text is divided into "Phonological Words" (PW), defined as a phonetic unit com-posed by the subset of words which is uttered as it were a single word. The PW contains only one principal stress. The PWs are classified in terms of 'gv' (verbal group), 'gn' (noun group), 'gp' (prepositional group), 'ga' (adjunt group), 'fr' (relative phrase) and 'fs' (secondary phrase).

4.3   Determination of the BPGs in the Input Text

As introduced before, the meta-text produced so far has to be segmented into BPGs, defined in Section 2. The segmentation has been realized with a grammar which classify a set of PW as the appropriate BPG according to the structure

$$[\langle nominal\ group \rangle] \langle verbal\ group \rangle [\langle nominal\ group \rangle] \langle prepositional\ group \rangle^*.$$

We now describe the syntax for the declarative phrases, which has been derived through the analysis of many sentences. Slight modifications are required for the interrogative phrases.

Definition 2 *The grammar used for the segmentation into BPG is a set* $G = \{V_N, V_T, P, S\}$, *where the nonterminal symbols are* $V_N = \{\langle s_i \rangle, \langle PF_j \rangle, \langle p \rangle, \langle FALL \rangle\}$, for $i = 20, 40$ and $j = 0, 10 \ldots 80$ and the set of terminal symbols is $V_T = T_1 \cup \{PI, PNI, SI, SNI, FP\} \cup \{:, ., , , \{, \}\}$. The initial symbol is S. The set of production rules P is given below in BNF.

1. $S ::= (\{(gav|ga|fs|fsv|gp|gpv|frv|fr)\langle PF0\rangle\langle SI\rangle\langle s20\rangle)|(\{(gn|gv|gnv)\langle PF0\rangle$
   $\langle PI\rangle\langle s40\rangle)$
2. $p ::= , | :$
3. $fr\langle s20\rangle ::= fr\langle PF0\rangle\langle PSNI\rangle\langle s20\rangle$, same for $fsv, frv, fs, ga, gav, gp, gpv$
4. $gn\langle s20\rangle ::= gn\langle PF0\rangle\langle PNI\rangle\langle s40\rangle$, same for gv, gnv
5. $\langle p\rangle\langle s20\rangle ::= \{\langle p\rangle(t, t \in T1)\langle PF0\rangle\langle SNI\rangle\langle s20\rangle$
6. $\langle s40\rangle ::= \{(t, t \in T1 \text{ or } T2)\langle PF0\rangle\langle SNI\rangle\langle s40\rangle$
7. $.\langle FALL\rangle ::= .\}$
8. $.\}(\langle PSI\rangle\langle s20\rangle|\langle PI\rangle\langle s40\rangle|\langle SNI\rangle\langle s20\rangle|\langle SNI\rangle\langle s40\rangle|\langle PNI\rangle\langle s40\rangle) ::= .\}\langle PF\rangle$
9. $\langle p\rangle\langle FALL\rangle ::= \langle p\rangle\}$
10. $gv\langle PF0\rangle ::= gv\langle PF10\rangle$
11. $gpv\langle PF0\rangle ::= gpv\langle PF20\rangle$, same for fsv, frv, gav
12. $gn\langle PF0\rangle ::= gn\langle PF30\rangle$, same for fr, fs, ga, gp
13. $\langle PF10\rangle ::= (gv\langle PF10\rangle)|(gp\langle PF70\rangle)|((gn|gnv|gpv|ga|gav|fr|frv|fs|fsv)\langle PF40\rangle)$
14. $\langle PF20\rangle ::= (gv\langle PF10\rangle)|(fsv\langle PF20\rangle)|((gn|gnv|ga|gav)\langle PF40\rangle)|$
    $(gp\langle PF70\rangle)|((sf|fr|gpv|frv)\langle PF0\rangle\langle SNI\rangle\langle PF70\rangle))$
15. $\langle PF30\rangle ::= ((ga|gn|gp)\langle PF30\rangle)|((gv|gav|gnv)\langle PF40\rangle)|((gpv|fr|frv|fs|$
    $fsv)\langle PF0\rangle\langle SNI\rangle\langle PF10\rangle))$
16. $\langle PF40\rangle ::= ((gv|gav|gn)\langle PF40\rangle)|(gp\langle PF50\rangle)|(\})$
17. $\langle PF50\rangle ::= ((gv|gav)\langle PF60\rangle)|(gp\langle PF50\rangle)|(\})$
18. $\langle PF60\rangle ::= ((ga|gp|gav)\langle PF60\rangle)|(\})$
19. $\langle PF70\rangle ::= ((ga|gp|gav)\langle PF70\rangle)|(gn\langle PF80\rangle)|(\})$
20. $\langle PF80\rangle ::= ((ga|gav)\langle PF60\rangle)|(\})$
21. $(n, n \in N2 - \{\langle PF0\rangle\})|(.\langle PF0\rangle) ::= .\langle FALL\rangle$
22. $(n, n \in N2 - \{\langle PF0\rangle\})|(\langle p\rangle\langle PF0\rangle) ::= \langle p\rangle\langle FALL\rangle$

A parser has been realized by means of a small ATN built according to the described grammar.

Example Let us consider, as an example, the following Italian phrase: '*Il satellite contiene un orologio ed una stazione trasmittente che permettono di sincronizzare i tempi con grande precisione.*'. This phrase is transformed, at the output of the syntactical analysis of Section 4.2, in the following string: '*gn gv gn frv gp gn gp.*' which is left-to-right analysed with the grammar described above. The results of the analysis are reported below, where the employed production rules and the output strings are indicated.

$P1, P12 \rightarrow \{gn\ PF30\ PI\ s40$
$P15, P16 \rightarrow \{gn\ gv\ gn\ PF40\ PI\ s40$
$P16, P6 \rightarrow \{gn\ gv\ gn\}PI\{frv\ PF0\ SNI\ s40$
$P19, P20 \rightarrow \{gn\ gv\ gn\}PI\{frv\ gp\ gn\}SNI\ s40$
$P6, P8 \rightarrow \{gn\ gv\ gn\}PI\{frv\ gp\ gn\}SNI\{gp.\}PFIN$

Of course, the use of the syntactical model in text-to speech systems can be performed by determining the sequence of elementary curves needed to model the text. The suitable BPGs are then concatenated and superimposed to the synthetised signal.

5   Final Remarks and Conclusions

Twenty sentences have been used to test the algorithm. Such sentences were available in spoken as well as in written form. All the phrases in the test set were correctly segmented, using One Stage DPA and the BPG derived as described above. A further test was carried out to verify the correctness of the results from a perceptual point of view, giving a success of about 70%.

The test performed with the written form of the utterances gave good results either: the segmentation into BPG was 50% correct, but in additional 40% cases, it gave acceptable results. Clearly, a refinement of the morphological analyser would lead to an overall improvement. The algorithm has been integrated into a real time TTS system and it was observed that it improved the naturalness of the spoken utterances.

References

1. E. Mumolo, M. Nolich, G. Vercelli, "Algorithms and Architectures for Acoustic Localisation based on Microphone Array in Service Robotics", *IEEE Int. Conference on Robotics and Automation*, Stanford, CA, 2000.
2. R. Gretter, G. Mian, R. Rinaldo, M. Salmasi, "Linguistic Processing for an Italian Text-to-Speech System", in Proc. of *Int. Conf. on Speech Tech. VERBA '90*, 1990, Rome, Italy.
3. P. Bagshaw, S. Hiller, Jack, "Enhanced pitch tracking and the processing F0 contours for computer aided intonational teaching", in *Proceedings of Eurospeech '93*, Berlin.
4. W. A. Woods, "Cascaded ATN Grammars", *American Journal of Comp. Linguistics*, vol. 16, N. 1, 1980.
5. S. Quazza, P. L. Salza, S. Sandri, A. Spini, "Prosodic control in a text to speech system for Italian", in Proc. of *ESCA Workshop on Prosody*, Lund, Sept. 1993.
6. L. F. M. ten Bosch, "Automatic Classification of Pitch Movements via MLP-Based Estimation of Class Probabilities", ICASSP '95.
7. M. Nakei, H. Singer et al., "Automatic Prosodic Segmentation by F0 Clustering Using Superpositional Modelling", ICASSP '95.
8. J. t'Hart, R. Collier, A. Cohen, "A perceptual study of intonation: an experimental-phonetic approach to speech melody", *Cambridge University Press*, 1990.

What Do You Mean by "What Do You Mean"?
A Formal Representation and Its Dynamic Semantics of Meta-expressions in Conversations

Norihiro Ogata

Faculty of Language and Culture, Osaka University
1-8 Machikaneyama, Toyonaka, Osaka, Japan
ogata@lang.osaka-u.ac.jp

Abstract. This paper investigates dynamic semantics of conversations from the point of view of semantical closedness, presuppositions and shared belief/common knowledge updates, by analysing the meta-expression "what do you mean (by X)?" into three major usages: *semantic repair initiation*, *intentional repair initiation*, and *inferential repair initiation*, since these three usages are deeply related to three types of semantical closedness: *closedness of denotations*, *closedness of intention* and *closedness of inference* of conversations. As a result, the proposed dynamic semantics of conversations is semantically closed in terms of shared beliefs of the conversants.

1 Introduction

A conversation can be regarded as a cooperative social action that forms and updates the common knowledge of the society, community, or group. Therefore, to answer the question of how conversations can form or update the common knowledge of the community is to propose dynamic semantics of conversations. As a step towards proposing dynamic semantics of conversations, we will concentrate on the meaning of the phrase "what do you mean (by X)?". This phrase can be interpreted in at least three ways that are deeply relevant to forming or updating the common knowledge of the community. This means that analyses of this phrase can give a hint on modelling of formations and updates of the common knowledge of a community and conversants' commitment to the processes.

In Section 2, an analysis of three interpretations of the phrase "what do you mean (by X)?" will be shown, and a formal language modelling conversations will be defined. In Section 3, dynamic semantics of conversation will be defined.

2 *What Do You Mean* Means Three Types of Triggers of Updates of Common Knowledge

The phrase "what do you mean (by X)?", which functions as an initiation of repairs in the sense of conversational analysis ([9], etc.), is a typical phrase used in conversation. A consideration of its semantics is useful for proposing semantics of conversations, since the phrase has at least three uses:

P. Sojka, I. Kopeček, and K. Pala (Eds.): TSD 2000, LNAI 1902, pp. 393–398, 2000.
© Springer-Verlag Berlin Heidelberg 2000

(I) asking what the phrase X denotes (*semantic repair initiation*),

(II) asking what the previous speaker intends by saying the phrase X (*intentional repair initiation*), and

(III) asking what grounds of the previous speaker's statement (*inferential repair initiation*),

and all three meanings are deeply relevant to the formation or update of the common knowledge of a community, since (I) implies that in the community, the denotation of X is not defined as common knowledge but as the previous speaker's private knowledge, (II) implies that in the community, the implication relation between X and its intended content is not shared, and (III) implies that in the community, the deduction of X from some bases is not shared.

We can find examples of all three interpretations of the phrase in documents distributed over the WWW, as follows:

(1) a. A: ... Because the country is so different today from then. It's a different world entirely. Then you didn't have wages or crisis ...

B: And *what do you mean by then*?

A: Back in the 30s. Let's take 60 years.

B: Okay.

   b. A: *What do you mean by* saying that our sorrow should be interior?

B: When I say that our sorrow should be interior,

I mean that it should come from the heart,

and not merely from the lips.

   c. A: ... Why do you want the dog to stop?

it's not perverted - it's dog language. ...

B: *What do you mean* why do I want it to stop???

It's freaking embarrassing if guests come over and my dog humps them.

I do not want it.

(1a-c) can be represented in formal schemata, as follows:

(2) a. $p[x]; ?y.denotes(x, y)$

  b. $p; ?q.p \Rightarrow q$

  c. $p; ?y.y \vdash p$

where $p[x]$ is an atomic move which transmits the proposition p with an argument x, ";" means a turn exchange (i.e., conversational dynamic conjunction in the sense of dynamic semantics [10,7]), $?x.p$ means "in the previous expression p, what does x means?", $denotes(x, y)$ means x denotes y, $\Rightarrow$ means an implication, $x_1, \ldots, x_n \vdash p$ means that p is deducible from the context $x_1, \ldots, x_n$.

Since, by the deduction theorem, $x_1, \ldots, x_n \vdash p$ is equivalent to $\vdash x_1 \wedge \ldots \wedge x_n \Rightarrow p$, (2c) is reformulated as follows:

(3) $p; ?y.y \Rightarrow p$

These formulas (i.e., (2a-b) and (3)) are defined by a BNF-grammar as in the following definition.

Definition 1.

$$v \in Var_{INDIV} \qquad\qquad p \in Var_{PROP}$$

$$\tau \in TERM \qquad\qquad \phi \in \Phi$$

$$\varphi \in FORM_\Phi \qquad\qquad m \in MOVE_\Phi$$

$$\phi ::= \pi(\tau_1,\dots,\tau_n)|denotes(\tau_1,\tau_2)|\tau_1 = \tau_2$$

$$\varphi ::= \phi|\varphi_1 \Rightarrow \varphi_2|\varphi_1 \wedge \varphi_2|\bot$$

$$m ::= \varphi|?x.\varphi|agree|m_1; m_2$$

where Var_{INDIV} is a set of individual variables, Var_{PROP} a set of propositional variables, $TERM$ a set of terms, Φ a set of atomic formulas, $FORM_\Phi$ a set of formulas, $MOVE_\Phi$ a set of sequences of moves, $\pi \in PRED$ an n-place predicate, $denotes(\tau_1,\tau_2)$ means that τ_1 denotes τ_2, x is a propositional variable or an individual variable, and $agree$ means an assent move.

This language contains a semantic predicate $denotes$ and an implication $\Rightarrow$ which means both of an implication and a deductive relation. That is, this language is semantically, intentionally and inferentially closed in the sense that the denotation of terms, intention, which is treated as an implication, and inference, which is also treated as an implication, can be described within the language.

Intuitively, the semantics of each move is defined as a kind of conditional, since its semantics cannot be defined independently of its context as the following observation:

(4)   a. $p[x]$; $agree$ iff $(denotes(x,y) \wedge p[x] \wedge p[y])$ is shared in the community ... (2a)
      b. p; $agree$ iff $((p \Rightarrow y) \wedge p \wedge y)$ is shared in the community ... (2b)
      c. p; $agree$ iff $((\Gamma \Rightarrow p) \wedge \Gamma \wedge p)$ is shared in the community ... (3)

That is to say, assertive move p can change the community's shared knowledge if it is accepted in the community, and for the acceptance in Case (2a) $denotes(x,y)$ must be shared as its common presupposition, in Case (2b) $p \Rightarrow y$ for some "y" in the context, and in Case (3) $\Gamma \Rightarrow p$ for some context Γ, respectively.

Conversely, when we say "what do you mean (by X)?", we consider such presuppositions as possibly undefined, and this means, the phrase pragmatically urges re-sharing of such presuppositions, or testing of sharing of the presuppositions.

To sum up, the move p means a conditional "if the presupposition of p for its understanding is defined or shared in the community, update the common knowledge of the community by adding proposition what p means to the common knowledge", and "what do you mean (by X)?" means a declaration of undefinedness of such presuppositions.

3   A Dynamic Semantics of Conversations

More formally, exploiting the idea of update semantics [11], Discourse Representation Theory-based dynamic semantics of dialogue [8], and dynamic epistemic semantics [4,3,2], dynamic semantics of each sequence of moves m is defined in the basis of conditional updates discussed in Section 2.

Definition 2. Given a Kripke model of an epistemic logic
$(W, (R_a)_{a \in Agent}, (D_w)_{w \in W}, I)$, where W is a set of states, $Agent$ a set of agents,
$R_a \subseteq W \times W$, D_w is the set of individuals in state w, and
$I : W \times TERM \to D_w \cup W \times PRED \to pow(D_w^n)$, a dynamic interpretation of
$MOVE_\Phi \, [\![\,]\!] : CONTEXT \times W \to CONTEXT \times W$ is defined by induction of the
complexity of $m \in MOVE_\Phi$, as follows:

- $[\![\varphi]\!](c, X) = (c', P)$, where $c' = c[\varphi/c(prev), P/c(prevw)]$,
  $P = \{w \in Y | Presup(\varphi, w, c) =! \text{ implies } w \models shared(c(cm), \varphi)\}$ and if
  $top(c(world)) \neq \Lambda$, then $Y = top(c(world))$ and $c'(world) = pop(c(world))$,
  otherwise $Y = X$,
- $[\![?x.\varphi]\!](c, X) = (c', P)$, where $P = \{w \in X | Presup(\varphi, w, c) =?\})$ and
  $c' = c[\varphi/c(prev), push(c(prev), c(foc))/c(foc), P/c(prevw),$
  $push(c(world), c(prevw))/c(world)]$,
- $[\![agree]\!](c, X) = (c', \{w \in X | Presup(top(c(foc)), w, c) =!\})$, where
  $c' = c[pop(c(foc))/foc(c)]$,
- $[\![m_1; m_2]\!](c, X) = [\![m_2]\!](ex(c), [\![m1]\!](c, X))$.

where c is a contextual index and $ex(X)$ are operations of contextual indices, $push(X)$
and $pop(X)$ are operations of the *focus stack* of a context, defined in Definition 3,
$Presup(X, Y, Z)$ are also defined in Definition 4, and $w \models X$ (X is true at w), meta-
languages $shared(cm, Y)$ (Y is shared among the members of the community cm) is
defined in Definition 5.

Definition 3. $c \in CONTEXT = \{cm, spk, hrr, foc\} \hookrightarrow Agent \cup pow(Agent) \cup$
$Stack(FORM_\Phi)$ is a contextual index satisfying the following conditions:

- $c(cm) \subseteq Agent$, i.e., the community in the context c,
- $c(spk) \in Agent$ and $c(hrr)$ are the speaker and the hearer in the context c, where
  $c(spk) \neq c(hrr)$, respectively,
- $c(prevw) \in pow(W)$, $c(world) \in Stack(pow(W))$,
- $c(prev) \in FORM_\Phi$, $c(foc) \in Stack(FORM_\Phi)$,
- $ex : CONTEXT \to CONTEXT$ such that $spk(ex(c)) = c(hrr)$, $hrr(ex(c)) =$
  $c(spk)$, and $ex(c(foc)) = c(foc)$,

where $Stack(X)$ is a class satisfying the following conditions:
$\Lambda \in Stack(X)$,
if $s \in Stack(X)$ and $x \in X$ then $push(s, x) \in Stack(x)$,
if $s \in Stack(X)$, then $top(push(s, x)) = x$,
if $s \in Stack(X)$, then $pop(push(s, x)) = s$.

We can handle nested conversations such as (5) by the focus stack in the above definition.

(5) A: Hallowed be thy name ... B: Hold it. *What do you mean by that?* A: *By what?*
    B: By "hallowed be thy name"? A: It means ...

Definition 4. $Presup : (FORM_{\varPhi} \cup TERM_{\varPhi}) \times W \times CONTEXT \rightarrow \{!, ?\}$ ('!' means 'defined' and '?' 'undefined') is a check function of presuppositions[1] of expressions at a state and a context which is shared among the members of the community, and defined by induction on the complexity of φ as follows:

- $Presup(\tau, w, c) =!$ iff $w \models shared(c(cm), \tau = \tau')$ and $Presup(\tau', w, c) =!$,
- $Presup(denotes(\tau_1, \tau_2), w, c) =!$ iff $w \models shared(c(cm), \tau_1 = \tau_2)$
  and $Presup(\tau_2, w, c) =!$,
- $Presup(\pi(\tau_0, \ldots, \tau_{n-1}), w, c) =!$ iff for all $i < n$, $Presup(\tau_i, w, c) =!$
  and $Ground(\pi(\tau_0, \ldots, \tau_{n-1}), w, c) =!$,
- $Presup(\varphi_1 \Rightarrow \varphi_2, w, c) =!$ iff $Ground(\varphi_1 \Rightarrow \varphi_2, w, c) =!$, $Presup(\varphi_1, w, c) =!$
  and $Presup(\varphi_2, w, c) =!$,
- $Presup(\varphi_1 \wedge \varphi_2, w, c) =!$ iff $Presup(\varphi_1, w, c) =!$ and $Presup(\varphi_2, w, c) =!$,
- $Ground(\varphi, w, c) =!$ iff $w \models shared(c(cm), \varphi)$ or $((w \models shared(c(cm), p \Rightarrow \varphi)$
  or $w \models shared(c(cm), \varphi \Rightarrow p))$ and $Presup(p, w, c) =!)$.

The definition of $Presup(denotes(\tau_1, \tau_2), w, c)$ in the above definition means that τ_1 is defined as the other term which is already shared in the community, that is, $denotes$ is defined not as a purely semantic predicate, but as a kind of *renaming* predicate.

Definition 5. Given a Kripke model of an epistemic logic $(W, (R_a)_{a \in Agent}, (D_w)_{w \in W}, I)$, $w \models \varphi$ means that p is true at $w \in W$, satisfying the following conditions:

- $w \not\models \bot$
- $w \models \pi(\tau_1, \ldots, \tau_n)$ iff $(I_w(\tau_1), \ldots, I_w(\tau_n)) \in I_w(\pi)$
- $w \models denotes(\tau_1, \tau_2)$ iff $I_w(\tau_1) = I_w(\tau_2)$
- $w \models \tau_1 = \tau_2$ iff $I_w(\tau_1) = I_w(\tau_2)$
- $w \models \varphi_1 \wedge \varphi_2$ iff $w \models \varphi_1$ and $w \models \varphi_2$
- $w \models \varphi_1 \Rightarrow \varphi_2$ iff $w \models \varphi_1$ implies $w \models \varphi_2$
- $w \models shared(cm, \varphi)$ iff the largest fixed point of equation

$$q = \bigcap_{a \in cm} Bel(a)(\llbracket \varphi \rrbracket \cap q)$$

where $\llbracket \varphi \rrbracket = \{w \in W | w \models \varphi\}$, and

$$Bel(a)(X) = \{w \in W | wR_a u \text{ implies } u \in X\}.$$

The following example is the interpretation of the formalised conversation of a conversation such as (1a).

Example 1.

$$\llbracket \pi(a, b); ?x.denotes(b, x); denotes(b, d); agree \rrbracket(c, X)$$
$$= \llbracket agree \rrbracket(\llbracket denotes(b, d) \rrbracket(c', \{w | Presup(denotes(b, x), c, w) =?, P_1(w)\})$$
$$= (c'', \{w \in top(c'(world)) | Presup(denotes(b, d), c', w) =$$
$$w \models shared(c'(cm), denotes(b, d))\})$$

---

[1] This meaning of the term 'presuppositions' has a sense wider than a usual sense of the term which can be found in [5,1,6].

where $c' = c[push(pop(foc(c)), \pi(a,b))/foc(c), push(\{w \in X|P_1(w)\}, c(world))/$
$c(world), \ldots]$,
$c'' = c'[push(pop(foc(c)), denotes(b,d))/foc(c), push(\{w \in top(c'(world))|$
$P_2(w)\}, c(world))/ c(world), \ldots], P_1(w) = Presup(\pi(a,b), c, w) =! \rightarrow w \models$
$shared(c(cm), \pi(a,b))$, and $P_2(w) = Presup(denotes(b,d), c', w) =! \rightarrow w \models$
$shared(c'(cm), denotes(b,d))$.

In this conversation, if intentional or inferential presuppositions of the first move are shared, the content of the first move is shared, and this property is reflected in Example 1.

4   Conclusion

We have discussed the meaning of "what do you mean (by X)?" and its dynamic semantics based on updates of the common knowledge of the community. To clarify the meaning of "what do you mean (by X)?", a new concept of presuppositions has been defined in terms of shared beliefs among the members of the conversation. As a result, we could propose dynamic semantics and representation that can grasp the semantically-closed or meta-linguistic closed character of conversation, i.e., closedness on denotation and inference. Furthermore, we have been able to treat nested structures of conversations introduced by "what do you mean (by X)?" and other repair initiation moves by defining contexts by a kind of stack structure.

References

1. David Ian Beaver. Presupposition. In Johan van Benthem and Alice ter Meulen, editors, *Handbook of Logic and Language*. Elsevier Science B.V., Amsterdam, 1997.
2. Jelle Gerbrandy. Dynamic epistemic logic. In Lawrence S. Moss, Jonathan Ginzburg, and Maarten de Rijke, editors, *Logic, Language and Computation: vol. 2*, pages 67–84. CSLI Publications, Stanford, 1999.
3. Jelle Gerbrandy and Willem Groeneveld. Reasoning about information change. *Journal of Logic and Computation*, 23:267–306, 1997.
4. Willem Groeneveld. *Logical Investigations into Dynamic Semantics*. Ph.D. thesis, University of Amsterdam, 1995. published by ILLC-Publications.
5. Irene Heim. On the projection problem for presuppositions. In D. Flickinger et al., editors, *Proceedings of the Second West Coast Conference on Formal Linguistics*, pages 114–125. Stanford, 1988.
6. Emiel Krahmer. *Presupposition and Anaphora*. CSLI Publications, Stanford, 1998.
7. R. Muskens, J. van Benthem, and A. Visser. Dynamics. In Johan van Benthem and Alice ter Meulen, editors, *Handbook of Logic and Language*, pages 587–648. Elsevier Science B.V., Amsterdam, 1997.
8. Norihiro Ogata. Formal semantics of dialogues based on belief sharing and observational equivalence of dialogues. *Journal of Natural Language Processing*, 6(4):93–115, 1999.
9. Emanuel A. Schegloff, Gail Jefferson, and Harvey Sacks. The preference for self-correction in the organization of repair in conversation. *Language*, 53(2):361–382, 1977.
10. Johan van Benthem. *Exploring Logical Dynamics*. CLSI Publications, Stanford, 1996.
11. Frank C. Veltman. Defaults in update semantics. *Journal of Philosophical Logic*, 8:73–80, 1996.

Simplified Processing of Elliptic and Anaphoric Utterances in a Train Timetable Information Retrieval Dialogue System*

Václav Matoušek

Department of Computer Science and Engineering
Faculty of Applied Sciences, University of West Bohemia
Univerzitní 22, CZ – 306 14 Plzeň, Czech Republic
matousek@kiv.zcu.cz

Abstract. This paper presents a simplified approach to processing of ambiguous requests in spoken dialogues in information train timetable service systems. The simplified processing of ambiguous and incomplete utterances is based on a simple representation of the semantics of analyzed utterances by specially constructed frames, on the special representation and storage of facts extracted from the previous steps of dialogue (dialogue path, or dialogue history), and on the creation of the simple knowledge base containing the reasoning rules linking the meaning detected in the analyzed user's utterance with the facts stored in the dialogue path or in the system knowledge base. Some aspects of the implementation of utterance internal representing frames completion and their evaluation are discussed in the concluding part of this paper.

1 Introduction

The specific feature of standard dialogues conducted in information offices of railway stations can be seen in the presumption that both participants in the dialogue have approximately equal knowledge about the object of the dialogue conducting. Based on this fact, the speaking human does not need to express some essential information because this information is deduced from the receiver's knowledge and the context of the dialogue. The main problem of human-machine interaction in "machine-based" information retrieval systems consists in the fact that intelligent systems have to simulate such behavior of the human being and they have to combine the incomplete semantic information extracted from the analyzed utterance with the previous data stored in the dialogue history path or in the system knowledge base. It means that these systems must be able to process and also "understand" the utterances (queries) which we call incomplete or ambiguous.

---

* The work presented in this paper was partly supported by the Grant Agency Research Project No. 201/1248/99 and by the Czech Ministry of Education under contract number MSM 2352 00005. The author would also like to sincerely thank the colleagues from the University of Erlangen for valuable suggestions and discussions.

P. Sojka, I. Kopeček, and K. Pala (Eds.): TSD 2000, LNAI 1902, pp. 399–404, 2000.

The following four kinds of sentence ambiguities have to be processed in the phase of user's utterance understanding [10]:

1. *Lexical Ambiguities* – Most of the words have multiple meanings, e. g., if we look up the czech word psaní in a dictionary, we find that it can be either a verb (to write) or a noun (letter); determining the correct syntactic category poses a problem of lexical syntactic ambiguity. Having determined the correct syntactic category, we have to further decide what semantic concept a word represents. The meaning behind the noun jezdec, for example, can be either a person who rides on the horse or bicycle, a special toy, a sculpture, or an electric (electronic) control element. Deciding which of these meanings is correct (based on the utterance context) constitutes the goal of the lexical semantic ambiguity resolution.

2. *Structural Ambiguities* – Two or more different corresponding syntactic trees can be generated for one simple utterance. The system has to determine the relations between the individual words. The identification of the relations among the words is based on our knowledge of the concepts they represent.

3. *Ambiguity of Reference* – The short utterance refers to more objects (e. g. nouns) mentioned in the previous dialogue steps. A human would not have a problem to understand this reference, it results mostly from the listener's experience or the common knowledge.

4. *Ellipsis and Anaphoras* – Many user's queries appear to be ill-formed because they do not form complete sentences. Typically the parts that are missing can be extracted from the previous utterances. An elliptical utterance (the input fragment) must correspond in structure to a sub-constituent in the previous sentence (the target fragment). The final syntactic structure of the utterance is usually constructed by replacing the target fragment in the previous sentence with the input fragment. In this sense, ellipsis resolution is similar to anaphora resolution, where we also have to search for appropriate constituents in the previous sentences, and both ellipsis and anaphora resolution are heavily dependent on the context and general knowledge.

Since the last mentioned kind of ambiguities appears in approximately 54% of user's queries to the train timetable information dialogue system, we will deal with this problem in the following paragraphs.

2   Structure of a Dialogue Manager

A dialogue manager for the train timetable information retrieval dialogue system was designed by incorporating in the system pragmatic interpretation formation, formulas describing the database relating to the application, interpretation rules of earlier history of the current dialogue and their relationships (dialogue model), as well as a set of dialogue goals representing intentions of the system. The following basic program modules were incorporated in the developed dialogue manager:

- linguistic interface module for providing the communication with the parser,
- interpretation module for setting user utterance interpretation in the current dialogue context,

- task module for handling with database query and language adaptation task performance,
- dialogue module for planning system utterance formulation within the pragmatic information context and interpretation, and
- message planning module for generating the system message and protocols.

The structure of the dialogue manager is made fully open to enable the system extension by new modules. Their incorporation is performed under the control of the dialogue control module in which the message passing protocol was used to provide the communication among the modules. The more detailed description of the developed dialogue manager can be found in [5,6,7].

3   Internal Utterance Representation

Each system which analyses sentences of a natural language has to deal with a problem of sentence representation. Every sentence, represented in the input by a string of words, has to be converted into an internal representing structure. This internal structure has to be well defined and must distinguish all alternative meanings of the original sentence. It means that an adequate and flexible internal representation structure must be derived for each concrete implementation, and furthemore, it must be rather simple to achieve the real-time processing of user's utterances.

Queries to the information retrieval dialogue system covering the information about train departures and arrivals consist mainly of six essential parts of information – source (departure) city, source (departure) time, goal city, goal time, via-city (optional), and kind of train. All other information involved in the user's utterance seems (from the viewpoint of the required information) to be irrelevant. Then we can use the simplified internal representation in terms of frames involving six unstructured items, e. g.:

source-city	goal-city	source-time	goal-time	via-city	kind-of-train

Representing frames defined by this method are filled during the phase of linguistic and pragmatic analysis of the utterance and extraction of its essential meaning (see below).

4   Processing of Incomplete Utterances

Frame representation of the utterance semantics assumes the removal of all inadequate information from the utterance in the phase of linguistic analysis by specially structured linguistic analyzer [1,7]. The linguistic analyzer parses the best word sequence appearing in the output of the word recognizing module and interprets the meaning of the basic utterance at the same time. The meaning of the interpreted utterance is filled into the above described frame structure. Query to the database is composed if an adequate information has been extracted from the user's utterance, or else a clarifying question to the user has to be generated with the aim to complete the information for the database query completion in more composition steps and the incomplete representing frame is stored into the dialogue history path implemented as a classical chained list. The user's answer to the clarifying question is processed in the same way like his initial query, e. g.

the adequate information is extracted to the new utterance representing frame. This new generated frame is then overlapped (inclusive-or added) with the last one stored in the dialogue history pathlist. This loop has to be repeated until the representing frame is complete and the query to the database can be successfully composed.

In the second case, the user's query to the information system arises from the presumption, that both participants in the dialogue have approximately equal knowledge and experience in the dialogue domain. That means, the user assumes some general knowledge in the real life. Therefore, this knowledge has to be included into the system's knowledge base in the phase of the dialogue system development or system functional features enhancement (refinement). The utterance representing frames are then completed using this knowledge base. The created knowledge base has about 350 stored general rules, by which the internal sentence meaning frames can be completed. The rules were derived from a huge set of real dialogues recorded in 73 information offices in the Czech Republic. These real dialogues were digitalized and analyzed by a special quantitative linguistic analysis method [2,8].

5   Implementation

The processing of sentences of all kinds, including the incomplete sentences, is controlled by the dialogue module of the dialogue manager [5,6]. The internal representing frames are implemented by using a simple record data structure. To preserve the dialogue history, all analyzed and step-by-step completed semantic frames are stored in the special dialogue history path (temporary storage area of the dialogue module [6]) which is dynamically created as a simple chained reference list of elements containing at most seven contextual items with the aim to obtain an efficient implementation, to save the memory space, and to achieve the utterance processing in the shortest (real) time.

If the last analyzed sentence is classified as an incomplete one, its representing frame is compared with all temporary stored frames of previously analyzed sentences (the dialogue history pathlist is searched from the last stored frame to the first stored one), the frame is "overlapped" with the semantically most corresponding "elder" frame and completed for all missing data. If no corresponding frame is found in the temporary storage (in the dialogue history pathlist), i.e. the analyzed sentence is an anaphoric one, the dialogue module hands over the sentence analysis to the interpretation module, which attempts to complete the missing data with the help of a set of specially created and organized domain dependent reasoning rules stored as simple "$E \rightarrow H$" production rules of the general knowledge base (the rule which corresponds to the sentence most is applied on the last created representing frame). If this second analysis phase is unsuccessful too, only then the clarifying question is uttered. Finally, all sentence frames representing the saved dialogue history are immediately cleared after the ceremony closing the sequence of dialogue acts.

The program package for the processing of incomplete and ambiguous utterances was completely written in Quintus Prolog v. 3.2 as the separate (separately compiled) program module and included into the open modular program system of the dialogue manager.

6   Conclusion

The second version of the "Czech natural speaking" train timetable information retrieval dialogue system was developed and successfully implemented in last two years. The functional features of the developed dialogue manager involving the program package for the processing of incomplete and ambiguous user's utterances were tested and evaluated by the group of "semi-naive" users (students and laboratory staff). The results of this evaluation are summarized in the following table:

Number of users	58
Number of realized dialogues	580
Excellent dialogues	178
Dialogues with troubles *)	215
Unsuccessful dialogues	187
Successful dialogues total	393
in %	67.75

*) Dialogue with troubles means the dialogue with information repetitions, corrections, misunderstandings, additions, etc.

Summarizing the above presented method and results (features of the simplified processing of ambiguous and incomplete utterances), we can conclude that the presented method is based:

- on the simple representation of semantics of analyzed utterances by specially constructed representation frames,
- on the special representation and storage of facts extracted from the previous steps of dialogue (dialogue path, or dialogue history), and
- on the creation of the simple knowledge base containing the reasoning rules linking the meaning detected in the analyzed user's utterance with the facts stored in the dialogue path or in the system knowledge base.

In the process of further system testings, the knowledge base will be primarily extended for new extracted (formulated) reasoning rules inferred by testing and feature enhancement loop [7]. The extension of the knowledge base carried out in last nine months caused an increase of the relative number of successful dialogues (in comparison with the results presented in [7]) by 5.75%. We expect that – depending on the extension of the dialogue manager knowledge base in future and better organization of the dialogue history path – the number of successfully realized dialogues (dialogue act accuracy) will significantly increase. The application of the developed information retrieval dialogue system in other application areas (primarily in e-commerce) is expected as well.

References

1. Aretoulaki, M.; Gallwitz, F.; Harbeck, S.; Ipšić, I.; Ivanecký, J.; Matoušek, V.; Niemann, H.; Nöth, E.; Pavešić, N.: SQEL: A Multilingual and Multifunctional Dialogue System. In: Proceedings of the 5th International Conference on Spoken Language Processing (ICSLP '98), Sydney, Australia, 1998, paper No. 329.

2. Dialoganalyse VI: Referate der 6. Arbeitstagung in Prag 1996 (Hrsg. Čmejrková, S.; Hoffmanová, J.; Müllerová, O.; Světlá, J.), Teil I. Niemeyer Verlag, Tübingen, 1998.

3. Gibbon, D.; Moore, R.; Winski, R.: Handbook of Standards and Resources for Spoken Language Systems. Mouton de Gruyter Verlag, Berlin, New York, 1997.

4. Kosta P.: Gliederungssignale in tschechischen umgangssprachlichen und literarischen Texten. In: Zeitschrift für Slawistik 40 (1995), pp. 181–201.

5. Krutišová, J.; Matoušek, V.; Ocelíková, J.: Development of an One-Purpose Dialog Manager. In: Proc. of the Int. Workshop SPECOM '98, St. Petersburg, 1998, pp. 131–134.

6. Matoušek, V.; Krutišová, J.; Mautner, P.; Ocelíková, J.: A Dialog Module for the Information Retrieval System. In: Proc. of the AIII Int. Conference on Artificial Intelligence Applications in Industry, Košice, 1998, pp. 469–478.

7. Matoušek, V.; Ocelíková, J.: Managing Spoken Dialogues in Information Services. In: Proceedings of the IFIP TC.13 Int. Conference INTERACT '99, Edinburgh, 1999, pp. 141–148.

8. Matoušek, V.; Schwarz, J.: Creation and Use of a Digitalized Corpus of Spoken Dialogues. Technical Report No. 1 to the Bilateral Cooperation Project No. CZE-00-034, University of West Bohemia, Plzeň, 2000.

9. Ocelíková, J.; Matoušek, V.: Processing of Anaphoric and Elliptic Sentences in a Spoken Dialogue System. In: Proceedings of the European Conference EuroSpeech '99, Budapest, 1999, pp. 1185–1188.

10. Štětina, J.: Corpus Based Natural Language Ambiguity Resolution. Ph.D. Thesis, CTU Prague, 1997.

Pragmatic and Grammatical Aspects
of the Development of Dialogue Strategies

James Monaghan

Linguistics, University of Hertfordshire, Hatfield, Herts, England
linqjm@herts.ac.uk

Abstract. Technological developments in telephone-based dialogue systems have led to a situation where the main hindrance to progress is our lack of understanding of how dialogues work. The challenge to us is to understand dialogues in order to design efficient automated systems which take account of what users instinctively need. Two areas are addressed. Firstly, there is the fact that users automatically relate to the interpersonal aspect of each others participant role. The other one is that dialogue sequences are joint productions and grammatical expectations are exchanged in a way not immediately intuitive to the observer. Examples are presented and possible ways forward discussed.

1 Introduction

The current increase in the use and availability of telecomms-based information systems is largely technology-driven and as a result has thrown up many problems at the user interface. Speech interfaces, hand-held display systems, whether text or graphics-based, speed of accessing and processing information have all improved exponentially in availability as well as in reliability.

A case in point is automatic speech recognition. This has been possible for over forty years but it is only in the last five years that cheap, accurate and almost universally compatible speech recognition systems have been widely available for accessing remote information sources. Unfortunately, as is often the case, what improved hardware and software design can deliver often comes to a halt when we ask what the most effective and appropriate dialogue design is for a given purpose. This is the problem we want to begin to address.

This paper will concentrate on some typical aspects of linguistic activity that can underlie the design of information retrieval dialogues. These are dialogues where one agent (the source) has access to information in a specific domain and has to be able to interpret the input of a second agent (the client) so as to produce a relevant subset of its knowledge base to fulfil the information needs of the client. Theoretically, the two agents could be themselves automated expert systems. Examples would include market tracking software that is programmed to react to certain types of share movements, road navigation systems that compare knowledge of a vehicle's movements against updates on traffic problems on local roads, and naval and aeronautical systems that optimise course choices in terms of changes in meteorological factors.

P. Sojka, I. Kopeček, and K. Pala (Eds.): TSD 2000, LNAI 1902, pp. 405–409, 2000.
© Springer-Verlag Berlin Heidelberg 2000

Expert systems are relatively well-understood, because the underlying logic of the source information base and the executive client is the same. Human clients are, ironically, less well understood in the sense that they do not naturally query the source in a completely transparent and logical way. The same holds for human sources. They interact with the other participant as a fellow interlocutor while trying to achieve the transactional goal of the information exchange and, far from holding up the information exchange, this seems to optimise the speed of getting the required information transferred.

The approach of human participants is not so much reactive to explicit cues but is rather based on tacitly agreeing reciprocal roles in the encounter, on what the common task is, and on what the goals and the information status of the other participant are. These goals are, therefore, as much interpersonal as to do with achieving the transaction of information transfer. Sometimes the responses can be seen as coherent – in that they make sense in the task context – rather than cohesive – meaning that the sequence is signalled in dialogue terms. We will return to this below.

As a result, it is important to start by looking at evidence based on human-human knowledge elicitation. When we do this, we see that the outcome is very much attuned to the mutual understanding between client and source – often without subtasks being explicitly stated. The specific dialogue type which we are concentrating on is where the source is an interface to an intelligent knowledge-based system and the client is an untrained human user with an interest in accessing one piece of specific kind of information in a fixed domain. All of the data I draw on is derived from BT's VODIS corpus, an extensive series of information request transcripts where a user telephones one of a variety of sources and attempts to elicit information to do with travel needs, including coach and train services, restaurants, sightseeing, etc.

The most striking characteristic – obvious after even a cursory examination – is that there are two main intertwined activities going on. From the start, the two interactants assume congruent roles and automatically ascribe to each other motives derived from their own experience. This runs parallel to the most high profile task of information transfer, and is maintained and checked on an ongoing basis. Thus as well as transacting an information exchange, the interactants are also collaborating in generating a collaborative environment, mutually protecting and assigning what Goffman calls face [6]. By intruding on the space of another person – for example by telephoning – this needs propitiatory rituals such as asking if the other could tell you something other than ordering them to tell you.

All of this can be characterised in the relevant situational context in terms of *field*, *mode* and *tenor* [7]. The field of the information request dialogue is defined by what the relevant information is and the processes that are used to elicit it. The mode is a description of the channel of communications that apply – in this case non-face-to-face spoken dialogue. The tenor encodes the role relationship between the participants in the activity. We will address this last first.

2   Tenor and Transactional and Interactional Goals

Face has to do with the duty on each participant to recognise the other's underlying role in terms of the transaction the dialogue is designed to fulfil. It is then incumbent on each speaker to cooperate in recognising and trying to fulfil the other's goals. This applies not only to the long-term strategic goals of the whole transaction, but also the short-term tactical goals designed to facilitate each phase of the process of defining what the client wants and what the system can provide. Each participant has a status in relation to the other. The source has the status of access to information valuable to the client and the client has the status of customer, who ultimately pays the bill. Both owe to each other the respect based on their mutual status and above the bare necessities of the transaction. Failure on either party's part to know their place could result in the discourse being abruptly curtailed.

In the following dialogue, for example, the transaction would be fulfilled by the response 2:17, but what in fact happened was as follows:

Railway Company.

Oh yes, could you tell me when the next train from Trimley to Felixstowe is?

Trimley to Felixstowe

Yes.

What's the time now? Ten past one. Oh dear, it's not for an hour, I'm afraid. 2:17.

2:17. Okay, thanks a lot.

'Bye.

'Bye.

Here the client uses a rather complicated form of words to avoid asking the question in blunt terms. The source then takes on, unasked, the responsibility for the inconvenience of there not being an earlier train *Oh dear . . .   I'm afraid.* This is very common in the data, and is classed as interactional since it is not central to the transaction, which is about finding out a train time. There are of course some grey areas as for instance if the dialogue was a formal complaint. In this case, the goal of the transaction is to address the grievance and so *Sorry* and *I'm afraid* could legitimately be regarded as transactional.

The corollary for automated systems is that we must be aware of such expectations on behalf of the client, and at the very least, not run counter to them. How far we should attempt to emulate expressions of solidarity such as the above on non-human interactants is probably a matter for further study.

3   Dialogue Sequences

In addition to the importance of appreciating the tenor of a dialogue, there are several important aspects of the structure of the usual transactional dialogue. At the macrostructural level, dialogues can be seen as consisting of, firstly, a boundary phase of two parts – opening and closing – , and, more importantly, the medial phase or body where the crucial information is elicited and provided. In both boundary and medial phases, the dual view of language in the construction of reality, and language in the negotiation of participant face can be seen. Unlike a single person reading a timetable for their own information, where the process is purely transactional, as soon as another person is involved at least some language is required to oil the interpersonal wheels. From a functional point of view, the interactants' behaviour is highly constrained in terms of the overall goals of the interaction, as we have seen above, but it has not been widely appreciated that the interactants enter into a collaboration in attacking the problem posed.

The source and the client, often explicitly, reinterpret the problem to be solved as a mutual task not just in the business sense of trying to solve it, but also in the sense that they engage in mutually congruent evaluation of it. It becomes a joint problem where the source apologises for its existence and the client apologises for having inflicted the problem on the source, as we saw in the previous section.

This collaborative principle extends to relatively low level aspects of the lexicogrammar. Grammatical sequences have tended to be seen as confined to the sentence but, because of the collaboration of the participants in the joint production of the dialogue, the role of sequences running over the grammatical boundaries of clauses sentences is crucial. Questions, for example, are not sentences but demands for a completion which gives the equivalent of a sentence. All questions have built-in incompleteness. Polar questions have the positive-negative axis unspecified. Constituent questions have a constituent lexically unfulfilled. In the second part of the question-answer sequence which is characteristically produced by the other participant, the unfulfilled constituent symbol such as *What time would you like to be at Swindon by?* is replaced by a referential symbol such as *Well, around 9 to 10*. The answer is characteristically 'ungrammatical' if taken in isolation, but not in combination. The phrase *around 9 to 10* replaces *What time*.

Sensitivity to the importance of completing such user gambits appropriately is crucial to efficient dialogue design. Other sequences which relate to the overall task scheme of the dialogue as a whole include as well as Question-Answer, Problem-Solution, General-Specific and Situation-Evaluation. These key words are signals of Clause Relations – the building blocks of discourse in general and dialogues in particular. Different grammatical configurations of the same ideational content are related to different types of contextual meaning. The problem is recognising them, since the logic of clause relations is often based on the pragmatics of the task rather than how one word relates to the next. The human user, once engaged on the task automatically commits to the joint project.

In transactional dialogues like these, a statement of a need – *I want . . .* or *I'm interested in finding out . . .* , etc. – is treated as a formal request. Also the source often asks questions of the client, such as in the following excerpt:

Could you please tell me the time of a train to Fairford.

Fairford? There's no station there, I'm afraid. You are trying to get to the air show are you?

How far such interpersonal interchanges are worth building into automated interfaces is still a matter for study but some clarificatory initiatives will be necessary to tailor the transactional information to the client's needs. Certainly we need a better appreciation of the way people see interpersonal dialogues before we can have any confidence in being able to automate them successfully.

References

1. Cheepen, C.: The Predictability of Informal Conversation, Pinter, London (1988).
2. Cheepen, C.: 'Phonological Signalling of Topic Movement in Conversational Discourse: Automatic Tagging in Spoken Language Corpora', Proceedings of the Institute of Acoustics, 16: (1994), 483–491.
3. Cheepen, C., Monaghan, J. 'Spoken English: A Practical Guide', Pinter, London (1990).
4. Cheepen, C., Monaghan, J. 'Linguistic Signalling and Topic Management' in Interviews: Automatic tagging in spoken language corpora. Proceedings of the Institute of Acoustics, (1996) 273–278.
5. Cheepen, C. and Monaghan, J. 'Designing for naturalness in automated dialogues.' In: Wilks, Y. (Ed.): Machine Conversations Kluwer Academic, Boston & Dordrecht (1999).
6. Goffman, E. 'On Face Work: an analysis of ritual elements in social interaction'. In: Laver J., Hutcheson, S. (Eds.) 1972 Communication in Face to Face Interaction, Penguin, Harmondsworth (1955).
7. Monaghan, J.: 'The Neo Firthian Tradition', Niemeyer, Tübingen, (1979).
8. Monaghan, J., Cheepen, C. 'Dialogue Design for Speech Interfaces in the Office Context', In: H.-J. Bullinger (Ed.) Human Aspects in Computing: Design and Use of Interactive Systems and Work with Terminals, Elsevier Science Publishers, Amsterdam (1991).
9. Schegloff, E. & H. Sacks 'Opening up Closings'. In: Turner, R. (Ed.) Ethnomethodology, Penguin, Harmondsworth (1973).
10. Wilson, J. 'On the Boundaries of Conversation', Pergamon, Oxford (1989).

An Annotation Scheme for Dialogues
Applied to Anaphora Resolution Algorithms

Patricio Martínez-Barco and Manuel Palomar

Departmento de Lenguajes y Sistemas Informáticos
Universidad de Alicante
Carretera de San Vicente del Raspeig - Alicante - Spain
Tel. +34965903653, Fax +34965909326
patricio@dlsi.ua.es, mpalomar@dlsi.ua.es

Abstract. Usually, anaphora resolution researchers focus their works on defining a set of sources to extract useful information that helps anaphora resolution. Other works base their research on extracting relationships between utterances and anaphors obtaining satisfactory results working on languages with short anaphoric accessibility spaces like English. In this work, we state that anaphora resolution in Spanish needs an adequate definition of accessibility spaces and then we propose an annotation scheme for dialogue structure to define these spaces. This proposal has been tested achieving successful results when it is applied to real man-to-man telephone conversations.

1 Introduction

In this paper, an annotation scheme for dialogues applied to anaphora resolution algorithms is presented. This annotation scheme for Spanish dialogues is based on the theories about the taking of speaking turns. This scheme is oriented to the definition of an anaphoric accessibility space where the antecedents of an anaphora can be found. The adequate definition of this space allows the optimisation of the anaphora resolution algorithm.

According to Dahlbäck [4], the efforts made so far towards resolving anaphora can be divided into two basic approaches: Traditional and Discourse-oriented. The traditional approach generally depends on linguistic knowledge. In the discourse-oriented approach, however, the researcher tries to model the complex structure of discourse. Anaphora, accepted as discourse phenomena, is resolved with the help of that complex structure. These works are mostly focussed on defining anaphora resolution algorithms, both the traditional approaches (Hobbs [8], Baldwin [1], Mitkov [11]) and the discourse-oriented ones (Grosz et al. [7], Strube [17]).

However, the former do not perform a defined proposal about anaphoric accessibility space, and the latter constraint the space for possible antecedents to the previous utterance. Although, this strategy is adequate for English processing, its application to other languages such as Spanish is not so suitable. For instance, Spanish personal pronouns contain more morphological information than English ones. This makes

P. Sojka, I. Kopeček, and K. Pala (Eds.): TSD 2000, LNAI 1902, pp. 410–414, 2000.

Spanish speakers to expect larger anaphoric accessibility spaces. Also, Spanish free-word-order causes problems when grammatical role information must be used.

Following the idea that any treatment of anaphora must consider the structure of its source text-types, Fox [5] investigated anaphora looking for an adequate accessibility space on the basis of the relationship between discourse structure and this phenomena. In this work, Fox used the theories of conversational analysis by Sacks, Schegloff and Jefferson [15] to define the structure of discourse. According to this approach, the adjacency pair is the basic structural unit of dialogues. Thus, a close relationship between adjacency pairs and anaphoric accessibility space is shown.

In the next section, an annotation scheme for Spanish dialogue structure is proposed. After that, a brief survey of the anaphora resolution algorithm is shown, and finally, the evaluation of the annotation scheme applied to the anaphora resolution algorithm is presented.

2   An Annotation Scheme for Dialogue Structure

For the successful processing and resolution of anaphora in dialogues, we believe that a proper annotation of the dialogue structure is necessary. With such a view, we propose an annotation scheme, for Spanish dialogues, which is based on the work carried out by Gallardo [6], who applies, to Spanish dialogues, the theories put forward by Sacks, Schegloff and Jefferson [15] about the taking of speaking turns (conversational). According to these theories, the basic unit of knowledge is the *move* that can inform the listener about an action, request, question, etc. These moves are carried out by means of *utterances*. Therefore, utterances are joined together to become *turns*.

Since our work was done on spoken dialogues that have been written (transcribed), the turn appears annotated in the texts and the utterances are delimited by the use of punctuation marks. The reading of a punctuation mark (., ?, !, ...) allows us to recognise the end of an utterance.

As a conclusion, therefore, we propose the following annotation scheme for a dialogue structure based on the structure defined by Gallardo [6]. This proposal is justified on the studies by Fox [5] about discourse structure and anaphora resolution:

Turn (T) is identified by a change of speaker in the dialogue; each change of speaker supposes a new speaking turn. On this point, Gallardo makes a distinction between two different kinds of turns:

- An **Intervention Turn (IT)** is one that adds information to the dialogue. Such turns constitute what is called *the primary system of conversation*. Speakers use their interventions to provide information that facilitates the progress of the topic of conversation. Interventions may be **initiatives (IT_I)** when they formulate invitations, requirements, offers, reports, etc., or **reactions (IT_R)** when they answer or evaluate the previous speaker's intervention. Finally, they can also be **mixed interventions ($IT_{R/I}$)**, meaning a reaction that begins as a response to the previous speaker's intervention, and ends as an introduction of new information.

- A **Continuing Turn (CT)** represents an empty turn, which is quite typical of a listener whose aim is the formal reinforcement and ratification of the cast of conversational roles. Such interventions lack information.

Adjacency Pair or **Exchange (AP)** is a sequence of turns T headed by an initiation intervention turn (IT_I) and ended by a reaction intervention turn (IT_R). One form of anaphora which appears to be very common in dialogues is the reference within an adjacency pair [5].

Topic (TOPIC) is the main entity in the dialogue. According to Rocha [14], four features are taken into account in the selection of the best candidate for discourse topic: frequency, even distribution, position of first token, and semantic adequacy. The topic must be a lexical item which is frequently referred to.

According to the above-mentioned structure, the following set of tags is considered necessary for dialogue structure annotation: IT_I, IT_R, $IT_{R/I}$, CT, AP and TOPIC. AP and TOPIC tags will be used to define the anaphoric accessibility space and the remaining will be used to obtain the adjacency pairs.

For this experiment, the corpus has been manually annotated. However, nowadays there are some works performing an automatic adjacency pair tagging, such as the *Basurde* project [2]. On the other hand, there are other works performing automatic topic tagging (e.g. Reynar [13]) or automatic topic extraction (e.g. the method for anaphora resolution shown in Martínez-Barco et al. [9]).

The annotation of conversational dialogues is carried out, as shown above, and the evaluation of the proposed anaphoric accessibility space accomplished. An important aspect of this type of annotation is the training phase, which assures the reliability of the annotation.

The annotation phase is accomplished in the following way: a) two annotators are selected, b) an agreement is reached between the two annotators with regard to the annotation scheme using 5 dialogues (training corpus), c) the annotation is then carried out by both annotators in parallel over the remaining 35 dialogues (test corpus) and, d) finally, a reliability test is done on the annotation (see Carletta et al. [3]) in order to guarantee the results. The reliability test uses the *kappa* statistic that measures the affinity between the annotations of the two annotators by making judgements about categories. See Siegel and Castellan [16] for *kappa* statistic (k) computing.

According to Carletta, a k measurement such as $0.68 < k < 0.8$ allows us to make encouraging conclusions, and $k > 0.8$ means total reliability between the results of both annotators.

Once both annotators have carried out the annotation, the reliability test of the annotation has been run, with a *kappa* measurement of $k = 0.91$. We therefore consider the annotation obtained for the evaluation to be totally reliable.

3   A Brief Survey of the Algorithm

Based on the above-mentioned dialogue structure, an algorithm that combines several kinds of knowledge must be proposed. Concretely, it must use and combine: a) linguistic knowledge such as lexical, morphological, syntactic and semantic knowledge; and

b) knowledge from the dialogue structure itself, which is based on the annotation previously proposed, and knowledge taken from the topic of the dialogue.

Following the previous directives, an anaphora resolution algorithm for dialogues was proposed by Palomar and Martínez-Barco [12]. This algorithm was based on the following three steps:

1. All possible antecedents are obtained from the structure and topic of dialogue texts.
2. Linguistic constraints are applied on the previously selected antecedents, with the aim of discarding incompatible antecedents:
3. If there are more than one antecedent left after applying the previous constraints, then a set of linguistic and dialogue structure preferences are applied.

4   Evaluation of the Annotation Scheme

In order to carry out the evaluation of this scheme, we had 200 transcribed spoken dialogues (*Corpus InfoTren: Person*) at our disposal, afforded us by the project *Basurde*, from which we selected and POS-tagged 40. The tagging provides lexical and morphological knowledge for each word of the text. Afterwards, the structure of the dialogue was manually annotated, following the directives previously presented. From the 40 POS-tagged dialogues, 5 were randomly selected for the training of the algorithm and the remaining 35 were reserved in order to carry out the final evaluation. As a result, 73.8% precision for pronominal anaphora resolution and 78.9% for adjectival anaphora resolution was achieved.

An empirical study about the precision of the anaphoric accessibility space using this schema is shown in Martínez-Barco and Palomar [10].

5   Conclusions

In this paper, we have proposed an annotation scheme of dialogue structure that helps to anaphora resolution in Spanish dialogues. This annotation scheme has been developed on the basis of works by Gallardo [6] who applied the theory of conversational analysis to Spanish dialogues and the studies by Fox [5] about the relationship between this theory and anaphora. Furthermore, an evaluation of this proposal over an anaphora resolution algorithm has been shown with successful results.

Acknowledgements

The authors wish to thank N. Prieto, F. Pla and A. Molina (Universitat Politecnica de Valencia) for having contributed their tagger and E. Segarra (Universitat Politecnica de Valencia) for affording us the *Corpus InfoTren: Person* from the BASURDE Project.

This paper has been supported by the Spanish Government under grant HB1998-0068.

References

1. B. Baldwin. CogNIAC: high precision coreference with limited knowledge and linguistic resources. In *Proceedings of ACL/EACL workshop on Operational factors in practical, robust anaphora resolution*, Madrid (Spain), July 1997.
2. Proyecto BASURDE. *Spontaneus-Speech Dialogue System in Limited Domains*. CICYT (TIC98-423-C06), 1998-2001. http://gps-tsc.upc.es/veu/basurde/Home.htm.
3. J. Carletta, A. Isard, S. Isard, J.C. Kowtko, G. Doherty-Sneddon, and A.H. Anderson. The Reliability of a Dialogue Structure Coding Scheme. *Computational Linguistics*, 23(1):13–32, 1997.
4. N. Dahlbäck. *Representations of Discourse-Cognitive and Computational Aspects*. Ph.D. thesis, Department of Computer and Information Science, Linköping University, Linköping, Sweden, 1991.
5. B. Fox. *Discourse Structure and Anaphora*. Written and conversational English. Cambridge Studies in Linguistics. Cambridge University Press, Cambridge, 1987.
6. B. Gallardo. *Análisis conversacional y pragmática del receptor*. Colección Sinapsis. Ediciones Episteme, S.L., Valencia, 1996.
7. B. Grosz, A. Joshi, and S. Weinstein. Centering: a framework for modeling the local coherence of discourse. *Computational Linguistics*, 21(2):203–225, 1995.
8. J. Hobbs. Resolving pronoun references. In B. Grosz B.L. Webber and K. Jones, editors, *Readings in Natural Language Processing*. Morgan Kaufmann, Palo Alto, CA, 1986.
9. P. Martínez-Barco, R. Muñoz, S. Azzam, M. Palomar, and A. Ferrández. Evaluation of pronoun resolution algorithm for Spanish dialogues. In *Proceedings of the Venezia per il Trattamento Automatico delle Lingue (VEXTAL '99)*, pages 325–332, Venice (Italy), November 1999.
10. P. Martínez-Barco and M. Palomar. Empirical study of the anaphoric accessibility space in Spanish dialogues. In *Proceedings of the Fourth Workshop on the Semantics and Pragmatics of Dialogue (GÖTALOG '2000)*, Göteborg, Sweden, June 2000.
11. R. Mitkov. Robust pronoun resolution with limited knowledge. In *Proceedings of the 36th Annual Meeting of the Association for Computational Linguistics and 17th International Conference on Computational Linguistics (COLING-ACL'98)*, Montreal (Canada), August 1998.
12. M. Palomar and P. Martínez-Barco. Anaphora Resolution through Dialogue Adjacency Pairs and Topics. In D.N. Christodoulakis, editor, *Natural Language Processing – NLP 2000*, volume 1835 of *Lecture Notes in Artificial Intelligence*, pages 196–203, Patras, Grece, June 2000. Springer-Verlag.
13. Jeffrey C. Reynar. Statistical Models for Topic Segmentation. In *Proceedings of 37th Annual Meeting of the Association for Computational Linguistics*, pages 357–364, Maryland, USA, June 1999.
14. M. Rocha. *A corpus-based study of anaphora in dialogues in English and Portuguese*. Ph.D. thesis, University of Sussex, Sussex. UK, 1998.
15. H. Sacks, E. Schegloff, and G. Jefferson. A simplest systematics for the organization of turn taking for conversation. *Language*, 50(4):696–735, 1974.
16. S. Siegel and J. Castellan. *Nonparametric Statistics for the Behavioral Sciences*. McGraw-Hill, 2nd edition, 1988.
17. M. Strube and U. Hahn. Functional Centering – Grounding Referential Coherence in Information Structure. *Computational Linguistics*, 25(5):309–344, 1999.

Cooperative Information Retrieval Dialogues through Clustering

Paulo Quaresma and Irene Pimenta Rodrigues

Departamento de Informática, Universidade de Évora,
7000 Évora, Portugal
pq@di.uevora.pt, ipr@di.uevora.pt

Abstract. In this paper, we present some aspects of a cooperative web information retrieval system in the law domain. Our system is able to infer the user intentions and to keep the context of the user interaction in order to supply suggestions for further refinement of the user query. One important aspect of our system is its ability to compute clusters of documents associating a keyword to each cluster. A detailed example of an interaction with the system is presented.

1 Introduction

In this paper, we present some aspects of a cooperative web information retrieval system for juridical documents based on SINO, a boolean text search engine from the AustLII Institute [5].

During an interaction when a user poses a query, we want our system to be able:

- To infer what the user intentions with the queries are [7,10,9,8].
  When a user asks for documents with a particular keyword, usually he is interested in documents that may not have that keyword and he is not interested in all documents with that keyword.
- To supply pertinent answers or questions as a reply to a user question.
  The system must supply some information on the set of documents selected by the user query in order to help the user in the refinement of his query.

  In order to accomplish these goals, we need:

- To record the previous user interaction with the system (user questions and the system answers).
  This record will play the role of a dialogue structure [4,11]. It provides the context of sentences (questions and answers) [1], allowing the system to solve some discourse phenomena such as anaphoras and ellipses. Since our system is multi-modal, other user acts such as button clicks and menu choices are also represented in our dialogue structure.
- To obtain new partitions (clusters labelled with a topical keyword) of the set of documents that the user selected with his query(ies).

P. Sojka, I. Kopeček, and K. Pala (Eds.): TSD 2000, LNAI 1902, pp. 415–420, 2000.

– To use domain knowledge whenever the system has it.

In our system, each event (utterance) is represented by logic programming facts that are used to dynamically update the previous model. Using this approach, it is possible to represent new events as logic programs and to obtain the new states. Moreover, it is possible to reason about past events and to represent non-monotonic behaviour rules.

Each utterance will trigger the inference of the user intentions, taking into account the user attitudes (such as his beliefs and the user profile). The results of the inference of the user intentions are:

– A new set of user and system beliefs and intentions (such as the intention of the user to be informed of something by the system).
– A new dialogue structure. This structure keeps the dialogue context allowing for the interpretation of user acts in its occurrence context. The dialogue structure constraints the interpretation of user intentions and it is built as a result of the intentions inference.

2   Information Retrieval System

During an interaction, the user wants to look for some documents and his queries are ways of selecting sets of documents. The system's questions and answers always intend to help the user in his search of documents by supplying information on subsets of documents in the text database.

After a user query, the system may:

– Show the set of documents selected by the query.
– Present a set of keywords that may help the user to refine his query. In order to build a set of keywords, the system may build groups of documents (clusters) from the initial set selected by the user query (with or without expanding).
– Present a set of concepts that may help the user to refine his query. In cases where the system has knowledge about some of the documents' subject, it is possible to build groups of documents using that knowledge, and to provide the user concepts for refining its query.
– Explain to the user why his query does not select any document, providing suggestions for other queries.

2.1   An Interaction Example

Suppose that the user is a retired fireman who has saved a child from drowning in a river during his holidays by putting his life at risk. Since he has caught a pneumonia as a consequence, he wants to know if he can get a pension for relevant services to his country.

[User - Q1:] Documents about pensions for relevant services?

[System - Q2:] There are 243 documents, listed in the right frame. For further refinement, you may choose one (or none) option in each column:

Pensions that were:	Pensions for:	Documents with keyword:
given	militaries	drowning
or refused	or civilians	or medal
		or in duty
		or ...

Options in Columns 1 and 2 are obtained using rules that model legal knowledge on legislation on pensions for relevant services. Options on Column 3 are obtained by clustering the set of 243, using the method described in Section 4.

[User - Q3:] chooses: civilians and drowning.

[System - Q4:] There are 45 documents, listed in the right frame. For further refinement, you may choose one (or none) option in each column:

Documents with keyword:
death
or accident
or ...

Options in this column are obtained by reclustering the 45 documents.

[User - Q5:] Documents where there was a drowning in a river.

[System - Q6:] Since there are 13 documents of the 45 above that match the concept, I've listed them in the usual frame. For further refinement, you may choose one (or none) option in each column:

Documents with keyword:
car crash
or bridge
or ...

[User - Q7:] Where there was someone swimming?

[System - Q8:] Since there are no documents of the 13 above that match your new constraint. I assume that you want your query confines to Q3, i.e. you are looking for documents with the concept swimming, and drowning and pensions for relevant services for civilians. Do you want to see these documents?

[User - Q9:] Yes. .....

3   Interaction Context

The interaction structure supplies the context for the user and system actions. This representation structure takes into account that an utterance may: specify the information contained in a set of previous utterances; or to open a new context, when the user does not intend to continue refining its query and desires to start a new one.

The Interaction structure (IS) is made of segments that group sets of acts (user and system sentences). The Interaction structure reflects the user intentions; it is built by taking into account the user and system intentions. The Interaction segments have precise inheritance rules defining how segments inherit their attributes from the attributes of their multimodal actions.

An example of the interrogation context for the dialogue from Subsection 2.1 is shown in Figure 1.

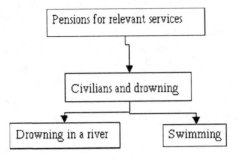

Fig. 1. Interrogation context after utterance Q7

4   Intelligent Clustering

Clustering is a complex process [12] since it involves: the choice of a representation for the documents, a function for associating documents (measures for similarity of documents with the query or between them) and a method with an algorithm to build the clusters. One of the best clustering methods is the Scatter/Gather browsing paradigm [2,3,6] which clusters documents into topically-coherent groups. It is able to present descriptive textual summaries that are built with topical terms that characterise the clusters. The clustering and reclustering can be done on-the-fly, so that different topics are seen depending on the subcollection clustered.

4.1   Clustering and Reclustering

Given a set of documents selected by a user query, a structure associating a set of descriptors to each document (the document classification) is built: structure 1, with a linear ($O(n)$, where n is the number of texts) procedure. This structure is transformed to another structure, structure 2, that associates to each descriptor in the first structure a set of documents, with a procedure that has complexity $O(n * m)$, where m is the number of descriptors in the structure. These structures are shown in Figure 2.

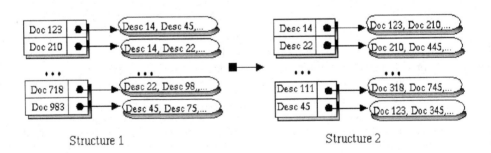

Fig. 2. Document structure

Finally we must choose a set of descriptors such that:

1. The union of the set of documents associated to the descriptors is the initial set of documents.
2. The intersection of the set of documents associated to any two descriptors is empty.

These two conditions cannot be satisfied always, when this is the case, the first one is dropped.

However, there are other proprieties that the set of descriptors should have:

1. Its cardinality should be between 10 and 20.
2. The cardinality of each document set should be similar.
3. Descriptors with only one document associated should be ignored.

Our search space, for m descriptors in structure 2, will have $2m$ states that should be tested. Since it is not possible to search all the state space in a reasonable time, we have to use some heuristics in order to cut off part of the search space, and we use an informed search algorithm, a best first search with an evaluation function specially designed for this problem.

This procedure will start as follows:

- Sort structure 2 by descendent order of the cardinality of the document set.
- To eliminate the descriptors with only one document associated.
- To represent each set of documents in a bit table, to simplify the test for inclusion of document (it will become $O(1)$).

Then the best first search will be guided by an evaluation function which always choose to add a descriptor as a set of documents with its cardinal as near as possible to the interval $[10, 20]$.

The search ends with success when:

- All documents are selected, the union of the sets associated with the selected descriptors is the set of selected documents.
- The cardinal of the set of descriptors reaches 30, and the cardinal of the union of the sets of documents is greater then 70% of the initial number of documents.

Evaluations of this algorithm grant that it will take $O(n \cdot m)$, where n is the number of documents and m is the number of descriptors in structure 2 without those eliminated in the first step. For 10000 documents and 2000 descriptors, it will take 100 milliseconds, which is a reasonable time for a search in the World Wide Web.

The reclustering can be done by modifying structure 2, taking out the documents that are not selected in the refinement, and resorting this structure. Normally reclustering is must faster than the initial clustering, since the input is smaller, and structure 2 is already there.

5   Conclusions and Future Work

We aim to build a cooperative IR system for juridical information. In order to be cooperative, to help the user to find a specific set of documents, our system needs to represent some knowledge about the database documents. One important source of knowledge is obtained by clustering sets of documents and labelling each cluster with a topical term resulting from a document juridical analysis.

By now the evaluation of our system has been performed by a set of users, mainly law students, who think that the system's suggestions are helpful to their searches. We hope to use other evaluation criteria that may quantify how helpful can the system suggestions be, but by now we only have a quality evaluation.

References

1. J. Chu-Carroll and S. Carberry. Response generation in planning dialogues. *Computational Linguistics*, 24(3), 1998.
2. D. R. Cutting, J. O. Pedersen D. R. Karger, and J. W. Tukey. Scatter/gather: A cluster-based approach to browsing large document collections. In *Proc. 15th Annual Int'l ACM SIGIR Conf. on R&D in IR*, June 1992.
3. D. R. Cutting, D. Karger, and J. Pedersen. Constant interaction-time scatter/gathern browsing of very large document collections. In *Proc. of the 16th Annual Int. ACM/SIGIR Conf.*, Pittsburgh, PA, 1993.
4. Sandra Carberry and Lynn Lambert. A process model for recognizing communicative acts and modelling negotiation subdialogs. *Computational Linguistics*, 25(1), 1999.
5. G. Greenleaf, A. Mowbray, and G. King. Law. On the net via austlii-14m hypertext links can't be right? In *In Information Online and on Disk '97 Conference*. Sydney, January, 1997.
6. M. A. Hearst and J. O. Pedersen. Reexamining the cluster hypothesis:scatter/gather on retrieval results. In *Proceedings of the Nineteenth Annual International ACM SIGIR Conference*, Zurich, June 1996.
7. Karen E. Lochbaum. A collaborative planning model of intentional structure. *Computational Linguistics*, 24(4), 1998.
8. Martha Pollack. Plans as complex mental attitudes. In Philip Cohen, Jerry Morgan, and Martha Pollack, editors, *Intentions in Communications*. MIT Press Cambridge, 1990.
9. P. Quaresma and J. G. Lopes. Unified logic programming approach to the abduction of plans and intentions in information-seeking dialogues. *Journal of Logic Programming*, 54, 1995.
10. P. Quaresma and I. P. Rodrigues. Keeping context in web interfaces to legal text databases. In *Proc. of the 2nd French-American Conf. on AI&LAW*, Nice, France, 1998.
11. I. P. Rodrigues and J. G. Lopes. Building the text temporal structure. In *Progress in Artificial Intelligence: 6th EPIA*. Springer-Verlag, 1993.
12. Gerard Salton. *Automatic text processing: the transformation, analysis, and retrieval of information by computer*. Addison-Wesley, 1989. Reading, MA.

Acoustic Cues for Classifying Communicative Intentions in Dialogue Systems

Michelina Savino and Mario Refice

D.E.E. – Politecnico di Bari, Italy
esavino@poliba.it, refice@poliba.it

Abstract. Filled pauses are normally used as a planning strategy: they signal speaker's intention to hold the floor in a conversation. They are normally realised by inserting a vowel (optionally followed by a nasal), but in Italian they can be produced by lengthening the final vowel of a word. Word final lengthening filled pauses are then an intermediate category between lexical and non-lexical speech event. In human machine interaction, the system should be able to discriminate between a "default" lexical speech event and one characterised by a word final lengthening for planning strategy: in this second case, the related communicative intention has to be additionally recognised. Our preliminary investigation shows that duration and F0 shape are reliable acoustic cues for identifying word final lengthening filled pauses in a variety of Italian.

1 Introduction

One of the main challenge in the development of dialogue systems is the attempt to "naturalising" interaction as much as possible, i.e. allowing stronger control of dialogue modality by the human being and not by the system (as it is presently the case). For example, in turn-taking the system should be able to "recognise" speech events signalising human communication intentions of "giving the floor" from those which are simply pauses within a turn. Most of these phenomena are not reliably predictable, and therefore not easily managed if the system lacks the needed knowledge. Most of the present dialogue systems make use of pauses (i.e. no speech production by the user) as a "signal" for switching the floor back to the system itself. This simple technique results, in several cases, in the overlapping of human and machine speech, with the consequent loss of control of the planned interaction process. On the other hand, filled pauses are not "interpreted" as user's intention of "holding the floor", but simply as lexical speech items in themselves.

The purpose of this paper is to discuss possible solutions for coping with the mentioned problem, trying to discriminate between different uses of pauses. In particular, preliminary results on attempt of modelling (a special type of) filled pauses will be given, basing on data collected and properly annotated in a spontaneous, dialogue-based speech database of Italian regional varieties under development within a national project.

P. Sojka, I. Kopeček, and K. Pala (Eds.): TSD 2000, LNAI 1902, pp. 421–426, 2000.

2   Communicative and Non-communicative Speech Events

In human verbal communication, it is possible to identify two main typologies of speech events: lexical speech events and non-lexical speech events. The latter can be further classified in:

1. Non-lexical speech events conveying communicative intentions like feedback and turn-taking, such as filled pauses;
2. Non-lexical speech events which do not convey any communicative intentionality, such as coughing, sneezing, etc.

Despite this clearly different function, most of the traditional work (expecially in ASR and man-machine interaction in general) has considered both classes as one category, that of "disfluency phenomena", sharing the same function of class 2, and, as such, of less interest in terms of modelling with respect to that of lexical speech events. Only recently, attention has been paid to the description, classification and formalisation of the above mentioned non-lexical communicative speech events [1], mainly with reference to ASR performance improvement [2,3]. In this work we try to make a step further in modelling filled pauses, by recovering additional information, in terms of communicative intentionality conveyed by this kind of disfluency, in dialogue system applications.

3   "Word Final Lengthening" Filled Pauses

Filled pauses are normally used as a planning strategy: they signal speaker's intention of holding the floor in a conversation. From the segmental/acoustic point of view, they are realised by inserting a central vowel, optionally followed by a nasal (less common), but their segmental realisations may be language-specific. For example, in Italian – where almost all words end by a vowel – speaker do not need to insert a "spurious" vowel-like segment in their speech: they can achieve the same by simply lengthening a word ending vowel. For the same fonotactic reasons, if the word ends by a consonant, then a central vowel schwa is added and prolonged. "Word final lengthening" filled pauses are then a sort of intermediate category, half way between lexical and non-lexical speech events, since they consist of a lexical event being "affected" by a non-lexical speech phenomenon. In human-machine interaction for Italian, then, the system should be able to distinguish between a "default" lexical speech event and a lexical speech event characterised by a "word final lengthening" filled pause. In the latter case, a particular communicative intention (i.e. holding the floor) has to be additionally recognised by the system.

At a first glance, duration seems to be the main acoustic cue to be used in the above mentioned classification task. Yet duration reliability cannot be taken for granted without detailed investigations, since in determining threshold values one has to consider other possible cases of word final lengthening, i.e. those occurring at (major) prosodic boundaries, and conveying intentionality of different types. With this respect, we hypothesised also that an additional acoustic cue which might be relevant for discriminating word final lengthening filled pause is F0 shape.

4 "Word Final Lengthening" at Prosodic Boundaries

Word final lengthening is also possible, with different degrees of prolongation, at (major) prosodic boundaries. The higher degrees of lengthening are normally associated to cases of phrase final nuclear stressed syllables, i.e. when a complex tonal sequence (pitch accent + boundary tones) has to be realised on one syllable (tonal crowding). Theoretically, it may be postulated that the more complex the movement to be realised, the stronger the degree of lengthening to be found. Actually, languages may adopt either a compression strategy (i.e. realisation of the whole complex tonal sequence on one syllable with its consequent prolongation) or a partial/total truncation one (i.e. partial/total truncation of the sequence: in this case the movement is not completely realised) [4]. In Italian, prevailing of one or the other strategy is variety-depending. Bari Italian speakers – being the regional variety under investigation that of Bari – may use both of them, depending on speaking style, speaking rate, or some added paralinguistic meaning —cite63bib5. In analysing our Bari Italian speech material, then, we expect to find cases of phrase final stressed syllable with (possibly) different degrees of prolongation. In this preliminary analysis, we considered them as belonging to one broad category.

5 Method

In order to discriminate between "default" lexical speech events and those characterised by the lengthening of the word ending vowel, a number of duration measurements has been carried out. In our analysis, default or unmarked cases of vowel duration at the end of a word are those in stressed open syllables which are not phrase final. Such default durations have been compared with those in two marked contexts: a) (degrees of) prolongation at prosodic boundary, and b) prolongation for planning strategies. Therefore, duration measurements have been performed on the following types:

1. vowels in word (but not phrase) final stressed open syllables ("default");
2. vowels in phrase final stressed open syllables;
3. vowels in word final stressed and unstressed open syllables with "planning lengthening".

Moreover, F0 shapes of the three above mentioned typologies have been described and compared. In our analysis, both monosyllabic and polysyllabic words have been taken into account.

6 Speech Material

Analysed speech material consists of three spontaneous Map Task [6] dialogues between pairs of Bari Italian speakers, which is a subset of a corpus of some regional varieties of Italian (namely those of Bari, Naples and Pisa) under development within the national project AVIP (Archivio di Varietà dell'Italiano Parlato, Spoken Italian Varieties Archive). The speech material has been orthographically transcribed, segmented and annotated (both at segmental and suprasegmental levels), including non-lexical speech events. A special label was used for coding cases of "word final lengthening for planning purposes".

7   Preliminary Results

7.1   Duration

Duration mean values of all five vowel types (in stressed open syllable) in the three above mentioned contexts for the six speakers are shown in Figures 1, 2, 3, respectively. Letters G and F identify speaker role within each dialogue (instruction Giver or instruction Follower), and number refer to the pair of maps used (each pair of map having different path and different landmarks names).

Preliminary results, within the statistical significance of the available data, confirm that mean duration of phrase final stressed vowels are systematically higher than those in "default" position for all speakers. Some inter- and intra-speaker variability within the category "final lengthening at prosodic boundaries" is to be noted, which can be related to the different degrees of prolongation, as discussed in Section 4. Since we are interested, at this stage, in determining a threshold value between the two broad categories "word final lengthening at prosodic boundaries" and "word final lengthening as filled pauses", a further sub-classification within such variability has not been considered in the present work.

Our results show also that mean duration values of word ending vowels with "planning lengthening" are systematically higher than those in the two remaining categories, for all vowel types.[1] As vowel /u/ is concerned, no cases of final lengthening caused by planning strategies was found in our dialogues. This is not surprising, since /u/ ending words are less common in Italian. On the basis of these results, we can give some indications of duration ratios among the three categories considered. Figure 4 (left) shows ratio, for each vowel type, between mean duration of category "word final lengthening for planning strategies" and the default category "word (but not phrase) final", for all speakers: vowels in word final stressed and unstressed open syllables can be classified as a "planning lengthening" phenomenon if they are at least three times longer than in "default" cases. Figure 4 (right) shows ratio, for each vowel types, between mean duration of category "word final lengthening for planning strategies" and "word final lengthening at prosodic (major) boundaries", for all speakers: in this last case, vowel with planning lengthening are at least two times longer than those at prosodic boundaries.

Table 1. % of F0 shape types in filled pauses and phrase final vowels for all speakers (R=Rise, F=Fall)

	R,F	RF, FR, RFR	LEVEL
phrase-final	76%	22%	2%
filled pauses	–	–	100%

---

[1] Stressed and unstressed vowels mean durations for this category were first computed separately; since they did not show any statistically significant difference, both types have been merged into one group.

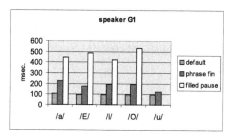

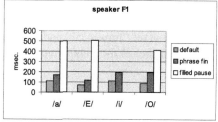

Fig. 1. Mean durations, for all vowel types (when found), in word final ("default"), at prosodic boundary ("phrase fin") and as filled pause positions for Giver (G1) and Follower (F1) in Map Task dialogue n. 1

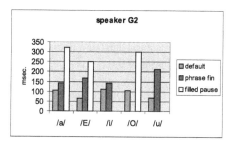

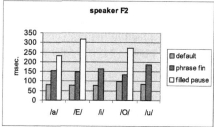

Fig. 2. Mean durations, for all vowel types (when found), in word final ("default"), at prosodic boundary ("phrase fin") and as filled pause positions for Giver (G2) and Follower (F2) in Map Task dialogue n. 2

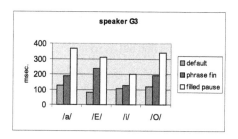

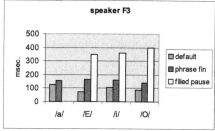

Fig. 3. Mean durations, for all vowel types (when found), in word final ("default"), at prosodic boundary ("phrase fin") and as filled pause positions for Giver (G3) and Follower (F3) in Map Task dialogue n. 3

7.2 F0 Shape

We considered also F0 shape as a possible additional acoustic cue in classifying the above mentioned types of filled pauses, expecially with respect to that of lengthening at prosodic boundaries. Results of our F0 shape analysis for both the above mentioned categories are shown in Table 1. It can be noticed that a level melodic contour (i.e. continuity of F0 values throughout vowel duration) strongly characterises vowels lengthened for planning strategies, in contrast with the variability (also in terms of complexity of the shape) of the "prosodic boundary lengthening" category, where this variability is related to a number of different communicative functions.

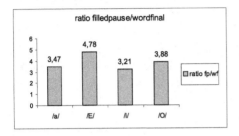 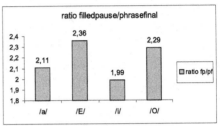

Fig. 4. Ratio of filled pauses on word-final (default) vowels mean duration values (left) and ratio of filled pauses on phrase-final vowels mean duration values (right)

8   Conclusion and Future Work

Our preliminary results suggest that – by means of simple decision rules in a man-machine dialogue system – duration and F0 shape can be used as reliable acoustic parameters in classifying communicative intentions at least in some broad classes. More specifically, these cues can help in detecting and interpreting typical Italian word final lengthening filled pauses as the intention of "holding the floor" by the speaker. A further sub-classification of communicative intentionality, within the broad category "final lengthening at prosodic boundaries" will be carried out as soon as a larger corpus will be available.

References

1. Gybbon D. & Shu-Chuan Tseng: Toward a formal characterisation of disfluency processing, in: ICPhS99 sat. meet "Disfluency in Spontaneous Speech" Proc. (1999) 35–38.
2. O'Shaughnessy D.: Better detection of hesitations in spontaneous speech, in: ICPhS99 satellite meeting "Disfluency in Spontaneous Speech" Proc. (1999) 39–42.
3. Pakhomov S. & Savova G.: Filled pause distribution and modelling in quasi-spontaneous speech, in: ICPhS99 sat. meeting "Disfluency in Spontaneous Speech" Proc. (1999) 31–34.
4. Ladd R.D.: Intonational phonology, Cambridge Univ. Press, Cambridge, (1996).
5. Refice M, Savino M, Grice M.: A contribution to the estimation of naturalness in the intonation of Italian spontaneous speech, in: Eurospeech 97 Proc. (1997) 783–786.
6. Brown G., Anderson A., Yule G., Shillcock R.: Teaching talk, Cambridge Univ. Press, Cambridge (1983).

Active and Passive Strategies
in Dialogue Program Generation

Ivan Kopeček

Faculty of Informatics, Masaryk University
Botanická 68a, 602 00 Brno, Czech Republic
kopecek@fi.muni.cz
`http://www.fi.muni.cz/~kopecek/`

Abstract. An application of dialogue systems for developing computer programs is described and discussed in this paper. The concept of generating program source code by means of a dialogue involves combining strategies with system and user initiative. The strategy with system initiative safely navigates the user, whereas the strategy with user initiative enables a quick and effective creation of the desired constructions of the source code and collaboration with the system using obtained knowledge to increase the effectiveness of the dialogue. The described system, which was initially developed for visually impaired users, can also be used by novice programmers as a tool for learning programming languages.

1 Introduction

The idea of generating source code by means of dialogue systems was initially connected with the problem on how to help blind and visually impaired programmers to create computer programs [1,2,3,6]. The asset of this approach lies in eliminating most of the syntactic errors that can appear in standard programming languages like C++, Java and Prolog by means of inquiring the user to obtain the necessary information. The system also supports automatic generation of some parts of the program (e.g. declarations of variables, parts of the programming language that can be derived from given parameters, etc.).

Dialogue strategy based on inquiring (passive strategy from the user's point of view) is a strategy with the initiative of the system. The user plays a passive role in answering the inquiries of the system. In the system, which is created for generating program source code, such a strategy is derived from a description of the programming language (a context-free grammar, a flowchart definition, etc.).

Passive dialogue strategy ensures the generation of correct statements. However, as it can be demonstrated by simulations, using this strategy in all situations would be cumbersome, and therefore this strategy has to be combined with other approaches.

The basic feature of active strategy (strategy with the initiative of the user) consists in determining the structure of the generated statement by user description, which can be done either directly in a natural language, or (if we cannot master this problem fully) by describing the generated structure by appropriate keywords.

P. Sojka, I. Kopeček, and K. Pala (Eds.): TSD 2000, LNAI 1902, pp. 427–432, 2000.
© Springer-Verlag Berlin Heidelberg 2000

Active and passive strategies can be combined effectively with adaptive approaches, like estimating the user's skill and using it for adaptation of the system, and for adaptation of the system by learning. In what follows, we will discuss it in more detail.

2   Generating the Dialogue Strategy with System Initiative

Suppose we have a context-free grammar $G = (V, T, S, P)$ (V is a finite set of nonterminals, T a finite set of terminals, S the start nonterminal and P a finite set of productions of the form $u \rightarrow v$, where $u \in V$, $v \in (V \cup T)^*$. (In this section we use standard terminology of the theory of formal languages, see e.g. [5].)

Our goal is to assign to G a dialogue strategy that enables to generate an element from $L(G)$. Let $\Rightarrow$ be the derivation relation of the grammar G (see e.g. [5]) and let $S \Rightarrow w(i)$, where $w(i)$ is the sequence which is derived from the start nonterminal S at a time point i. Suppose that

$$w(i) = a_1 u_1 a_2 u_2 a_3 \ldots a_t u_t a_{t+1} \quad (*)$$

where $u_r \in V$, $a_r \in T^*$. The generated dialogue strategy first chooses a nonterminal u_j belonging to the sequence. This can be based on the natural ordering of nonterminals (i.e., from left to right) or it can be, for instance, based on the expected depth of the derived tree (for which the nonterminal is the root). Another possibility is to let the user choose the nonterminal.

Now, suppose that all the productions that have u_j on the left side are as follows:

$$u_j \rightarrow c_{11} v_{11} c_{12} v_{12} \ldots c_{1m} v_{1m} c_{1m+1}$$

$$\vdots$$

$$u_j \rightarrow c_{k1} v_{k1} c_{k2} v_{k2} \ldots c_{kn} v_{kn} c_{kn+1}$$

where $v_{rs} \in V$, $c_{rs} \in T^*$.

The dialogue strategy then inquires the user to determine what next production will be used. If the user chooses the production with the index p, the nonterminal u_j in the expression $(*)$ will be overwritten by $c_{p1} v_{p1} c_{p2} v_{p2} \ldots c_{pn} v_{pn} c_{pn+1}$ and the process continues at the time point $i + 1$.

Although this strategy generates a code free of syntactic errors, simulations of the dialogues show that it can be slow and ineffective in some cases. Let us see the following simplified example of a possible communication between the user (U) and the dialogue system (S) by generating a single C (C++) statement $s = 0$; (the braces enclose the possible choices):

S: {labelled-statement; expression-statement; compound-statement;
     selection-statement; iteration-statement; jump-statement} ?
U: expression-statement;
S: {assignment-expression; expression, assignment-expression} ?
U: assignment-expression;
S: {non-conditional-assignment-expression; conditional-expression} ?

U: non-conditional-assignment-expression;
S: /definition of non-conditional-assignment-expression/
   Left hand side is: {identifier; unary expression} ?
U: identifier;
S: /definition of non-conditional-assignment-expression/ input identifier!
U: s
S: OK /definition of non-conditional-assignment-expression/
   assignment operator is: { =; *=; /=; %=; +=; -=; <<=; >>=; % &= ; ^=; } ?
U: =
S: OK
   /definition of non-conditional-assignment-expression/
   Right hand side is: {identifier; constant; string; expression; assignment-expression} ?
U: constant;
S: /definition of non-conditional-assignment-expression/ input constant!
U: 0
S: OK
   /definition of non-conditional-assignment-expression is completed/
   The assignment is: s = 0;
   /coming back to defining next block: name-of-the-block statement/

In this example, the formal form of the dialogue described above is enriched with simple system descriptions and messages that should help the user in generating the program. Also, the passive generating of the code stops when it is clearly not effective (in our example it is on the level when the user should define the left hand side variable and the right hand side constant. This example demonstrates the basic idea of the passive way of program generating and also clearly indicates that this approach has to be complemented by a strategy with user initiative.

3   Dialogue Strategy with User Initiative

The strategy with user initiative tries to determine the structure of the generated statement by user description, which can be formulated in natural language by means of appropriate keywords. The above presented example can be shortened using this strategy as follows:

U: * assign simple
S: /definition of non-conditional-assignment-expression/
   input left hand side in the form of identifier!/
U: s
 . . .

The character * indicates that the user takes initiative. This can be signalled by pressing a key or by a keyword. 'assign' is a keyword describing the chosen statement. 'simple' is a keyword which, in this case, says that the user demands the simple form of the corresponding construction. Hence, 'simple' is a keyword that belongs to the category of the keywords with general meaning. Other keywords in this category are, for instance:

  – 'general' – demanding the general form of the specified construction,

- 'more simple' – demanding a simpler form of the specified construction,
- 'more general' – demanding a more general form of the specified construction,
- 'the same' – demands a repetition of the previously specified construction,
- 'often used' – demands a choice from the list of often used constructions,
- etc.

Using the active strategy, the user tries to find a sufficiently precise characterisation of the generated statement and the system tries to guess a probable type of the statement, which is characterised by the given keywords. Both the user and the system have to be ready to face a possible misunderstanding or inaccuracy by determining the statement. Possible ways to handle these situations are as follows:

A: If the system guessed a false type of the generated statement:

- add new keywords to the given ones and demand a new guess,
- cancel the turn and give another keywords,
- cancel the turn and switch to the "passive" way of generation.

B: If the system guessed an inaccurate type of the generated statement:

- add new keywords to the given ones and demand a new guess,
- demand a more general guess and then specify the right form,
- specify a correction (for instance, if one needs a labelled statement, specify "label"),
- cancel the turn and switch to the "passive" way of generation.

Direct definition of the source code, which is a special case of the user initiative strategy, allows the user to create some constructions directly (without being navigated by the system). Using this strategy, the user is neither navigated nor has to use keywords, just simply defines the statement directly. The system checks the correctness of the statement and acknowledges it. If the statement is not correct, the user has to make corrections or switch to other modes. The above example is then maximally shortened into just typing the statement. Clearly, this mode is effective provided that either the generated statement is very simple or the user is sufficiently experienced. On the other hand, this mode can be risky for more complex statements.

4   Adaptation of the Dialogue Strategies

The adaptation of dialogue strategies that are based on an estimation of the user's skill utilises either a direct proclamation of the user (by setting an appropriate option indicating his or her skill and experiences) or the analysis of the user's behaviour during the session.

Based on this estimation, the system may adapt its dialogue strategies, especially those that are related to on-line and context-sensitive help, to the structure of the list of offered possibilities, and to the type of guessed statements for the active generation.

Adaptation by learning is a method of restructuring the grammar (or assigning weights to some paths that appear to be more frequently used) and making shortcuts by learning from the previous sessions. An observed high frequency for a path indicates a need to create a shortcut.

On the other hand, it is clear that the number of shortcuts in the grammar has to be kept reasonable. To comply with this requirement, we can dynamically update active and passive (not allowed) shortcuts by allowing only a priori estimated number of active shortcuts and by switching the "activity" or "passivity" of a shortcut depending on the observed frequency.

Adaptation by estimation of the probable next statement is a strategy based on the prediction of the next statement. It seems to be obvious that the probability of what statement will be generated for a correct program depends on the previously used statements (more generally on the context). This can be used to make the estimation of the next statement more precise.

5   Implementation and Applications

The system has been developed as a multi-modal dialogue system supported by a universal speech interface (allowing direct speech input and output).

An important feature of the system is using the informative speech and non-speech [8] sounds to enable the user to be informed appropriately at each level of program generation. This is supported by a sophisticated multi-structural organisation of the help and by adaptation of the system to the user abilities and practice.

The created data involve at any moment their whole history so that they can be edited in the same mode. Of course, the user can export them to usual text form which may be further processed by standard integrated environments.

Even though the system was initially developed for visually impaired users, it can also be used by novice programmers and for teaching and learning programming languages.

The effect of learning by using the system (see also [7]) is related to the following aspects:

- in the passive mode: this mode is used very frequently by inexperienced users who do not know properly the basic structure of the grammar and have to be navigated. The important feature is that the navigation also requires active participation of the user and that he gets a new relevant information in this context. Simultaneously, the user naturally aims to use more frequently the more effective active mode (which is however reachable only with some experience). Those features create feedback effect which strongly motivates the user.
- in the active mode: this mode is more frequently used by more experienced users. Using this mode, the user learns by repetition of the relevant knowledge obtaining simultaneously new relevant information whenever he or she errs. The background of the system assistance encourages the user to use new statements and techniques.

6   Conclusions

Development of the dialogue systems oriented to generating program source code raises specific problems that can be partially solved by adaptive dialogue strategies. In the future work, we would like to perform further testing on the possible extensions and modification of the method described in this paper (also by WOZ simulation) to verify and enhance the effectiveness of the method. The further development of the dialogue strategies is directed especially towards enabling as much freedom in communication as possible.

Acknowledgement

This research has been partially supported by the Czech Ministry of Education under the Grant VS97028 and by the Grant Agency of the Czech Republic under the Grant 201/99/1248.

References

1. Batušek, R., Kopeček, I.: User Interfaces for Visually Impaired People; in Proceedings of the 5th ERCIM Workshop on User Interfaces for All, Dagstuhl, 1999, pp. 167–173.
2. Kopeček, I., Jergová, A.: Programming and Visually Impaired People; in Proceedings of the XV. World Computer Congress, ICCHP '98, Wien-Budapest, September 1998, pp. 365–372.
3. Kopeček, I.: Dialog Based Programming; Proceedings of the First Workshop on Text, Speech and Dialogue – TSD '98, 1998, pp. 407–412.
4. Kopeček, I.: Modelling the Information Retrieval Dialogue Systems; in Proceedings of the Workshop on Text, Speech and Dialogue – TSD '99, Lectures Notes in Artificial Intelligence 1692, Springer-Verlag, 1999, pp. 302–307.
5. Gruska, J: Foundations of Computing, International Thompson Computer Press, London, New York, 1997.
6. Kopeček, I.: Speech Sciences and Visually Impaired Students; In Proceedings of the ESCA Workshop on Method and Tool Innovations for Speech Science Education, University College London, April 1999, pp. 69–72.
7. Kopeček, I.: Generating Source Code by Means of Dialogue and Applications for Learning and Teaching Programming Languages. In Proceedings of the Conference EUNIS 2000, Poznań, pp. 60–67.
8. Stevens, R.D., Wright, P.C., Edwards, A.D.N., Brewster, S.A. (1996) An Audio Glance at Syntactic Structure Based on Spoken Form; Proceedings of the conference ICCHP '96 1996, Wien-Budapest, pp. 627–635.
9. Smith, R.W., Hipp, R.D.: Spoken Natural Language Dialog Systems: A Practical Approach. Oxford University Press, 1994.

Architecture of Multi-modal Dialogue System

Martin Fuchs, Petr Hejda, and Pavel Slavík

Department of Computer Science and Engineering,
FEE, Czech Technical University,
Karlovo nám. 13,
12 135 Praha 2, Czech Republic
slavik@cslab.fel.cvut.cz, phejda@ra.rockwell.com
http://www.cgg.cvut.cz

Abstract. This article describes an architectural framework of a multi-modal dialogue system. The framework is based on separation between the semantic and the syntactic parts of the dialogue. The semantics of the human-computer conversation is captured using a formal language. It describes the conversation by means of sequences of dialogue elements. The paper further elaborates how to derive the syntactic features of the conversation. A two-layer architecture has been proposed for the dialogue system. The upper layer, called sequencer, works with the description of the whole dialogue. The lower layer (driver dock) deals with individual dialogue elements.

A prototype has been implemented to demonstrate the main benefits of our framework. These are adaptability and extensibility. The adaptability involves multiple modes of communication, where the modalities can be changed even during the course of a dialogue. Due to layering, the applications can be easily extended to additional modes and user interface devices.

1 Introduction

This article describes an architecture framework of a multi-modal dialogue system. In general, a multi-modal dialogue system takes advantage of the multi-sensory nature of humans. It can utilise more than one sense for communication. Traditionally, applications are based on visual modes. Additional modes can be, for example, speech, gesture, and tactile input/output modes. The multi-modal approach increases the bandwidth of human-computer interaction and it may improve the interactive nature of the system. Also, it allows for deployment of the system in various environments.

Multi-modal systems may find their applications in a number of fields. To name only a few examples, they proved to be a viable aid for visually impaired users, an alternative to WIMP[1] interfaces in mobile computing, or an entertaining extension of computer games.

The functionality of a multi-modal system can be fairly extensive. We have focussed on a simple, yet extensible dialogue-based system. The main purpose of the system is to present information to the user and to query him for data. The challenge was to build a system with the following features:

---

[1] Windows, Icon, Menu, and Pointer based interfaces

P. Sojka, I. Kopeček, and K. Pala (Eds.): TSD 2000, LNAI 1902, pp. 433–438, 2000.
© Springer-Verlag Berlin Heidelberg 2000

- **Simple Architecture** The architecture should be as simple as possible. It has to specify function blocks, their roles and type of data the blocks exchange.
- **Extensible** The system should be open to new communication devices. Once there is a need to connect a new device or use a new mode, the system should **not** be re-implemented.
- **Adaptive** The system should allow for changing of modalities. These changes should be possible even during the run-time of the system.

The text of this article is structured as follows. Section 2 introduces formal description of a human-computer conversation utilised in our approach. This formal description is used in the architecture as described in Section 3. Section 4 gives details of our system prototype. The last section summarises our ideas and deals with the future development.

2   Formal Description of a Dialogue

The framework focusses on multi-modal dialogue systems in which the dialogue consists of a finite number of dialogue element types. In our previous work, we have shown that a class of dialogues can be described via sets of predefined, parameterised dialogue elements [3]. These elements capture the semantics of the human-computer conversation. The elements can be divided into classes according to the type of information which is expected as the result of the conversation with the user.

An example of an element can be a simple question, such as *"Would you like to continue?"*. It can be captured by a dialogue element with the following formal description[2]:

```
<question id="2" default="yes">
    Would you like to continue?
</question>
```

The description captures three pieces of information:

1 The **request** is a question sentence *"What ... "*
2 The **answer** *"yes"* or *"no"* is expected
3 The **default value** is *"yes"*

These three pieces capture the semantics of the dialogue element.

The dialogue system has to add syntax of the actual conversation with the user. This may vary according to the device and mode used for the communication with the user. For example, the **request** can be displayed together with a check box. The check box is initially checked to reflect the **default value**. In another situation, the speech recognition and synthesis is used. In that case, the system voices the request to the user and expects one of the words *"yes"*, *"no"*, *"default"*, *"whatever"*, *"yep"*, *"o.k."*, etc. As a result, the dialogue system can have some freedom in interpreting the dialogue elements and handling the actual conversation with the user.

---

[2] This example uses XML, see below.

As mentioned above, the dialogue system receives the formalised dialogue description. In our prototype, Dialogue Markup Language version 2.0 (DML2.0) was used [1]. It can describe the following types of dialogue elements:

1 **Message.** It presents some information to the user.
2 **Question.** A yes/no answer is expected.
3 **Choice.** An array of choices. The user can choose one or several of them.
4 **Text.** Single-line text. Allows the editing of linear text.
5 **TextEdit.** Multi-line text.
6 **Number.** A number is expected as a result.
7 **Program.** Any sequence of simple dialogue elements.
8 **Dialogue.** Any sequence of simple dialogue elements and programs.

Each simple dialogue element (elements 1–6) represents a part of a conversation focussed on delivering or obtaining a basic piece of information, such as a number or a text string. Their semantics is standardised. The last two items in the list describe sequences of simple dialogue elements. Their semantics is defined as a sequence of joint semantics of used elements. Hence, the structure and the semantics of the whole dialogue are described in a formal way [2].

3   Architecture of the System

The formal description of the dialogue can be used for communication between the user interface part and the application part of the system. This creates a natural division of the application in two sub-systems. The **application side** generates a dialogue to obtain some data from the user, for example what to do next, name of a command or its parameters. The **user side** is then responsible for effective interpretation of the formal description. This section focusses on the architecture of the user side (see Figure 1).

The formalised description of the dialogue is processed by the user part to work out the details of the conversation. During this process, it can be decided which modalities to use for which parts of the dialogue.

The key concept of our architecture is the definition of higher and basic processing layers: the **sequencer** and the **low-level dock**. The sequencer transforms the DML dialogue description into the description of single dialogue elements. It processes the whole dialogue at once, breaking it into dialogue elements. This solves the counteracting nature of linear and non-linear conversation. The linear conversation requires processing of one dialogue element at one time. An example can be voice-based conversation. The non-linear conversation, on the other hand, processes dialogue elements in parallel, as in case of a formular. The user is free to process the elements in any order [4]. The sequencer is the part of the dialogue system responsible for making the conversation either linear or non-linear.

Figure 2 depicts a simple dialogue which is processed in two ways. On the left-hand side, there is a non-linear conversation. The user is free to choose where to start. The right-hand side shows a sequence of frames featuring the same conversation in a linear fashion. Due to limitations of the small display, the dialogue is broken into small pieces. These pieces are processed one by one, in a linear fashion. The figure was rendered by our prototype [1].

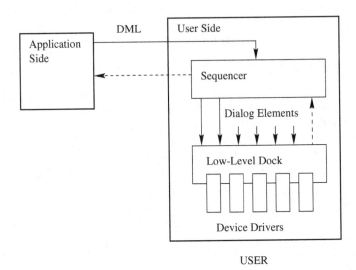

Fig. 1. The architecture of the framework

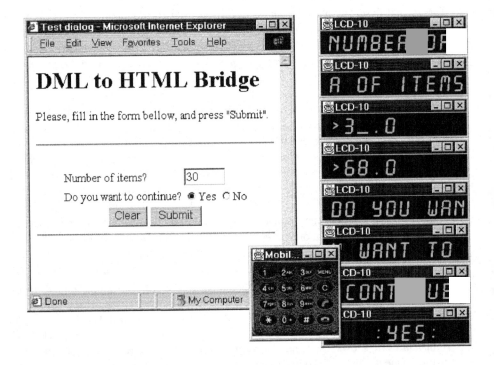

Fig. 2. The effect of the sequencer on the dialogue structure

Even though the whole dialogue system can be based on the sequencer layer, additional benefits are gained by employing the second layer, low-level dock. It defines a plug-and-play interface for software components processing the dialogue elements on various devices using various modalities. The set of plug-ins defines an interface between device independent and device dependent parts of the user part.

For example, there are two modules allowing for the output to either an LCD display (as in Figure 2) or to a speaker (not depicted). The LCD module breaks any output message into small pieces which can fit the size of the display. To be able to use a speaker as an output, a voice synthesis module has to be used. Its main task is to transform all messages to speech and to repeat the missing parts.

4   The Prototype

To prove our ideas workable, we have implemented a working prototype of the application framework. Its structure reflects the architectural model described above. The framework is divided in two parts, the application and user sides. For testing purposes, the application side implements two applications.

The first application is a reader of e-mail. It generates dialogues for reading and sending e-mail messages. The second is an automatic teller machine (ATM) simulator. The dialogues generated by this application mirror the functionality of a real ATM.

The user side was implemented according to the two-layer architecture. Where the sequencer provides the dialogue sequencing, the low-level dock and its drivers process the dialogues and allow for various modes. The capabilities of this part are crucial to the functionality of the application.

The following drivers have been implemented for both applications:

- Term - text-based mode only. The processing is linear.
- HTML - text with more formatting. The processing is non-linear.
- Applet - widget-based interface. The processing is non-linear.
- Keyboard - driver for text input.
- MobileKeys - driver simulating phone keyboard.
- Mouse - driver for input using a mouse.
- X-Key - driver for a joystick-like device with two buttons.
- SmallLCD - driver for a small alphanumeric display.
- SmallBitmap - driver for a small bit mapped display.
- Voice - driver for speech synthesis and recognition.

The drivers allow for mutual combination and switching during the execution of the application. This results in a highly flexible user interface, which is capable of changing modes of interaction. The drivers cover only a small portion of possible input/output devices. Therefore, it is apparent that the drivers are fairly small and easy to implement components.

The implementation of the prototype was done using the Java 1.1 (http://java.sun.com/) and Extensible Markup Language (XML) technologies (http://www.w3.org/XML/). The Java language brings additional benefits of portability and platform independence. Both the application and the user side were implemented as separate components connected via a data stream.

DML was implemented as an application of XML. This allowed for fast prototyping using the SAX compliant XML parser Aelfred. Speech synthesis and recognition was implemented with IBM's ViaVoice (`http://www-4.ibm.com/software/speech/`) and SpeechForJava API (`http://www.alphaworks.ibm.com/tech/speech`).

5   Summary and Future Work

We have described an architectural framework of a multi-modal dialogue system. It is based on the formal dialogue description in DML. The formal description captures the semantics of the conversation using dialogue elements. The syntactic features are delivered by our two-layer architecture of the dialogue system. The upper layer, called sequencer, works with the description of the whole dialogue. The lower layer deals with individual dialogue elements. As a result, we have got an application framework which allows for changes of modalities even during the processing of a dialogue. The other benefit is that the applications can be easily extended to additional modes and user interface devices.

In the future, we would like to extend the framework to cover a wider set of applications and drivers. The other issue is usability testing and evaluation of the framework.

References

1. Fuchs, M.: Multi-modal user interface (in Czech). Master thesis, Department of Computer Science and Engineering, FEE, Czech Technical University Prague (1999).
2. Hejda, P.: Dialog Markup Language. Poster99, FEE, Czech Technical University in Prague (1999) IC8.
3. Hejda, P.: Situations in Dialogue. In Text, Speech and Dialogue. Springer-Verlag, Berlin Heidelberg New York (1999) 290–295.
4. Larson, J. A.: Interactive Software. Yourdon Press (1992).

The Utility of Semantic-Pragmatic Information and Dialogue-State for Speech Recognition in Spoken Dialogue Systems

Georg Stemmer, Elmar Nöth, and Heinrich Niemann

University of Erlangen-Nürnberg, Chair for Pattern Recognition, Martensstrasse 3,
D-91058 Erlangen, Germany
stemmer@informatik.uni-erlangen.de,
http://www.mustererkennung.de

Abstract. Information about the dialogue-state can be integrated into language models to improve performance of the speech recogniser in a dialogue system. A dialogue state is defined in this paper as the question, the user is replying to. One of the main problems in dialogue-state dependent language modelling is the limitation of training data. In order to obtain robust models, we use the method of rational interpolation to smooth between a dialogue-state dependent and a general language model. In contrast to linear interpolation methods, rational interpolation weights the different predictors according to their reliability. Semantic-pragmatic knowledge is used to enlarge the training data of the language models. Both methods reduce perplexity and word error rate significantly.

1 Introduction

Current spoken dialogue systems usually have a modular architecture. In most systems, the understanding of the user's utterances is done by several components, which usually form a processing pipeline: A speech recogniser generates one or several hypotheses of the spoken word sequence, which are transformed into a semantic-pragmatic representation by a language understanding unit. In combination with the actual dialogue-state, the semantic-pragmatic representation is used by the dialogue management for system-user interaction and communication with external systems, e.g. a database.

This paper addresses an approach to increase the performance of the speech recogniser of a spoken dialogue system by additional information sources. This is motivated by the observation that errors during speech recognition often conflict with the current dialogue-state. E.g. for a train timetable information system, if the system asks for the city of departure, *yes* or *no* do not have a very high probability to occur in the spoken utterance. In literature, several approaches to use the dialogue-state as a predictor of the user response can be found. The training corpus is split into partitions, which correspond to the dialogue-states. Each partition is used to estimate a separate, dialogue-state dependent language model. As the partitioning reduces the amount of training data for each language model, interpolation or fall back strategies have to be

P. Sojka, I. Kopeček, and K. Pala (Eds.): TSD 2000, LNAI 1902, pp. 439–444, 2000.

applied in order to get robust language models. In [1], dialogue-states are generalised until the training data is sufficient. In the work of Riccardi et al. [3] the dialogue-state dependent language models are interpolated with a general language model. Wessel et al. [5] use interpolation to combine the dialogue-state dependent language models with each other. In the following, we basically propose two approaches in the field of dialogue-state dependent language modelling. First, we describe a new strategy for the interpolation between specialised and general language models, rational interpolation. In contrast to linear interpolation schemes, rational interpolation weights the different predictors with their reliability. Second, we show how to utilise semantic-pragmatic knowledge to find suitable backing-off data for the language models of rare dialogue-states.

2   Data

All evaluations were done on 20678 utterances, which have been recorded with the conversational train timetable information system EVAR, as it is described in [2]. Nearly all utterances are in the German language. The total amount of data is 23 hours, the average length of an utterance is four seconds. 16767 utterances have been selected randomly for training and validation (15745 for training, 1022 for validation), the remainder of 3911 utterances is available for testing.

3   Semantic Attributes and Dialogue-States

The corpus is transcribed with a set of 58 semantic-pragmatic attributes, which give a formatted description of the meaning of the user's utterance in the context of train timetable information. The most important attributes are *time*, *date*, *sourcecity* (city of departure), *goalcity* (destination), *no* and *yes*.

As in the work of Eckert et al. [1], we define the dialogue-states by the question the user is replying to. Examples for the questions are *what information do you need?* or *where do you want to go?*. We only take the six most frequent questions into account, and map the less frequent questions to the more frequent ones.

4   Evaluation of the Baseline System

The baseline system has a word error rate of 21.2%. As integration of additional information will be used to increase the performance of semantic-pragmatic attribute recognition, we evaluate the semantic-pragmatic attribute accuracy of the baseline system. The attribute accuracy of the system is evaluated on 2000 utterances of the test data set, for which a manual transcription with semantic-pragmatic attributes is available. The attribute accuracy is defined similar to the word accuracy as the number of substituted, inserted or deleted attributes, subtracted from the number of attributes in the reference, relative to the number of attributes in the reference. Please note that we do not compute a semantic concept accuracy here, i.e. if the recogniser intermixes two city names, there may be no influence on the attribute accuracy, because the correct attribute *goalcity* can still be generated by the language understanding component. If the language understanding component of the dialogue system is applied to the spoken word sequence, the attribute accuracy for the attributes *time*, *date*, *sourcecity*, *goalcity*, *yes*, and *no* is 90.8%. This value drops to 86.0%, if the language understanding component is applied to the output of the speech recogniser. The following experiments investigate, to which extent the loss in semantic-pragmatic attribute accuracy may be reduced by the integration of new information sources.

5 Description of the Language Models

5.1 Rational Interpolation

The method of rational interpolation for language modelling has been proposed by Schukat-Talamazzini et al. [4] for the task of combining a set of conditional n-gram word probability predictors. The approach was to find a good approximation $\tilde{P}(w_t|v)$ of the conditional probability $P(w_t|v)$, that a word w_t occurs given a sentence history v. The approximation is based on the maximum likelihood estimates

$$\hat{P}_i(w_t|v) = P'(w_t|w_{t-i+1}, \dots, w_{t-1}) = \frac{\#(w_{t-i+1}, \dots, w_t)}{\#(w_{t-i+1}, \dots, w_{t-1})} \qquad (1)$$

where the function $\#(\cdot)$ counts the frequence of occurrence of its argument. A set of predictors $\hat{P}_i(w_t|v)$, $i \in I$, results from assigning different values to i, i.e. looking at different portions of the sentence history v. All predictors $\hat{P}_i$ are combined in the following interpolation scheme:

$$\tilde{P}(w_t|v) = \frac{\sum_{i \in I} \lambda_i \cdot g_i(v) \cdot \hat{P}_i(w_t|v)}{\sum_{i \in I} \lambda_i \cdot g_i(v)} \qquad (2)$$

The λ_i represent the interpolation factors, the function $g_i(\cdot)$ weights the predictor $\hat{P}_i$ with its reliability. The reliability is given by a hyperbolic weight function which is high for large values of $\#_i(v)$ and low for small values of $\#_i(v)$. The denominator is for normalisation. The optimisation of the λ_i is done by Newton iteration on a cross-validation data set. It is not possible to apply the EM-Algorithm here, because – in contrast to linear interpolation schemes – Eq. (2) cannot be interpreted as a stochastic process. In the following, the language model defined by Eq. (2) will be referred to as $\mathcal{L}_0$, it is a general model that is independent of the dialogue-state.

5.2 Rational Interpolation for Dialogue-State Dependent Models

Rational interpolation is basically a method for the combination of different predictors for the approximation of $P(w_t|v)$. Dialogue-state dependent modelling is based on the assumption, that the dialogue-state is a good predictor for what the user says. Instead of approximating $P(w_t|v)$, we want to find an estimation of $P_d(w_t|v)$, where d stands for the current dialogue-state. The first approach is to combine only the dialogue-state dependent predictors $\hat{P}_{i,d}(w_t|v)$ for the language model of one specific dialogue state d. In the following, the resulting model is called $\mathcal{L}_1$. Since the predictors $\hat{P}_{i,d}(w_t|v)$

are estimated only on a fraction of the original dialogue-state independent training data, the reliability of most predictors is much lower. Rational interpolation enables us to combine the predictors $\hat{P}_{i,d}(w_t|v)$ with the predictors $\hat{P}_i(w_t|v)$ to increase robustness of the language model. The resulting language model will be called $\mathcal{L}_2$:

$$\tilde{P}_{\mathcal{L}_2,d}(w_t|v) = \frac{\sum_{i\in I} \lambda_{i,d} \cdot g_{i,d}(v) \cdot \hat{P}_{i,d}(w_t|v) + \gamma \cdot \sum_{i\in I} \lambda_i \cdot g_i(v) \cdot \hat{P}_i(w_t|v)}{\sum_{i\in I} \lambda_{i,d} \cdot g_{i,d}(v) + \gamma \cdot \sum_{i\in I} \lambda_i \cdot g_i(v)} \quad (3)$$

The γ is the interpolation factor between the dialogue-state dependent and the general language model. For parameter adjustment, the $\lambda_{i,d}$ and γ are optimised jointly, the λ_i are the same parameters, that have been calculated for the general language model $\mathcal{L}_0$, and do not underlie any further optimisation.

5.3   Incorporating Semantic-Pragmatic Knowledge

It is obvious, that the current dialogue-state primarily determines the meaning of the user's utterance. There is only a minor influence on the syntactical structure of the sentence. There is, for example, a high similarity between utterances, that contain information about the time of departure. This similarity is not influenced by the dialogue-state, in which a sentence was uttered. This observation can be expressed by the following simplified model of utterance production:

$$P_d(w_1, .., w_t) = \sum_s P_d(w_1, .., w_t|s) \cdot P_d(s) \approx \sum_s P(w_1, .., w_t|s) \cdot P_d(s) \quad (4)$$

The semantic-pragmatic content s of the utterance $w_1, .., w_t$ depends on the dialogue-state d, while the influence of the dialogue state on the syntactical realization of the utterance is neglected. A consequence of Eq. (4) is to integrate semantic-pragmatic predictors $\hat{P}_{i,s}(w_t|v)$ in the language model. These do not depend on a dialogue-state, the predictor $\hat{P}_{i,s}(w_t|v)$ is estimated on all sentences in the training corpus, that have the semantic transcription s, e.g. *goalcity*. The resulting language model will be referred to as $\mathcal{L}_3$:

$$pred_0 = \sum_{i\in I} \lambda_i \cdot g_i(v) \cdot \hat{P}_i(w_t|v) \quad (5)$$

$$pred_1(d) = \sum_{i\in I} \lambda_{i,d} \cdot g_{i,d}(v) \cdot \hat{P}_{i,d}(w_t|v) \quad (6)$$

$$pred_2(s) = \sum_{i\in I} \lambda_{i,s} \cdot g_{i,s}(v) \cdot \hat{P}_{i,s}(w_t|v) \quad (7)$$

$$\tilde{P}_{\mathcal{L}_3,d}(w_t|v) = \frac{\gamma_0 \cdot pred_0 + \gamma_1 \cdot pred_1(d) + \sum_{s\in S} \gamma_{2,s} \cdot pred_2(s)}{norm} \quad (8)$$

Model $\mathcal{L}_3$ integrates the dialogue-state dependent, general and semantic-pragmatic predictors. *norm* is the normalisation factor given by the sum of all interpolation and weighting factors. S is a set of semantic-pragmatic attributes, which have a high probability to occur in d. For our experiments, $\mathcal{L}_3$ only uses semantic predictors for the model of dialogue-state three, which is the state with the lowest amount of training data. S contains only one semantic-pragmatic attribute here, *goalcity*, which is the most frequent attribute in dialogue-state three. All other dialogue-states are represented as in language model $\mathcal{L}_2$. To keep the number of parameters that are subject to optimisation low, only the γ factors are optimised jointly, all λ factors can be optimised with separate (dialogue-state or attribute dependent) language models.

6   Experimental Results

For evaluation, we have measured the perplexities and the word error rates on the test sentences. Table 1 shows the amount of training and test sentences, that were available for the different language models and the perplexities. As can be seen from columns four and five, dialogue-state dependent modelling without interpolation can increase perplexities, if the training data is not sufficient. The same effect influences also model $\mathcal{L}_2$, because the optimisation algorithm does not allow the weights to become zero. In model $\mathcal{L}_3$ the perplexity in all dialogue-states is reduced, even in dialogue-state three, mainly because additional training data becomes available for the model of state three (3131 sentences from the training corpus, which are labelled with *goalcity*).   For the

Table 1. Number of sentences for each dialogue-state in the training and test corpus and perplexities for the different language models on the test corpus

dialogue-state	train	test	$\mathcal{L}_0$	$\mathcal{L}_1$	$\mathcal{L}_2$	$\mathcal{L}_3$
0	8550	1957	13.0	12.4	12.3	12.3
1	1975	566	13.5	11.9	11.3	11.3
2	1397	379	16.5	13.8	12.1	12.1
3	763	219	17.1	44.2	21.2	14.3
4	1321	373	18.1	13.6	12.3	12.3
5	1739	417	21.8	16.3	14.7	14.7

application of the models in our dialogue system, we integrated the new interpolation methods into the bigram model of the forward search of the recogniser and into the 4-gram model that is used for the rescoring of the word lattice during the $A^\star$ search. Table 2 shows the word error rates for the different models. The best word error rate reduction is 3.8% relative, while the attribute accuracy increases by 0.8% absolute.

7   Conclusion

Errors of the word recogniser cause a loss in speech understanding performance. We presented two new models which apply the method of rational interpolation to the problem of smoothing between language models. Additional training data becomes available by the incorporation of semantic-pragmatic knowledge. Sentences which have a similar meaning can be used for the estimation of backing-off statistics of a model for a

Table 2. Word error rate (WER) and attribute accuracy (AA) for the different language models

model	WER [%]	AA [%]
$\mathcal{L}_0$	21.2	86.0
$\mathcal{L}_1$	20.9	86.1
$\mathcal{L}_2$	20.5	86.8
$\mathcal{L}_3$	20.4	86.8

dialogue-state. We showed that the integration of our dialogue-state dependent language models into the speech recogniser improves performance: The word error rate is reduced by 3.8% relative, there is also an increase in speech understanding performance. Further experiments will investigate into a more sophisticated definition of the dialogue-state.

References

1. W. Eckert and F. Gallwitz and H. Niemann: Combining Stochastic and Linguistic Language Models for Recognition of Spontaneous Speech. Proc. IEEE Int. Conf. on Acoustics, Speech and Signal Processing, Atlanta, USA (1996) 423–426.
2. F. Gallwitz and M. Aretoulaki and M. Boros and J. Haas and S. Harbeck and R. Huber and H. Niemann and E. Nöth: The Erlangen Spoken Dialogue System EVAR: A State-of-the-Art Information Retrieval System. Proceedings of 1998 International Symposium on Spoken Dialogue, Sydney, Australia (1998) 19–26.
3. G. Riccardi and A. L. Gorin: Stochastic Language Adaptation Over Time and State in a Natural Spoken Dialog System. IEEE Trans. on Speech and Audio Proc., Vol. 8, No. 1, January 2000 3–10.
4. E.G. Schukat-Talamazzini and F. Gallwitz and S. Harbeck and V. Warnke: Rational Interpolation of Maximum Likelihood Predictors in Stochastic Language Modeling. Proc. European Conf. on Speech Communication and Technology, Rhodes, Greece, (1997) 2731–2734.
5. F. Wessel and A. Baader: Robust Dialogue–State Dependent Language Modeling Using Leaving–One–Out. Proc. IEEE Int. Conf. on Acoustics, Speech and Signal Processing, Phoenix, USA (1999) 741–744.

Word Concept Model for Intelligent Dialogue Agents

Yang Li, Tong Zhang, and Stephen E. Levinson

Beckman Institute, 405 North Mathews, Urbana, IL 61801, USA
yangli@ifp.uiuc.edu, tzhang1@ifp.uiuc.edu, sel@ifp.uiuc.edu

Abstract. Information extraction is a key component in dialogue systems. Knowledge about the world as well as knowledge specific to each word should be used for robust semantic processing. An intelligent agent is necessary for a dialogue system when meanings are strictly defined by using a world state model. An extended concept structure is proposed to represent knowledge associated with each word in a "speech-friendly" way. By considering knowledge stored in the word concept model as well as knowledge base of the world model, meaning of a given sentence can be correctly identified. This paper describes the extended concept structure and how knowledge about words can be stored in this concept model.

1   Introduction

With the recent progress in speech recognition techniques, it is practical now to build spoken dialogue systems that can accept relatively large number of vocabularies. Researchers have built many spoken dialogue systems [1,2,3]. With the increased complexity of tasks, however, there are several limitations for currently used methods. Building spoken dialogue systems requires a lot of manually transcribed data, and the system are usually not robust and flexible enough in dealing with unexpected sentence styles. More importantly, information extraction has to be built according to a specific domain. There is no systematical approach that we can use to build spoken dialogue systems in a fast and automatic way. Although there are many aspects to be considered, we claim that meanings of each word in an input sentence have not been given enough emphasis when semantic processing is done using current methods.

For human, there is knowledge associated with every word he knows. We know a book is something composed of pages and made of paper. We also know there are words printed in a book. There may be other information. All these knowledge composes the concept of "book". Human uses the knowledge behind the concept to interpret the meaning of sentences. There may be techniques for computer to extract information embedded in a sentence without implementing the knowledge associated with each word, but the limitations are clear as we can find from currently built systems. We shall have a much better chance of success if we explicitly implement into our system the knowledge associated with each word, and each of those word phrases whose meanings are different from the original words. This knowledge will help us to extract information with more robustness and flexibility if we build powerful reasoning tools at the same time.

P. Sojka, I. Kopeček, and K. Pala (Eds.): TSD 2000, LNAI 1902, pp. 445–449, 2000.

The knowledge associated with words are actually not knowledge about the "word", it is about the "world". Each sentence has a meaning where the meaning is about the "world". According to Schank's Conceptual Dependency Theory, [4] there is a unique representation for meaning behind any sentences that convey the exact message, regardless of language. This is absolutely true. However, Schank's scheme of meaning representation doesn't define meaning in a strict way. Further, Schank's conceptualization doesn't employ knowledge behind each word and therefore, doesn't cover the meanings of a given sentence accurately.

We claim that strict meaning can only be defined in a given "world". Meanings in different "worlds" may have different representations. Therefore, it is necessary to have a "world model" before any meaning can be defined. As Woods suggested, an intelligent system will need to have some internalized "notation" or "representation" for expressing believed and hypothesized facts about the world [5]. Once we have a world model, representation of meaning is clear and unique: descriptions of the world states are the stative conceptualizations of Schank, and changes of the world states are the active conceptualizations. This meaning representation is coherent to the world model and has nothing to do with any specific language. We can easily describe the world in formal languages, but the difficult task is how to describe it in natural languages and how to understand the natural languages used to describe it.

If a world model is used in a dialogue system, it will be convenient to use an intelligent agent who responses to changes in the world state and acts to achieve some ideal world state. An intelligent agent is a software that has its own goals and can reason and plan according to its world state or simple environmental variables. Intelligent agents are capable of completing complicated tasks.

As we mentioned earlier, knowledge behind each word – the concept is important for semantic processing. However, no current knowledge representation method is good for storing information associated with each word. The procedural semantics suggested by Woods cannot describe all the knowledge associated with each word accurately. Researchers have tried to build universal methods for knowledge representation. These methods only represent the knowledge by using highly abstracted symbol languages. They are not suitable for storing information related to a specific word. In order to build a structure that can store the associated concept of each word, we propose a word concept model to represent knowledge in a "speech-friendly" way. Our goal should be to establish a universal knowledge representation method so that a system can use the knowledge to extract information from a sentence as well as to learn new words and knowledge by simply filling the newly acquired information into existing structures. The motivation behind this is that we want to build a system that can grow automatically through interaction with its environments and users. In Section 2, we propose an Extended Concept Structure that can be used to store information related to each word. In Section 3, we describe how knowledge about words can be stored in the proposed concept structure. A discussion is given in Section 4.

2 Extended Concept Structure (ECS)

Currently, a concept can be formally defined as specific regions in an attribute space. Each dimension of an attribute space is a specific attribute that can take continuous or discrete, finite or infinite values. In this formal concept description, an attribute space is required first. Selection of this attribute space is determined by the specific application. However, for speech capable intelligent agent, the attribute space should be universal if we want the agent to have growth potentials. Therefore, no specific domain should be defined though we may start from certain applications. Given the tremendous varieties of everyday life, it is impossible to select an attribute space on which all the possible words can be defined in. Furthermore, new types of words may not be incorporated into this attribute space properly. On the other hand, concepts in an intelligent agent should be layered. Concepts in different layers may have different attributes. For a fixed task intelligent agent, we can manually set the attributes for different layers. But for a learning agent, such structure will fundamentally limit the agent's abilities.

In order to conquer the fixed attributes problem, we propose a new type of concept description: extended concept structure (ECS). Key features of ECS are: an attribute can be another concept; an attribute and the concept it belongs to is linked by "relations"; there is no fixed attribute list, concepts are described by attribute-on-demand.

The key idea here is not to limit a concept to only several possible attributes. We may view all the possible concepts as potential attributes to a specific concept. The problem is that the concept of everyday life is an almost infinite complex network. Apparently, concepts are layered. Explanation of "book" requires knowledge of "paper", "text", etc. Ultimately, all concepts are explained by a primitive concept set that is directly explained by input signal patterns from sensory motors. Therefore, we can view the perceptual space as the fixed part of the attribute space of our concept model. Primitive concepts built directly on this fixed attribute space can be used as attributes of other concepts. For example, the concept of "color" can be built directly on the perceptual space while the concept of "Sun" requires "color" as one of its attributes. It is not necessary to list all the possible attributes the concept of "sun" might have because all the concepts are possible attributes. We only list them when the agent knows there is connection between concept and a possible attribute.

In order to correctly reflect the relation between a concept and an attribute or another concept, a set of basic relations should be defined. "Sun" "has" the "color" of "red" while "door" is "part of" a "room". Here, "has" and "part of" are different relations. We shall distinguish such relations so that we know "color" is applied to the entire part of "Sun" while "door" may not appear anywhere in a "room". Fortunately, the number of basic relations is limited. We can fix the basic relation set without losing too much understanding abilities of the intelligent agent. Ways to automatically learn basic relations may also be explored. However, we shall not worry about that at this stage.

By extending the ideas of concept and attribute, ECS views all concepts as possible attributes for a specific concept. Therefore, layered concepts are linked by the basic relations. The base attributes comes from the perceptual space. In this way, ECS has the capability to universally store knowledge in a similar way used by human minds.

Obviously, many problems arise when we want to utilize ECS in an intelligent agent. Problems in the formal concept description such as learning new concept from examples or discovering new conclusion from knowledge base may be reinvestigated here. However we may want to focus on building the word concept model by using ECS and come back to these problems when necessary.

3   Word Concept Model

In a human mind, complex concepts are explained by simple concepts. We need to understand the concept of "door" and "window" before we understand the concept of "room". The concept of "window" is further explained by "frame", "glass" and so on. Ultimately, all the concepts are explained based on the input signal patterns perceived by the human sensory motors. This layered abstraction is the key to fast processing of information. When reasoning is being done, only related information is pulled out. Lower layered information may not appear in a reasoning process. In our word concept model, such layered concept abstraction should also be used. We should build complex concepts by using simple concepts.

As we started to map word into this concept structure, it is necessary to treat different types of words differently. Since the most basic type of concept in the world are physical matters, we should first map nouns and pronouns into the concept space. We call this types of words solid word. For solid words, we can find the mapping on the concept space quite easily since they refer to specific types of things in the physical world. There may be multiple definitions for one word because one word can have many meanings. The agent can decided which definition to use by combining context information. Solid words are the basic building blocks for word concept modeling. Each solid word can be stored in an extended concept structure or ECS.

After we have defined the solid words, other types of words can be defined around solid words instead of in the concept space. However, their definitions are closely coupled with the concept space.

For verbs, we can first define the positions where solid word can appear around this verb. For example, a solid word can appear both before and after the verb "eat". For some verb, more than one solid word can appear after the verb. In all cases, the positions where a solid word can appear are numbered. Then, definition of this verb is described by how the attribute of each solid word should change. For example, if "Tom" is the solid word before "go" and "home" is the solid word after "go", then the "position" attribute of "Tom" should be set to "home" or the location of "home". Of course, there are complex situations where this simple scheme doesn't fit. However, more techniques can be developed by using the same idea.

For adjectives, definitions are described as values of the attributes. "Big" may be defined as "more than 2000 square feet" for the "size" attribute if it is used for houses. Obviously, multiple definitions are possible and should be resolved by context. Also, since there is a link between a concept and an attribute, we can put an extended field in the link of ECS to locally limit the relation. Obviously, there are many options to solve this ambiguity problem, we can go back and attach them when necessary. Adverbs can be defined in a similar fashion. Though adverbs are to limit adjectives and verbs, the limitations are ultimately reflected in the attributes of solid words. For example, "quickly" may mean the position of some object changes a large amount in a short time. If we define basic relations to reflect changes in time, then "quickly" can be modeled.

For prepositions, we should define them by using the basic set of relationships. These include "in", "on", "in front of", "at left of", "include", "belong to", etc. Then prepositions can be defined by using these basic relationships.

There are other types of words, but most of them are grammar words and can be dealt with by a language parser. We should solve many miscellaneous tasks when we are building the system.

4   Discussion

An intelligent system can be built in two ways: one is to build all parts of the system manually. We can put all the necessary algorithm and knowledge into the system and fine-tune it when we see problems. Another approach is to build a suitable structure and then the system can learn from the environment and grow on its own. The first approach may fail when the task is so complex that the designers are unable to control over so many details. The second approach is attractive but maybe difficult to start. We hope that we can design a proper structure and implement some core knowledge into the system for learning. Then the system can grow from that point. The word concept model is one small step towards building the universal learning structure for intelligent systems as we see language capability plays a key role in intelligence. Actually, there are already excellent theories in the field of artificial intelligence. The lack of speech capability for current intelligent agents may be the crucial reason why real applications of artificial intelligence are not so fruitful. We hope, that giving intelligent agents natural language capability can help to provide better solutions. Given the scope of the work involved, the authors were unable to exhaust all possible references at this time. The readers may forgive us for this matter.

Acknowledgement

This work was supported in part by Yamaha Motors Corporation and in part by National Science Foundation Grant CDA 96-24396.

References

1. Zue, V., et al., JUPITER: A Telephone-Based Conversational Interface for Weather Information, *IEEE Transactions on Speech and Audio Processing*, 8(1), 85–96, 2000.
2. Baggia, P., G. Castagneri, and M. Danieli, Field Trials of the Italian ARISE train timetable system, in *Proceedings of the 1998 IEEE 4th Workshop on Interactive Voice Technology for Telecommunications Applications*, New York, NY 1998.
3. Sourvignier, B. et al., The Thoughtful Elephant: Strategies for Spoken Dialog Systems, *IEEE Transactions on Speech and Audio Processing*, 8(1), 51–62, 2000.
4. Schank, R. C., Conceptual Information Processing. North Holland, Amsterdam. 1975.
5. Woods, W. A., Procedural Semantics as A Theory of Meaning, in Elements of Discourse Understanding, Ed. By A. K. Joshi, B. L. Webber and I. A. Sag., Cambridge University Press, 1981.

Author Index

Subject Index